Creative
NEEDLE
CRAFTS

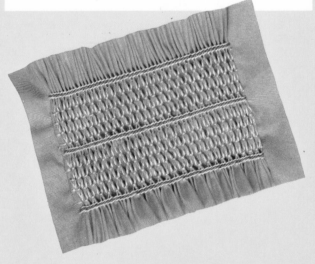

Creative NEEDLE CRAFTS

Exeter Books

NEW YORK

First published in 1989 by Exeter Books
Distributed by Bookthrift
Exeter is a trademark of Bookthrift Marketing Inc.
Bookthrift is a registered trademark of
Bookthrift Marketing, New York, New York.

Original material © Marshall Cavendish Ltd
This arrangement © 1987 Marshall Cavendish Ltd
Prepared by Marshall Cavendish Books Ltd
58 Old Compton St. London W1V 5PA.

Printed in Portugal
ISBN 0 671 09231 6

Printed in Portugal by Resopal

Contents

Introduction

Knitting, crochet, embroidery, quilting, patchwork or appliqué – whichever of these you prefer, or indeed if you enjoy experimenting with several of these rewarding pastimes, you will find that this book is filled with unusual and innovative designs, including fashionable clothes for you and your family as well as delightful soft furnishings for your home. It does not matter whether you are a beginner at any particular craft or a skilled amateur, there is plenty here to interest you and increase your skills, and the results are bound to win admiration.

There are lots of patterns for women, ranging from very stylish, high-fashion clothing, to sophisticated classics that underpin any versatile wardrobe, to attractive and practical sportswear. If you are looking for presents to make for the men in your life, you will find knitted or crocheted sweaters, cardigans, pullovers and T-shirts, again with plenty of style choice, including a classic Fair Isle pullover, and an Aran sweater, as well as a smart crocheted vest or a maxi-knit jacket for the less conventional male. And there are plenty of patterns – knitted, crocheted or embroidered – for babies and children, including a stunning, embroidered christening gown, which would surely become a treasured family heirloom to greet the arrival of each new generation.

One very important – and unusual – feature of this book is the range of patterns in the Pattern Library that accompanies many of the designs.

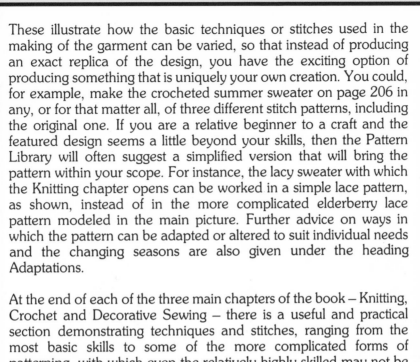

These illustrate how the basic techniques or stitches used in the making of the garment can be varied, so that instead of producing an exact replica of the design, you have the exciting option of producing something that is uniquely your own creation. You could, for example, make the crocheted summer sweater on page 206 in any, or for that matter all, of three different stitch patterns, including the original one. If you are a relative beginner to a craft and the featured design seems a little beyond your skills, then the Pattern Library will often suggest a simplified version that will bring the pattern within your scope. For instance, the lacy sweater with which the Knitting chapter opens can be worked in a simple lace pattern, as shown, instead of in the more complicated elderberry lace pattern modeled in the main picture. Further advice on ways in which the pattern can be adapted or altered to suit individual needs and the changing seasons are also given under the heading Adaptations.

At the end of each of the three main chapters of the book — Knitting, Crochet and Decorative Sewing — there is a useful and practical section demonstrating techniques and stitches, ranging from the most basic skills to some of the more complicated forms of patterning, with which even the relatively highly skilled may not be entirely familiar.

All the designs in this book are fully and clearly described, step by step, with additional drawings demonstrating a Special Technique, in each case, and drawings showing the stitches used, where relevant. Whatever your level of skill, you can use this book to brighten up your wardrobe, beautify your home or make handcrafted gifts with a personal touch. You can follow the patterns to the letter, or use them as a spring board to a host of entirely new designs. The choice is up to you, for this book is designed to be used in many ways — all of them enjoyable and creative!

Knitting

This exclusive knitwear collection offers a full range of garments suited to every season of the year and to every sort of occasion, from casual, everyday wear to luxurious evening clothes. It opens with a section for women that includes warm winter sweaters, cool, loose-fitting summer wear, daytime dresses, a chic cocktail dress, two evening tops and, in contrast, a selection of smart outer wear. The men's section, which follows, includes something to please most men, from the ultra-conventional to the more adventurous, and the children's section contains some delightful patterns for babies, including a flower-stitch christening gown, sweaters for older children, and an enchanting party dress for a small girl.

Yarns, and the colors in which they are available, tend to change with the seasons, and it may be that some of the yarns used are not readily available. If you are substituting another yarn for that specified in the pattern, it is extremely important to knit up a gauge sample. If your sample is too tight, change to larger needles, if it is too loose, change to smaller ones. In either case, knit a second sample to make sure that the gauge is now correct before embarking on the pattern.

In the same way, do not worry if the suggested colors are no longer available; it is in any case preferable to make your own choice, for you know that is best suited to your own personality and coloring and what will coordinate with existing clothes or decor.

KNITTING FOR WOMEN
All-over lace

Skills you need

*Decreasing purlwise
*Decreasing knitwise
*Twisting stitches

If you do not know these skills refer to page 175.

Materials

All-over lace knitting is very effective when worked in fine delicate yarn. Chunky, textured yarns tend to obscure the lacy pattern. A touch of glitter yarn, however, produces sparkling highlights that enhance the luxurious appeal of these patterns. If you cannot find a yarn in the desired color, knit glitter embroidery thread in with the chosen yarn. The yarn used here is a mixture of acrylic, wool and mohair of approximately four-ply weight.

Special technique – working a crew neckband

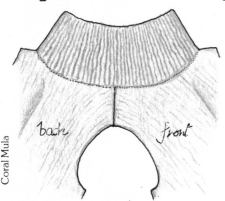

1 *Join the right shoulder seam. Pick up the number of stitches specified in the pattern around the neck edge. Work the ribbing to twice the required depth of neckband. Bind off very loosely in ribbing.*

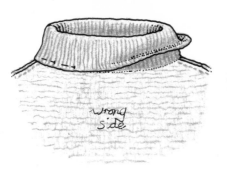

2 *Join the left shoulder seam and the neckband seam. Fold the neckband in half to the wrong side of the garment. Pin the bound-off edge to the inner neck edge.*

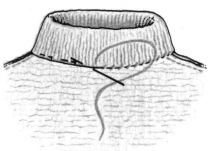

3 *Using matching yarn, thread a tapestry needle and slipstitch the bound-off edge in position.*

Coral Mula

The basic lacy sweater

A fluffy sweater knitted in an elderberry lace pattern that's delicious enough to make your mouth water. It looks equally good with dressy or casual clothes.

Sizes
To fit 32-34[36-38] in. bust.
Length 23[25] in.
Sleeve seam 17 in.
Note: Instructions for larger sizes are in square brackets []; where there is only one set of figures it applies to all sizes.

Gauge
28 sts and 38 rows to 4 in. in pat on size 2 needles

Materials
13 [15] oz lightweight/mohair-blend yarn
1 pair each sizes 1 and 2 knitting needles

Back
**Using smaller needles, cast on 120 [150] sts.
Next row (RS) (K1, P1) to end.
Next row (K1, P1) to end.
Cont in K1, P1 ribbing until work measures 3 in. from beg, ending with a RS row.
Next row Rib 12[15], pick up loop lying between needles and K tbl (called make 1 or M1), (rib 24[30], M1) 4 times, rib to end. 125[155] sts. Change to larger needles, begin pat.
1st row (RS) K3, *K2 tog, P3, K1, yo, P8, (K1, yfwd, K1, yfwd, K1) all into next st, turn, P5, turn, K2 tog tbl, K3 tog, pass first st over 2nd (called make bobble or MB), P8, yo, K1, P3, ybk, sl 1 P-wise, K1, psso, K1, rep from * to last 2 sts, K2.
2nd row K2, P2, *K3, P2, K8, P1 tbl, K8, P2, K3, P3, rep from * to last 4

10

Victor Yuan

sts, P2, K2 instead of P3.
3rd row K4, *P2 tog, P1, K1, yo, P5, MB, P3, K1, P3, MB, P5, yo, K1, P1, P2 tog, K3, rep from * to last st, K1.
4th row K2, P2, *K2, P2, K5, P1 tbl, K3, P1, K3, P1 tbl, K5, P2, K2, P3, rep from * to last 4 sts, P2, K2 instead of P3.
5th row K4, *P2 tog, K1, yo, P2, MB, (P3, K1) 3 times, P3, MB, P2, yo, K1, P2 tog, K3, rep from * to last st, K1.
6th row K2, P2, *K1, P2, K2, P1 tbl, (K3, P1) 3 times, K3, P1 tbl, K2, P2, K1, P3, rep from * to last 4 sts, P2, K2

instead of P3.
7th row K4, *K2 tog, yo, (P3, K1) 5 times, P3, yo, sl 1 P-wise, K1, psso, K3, rep from * to last st, K1.
8th row K2, P4, *(K3, P1) 5 times, K3, P7, rep from * to last 6 sts, P4, K2 instead of P7.
9th row K3, *K2 tog, yo, P4, yo, K1, P3, K1, P1, P2 tog, K1, P2 tog, P1, K1, P3, K1, yo, P4, yo, sl 1 P-wise, K1, psso, K1, rep from * to last 2 sts, K2.
10th row K2, P3, *K4, P2, K3, (P1, K2) twice, P1, K3, P2, K4, P5, rep

from * to last 5 sts, P3, K2 instead of P5.
11th row K2, K2 tog, * yo, P6, yo, K1, P3, (K1, P2 tog) twice, K1, P3, K1, yo, P6, yo, sl 1 P-wise, K2 tog, psso, rep from * to last 4 sts, sl 1 P-wise, K1, psso, K2.
12th row K10, *P2, K3, (P1, K1) twice, P1, K3, P2, K15, rep from * to last 10 sts, K10 instead of K15.
13th row K2, *MB, P8, yo, K1, P3, ybk, sl 1 P-wise, K1, psso, K1, K2 tog, P3, K1, yo, P8, rep from * to last 3 sts, MB, K2.

11

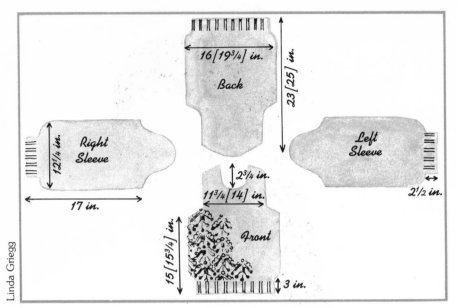

Linda Griegg

14th row K2, *P1 tbl, K8, P2, K3, P3, K3, P2, K8, rep from * to last 3 sts, P1 tbl, K2.

15th row K3,*P3, MB, P5, yo, K1, P1, P2 tog, K3, P2 tog, P1, K1, yo, P5 MB, P3, K1, rep from * to last 2 sts, K2.

16th row K2, *P1, K3, P1 tbl, K5, P2, K2, P3, K2, P2, K5, P1 tbl, K3, rep from * to last 3 sts, P1, K2.

17th row K3, *P3, K1, P3, MB, P2, yo, K1, P2 tog, K3, P2 tog, K1, yo, P2, MB, (P3, K1) twice, rep from * to last 2 sts, K2.

18th row K2, * (P1, K3) twice, P1 tbl, K2, P2, K1, P3, K1, P2, K2, P1 tbl, K3, P1, K3, rep from * to last 3 sts, P1, K2.

19th row K3, *(P3, K1) twice, P3, yo, sl 1 P-wise, K1, psso, K3, K2 tog, yo, (P3, K1) 3 times, rep from * to last 2 sts, K2.

20th row K2, * (P1, K3) 3 times, P7, (K3, P1) twice, K3, rep from * to last 3 sts, P1, K2.

21st row K3, *P2 tog, P1, K1, P3, K1, yo, P4, yo, sl 1 P-wise, K1, psso, K1, K2 tog, yo, P4, yo, K1, P3, K1, P1, P2 tog, K1, rep from * to last 2 sts, K2.

22nd row K2, *P1, K2, P1, K3, P2, K4, P5, K4, P2, K3, P1, K2, rep from * to last 3 sts, P1, K2.

23rd row K3, *P2 tog, K1, P3, K1, yo, P6, yo, sl 1 P-wise, K2 tog, psso, yo, P6, yo, K1, P3, K1, P2 tog, K1, rep from * to last 2 sts, K2.

24th row K2, *P1, K1, P1, K3, P2, K15, P2, K3, P1, K1, rep from * to last 3 sts, P1, K2.

These 24 rows form the elderberry lace pat. Cont in pat until work
12

measures 15[15¾] in. from beg, ending with a WS row.
Shape armholes
Keeping pat correct, bind off 6 sts at beg of next 2 rows. Dec 1st at each end of next 5[9] rows, then dec 1 st at each end of every foll alt row until 93[111] sts rem.**
Cont without shaping until work measures 23[25] in. from beg, ending with a WS row.
Shape shoulders
Keeping pat correct, bind off 8[9] sts at beg of next 4 rows, then 9[10] sts at beg of next 2 rows. Leave rem 43[55] sts on a spare needle.

Front
Work as given for back from ** to **
Cont without shaping until work measures 20[22½] in. from beg, ending with a WS row.
Shape left front neck
Next row Work in pat 35[44] sts, P2 tog, turn, leaving rem sts on a spare needle. Dec 1st at neck edge on every foll row until 25[28] sts rem. Cont without shaping until front matches back to shoulder ending with a WS row.
Shape shoulder
Bind off 8[9] sts at beg of next and every other row once. Work 1 row. Bind off rem 9[10] sts.
Shape right front neck
Return to sts on spare needle, beg at neck edge, sl 19 sts onto a holder. Rejoin yarn to rem sts, P2 tog, pat to end. Complete to match left side, reversing shapings.

Sleeves (alike)
Using smaller needles, cast on 56[62]

sts and work in K1, P1 ribbing as given for back for 2½ in.
Next row Rib 9[15], M1, (rib 1, M1) 38[32] times, rib to end. 95 sts. Change to larger needles and cont in pat as given for back until work measures 17 in. from beg, ending with a WS row.
Shape top
Keeping pat correct, bind off 6 sts at beg of next 2 rows. Dec 1 st at each end of next and foll 4th rows until 79[65] sts rem. Work 1 row. Dec 1 st at each end of next and every other row until 31 sts rem. Work 1 row. Bind off.

To finish
Do not press. Join right shoulder seam.

Neck Border
Using smaller needles and with RS facing, pick up and K 24 sts down left neck, K19 sts from holder, pick up and K 24 sts up right neck, then K43[55] from spare needle. 110[122] sts. Work in K1, P1 ribbing for 2¾ in. Bind off in ribbing. Join left shoulder and neck border fold in half to WS and slip stitch. Set in sleeves. Join side and sleeve seams.

Adapting the lacy sweater

The stitch patterns on the opposite page can be adapted to the lacy sweater pattern or to other patterns you may have.
Choosing a stitch
The row-by-row instructions for the stitch patterns will tell you how they can be adapted to the sweater. In such cases the number of cast-on stitches for the back, front and sleeves, and the shaping instructions for the waistband, armhole and neck edges remain the same. When adapting stitches for other patterns, check that the number of stitches in the pattern repeat is divisible into the number of cast-on stitches, allowing for edge stitches.

Gauge
Work a gauge square in the new stitch pattern. The gauge should match the pattern you are using. Adjust the needle size if necessary. If both row and stitch gauge cannot be matched, use a needle size that will achieve the correct stitch gauge and follow the measurement diagram for length. All-over lace patterns cannot easily be adapted to plain garment patterns.

All-over lace patterns

1 Simple lace

This stitch usually repeats over 6 stitches plus 1 extra.
By adding 4 edge stitches it can be adapted for the sweater pattern as follows:
Cast on a multiple of 6 sts, plus 5 extra.

1st and 3rd rows (WS) P2 tbl, *P2 tbl, P3, P1 tbl, rep from * to last 3 sts, P3 tbl.

2nd row K2 tbl,*K2 tbl, yfwd, sl 1, K2 tog, psso, yfwd, K1 tbl, rep from * to last 3 sts, K3 tbl.

4th row K2 tbl, *K2 tbl, K3, K1 tbl, rep from * to last 3 sts, K3 tbl.
These 4 rows form the pattern repeat.

2 Dewdrop

This stitch usually repeats over 6 stitches plus 1 extra. By adding 2 edge stitches on either side it can be adapted to the sweater pattern as follows:
Cast on a multiple of 6 sts, plus 5 extra.

1st row K2, K2 tog, yfwd, *K3, yfwd, sl 1, K2 tog, psso, yfwd, rep from * to last st, K1.

2nd and 4th rows K4, *P3, K3, rep from * to last st, K1.

3rd row P4, *K3, P3, rep from * to last st, P1.

5th row P4, *yo, sl 1, K2 tog, psso, yo, P3, rep from * to last st, P1.
These 5 rows form the pattern repeat.

3 Florette

This stitch is adaptable to the basic sweater pattern. Cast on a multiple of 6 stitches, plus 5 extra.

1st row K2, *K1, yfwd, K2 tog tbl, K1, K2 tog, yfwd, rep from * to last 3 sts, K3.

2nd and every other row P across sts.

3rd row K2, *K2, yfwd, K3, yfwd, K1, rep from * to last 3 sts, K3.

5th row K2, K2 tog, *yfwd, K2 tog tbl, K1, K2 tog, yfwd, sl 1, K2 tog, psso, rep from * to last 9 sts, yfwd, K2 tog tbl, K1, K2 tog, yfwd, K2 tog tbl, K2.

7th row K2, *K1, K2 tog, yfwd, K1, yfwd, K2 tog tbl, rep from * to last 3 sts, K3.

8th row P across sts.
These 8 rows form the pattern repeat.

4 Grape hyacinth

This stitch usually repeats over 6 stitches plus 1 extra. By adding 2 edge stitches either side it can be adapted for the sweater pattern as follows:
Cast on a multiple of 6 sts, plus 5 extra.

1st, 3rd, 5th, 7th, 9th and 11th rows K2, *K1, K2 tog, yfwd, K1, yfwd, sl 1, K1, psso, rep from * to last 3 sts, K3.

2nd and every other row P across sts.

13th, 15th, 17th, 19th, 21st and 23rd rows K2, * K1, yfwd, sl 1, K1, psso, K1, K2 tog, yfwd, rep from *to last 3 sts, K3.

24th row P across sts.
These 24 rows form pattern repeat.

1

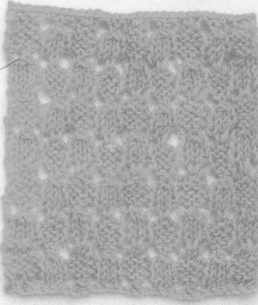

2

3

4

Op-art patterns

Intricate eye-catching geometric patterns translate well into knitted fabrics and make for smooth smart garments that are eminently wearable.

Skills you need

*Decreasing
*Simple increasing
*Working with color

If you do not know these skills refer to pages 174 and 175.

Materials

Op-art designs are generally thought of as being in black and white only but the term can be used to describe any visually striking geometric pattern that has some element of optical illusion. The most suitable yarn for such pat-terns are the smooth plain types in which the sharp outlines and angles can be emphasized. The basic cardigan is worked in pure wool knitting worsted and the vest in sport-weight yarn.

Special technique – working an armband

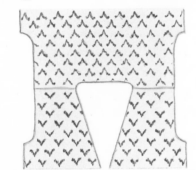

1 *The basic vest has armbands that are knitted onto the main pattern pieces. Begin by joining the shoulder seams.*

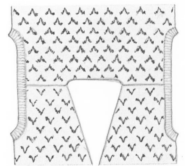

2 *With right side of work facing, pick up and knit the required number of stitches evenly around armhole edge. Work in single ribbing as required. Bind off in ribbing.*

3 *Finish by joining the side seams. Join the ribbed waistband and armband with a flat seam. Join the stockinette stitch parts with an invisible seam.*

Coral Mula

The basic op-art twinset

Put on the style in this super-sophisticated but unusual two-piece combining a pocketed vest and classic cardigan in an interesting positive-negative color scheme.

Sizes
To fit 32[34:36:38] in. bust
Vest length 22[22½:23:23½] in.
Cardigan length 26[26½:27:27½] in.
Sleeve seam 17[17:17¼:17¼] in.

Note: Instructions for larger sizes are in square brackets []; where there is only one set of figures it applies to all sizes.

Gauge
Vest:
31 sts and 34 rows to 4 in. over pat on size 3 needles
Cardigan:

14

19 sts and 24 rows to 4 in. over pat on size 6 needles

Materials
Vest:
9[10:10:12] oz sport-weight yarn in main color (A)
3[3:5:5] oz in contrasting color (B)
1 pair each sizes 2 and 3 knitting needles
6 buttons
Cardigan:
21[21:23:23] oz of knitting worsted in main color (C)
7[7:8:8] oz in contrasting color (D)
1 pair each sizes 4 and 6 knitting

needles
7 buttons

Vest
Back
Using smaller needles and A, cast on 103[109:115:123] sts.
Work in K1, P1 ribbing as foll:
1st row (RS) K1, *P1, K1, rep from * to end.
2nd row P1, *K1, P1, rep from * to end.
Rep the last 2 rows for 3 in. ending with a first row.
Next row Rib 11[12:13:15], pick up loop between last st worked and next st and work into back of it (called M1), (rib 2, M1) 41[43:45:47] times, rib to end. 145[153:161:171] sts.
Change to larger needles and work in

Chris Davies

stockinette st foll pat from Chart 1, working edge sts as shown and rep the 12 pat sts across the row.
Cont in pat until work measures 13½[13½:13½:13¾] in. from cast-on edge, ending with a WS row.

Shape armholes
Keeping pat correct, bind off 7 sts at beg of next 2 rows.
Dec 1 st at each of the next 9[9:11:11]

rows, then at each end of every other row until 99[103:105:113] sts rem.
Cont without shaping until work measures 22[22½:23:23½] in. from cast-on edge, ending with a WS row.

Shape shoulders
Bind off 8[9:8:9] sts at beg of next 4 rows and 9[8:9:10] sts at beg of foll 2 rows.
Bind off rem 49[51:55:57] sts.

Pocket lining
Using larger needles and A, cast on 31 sts. Beg with a K row cont in stockinette st until work measures 4 in. from beg, ending with a P row.
Leave these sts on a spare needle.

Left front
**Using smaller needles and A, cast on 51[55:57:61] sts.

15

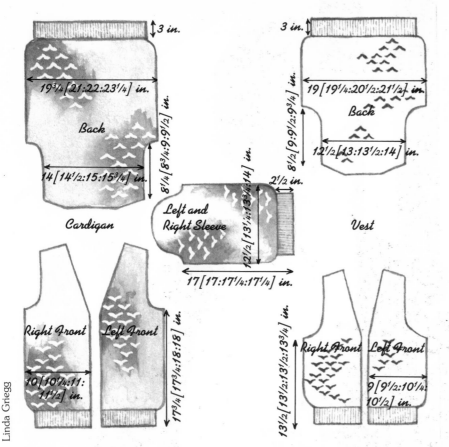

Back

19¾[21:22:23¼] in.

Cardigan

14[14½:15:15¾] in.

8¼[8¾:9:9½] in.

Left and Right Sleeve

12½[13½:13¾:14] in.

17[17:17¼:17¼] in.

3 in.

Back

Vest

19[19¼:20½:21½] in.

12½[13:13½:14] in.

8½[9:9½:9¾] in.

2½ in.

3 in.

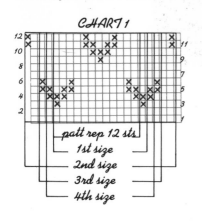

Right Front   Left Front

10[10¼:11:11½] in.

17¾[17¾:18:18] in.

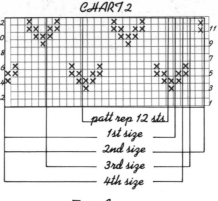

Right Front   Left Front

9[9½:10¼:10½] in.

13½[13½:13½:13¾] in.

Work in K1, P1 ribbing as given for back for 3 in. ending with a 1st row.
Next row Rib 6[8:7:8], M1, (rib 2, M1) 20[20:22:23] times, rib to end. 72[76:80:85] sts. **
Change to larger needles and work in stockinette st foll pat from Chart 2.
Cont in pat until work measures 7 in. from cast-on edge, ending with a WS row.

Place pocket
Next row Work in pat on 16[18:20:22] sts, sl next 41 sts onto a stitch holder, pat across 31 sts of pocket lining *at same time* inc 10 sts evenly, work in pat to end.
Cont in pat until work matches back

to underarm, ending with a WS row.
Shape armhole and neck
Next row Bind off 7 sts, work in pat to last 2 sts, K2 tog.
Next row Work in pat to end.
Dec 1 st at armhole edge on next 9[9:11:11] rows then on every other row and *at the same time*, dec 1 st at neck edge on the next and every other row until 36[36:35:38] sts rem.
Keeping armhole edge straight cont to dec at neck edge on every 3rd row until 25[26:25:28] sts rem.
Cont without shaping until work matches back to shoulder shaping ending with a WS row.
Shape shoulder

Bind off 8[9:8:9] sts at beg of next and every other row. Work 1 row. Bind off rem 9[8:9:10] sts.

Right front
Work as given for left front from ** to **.
Change to larger needles and work in stockinette st foll pat from Chart 3. Complete to match left front, omitting pocket and reversing shapings.

To finish
Do not press.
Join shoulder seams.
Pocket edging
With RS of work facing, using smaller needles, join in A to 41sts on stitch holder.
1st row K1, *P1, K1, rep from * to end.
2nd row P1, *K1, P1, rep from * to end.
Rep the last 2 rows 3 times more.
Bind off in ribbing.
Tack down pocket edging and pocket lining.
Buttonband
Using smaller needles and A, cast on 11 sts.
1st row (RS) K2, *P1, K1, rep from * to last st, K1.
2nd row *K1, P1, rep from * to last st, K1.
Rep the last 2 rows until band, when slightly stretched, fits up left front edge to centre back neck.
Bind off in ribbing.
Buttonhole band
Sew on buttonband. Mark the position of six buttonholes, the first to come ¾ in. from lower edge, the last ¾ in. below front neck shaping, with the others evenly spaced between.
Using smaller needles and A, cast on 11 sts.
Work as given for button band making buttonholes opposite markers as foll:

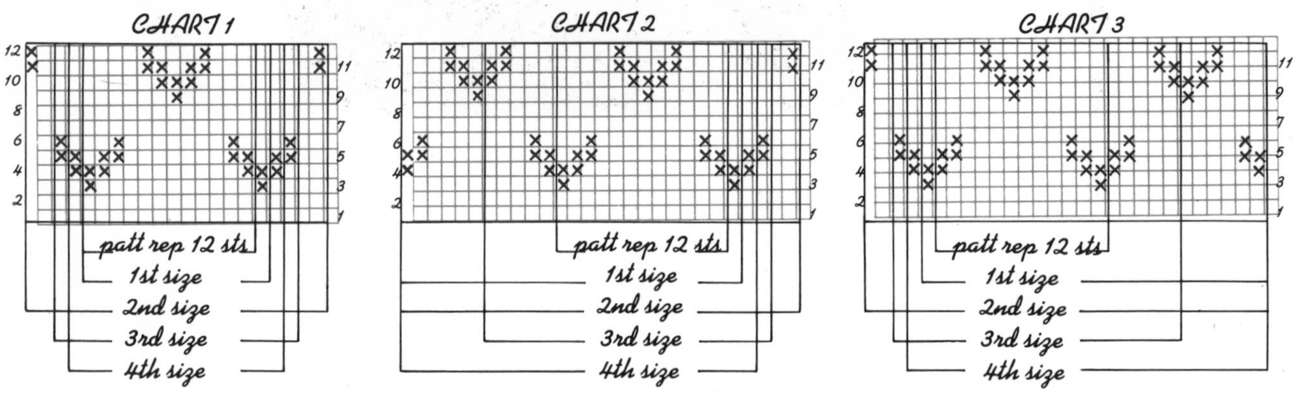

CHART 1

patt rep 12 sts
1st size
2nd size
3rd size
4th size

CHART 2

patt rep 12 sts
1st size
2nd size
3rd size
4th size

CHART 3

patt rep 12 sts
1st size
2nd size
3rd size
4th size

□ = A
× = B   *Vest Key*

Linda Griegg

Dennis Hawkins

1st row (RS) Rib 5, bind off 2, rib 4.
2nd row Rib 4, cast on 2, rib 5.
Sew on buttonhole band, joining to
buttonband at center back neck.

Armbands

With RS of working facing, using
smaller needles and A, pick up and K
114[118:124:130] sts evenly around
the armhole edge.
Work 10 rows of K1, P1 ribbing. Bind
off in ribbing.
Join side seams. Sew on buttons.

Cardigan

Back

Using smaller needles and C, cast on
81[85:91:97] sts and work in K1, P1
ribbing as given for vest back for 3 in.
ending with a first row.
Next row Rib 8[5:8:4], M1, (rib
5[5:5:6], M1) 13[15:15:15] times, rib
to end. 95[101:107:113] sts.
Change to larger needles and work in
stockinette st foll pat from Chart 4.
Cont in pat until work measures
approx 17¾[17¾:18:18] in. from
cast-on edge, ending with a WS row.

Shape armholes

Keeping pat correct, bind off 5 sts at
beg of next 2 rows. Dec 1 st at each
end of the next 3[3:5:5] rows, then on
every other row until 69[71:73:77] sts
rem.
Cont without shaping until work
measures 26[26½:27:27½] in. from
cast-on edge, ending with a WS row.

Shape shoulders

Bind off 6[6:6:7] sts at beg of next 4
rows and 7[7:7:6] sts at beg of next 2
rows.
Bind off rem 31[33:35:37] sts.

Left front

***Using smaller needles and C, cast
on 39[41:45:47] sts and work in K1,
P1 ribbing as given for vest back for 3
in. ending with a first row.
Next row Rib 2[5:5:4], M1, (rib
5[4:5:5], M1) 7[8:7:8] times, rib to
end. 47[50:53:56] sts. ***
Change to larger needles and work in
stockinette st as foll pat from Chart 5.
Cont in pat until work matches back
to underarm, ending with a WS row.

Shape armhole and neck

Next row Bind off 5 sts, work in pat to
last 2 sts, K2 tog.
Next row Work in pat to end.
Dec 1 st at armhole edge on the next
3[3:5:5] rows then on every other row
at the same time, dec 1 st at neck edge
on the next and every other row until
19[19:19:20] sts rem. Cont without
shaping until work matches back to

shoulder shaping, ending with a WS
row.

Shape shoulder

Bind off 6[6:6:7] sts at beg of next and
every other row.
Work 1 row.
Bind off rem 7[7:7:6] sts.

Right front

Work as given for left front from ***
to ***.
Change to larger needles and working
in pat from Chart 6 complete to match
left front, reversing shapings.

Sleeves

Using smaller needles and C, cast on
38[40:42:44] sts and work in K1, P1
ribbing for 2½ in.
Next row Rib 8[8:9:10], M1, (rib 1,
M1) 22[24:24:24] times, rib to end.
61[65:67:69] sts.
Change to larger needles and work in
stockinette st foll pat from Chart 7.
Cont in pat until work measures
approx 17[17:17¼:17¼] in. from
cast-on edge, ending with a
6th[6th:8th:8th] pat row.

Shape top

Keeping pat correct, bind off 5 sts at
beg of next 2 rows.

First size only

Dec 1 st at each end of the next and
foll 4th row. Work 1 row. 47 sts.

All sizes

Dec 1 st at each end of the next and
every other row until 21 sts rem,
ending with a WS row. Bind off.

To finish

Do not press.
Join shoulder, side and sleeve seams.
Set in sleeves.

Buttonband

Using smaller needles and C, cast on
9 sts.
Work as given for buttonband of vest.

Buttonhole band

Sew on buttonband. Mark the position
of seven buttonholes, the first to come
¾ in. from lower edge, the last ¾ in.
below front neck shaping, with the
others evenly spaced between.
Using smaller needles and C, cast on
9 sts.
Work as given for buttonband, making
buttonholes opposite markers as foll:
1st row (RS) Rib 4, bind off 2, rib 3.
2nd row Rib 3, cast on 2, rib 4.
Sew on buttonhole band, joining to
buttonband at center back neck.
Sew on buttons.

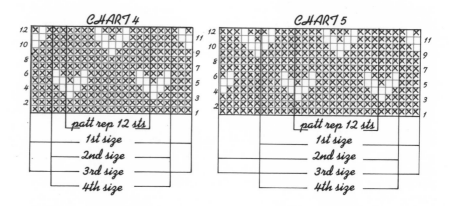

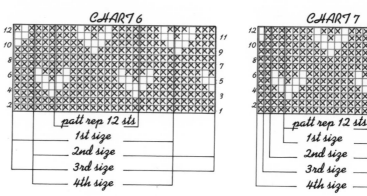

Cardigan Key   × = C
□ = D

Checked patterns

Checks are found among the traditional patterns of almost every country. The simple grid format offers great potential for color variation whether bold, subtle or beautifully intricate.

Skills you need

*Decreasing
*Simple increasing
*Working with color

If you do not know these skills refer to pages 174 and 175.

Materials

Large checked patterns can be worked in any type of yarn and lend themselves well to combinations of smooth and fancy yarns. The fine details of color and line in small checks are best expressed in smooth plain yarns such as the pure wool sport-weight yarn used in the basic checked sweater. Such yarns tend to emphasize the essentially countrified appeal of checked patterns. The same patterns worked in glitter yarns are beautifully glamorous.

Special technique – fitting shoulder pads

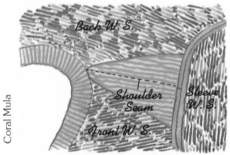
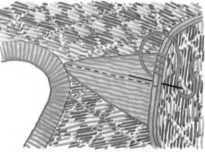
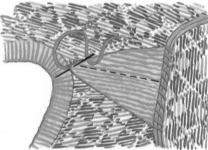

Coral Mula

1 *Place the center of the base of the shoulder pad to the join of the shoulder seam and sleeve cap on the wrong side of the work. Place the apex at the other end of the shoulder seam.*

2 *Thread a tapestry needle with matching yarn and sew the base of the shoulder pad around the sleeve seam.*

3 *Catchstitch the apex of the shoulder pad to the other end of the shoulder seam.*

The basic checked sweater

The clear lines of a traditional argyle pattern from Scotland are displayed to perfection on this slinky V-necked sweater.

Sizes
To fit Misses' size 10[12:14]
Length 22¾[23½:24] in.
Sleeve seam 17 in.
Note: Instructions for larger sizes are in square brackets []; where there is only one set of figures it applies to all sizes.

Gauge
32 sts and 32 rows to 4 in. over pat on size 3 needles

Materials
11[11:13] oz of a sport-weight yarn in camel, main color (A)
6[6:7] oz in dark chocolate, contrasting color, (B)
2[4:4] oz in blue jay, contrasting color (C)
4[4:6] oz in claret, contrasting color (D)
1 pair each size 2 and 3 knitting needles

Back
***Using smaller needles and A, cast on 133[140:148] sts.
Next row *K1, P1, rep from * to last 1[0:0] sts, K1[0:0].
Next row P1[0:0], *K1, P1 rep from * to end.
Rep the last 2 rows for 2¼ in. ending with a RS row.

Next row Rib 6[4:8], pick up loop lying between needles and work into back of it – called make one (M1), (rib 11[12:12], M1) 11 times, rib to end. 145[152:160] sts.
Change to larger needles. Working in stockinette st, begin pat from chart. Work rows 1-38 inclusive once. Now rep rows 1-38 inclusive using C instead of D. Cont in this way, repeating the last 76 rows, until work measures 15 in. from cast-on edge, ending with a WS row.**
Shape armholes
Bind off 3 sts at beg of next 2 rows. Dec 1 st at each end of every row until 119[126:134] sts rem, then dec 1 st at each end of every other row until 105[110:116] sts rem. Cont without shaping until work measures

18

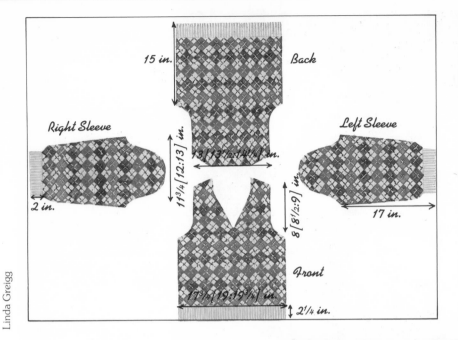

Right Sleeve
15 in.
Back
2 in.
11¾[12:13] in.
13[13½:14¼] in.
Left Sleeve
17 in.
8[8½:9] in.
Front
17¾[19:19¾] in.
2¼ in.

Complete to match first side of neck, reversing all shapings.

Sleeves

Using smaller needles and A, cast on 66[68:70] sts, work in K1, P1 ribbing for 2 in., ending with a RS row.

Next row Rib 4, M1, rib 5[6:7], M1, (rib 7, M1) 7 times, rib 5[6:7], M1, rib to end. 76[78:80] sts.

Change to larger needles and stockinette st.

Beg with the 21st row, begin pat from chart, *at the same time*, inc 1 st at each end of every 10th[9th:8th] row until there are 96[100:104] sts. Cont without shaping until work measures approx 17 in. from beg, ending with the same pat row as back.

Shape top

Bind off 3 sts at beg of next 2 rows. Dec 1 st at each end of every foll 4th row until 86[90:94] sts rem, then dec

22¾[23½:24] in. from beg, ending with a WS row.

Shape shoulders

Bind off 10 sts at beg of next 4 rows and 10[12:14] sts at beg of foll 2 rows. Leave rem 45[46:48] sts on spare needle.

Front

Work as given for back from ** to **.

Shape armholes and divide for neck

Next row Bind off 3, work in pat 67[71:75] sts, K2 tog and turn, leave rem sts on a spare needle.

Work 1 row. Cont on these 68[72:76] sts for first side of neck.

Dec 1 st at neck edge on next and every other row and *at the same time* dec 1 st at armhole edge on every row until 53[57:61] sts rem then on every other row until 39[41:43] sts rem. Keeping armhole edge straight, cont to dec at neck edge on every 3rd row until 30[32:34] sts rem.

Cont without shaping until work matches back to shoulder shaping, ending with a WS row.

Shape shoulder

Bind off 10 sts at beg of next and every other row once. Work 1 row. Bind off rem sts. Return to sts on spare needle.

First size only

Sl first st onto a safety pin for front neck, rejoin yarn to next st, work 2 tog, work in pat to end.

2nd and 3rd sizes

Rejoin yarn to next st, work 2 tog, work in pat to end.

All sizes

Next row Bind off 3, work in pat to end.

20

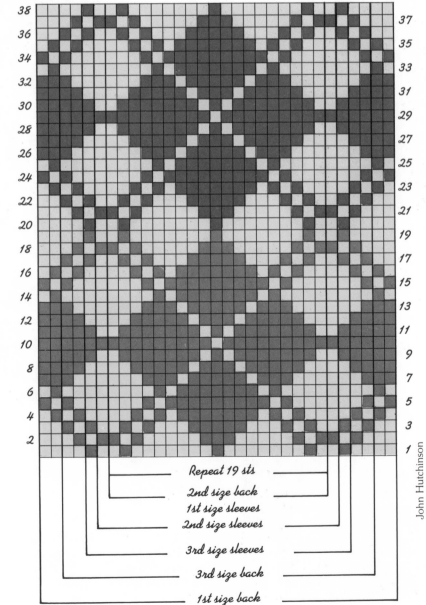

38 36 34 32 30 28 26 24 22 20 18 16 14 12 10 8 6 4 2

37 35 33 31 29 27 25 23 21 19 17 15 13 11 9 7 5 3 1

Repeat 19 sts
2nd size back
1st size sleeves
2nd size sleeves
3rd size sleeves
3rd size back
1st size back

1 st at each end of every other row until 48 sts rem. Bind off.

Shoulder pads (make 2)
Using larger needles and A, cast on 30 sts.
Work in K1, P1 ribbing for 2 rows.
Cont in K1, P1 ribbing dec 1 st at each end of the next and every foll 3rd row until 20 sts rem.
Work 1 row.
Dec 1 st at each end of the next and every other row until 2 sts rem.
Lift the 2nd st over the 1st st and off the needle. Fasten off.

To finish
Press lightly with a warm iron over a damp cloth. Join right shoulder seam.
Neck border
With RS facing, using smaller needles and A, pick up and K 70[74:78] sts down left side of neck, K1[M1:M1],

(mark this st), pick up and K 70[74:78] sts up right side of neck, K across back neck sts, dec 1 st on *first size only.* 185[195:205] sts.

Next row (WS) Work in K1, P1 ribbing to within 2 sts of center marked st, K2 tog, P1, K2 tog, rib to end.
Next row Rib to within 2 sts of center st, P2 tog, K1, P2 tog, rib to end.
Rep the last 2 rows 4 times more.
Bind off in ribbing, dec on this row as before.
Join left shoulder seam and neck border. Set in sleeves easing fullness evenly around sleeve cap. Join side and sleeve seams. Sew shoulder pads in position.

Adapting the check sweater

Experiment with other checked patterns.

Ideally, checked patterns should match perfectly at the side seams. The staggered-checked pattern can be used on the basic sweater by working the back and front with the four-stitch repeat and only one edge stitch for the back and front of the first size, none for

the second and third sizes; none on the sleeve of the first and third sizes and two for the second size. Both charts show the basic pattern repeat plus edge stitches and the diamond-check pattern has a centralizing stitch (the stitch immediately to the left of the pattern repeat). If the whole chart cannot be fitted into the pattern, work the repeat without edge stitches.

Check patterns

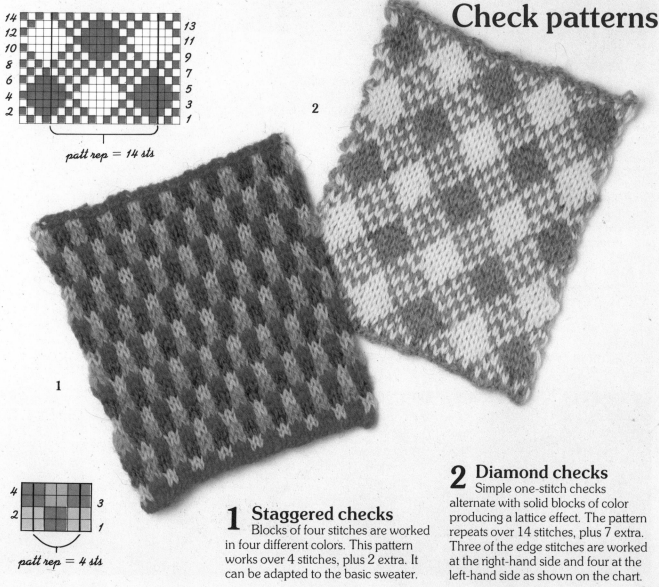

patt rep = 14 sts

patt rep = 4 sts

1 Staggered checks
Blocks of four stitches are worked in four different colors. This pattern works over 4 stitches, plus 2 extra. It can be adapted to the basic sweater.

2 Diamond checks
Simple one-stitch checks alternate with solid blocks of color producing a lattice effect. The pattern repeats over 14 stitches, plus 7 extra. Three of the edge stitches are worked at the right-hand side and four at the left-hand side as shown on the chart.

Steve Campbell

Grundy & Northedge

All measurements in inches.
Size 34/36 [38/40]

5½[8]

2¼[2½]
5½[6¼]

Left Front   Back   Right Front

15¾[17¾]
Sleeve

15[16½]

15¾[19]

10½[11¾]   20½[23½]   10½[11¾]

3

9¾[10½]

2

Unisex jacket

Quick-to-knit, chunky, unisex jacket featuring gray, black and orange cats.

Sizes
Chest 34/35¾[37½/39½] in.
Length 26¾[28¾] in.
Sleeve length 17¾[21] in.

Gauge
15 sts and 17 rows to 4 in. over stockinette st on size 8 needles

Materials
18 oz of a semi-bulky Shetland-type yarn in MC
2 oz each of contrasting colors (A), (B) and (C)

1 pair each size 6 and 8 circular needles 30 in. long
1 pair each size 6 and 8 needles
One 23½[25½] in heavyweight black zipper

Fronts and back (knitted in one)
Using smaller circular needle, cast on 145[165] sts in MC. Knit 20 rows of K1, P1 ribbing. Change to larger needle and K to end, inc 15 sts evenly across to 160[180] sts. Purl next row.
23rd row Cont in stockinette st, mark off the fronts and back sections as in diagram (spread out additional sts for larger sizes evenly across the design). Working from chart and changing direction line of cats and color cont until 88[94] rows have been completed. Divide the work for armholes.

Fronts
Work 24[28] rows following chart and knit in triangles as shown in alternating lines of A, B and C. To shape the neck, bind off 6 sts at beg of next row, 2 sts at beg of every other row until 29 sts rem. Work straight to end of chart, leave sts on a needle.

Back
Work 34[38] rows. Work straight to end of chart, leave sts on a needle.

Sleeves (knitted flat)
Using smaller needles, cast on 32[38] sts in MC. Work 14 rows of K1, P1 ribbing. Change to larger needles and knit to end, inc 6[4] sts evenly across to 38[42] sts. Purl next row.
17th row Following triangles only on chart, cont in stockinette st inc 1 st at each end of every 8th[10th] row. Work without shaping to 80[94] rows from beg. Bind off.

To finish
Join shoulder seams. Join sleeve seams and sew in. With RS of work facing, pick up and K 16 sts from right front neck, 21 sts from back and 16 sts from left front neck. Work in K1, P1 ribbing for 16 rows. Bind off. Sew in the zipper, turn the neckband over and slipstitch to the inside of the jacket.

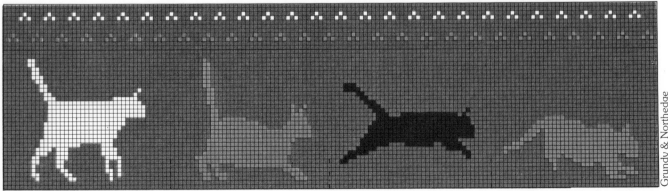

Grundy & Northedge

Smocking

Smocking effects can be achieved in knitted fabrics in a number of ways. There are several stitch patterns that have a smocked look and it is also possible to knit a background fabric that can then be smocked with simple embroidery stitches to give the familiar honeycomb pattern.

Ron Kelly

Skills you need

*Decreasing
*Simple increasing
*Smocking

If you do not know these skills refer to pages 174, 175 and 184.

Materials

Smocking can be worked with almost any type of yarn. Heavy bouclé or slub yarns are unsuitable but fluffy angora and mohair can produce particularly pretty smocked fabrics, especially when further decorated with small beads or seed pearls. Fine cotton yarns are the most successful materials for the traditional smocked effect, but chunky wool produces interesting three-dimensional fabrics. The basic sweater is made in a smooth sport-weight yarn that is composed of wool and alpaca fibers.

Special technique – working the smocking

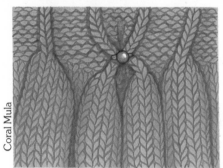

Coral Mula

1 *The smocking is worked over the center ten knit ribs on the front of the sweater. Begin with the center two ribs. Use a needle threaded with matching yarn. Secure the yarn at the back of the work. Bring the needle through to the front on the left of the pair. Take it through to the back on the right, then to the front again. Thread a bead onto the yarn and push it up to the work, drawing the ribs together. Take the yarn through to the back.*

2 *Leaving four rows between, draw together the pairs of ribs on either side of the first pair as shown, placing a bead on each one as before.*

3 *Leaving four rows between, draw together the middle pair of ribs and two pairs on either side of the middle pair. Carry on in this way, smocking alternate pairs of ribs to produce a honeycomb effect, working evenly from right to left on each smocking row.*

The basic smocked sweater

A prettily pointed frill and a beaded smocked front panel give this beautifully shaped sweater a romantic medieval look.

Sizes
To fit 34[36:38] in. bust
Length (including ruffle)
21¼[21¾:22½] in.
Sleeve seam (including ruffle) 18 in.

Note: Instructions for the larger sizes are in square brackets []; where there is only one set of figures it applies to all sizes.

Gauge
24 sts and 30 rows to 4 in. measured over main rib pat on size 5 needles

Materials
23[25:27] oz alpaca-blend sport-weight yarn or 27[29:31] oz knitting worsted
1 pair each size 3 and 5 knitting
1 size 5 circular needle
approx 110 small beads

Front
Using larger needles, cast on 3 sts.
Begin shaping.
1st row K3.
2nd row (RS) Cast on 4 sts and work across sts as foll: P2, K1, P4.
3rd row Cast on 4 sts and work as foll: K2, P1, K5, P1, K2.
4th row Cast on 5 sts and work as foll: P1, K1, (P5, K1) twice, P2.
5th row Cast on 5 sts and work as foll: K1, P1, (K5, P1) 3 times, K1.
6th row Cast on 5 sts and work as foll: K1, (P5, K1) 4 times, P1.
7th row Cast on 5 sts and work as foll: P1, (K5, P1) 5 times.

Cont in this way, casting on 5[6:6] sts at beg of next 4[8:6] rows, working extra sts into pat. Then cast on 6[7:7] sts at beg of foll 6[8:8] rows.
First and 3rd sizes only
Cast on 7[8] sts at beg of next 6[4] rows.
All sizes
Cont in pat as set on these 129[135:141] sts until work measures 11½[11½:12] in. measured at side edge, ending with a WS row.
Shape armholes and divide for neck
Next row Bind off 4[5:6] sts, work in pat for 58[60:62] sts including st used in binding off, K2 tog and turn, leaving rem sts on a spare needle.
Complete left side of neck first.
Work 1 row.
**Dec 1 st at armhole edge on next 3[5:5] rows, then on every other row, *at the same time*, dec 1 st at neck edge

24

on next and every other row until 40[41:43] sts rem.

Keeping armhole edge straight, cont to dec at neck edge only as before until 20[20:21] sts rem, ending with a RS row.

Cont without shaping. Work 3 rows.

Shape shoulder

Bind off 7 sts at beg of next and every other row.

Work 1 row.

Bind off rem 6[6:7] sts. **

With RS of work facing, return to sts on spare needle, Sl center st onto a safety pin, join in yarn to rem sts, K2 tog, work in pat to end.

Next row Bind off 4[5:6], work in pat to end.

Complete to match first side of neck, work from ** to **, reversing shapings, and working 4 rows before shoulder shaping.

Front lower edge frill

With RS of work facing, using circular needle, pick up and K 129[135:141] sts around lower edge. Work in rows.

1st row (WS) K1[4:1], *P1, K5, rep from * to last 2[5:2] sts, P1, K1[4:1].

2nd row P1[4:1], pick up loop between last st and next st on LH needle and work into the back of it (called M1), *K1, M1, P5, M1, rep from * to last 2[5:2] sts, K1, M1, P1[4:1].

3rd row K1[4:1], *P3, K5, rep from * to last 4[7:4] sts, P3, K1[4:1].

4th row P1[4:1], M1, *K3, M1, P5, M1, rep from * to last 4[7:4] sts, K3, M1, P1[4:1].

5th row K1[4:1], *P5, K5, rep from * to last 6[9:6] sts, P5, K1[4:1].

6th row P1[4:1], M1, *K5, M1, P5, M1, rep from * to last 6[9:6] sts, K5, M1, P1[4:1].

7th row K1[4:1], *P7, K5, rep from * to last 8[11:8] sts, P7, K1[4:1].

8th row P1[4:1], M1, *K7, M1, P5, M1, rep from * to last 8[11:8] sts, K7, M1, P1[4:1].

9th row K1[4:1], *P9, K5, rep from * to last 10[13:10] sts, P9, K1[4:1].

10th row P1[4:1], M1, *K9, M1, P5, M1, rep from * to last 10[13:10] sts, K9, M1, P1[4:1].

11th row K1[4:1], *P11, K5, rep from * to last 12[15:12] sts, P11, K1[4:1].

12th row P1[4:1], *K11, P5, rep from * to last 12[15:12] sts, K11, P1[4:1].

Rep last 2 rows until frill measures 2 in. from beg. ending with a WS row.

Bind off in ribbing as set.

Back

Using larger needles, cast on 105[111:117] sts.

Begin pat.

1st row (RS) P1[4:1], *K1, P5, rep from * to last 2[5:2] sts, K1, P1[4:1].

2nd row K1[4:1], *P1, K5, rep from * to last 2[5:2] sts, P1, K1[4:1].

These 2 rows form the rib pat. Cont in pat until work measures same as front to underarm at side seam, ending with a WS row.

Shape armholes

Keeping pat correct, bind off 4[5:6] sts at beg of next 2 rows.

Dec 1 st at each end of next 3[5:5] rows, then on every other row until 77[79:83] sts rem.

Cont without shaping until work matches front to shoulder shaping, ending at armhole edge.

Shape shoulders

Bind off 7 sts at beg of next 4 rows, then 6[6:7] sts at beg of foll 2 rows.

Leave rem 37[39:41] sts on a spare needle.

Back lower edge frill

With RS of work facing, using circular needle, pick up and K 105[111:117] sts around lower edge.

Work as given for front lower edge frill

Sleeves

Using smaller needles, cast on 51[51:57] sts.

1st row K1, *P1, K1, rep from * to end of row.

2nd row P1, *K1, P1, rep from * to end.

Rep the last 2 rows for ¾ in., ending with a 2nd row.

Change to larger needles and begin pat as given for back. Inc and work into pat 1 st at each end of the 5th and every foll 8th row until there are 75[75:81] sts.

Cont without shaping until work measures 16 in. from cast-on edge, ending with a WS row.

Shape top

Bind off 4[5:6] sts at beg of next 2 rows. Dec 1 st at each end of next and every foll 4th row until 51[45:49] sts rem, then at each end of every other row until 37 sts rem, ending with a WS row.

Next row K2 tog, K2, *(K2 tog) twice, K2, rep from * to last 3 sts, K2 tog, K1, 25 sts.

Bind off.

Sleeve frills

With RS of work facing, using larger needles, pick up and K 51[51:57] sts along lower edge of sleeve.

Work as given for front lower edge frill.

To finish

Do not press.

Work smocking over central panel of 55 sts. (See Special Technique page 24).

Join right shoulder.

17¼[18:19¼] in.

11½[11½:12] in.

Back

12½[13:13¾] in.

8¼[8¼:9½] in.

Right Sleeve

12¼[12¼:13¾] in.

Left Sleeve

16 in.

8[8¼:8½] in.

Front – before smocking

21¼[22:23¼] in.

Jan Mason

Neck frill
With WS of work facing, using larger needles, K across 37[39:41] sts on back, pick up and K 49[54:60] sts down right side of neck, K center st, pick up and K 50[55:59] sts up left side of neck. 137[149:161] sts.
1st row (WS) K2[2:5], *P1, K5, rep from * to last 3[3:6] sts, P1, K2[2:5].
2nd row P2[2:5], M1, *K1, M1, P5, M1, rep from * to last 3[3:6] sts, K1, M1, P2[2:5].
3rd row K2[2:5], *P3, K5, rep from * to last 5[5:8] sts, P3, K2[2:5].

4th row P2[2:5], M1, *K3, M1, P5, M1, rep from * to last 5[5:8] sts, K3, P2[2:5].
5th row K2[2:5], *P5, K5, rep from * to last 7[7:10] sts, P5, K2[2:5].
6th row P2[2:5], M1, *K5, M1, P5, M1, rep from * to last 7[7:10] sts, K5, M1, P2[2:5].
7th row K2[2:5], *P7, K5, rep from * to last 9[9:12] sts, P7, K2[2:5].
8th row P2[2:5], M1, *K7, M1, P5, M1, rep from * to last 3[3:6] sts, K1, M1, P2[2:5].
9th row K2[2:5], *P9, K5, rep from *

to last 11[11:14] sts, P9, K2[2:5].
10th row P2[2:5], M1, *K9, M1, P5, M1, rep from * to last 11[11:14] sts, K9, M1, K2[2:5].
11th row K2[2:5], *P11, K5, rep from * to last 13[13:16] sts, P11, K2[2:5].
12th row P2[2:5], *K11, P5, rep from * to last 13[13:16] sts, K11, P2[2:5].
Rep last 2 rows until frill measures 2 in., ending WS. Bind off in rib as set. Join left shoulder, neck frill, side and sleeve seams. Set in sleeves.

Adapting the smocked sweater

The Pattern Library samples suggest some new ways to decorate the smocked panel to give the sweater a different look.

The stitch tension of smocking patterns varies considerably so it is advisable to restrict adaptations of the sweater to surface decoration on the knitted fabric. As the Pattern Library samples show, the smocking itself can be carried out in different colors or textures of yarn or contrasting colors can be introduced in the knitting. Various embroidery stitches can also be used — chain stitch on the ribs or French knots in the hollows of the pattern.

1 Smocking stitch
This pattern is worked over a multiple of 8 stitches, plus 2 extra.
1st and every other row (WS) K2, *P2, K2, rep from * to end.
2nd row P2, *K2, P2, rep from * to end.
4th row P2, *ybk, insert RH needle from front to back between 6th and 7th sts on LH needle, take the yarn under and over the needle and draw a loop through to RS, place loop on LH needle and K it tog with next st (called smock 1), K1, P2, K2, P2, rep from * to end.
6th row As 2nd row.
8th row P2, K2, P2, *smock 1, K1, P2, K2, P2, rep from * to last 4 sts, K2, P2.
These 8 rows form the pattern repeat.

Smocking patterns

1

2

2 Glitter smocking
Glitter threads and sequins have been used to decorate this sample. Work the background fabric as given for smocked chain stitch. Use a glitter thread to smock the ribs and place a sequin or sparkling bead in the hollows of the honeycomb.

3 Basic smocking

This stitch is worked over a multiple of 8 stitches, plus 3 extra.

1st row (RS) P3, *K1, P3, rep from * to end.

2nd row K3, *P1, K3, rep from * to end.

These 2 rows form the pattern repeat. When the knitting is complete, smock the fabric by gathering together pairs of ribs every 4 rows as shown in the sample. The yarn used for embroidery can be the same as the background fabric or (as here) in a contrasting color.

4 Mock smocking stitch

This pattern is worked over a multiple of 6 stitches, plus 2 extra.

1st row (WS) P2, *K into front and back of next st twice (called 4 from 1), P2, K1, P2, rep from * to end.

2nd and 4th rows *K2, P1, K2, K4 winding yarn twice around needle on each st, rep from * to last 2 sts, K2.

3rd and 5th rows P2, *K4 dropping extra loops, P2, K1, P2, rep from * to end.

6th row *K2, P1, K2, P4 tog, rep from * to last 2 sts, K2.

7th row P2, *K1, P2, 4 from 1, P2, rep from * to end.

8th and 10th rows *K2, K4 winding yarn twice around needle on each st, K2, P1, rep from * to last 2 sts, K2.

9th and 11th rows P2, *K1, P2, K4 dropping extra loops, P2, rep from * to end.

12th row *K2, P4 tog, K2, P1, rep from * to last 2 sts, K2.

These 12 rows form the pattern repeat. Work smocked effect by drawing together vertical ribs as shown in sample.

5 Smocked chain stitch

This pattern is worked over a multiple of 6 stitches, plus 5 extra.

1st row (RS) P5, *K1, P5, rep from * to end.

2nd row K5, *P1, K5, rep from * to end.

These 2 rows form the pattern repeat. Continue until work is required depth. Using a contrasting color, work chain stitch over the knit ribs on the right side then smock them on every 4th row as shown.

Simon Butcher

27

Plaid patterns

Traditional Highland dress included a belted cloak or shawl woven from wool or, occasionally, silk. Strictly speaking, "plaid" refers to this garment but it has also come to mean the checked patterns with which the plaids were decorated.

Skills you need

*Decreasing
*Simple increasing
*Working with color

If you do not know these skills refer to pages 174 and 175.

Materials

Pure wool spun from the fleeces of local sheep and dyed with natural vegetable dyes is the material from which traditional Scottish tartans were woven. Nowadays the dyes are likely to be chemical but Scottish spinners still produce fine quality wool in the most beautiful colors. This is ideal for plaid patterns, as is shown by the Pattern Library samples, all knitted in Shetland yarn. They would also look good in fine cottons or even silks. The bold lines of plaid patterns also make them suitable for textured yarns like the fluffy mohair, wool and synthetic mixture used for the basic jacket.

Special technique – attaching a ribbon facing

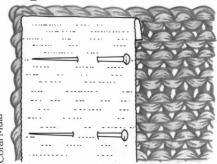

1 *The inside edges of the front opening on the basic jacket are faced with ribbon. Turn under a hem on one end of the ribbon. Begin by pinning it on the wrong side of one end of the front opening, then pin it evenly along the edge, taking care not to stretch the ribbon. At the other end trim the ribbon and turn under a hem.*

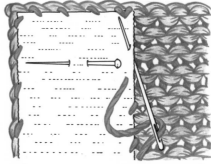

2 *Using sewing thread, overcast the facing to the garment around all the edges.*

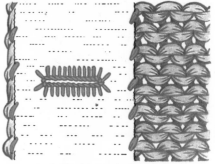

3 *Mark the buttonholes with pins, checking that they are evenly spaced along the ribbon. Cut through the ribbon to the buttonholes. Overcast the cut edges to prevent fraying. Work buttonhole stitch (see page 397) over both ribbon and knitted edges around the buttonhole.*

Coral Mula

The basic plaid jacket

Glowing colors in soft flattering mohair are perfectly combined in this pretty puff-sleeved jacket with a jaunty bow-tie finish at the neck. Add a belt in a toning color.

Sizes
To fit 30[32:34] in. bust
Length 22¾[24½:26] in.
Sleeve seam 17[17¼:17¾] in.
Note: Instructions for larger sizes are in square brackets []; where there is only one set of figures it applies to all sizes.

Gauge
17 sts and 14 rows to 4 in. over pat on size 9 needles

Materials
5[6:7] oz mohair-blend worsted-weight yarn in main color (A)
5[5:6] oz in contrasting color (B)
3[4:5] oz in contrasting color (C)
2[3:3] oz in contrasting color (D)
1[2:2] oz in contrasting color (E)
1 pair each size 6 and 9 knitting needles
8 buttons
Approx 48 in. of ribbon for facing

Back
**Using larger needles and B, cast on 67[71:75] sts.
K 1 row. P 3 rows. K 1 row.

28

Next row (form hem) *P next st tog with corresponding st from cast-on edge to make one st, rep from * to end. ** Begin pat.
1st row K0[2:4]A, 1B, 1A, 1B, * 4A, 3C, 5A, 1E, 5A, 3C, 4A, * 4A, 1B, 1A, 1B, 4A, rep from * to * once, 1B, 1A, 1B, 0[2:4]A.
2nd row P0[2:4]A, 1B, 1A, 1B, * 4A, 3C, 5A, 1E, 5A, 3C, 4A, * 4A, 1B, 1A, 1B, 4A, rep from * to * once, 1B, 1A, 1B, 0[2:4]A.
3rd-4th rows As 1st-2nd rows.
5th row K in B.
6th row P in B.
7th-8th rows As 1st-2nd rows.
9th-10th rows As 5th-6th rows.
11th-18th rows Rep 1st-2nd rows 4 times, using D instead of A.

19th-20th rows As 5th-6th rows.
21st-28th rows As 1st-8th rows.
29th row K15[17:19]C, 1E, 35C, 1E, 15[17:19]C.
30th row P15[17:19]C, 1E, 35C, 1E, 15[17:19]C.
31st-32nd rows As 29th-30th rows.
33rd-40th rows As 1st-2nd rows 4 times.
41st-42nd rows As 5th-6th rows using E instead of B.
43rd-48th rows As 1st-6th rows. These 48 rows form the pat. Cont in pat until work measures 13[14½:16] in. from hem, ending with a P row.
Shape armholes
Keeping pat correct, bind off 5 sts at beg of next 2 rows, 3 sts at beg of foll 4 rows. 45[49:53] sts.

Cont without shaping until work measures 9¾ in. from beg of armhole shaping, ending with a P row.
Shape shoulders
Bind off 11[12:13] sts at beg of next 2 rows.
Bind off rem 23[25:27] sts.

Left front
Using larger needles and B, cast on 38[40:42] sts.
Work as given for back from ** to **. Begin pat.
1st row K1[2:3]A, 1B, 1A, 1B, 4A, 3C, 5A, 1E, 5A, 3C, 8A, 1B, 1A, 1B, 2[3:4]A.
2nd row P2[3:4]A, 1B, 1A, 1B, 8A, 3C, 5A, 1E, 5A, 3C, 4A, 1B, 1A, 1B, 1[2:3]A.

29

3rd-4th rows as 1st-2nd rows.
5th row K in B.
6th row P in B.
7th-10th rows As 3rd-6th rows.
11th-18th rows Rep 1st-2nd rows 4 times, using D instead of A.
19th-20th rows As 5th-6th rows.
21st-28th rows As 1st-8th rows.
29th row K16 [17:18]C, 1E, 21[22:23]C.
30th row P21[22:23]C, 1E, 16[17:18]C.
31st-32nd rows As 29th-30th rows.
33rd-40th rows Rep 1st-2nd rows 4 times.
41st-42nd rows As 5th-6th rows using E instead of B.
43rd-48th rows As 1st-6th rows.
These 48 rows form the pat. Cont in pat until work matches back to armhole shaping, ending at side edge.
Shape armhole
Next row Bind off 5 sts, work in pat to end.
Next row Work in pat to end.
Next row Bind off 3 sts, work in pat to end. Rep the last 2 rows once more. 27[29:31] sts.
Cont without shaping until work measures 6¾ in. from beg of armhole, ending at front edge.
Shape neck
Next row Bind off 11[12:13] sts, work in pat to end.
Next row Work in pat to end.
Next row Bind off 2 sts, work in pat to end. Rep the last 2 rows once more.
Next row Work in pat to end.
Next row Work 2 tog, work in pat to end. 11[12:13] sts.
Cont without shaping until work matches back to shoulder, ending at armhole edge.
Shape shoulder
Bind off rem 11[12:13] sts.

Right front
Using straight pins mark the position of 8 buttons on left front edge, the first to come ¾ in. below neck edge, the last 1½ in. from hem with the other 6 spaced evenly between.
Using larger needles and B, cast on 38[40:42] sts.
Work as given for back from ** to **.
Work in pat as foll, *at the same time* working buttonholes as markers are reached.
1st buttonhole row (RS) Work in pat 3, bind off 2, work in pat to end.
2nd buttonhole row Work in pat to end, casting on 2 sts over those bound off in previous row.
Begin pat.
30

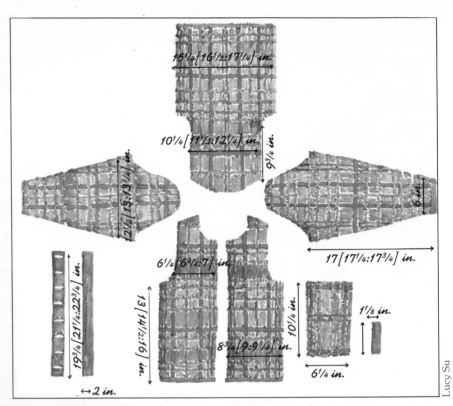

15¼ [16½:17¼] in.

10¼ [11½:12¼] in.

9¾ in.

12½ [13:13¾] in.

6 in.

17 [17¼:17¾] in.

6¼ [6¾:7] in.

13 [14½:16] in.

10¼ in.

8¾ [9:9¾] in.

19¾ [21¼:22¾] in.

1⅛ in.

6¼ in.

↔ 2 in.

Lucy Su

1st row K2[3:4]A, 1B, 1A, 1B, 8A, 3C, 5A, 1E, 5A, 3C, 4A, 1B, 1A, 1B, 1[2:3]A.
2nd row P1[2:3]A, 1B, 1A, 1B, 4A, 3C, 5A, 1E, 5A, 3C, 8A, 1B, 1A, 1B, 2[3:4]A.
3rd-4th rows As 1st-2nd rows.
5th row K in B.
6th row P in B.
7th-10th rows As 3rd-6th rows.
11th-18th rows Rep 1st-2nd rows 4 times, using D instead of A.
19th-20th rows As 5th-6th rows.
21st-28th rows As 1st-8th rows.
29th row K21[22:23]C, 1E, 16[17:18]C.
30th row P16[17:18]C, 1E, 21[22:23]C.
31st-32nd rows As 29th-30th rows.
33rd-40th rows Rep 1st-2nd rows 4 times.
41st-42nd rows As 5th-6th rows using E instead of B.
43rd-48th rows As 1st-6th rows.
These 48 rows form the pat. Complete to match left front, reversing all shapings.

Sleeves
Using larger needles and B, cast on 25 sts. Work as given for back from ** to **.
Begin pat.
1st row Work as given for 1st row of back from * to *.
2nd row Work as given for 2nd row of back from * to *.

Rep the last 2 rows 3 times more.
These 8 rows establish the pat. Cont in pat as given for back working from 41st row, *at the same time* inc and work into pat 1 st at each end of the next and every foll 3rd row until there are 55[57:59] sts.
Cont without shaping until work measures 17[17¼:17¾] in. from hem edge, ending with a P row.
Shape top
Keeping pat correct, bind off 5 sts at beg of next 2 rows and 3 sts at beg of foll 2 rows.
Dec 1 st at beg of foll 8 rows.
Work 2 rows.
Dec 1 st at beg of foll 2 rows.
Rep the last 4 rows twice more.
Dec 1 st at beg of next 10 rows.
Bind off rem 15[17:19] sts.

Bow
Using larger needles and B, cast on 27 sts. Begin pat.
1st row K1A, 3C, 8A, 1B, 1A, 1B, 8A, 3C, 1A.
2nd row As 1st row reading P for K.
3rd-4th rows As 1st-2nd rows.
5th row K in B.
6th row P in B.
7th-8th rows As 1st-2nd rows.
9th-10th rows As 5th-6th rows.
11th-12th rows As 1st-2nd rows using D instead of A.
Rep the last 2 rows 12 times more.
Bind off.

Bow Center
Using larger needles and A, cast on 6 sts.
Work 4 in. stockinette st. Bind off.
To finish
Join shoulder seams.
Neckband
With RS of work facing, using smaller needles and B, pick up and K75 [77:79] sts evenly around neck edge.
Beg with a P row work 4 rows stockinette st.
Next row K to form fold-line.
Beg with a K row work 2 rows stockinette st. K 2 rows. Bind off.
Fold neckband in half onto WS and tack down.

Pocket linings (alike)
Place a marker 6 in. above hem edge on back side seam, and another above hem. With RS of work facing, using larger needles and A, pick up and K 14 sts between markers.
Beg with a P row work 11¾ in. stockinette st.
Bind off.
Sew bound – off edge to front side seam to form pocket bag. Catch lower edge of lining to top of hem.
Join side and sleeve seams. Set in sleeves, matching pat and gathering top to form puff.
Make front edge ribbon facings as given in Special Technique (page 28)

or make knitted facings as folls:
Buttonhole facing (optional)
Using larger needles and A, cast on 8 sts. Beg with a K row cont in stockinette st, making buttonholes to correspond with those on right front.
When facing matches front to neck edge, ending with a P row, bind off.
Button facing (optional)
Work to match buttonhole facing omitting buttonholes. Using a flat seam join facings to front edges. Fold back onto WS and tack down.
Fold bow in half, cast-on edge to bound-off edge. Join sides. Join bow center into a ring to gather bow.
Sew on bow and buttons.

Adapting the plaid jacket

Plaid patterns may look complicated but they are basically simple stripes, which makes it easy to invent numerous new variations.

The Pattern Library samples are all inspired by authentic Scottish clan tartans though knitted fabrics can never match exactly the intricacies of the woven cloth. However, they do show how the interweaving effect of the horizontal and vertical stripes can be achieved. The samples are all worked in stockinette stitch but the single-stitch vertical stripes can be Swiss-darned.

Plaid patterns

1 Johnston
This pattern is worked over a multiple of 32 stitches, plus 1 extra. Work in stockinette stitch using 5 contrasting colors in sequence as folls:
1st-8th rows 1A, *1B, 1C, 6B, 5D, (1E, 1D) twice, 1E, 5D, 6B, 1C, 1B, 1A, rep from * to end.
9th row 1A, *31C, 1A, rep from * to end.
10th row As 1st row.
11th row A to end.
12th row As 1st row.
13th row As 9th row.
14th-21st rows As 1st-8th rows.
22nd-27th rows 1A, *1D, 1C, 6D, 5C, (1E, 1C) twice, 1E, 5C, 6D, 1C, 1D, 1A, rep from * to end.
28th row 1A, *1E, 1C, 27E, 1C, 1E, 1A, rep from * to end.
29th row As 22nd row.
30th-31st rows As 28th-29th rows.
32nd row As 28th row.
33rd-38th rows As 22nd-27th rows.
These 38 rows form the pattern repeat.

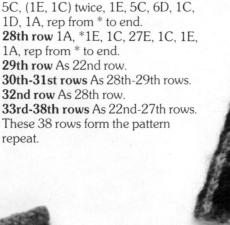

2 Macleod
This pattern is worked over a multiple of 27 stitches. Work in stockinete stitch, using five contrasting colors in sequence as folls:
1st-6th rows *2A, 1B, 4A, 6B, 1A, 6B, 4A, 1B, 2A, rep from * to end.
7th row *2C, 1D, 4C, 6D, 1E, 6D, 4C, 1D, 2C, rep from * to end.
8th-14th rows As 1st-7th rows.
15th-20th rows As 1st-6th rows.
21st-28th rows As 7th row.
29th row *2A, 1E, 4A, 13E, 4A, 1E, 2A, rep from * to end.
30th-37th rows As 7th row.
These 37 rows form the pattern repeat.

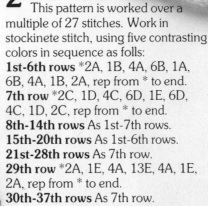

1

2

Simon Wheeler

4 Lamont

This pattern is worked over a multiple of 32 stitches, plus 1 extra. Work in stockinette stitch, using four contrasting colors in sequence as folls:

1st-6th rows 1A, *5B, 5C, 5D, 1E, 5D, 5C, 5B, 1A, rep from * to end.
7th row 1A, *15A, 1E, 16A, rep from * to end.
8th-13th rows As 1st-6th rows.
14th-19th rows 1A, *5C, 5E, 5F, 1E, 5F, 5E, 5C, 1A, rep from * to end.
20th-25th rows 1A, *5D, 5F, 5G, 1E, 5G, 5F, 5D, 1A, rep from * to end.
26th row 1A, *15E, 1G, 15E, 1A, rep from * to end.
27th-32nd rows As 20th-25th rows.
33rd-38th rows As 14th-19th rows.
These 38 rows form the pattern repeat.

3 Cameron

This pattern is worked over a multiple of 30 stitches. Work in stockinette stitch, using seven contrasting colors in sequence as folls:

1st-7th rows *1A, 4B, 1A, 1C, 1D, 1C, 5A, 2B, 5A, 1C, 1D, 1C, 1A, 4B, 1A, rep from * to end.
8th-10th rows *1B, 4C, 1B, 1C, 1E, 1C, 5B, 2C, 5B, 1C, 1E, 1C, 1B, 4C, 1B, rep from * to end.
11th-17th rows As 1st-7th rows.
18th row *7C, 1E, 14C, 1E, 7C, rep from * to end.
19th row *1D, 4E, 1D, 1E, 1F, 1E, 5D, 2E, 5D, 1E, 1F, 1E, 1D, 4E, 1D, rep from * to end.
20th row As 18th row.
21st row As 1st row.
22nd-27th rows *1B, 4G, 1B, 1C, 1E, 1C, 5B, 2C, 5B, 1C, 1E, 1C, 1B, 4G, 1B, rep from * to end.
28th-30th rows As 1st row.
31st-36th rows As 22nd-27th rows.
37th row As 1st row.
38th-40th rows As 18th-20th rows.
These 40 rows form the pattern repeat.

5 Wallace

This pattern is worked over a multiple of 26 stitches, plus 1 extra. Work in stockinette stitch using four contrasting colors in sequence as folls:
1st-8th rows 1A, *6B, 6C, 1D, 6C, 6B, 1A, rep from * to end.
9th-16th rows 1A, *6C, 6A, 1D, 6A, 6C, 1A, rep from * to end.
17th row 1A, *25D, 1A, rep from * to end.
18th-25th rows As 9th-16th rows.
26th-33rd rows As 1st-8th rows.
34th row 1A, *12A, 1D, 13A, rep from * to end.
These 34 rows form pattern repeat.

Simon Wheeler

Paisley patterns

The curly motif typical of Paisley patterns was copied by the
Victorians from imported Kashmiri shawls. The textile industry in
Paisley, Scotland, became known for its fine imitations of these
designs which from then on were named after that town.

Eamonn McCabe

Skills you need

*Decreasing
*Simple increasing
*Working with color

If you do not know these skills refer to pages 174 and 175.

Materials

Intricate jacquard patterns such as these Paisley motifs should always be worked in smooth yarns. Fine cottons and silks would be very much in keeping with traditional Paisley textiles but the Shetland yarn used in the basic cardigan is also appropriate. Although technically "two-ply" in that only two strands of wool are twisted together to make the yarn, jumper weight Shetland yarn is approximately equivalent to a sport-weight yarn.

Special technique – picking up stitches from shaped and vertical edges

1 On a shaped edge, insert a needle from front to back through a bound-off stitch or the last stitch in a row. Take the yarn knitwise around the point of the needle and draw a loop through. On shaped edges one stitch is picked up for every two rows.

2 On vertical edges, insert a needle from front to back through the first stitch in a row. Take the yarn around the point of the needle knitwise and draw a loop through. Generally, on vertical edges, one stitch is picked up for every row.

3 Similarly, stitches can be picked up and purled along shaped or vertical edges. In this case work with the wrong side of the fabric facing.

The basic Paisley cardigan

A string of tiny flowers buttons up this scoop-necked cardigan.
The sleeves are beautifully puffed at the top and taper to the wrist.

Sizes
To fit 30[32:34:36] in. bust
Length 19½[19½:21:21] in.
Sleeve seam 15 [15¾:16½:17½] in.

Note: Instructions for the larger sizes are in square brackets []; where there is only one set of figures it applies to all sizes.

Gauge
29 sts and 29 rows to 4 in. over pat on size 3 needles

Materials
8[8:9:11] oz Shetland wool in main color (A)
4[4:5:5] oz in first contrasting color (B)
5[5:6:6] oz in 2nd contrasting color (C)
1 pair each sizes 2 and 3 knitting needles
13[13:14:14] buttons

34

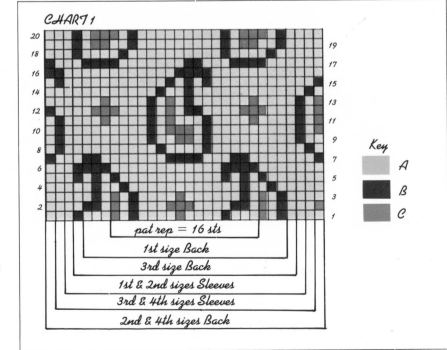

CHART 1

pat rep = 16 sts
1st size Back
3rd size Back
1st & 2nd sizes Sleeves
3rd & 4th sizes Sleeves
2nd & 4th sizes Back

Key
A
B
C

Coral Mula

Murray West

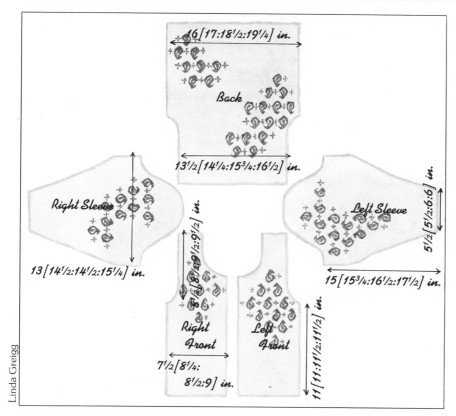

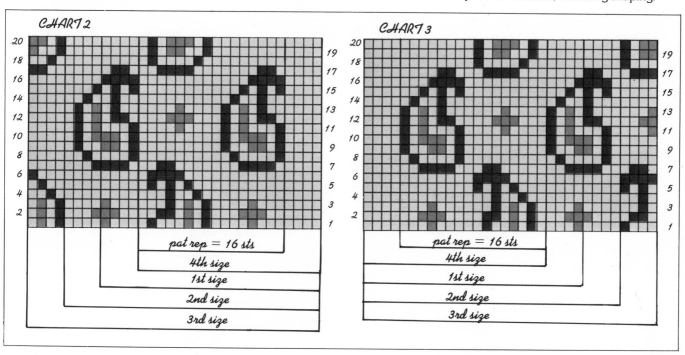

Right front
Using larger needles and A, cast on 56[60:64:68] sts.
Work as given for back from ** to ** working pat from Chart 2.
Shape armhole
Next row Bind off 4 sts, work in pat to end.
Next row Work in pat to end.
Next row Bind off 3 sts, work in pat to end.
Next row Work in pat to end.
Next row Bind off 2 sts, work in pat to end.
Next row Work in pat to end.
Next row Work 2 tog, work in pat to end. 46[50:54:58] sts.
Cont without shaping until work measures 15[15:15¾:15¾] in. from cast-on edge, ending with a K row.

Shape neck
Next row Bind off 9 sts, work in pat to end.
Next row Work in pat to end.
Next row Bind off 7[7:6:7] sts, work in pat to end.
Next row Work in pat to end.
Next row Bind off 6 sts, work in pat to end. 24[28:33:36] sts.
Cont without shaping until work matches back to shoulder shaping, ending at armhole edge.
Shape shoulder
Bind off rem sts.

Left front
Work as given for right front working pat from Chart 3, reversing shaping.

Back
Using larger needles and A, cast on 118[126:136:142] sts.
**Work 6 rows K1, P1 ribbing.
Beg with a K row cont in stockinette st and pat from chart 1. Read K rows from right to left, P rows from left to right.
Cont until work measures 11[11:11½:11½] in. from cast-on edge, ending with a P row.**
Shape armholes

Keeping pat correct, bind off 4 sts at beg of next 2 rows, 3 sts at beg of foll 2 rows and 2 sts at beg of next 2 rows.
Dec 1 st at beg of next 2 rows. 98[106:116:122] sts.
Cont without shaping until work measures 19½[19½:21:21] in. from cast-on edge, ending with a P row.
Shape shoulders
Bind off 24[28:33:36] sts at beg of next 2 rows.
Bind off rem 50 sts.

Sleeves

Using larger needles and A, cast on 42[42:44:44] sts. Work 6 rows ribbing. Change to stockinette st and work in pat from Chart 1. Inc 1 st at each end of every foll 4th row until there are 60[60:64:64] sts. Now inc 1 st at each end of every other row until there are 102[108:108:112] sts. Cont without shaping until work measures 15[15¾:16½:17¼] in. from cast-on edge, ending with a P row.

Shape sleeve top
Bind off 4 sts at beg of next 2 rows and 2 sts at beg of foll 2 rows. Dec 1 st at each end of next and every other row until 54[66:54:62] sts rem, ending with a P row. Bind off 2 sts at beg of next 8[14:8:12] rows, then 4 sts at beg of next 2 rows. Bind off rem 30 sts.

To finish

Join shoulder seams.

Neckband

With RS of work facing, using smaller needles and A, pick up and K 53[53:55:55] sts up right neck, pick up and K 50 on back neck, pick up and K 53[53:55:55] sts down left neck. 156[156:160:160] sts. Work 5 rows K1, P1 ribbing. Bind off in ribbing.

Buttonhole band

With RS of work facing, using smaller needles and A, pick and K 115[115:123:123] sts evenly along front and neckband edge.
1st row (WS) P1, (K1, P1) to end.
2nd row K1, (P1, K1) to end.
Rep the 1st row again.
Buttonhole row Rib 3, (yo, work 2 tog, rib 7) 12[12:13:13] times, yo, work 2 tog, rib to end.
Rib 4 more rows. Bind off in ribbing.

Buttonband

Work as buttonhole band omitting buttonholes. Join side and sleeve seams. Set in sleeves, gathering top. Sew on buttons.

Adapting the Paisley cardigan

Steve Tanner/Murray West

Use any of the charts in the Pattern Library to transform the basic cardigan.

All the motifs in the Pattern Library are based on charts that have a 16-stitch pattern repeat, as do the charts for the basic cardigan. Using the basic charts as examples, extend the substitute chart to include the correct number of edge stitches for your size. To ensure a neat finish on the center front do not work half motifs at the opening edges of the left and right fronts.

Reading the charts

Work all the charts in stockinette stitch reading odd-numbered (knit) rows from right to left and even-numbered (purl) rows from left to right.

Paisley patterns

1 Floral paisley

The basic Paisley motif is usually elaborated in various ways, sometimes with geometric shapes or "pips" or, as here, with tiny flowers.

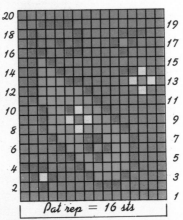

Pat rep = 16 sts

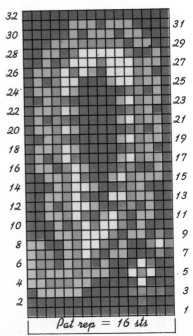

Pat rep = 16 sts

2 Pine cone

There are many theories about the derivation of the Paisley motif. One that seems plausible suggests that the original inspiration was a pine cone. This chart repeats over 16 stitches and 32 rows.

36

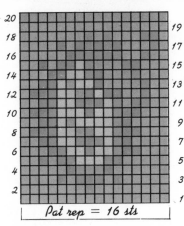

3 Basic Paisley motif

This chart repeats over 16 stitches and 20 rows. Try working the chart by reading it upside down on every alternate row-repeat.

Pat rep = 16 sts

3

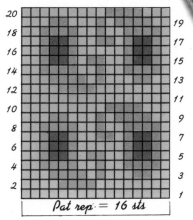

Pat rep = 16 sts

4 Simple Paisley motifs

These simple shapes are the basic form of most Paisley motifs although they are often filled with intricate ornamentation and the spaces between them are similarly highly decorated. This all-over pattern repeats over 16 stitches and 20 rows.

4

5 Multi-colored Paisley

These tiny shapes owe little except their basic form to traditional Paisley patterns, but they would make a very pretty substitute for the pattern on the basic cardigan. The chart repeats over 16 stitches and 16 rows.

5

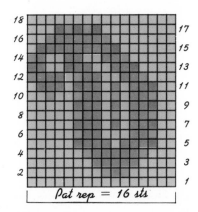

Pat rep = 16 sts

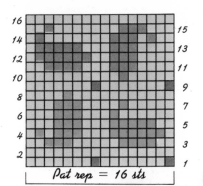

Pat rep = 16 sts

6 Boteh

This Persian word meaning "tree" or "shrub" is the term used to describe the characteristic pear-shaped Paisley motif. The chart repeats over 16 stitches and 20 rows. Work it as usual or on each alternate row – repeat, reading the chart upside down as shown in this sample.

6

Zigzag patterns

These can be some of the boldest, most dramatic patterns and they are easily translated into knitting designs. Different combinations of scale and color scheme can alter the mood from jazzy to cool and sophisticated.

Skills you need

*Decreasing
*Making buttonholes

If you do not know these skills refer to pages 162 and 175.

Materials

Delicate, finely drawn patterns should be worked in plain yarns but where the zigzags are broader and bolder it may well be possible to incorporate certain textured yarns. Touches of mohair or angora can be particularly effective. The basic jacket is worked in a smooth pure wool yarn in a worsted weight. As an alternative, the fourth and fifth contrasting colors could be replaced by an equivalent mohair or glitter yarn.

Special technique – reinforcing buttonholes

1 *Where large buttonholes have been worked, or where there is likely to be more than the usual strain on a buttonhole, as on heavy jackets or coats, it is advisable to reinforce them. This can be done by working ordinary buttonhole stitch around the edges. Use the same yarn as the garment or a finer one in an exactly matching color.*

2 *Alternatively, bind the buttonhole with a strip of bias knitting either in the same color as the garment or in a contrasting color for decorative effect. To make the strip, cast on the required number of stitches and work in stockinette stitch. Decrease one stitch at the beginning of knit rows and increase one stitch at the end.*

3 *When the strip is long enough to fit around the buttonhole bind off. Fold it in half and stitch it neatly around the buttonhole on both sides of the fabric.*

Coral Mula

The basic zigzag jacket

Make yourself a genuine coat of many colors in a sizzling zigzag pattern. This one has an interesting double-breasted front and a cozy shawl collar.

Sizes
To fit 32-34[36-38] in. bust
Length 25[26] in.
Sleeve seam 17 in.
Note: Instructions for larger size are in square brackets []; where there is only

38

one set of figures it applies to both sizes.

Gauge
21 sts and 23 rows to 4 in. over pat on size 5 needles

Materials
17[19] oz of knitting worsted in main color (A)
6[9] oz, respectively, in each of contrasting colors (B) and (C)

4 oz, respectively, each of contrasting colors (D) and (E)
1 pair each sizes 4 and 5 knitting needles
4 buttons

Back
Using smaller needles and A, cast on 104[114] sts. Work 2 in. K1, P1 ribbing.
Change to larger needles.
Beg with a K row cont in stockinette st

Victor Yuan

and pat from chart. Use small, separate balls of yarn for each color area, twist yarns when changing color to avoid a hole.
Work 90 rows

Shape armholes
Bind off 4[5] sts at beg of next 2 rows. Dec 1 st at each end of next and every other row until 82[88] sts rem. Cont without shaping until work measures 7¾[8¾] in., ending with a WS row.

Shape shoulders
Bind off 9 sts at beg of next 4 rows at

7[10] sts at beg of foll 2 rows. Bind off rem 32 sts.

Pocket linings (make 2)
Using larger needles and A, cast on 24 sts. Work in stockinette st for 4¾ in., ending with a P row. Leave these sts on a spare needle.

Left front
Using smaller needles and A, cast on 36[41] sts. Work 2 in. K1, P1 ribbing.
Change to larger needles.

Beg with a K row cont in pat from chart until work measures 6¾ in., ending with a WS row.

Place pocket
Next row Work in pat 6 sts, sl next 24 sts onto a st holder and pat across pocket lining sts on spare needle, work in pat to end.
Cont in pat until work matches back to armhole, ending with a P row.

Shape armhole
Bind off 4[5] sts at beg of next row. Dec 1 st at armhole edge on every other row until 25[28] sts rem.

39

Cont without further shaping until work matches back to shoulder shaping, ending at armhole edge.

Shape shoulder
Bind off 9 sts at beg of next and foll alt row.
Work 1 row. Bind off rem 7[10] sts.

Right front
Work as given for left front from ** to **.
Change to larger needles.
Beg with a K row cont in stockinette st and pat from chart until work measures 6¾ in., ending with a WS row.

Place pocket
Next row Work in pat 6[11] sts, sl next 24 sts onto a st holder, work in pat across pocket lining sts on spare needle, work in pat to end.
Cont in pat until work matches back to armhole, ending with a K row.

Shape armhole
Bind off 4[5] sts at beg of next row.
Dec 1 st at armhole edge on next and every other row until 25[28] sts rem.
Complete to match left front.

Sleeves
Using smaller needles and A, cast on 62 sts. Work 1½ in. K1, P1 ribbing.
Change to larger needles.
Beg with a K row cont in stockinette st and pat from chart. Inc and work into pat 1 st at each end of the 11th and every foll 12th[9th] row until there are 74[80] sts. Cont without shaping until work measures approx 17 in., ending with an 18th pat row.
Shape top

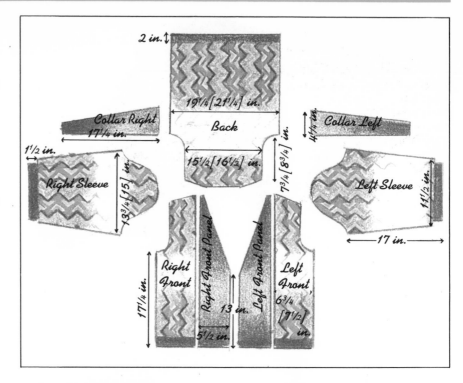

Bind off 4[5] sts at beg of next 2 rows.
Dec 1 st at each end of next and every other row until 50 sts rem, then at each end of every row until 18 sts rem. Bind off.

Right front panel
Using smaller needles and A, cast on 36 sts.
Work 4¾ in. K1, P1 ribbing.
1st buttonhole row Rib 7, bind off 2 sts, rib 18 including st used in binding off, bind off 2 sts, rib to end.
2nd buttonhole row Rib to end, casting on 2 sts over those bound off in previous row.

Cont in ribbing until work measures 8¾ in. from cast-on edge.
Work 1st and 2nd buttonhole rows again.
Now cont in ribbing until work measures 13 in. from cast-on edge, ending at front edge.

Shape front edge
Bind off 12 sts at beg of next row.
Dec 1 st at front edge on 3 foll 4th[6th] rows, then on every foll 4th row until 2 sts rem.
Work 2 tog and fasten off.

Left front panel
Work to match right front panel, omitting buttonholes.

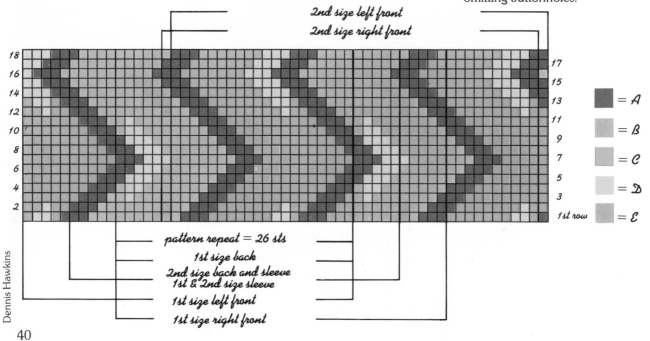

Collar (make 2 pieces)
Using smaller needles and A, cast on 106[110] sts.
Work 14 rows in K1, P1 ribbing.
Next row Rib to last 2 sts, turn.
Next row Sl 1, rib to end.
Next row Rib to last 4 sts, turn.
Next row Sl 1, rib to end.
Cont in this way until the row "rib to last 10 sts, turn" has been worked.
Next row Sl 1, rib to end.
Next row Rib to last 20 sts, turn.
Next row Sl 1, rib to end.
Next row Rib to last 30 sts, turn.
Next row Sl 1, rib to end.
Next row Rib to last 40 sts, turn.
Next row Sl 1, rib to end.
Next row Rib to end across all sts on needle.
Bind off.

To finish
Press with a warm iron over a damp cloth.
Pocket edgings
Using smaller needles and A, K across 24 sts left on st holder. Work ¾ in. K1, P1 ribbing. Bind off in ribbing. Sew down pocket linings on WS and edgings on RS.

Join shoulder, side and sleeve seams. Set in sleeves. Sew front panels to front edges. Join center back neck seam of collar. Sew shaped edge of collar to neck edge, joining short ends to bound-off sts at front edge. Sew on buttons. Reinforce buttonholes, if required, as shown in Special Technique, page 38.

Adapting the zigzag jacket

The Pattern Library provides several dazzling alternatives to the basic pattern.

The basic pattern is fairly intricate and quite difficult to knit but there are several simpler designs in the Pattern Library that could be substituted for it. Some of them are designed as all-over repeating patterns as in samples 1, 2 and 3. Others are more like panel patterns with a single motif worked vertically. These could be combined by working them side by side.

Zigzag patterns

1 Striped zigzag
This multicolored pattern is a perfect vehicle for using up odd balls of yarn and for mixing plain and textured fibers. The chart repeats over 5 stitches and, if required, different contrasting colors could be used on each row repeat, as in this sample.

2 Op-art zigzag
This pattern repeats over 7 stitches and is worked in two colors only. Nevertheless it is surprisingly difficult to work.

pat rep = 7 sts

pat rep = 5 sts

3 Bordered zigzag
Four colors are used in this pattern, which repeats over 13 stitches and can be used on the basic jacket.

pat rep = 13 sts

4 Interlocking zigzags
This pattern repeats over 13 stitches. It can be used on the basic jacket as an all-over pattern or single repeats could be worked up the center of sleeves, or on the back and front of any suitable garment.

pat rep = 13 sts

5 Three-dimensional zigzag
A clever *trompe l'oeil* effect is achieved in this pattern with three colors only. The pattern repeats over 13 stitches and can be used on the basic jacket.

pat rep = 13 sts

Lattice patterns

Interlocking lattice patterns can be worked very effectively in knitting using a variety of techniques including twisting stitches and cabling. The textures are usually subtle and there are opportunities for incorporating color, embroidery and other surface decoration.

Skills you need

*Decreasing
*Using a cable needle
*Making bobbles

If you do not know these skills refer to pages 175, 178 and 179.

Materials

Stitches with a definite surface texture are best worked in fairly thick plain yarns like Aran-weight yarn used in the basic sweater. Worked in finer yarns, some of the three-dimensional qualities of the stitches are inevitably lost, but there is often a rather pleasing brocade-like texture in the resulting fabric. Fluffy mohair-type yarns can also work well.

Special technique – working the lattice

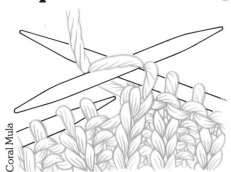

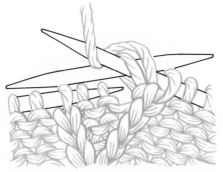

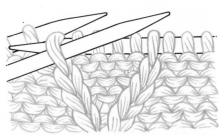

Coral Mula

1 *The lattice pattern is worked by cabling techniques. On the first row work a two-stitch cable back. Slip the next stitch onto a cable needle and hold at back of work. Knit one, then knit the stitch on the cable needle. The cable front on the 9th row is worked in the same way but the cable needle is held at the front.*

2 *A two-stitch back cross, found on the 3rd, 5th, 7th, 11th, 13th and 15th rows, is worked as follows: Slip the next stitch onto a cable needle and hold at back of work. Knit one, then purl the stitch on the cable needle.*

3 *A two-stitch front cross, found on on the 3rd, 5th, 7th, 11th, 13th and 15th rows, is worked as follows: Slip the next stitch onto a cable needle and hold at front of work. Purl one, then knit the stitch on the cable needle.*

The basic lattice sweater

A crisp diamond lattice on the sleeves and collar, a crunchy bobble stitch on the back and front and a simple classic sweater is transformed into something special.

Sizes
To fit 34¼[36¼:38¼] in. bust
Length 21¼[21½:22] in.
Sleeve seam 16½ in.

Note: Instructions for larger sizes are in square brackets []; where there is only one set of figures it applies to all sizes.

Gauge
20 sts and 30 rows to 4 in. over stockinette st on size 5 needles

Materials
27[28:30] oz of a worsted-weight yarn
1 pair each size 4 and 5 needles
Cable needle

Nosegay pat
1st row (WS) K7, P2, K7.
2nd row P6, sl next st onto cable needle and hold at back of work, K1, then K1 from cable needle (called

C2B), sl next st onto cable needle and hold at front of work, K1, then K1 from cable needle (called C2F), P6.
3rd row K5, sl next st onto cable needle and hold at front of work, P1, then K1 from cable needle (called Cr2F), P2, sl next st onto cable needle and hold at back of work, K1, then P1 from cable needle (called Cr2B), K5.
4th row P4, Cr2B, C2B, C2F, Cr2F, P4.
5th row K3, Cr2F, K1, P4, K1, Cr2B, K3.
6th row P2, Cr2B, P1, Cr2B, K2, Cr2F, P1, Cr2F, P2.
7th row (K2, P1) twice, K1, P2, K1, (P1, K2) twice.
8th row P2, (K1, P1) twice into next st, turn, P4, turn, K4 turn, (P2 tog) twice, turn, K2 tog, (called MB), P1, Cr2B, P1, K2, P1, Cr2F, P1, MB, P2.
9th row K4, P1, K2, P1, K2, P1, K4.
10th row P4, MB, P2, K2, P2, MB, P4.

These 10 rows form the nosegay pat.

Lattice pat
1st row (RS) P3, C2B, *P6, C2B, rep from * to last 3 sts, P3.
2nd and every other row P the K sts and K the P sts of previous row.
3rd row P2, *Cr2B, Cr2F, P4, rep from * to last 6 sts, Cr2B, Cr2F, P2.
5th row P1, *Cr2B, P2, Cr2F, P2, rep from * to last 7 sts, Cr2B, P2, Cr2F, P1.
7th row *Cr2B, P4, Cr2F, rep from * to end.
9th row K1, *P6, C2F, rep from * to last 7 sts, P6, K1.
11th row *Cr2F, P4, Cr2B, rep from * to end.
13th row P1, *Cr2F, P2, Cr2B, P2, rep from * to last 7 sts, Cr2F, P2, Cr2B, P1.
15th row P2, *Cr2F, Cr2B, P4, rep from * to last 6 sts, Cr2F, Cr2B, P2.
16th row As 2nd row.

These 16 rows form the lattice pat.

44

Back

**Using smaller needles, cast on 84[90:96] sts and work 17 rows in K1, P1 ribbing.

Next row Rib 11[7:10], (work twice into next st – called inc 1 – rib 3[4:4]) 15 times, inc 1, rib to end. 100[106:112] sts.

Change to larger needles and begin pat.

1st row (WS) K14[15:16], (work first row of nosegay pat, K12[14;16]) twice, work first row of nosegay pat, K14[15:16].

2nd row P14[15:16], (work 2nd row of nosegay pat, P12[14:16]) twice, work 2nd row of nosegay pat, P14[15:16].

These 2 rows establish the pat, three panels of nosegay pat on reverse stockinette st. Cont in pat until work measures approx 14¼ in. from cast-on edge, ending with a 10th pat row.

Shape armholes

Bind off 6 sts at beg of next 2 rows and 2 sts at beg of foll 2 rows. Dec 1 st at each end of the next 6 rows, ending with a 10th pat row. 72[78:84] sts.

Next row (WS) K7[8:9], (P2 tog, K26[28:30]) twice, P2 tog, K7[8:9].

Next row P7[8:9], (MB, P26[28:30]) twice, MB, P7[8:9]. 69[75:81] sts.**

Beg with a K row cont in reverse stockinette st until work measures 6[6¼:6¾] in. from beg of armhole shaping, ending with a P row.

Shape neck

Next row K25[28:31], bind off 19 sts, K to end.

Complete right side of neck first.

Dec 1 st at neck edge on every row until 17[20:23] sts rem. Bind off.

Return to sts for left side of neck. With RS facing, rejoin yarn to neck edge. Complete to match first side of neck.

Front

Work as given for back from ** to **.

Beg with a K row cont in reverse stockinette st until work measures 4¼[4¾:5] in. from beg of armhole shaping, ending with a K row.

Shape neck

Next row P24[27:30], bind off 21 sts, P to end.

Complete right side of neck first.

Dec 1 st at neck edge on every other row until 17[20:23] sts rem. Cont without shaping until work measures same as back to shoulder, ending at armhole edge. Bind off.

Return to sts for left side of neck. With WS of work facing, rejoin yarn at neck edge and work to match first side.

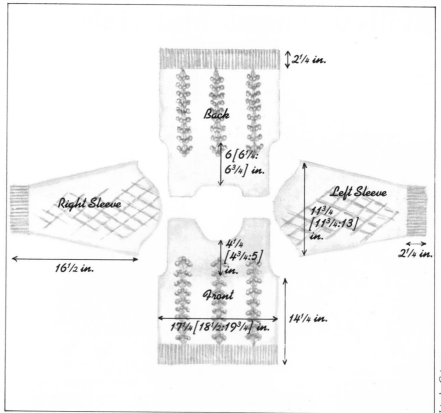

Linda Griegg

Sleeves

Using smaller needles, cast on 48[48:54] sts and work 17 rows in K1, P1 ribbing.

Next row *Rib 2, inc 1, rep from * to end. 64[64:72] sts.

Change to larger needles and work in lattice pat as given above. Inc and work into pat 1 st at each end of every 10th row until there are 78[78:86] sts. Cont without shaping until work measures 16½ in. from cast-on edge, ending with a WS row.

Shape top

Keeping pat correct, bind off 6 sts at beg of next 2 rows.

Next row P2 tog, Cr2F, work in pat to last 4 sts, Cr2B, P2 tog.

Next row Work in pat to end.

Rep the last 2 rows until 24 sts rem. Bind off 5 sts at beg of next 2 rows. Bind off rem sts.

To finish

Press lightly with a warm iron over a damp cloth, avoiding nosegay pat. Join right shoulder seam.

Collar

With RS of work facing, using smaller needles, pick up and K 80 sts around front neck edge, and 40 sts from back neck edge. 120 sts. Begin lattice pat. Work 1st-16th rows twice, then 1st-7th rows again. Knit 3 rows. Bind off. Join left shoulder seam and collar. Join side and sleeve seams. Set in sleeves.

Adapting the lattice sweater

Lattice patterns are so simple they can be adapted in a number of ways. Try one of the variations on the sweater.

Surface decoration

The lattice pattern on the sleeves and collar of the basic sweater makes a perfect background for various kinds of decoration. Several of the Pattern Library samples show how the pattern can be beaded. The "windows" of the lattice could also be used as a frame for embroidery, for example, tiny flowers made of lazy-daisy stitches or bullion knots. Alternatively, the bobbles on the nosegay pattern on the back and front could be worked in a contrasting color for added interest.

Lattice patterns

1 Beaded lattice

This pattern is an adaptation of the basic lattice pattern. Thread beads onto yarn and continue as given for the lattice pattern working 1st and 9th rows as foll:

1st row P3, C2B, *P3, bring a bead up close to work, P3, C2B, rep from * to last 3 sts, P3.

9th row K1, *P3, bring a bead up close to work, P3, C2F, rep from * to last 7 sts, P3, bring a bead up close to work, P3, K1.

3

1

2

2 Bobbled lattice

This pattern works over a multiple of 8 stitches and can be used instead of the lattice pattern on the basic sweater. Here it is worked in main color A with bobbles in rows of contrasting colors (B, C, D).

1st row With A, P3, *sl next st onto cable needle and leave at front of work, K1, with B (K1, yfwd, K1, yfwd, K1) all into st on cable needle, turn, P5, turn, K5, sl 2nd, 3rd, 4th and 5th sts over 1st st (called MB) with A, P6, rep from * to last 5 sts, sl next st onto a cable needle and leave at front of work, K1, with B, MB, P3.

2nd and every other row. With A, P the K sts and K the P sts of previous row.

3rd row With A, P2, *sl next st onto cable needle and hold at back of work, P1, then K1 from cable needle (called Cr2B), sl next st onto cable needle and leave at front of work, K1, then P st from cable needle (called Cr2F),

P4, rep from * to last 6 sts, Cr2B, Cr2F, P2.

5th row With A, P1, *Cr2B, P2, Cr2F, P2, rep from * to last 7 sts, Cr2B, P2, Cr2F, P1.

7th row With A, *Cr2B, P4, Cr2F, rep from * to end.

9th row With A, K1, *P6, sl next st onto cable needle and hold at front of work, K1, with C, MB, rep from * to last 7 sts, P6, K1.

11th row With A, *Cr2F, P4, Cr2B, rep from * to end.

13th row With A, P1, *Cr2F, P2, Cr2B, P2, rep from * to last 7 sts, Cr2F, P2, Cr2B, P1.

15th row With A, P2, *Cr2F, Cr2B, P4, rep from * to last 6 sts, Cr2F, Cr2B, P2.

16th row As 2nd row.

These 16 rows form the pattern repeat. Use color D for the next row of bobbles, then B, C and D in sequence.

3 Lattice with diagonal beads

This is an adaptation of the basic lattice pattern and can be used on the basic sweater. Thread beads onto yarn and continue as given for the lattice pattern, working the 1st, 5th, 9th and 13th rows as foll:

1st row P2, bring a bead up close to work, P1, C2B, *P5, bring a bead up close to work, P1, C2B, rep from * to last 3 sts, P3.

5th row Bring a bead up close to work, P1, *Cr2B, P2, Cr2F, P1, bring a bead up close to work, P1, rep from * to last 7 sts, Cr2B, P2, Cr2F, P1.

9th row K1, *P5, bring a bead up close to work, P1, C2F, rep from * to last 7 sts, P5, bring a bead up close to work, P1, K1.

13th row P1, *Cr2F, P1, bring a bead up close to work, P1, Cr2B, P2, rep from * to last 7 sts, Cr2F, P1, bring bead up close to work, P1, Cr2B, P1.

4 Moss stitch lattice

This pattern works over a multiple of 8 stitches and can be used instead of the lattice pattern on the basic sweater.

1st row (RS) P3, sl next st onto a cable needle and hold at back of work, K1, then K1 from cable needle (called C2B), *P6, C2B, rep from * to last 3 sts, P3.

2nd row P the K sts and K the P sts of previous row.

3rd row P2, *C2B, sl next st onto cable needle and hold at front of work, P1, then K1 from cable needle (called

4

5

5 Fractured lattice

This works over a multiple of 8 stitches and can be used instead of the lattice on the basic sweater.

1st and every other row (WS) P across row.

2nd row *K tbl 2nd st on LH needle then K 1st st (called left twist, LT). K2, LT, K 2nd st on LH needle then K. first st (called right twist, RT), rep from *.

6th row *RT, LT, RT, K2, rep from *.

8th row K3, *LT, K2, RT, K2, rep from * to last 5 sts, LT, K3.

These 8 rows form the pattern repeat.

Cr2F), P4, rep from * to last 6 sts, C2B, Cr2F, P2.

4th row K2, *P2, K1, P1, K4, rep from * to last 6 sts, P2, K1, P1, K2.

5th row P1, *sl next st onto cable needle and leave at back of work, K1, then P1 from cable needle – (called Cr2B), K1, P1, sl next st onto cable needle and hold at front of work, K1, then P1 from cable needle (called C2F), P2, rep from * to last 7 sts, Cr2B, K1, P1, C2F, P1.

6th row K1, *(P1, K1) twice, P2, K2, rep from * to last 7 sts, (P1, K1) twice, P2, K1.

7th row *C2B, (P1, K1) twice, Cr2F, rep from * to end.

8th and 10th rows *P2, (K1, P1) 3 times, rep from * to end.

9th row K1, *(K1, P1) 3 times, C2B, rep from * to last 7 sts, (K1, P1) 3 times, K1.

11th row *Cr2F, (P1, K1) twice, Cr2B, rep from * to end.

12th row *K1, (P1, K1) twice, P2, K1, rep from * to end.

13th row P1, *Cr2F, K1, P1, Cr2B, P2, rep from * to last 7 sts, Cr2F, K1, P1, Cr2B, P1.

14th row K2, *P2, K1, P1, K4, rep from * to last 6 sts, P2, K1, P1, K2.

15th row P2, *Cr2F, Cr2B, P4, rep from * to last 6 sts, Cr2F, Cr2B, P2.

16th row As 2nd row.

These 16 rows form the pattern repeat.

6 Detached lattice

This stitch works over a multiple of 8 stitches, plus 4 extra. It is worked in three colors, B, C, and D on main color A.

1st row K3A, *(with B, cast on 7 sts, bind off 7 sts – called make a strip) twice, K6A, rep from * ending last rep K1A.

2nd row With A, K across row.

3rd-10th rows Beg with a K row work 8 rows stockinette st in A.

11th row With A, pick up and K 1 st from end of 2nd strip, sl onto LH needle and K2 tog. *K6, pick up and K 1 st from end of 4th strip, sl onto LH needle and K2 tog. pick up and K 1 st from end of first strip and K2 tog, rep from * keeping order of strips correct ending last rep K3.

12th row With A, K across row.

13th row With C, make a strip, *K6A,

with C make a strip twice, rep from * ending last rep K3.

14th row With A, K across row. Beg with K row, work 8 rows stockinette st in A.

23rd row With A, K3, *pick up and K 1 st from end of 3rd strip, sl onto LH needle, K2 tog, pick up and K 1 st from end of first strip, sl onto LH needle, K2 tog, K6, rep from * keeping sequence of strips correct, ending last rep pick up and K 1 st from end of last strip, sl onto LH needle, K2 tog.

24th row With A, K across row. These 24 rows form pattern repeat.

47

Traditional Shetland patterns

The Shetland Islands are famous not only for exquisite lace but also for elaborate color-patterned knitting which, though similar to Fair Isle, has its own distinctive features such as the use of all-over patterns as well as banded designs.

Skills you need

*Decreasing
*Simple increasing
*Working with color

If you do not know these skills refer to pages 174 and 175.

Materials

Traditional Shetland knitting was worked in wool from local sheep, which was carded and spun by hand, and dyed, if at all, with natural vegetable dyes. The softness and fineness of the yarn and the beauty and subtlety of the colors are responsible for much of the perennial appeal of Shetland patterns. Although chemical dyes are used these days they still retain the natural tones of vegetable dyes. The basic garments are worked in fingering yarn (which knits the same as sport weight) from the Shetland Isles.

Special technique – shaping with turning rows

 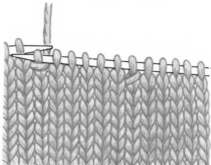 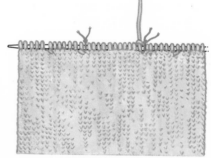

Coral Mula

1 The shoulders of the basic garments are shaped by working turning rows. On the first row of shoulder shaping purl the required number of stitches then turn the work so that the knit side is facing you, leaving the remaining stitches on the right-hand needle. Wrap yarn around first stitch on right-hand needle thus: yarn forward, slip one from right-hand needle, yarn back, slip stitch back on right-hand needle.

2 Knit the required number of stitches, then turn work so that the purl side is facing leaving the remaining stitches on the end of the needle. Wrap yarn around first stitch on right-hand needle thus: yarn back, slip one from right-hand needle, yarn forward, slip stitch back on right-hand needle. Purl the required number of stitches back to right shoulder, turn again, wrapping yarn around first stitch on right-hand needle.

3 Knit the required number of stitches back. This point marks the inner edge of the left shoulder. Now turn, wrap yarn around first stitch on right-hand needle as before and purl the required number of stitches back. This point marks the inner edge of the right shoulder. Leave the stitches on a spare needle. Working turning rows in this way makes it possible to graft the shoulders invisibly in the finishing.

The basic Shetland garments

You can put together a whole wardrobe of beautiful classics from this cleverly constructed composite pattern. A back, front and sleeves (long or short) makes a sweater; with armbands instead of sleeves it's a pullover; with a front opening it's a vest.

Sizes
To fit 32[34:36:38] in. bust
Length 21[21¼:22:22½] in.
Long sleeve seam 17¼ in.
Short sleeve seam 6 in.

Note: Instructions for larger sizes are in brackets []; where there is only one set of figures it applies to all sizes.

Gauge
30 sts and 29 rows to 4 in. over pat on size 3 needles

Materials
Vest
6[6:8:8] oz Shetland fingering yarn in main color (A)

3 oz in contrasting color (B)
1 oz in each of 9 contrasting colors (C, D, E, F, G, H, J, L, M)
Cardigan
9[9:10:10] oz in main color (A)
2 oz in contrasting color (B)
1 oz in each of 9 contrasting colors (C, D, E, F, G, H, J, L, M)
Short-sleeved pullover
10[10:11:11] oz in main color (A)
2 oz in contrasting color (B)
1 oz in each of 9 contrasting colors (C, D, E, F, G, H, J, L, M) (add 3 oz in main color for long-sleeved version)
1 pair each sizes 2 and 3 knitting needles
10[10:11:11] buttons (for vest or cardigan)

Vest
Back
** Using smaller needles and A, cast on 113[121:129:135] sts. Work in K1, P1 ribbing as foll:
1st row (RS) K1, *P1, K1, rep from * to end.
2nd row P1, *K1, P1, rep from * to end.
Rep the last 2 rows for 2¾ in. ending with a 1st row.
Next row Rib 4[8:4:7], (work twice into next st – called inc 1), rib 6[6:7:7] 15 times, inc 1, rib to end. 129[137:145:151] sts.
Change to larger needles and beg with a K row cont in stockinette st working Fair Isle pat from chart. Read K rows from right to left and P rows from left to right. Cont in pat until work measures 13 in. from cast-on edge, ending with a P row.

Shape armholes

Keeping pat correct, bind off 8[8:10:10] sts at beg of next 2 rows. Dec 1 st at each end of next and every other row until 101[107:107:113] sts rem.

**Cont without shaping until work measures 8[8¼:9:9½] in. from beg of armholes, ending with a K row.

Shape shoulders

Next row P86[91:91:96], turn.
Next row K71[75:75:79], turn.
Next row P55[58:58:61], turn.
Next row K39[41:41:43], turn.
Next row P39[41:41:43]. Leave these sts on a spare needle.

Pocket linings (make 2)

Using larger needles and A, cast on 25 sts. Beg with a K row cont in stockinette st. Work 23 rows, inc 1 st at each end of last row. 27 sts. Leave these sts on a spare needle.

Left front

Using smaller needles and A, cast on 67[71:75:77] sts. Work K1, P1 ribbing as for back for 2¾ in. ending with first row.

Next row Rib 11 and sl these sts onto a safety pin, rib 4[6:8:6], (inc 1, rib 5) 8[8:8:9] times, inc 1, rib to end. 65[69:73:76] sts.

Change to larger needles and beg with a K row cont in stockinette st and pat from chart thus: Begin reading chart at S[T:U:V], work 1[5:9:2] sts at beg of row, then rep 32 pat sts twice. Cont until work measures 5 in. from cast-on edge, ending with a P row.

Place pocket

Next row Work in pat 19[21:23:24], with A, K1, (P1, K1) 13 times, work in pat to end.

Next row Work in pat 19[21:23:25], with A, P1, (K1, P1) 13 times, work in pat to end.

Rep the last 2 rows once more.

Next row Work in pat 19[21:23:24],

with A, bind off in ribbing 27 sts, work in pat to end.

Next row Work in pat 19[21:23:25], work in pat across sts of one pocket lining, work in pat to end. Cont in pat until work measures same as back to underarm, ending at side edge.

Shape armhole

Bind off 8[8:10:10] sts at beg of next row. Dec 1 st at armhole edge on every other row until 51[54:54:57] sts rem. Cont without shaping until work measures 5½[6:6¾:7] in. from beg of armhole shaping, ending at front edge.

Shape neck

Next row Bind off 11 sts, work in pat to end.

Dec 1 st at neck edge on every row until 31[33:33:35] sts rem. Cont without shaping until work matches back to shoulder shaping, ending at neck edge.

Shape shoulder

Next row Work in pat 16[17:17:18], turn.

Next row Work in pat to end. Leave these sts on a spare needle.

Right front

Using smaller needles and A, cast on 67[71:75:77] sts.

Work in K1, P1 ribbing as given for back for ⅜ in., ending with a 2nd row.

1st buttonhole row Rib 4, bind off 3 sts, rib to end.

2nd buttonhole row Rib to end, casting on 3 sts over those bound off in previous row.

Cont in ribbing until work measures 2 in. from base of previous buttonhole, ending with a 2nd row. Work the 2 buttonhole rows again, then cont in ribbing until work measures 2¾ in. from cast-on edge, ending with a 1st row.

Next row Rib 3[5:7:5], (inc 1, rib 5) 8[8:8:9] times, inc 1, rib 4[6:8:6], turn and leave rem 11 sts on a safety pin. 65[69:73:76] sts.

Change to larger needles, beg with a K row, cont in stockinette st and pat from chart thus: begin reading chart at S, work 1 st at beg of row, rep 32 pat sts twice, then work 0[4:8:11] sts, finishing at W[X:Y:Z].

Complete to match left front, reversing placing of pocket on 4th size and all shapings.

To finish

Graft shoulder seams.

Armbands

With RS of work facing, using smaller needles and A, pick up and K 117[123:133:139] sts evenly around armhole edge.

Beg with a 2nd row work in K1, P1 ribbing as given for back for 9 rows. Bind off in ribbing.

Buttonband

With RS of work facing, using smaller needles and A, join in yarn to inner edge of sts on safety pin on left front. Work in K1, P1 ribbing as set until band is long enough, when slightly stretched, to fit up front edge to neck, ending with a WS row. Break yarn, leave these sts. Mark position of 9[9:10:10] buttons, two on band opposite buttonholes already worked, one 1½ in. above band, one 1½ in. below neck edge and others evenly spaced between.

Buttonhole band

With WS of work facing, using smaller needles and A, join in yarn to inner edge of sts on safety pin. Cont in ribbing as set making buttonholes

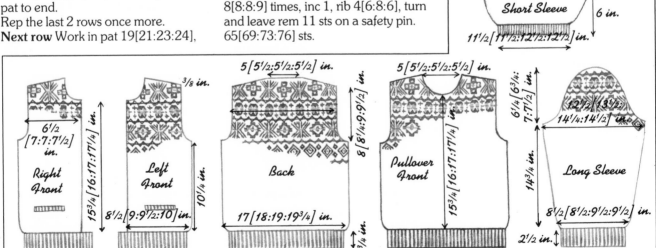

Ingrid Jacob

opposite markers until band measures same as buttonband, ending with WS row. Do not break yarn.

Neckband

With RS of work facing, using smaller needles and A, rib across sts of buttonhole band, pick up and K 26 sts up right side of neck, K across 39[41:41:43] sts on back neck, pick up and K 26 sts down right side neck, then rib across 11 sts on buttonband. 113[115:115:117] sts. Beg with 2nd row work 3 rows ribbing as given for back. Work 2 buttonhole rows again. Rib 4 more rows. Bind off in ribbing. Join side seams. Tack down pocket linings. Sew on front bands and buttons.

Cardigan

Back, pocket linings, left front and right front

Work as given for vest.

Long sleeves

Using smaller needles and A, cast on 57[59:61:63] sts.
Work in K1, P1 ribbing as given for back for 2¼ in. ending with a 1st row.
Next row Rib 4[7:3:4], *inc 1, rib 6[8:4:5], rep from * to last 4[7:3:5] sts, inc 1, rib to end. 65[65:73:73] sts.
Change to larger needles and beg with a 129th row cont in stockinette st and pat from chart, inc and work into pat 1 st at each end of 6th[9th:5th:5th] row and every foll 6th[5th:5th:5th] row until there are 97[101:107:111] sts.
Cont without shaping until work measures approx 17¼ in. from cast-on edge, ending with same pat row as back at underarm.

Shape top

Keeping pat correct, bind off 8[8:10:10] sts at beg of next 2 rows. Dec 1 st at each end of next and every foll 4th row until 77[81:81:85] sts rem, then at each end of every other row until 55[55:53:57] sts rem. Now dec 1 st at each end of every row until 25[25:27:27] sts rem.
Bind off.

To finish

Graft shoulder seams. Join side and sleeve seams. Set in sleeves. Tack down pocket linings. Sew on front bands and buttons.

Sweater

Back

Work as given for back of vest.

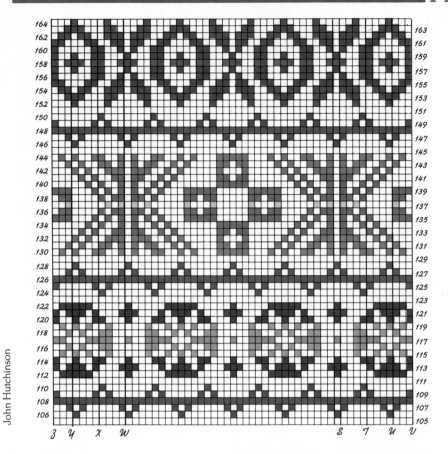

John Hutchinson

Front

Work as given for back of vest from ** to **.

Cont without shaping until work measures 5½[6:6¾:7] in. from beg of armholes, ending with a P row.

Shape neck

Next row Work in pat 38[40:40:42] and turn, leaving rem sts on a spare needle.

Complete left side of neck first. Dec 1 st at neck edge on every row until 31[33:33:35] sts rem.

Cont without shaping until work matches back to shoulder shaping, ending at neck edge.

Shape shoulder

Next row Work in pat 16[17:17:18], turn.

Next row Work in pat to end.

Leave these sts on a spare needle. With RS of work facing return to sts for right side of neck. Sl center 25[27:27:29] sts onto a spare needle, join in yarn to next st, work in pat to end.

Complete to match first side of neck.

Short sleeves

Using smaller needles and A, cast on 78[81:89:91] sts. Work in K1, P1 ribbing as given for back for 1¼ in. ending with a first row.

Next row Rib 4[8:6:5], *inc 1, rib

52

9[12:10:15], rep from * to last 5[8:6:6] sts, inc 1, rib to end. 87[87:97:97] sts.

Change to larger needles and beg with a 41st row cont in pat from chart, inc and work into pat 1 st at each end of the 5th and every foll 4th row until there are 97[101:107:111] sts.

Cont without shaping until work measures approx 6 in. from cast-on edge, ending with same pat row as back at underarm.

Shape top

Work as given for long sleeves on cardigan.

Should pads (make 2)

Using larger needles and A, cast on 38 sts.

Work in K1, P1 ribbing dec 1 st at each end of the 3rd and every other row until 2 sts rem.

Work 2 tog and fasten off.

To finish

Neckband

Graft right shoulder seam.

With RS of work facing, using smaller needles and A, pick up and K 19 sts down left side of neck, K across 25[27:27:29] sts at center front, pick up and K 19 sts up right side of neck, K across 39[41:41:43] sts on back neck, inc 1 st at center. 103[107:107:111] sts.

Beg with a 2nd row work in K1, P1 ribbing as given for back. Work 9 rows. Bind off in ribbing.

Graft left shoulder seam and join neckband.

Join side and sleeve seams. Set in sleeves. Sew in shoulder pads.

Adapting the Shetland garments

With the Pattern Library and a huge choice of shapes in the basic pattern, there really are endless possibilities for variations on the basic garments.

All the component parts of the garments in the basic pattern have been designed to fit together perfectly so they can be combined to make any number of different garments. Some of the possibilities are shown in the photograph but there are many others. The sweater, for example, can be made up with the long sleeves of the cardigan pattern, the instructions for armbands on the vest also apply to a sleeveless pullover made from the back and front of the sweater pattern, and the shoulder pads from the sweater are just as appropriate to the cardigan.

Shetland patterns

Hand knitting has been a cottage industry in the Shetland Islands for at least 500 years, and very probably much longer than that. The traditions of fine lace knitting associated with the Shetlands, and of color-patterned knitting from Fair Isle (generally considered to be part of the Shetland Island group) are justly famous but have tended to overshadow the equally strong tradition of multi-colored knitting found in the rest of the Shetland Islands.

At first glance these patterns are, as one would expect, very similar to Fair Isle patterns. However, there are some important differences. Banded designs are used, as in Fair Isle, and often employ the same basic motifs (the

OXO designs, Norwegian stars, and so on) but these are frequently worked on a constant background color as in the basic garments on page 48. Also, there is far more use of all-over patterns such as those on samples 1 and 3. Often a banded effect is imposed on these strongly geometric patterns by working the basic design alternately with a dark contrast on a light background, then a light contrast on a dark background (see sample 3). Sample 4 shows some of the small patterns (known locally as "peerie" patterns) that are used for borders or vertical "filling" motifs or, sometimes, on small items as all-over patterns. The coloring of traditional Shetland work also differs from classic Fair Isle knitting in that it is generally more subdued and certainly less intricate. Sample 1 shows a typical traditional color scheme.

Simon Wheeler/Murray West

repeat 12 sts

repeat 26 sts

repeat 10 sts

repeat 12 sts

Woven-look patterns

Knitting techniques can imitate the appearance and textures of woven fabric surprisingly successfully. A wide range of effects can be achieved using yarns of varying thickness and in contrasting colors and textures.

Skills you need

*Using a cable needle
*Traveling stitches

If you do not know these skills refer to pages 174 and 185.

Materials

The basic dress is worked in a plain worsted-weight yarn that makes it very quick to knit up yet still relatively light for this type of garment. The contrasting yarns are of the same type but they could be replaced with, for example, mohair if a more elaborate texture is required. In fact, woven-look patterns in general are excellent vehicles for mixing different types of yarn.

Special technique – knitting in weaving threads

1 The woven-look effect on the patchwork cable is achieved by weaving in contrasting yarns as you knit. On right-side rows secure the end of the weaving thread at the back of the work, bring it to the front then work the next stitch in the main color. Take the weaving thread to the back.

2 On wrong-side rows the weaving thread begins at the front of the work. Take it through to the back (the right side of the work), work the next stitch in the main color, then bring the weaving thread back to the front. The contrasting yarns are thus woven from back to front of the work but never actually knitted.

3 The weaving threads are arranged in two different ways in the basic pattern. On one section of the cable the threads on the right side are staggered above each other. On the other section they lie directly above each other.

Coral Mula

The basic woven-look dress

Interlaced cables woven through with contrast-colored threads add an original touch to an attractive Aran-knit sweater dress that's both warm and stylish.

Sizes
To fit 32[34:36] in. bust
Length 35½[36:36½] in.
Sleeve seam 17¾[18:18½] in.

Note: Instructions for larger sizes are in square brackets []; where there is only one set of figures it applies to all sizes.

Gauge
20 sts and 24 rows to 4 in. over seed
54

st on size 6 needles
28 sts and 24 rows to 4 in. over central cable panel on size 6 needles

Materials
53[57:60] oz of knitting worsted in main color (A)
3 oz in each of two contrasting colors (B) and (C)
1 pair each sizes 5 and 6 knitting needles

Size 5 circular needle 16 in. long
Cable needle

Special note: When weaving contrasting yarns on patchwork panels, use separate balls of yarn for each panel, carrying yarn up WS of work when not in use. See also Special technique above.

Patchwork cable panel pat
(worked over 19 sts)
1st row (RS) P2, K2 (K1 weaving B on RS, thus, bring contrasting yarn B to RS, K1A, take B to WS – called

Eamonn McCabe

K1wB –, P1) 3 times, K1wB, K4, P4.

2nd row K4, P4, (K1, P1 weaving B on RS thus, take contrasting yarn B to RS, P1A, bring B to WS, called P1wB), 3 times, K1, P2, K2.

3rd row P2, sl next 2 sts onto cable needle and hold at front of work, P1, then K2 from cable needle – called Tw3F –, (P1, K1wB) 3 times, sl next 2 sts onto cable needle and hold at front of work, K2, then K2 from cable needle (called C4F), P4.

4th row K4, P4, (K1, P1wB), 3 times, P2, K3.

5th row P3, Tw3F, K1wB, P1, K1wB, sl next 2 sts onto cable needle and hold at back of work, K2, then P2 from cable needle – called Tw4B –, sl next 2 sts onto cable needle and hold at front of work, K1, then K2 from cable needle (called C3F), P3.

6th row K3, P2, P1 tbl weaving C on RS thus, take contrasting yarn C to RS, P1A tbl, bring C to WS (called P1 tblwC), K1, P1 tblwC, P2, K1, P1wB, K1, P2, K4.

7th row P4, Tw3F, Tw4B, K1 tbl weaving C on RS thus, bring contrasting yarn C to RS, K1 tbl, take C to WS (called K1 tblwC), P1, K1 tblwC, Tw3F, P2.

8th row K2, P2, (K1, P1 tblwC) 3 times, P4, K5.

9th row P5, Tw4B, (K1 tblwC, P1) 3 times, K2, P2.

10th row K2, P2, (K1, P1 tblwC) 4 times, P2, K5.

11th row P3, Tw4B, (K1 tblwC, P1) 3 times, K1 tblwC, sl next st onto cable needle and hold at back of work, K2, then P1 from cable needle (called Tw3B), P2.

12th row K3, P2, (P1 tblwC, K1) 4 times, P1 tblwC, P2, K3.

13th row P2, Tw3B, (K1 tblwC, P1) 3 times, K1 tblwC, Tw4B, P3.

14th row K5, P2, (P1 tblwC, K1) 4 times, P2, K2.

15th row P2, K2, (P1, K1 tblwC) 3 times, sl next 2 sts onto cable needle and hold at back of work, K2, then K2 from cable needle (called C4B), P5.

16th row K5, P4, (P1 tblwC, K1) 3 times, P2, K2.

17th row P2, Tw3F, K1 tblwC, P1, K1 tblwC, Tw4B, C3F, P4.

18th row K4, P2, K1, P1wB, K1, P2, P1 tblwC, K1, P1 tblwC, P2, K3.

19th row P3, Tw3F, Tw4B, K1wB, P1, K1wB, Tw3F, P3.

20th row K3, P2, (P1wB, K1) 3 times, P4, K4.

21st row P4, C4F, (K1wB, P1) 3 times, C3F, P2.

22nd row K2, P2, (K1, P1wB) 3 times, K1, P4, K4.

23rd row P4, K4, (K1wB, P1) 3 times, K1wB, K2, P2.

24th row K2, P2, (K1, P1wB) 3 times, K1, P4, K4.

25th row P4, C4F, (K1wB, P1) 3 times, Tw3B, P2.

26th row K3, P2, (P1wB, K1) 3 times, P4, K4.

27th row P3, sl next st onto cable needle and hold at back of work, K2, then K1 from cable needle (called Cr3B), sl next 2 sts onto cable needle and hold at front of work, P2, then K2 from cable needle (called Tw4F), K1wB, P1, K1wB, Tw3B, P3.

28th row K4, P2, K1, P1wB, K1, P2, P1 tblwC, K1, P1 tblwC, P2, K3.

29th row P2, Tw3B, K1 tblwC, P1, K1 tblwC, Tw4F, Tw3B, P4.

30th row K5, P4, (P1 tblwC, K1) 3 times, P2, K2.

31st row P2, K2, (P1, K1 tblwC) 3 times, Tw4F, P5.

32nd row K5, P2, (P1 tblwC, K1) 4 times, P2, K2.

33rd row P2, Tw3F, (K1 tblwC, P1) 3 times, K1 tblwC, Tw4F, P3.

34th row K3, P2, (P1 tblwC, K1) 4 times, P1 tblwC, P2, K3.

35th row P3, Tw4F, (K1 tblwC, P1) 3 times, K1 tblwC, Tw3F, P2.

36th row K2, P2, (K1, P1 tblwC) 4 times, P2, K5.

37th row P5, C4F, (K1 tblwC, P1) 3 times, K2, P2.

38th row K2, P2, (K1, P1 tblwC) 3 times, P4, K5.

39th row P4, Cr3B, Tw4F, K1 tblwC, P1, K1 tblwC, Tw3B, P2.

40th row K3, P2, P1 tblwC, K1, P1 tblwC, P2, K1, P1wB, K1, P2, K4.

41st row P3, Tw3B, K1wB, P1, K1wB, Tw4F, Tw3B, P3.

42nd row K4, P4, (K1, P1wB) 3 times, P2, K3.

43rd row P2, Cr3B, (P1, K1wB) 3 times, C4F, P4.

44th row K4, P4, (K1, P1wB) 3 times, K1, P2, K2.

These 44 rows form patchwork cable panel pat, referred to throughout as "cable 19".

Central cable panel pat (worked over 31 sts)

1st row (RS) K2, P1, K3, (P4, K6) twice, P3, K2.

2nd and every other row K the P sts and P the K sts of previous row.

3rd row K2, P1, K3, (P4, sl next 3 sts onto cable needle and hold at front of work, K3, then K3 from cable needle) twice, P3, K2.

5th row K2, P1, (sl next 3 sts onto cable needle and hold at front of work, P2, then K3 from cable needle (called C5F), sl next 2 sts onto cable needle and hold at back of work, K3, then P2 from cable needle (called C5B) twice, C5F, P1, K2.

7th row K2, P3, (sl next 3 sts onto cable needle and hold at back of work, K3, then K3 from cable needle, P4) twice, K3, P1, K2.

9th row K2, P1, (C5B, C5F) twice, C5B, P1, K2.

10th row As 2nd row.

These 10 rows form the central cable panel pat, referred to throughout as "cable 31".

Back

**Using smaller needles and A, cast on 114[118:122] sts. Work in twisted K1, P1 ribbing as foll:

1st row (RS) *K1 tbl, P1, rep from * to end.

2nd row *K1, P1 tbl, rep from * to end.

Rep the last 2 rows until work measures 1⅛ in. from cast-on edge, ending with a WS row.

Next row Rib 29[30:31], (work twice into next st – called inc 1 –, rib 27[28:29]) twice, inc 1, rib to end. 117[121:125] sts.

Next row K across row.

Change to larger needles and commence pat.

1st row (RS) (K1, P1) 11[12:13] times, K2, work first row of cable 19, first row of cable 31, first row of cable 19, K2, (P1, K1) 11[12:13] times.

2nd row (K1, P1) 11[12:13] times, P2, work 2nd row of cable 19, 2nd row of cable 31, 2nd row of cable 19, P2, (P1, K1) 11[12:13] times.

These 2 rows establish the pat of cable panels between stockinette st borders and seed st edge sts.

Keeping pat correct, inc and work into seed st 1 st at each end of 18th and every foll 20th row until there are 125[131:137] sts. Cont in pat until work measures 25½[26:26½] in. ending with a WS row.

Shape armholes

Next row Work in pat 26[29:32] sts and sl onto a st holder, work in pat 73, turn, sl last 26[29:32] sts onto a st holder. **

Cont in pat until work measures 35½[35¾:36¼] in. from cast-on edge, ending with a RS row.

Next row P3, K to last 3 sts, P3.

Leave these sts on a spare needle.

Front

Work as given for back from ** to **.

Cont in pat until work measures 5 rows less than back.

Shape neck

Next row (WS) P2, K2 tog, turn.

Next row P1, K2, turn.

Next row P1, P2 tog, turn.

Next row K2, turn.

Next row P2 tog, K65 sts at center, K2 tog, P2, turn.

Next row K2, P1, turn.

Next row P2 tog, P1, turn.

Next row K2, turn.

Next row P2 tog.

Break off yarn, leave rem 67 sts on a spare needle.

Left sleeve

*** Using smaller needles and A, cast on 50[52:54] sts. Work 1⅛ in. twisted K1, P1 ribbing as given for back, ending with a WS row.

Next row Rib 3[2:14], *inc 1, rib 1[1:0], rep from * to last 3[2:14] sts, inc 1, rib to end. 73[77:81] sts.

Next row K across row.

Change to larger needles and commence pat.

First size only

1st row K2, cable 19, cable 31, cable 19, K2.

2nd row P2, cable 19, cable 31, cable 19, P2.

These 2 rows establish the pat.

2nd and 3rd sizes only

1st row (K1, P1) [1:2] times, K2, cable 19, cable 31, cable 19, K2 (P1, K1) [1:2] times.

2nd row (K1, P1) [1:2] times, P2, cable 19, cable 31, cable 19, P2 (P1, K1) [1:2] times.

These 2 rows establish the pat.

All sizes

Keeping pat correct, inc and work into seed st, 1 st at each end of the 2nd[4th:4th] and every foll 4th row until there are 121 sts. ***

Cont without shaping until work measures 17¾[18¼:18½] in. from cast-on edge, ending with a RS row.

Shape pocket lining

Next row Cast on 20 sts, P20, work in pat to end.

Next row Work in pat to last 20 sts, K20.

Rep the last 2 rows until work measures 5[5½:6¼] in. from beg of pocket lining, ending with a RS row.

Next row K across row.

Bind off loosely.

Right sleeve

Work as given for left sleeve from *** to ***. Cont without shaping until work measures 17¾[18¼:18½] in. from cast-on edge, ending with a WS row.

Shape pocket lining

Next row Cast on 20 sts, K20, work in pat to end.

Next row Work in pat to last 20 sts, P20.

Complete to match left sleeve.

To finish

Join side seams

Left pocket border

Using smaller needles and A, with WS of work facing, K across the 26[29:32] sts left on stitch holder at left front

armhole, then K across the 26[29:32] sts on stitch holder at left back armhole. 52[58:64] sts. Work 8 rows twisted K1, P1 ribbing as given for back, beg with a 2nd row. Bind off in ribbing.

Right pocket border
Work as given for left pocket border but K across sts on holder at right back armhole, then across sts on holder at right front armhole. 52[58:64] sts. Complete as for left pocket border.

Join underarm seams to pocket lining. Fold pocket borders onto RS and tack down sides. Set in sleeves. Tack down pocket linings to WS.

Collar
Using circular needle, with RS of work facing, pick up and K 4 sts from left side of neck, K across 67 sts at center front, pick up and K 4 sts up right side of neck, K across 73 sts on back neck. 148 sts. Work in rounds.

1st round *P1 tbl, K1, rep from * to end.

Rep this round until work measures 11 in. from beg.
Bind off in ribbing.

Adapting the woven-look dress

Contrasting weaving threads can be knitted into the fabric in lots of ways to give your dress a touch of individuality.

The patterns created by weaving threads can be endlessly varied and almost any stitch can provide a suitable base for them. It would even be possible to work motifs by plotting the stitches carefully. The Special Technique on page 54 describes the basic principles of knitting in weaving threads and these can be applied to this or any other pattern you may have. Do not leave too great a gap before bringing the yarn to the right side again or you will have long untidy (and uncomfortable) "floats" on the wrong side of the work where the yarn has been carried across the back.

Woven-look patterns

1 Turned check
This pattern is worked over an odd number of stitches, and in two colors (A and B).
1st row (WS) With A, K across row.
2nd row With B, K1, *insert RH needle into next st tbl from left to right and sl it onto RH needle, K1, rep from * to end.
3rd row With B, K1, *yfwd, sl 1, ybk, K1, rep from * to end.
4th row With A, K1, *K1 tbl, K1, rep from * to end.
5th row With A, K across row.
6th row With B, K2, *insert RH needle into next st tbl from left to right and sl it onto RH needle, K1, rep from * to last st, K1.
7th row With B, K2, *yfwd, sl 1, ybk, K1, rep from * to last st, K1.
8th row With A, K2, *K1 tbl, K1, rep from * to last st, K1.
These 8 rows form the pattern repeat.

2 Tweed knot stitch
This pattern is worked over an odd number of stitches and in two colors (A and B).
1st row (WS) With A, K across row.
2nd row With B, K1, *K next st in row below, K1, rep from * to end.
3rd row With B, K across row.
4th row With A, K2, *K next st in row below, K1, rep from * to last st, K1.
These 4 rows form the pattern repeat.

3 Woven slip stitch

This pattern is worked over an even number of stitches and in three colors (A, B and C).

1st row (RS) With A, K across row.
2nd row With A, P across row.
3rd row With B, *ybk, sl 1, yfwd, sl 1, rep from * to end.
4th row With B, *yfwd, sl 1, ybk, sl 1, rep from * to end.
5th-8th rows As 1st-4th rows using C instead of B.
These 8 rows form the pattern repeat.

4 Tassel weave

This pattern is worked over a multiple of 6 stitches, plus 1 extra, and in three colors, (A, B and C).

1st row (RS) With A, *K4, P2, rep from * to last st, K1.
2nd row With A, P1, *K2, P4, rep from * to end.
3rd row As 1st row.
4th row As 2nd row.
5th row *Insert RH needle between 4th and 5th sts on LH needle, wind B around point of RH needle and draw loop through to RS, with A, K1, P2, K3, rep from * to last st, K1.
6th row With A, P1, *P3, K2, P2 tog, rep from * to end.
7th and 9th rows With A, K1, *P2, K4, rep from * to end.
8th and 10th rows With A, *P4, K2, rep from * to last st, P1.
11th row With A, K3, *insert RH needle between 4th and 5th sts on LH needle, wind C around point of RH needle and draw loop through to RS, with A, K1, P2, K3, rep from * ending last rep, K1, P2, K1.
12th row P1, K2, P2 tog, *P3, K2, P2 tog, rep from * to last 3 sts, P3.
These 12 rows form the pattern repeat.

5 Ribbon bow

This pattern is worked over a multiple of 4 stitches, plus 3 extra, and in two colors (A and B).

1st row (WS) With A, P across row.
2nd row With B, K1, *sl 1, K3, rep from * to last 2 sts, sl 1, K1.
3rd row With B, K1, *yfwd, sl 1, ybk, K1, K1 winding yarn 4 times around needle, K1, rep from * to last 2 sts, yfwd, sl 1, ybk, K1.

4th row With A, K3, *sl 1 dropping extra loops, K3, rep from * to end.
5th row With A, P3, *ybk, sl 1, yfwd, P3, rep from * to end.
6th row With A, K3, *sl 1, K3, rep from * to end.
7th row As 5th row.
8th row As 6th row.
9th row As 5th row.
The 2nd-9th rows form pattern repeat.

3

4

Steve Tanner

5

Garter stitch variations

Garter stitch is the simplest, most basic knitting pattern, being composed entirely of either knit or purl stitches. Even so, by combining it with other stitches, a surprisingly wide range of textures can be constructed.

Skills you need

*The knit stitch
*The purl stitch

If you do not know these skills refer to pages 172 and 173.

Materials

Garter stitch and its variations can be worked in any type of yarn. The subtle horizontal corrugated texture is more pronounced when a smooth plain yarn is used. Garter stitch itself is also suitable for very fancy yarns where the special characteristics of the yarn are the main design feature and a plain stitch pattern is required. The variations on garter stitch are best worked in plain yarns like the knitting worsted used for the basic sweater and dress.

Special technique – setting sleeves in flat

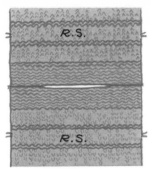
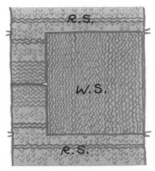
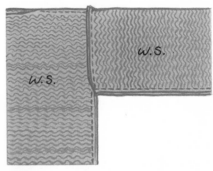

1 *Join the shoulder seam. Place a marker on the front and back of the garment at the distance from the shoulder seam given in the pattern.*

2 *With right sides together, place the center of the bound-off edge of the sleeve to the shoulder seam.*

3 *Join the seam between the markers. Join the side and sleeve seams.*

Coral Mula

The basic garter-stitch dress and sweater

This simple sporty dress and sweater are both so easy to knit. Made from basic rectangular shapes in stockinette stitch with garter stitch ridges and borders, they are ideal garments for beginners.

Sizes
To fit 32[34:36:38] in. bust
Sweater length 28[28:30:30] in.
Dress length 36[36:38:38] in.
Sleeve seam 14 in.
Note: Instructions for larger sizes are in brackets []; where there is only one set of figures it applies to all sizes.

Gauge
22 sts and 30 rows to 4 in. over stockinette st on size 5 needles

Materials
Pullover
25[25:29:29] oz knitting worsted
Dress
29[33:37:37] oz knitting worsted
1 pair each sizes 3 and 5 knitting needles

Sweater
Back
Using smaller needles, cast on 108 [114:120:126] sts.
Next row (WS) K across row.

Next row K across row.
Cont in garter st (every row K). Work 45[45:39:39] rows.
Change to larger needles.
* Beg with a K row work 15 rows in stockinette st.
Next row (WS) K across row.
Next row K across row.
Next row K across row.*
Rep from * to * 7[7:8:8] times more.
Work 15 rows stockinette st, ending with a K row.
Change to smaller needles
Work 35 rows garter st.
Bind off.

Front
Work as given for back.

Sleeves
Using smaller needles, cast on 82 [88:94:100] sts.
Work 23 rows in garter st.
Change to larger needles.
Work as given for back from * to * 3 times.
Work 15 rows stockinette st, ending with a K row.
Change to smaller needles.
Work 35 rows garter st.
Bind off.

To finish

Press lightly, omitting garter st borders. Using a back-stitch seam, join shoulder seams, leaving the center 9¾ in. free for neck opening. Mark down 7½ [8:8¾:9] in. from shoulder on back and front. Placing the center of bound-off edge of sleeve to shoulder seam, set in sleeves between markers. Join sleeve and side seams leaving garter st border at hem free to form slits.

Spike Powell

Dress
Back

Using smaller needles, cast on 108 [114:120:126] sts.
Next row (WS) K across row.
Next row K across row.
Cont in garter st (every row K). Work 51[51:49:49] rows.
Change to larger needles.
Work as given for back of sweater from * to * 11[11:12:12] times. Work 15 rows in stockinette st, ending with a K row.
Change to smaller needles.
Work 35 rows in garter st.
Bind off.

Front

Work as given for back.

Sleeves

Work as given for sweater.

To finish

Complete as given for sweater, but join garter stitch border to hem omitting slits.

62

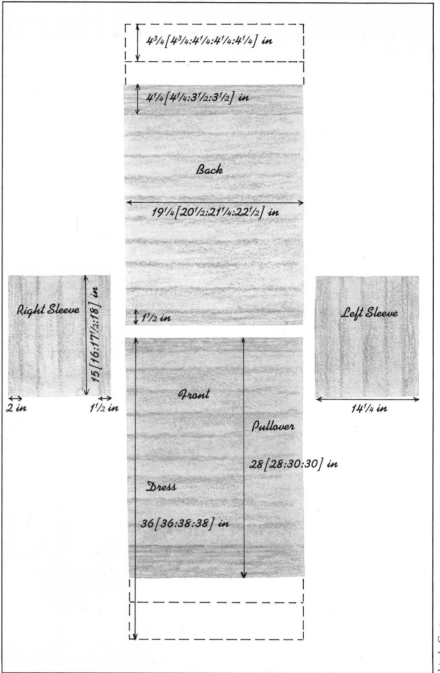

4¾[4¾:4¼:4¼:4¼] in

4¼[4¼:3½:3½] in

Back

19¼[20½:21¼:22½] in

Right Sleeve

15[16:17½:18] in

1½ in

2 in   1½ in

Front

Pullover

28[28:30:30] in

Dress

36[36:38:38] in

Left Sleeve

14¼ in

Linda Greigg

Adapting the basic dress

Simple shapes like those in the dress are easy to adapt to new stitch patterns.

Adding color

Give the dress or sweater a genuine nautical flavor by striping them. Work the garter stitch ridges and borders in a contrasting color. For a smooth unbroken line between the ridge and the stockinette stitch band, work the 15th row of stockinette stitch in each pattern repeat in the same color as the ridge (that is, the following three knit rows). Alternatively the ridges can be worked much closer together to give the garments a more densely textured look or made wider by working more knit rows between the bands of stockinette stitch. When varying the pattern in this way, follow the measurement diagram for length.
Color can also be added by treating the plain stockinette stitch bands as a background for simple surface embroidery. Stockinette stitch provides a natural "grid" that is especially suitable for working cross-stitch patterns.

Transferred patterns

Almost anything can be used as inspiration for knitting designs but printed fabrics are particularly appropriate since you can use the fabric to make up a matching garment. Transferring patterns in this way from one fabric to another makes it possible to coordinate your wardrobe in an entirely new way.

Ray Moller

Skills you need

*Decreasing
*Working with color

If you do not know these skills refer to pages 174 and 175.

Materials

When choosing fabric designs suitable for translation into knitting patterns, look for fairly simple ones as it is not possible to copy the lines of intricate printed motifs exactly onto knitted fabrics. Geometric designs are generally the easiest to imitate successfully though you may need to scale the pattern down or up, as in the case of the basic top. Simple floral motifs such as those in the Pattern Library are also possibilities. Matching the colors of the knitted pattern to the original is important and may dictate the choice of yarn. The basic top is worked in a fine cotton in eight colors.

Special technique – diagonal color changes

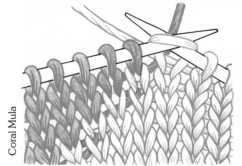

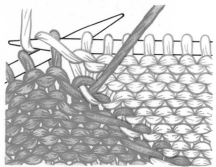

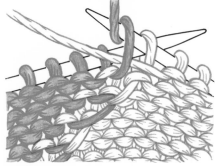

Coral Mula

1 When working with different blocks of color in a row it is often not practical to strand or weave yarns across the back. They must therefore be twisted together, otherwise holes will appear between color blocks. When the design moves diagonally to the right, twist colors together on knit rows as shown.

2 On purl rows it is not necessary to twist the colors as they are automatically twisted in the course of working the pattern as usual.

3 When the diagonal moves to the left on the right side of the work the colors must be twisted on purl rows only crossing the yarns as shown.

The basic patterned top

Bold geometrics and glowing colors make this stunning cotton top a perfect translation of the silky fabric of the trousers. Tricky to knit but the end result is definitely worthwhile!

Sizes
To fit 32[34:36:38] in. bust
Length 18[18:18½:18½] in.

Note: Instructions for larger sizes are in square brackets []; where there is only one set of figures it applies to all sizes.

Gauge
33 sts and 39 rows to 4 in. over pat on size 2 needles

Materials
6[7:9:11] oz of fingering-weight cotton yarn in main color (A)
2 oz in each of 7 contrasting colors (B, C, D, E, F, G, H)
Size 00 and 2 long knitting needles
8 buttons
64

Special note:
Use small separate balls of yarn for each color area, twisting yarns tog with changing color to avoid a hole (see Special technique).

Front and backs (worked in one piece)
Using smaller needles and A, cast on 291[309:327:349] sts.
1st row K1, *P1, K1, rep from * to end.
2nd row P1, *K1, P1, rep from * to end.
Rep the last 2 rows for 2¼ in., ending with a first row.
Next row Rib 13[11:15:15], pick up loop between last st worked and next st on LH needle and work into the back of it (called M1), *rib 24[26:27:29], M1, rep from * to last

14[12:15:15] sts, rib to end.
303[321:339:361] sts.
Change to larger needles.
Beg with a K row cont in stockinette st, working pat from chart (read K rows from right to left and P rows from left to right).
Cont in this way until work measures 11¾ in. from cast-on edge, ending with a P row.
Divide for armholes
Next row Work in pat 65[68:72:76], bind off 22[24:26:28], work in pat 129[137:143:153] including st used in binding off, bind off 22[24:26:28], work in pat to end.
Cont on last set of 65[68:72:76] sts for right back.
Shape armhole and back neck
Next row Work 2 tog, work in pat to end.
Dec 1 st at each end of next 9[11:11:13] rows, then on every other row until 32[31:33:31] sts rem.
Keeping armhole edge straight, cont to dec at neck edge as before on every other until 13[13:14:14] sts rem, ending with a P row.

Shape shoulder

Bind off 4[4:5:5] sts at beg of next and foll alt row.
Work 1 row. Bind off rem 5[5:4:4] sts.

Work front

With WS of work facing, join in appropriate yarn to center 129[137:143:153] sts for front and work in pat to end.
Dec 1 st at each end of next 9[11:11:13] rows, then on every other row until 97[101:105:109] sts rem.
Cont without shaping until work measures 23 rows fewer than right back to shoulder shaping, so ending with a K row.

Shape front neck

Next row Work in pat 22[22:23:23] sts, bind off 53[57:59:63] sts, work in pat to end.
Cont on last set of 22[22:23:23] sts for left side of front neck.
Dec 1 st at neck edge of next 5 rows then on every other row until 13[13:14:14] sts rem.
Cont without shaping until work measures same as right back to shoulder shaping, ending with a P row.

Shape shoulder

Bind off 4[4:5:5] sts at beg of next and foll alt row. Work 1 row. Bind off rem 5[5:4:4] sts.
With RS of work facing, return to sts for right side of front neck. Join in appropriate yarn to next st and work in pat to end.
Complete to match first side of neck, reversing all shapings.

Work left back

With WS of work facing, return to 65[68:72:76] sts for left back.

Shape armhole and back neck

Complete to match right back, reversing all shapings.

Armbands

With RS of work facing, using smaller needles and A, pick up and K 166[168:176:178] sts around armhole edge. Work 7 rows K1, P1 ribbing. Bind off in ribbing.

Buttonband

With RS of work facing, using smaller needles and A, pick up and K 118 sts up left back to beg of neck shaping, and 74[74:78:78] sts up left back neck to shoulder. 192[192:196:196] sts.
Work 7 rows K1, P1 ribbing. Bind off in ribbing.

Buttonhole band

With RS of work facing, using smaller

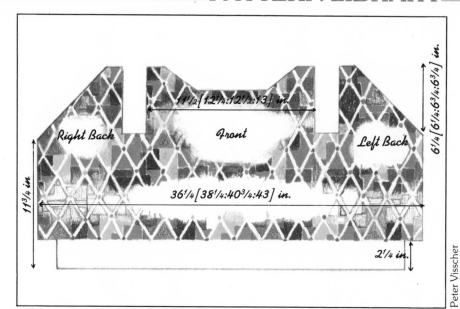

needles and A, pick up and K 74[74:78:78] sts down right back neck from shoulder to beg of neck shaping, and 118 sts down right back. 192[192:196:196] sts. Work 3 rows K1, P1 ribbing.
Buttonhole row Rib 74[74:78:78], work 2 tog, yo, (rib 14, work 2 tog, yo) 7 times, rib 4.
Rib 3 more rows. Bind off in ribbing.

Front neckband

With RS of work facing, using smaller needles and A, pick up and K 100[104:108:112] sts evenly around neck edge.
Work 7 rows K1, P1 ribbing.
Bind off in ribbing.

To finish

Press with a warm iron.
Join shoulder seams.
Sew on buttons.

Adapting the patterned top

The pattern on the top presents a challenge even to experienced knitters but there are some ways in which it could be simplified.

The simplest of all variations would be to knit an entirely plain version of the sweater, following the shaping instructions of the basic pattern but ignoring the chart. Alternatively, try a straightforward harlequin version. Work the basic white diagonals from the chart but use one color for each diamond instead of the multicolors of the original. The tiny diamonds that occur where the diagonals cross could also be ignored if desired.

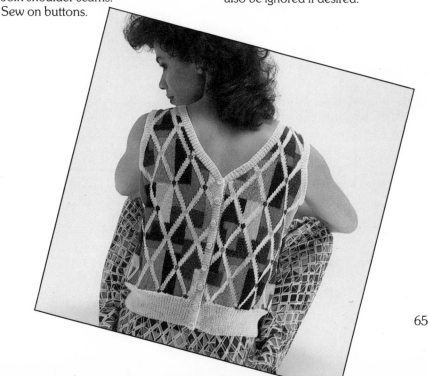

Chart for patterned top

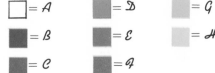

☐ = A   ▨ = D   ▨ = G

▨ = B   ▨ = E   ▨ = H

▨ = C   ▨ = F

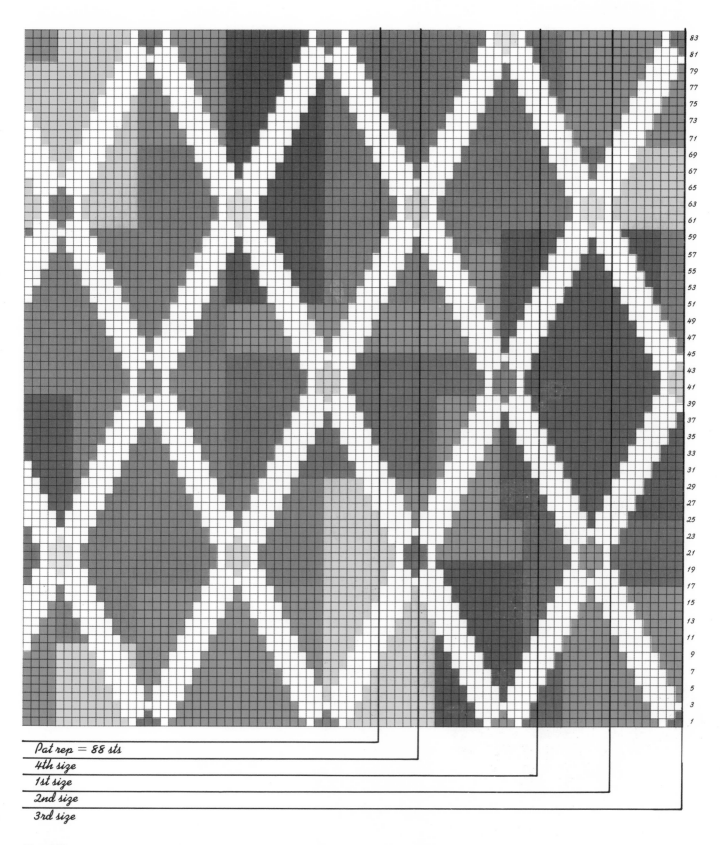

Pat rep = 88 sts
4th size
1st size
2nd size
3rd size

Read K rows from right to left and P rows from left to right, following the two halves of the chart consecutively thus: beg with RH side of chart K edge sts for your size as set, then first 44 pat sts, cont to LH side of chart, K rem 44 pat sts, rep 88 pat sts 2[2:2:3] times more, K edge sts on LH side of chart. Work in reverse for P rows.

Transferred patterns

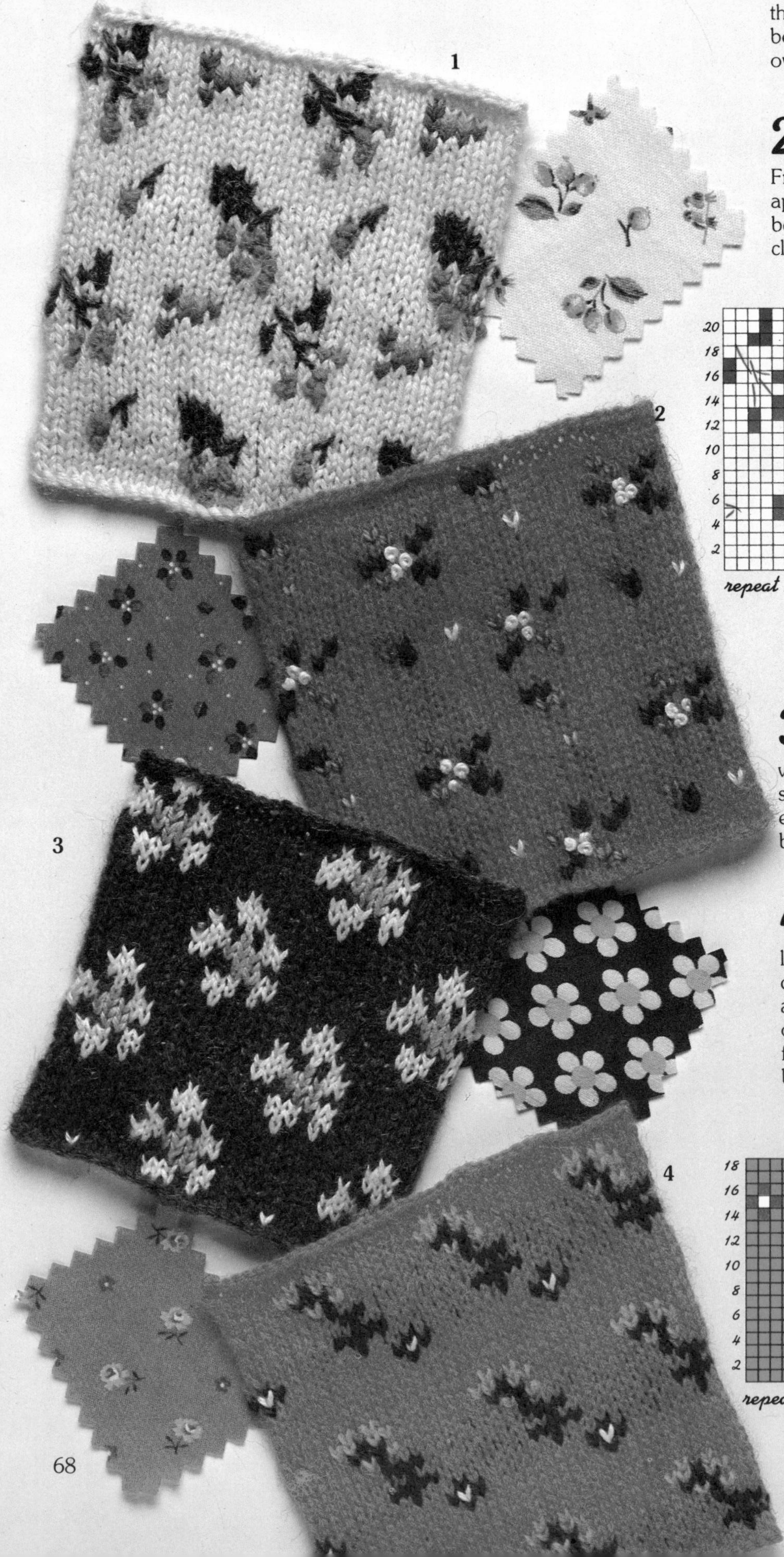

1 Rose hips
Simple straight-stitch embroidery for the stems completes the motifs on this sample. Although the motifs have been considerably simplified, the overall feeling of the fabric is retained.

2 Holly
Tiny single-stitch holly leaves and French knots for berries add up to an appealing all-over pattern that would be particularly suitable for children's clothes.

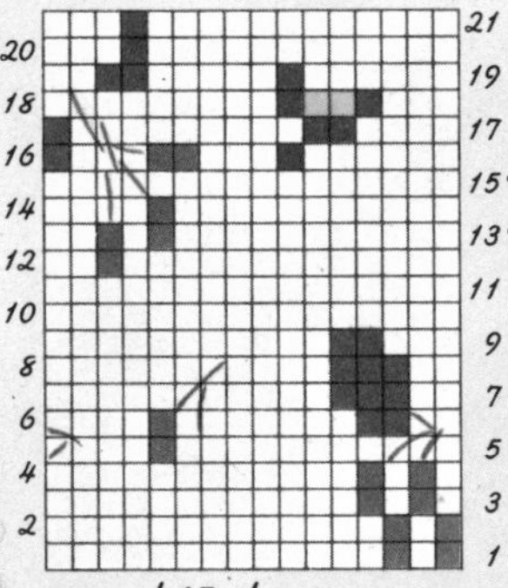

repeat 15 sts

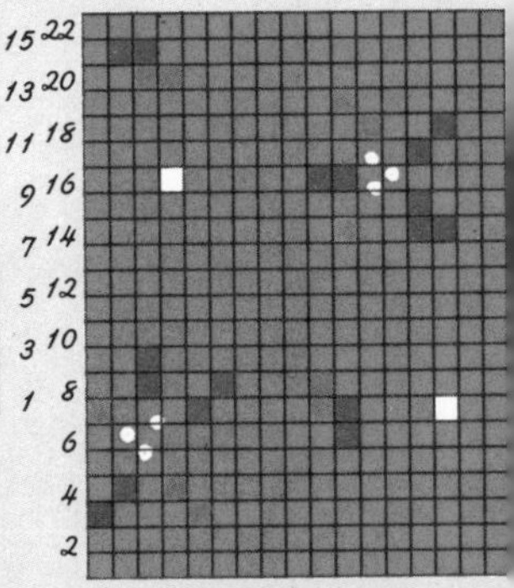

repeat 17 sts

3 Daisy
A scattering of daisies is here worked into an all-over pattern but single motifs could also be worked either alone or strung into chains as a border design.

4 Texas roses
Much of the appeal of this sample lies in its vivid color scheme. The motif can be worked as a repeating pattern, as here, or simply strewn at random over the background color. If only a few motifs are being worked it would be more practical to Swiss-darn them.

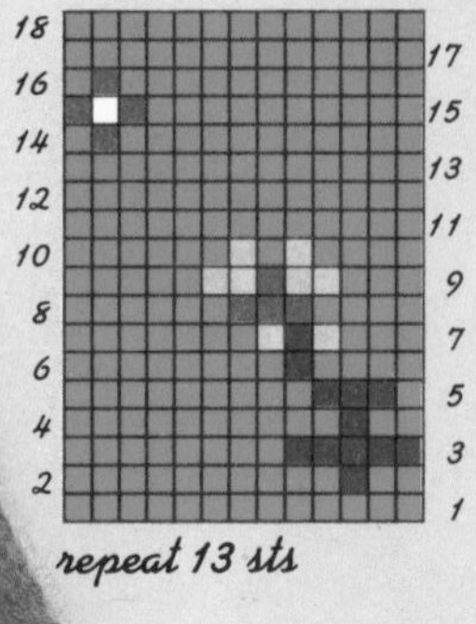

repeat 13 sts

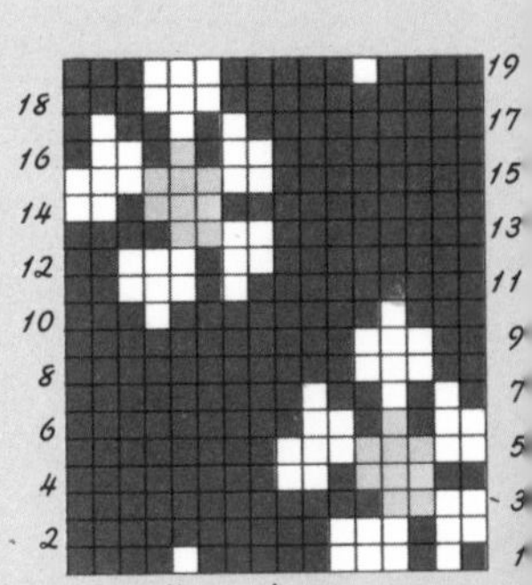

repeat 16 sts

68

Vertical stripes

Vertical stripes can be wide, narrow, plain or textured. They can also incorporate cables, eyelets, bobbles and lacy stitches in patterns ranging from jazzy to delicate.

Eammon McCabe

Skills you need

*Simple increasing
*Eyelets

If you do not know these skills refer to pages 174 and 182.

Materials

The bold simple lines of vertical-stripe patterns show up well in almost any type of yarn. Combinations of different textured yarns can also be used very successful as is shown by many of the samples in the Pattern Library. Providing that all the fibers are compatible for cleaning purposes you can mix wool with cotton or bouclé, or mohair with glitter or slubbed yarns. The basic sweater is worked in a plain cotton yarn in four colors approximating knitted worsted in thickness.

Special technique – edge-to-edge seam selvege

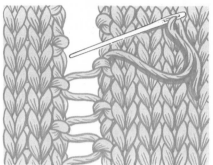

1 Thick yarns like the worsted-weight cotton used for the basic sweater can produce bulky seams. These can be avoided by working an edge-to-edge seam. This requires a special selvege to be knitted in as the work progresses. Knit the first and last stitches on both right-side and wrong-side rows thus producing a line of "pips" on both edges.

2 When the time comes to finish the garment, place the edges of the pieces to be joined facing each other matching row to row. Thread a needle with matching yarn and secure it at one side of the bottom of the seam. Insert the needle up through the pip immediately above, then up through the pip opposite. Continue lacing the thead from side to side.

3 Pull the thread to tighten and close up the seam as you work. Fasten it off securely when the seam is complete. This seam, which is almost invisible, can be worked with either the right or wrong side of the work facing.

The basic striped sweater

This pretty pastel-striped sweater, perfect for summer, can be worn on or off the shoulder, and it is made in a marvelously practical thick cotton yarn.

Sizes
To fit 34[36:38] in. bust
Length 21½[22:22] in.

Note: Instructions for larger sizes are in brackets []; where there is only one set of figures it applies to all three sizes.

Gauge
20 sts and 28 rows to 4 in. over stockinette st on size 5 needles

Materials
13[16:20] oz thick cotton yarn in main color (A)
5[8:8] oz in contrasting color (B)
8[8:12] oz in contrasting color (C)
8[12:12] oz in contrasting color (D)
1 pair each sizes 3 and 5 knitting needles
1 pair each sizes 3 and 5 circular needles

70

Back and front (alike)
Using smaller needles and A, cast on 96[102:106] sts.
Work 3 in. in K1, P1 ribbing.
Next row Rib 9[12:14], *work twice into next st, rib 18, rep from * ending last rep rib 10[13:15]. 101[107:111] sts.
Change to larger needles and begin pat. Use small separate balls of yarn for each color section, twist yarns when changing color to avoid a hole.
1st row (RS) K4[7:9]C, K2A, * with B, K5, yfwd, sl 1, K1, psso, K4, K2A*, rep from * to * using D instead of B, rep from * to * using C instead of B, rep from * to *, rep from * to * using C instead of B, rep from * to * using D instead of B, rep from * to *, K4[7:9]C.
2nd and every other row K1, P to last st, K1 keeping sections of color as set.
3rd row K4[7:9]C, K2A, * with B, K3, K2 tog, yfwd, K1, yfwd, sl 1, K1, psso, K3, K2A*, rep from * to * using D instead of B, rep from * to * using C instead of B, rep from * to *, rep from * to * using C instead of B, rep from * to * using D instead of B, rep from * to *, K4[7:9]C.
5th row K4[7:9]C, K2A, *with B, K2, K2 tog, yfwd, K3, yfwd, sl 1, K1, psso, K2, K2A*, rep from * to * using D instead of B, rep from * to * using C instead of B, rep from * to *, rep from * to * using C instead of B, rep from * to * using D instead of B, rep from * to * K4[7:9]C.
7th row K4[7:9]C, K2A, * with B, K1, K2 tog, yfwd, K5, yfwd, sl 1, K1, psso, K1, K2A *, rep from * to * using D instead of B, rep from * to * using C

instead of B, rep from * to *, rep from * to * using C instead of B, rep from * to * using D instead of B, rep from * to *, K4[7:9]C.

8th row As 2nd row.

These 8 rows form the pat. Cont in pat until work measures about 12½ in. from cast-on edge, ending with a 4th pat row.

Shape sleeves

Next row Cast on 21[18:16] sts, work across these sts as foll:

K1D, using D instead of B, work as given for 5th row from * to *, using C instead of B work as given for 5th row from * to *, work in pat to end.

Next row Cast on 21[18:16] sts, work across these sts as foll:

K1D, P11D, P2A, P11C, work in pat to end.

143 sts.

Keeping pat correct, cont without shaping until work measures 4¾ in. from beg of sleeve shaping, ending with a WS row.

Shape neck

Next row Work in pat on 56 sts, turn, leaving rem sts on a spare needle. Complete left side of neck first.

Keeping pat correct, dec 1 st at neck edge on foll 10 rows. 46 sts.

Cont without shaping until work measures 9[9½:9½] in. from beg of sleeve shaping, ending with a WS row. Bind off.

Return to sts on spare needle. Sl center 31 sts onto a st holder, join in appropriate yarn to next st, work in pat to end.

Complete to match first side of neck.

To finish

Join shoulder seams.

Collar

With RS of work facing, using smaller circular needle and A, pick up and K 30[32:32] sts down left side of front neck, K31 sts from front neck, pick up and K 30[32:32] sts up right side of front neck, 30[32:32] sts down right back neck, K31 from center back neck, and pick up and K 30[32:32] sts up left back neck. 182[190:190] sts. Work in rounds of K1, P1 ribbing for 3 in.

Change to larger circular needle and cont in rounds of ribbing until work measures 6 in. from beg.

Bind off loosely in ribbing.

Sleeve edgings

Using smaller needles and A, with RS of work facing, pick up and K 128[132:136] sts evenly around sleeve edge.

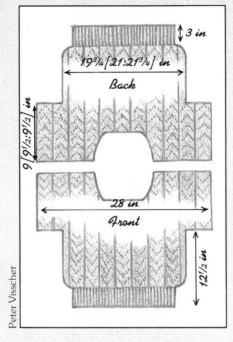

Peter Visscher

Next row *K2 tog, P2 tog, rep from * to end. 64[66:68] sts.

Work 6 rows K1, P1 ribbing.

Bind off loosely in ribbing.

Join side and underarm seams (see Special technique opposite).

Roll collar to RS.

Adapting the striped sweater

The stripy samples in the Pattern Library should give you endless ideas for varying the basic sweater.

The sweater is very easy to adapt in many different ways. The shape is extremely simple, the sleeves being worked as part of the back and front pieces. The striped pattern consists of a wide stripe with a faggoting motif alternating with a narrower plain one. If you prefer, the patterned stripe could be knitted plain (this should not alter the tension to any noticeable extent). Alternatively, you could cross it with horizontal stripes at intervals, or add texture with bobbles, or vary the width of the stripes (by working pin stripes, for example) to give it a completely new look. A much simpler but very elegant version could be made by working the vertical chevron pattern as set but in one color only.

Vertical stripes

1 Pin stripes

This pattern is worked over a multiple of 16 stitches, plus 9 extra, and in 2 colors (A, B).

1st row (RS) K1A, *(P1B, K2A) twice, (P1B, K4A) twice, rep from * to last 8 sts, (P1B, K2A) twice, P1B, K1A.

2nd row P1A, *(K1B, P2A) twice, (K1B, P4A) twice, rep from * to last 8 sts, (K1B, P1A) twice, K1B, P1A.

These 2 rows form the pattern repeat.

2

2 Cabled stripes

This pattern is worked over a multiple of 28 stitches and in four colors (A, B, C, D).

1st row (RS) *P4A, K2B, K2C, K2D, P8A, K2D, K2C, K2B, P4A, rep from * to end.

2nd row *K4A, P2B, P2C, P2D, K8A, P2D, P2C, P2B, K4A, rep from * to end.

3rd row *P4A, sl next 2 sts onto cable needle and hold at front of work, K2C, K2B from cable needle, K2D, P8A, K2D, sl next 2 sts onto cable needle and hold at back of work, K2B, K2C from cable needle, P4A, rep from * to end.

4th row *K4A, P2C, P2B, P2D, K8A, P2D, P2B, P2C, K4A, rep from * to end.

5th row *P4A, K2C, sl next 2 sts onto cable needle and hold at back of work, K2D, K2B from cable needle, P8A, sl next 2 sts onto cable needle and hold at front of work, K2B, K2D from cable needle, K2C, P4A, rep from * to end.

6th row *K4A, P2C, P2D, P2B, K8A, P2B, P2D, P2C, K4A, rep from * to end.

7th row *P4A, sl next 2 sts onto cable needle and hold at front of work K2D, K2C from cable needle, K2B, P8A, K2B, sl next 2 sts onto cable needle and hold at back of work, K2C, K2D from cable needle, P4A, rep from * to end.

8th row *K4A, P2D, P2C, P2B, K8A, P2A, P2C, P2D, K4A, rep from * to end.

9th row *P4A, K2D, K2C, K2B, P8A, K2B, K2C, K2D, P4A, rep from * to end.

10th row As 8th row.

11th-24th rows Rep 9th-10th rows 7 times more.

25th-48th rows Rep 1st-24th rows reading A instead of C, and C instead of A.

These 48 rows form the pattern repeat.

3

3 Multi-colored verticals

This pattern is worked over a multiple of 18 stitches, plus 3 extra, and in four colors (A, B, C, D).

1st row (RS) *(K3A, K1B) twice, (K1A, K1B) twice, K3A, K1B, K1A, K1B, rep from * to last 3 sts, K3A.

2nd row P3A, *P1B, P1A, P1B, P3A, (P1B, P1A) twice, (P1B, P3A) twice, rep from * to end.

3rd-4th rows As 1st-2nd rows.

5th row As 1st row.

6th row As 2nd row using C instead of B.

7th row As 1st row using C instead of B.

8th row As 6th row.

9th row As 1st row using D instead of B.

10th row P3A, *K1D, P1A, K1D, P3A, (K1D, P1A) twice, (K1D, P3A) twice, rep from * to end.

11th row *(K3A, P1D) twice, (K1A, P1D) twice, K3A, P1D, K1A, P1D,

4

rep from * to last 3 sts, K3A.

12th-13th rows As 10th-11th rows.

14th-16th rows As 6th-8th rows.

These 16 rows form pattern repeat.

4 Bouclé stripes

This pattern is worked over a multiple of 22 stitches, plus 5 extra, and in four colors (A, B, C, D).

1st row (RS) With A, K4, *(sl 1, K3) twice, (sl 3, K1) twice, sl 3, K3, rep from * to last st, K1.

2nd row With A, K1, P3, *(sl 3, P1) twice, sl 3, (P3, sl 1) twice, P3, rep from * to last st, K1.

3rd row With B, K1, sl 3, *(P1, ybk, sl 3) twice, (P3, ybk, sl 1) twice, P3, ybk, sl 3, rep from * to last st, K1.

4th row With B, K1, yfwd, sl 3, *(K3, yfwd, sl 1) twice, K3, (yfwd, sl 3, K1) twice, yfwd, sl 3, rep from * to last st, K1.

5th-8th rows As 1st-4th rows.

9th-16th rows As 1st-8th rows using C instead of B.

17th-24th rows As 1st-8th rows using D instead of B.

These 24 rows form the pattern repeat.

5

6

7

5 Woven vertical ladders

This pattern is worked over a multiple of 7 stitches.

1st row (RS) K2, *bind off 3 sts, K4 including st used in binding off, rep from * to last 5 sts, bind off 3, K to end.

2nd row P2, *pick up and K1 st over the bound-off sts of previous row, P4, rep from * to last 2 sts, pick up and K 1st, P2.

3rd row K2, P1, *K4, P1, rep from * to last 2 sts, K2.

4th row P2, K1, *P4, K1, rep from * to last 2 sts, P2.

Rep 3rd-4th rows to within 3 rows of required length.

1st bound-off row K2, *drop next st off needle and allow to run down to 1st row, cast on 3 sts onto RH needle, K4, rep from * to last 3 sts, drop next st, cast on 3 sts, K2.

2nd bound-off row P to end.

3rd bound-off row Bind off.

Weave strands of contrasting yarn through ladders as on sample.

6 Broken verticals

This pattern is worked over an odd number of stitches, and in three colors (A, B, C).

1st row (RS) With B, K1, *sl 1, K1, rep from * to end.

2nd row With B, K1, yfwd, *sl 1, P1, rep from * to last 2 sts, sl 1, ybk, K1.

3rd row With A, K2, *sl 1, K1, rep from * to last st, K1.

4th row With A, K1, P1, *sl 1, P1, rep from * to last st, K1.

5th-28th rows Rep 1st-4th rows 6 times more.

29th-40th rows Rep 1st-4th rows 3 times more, using C instead of B. These 40 rows form the pattern repeat.

7 Candy stripes

This pattern is worked over a multiple of 10 stitches, plus 7 extra, and in three colors (A, B, C).

1st row (RS) *K2A, 3B, 2A, 3C, rep from * to last 7 sts, 2A, 3B, 2A.

2nd row *P2A, 3B, 2A, 3C, rep from * to last 7 sts, 2A, 3B, 2A.

These 2 rows form the pattern repeat.

Simon Butcher

73

Oriental motifs

The Far East has for centuries provided a rich source of inspiration for European craftsmen and women. Characteristic motifs range from delicate floral studies to bold calligraphy.

Skills you need

* **Decreasing**
* **Working with color**

If you do not know these skills refer to pages 174 and 175.

Materials

Intricate motifs are best worked in farily plain yarn like the smooth wool and silk mixture used for the basic dress or a chunky wool in which individual stitches stand out. Bolder shapes like some of those used for the Pattern Library samples can incorporate fancier textures like glitter yarns and bouclé. The motifs are in stockinette stitch but embroidery could be added.

Special technique – working pleats

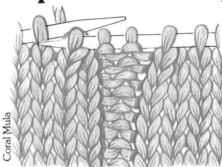

1 Make pleats by working flat ribbing as follows: work in knit ten, purl two ribbing to the required depth then, on the right side, decrease one stitch either side of the knit ribs.

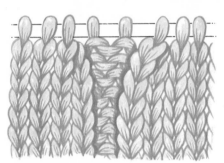

2 Work straight for the required number of rows then decrease one stitch on either side of the knit ribs as before.

3 Carry on in this way decreasing on either side of the knit ribs at given intervals until the ribs are two stitches wide.

The basic pleated dress

This silky flapper dress is pretty enough for any party.

Sizes
To fit 32[34] in. bust
Length from hem to waist 20 in.

Note: Instructions for larger size are in square brackets; where there is only one figure it applies to both sizes.

Gauge
32 sts and 40 rows to 4 in. over stockinette st on size 3 needles

Materials
14 [17]oz wool-silk blend fingering yarn in main color (A)
3 oz in contrasting color (B)

1 oz in contrasting color (C)
1 pair each size 00 and 3 knitting needles
1 each size 2 and 3 circular needles

Back
***Using larger circular needle and A, cast on 410[434] sts. Work in rows.
1st row (RS) *P2, K10, rep from * to last 2 sts, P2.
2nd row *K2, P10, rep from * to last 2 sts, K2.
3rd-26th rows Rep 1st-2nd rows 12 times more.
27th row *P2, K2 tog, K6, K2 tog, rep from * to last 2 sts, P2.
28th row *K2, P8, rep from * to last 2 sts, K2.

29th row *P2, K8, rep from * to last 2 sts, P2.
30th-53rd rows Rep 28th-29th rows 12 times more.
54th row *K2, P2 tog, P4, P2 tog, rep from * to last 2 sts, K2.
55th row *P2, K6, rep from * to last 2 sts, P2.
56th row *K2, P6, rep from * to last 2 sts, K2.
57th-80th rows Rep 55th-56th rows 12 times more.
81st row *P2, K2 tog, K2, K2 tog, rep from * to last 2 sts, P2.
82nd row *K2, P4, rep from * to last 2 sts, K2.
83rd row *P2, K4, rep from * to last 2 sts, P2.

Ron Kelly

84th-107th rows Rep 82nd-83rd rows 12 times more.

108th row *K2, (P2 tog) twice, rep from * to last 2 sts, K2. 138[146] sts.

109th row *P2, K2, rep from * to last 2 sts, P2.

110th row *K2, P2, rep from * to last 2 sts, K2.

Rep the last 2 rows until work measures 15 in. from cast-on edge. Change to smaller straight needles and rep last 2 rows for a further 5 in., ending with a WS row. (Adjust skirt length here.) Change to larger straight needles. Beg with a K row cont in stockinette st.

***Work 136 rows.

Shape back neck

Next row K61[65], sl next 16 sts onto a stitch holder, K to end.

Complete left side of back neck first.

Next row P to last 2 sts, P2 tog.

Next row Bind off 2 sts, K to end. Rep the last 2 rows twice more.

Next row P to last 2 sts, P2 tog.

Next row K2 tog, K to end. Rep the last 2 rows once more.

Next row P to last 2 sts, P2 tog.

Next row K across row.

Rep last 2 rows once. 46[50] sts.

Shape armhole

Next row Bind off 8 sts, P to last 2 sts, P2 tog.

Next row K to last 2 sts, K2 tog.

Next row Bind off 2 sts, P to last 2 sts, P2 tog.

Rep the last 2 rows once more.

Next row K to last 2 sts, K2 tog.

Next row P2 tog, P to last 2 sts, P2 tog.

Rep the last 2 rows twice more.

Next row K across row.

Next row P2 tog, P to last 2 sts, P2 tog.

Rep the last 2 rows until 8 sts rem. Cont without shaping until work measures 6[6¾]in. from beg of armholes, ending at armhole edge. Bind off. With WS of work facing return to sts for right side of neck, join in A and complete to match first side, reversing shapings.

Front

Work as given for back from *** to ***. Work 10 rows.

Next row K86[90] A, 1B, 2A, 1B, 4A, 1B, 1A, 1B, 2A, (1B, 1A) 3 times, 1A, 1B, 4A, 1B, 26[30] A.

Next row P26[30] A, 1B, 4A, 1B, 1A, (1A, 1B) 3 times, 2A, 1B, 1A, 1B, 4A, 1B, 2A, 1B, 86[90] A.

Rep last 2 rows 18 times more.

Cont in stockinette st working from

76

=A =B =C

John Hutchinson

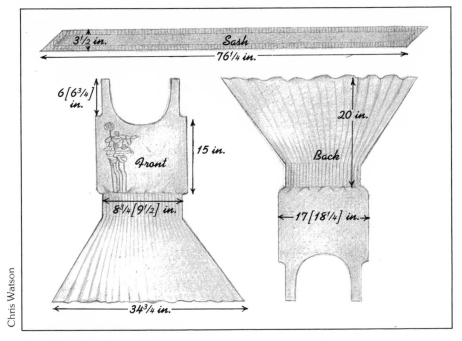

Chris Watson

chart as foll:
1st row K64[68]A, K first row from chart, K to end in A.
2nd row P14[18]A, P 2nd row from chart, P to end in A.
Cont in this way from chart until work matches back to underarm, ending with a P row.

Shape armholes
Keeping chart correct, bind off 8 sts at beg of next 2 rows.
Next row Bind off 2 sts, K to last 2 sts, K2 tog.
Next row Bind off 2 sts, P to last 2 sts, P2 tog.
Rep the last 2 rows once more.
Next row K2 tog, K to last 2 sts, K2 tog.
Next row P2 tog, P to last 2 sts, P2 tog.
Rep the last 2 rows twice more.
Next row K across row.
Next row P2 tog, P to last 2 sts, P2 tog.
Rep the last 2 rows twice more. 92[100] sts.

Shape neck
Next row K37[41], sl next 18 sts onto a stitch holder, K to end.
Complete right side of neck first.
Next row P2 tog, P to last 2 sts, P2 tog.
Next row Bind off 2 sts, K to end.
Rep the last 2 rows 2[4] times more.
Next row P to last 2 sts, P2 tog.
Next row K2 tog, K to end.
Rep the last 2 rows 5[3] times more. 13 sts.
Next row P to last 2 sts, P2 tog.
Next row K across row.
Rep the last 2 sts until 8 sts rem.

Cont without shaping until work matches to shoulder, ending at armhole edge.
Bind off.
With WS of work facing, return to sts for left side of neck, join in A, P to end. Complete to match first side of neck, reversing shapings.

Sash
Using larger needles and B, cast on 2 sts.
Next row (WS) K into front and back of st (called inc 1), K1. 3 sts.
Knit 2 rows.
Next row K to last st, inc 1.
Next row Inc 1, K to end.
Rep the last 4 rows 4 times more. 13 sts.
Next row K across row.
Next row K6, P1, K6.
Next row K to last st, inc 1.
Next row Inc 1, K4, P to last 6 sts, K6.
Next row K across row.
Next row K6, P to last 6 sts, K6.
Rep the last 4 rows 7 times more. 29 sts.
Next row K across row.
Next row K6, P17, K6.
Rep the last 2 rows until work measures 76¼ in. from cast-on edge, ending with a WS row.
Next row K6, sl 1, K1, psso, K to end.
Next row K6, P to last 8 sts, P2 tog tbl, K6.
Next row K across row.
Next row K6, P to last 6 sts, K6.
Rep the last 2 rows 7 times more. 13 sts.
Next row K6, sl 1, K1, psso, K to end.

Next row K to last 8 sts, K2 tog tbl, K6.
Knit 2 rows.
Rep the last 4 rows twice more. 7 sts.
Next row K to last 2 sts, K2 tog.
Next row K2 tog, K to end.
Knit 2 rows.
Rep the last 4 rows once more. 3 sts.
Next row K1, K2 tog.
Next row K2 tog and fasten off.

To Finish
Press motif lightly on wrong side.
Join right shoulder seam.
Neckband With RS of work facing, using smaller circular needle and A, pick up and K 54[58] sts down left side of neck, K across 18 sts on center front stitch holder, pick up and K 53[57] sts up right side of neck to shoulder, 72[76] sts down right side of back neck, K across 16 sts on center back stitch holder, pick up and K 72[76] sts up left side of back neck. 285[301] sts. Work in rows.
1st row (WS) P1, *K1, P1, rep from * to end.
2nd row K1, *P1, K1, rep from *.
Rep the last 2 rows once. Bind off loosely in ribbing.
Join left shoulder and neckband.
Armbands
With RS of work facing, using smaller circular needle and A, pick up and K 135[145] sts evenly around armhole edge.
Work in rows.
Complete as given for neckband.
Join side seams.

Adapting the pleated dress

Transform the mood of the dress with an entirely different motif or some embroidery.

The bodice of the basic dress is worked entirely in stockinette stitch which makes an ideal background for all kinds of embroidery stitches or for any of the motifs in the Pattern Library. These can be knitted in as you go along or, if you cannot decide where to place the design, work the bodice in the main color and add the motif in duplicate stitch afterwards.

Reading the charts
Work all charts in stockinette stitch reading right-side (knit) rows from right to left and wrong-side (purl) rows from left to right.

Oriental motifs

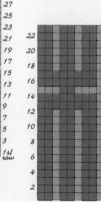

2

1 Plum blossom

The Japanese are renowned for their beautiful gardens full of flowering shrubs and trees which, in turn, inspired the designs and motifs of artists and craftsmen.

2 Waves

Both Japanese and Chinese art frequently feature wave motifs in more or less stylized form. They appear on many types of objects including ceramics, paintings and textiles. The chart can be used either as a single motif or for a repeating border pattern.

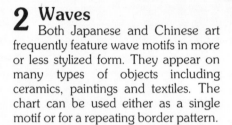

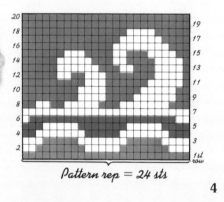

Pattern rep = 24 sts

1

4

3 Water

This Chinese character means "water".

4 Badge

Traditional Japanese costume was often marked with the family crest or emblem of the wearer. On the clothes of the wealthy these could be elaborate but more often than not they were bold, easily recognizable devices like this one.

3

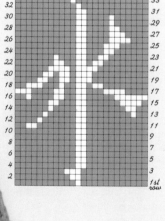

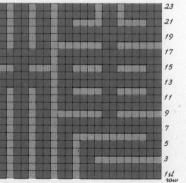

Dennis Hawkins/Steve Tanner

Picture eyelets

Eyelets have many different uses in knitting. They can be buttonholes, ribbon slots and part of all-over lacy fabrics; the arrangements of the eyelets can also form beautiful and most effective openwork pictorial motifs.

Skills you need

* **Decorative increasing**
* **Using a cable needle**
* **Making eyelets**

If you do not know these skills refer to pages 175, 178 and 182.

Materials

The motifs formed from eyelet holes are always rather subtle in their effects so it is generally inadvisable to use anything other than fairly plain yarns. Fine cotton and silk yarns show up eyelet patterns beautifully but wool and lightly fluffy yarns can look pretty. The basic evening sweater is worked in a fine smooth glitter yarn, approximately equivalent to a standard fingering yarn. It would show up any picture eyelet pattern beautifully.

Special technique – working a bold eyelet

1 *The knot on the bow motif of the basic sweater is made from a series of bold eyelets worked over four stitches and four rows. On the first row, knit two together, take the yarn around the needle twice, then slip one, knit one, then pass the slipped stitch over.*

2 *On the second row, purl together the first stitch and the first yarn over, knit together the second yarn over and the second stitch.*

3 *On the third row, knit one, yarn over twice, knit one. On the fourth row, purl together first stitch, first yarn over and the strand below, then knit one and purl one, into second yarn over and strand below at the same time, then purl one.*

Coral Mula

The basic eyelet evening sweater

Brighten up your nightlife in this gorgeous glittering sweater knitted in fine gold yarn. The central panel with its pretty eyelet bow motif is bordered by textured panels in cables and blackberry stitch.

Sizes
To fit 32[34:36]in. bust
Length 20 in.
Sleeve seam 6 in.

Note: Instructions for larger sizes are in brackets []; where there is only one set of figures it applies to all three sizes.

Gauge
38 sts and 48 rows to 4 in. over stockinette st on size 2 needles

Materials
11[12:12]oz fine metallic fingering yarn
1 pair each sizes 1 and 2 knitting needles
Cable needle
80

Back
***Using smaller needles, cast on 138[142:146] sts. Work in K2, P2 ribbing as folls:
1st row *K2, P2, rep from * to last 2 sts, K2.
2nd row *P2, K2, rep from * to last 2 sts, P2.
Rep the last 2 rows until work measures 4¼[4¾:4¾]in. from cast-on edge, ending with a 2nd row.
Next row P8[4:0], *P2, P twice into next st, rep from * to last 10[6:2] sts, P to end. 178[186:194] sts.
Begin pat.
1st row (WS) P1, *(K1, P1, K1) all into next st, P3 tog, rep from * to last st, P1.
2nd row K1, P to last st, K1.
3rd row P1, *P3 tog, *(K1, P1, K1) all into next st, rep from * to last st, P1.
4th row As 2nd row.
These 4 rows form the pat. Cont in pat for a further 118 rows, ending with a 2nd pat row.
Shape armholes
Keeping pat correct, bind off 20 sts at beg of next 2 rows. 138[148:154] sts.

Work 1st-2nd pat rows again.
Next row Bind off 4 sts, *P3 tog, (K1, P1, K1) all into next st, rep from * to last st, P1.
Next row Bind off 4 sts, P to last st, K1.
Rep the last 4 rows once more. 122[130:138] sts.
Cont without shaping, work a further 50 rows in pat.
Bind off.

Front
Work as given for back from *** to ***. Begin pat.
1st row (WS) P1, *(K1, P1, K1) all into next st, P3 tog*, rep from * to * 9[10:11] times more, K2, P10, K2, P68, K2, P10, K2, **P3 tog, (K1, P1, K1) all into next st **, rep from ** to **, 9[10:11] times more, P1.
2nd row K1, P42[46:50], K10, P2, K68, P2, K10, P42 [46:50], K1.
3rd row P1, *P3 tog, (K1, P1, K1) all into next st *, rep from * to * 9[10:11] times more, K2, P10, K2, P68, K2, P10, K2, ** (K1, P1, K1) all into next st, P3 tog **, rep from ** to **

9[10:11] times more.

4th row K1, P42[46:50], sl next 5 sts onto cable needle and hold at back of work, K5, then K5 sts from cable needle – called C10B, P2, K68, P2, sl next 5 sts onto cable needle and hold at front of work, K5, and K5 sts from cable needle – called C10F, P42[46:50], K1.

5th row As 1st row.
6th row As 2nd row.
7th row As 3rd row.
8th row As 2nd row.

These 8 rows establish the side panel pat with the central panel in stockinette st.

Work the first row again.

Now maintaining side panel pat as set, begin working picture eyelets from chart.

1st row Work in pat on 55[59:63] sts, work first row from chart as folls: K45, yfwd, K2 tog, K21, work in pat to end.

2nd row Work in pat on 55[59:63] sts, work 2nd row from chart as folls: P68, work in pat to end.

3rd row Work in pat on 55[59:63] sts, K68, work in pat to end.

4th row Work in pat on 55[59:63] sts, P68, work in pat to end.

5th-8th rows Rep 1st-4th rows again.

9th row Work in pat on 55[59:63] sts, K45, (yfwd, K2 tog) twice, K19, work in pat to end.

Cont in this way until 113 rows have been worked from chart. (On 107th row refer to Special technique on page 80.)

Shape armholes
Keeping pat and chart correct, bind off 20 sts at beg of next 2 rows. 138[148:154] sts.

Work 2 rows.

Bind off 4 sts at beg of next 2 rows. Rep the last 4 rows once more. 122[130:138] sts.

Work a further 7 rows until chart is completed.

Now cont with side panel pat as set and central panel in stockinette st.

Work 28 rows.

Shape neck
Next row Work in pat on 47[51:55] sts and turn, leaving rem sts on a spare needle.

Complete left side of neck first.

Bind off 4 sts at beg of next row and 2 sts at beg of foll alt row.

Work 1 row.

Dec 1 st at neck edge on next 5 rows and on foll alt row. 35[39:43] sts.

Cont without shaping until work matches back to shoulder, ending at armhole edge.

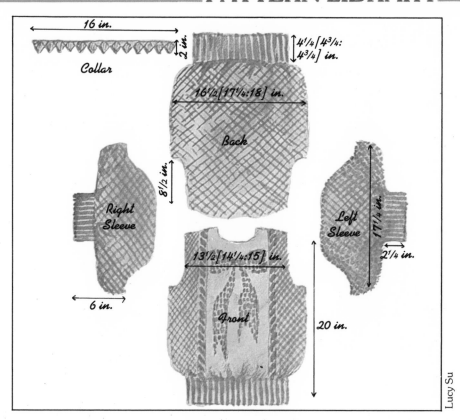

Collar

Back

Right Sleeve

Left Sleeve

Front

16 in.

2 in.

4¼[4¾:4¾] in.

16½[17¼:18] in.

8½ in.

13½[14¼:15] in.

6 in.

17¼ in.

2¼ in.

20 in.

Lucy Su

Bind off.

With RS of work facing return to sts on spare needle.

Join in yarn, bind off center 28 sts, work in pat to end.

Work 1 row.

Complete as given for first side of neck.

Sleeves
Using smaller needles, cast on 94 sts.

Work in K2, P2 ribbing as given for back for 2¼ in., ending with a 2nd row.

Change to larger needles.

Next row P1, *P twice into next st, rep from * to last st, P1. 186 sts.

Cont in pat as given for back until work measures 6 in. from cast-on edge, ending with a 2nd or 4th pat row.

Shape top
Keeping pat correct, bind off 20 sts at beg of next 2 rows. Bind off 4 sts at beg of every foll row until 106 sts rem.

Cont without shaping until work measures 9½ in. from cast-on edge, ending with a 2nd or 4th pat row.

Bind off 4 sts at beg of next 8 rows.

Next row P1, *P3 tog, rep from * to last st, P1.

Bind off.

Collar
Using larger needles, cast on 12 sts.

Knit 2 rows.

Begin pat.

1st row (RS) K twice into first st – called inc 1, K1, turn.

2nd and every other row K to end.

3rd row Inc 1, K3, turn.
5th row Inc 1, K5, turn.
7th row Inc 1, K7, turn.
9th row Inc 1, K9, turn.
11th row Inc 1, K11, turn.
13th row Inc 1, K13, turn.
15th row Inc 1, K15, turn.
17th row Inc 1, K17, turn.
19th row Inc 1, K19, turn.
21st row K22.
23rd row K2 tog, K19, turn.
25th row K2 tog, K17, turn.
27th row K2 tog, K15, turn.
29th row K2 tog, K13, turn.
31st row K2 tog, K11, turn.
33rd row K2 tog, K9, turn.
35th row K2 tog, K7, turn.
37th row K2 tog, K5, turn.
39th row K2 tog, K3, turn.
41st row K2 tog, K1, turn.
42nd-54th rows K across row.

These 54 rows form the pat. Rep them 12 times more. Bind off.

To finish
Join shoulder seams. Join side and sleeve seams. Set in sleeves, gathering to form a puff top. Join short ends of collar. Sew collar to neck edge, placing seam at center back neck. Do not press. Wash gently by hand in warm water and dry flat on a towel.

The chart on the left shows the central panel, with rows numbered 1 to 129 up both sides (even numbers on the left, odd numbers on the right). The eyelet symbols are arranged in the bow motif pattern described in the text.

Murray West

Key (below chart):

- ☐ K on R.S. rows P on W.S. rows
- ▫ yfwd
- ◩ K2 together
- ⊞ work bold eyelet

Adapting the evening sweate

The bow motif is worked from a chart that makes it very easy to substitute another design.

The chart represents the central panel on the front of the basic sweater. The position of the eyelets that make up the motif is indicated by stitch symbols, as shown in the key.

To adapt the chart for another design, simply copy the basic grid and plot a new arrangement of eyelets on it. Simple eyelets are worked over two stitches (see page 182), that is, two squares on the chart. Where they are arranged vertically above each other, there must be at least three rows of stockinette stitch between each eyelet. More complicated eyelets, like the bold eyelets used on the knot of the bow motif, may occupy more stitches and rows and this must be allowed for on the chart.

Using the Pattern Library

Any of the Pattern Library motifs can be plotted on to the chart. They can be positioned centrally or to one side or

1

corner of the panel as required. Take into account the total number of stitches and rows occupied by the new motif (given in the first and last lines of each pattern) and first plot this rectangle onto the grid. Then work out the position of the eyelets within it, using the written pattern.

Picture eyelet patterns

1 Butterfly

This motif is worked over 38 sts.
1st row K6, (yfwd, K2 tog) 4 times, K10, (yfwd, K2 tog) 4 times, K6.
2nd and every other row P across row.
3rd and every foll 4th row K across row.
5th row K4, (yfwd, K2 tog) 6 times, K6, (yfwd, K2 tog) 6 times, K4.
9th row K2, (yfwd, K2 tog) 8 times, K2, (yfwd, K2 tog) 8 times, K2.
13th row K4, (yfwd, K2 tog) 7 times, K2, (yfwd, K2 tog) 7 times, K4.
17th row K10, (yfwd, K2 tog) 4 times, K2, (yfwd, K2 tog) 4 times, K10.
21st row K6, (yfwd, K2 tog) 6 times, K2, (yfwd, K2 tog) 6 times, K6.
25th row As 9th row.
29th row (Yfwd, K2 tog) twice, K6, (yfwd, K2 tog) 3 times, K6, (yfwd, K2 tog) 3 times, K6, (yfwd, K2 tog) twice.
33rd row (Yfwd, K2 tog) 7 times, K10, (yfwd, K2 tog) 7 times.
37th row (Yfwd, K2 tog) 6 times, K14, (yfwd, K2 tog) 6 times.
41st row K2, (yfwd, K2 tog) 4 times, K18, (yfwd, K2 tog) 4 times, K2.
45th row K4, (yfwd, K2 tog) twice, K22, (yfwd, K2 tog) twice K4.
46th row P across row.
These 46 rows form the eyelet motif.

2 Cherries

This motif is worked over 36 sts.
1st row K21, (yfwd, K2 tog) 3 times, K9.
2nd and every other row P across row.
3rd and every foll 4th row K across row.
5th and 9th rows K19, (yfwd, K2 tog) 5 times, K7.
13th row K8, (yfwd, K2 tog) 3 times, K7, (yfwd, K2 tog) 3 times, K9.
17th row K6, (yfwd, K2 tog) 5 times, K7, yfwd, K2 tog, K11.
21st row K6, (yfwd, K2 tog) 5 times, K8, yfwd, K2 tog, K10.
25th row K8, (yfwd, K2 tog) 3 times, K11, yfwd, K2 tog, K9.
29th row K10, yfwd, K2 tog, K13, yfwd, K2 tog, K9.
33rd row (K11, yfwd, K2 tog) twice, K10.
37th row K12, yfwd, K2 tog, K9, yfwd, K2 tog, K11.
41st row K13, yfwd, K2 tog, K7, yfwd, K2 tog, K12.
45th row K4, (yfwd, K2 tog) 4 times,

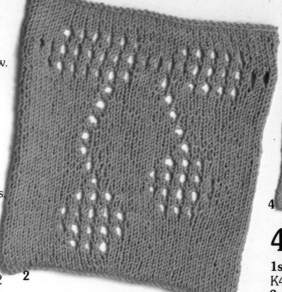

K2, yfwd, K2 tog, K4, (yfwd, K2 tog) 7 times, K2.
49th row (Yfwd, K2 tog,) 18 times.
53rd row K4, (yfwd, K2 tog) 5 times, K6, (yfwd, K2 tog) 6 times, K4.
54th row P across row.
These 54 rows form the eyelet motif.

3 Boat

This motif is worked over 34 sts.
1st row K4, (yfwd, K2 tog) 13 times, K4.
2nd and every other row P across row.
3rd and every foll 4th row K across row.
5th row K2, (yfwd, K2 tog) 15 times, K2.
9th row (Yfwd, K2 tog) 17 times.
13th row K15, yfwd, K2 tog, K17.
17th row K3, (yfwd, K2 tog) 14 times, K3.
21st row K5, (yfwd, K2 tog, K8) twice, K2, yfwd, K2 tog, K5.
25th row K7, (yfwd, K2 tog, K6) twice, K2, yfwd, K2 tog, K7.
29th row K9, (yfwd, K2 tog, K4) twice, K2 yfwd, K2 tog, K9.
33rd row K11, (yfwd, K2 tog, K2) twice, K2, yfwd, K2 tog, K9.
37th row K13, (yfwd, K2 tog) twice, K2, yfwd, K2 tog, K13.
41st row K15, (yfwd, K2 tog) twice, K15.
45th row K15, yfwd, K2 tog, K17.
46th row P across row.
These 46 rows form the eyelet motif.

4 House

This motif is worked over 40 sts.
1st row K2, (yfwd, K2 tog) 17 times, K4.
2nd and every other row P across row.
3rd and every foll 4th row K across row.
5th, 9th, 13th and 17th rows K2, yfwd, K2 tog, K10, (yfwd, K2 tog) 5 times, K10, yfwd, K2 tog, K4.
21st row K2, yfwd, K2 tog, K2, (yfwd, K2 tog) 5 times, K6, (yfwd, K2 tog) 5 times, K2, yfwd, K2 tog, K4.
25th row K2, yfwd, K2 tog, K2, (yfwd, K2 tog, K6) 3 times, (yfwd, K2 tog, K2) twice, K2.
29th row As 21st row.
33rd row As 25th row.
37th row (Yfwd, K2 tog) 20 times.
41st row (Yfwd, K2 tog) 19 times, K2.
45th row As 1st row.
49th row K8, (yfwd, K2 tog) twice, K28.
53rd row As 49th row.
54th row P across row.
These 54 rows form the eyelet motif.

Combining yarns

Impressive decorative effects can be achieved with the simplest stitch patterns by combining different types of yarn imaginatively in the same garment.

Skills you need

* **Decreasing**
* **Stranding yarn**
* **Simple increasing**

If you do not know these skills refer to pages 174 and 175.

Materials

Provided they can be knitted up to the same gauge, any number of fancy yarns can be used together. The range of yarns now available is so great that there are endless opportunities for experiment. Try mixing a glitter yarn with a fluffy one or a fine bouclé with mohair. Since the design feature is the yarn itself, choose a simple stitch pattern. The basic sweater is worked in two yarns: one a metallic yarn used double and the other a bouclé composed of four separate threads twisted together, namely, two different-colored soft fibers, a cotton thread and a gold glittery thread.

Special technique – using yarn double

1 *Wherever it is used in the pattern, the glitter yarn is worked double. Before beginning work wind the ball of glitter yarn into two balls.*

2 *To use the glitter take the yarn from both balls. Wind both strands of yarn together around the needles to knit the next stitch. Knit the next five stitches in the same way.*

3 *On the next pattern row the stitches worked in glitter yarn are again knitted using the yarn double, forming a low garter stitch ridge on the right side of the work.*

The basic textured sweater

The mixture of curly bouclé and metallic yarns transforms a simple stockinette stitch sweater into an exotic garment suitable for any occasion.

Sizes
To fit 32[34:38]in. bust.
Length 22¾[23¼:23½:24]in.
Sleeve seam 18 in.

Note: Instructions for larger sizes are in square brackets []; where there is only one set of figures it applies to all sizes.

Gauge
13 sts and 20 rows to 4in. over stockinette st on size 8 needles
84

Materials
16[18:20:21]oz semi-bulky glitter bouclé yarn (A)
1 oz glitter yarn, used double throughout (B)
1 pair each size 6 and 8 knitting needles

Back
**Using smaller needles and A, cast on 52[56:60:64] sts and work in K1, P1 ribbing for 2 in., ending with a RS row.

Next row Rib 6[7:7:8], inc 1 by picking up the bar between needles and working into it tbl, (rib 13[14:15:16], inc 1) 3 times, rib 7[7:8:8]. 56[60:64:68] sts.
Change to larger needles and pat.
1st row K1[0:0:1]A, K6[3:5:6]B, * K6A, K6B, rep from * to last 1[9:11:1]sts, K1[6:6:1]A, K0[3:5:0]B.
2nd row P1[0:0:1]A, K6[3:5:6]B, *P6A, K6B, rep from * to last 1[9:11:1]sts, P1[6:6:1]A, K0[3:5:0]B.
3rd-10th rows Beg with a K row with

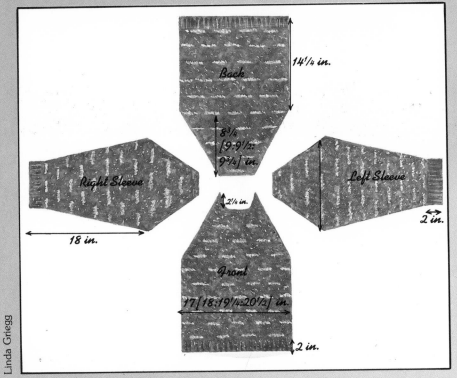

Linda Griegg

Back

14¼ in.

8¾
[9:9½:
9¾] in.

Right Sleeve

Left Sleeve

18 in.

2 in.

2¼ in.

Front

17[18:19¼:20½] in.

2 in.

To finish
Do not press.
Join raglan seams, leaving left back raglan open.
Neck border
Using smaller needles and A, with RS of work facing K6 sts from left sleeve top, pick up and K 12 sts down left side of neck, K8[8:10:10] sts from center front, pick up and K 12 sts up right side of neck, K6 sts from right sleeve top and 20[20:22:22] sts from back neck. 64[64:68:68] sts.
Work in K1, P1 ribbing for 2¼ in., ending with a WS row. Bind off loosely in ribbing using a larger needle.
Join left back raglan seam and neck border. Fold neck border in half to wrong side and slip stitch down. Join side and sleeve seams.

8 rows in stockinette st in A.
11th row K7[3:5:7]A, *K6B, K6A, rep from * to last 13[9:11:13] sts, K6B, K7[3:5:7]A.
12th row P7[3:5:7]A, *K6B, P6A, rep from * to last 13[9:11:13] sts, K6B, P7[3:5:7]A.
13th-20th rows Beg with a K row work 8 rows in stockinette stitch in A. These 20 rows form the pat. Cont in pat until work measures 14¼ in. from the beg, ending with a WS row.
Shape raglan armholes
Keeping pat correct, bind off 3 sts at beg of next 2 rows. Dec 1 st at each end of the next and every foll 4th row until 38[44:48:54] sts rem.
Work 3 rows straight. **
Dec 1 st at each end of the next and every other row until 20[20:22:22] sts rem, ending with a WS row.
Leave rem sts on a spare needle.

Front
Work as given for back from ** to **.
Dec 1 st at each end of the next and every other row until 32[32:34:34] sts rem, ending with a WS row.

Divide for neck
Next row K2 tog, work in pat on 8 sts, K2 tog, turn and leave rem sts on a spare needle.
Work this side of neck first.
Dec 1 st at neck edge on every row and *at the same time* dec 1 st at armhole edge on every other row until 4 sts rem.

Keeping neck edge straight dec as before at armhole edge until 2 sts rem, ending with a WS row.
Next row K2 tog and fasten off.
Return to sts on spare needle. With RS of work facing, sl the center 8[8:10:10] sts onto a spare needle, rejoin the yarn to next st, K2 tog, work in pat to last 2 sts, K2 tog.
Complete to match first side of neck, reversing shapings.

Sleeves
Using smaller needles and A, cast on 28[30:30:32] sts and work in K1, P1 ribbing for 2 in., ending with a RS row.
Next row Rib 3[8:2:4], inc 1, (rib 7[15:5:8], inc 1) 3[1:5:3] times, rib 4[7:3:4]. 32[32:36:36] sts.
Change to larger needles and work in pat as given for the 1st[1st:2nd:2nd] sizes of back. Inc and work into pat 1 st at each end of the 3rd and every foll 12th[9th:12th:10th] row until there are 44[48:48:50] sts. Cont without shaping until work measures 18 in. from the beg, ending with the same pat row as back.
Shape raglan sleeve top
Keeping pat correct, bind off 3 sts at the beg of the next 2 rows. Dec 1 st at each end of the next and every foll 4th row until 28[34:32:34] sts rem.
Work 3 rows straight.
Dec 1 st at each end of the next and every other row until 6 sts rem, ending with a WS row. Leave these sts on a spare needle.

Adapting the textured sweater

Take inspiration from the samples to create imaginative variations on the basic sweater.

Substituting yarns
Only the most experienced knitters should attempt to substitute a different yarn for the one specified in a pattern. Variations in gauge can be considerable even where yarns are apparently of the same thickness. In such cases the gauge must always be carefully checked against the pattern. The basic sweater can be varied by using the same yarn combination in a number of different ways. For example, you could use either the garter stitch bobbles or the garter stitch stripes, substituting the yarns from the basic pattern. Some of the other samples can be used in the same way or simply as a springboard for your own ideas on inventive yarn mixtures. Fine yarns can be used in combination with thick yarns by twisting together two strands of the fine yarn and knitting them as one thread — this has been done in the basic sweater. Very fine threads can be knitted together with thicker ones to make up the weight.

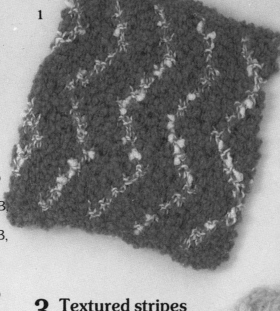

1 Garter stitch zigzags

This stitch is worked over a multiple of 6 stitches. The sample is knitted in bouclé (A) and a bi-color fancy yarn (B).

1st and 13th rows *K4A, K2B, rep from * to end of row.

2nd and 14th rows *K2B, P4A, rep from * to end of row.

3rd and 23rd rows *K1B, K4A, K1B, rep from * to end of row.

4th and 24th rows *K1B, P4A, K1B, rep from * to end of row.

5th and 21st rows *K2B, K4A, rep from * to end of row.

6th and 22nd rows *P4A, K2B, rep from * to end of row.

7th and 19th rows *K1A, K2B, K3A, rep from * to end of row.

8th and 20th rows *P3A, K2B, P1A, rep from * to end of row.

9th and 17th rows *K2A, K2B, K2A, rep from * to end of row.

10th and 18th rows *P2A, K2B, P2A, rep from * to end of row.

11th and 15th rows *K3A, K2B, K1A, rep from * to end of row.

12th and 16th rows *P1A, K2B, P3A, rep from * to end of row.

These 24 rows form the pattern repeat.

2 Garter stitch bobbles

This stitch repeats over 8 stitches. By adding 4 edge stitches for some sizes it can be adapted for the sweater pattern as follows: cast on a multiple of 8 sts [plus 4 extra for the 2nd and 4th sizes on the front and back, and for the 3rd and 4th sizes on the sleeve]. The sample is knitted in Shetland wool (A) and mohair (B).

1st row K0[2]A, *K3A, with B, K into front and back of next st twice, turn, K4, turn, K4, turn, K4, turn (K2 tog) twice, sl 1 st over 2nd st (called make bobble), K4A, rep from * to last 0[2] sts, K0[2]A.

2nd, 4th, 6th and 8th rows With A, P across row.

3rd and 7th rows With A, K across row.

5th row K0[2]A, *K7A, make bobble in B, rep from * to last 0[2]sts, K0[2]A.

These 8 rows form the pattern repeat.

3 Textured stripes

This sample is knitted in two colors of brushed, bulky yarn (A, B), a candlewick type yarn (C) and a slub yarn (D).

1st row With A, K across row.

2nd row With A, P across row.

3rd and 4th rows With C, K across row.

5th row With B, K across row.

6th row With B, P across row.

7th and 8th rows With D, K across row.

9th and 10th rows With D, P across row.

These 10 rows form the pattern repeat.

4 Garter stitch stripes

The sample is knitted in a multi-colored loop yarn (A) and a fine bouclé in four different colors (B).

1st and 3rd rows With A, K across row.

2nd and 4th rows With A, P across row.

5th and 6th rows With B, K across row.

Repeat these 6 rows alternating the bouclé colors on the 5th and 6th rows.

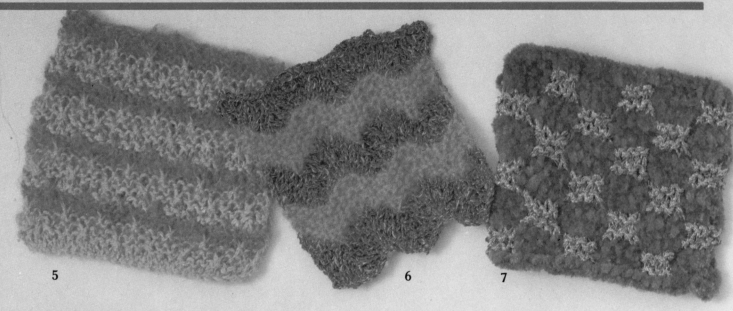

5 6 7

5 Tricolor stripes

This stitch is worked over a multiple of 4 stitches. The sample is knitted in a cotton and silk mixture (A), an acrylic and mohair mixture (B) and bouclé (C).

1st and 2nd rows With A, K across row.
3rd row *S1 1 P-wise, K3B, rep from * to end.
4th row *K3B, yfwd, sl 1 P-wise, ybk, rep from * to end.
5th and 6th rows With B, K across row.
7th row With C, *K2, sl 1 P-wise, K1, rep from * to end.
8th row With C, *K1, yfwd, sl 1 P-wise, ybk, K2, rep from * to end.
9th and 10th rows With C, K across row.
11th-14th rows As 3rd-6th rows but worked in A.
15th-18th rows As 7th-10th rows but worked in B.
19th-22nd rows As 3rd-6th rows but worked in C.
23rd-24th rows As 7th-8th rows but worked in A.
These 24 rows form the pattern repeat.

6 Garter stitch chevrons

This stitch is worked over a multiple of 9 stitches. The sample is knitted in a multi-colored bouclé glitter (A) and angora (B).

1st, 3rd and 5th rows With A, *K into front and back of next st, K2, sl 1, K2 tog, psso, K2, K into front and back of next st, rep from * to end.
2nd, 4th and 6th rows With A, P across row.
7th, 9th and 11th rows As 1st, 3rd and 5th rows but using B.
8th, 10th and 12th rows With B, K across row.
These 12 rows form the pattern repeat.

8 Glitter striped chevrons

This stitch is worked over a multiple of 13 stitches. The sample is knitted in acrylic bouclé (A), glitter (B) and mohair (C).

1st and 3rd rows *With A, K into front and back of next st, K4, sl 1, K2 tog, psso, K4, K into front and back of next st, rep from * to end of row.
2nd and 4th rows With A, P across row.
5th and 11th rows As 1st and 3rd rows but using B.
6th and 12th rows With B, K across row.
7th and 9th rows As 1st and 3rd rows but using C.
8th and 10th rows With C, P across row.
These 12 rows form the pattern repeat.

8

7 Garter stitch checks

This stitch is worked over a multiple of 8 stitches. The sample is knitted in chenille (A) and multi-colored four-ply glitter used double (B).

1st and 3rd rows *K4A, K4B, rep from * to end of row.
2nd and 4th rows *K4B, P4A, rep from * to end of row.
5th and 7th rows *K4B, K4A, rep from * to end of row.
6th and 8th rows *P4A, K4B, rep from * to end of row.
These 8 rows form the pattern repeat.

9 Raised ridges

This sample is knitted in random-dyed chunky bouclé (A) and sport-weight cotton yarn used double (B).

1st, 3rd and 5th rows With B, K across row.
2nd, 4th and 6th rows With B, P across row.
7th and 9th rows With A, P across row.
8th and 10th rows With A, K across row.
These 10 rows form the pattern repeat.

9

Tyrolean patterns

Cables, bobbles, traveling stitches and even eyelets are the building blocks of traditional knitting from the Austrian Tyrol. They combine to form beautifully textured panels that are then further decorated with embroidered flowers in vivid colors.

David Barnes

Skills you need

* Using a cable needle
* French knots
* Making bobbles
* Detached chain stitch

If you do not know these skills refer to pages 178, 179, 397 and 400.

Materials

Tyrolean knitting is worked in a medium-weight plain yarn such as the worsted knitting yarns used in the basic cardigan. Embroidery is worked in brightly colored tapestry yarns or oddments of knitting yarn of similar weight to that in the basic garment. There is very little scope for introducing fancy yarns, since the appeal of this type of knitting rests on the combination of strong stitch textures with the sharp colors of the embroidery.

Special technique – Tyrolean embroidery

1 Tyrolean embroidery stitches are simple ones like detached chain stitch and French knots. Work floral motifs to follow the lines of the stitch pattern. On the chevron panel work one flower in the point of each "V" and one above it on each side in a different color.

2 On the cable and bobble panel work three flowers and two leaves on each side of the bobbles, and one flower between each pattern repeat, alternating the contrasting colors as shown.

3 The medallion cable running along the center of the mitten backs makes a perfect "frame" for a string of lazy-daisy motifs in alternating contrasting colors.

Coral Mula

The basic Tyrolean cardigan

A profusion of flowers bloom on a brilliantly patterned cardigan. It has a traditional peplum, pompon ties and detachable collar.

Sizes
To fit 32[34:36:38]in. bust
Length 21½[22:22½:22½]in.
Sleeve seam 17[18:18:18½]in.

Note: Instructions for larger sizes are in brackets []; where there is only one set of figures it applies to all sizes.

Gauge
29 sts and 31 rows to 4 in. over pat on size 5 needles
22 sts and 31 rows to 4 in. over stockinette st on size 5 needles

Materials
Cardigan
35[37:39:41]oz knitting worsted
Collar
4 oz knitting worsted
Beanie
4 oz knitting worsted
Mittens
4 oz knitting worsted
1 pair each size 3 and 5 knitting
Cable needle

90

For embroidery
4 skeins tapestry yarn in red
3 skeins in blue
2 skeins each in yellow and green

Back
Using larger needles, cast on 152[156:160:164] sts. K 4 rows.
Work peplum
Begin pat.
1st row (RS) P1[3:5:7], *K the 3rd st on LH needle, then K the 1st and 2nd st (called TW3), K1, P2, sl next 3 sts onto cable needle and hold at back of work, K3, then K3 from cable needle (called C6B), K3, sl next 3 sts onto cable needle and hold at front of work, K3, then K3 from cable needle (called C6F), P2, K1, TW3 ***, K1, P5, K tbl 2nd st on LH needle then K 1st st (called TW2B), K1, (K1, P1, K1, P1, K1) all into next st, turn, P5, turn, K5, sl 4th, 3rd, 2nd and first st over 5th (called MB), K1, K 2nd st on LH needle, then K first st (called TW2F),

P5, K1 **, rep from * to *** once, P4, rep from * to ** once, rep from * to *** again, P1[3:5:7].
2nd row K1[3:5:7], *P3, K3, P6 tbl, P3, P6 tbl, K3, P3 ***, K6, P7, K6 **, rep from * to *** once, K4, rep from * to ** once, rep from * to *** again, K1[3:5:7].
3rd row P1[3:5:7], *K4, P2, K6 tbl, K3, K6 tbl, P2, K4 ***, K1, P4, TW2B, K5, TW2F, P4, K1 **, rep from * to *** once, P4, rep from * to ** once, rep from * to *** again, P1[3:5:7].
4th row K1[3:5:7], *P3, K3, P6 tbl, P3, P6 tbl, K3, P3 ***, K5, P9, K5 **, rep from * to *** once, K4, rep from * to ** once, rep from * to *** again, K1[3:5:7].
5th row P1[3:5:7], *TW3, K1, P2, K6 tbl, K1, MB, K1, K6 tbl, P2, K1, TW3 ***, K1, P3, TW2B, K1, MB, K3, MB, K1, TW2F, P3, K1 **, rep from * to *** once, P4, rep from * to ** once, rep from * to *** again, P1[3:5:7].
6th row K1[3:5:7], *P3, K3, P6 tbl, P3, P6 tbl, K3, P3 ***, K4, P11, K4,

, rep from * to * once, K4, rep from * to ***, rep from * to *** again, K1[3:5:7].

7th row P1[3:5:7], *K4, P2, K6 tbl, K3, K6 tbl, P2, K4 ***, K1, P2, TW2B, K9, TW2F, P2, K1 **, rep from * to *** once, P4, rep from * to ** once, rep from * to *** again, P1[3:5:7].

8th row K1[3:5:7], *P3, K3, P6 tbl, P3, P6 tbl, K3, P3 ***, K3, P13, K3 **, rep from * to *** once, K4, rep from * to ** once, rep from * to *** again, K1[3:5:7].

9th row P1[3:5:7], *TW3, K1, P2, K6 tbl, K1, MB, K1, K6 tbl, P2, K1, TW3 ***, K1, P1, TW2B, K1, MB, K7, MB, K1, TW2F, P1, K1 **, rep from * to *** once, P4, rep from * to ** once, rep from * to *** again, P1[3:5:7].

10th row K1[3:5:7], *P3, K3, P6 tbl, P3, P6 tbl, K3, P3 ***, K2, P15, K2 **, rep from * to *** once, K4, rep from * to ** once, rep from * to *** again, K1[3:5:7].

11th row P1[3:5:7], *K4, P2, K6 tbl, K3, K6 tbl, P2, K4 ***, K1, TW2B, K13, TW2F, K1 **, rep from * to *** once, P4, rep from * to ** once, rep from * to *** again, P1[3:5:7].

12th row K1[3:5:7], *P3, K3, P6 tbl, P3, P6 tbl, K3, P3 ***, K1, P17, K1 **, rep from * to *** once, K4, rep from * to ** once, rep from * to *** again, K1[3:5:7].

13th row P1[3:5:7], *TW3, K1, P2, K6 tbl, K1, MB, K1, K6 tbl, P2, K1, TW3***, TW2B, K1, MB, K11, MB, K1, TW2F **, rep from * to *** once, P4, rep from * to ** once, rep from * to *** again, P1[3:5:7].

14th row As 12th row.

15th row P1[3:5:7], *K4, P2, K6 tbl, K3, K6 tbl, P2, K4 ***, TW2F, K15, TW2B **, rep from * to *** once, P4, rep from * to ** once, rep from * to *** again, P1[3:5:7].

16th row As 12th row.

17th row P1[3:5:7], *TW3, K1, P2, K6 tbl, K1, MB, K1, K6 tbl, P2, K1, TW3 ***, K1, P5, TW2B, K1, MB, K1, TW2F, P5, K1 **, rep from * to *** once, P4, rep from * to ** once, rep from * to *** again, P1[3:5:7].

18th row As 2nd row.

19th row P1[3:5:7], *K4, P2, K6 tbl, K3, K6 tbl, P2, K4 ***, K1, P4, TW2B, K5, TW2F, P4, K1 **, rep from * to *** once, P4, rep from * to ** once, rep from * to *** again, P1[3:5:7].

20th row As 4th row.

21st row P1[3:5:7], *TW3, K1, P2, C6F, K3, C6B, P2, K1, TW3 ***, K1,

P3, TW2B, K1, MB, K3, MB, K1, TW2F, P3, K1 **, rep from * to *** once, P4, rep from * to ** once, rep from * to *** again, P1[3:5:7].

22nd row As 6th row.

23rd row P1[3:5:7], *K4, P2, K6 tbl, K3, K6 tbl, P2, K4 ***, K1, P2, TW2B, K9, TW2F, P2, K1 **, rep from * to *** once, P4, rep from * to ** once, rep from * to *** again, P1[3:5:7].

24th row As 8th row.

25th row P1[3:5:7], *K4, P2, K6 tbl, K3, K6 tbl, P2, K4 ***, K1, P1, TW2B, K1, MB, K7, MB, K1, TW2F, P1, K1 **, rep from * to *** once, P4, rep from * to ** once, rep from * to *** again, P1[3:5:7].

26th row As 10th row.

27th row P1[3:5:7], *K4, P2, K6 tbl, K3, K6 tbl, P2, K4 ***, K1, TW2B, K13, TW2F, K1 **, rep from * to *** once, P4, rep from * to ** once, rep from * to *** again, P1[3:5:7].

28th row As 12th row.

29th row P1[3:5:7], *K4, P2, K6 tbl, K3, K6 tbl, P2, K4 ***, TW2B, K1, MB, K1, MB, K1, TW2F **, rep from * to *** once, P4, rep from * to ** once, rep from * to *** again, P1[3:5:7].

30th row As 12th row.

31st row P1[3:5:7], *K4, P2, K6 tbl, K3, K6 tbl, P2, K4 ***, TW2F, K15, TW2B **, rep from * to *** once, P4, rep from * to ** once, rep from * to *** again, P1[3:5:7].

32nd row As 12th row.

These 32 rows form the pat.

Next row K1[3:5:7], *K2 tog, K1, rep

from * to last 1[3:5:7] sts, K to end. 102[106:110:114] sts.

Change to smaller needles and work 3 rows K1, P1 ribbing.

Next row (make eyelets) Rib 4[2:4:2], *yo, rib 2 tog, rib 2, rep from * to last 2[0:2:0] sts, rib to end.

Work 2 rows in ribbing.

Next row Rib 38[27:16:5], *work twice into next st, (called inc 1), rib 12, rep from * 1[3:5:7] times more, rib to end. 104[110:116:122] sts.

Change to larger needles, and restart pat as foll, working from corresponding rows of peplum.

1st row P1[4:7:10], TW3, work from *** to ** of peplum, then work from * to ***, P4, rep from * to ***, then from *** to ** again, TW3, P1[4:7:10].

2nd row K1[4:7:10], P3, work from *** to ** of peplum, then from * to ***, K4, rep from * to ***, then *** to ** again, P3, K1[4:7:10].

3rd row P1[4:7:10], *K3, work from *** to ** of peplum, then from * to **, P4, rep from * to ***, then from *** to ** again, K3, P1[4:7:10].

4th row As 2nd row.

5th row P1 [4:7:10], TW3, work from *** to ** of peplum, then from * to ***, P4, rep from * to ***, then *** to ** again, TW3, P1[4:7:10].

Cont working pat sections in this order, *at the same time*, inc and work into reverse stockinette st 1 st at each end of the next and every foll 6th row until there are 124[130:136:142] sts. Cont without shaping. Work 10 rows.

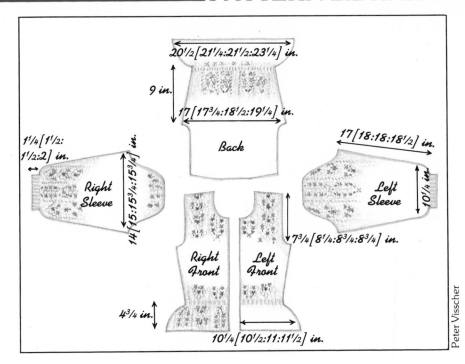

20½[21¼:21½:23¼] in.

9 in.

17[17¾:18½:19¼] in.

Back

1¼[1½: 1½:2] in.

17[18:18:18½] in.

Right Sleeve

Left Sleeve

14[15:15¾:15¾] in.

10¼ in.

Right Front

Left Front

7¾[8¼:8¾:8¾] in.

4¾ in.

10¼[10½:11:11½] in.

Peter Visscher

Shape armholes

Keeping pat correct, bind off 4 sts at beg of next 2 rows and 3 sts at beg of foll 2 rows.
Dec 1 st at each end of next 3[5:6:8] rows.
104[106:110:112] sts.
Cont without shaping until work measures 8[8¼:8¾:8¾]in. from beg of armholes, ending with a WS row.

Shape shoulders

Bind off 30[30:32:32] sts at beg of next 2 rows. Leave rem 44[46:46:48] sts on a spare needle.

Left front

Using larger needles, cast on 76[78:80:82] sts.
K 4 rows.
Begin pat as foll, working from corresponding rows of back peplum.
1st row P1[3:5:7], work as for back

from * to ** once, then from * to *** once, P1, K1.
2nd row K2, work as for back from * to **, then from * to *** once, K1[3:5:7].
3rd row P1[3:5:7], work as for back from * to ** once, then from * to *** once, P1, K1.
4th row K2, work as for back from * to ** once, then from * to *** once, K1[3:5:7].
Cont working in this way, work a further 28 rows.
Next row K1[3:5:7], *K2 tog, K1, rep from * to end. 51[53:55:57] sts.
Change to smaller needles.
Work in K1, P1 ribbing as foll:
Next row K1, *P1, K1, rep from * to end.
Next row P1, *K1, P1, rep from * to end.

Cont in ribbing as set. Work 1 more row.
Next row (make eyelets) Rib 4[2:4:2], *yo, work 2 tog, rib 2, rep from * ending last rep rib 1.
Work 3[2:2:2] rows in ribbing.
2nd, 3rd and 4th sizes only
Next row Rib [26:21:15], *inc 1, rib 12, rep from * [0:1:2] times more, rib to end. [54:57:60] sts.
All sizes
Change to larger needles and restart pat as foll working from corresponding rows of back peplum:
1st row P1[4:7:10], TW3, work as for back from *** to ** once, then from * to *** once, K1.
2nd row K1, work as for back from * to **, P3, K1[4:7:10].
3rd row P1[4:7:10], K3, work as for back from *** to ** once, then from * to ***, K1.
4th row K1, work as for back from * to **, P3, K1[4:7:10].
5th row P1[4:7:10], TW3, work as for back from *** to **, then from * to ***, K1.
Cont working in this way, *at the same time,* inc and work into reverse stockinette st 1 st at side edge on the next and every foll 6th row until there are 61[64:67:70] sts.
Cont without shaping. Work 10 rows.

Shape armholes

Keeping pat correct, bind off 4 sts at beg of next row and 3 sts at beg of foll alt row. Dec 1 st at armhole edge on foll 3[5:6:8] rows. 51[52:54:55] sts.
Cont without shaping until work measures 4¾[5:5:5]in. from beg of armhole, ending at front edge.

Shape neck

Bind off 8 sts at beg of next row and 4 sts at beg of foll alt row. Dec 1 st at neck edge on every row until 30[30:32:32] sts rem.
Cont without shaping until work matches back to shoulder shaping, ending at armhole edge.

Shape shoulder

Bind off rem sts.

Right front

Using larger needles, cast on 76[78:80:82] sts. K 4 rows.
Begin pat as foll working from corresponding rows of back peplum.
1st row K1, P1, work as for back from * to ** once, then from * to *** once, P1[3:5:7].
2nd row K1[3:5:7], work as for back from * to ** once, then from * to *** once, K2.
3rd row K1, P1, work as for back

from * to ** once, then from * to *** once, P1[3:5:7].
4th row K1[3:5:7], work as for back from * to ** once, then from * to *** once, K2.
Cont in this way, work another 28 rows.
Next row *K1, K2 tog, rep from * to last 1[3:5:7] sts, K to end. 51[53:55:57] sts.
Change to smaller needles. Work 3 rows in K1, P1 ribbing as given for left front.
Next row (make eyelets) Rib 1, work 2 tog, yo, *rib 2, work 2 tog, yo, rep from * to last 4[2:4:2] sts, rib to end.
Work 3[2:2:2] rows in ribbing.
2nd, 3rd and 4th sizes only
Next row Rib [26:21:15], *inc 1, rib 12, rep from * [0:1:2] times more, rib to end. [54:57:60] sts.
All sizes
Change to larger needles and restart pat as foll:
1st row K1, work as for back from * to ** once, TW3, P1[3:5:7].
2nd row K1[3:5:7], P3, work as for back from *** to **, then from * to ***, K1.
Complete to match left front, reversing all shaping.

Sleeves

Using smaller needles, cast on 52[54:56:58] sts.
Work in K1, P1 ribbing for 1¼[1½:1½:2] in.
Next row Rib 5[8:11:14], *inc 1, rib 1, rep from * to last 5[8:11:14] sts, rib to end. 73 sts.
Change to larger needles. Begin pat, working corresponding rows from back peplum as foll:

1st row K1, TW3, work as for back from *** to ** once, then from * to **, TW3, K1.

2nd row P4, work as for back from *** to ** once, then from * to **, P4.

3rd row K4, work as for back from *** to ** once, then from * to **, K4.

4th row P4, work as for back from *** to ** once, then from * to **, P4.

5th row K1, TW3, work as for back from *** to ** once, then from * to **, TW3, K1.

Cont working in this way, *at the same time,* inc and work into reverse stockinette st 1 st at each end of the next and every foll 6th row until there are 103 [109:113:113] sts. Work 34 [22:10:10] rows.

Shape top

Bind off 4 sts at beg of next 2 rows and 3 sts at beg of foll 2 rows. Dec 1 st at each end of next and every other row until 45 sts rem. Bind off.

Button band

Using smaller needles, cast on 6 sts. Work in K1, P1 ribbing until band, when slightly stretched, fits from beg of rib to neck edge of left front, ending at inner edge. Leave sts on a safety pin, Sew band in place. Mark 8 button positions on band, the first 1¼ in. from neck edge, the last ½ in. from cast-on edge with the others evenly spaced between.

Buttonhole band

Using smaller needles, cast on 6 sts. Work in K1, P1 ribbing for ½ in.

1st buttonhole row Rib 3, bind off 1, rib to end.

2nd buttonhole row Rib 2, cast on 1 rib to end.

Cont in ribbing, making buttonholes opposite markers, until band fits up right front edge, ending at outer edge. Do not break yarn. Sew band in place.

To finish

Join shoulder seams.

Neckband

Using smaller needles, rib across sts of buttonhole band, pick up and K 34[36:38:38] sts up right side of neck, K21[22:22:23], K2 tog, K21[22:22:23] across sts on back neck, pick up and K 34[36:38:38] sts down left side of neck, rib across buttonband. 123[129:133:135] sts. Beg with a 2nd row work 3 rows K1, P1 ribbing as given for left front. Work the 2 buttonhole rows again.

Rib 2 more rows. Bind off in ribbing. Work embroidery using 2 strands of yarn. (See Special technique, page 90.)

Join side and sleeve seams. Set in sleeves easing fullness at top. Sew on buttons.

Make a twisted cord and thread it through the waist eyelets, then make two small pompons and sew these to the ends of the cord.

Detachable collar

Using larger needles, cast on 244 sts. K 4 rows.

Begin pat, working from corresponding rows of back peplum.

1st row K1, work as for back from *

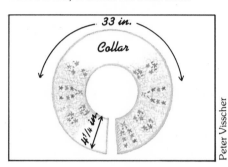

33 in.

Collar

4¼ in.

Peter Visscher

to ** twice, then from * to *** once, P4, rep from * to ** twice, then from * to *** again, K1.

2nd row K1, work as for back from * to ** twice, then from * to *** once, K4, rep from * to ** twice, then from * to *** again, K1.

Cont in this way. Work another 30 rows.

Next row (K2 tog) to end.

Next row (K2 tog) to end. 61 sts.

Make edging

1st row K across row.

2nd row K1, *yfwd, K2 tog, rep from * to end.

3rd row *K1, (K1, P1) all into yfwd of previous row, rep from * to last st, K1.

4th row Bind off 1, *insert LH needle into st below yfwd of 2nd row, draw through a loop and sl previous st over, bind off 3, rep from * to end.

Make a twisted cord and thread through at neck edge.

Beanie

Using larger needles, cast on 131 sts. Beg with a K row cont in stockinette st for 2¼ in. ending with a P row. Begin pat.

1st row K across row.

2nd and every other row P across row.

3rd row *K12, MB, rep from * to last st, K1.

4th row P across row.

Rep these 4 rows 4 times more. Begin shaping.

1st row *K2 tog, K11, rep from * to last st, K1.

2nd and every other row P across row.

3rd row *K2 tog, K9, MB, rep from * to last st, K1.

Keeping pat correct, cont to dec in this way on every other row until 11 sts rem.

Next row K2 tog, K to last st, K1. Break off yarn, thread through rem sts, draw up and fasten off securely.

To finish

Embroider flowers in "wedges" between rows of bobbles.

Join seam. Roll brim to RS and catch in place. Make a twisted cord, tie in a neat bow, sew to crown. Make two small pompons and sew to each end of cord.

Right mitten

**Using smaller needles, cast on 40 sts.

Work 9 rows K1, P1 ribbing.

Next row Rib 3, *work twice into next st (called inc 1), rib 6, rep from * to last 2 sts, rib 2. 45 sts. **

Begin pat and thumb gusset.

1st row *K1, P2, TW3, P2, sl next 2 sts onto cable needle and hold at back of work, then K2 from cable needle (called C4B), sl next 2 sts onto cable needle and hold at front of work, K2, then K2 from cable needle (called C4F), P2, TW3, P2, K1, P1, *K2, P1, K17.

2nd and every other row K1, P to last 24 sts, P1, K2, P3, K2, P8, K2, P3, K3.

3rd row *K1, P2, K3, P2, K8, P2, K3, P2, K1, P1, *work into front, back and front of next st, K1, P1, K17.

5th row K1, P2, TW3, P2, K8, P2, TW3, P2, K1, P1, K4, P1, K17.

7th row K1, P2, K3, P2, C4F, C4B, P2, K3, P2, K1, P1, (inc 1, K1) twice, P1, K17.

8th row As 2nd row.

These 8 rows establish the cable pat.

Next row As 1st row from * to *, K6, P1, K to end.

Next and every other row As 2nd row.

Next row As 3rd row from * to *, inc 1, K3, inc 1, K1, P1, K to end.

Cont in this way inc 1 st at each side of gusset on every foll 4th row until there are 55 sts.

Work 5 rows without shaping.

Divide for thumb
Next row Work in pat on 37 sts, turn leaving palm sts on spare needle.
Next row K1, P11, cast on 4 sts, turn.
Next row K16.
Next row K1, P to last st, K1.
Rep last 2 rows 8 times more.
Shape top
1st row (K2 tog) to end.
2nd row K1, P to last st, K1.
Break off yarn, thread through rem sts, draw up and fasten off securely. With RS of work facing, rejoin yarn to palm sts, K to end. 43 sts.
Dec 1 st at each end of next and every other row until 7 sts rem.
Bind off.

Left mitten
Work as given for right mitten from ** to **.
Begin pat and thumb gusset.

1st row K17, P1, K2, P1, K1, P2, TW3, P2, C4B, C4F, P2, TW3, P2, K1.
2nd and every other row K3, P3, K2, P8, K2, P3, K2, P3, K2, P to last st, K1.
3rd row K17, P1, work into front, back and front of next st, K1, P1, work in pat to last st, K1.
Cont in this way, inc 1 st at each side of gusset on every foll 4th row until there are 55 sts.
Work 5 rows without shaping.
Divide for thumb
Next row K30, cast on 4 sts, turn leaving back of hand sts on spare needle.
Next row K1, P14, K1, turn.
Complete as thumb of right mitten. With RS of work facing, rejoin yarn to sts for back of hand, work in pat to end.

Keeping pat correct, complete as given for right mitten reversing shaping.

Mitten edging
Using smaller needles and RS of work facing, pick up and K 39 sts along rib edge.
K 1 row.
Work edging as given for detachable collar.

To finish
Embroider mitten backs (see Special technique on page 90).
Join thumb and side seam.

Adapting the cardigan

Try some different embroidery stitches to give a new look to the basic outfit.

Tyrolean stitches are some of the most complicated and difficult to work so only the most experienced knitters will attempt to substitute new stitch patterns for those on the basic sweater. However, there is scope for variations on the basic makes in working alternatives to the embroidery stitches. The basic cardigan is very heavily decorated and some people may prefer a simpler look. For example, you could work the embroidery only on the cable and bobble panel or on the chevron panel rather than on both.

Tyrolean patterns

1 Tyrolean chevron

This pattern is worked over 51 stitches.
1st row K6, sl 1, K1, sl 1, K9, make bobble thus – (P1, K1, P1, K1) all into next st, turn, K4, turn, P4, lift 2nd, 3rd and 4th sts over 1st st and off needle (called MB), K2, MB, K2, yfwd, sl 1, K2 tog, psso, yfwd, (K2, MB) twice, K9, sl 1, K1, sl 1, K6.
2nd row P6, sl 1, P1, sl 1, P to last 9 sts, sl 1, P1, sl 1, P6.
3rd row K3, sl next 3 sts onto cable needle and leave at back of work, K1, then K3, from cable needle (called Cr4B), K1, sl next st onto cable needle and hold at front of work, K3, then K1 from cable needle (called Cr4F), K5,

(MB, K2) twice, K2 tog, yfwd, K1, yfwd, K2 tog tbl, (K2, MB) twice, K5, Cr4B, K1, Cr4F, K3.
4th row P across row.
5th row K6, sl 1, K1, sl 1, K7, (MB, K2) twice, K2 tog, yfwd, K3, yfwd, K2 tog tbl, (K2, MB), twice, K7, sl 1, K1, sl 1, K6.
6th row As 2nd row.
7th row K3, Cr4B, K1, Cr4F, K3, (MB, K2) twice, K2 tog, yfwd, K3, yfwd, K2 tog tbl, (K2, MB) twice, K3, Cr4B, K1, Cr4F, K3.
8th row P across row.
9th row K6, sl 1, K1, sl 1, K5, (MB, K2) twice, K2 tog, yfwd, K7, yfwd, K2 tog tbl, (K2, MB) twice, K5, sl 1, K1, sl 1, K6.
10th row As 2nd row.
11th row K3, Cr4B, K1, Cr4F, K1, (MB, K2) twice, K2 tog, yfwd, K9, yfwd, K2 tog tbl, (K2, MB) twice, K1, Cr4B, K1, Cr4F, K3.
12th row P across row.
13th row As 9th row.
14th row As 2nd row.
15th row As 7th row.
16th row P across row.
17th row As 5th row.
18th row As 2nd row.
19th row As 3rd row.
20th row P across row.
These 20 rows form the pattern repeat.

1

2 Tyrolean leaf

This panel is worked over 25 stitches.

1st row K1, K4 tbl, K1, P2 tog, P4, pick up loop between last st and next st and K it tbl – called make 1 (M1), K1, M1, P4, P2 tog, K1, K4 tbl, K1.
2nd row K1, P4 tbl, K6, P3, K6, P4 tbl, K1.
3rd row K1, K4 tbl, K1, P2 tog, P3, (K1, yfwd) twice, K1, P3, P2 tog, K1, K4 tbl, K1.
4th row K1, P4 tbl, K5, P5, K5, P4 tbl, K1.
5th row K1, sl next 2 sts onto cable needle and hold at front of work, K2 tbl, then K2 tbl from cable needle (called C4F tbl), K1, P2 tog, P2, K2, yfwd, K1, yfwd, K2, P2, P2 tog, K1, sl next 2 sts onto cable needle and hold at back of work, K2 tbl, then K2 tbl from cable needle (called C4B tbl), K1.
6th row K1, P4 tbl, K4, P7, K4, P4 tbl, K1.
7th row K1, K4 tbl, K1, P2 tog, P1, K3, yfwd, K1, yfwd, K3, P1, P2 tog, K1, K4 tbl, K1.
8th row K1, P4 tbl, K3, P9, K3, P4 tbl, K1.
9th row K1, K4 tbl, K1, P2 tog, K4, yfwd, K1, yfwd, K4, P2 tog, K1, K4 tbl, K1.
10th and 12th rows K1, P4 tbl, K2, P11, K2, P4 tbl, K1.
11th row K1, C4F tbl, K1, P1, K1, make bobble thus — (P1, K1, P1, K1) all into next st, turn, K4, turn, P4, lift 2nd, 3rd and 4th sts over first st and off needle (called MB), K7, MB, K1, P1, K1, C4B tbl, K1.
13th row K1, K4 tbl, K1, inc 1 P-wise, K4, sl 1, K2 tog, psso, K4, inc 1 P-wise, K1, K4 tbl, K1.
14th row As 8th row.

15th row K1, K4 tbl, K1, inc 1 P-wise, P1, K1, MB, K1, sl 1, K2 tog, psso, K1, MB, K1, P1, inc 1 P-wise, K1, K4 tbl, K1.
16th row As 6th row.
17th row K1, C4F tbl, K1, inc 1 P-wise, P2, K2, sl 1, K2 tog, psso, K2, P2, inc 1 P-wise, K1, C4B tbl, K1.
18th row As 4th row.
19th row K1, K4 tbl, K1, inc 1 P-wise, P3, K2 tog tbl, MB, K2 tog, P3, inc 1 P-wise, K1, K4 tbl, K1.
20th row As 2nd row.
21st row K1, K4 tbl, K1, inc 1 P-wise, P4, sl 1, K2 tog, psso, P4, inc 1 P-wise, K1, K4 tbl, K1.
22nd row K1, P4 tbl, K7, P1, K7, P4 tbl, K1.
23rd row K1, C4F tbl, K1, P13, K1, C4B tbl, K1.
24th row K1, P4 tbl, K15, P4 tbl, K1.
These 24 rows form pattern repeat.

3 Tyrolean diamond

This panel is worked over 21 stitches.

1st row (RS) P1, K second then first st on LH needle slipping both off needle together (called Tw2), P5, K2 tog, K into back of loop between next st and st just knitted (called make 1 K-wise), K1, make 1 K-wise, K2 tog tbl, P5, Tw2, P1.
2nd row P4, K4, P5, K4, P4.
3rd row P1, Tw2, P4, K2 tog, make 1 K-wise, K3, make 1 K-wise, K2 tog tbl, P4, Tw2, P1.
4th row P4, K3, P7, K3, P4.
5th row P1, Tw2, P3, K2 tog, make 1 K-wise, K5, make 1 K-wise, K2 tog tbl, P3, Tw2, P1.
6th row P4, K2, P9, K2, P4.

7th row P1, Tw2, P2, K2 tog, make 1 K-wise, K7, make 1 K-wise, K2 tog tbl, P2, Tw2, P1.
8th row P4, K1, P11, K1, P4.
9th row P1, Tw2, P1, K2 tog, make 1 K-wise, K9, make 1 K-wise, K2 tog tbl, P1, Tw2, P1.
10th row P across row.
11th row P1, Tw2, P into front and back of next st (called inc 1 P-wise), K1, (P1, K1, P1, K1) all into next st, turn, K4, turn, P4, lift 2nd, 3rd and 4th sts over first st and off needle (called MB), K3, sl 1, K2 tog, psso, K3, MB, K1, inc 1 P-wise, Tw2, P1.
12th row As 8th row.
13th row P1, Tw2, P1, inc 1 P-wise, K4, sl 1, K2 tog, psso, K4, inc 1 P-wise, P1, Tw2, P1.
14th row As 6th row.
15th row P1, Tw2, P1, inc 1 P-wise, P1, K1, MB, K1, sl 1, K2 tog, psso, K1, MB, K1, P1, inc 1 P-wise, P1, Tw2, P1.
16th row As 4th row.
17th row P1, Tw2, P1, inc 1 P-wise, P2, K2, sl 1, K2 tog, psso, K2, P2, inc 1 P-wise, P1, Tw2, P1.
18th row As 2nd row.
19th row P1, Tw2, P1, inc 1 P-wise, P3, K2 tog tbl, MB, K2 tog, P3, inc 1 P-wise, P1, Tw2, P1.
20th row P4, K5, P3, K5, P4.
21st row P1, Tw2, P1, inc 1 P-wise, P4, sl 1, K2 tog, psso, P4, inc 1 P-wise, P1, Tw2, P1.
22nd row P4, K6, P1, K6, P4.
23rd row P1, Tw2, P5, P2 tog, make 1 K-wise, K1, inc 1 K-wise, P2 tog, P5, Tw2, P1.
24th row P4, K5, P3, K5, P4.
These 24 rows form the pattern repeat.

2

3

Traveling stitches

Traveling stitch patterns are really an extension of cabling techniques. Knit stitches are crossed over purl stitches in such a way that they appear to meander in various directions over the background fabric. They combine well with more conventional cables and with Aran and bobble stitches.

David Barnes

96

Skills you need

* **Using a cable needle**
* **Making bobbles**

If you do not know these skills refer to pages 178 and 179.

Materials

Traveling stitches in general produce fairly heavily textured fabrics that look equally good in worsted-weight yarns like the tweedy wool used in the basic coat, and in yarns as fine as sport-weight Shetland-type wool or cotton. The chunkier the yarn the more pro-nounced the resulting three-dimensional effect of the fabric. These stitch patterns are usually worked in only one color though it is often possible to add touches of color with embroidery or, for example, by working contrasting bobbles or cables.

Special technique – sewing on a patch pocket

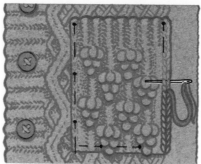
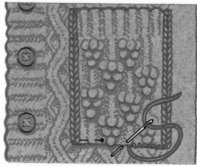

Coral Mula

1 Patch pockets can be sewn on with decorative embroidery stitches such as cross stitch or blanket stitch, or as on the basic coat, almost invisibly. First position the pocket on the coat, matching the pattern on the pocket to that on the coat, then pin it in place.

2 Thread a tapestry needle with matching yarn and, working through both layers, work a vertical line of duplicate stitch, as shown, through the edge stitches of the pocket on both sides.

3 Join the bottom edge of the pocket to the coat with neat over-stitching. (On plain stockinette stitch pockets this join can also be made with duplicate stitch.)

The basic traveling-stitch coat

Treat yourself to a warm winter in a beautiful tweedy coat encrusted with richly textured stitch patterns. Complete the picture with a snug ribbed hat to match.

Sizes
To fit 38[40:42]in. chest
Length 25[25:27]in.
Sleeve seam 20½ in.

Note: Instructions for larger sizes are in brackets []; where there is only one set of figures it applies to all sizes.

Gauge
12 sts and 20 rows to 4 in. over pat using size 10 needles

Materials
34[37:41]oz bulky yarn
1 pair each sizes 8 and 10 knitting needles
Size 8 circular needle
Cable needle
11 buttons

Back
Using smaller needles, cast on 66[70:74] sts.

Work in K2, P2 ribbing as foll:
1st row K2, *P2, K2, rep from * to end.
2nd row P2, *K2, P2, rep from * to end.
Rep the last 2 rows for 3 in., ending with a 1st row.
Next row Rib 8[10:10], pick up loop between last st worked and next st on LH needle and work into the back of it (called M1), (rib 2, M1) 25[25:27] times, rib to end.
92[96:102] sts.
Change to larger needles and begin pat.
1st row (RS) P4[6:2], K1 tbl, *P4, sl next 2 sts onto cable needle and leave at front of work, K2, then K2 from cable needle (called C4F), P4, sl next st onto cable needle and hold at front of work, K1 tbl, then K1 tbl from cable needle (called C2Ftbl), rep from * to last 17[19:15] sts, P4, C4F, P4,

K1 tbl, P4[6:2].
2nd and every other row K the P sts and P the K sts of previous row.
3rd row P4[6:2], *sl next st onto cable needle and hold at front of work, P1, then K1 tbl from cable needle (called Tw2F), P2, sl next st onto cable needle and hold at back of work, K2, then P1 from cable needle (called Tw3B), sl next 2 sts onto a cable needle and hold at front of work, P1, then K2 from cable needle, (called Tw3F), P2, sl next st onto cable needle and hold at back of work, K1 tbl then P1 from cable needle, (called Tw2B), rep from * to last 4[6:2] sts, P to end.
5th row P4[6:2] sts, *P1, Tw2F, Tw3B, P2, Tw3F, Tw2B, P1, rep from * to last 4[6:2] sts, P to end.
7th row P4[6:2], *P2, sl next st onto cable needle and hold at back of work, K2, then K1 tbl from cable needle (called Cr3B), P4, sl next 2 sts onto cable needle and hold at front of work, K1 tbl, then K2 from cable needle (called Cr3F), P2, rep from * to last 4[6:2] sts, P to end.

97

9th row P4[6:2], *P1, Tw3B, Tw2F, P2, Tw2B, Tw3F, P1, rep from * to last 4[6:2] sts, P to end.

11th row P4[6:2], *Tw3B, P2, Tw2F, Tw2B, P2, Tw3F, rep from * to last 4[6:2] sts, P to end.

13th row P4[6:2], K2, *P4, sl next st onto cable needle and hold at back of work, K1 tbl, then K1 tbl from cable needle (called C2Btbl), P4, sl next 2 sts onto cable needle and hold at back of work, K2, then K2 from cable needle (called C4B), rep from * to last 16[18:14] sts, P4, C2Btbl, P4, K2, P to end.

15th row P4[6:2], Tw3F, P2, Tw2B, Tw2F, P2, Tw3B, rep from * to last 4[6:2] sts, P to end.

17th row P4[6:2], *P1, Tw3F, Tw2B, P2, Tw2F, Tw3B, P1, rep from * to last 4[6:2] sts, P to end.

19th row P4[6:2], *P2, Cr3F, P4, Cr3B, P2, rep from * to last 4[6:2] sts, P to end.

21st row P4[6:2], *P1, Tw2B, Tw3F, P2, Tw3B, Tw2F, P1, rep from * to last 4[6:2] sts, P to end.

23rd row P4[6:2], *Tw2B, P2, Tw3F, Tw3B, P2, Tw2F, rep from * to last 4[6:2] sts, P to end.

24th row As 2nd row.
These 24 rows form the pat. Rep these 24 rows 4 times more.
Now cont in bobble pat as foll:

1st row (RS) P4[6:2], K1 tbl, *P5, K2, rep from * to last 10[12:8] sts, P5, K1 tbl, P4[6:2].

2nd and every other row K4[6:2], P1, *K5, P2, rep from * to last 10[12:8] sts, K5, P1, K4[6:2].

3rd row P4[6:2], K1 tbl, *P5, (K1, P1) twice into next st, P4, turn K4, turn, P2 tog, P2 tog tbl, turn, sl 1, K1, psso, (called make bobble, MB), K1, P5, K2, rep from * to last 17[19:15] sts, P5, MB, K1, P5, K1 tbl, P4[6:2].

5th row P4[6:2], K1 tbl, *P4, MB, K1, MB, P5, K2, rep from * to last 17[19:15] sts, P4, MB, K1, MB, P5, K1 tbl, P4[6:2].

7th row P4[6:2], K1 tbl, *P3, MB, P1, MB, K1, MB, P4, K2, rep from * to last 17[19:15] sts, P3, MB, P1, MB, K1, MB, P4, K1 tbl, P4[6:2].

9th row As 1st row.

11th row P4[6:2], K1 tbl, * P5, K2, P5, MB, K1, rep from * to last 17[19:15] sts, P5, K2, P5, K1 tbl, P4[6:2].

13th row P4[6:2], K1 tbl, * P5, K2, P4, MB, K1, MB, rep from * to last 17[19:15] sts, P5, K2, P5, K1 tbl, P4[6:2].

98

15th row P4[6:2], K1 tbl, P1, * P4, K2, P3, MB, P1, MB, K1, MB, rep from * to last 16[18:14] sts, P4, K2, P5, K1 tbl, P4[6:2].

16th row As 2nd row.
These 16 rows form bobble pat.

Shape armholes
Keeping pat correct, bind off 3 sts at beg of next 2 rows.
Dec 1 st at each end of next 7[7:5] rows and then on every other row until 62[62:76] sts rem.
Cont without shaping until work measures 38½[39:39½]in. from cast-on edge, ending with a WS row.

Shape shoulders
Keeping pat correct, bind off 8[8:11] sts at beg of next 2 rows and 8[7:10] sts at beg of foll 2 rows. Bind off rem 30[32:34] sts.

Left front
** Using smaller needles cast on 34[34:38] sts. Work 3 in. K2, P2 ribbing as given for back, ending with a first row.
Next row Rib 5[3:1], M1, (rib 2[2:3], M1) 12[14:12] times, rib to end. 47[49:51] sts. **
Change to larger needles and begin pat.

1st row (RS) P4[6:2], K1 tbl, * P4, C4F, P4, C2Ftbl, rep from * to last 14[14:20] sts, P4, C4F, P4, K1 tbl, P1[1:7].

2nd and every other row K the P sts and P the K sts of previous row.

3rd row P4[6:2], * Tw2F, P2, Tw3B, Tw3F, P2, Tw2B, rep from * to last 1[1:7] sts, P1[1:7].

5th row P4[6:2], * P1, Tw2F, Tw3B, P2, Tw3F, Tw2B, P1, rep from * to last 1[1:7] sts, P1[1:7].

7th row P4[6:2], * P2, Cr3B, P4, Cr3F, P2, rep from * to last 1[1:7] sts, P1[1:7].

9th row P4[6:2], * P1, Tw3B, Tw2F, P2, Tw2B, Tw3F, P1, rep from * to last 1[1:7] sts, P1[1:7].

11th row P4[6:2], * Tw3B, P2, Tw2F, Tw2B, P2, Tw3F, rep from * to last 1[1:7] sts, P1[1:7].

13th row P4[6:2], K2, * P4, C2Btbl, P4, C4B, rep from * to last 13[13:19] sts, P4, C2Btbl, P4, K2, P to end.

15th row P4[6:2], * Tw3F, P2, Tw2B, Tw2F, P2, Tw3B, rep from * to last 1[1:7] sts, P1[1:7].

17th row P4[6:2], * P1, Tw3F, Tw2B, P2, Tw2F, Tw3B, P1, rep from * to last 1[1:7] sts, P1[1:7].

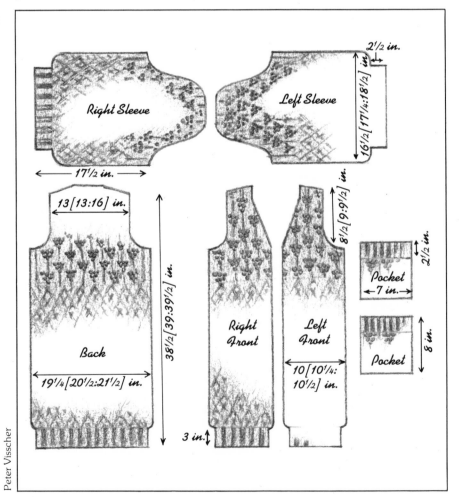

Peter Visscher

19th row P4[6:2], * P2, Cr3F, P4, Cr3B, P2, rep from * to last 1[1:7] sts, P1[1:7].

21st row P4[6:2], * P1, Tw2B, Tw3F, P2, Tw3B, Tw2F, P1, rep from * to last 1[1:7] sts, P1[1:7].

23rd row P4[6:2], * Tw2B, P2, Tw3F, Tw3B, P2, Tw2F, rep from * to last 1[1:7] sts, P1[1:7].

24th row As 2nd row.

These 24 rows form the pat. Rep these 24 rows 4 times more. Now cont in bobble pat as foll:

1st row (RS) P4[6:2], K1 tbl, * P5, K2, rep from * to last 7[7:13] sts, P5, K1 tbl, P1[1:7].

2nd and every other row K1[1:7], P1, K5, * P2, K5, rep from * to last 5[7:3] sts, P1, K4[6:2].

3rd row P4[6:2], K1 tbl, * P5, MB, K1, P5, K2, rep from * to last 14[14:20] sts, P5, MB, K1, P5, K1 tbl, P1[1:7].

5th row P4[6:2], K1 tbl, * P4, MB, K1, MB, P5, K2, rep from * to last 14[14:20]sts, P4, MB, K1, MB, P5, K1 tbl, P1[1:7].

7th row P4[6:2], K1 tbl, * P3, MB, P1, MB, K1, MB, P4, K2, rep from * to last 14[14:20] sts, P3, MB, P1, MB, K1, MB, P4, K1 tbl, P1[1:7].

9th row As 1st row.

11th row P4[6:2], K1 tbl, * P5, K2, P5, MB, K1, rep from * to last 14[14:20] sts, P5, K2, P5, K1 tbl, P1[1:7].

13th row P4[6:2], K1 tbl, * P5, K2, P4, MB, K1, MB, rep from * to last 14[14:20] sts, P5, K2, P5, K1 tbl, P1[1:7].

15th row P4[6:2], K1 tbl, P1, * P4, K2, P3, MB, P1, MB, K1, MB, rep from * to last 13[13:19] sts, P4, K2, P5, K1 tbl, P1[1:7].

16th row As 2nd row.

These 16 rows form bobble pat.

Shape armhole and neck

Next row Bind off 3 sts, work in pat to last 2 sts, P2 tog.

Work in pat 1 row.

Dec 1 st at neck edge on next and every other row, *at the same time,* dec 1 st at armhole edge on next 7[7:5] rows, then on every other row until 22[20:29] sts rem.

Keeping armhole edge straight cont to dec at neck edge as before until 16[15:21] sts rem. Cont without shaping until work matches back to shoulder shaping, ending at armhole edge.

Shape shoulder

Bind off 8[8:11] sts at beg of next row. Work 1 row. Bind off rem 8[7:10] sts.

Right front

Work as given for left front from ** to **. Change larger needles and begin pat.

1st row (RS) P1[1:7], K1 tbl, * P4, C4F, P4, C2Ftbl, rep from * to last 17[19:15] sts, P4, C4F, P4, K1 tbl, P4[6:2].

2nd and every other row K the P sts and P the K sts of previous row.

3rd row P1[1:7], * Tw2F, P2, Tw3B, Tw3F, P2, Tw2B, rep from * to last 4[6:2] sts, P4[6:2].

5th row P1[1:7], * P1, Tw2F, Tw3B, P2, Tw3F, Tw2B, P1, rep from * to last 4[6:2] sts, P4[6:2].

7th row P1[1:7], * P2, Cr3B, P4, Cr3F, P2, rep from * to last 4[6:2] sts, P4[6:2].

9th row P1[1:7], * P1, Tw3B, Tw2F, P2, Tw2B, Tw3F, P1, rep from * to last 4[6:2] sts, P4[6:2].

11th row P1[1:7], * Tw3B, P2, Tw2F, Tw2B, P2, Tw3F, rep from * to last 4[6:2] sts, P4[6:2].

13th row P1[1:7], K2, * P4, C2Btbl, P4, C4B, rep from * to last 16[18:14] sts, P4, C2Btbl, P4, K2, P to end.

15th row P1[1:7], * Tw3F, P2, Tw2B, Tw2F, P2, Tw3B, rep from * to last 4[6:2] sts, P4[6:2].

17th row P1[1:7], * P1, Tw3F, Tw2B, P2, Tw2F, Tw3B, P1, rep from * to last 4[6:2] sts, P4[6:2].

19th row P1[1:7], * P2, Cr3F, P4, Cr3B, P2, rep from * to last 4[6:2] sts, P4[6:2].

21st row P1[1:7], * P1, Tw2B, Tw3F, P2, Tw3B, Tw2F, P1, rep from * to last 4[6:2] sts, P4[6:2].

23rd row P1[1:7], * Tw2B, P2, Tw3F, Tw3B, P2, Tw2F, rep from * to last 4[6:2] sts, P4[6:2].

24th row As 2nd row.

These 24 rows form the pat. Rep these

24 rows 4 times more. Now cont in bobble pat as foll:

1st row (RS) P1[1:7], K1 tbl, * P5, K2, rep from * to last 10[12:8] sts, P5, K1 tbl, P4[6:2].

2nd and every other row K4[6:2], P1, K5, * P2, K5, rep from * to last 2[2:8] sts, P1, K1[1:7].

3rd row P1[1:7], K1 tbl, * P5, MB, K1, P5, K2, rep from * to last 17[19:15] sts, P5, MB, K1, P5, K1 tbl, P4[6:2].

5th row P1[1:7], K1 tbl, * P4, MB, K1, MB, P5, K2, rep from * to last 17[19:15] sts, P4, MB, K1, MB, P5, K1 tbl, P4[6:2].

7th row P1[1:7], K1 tbl, * P3, MB, P1, MB, K1, MB, P4, K2, rep from * to last 17[19:15] sts, P3, MB, P1, MB, K1, MB, P4, K1 tbl, P4[6:2].

9th row As 1st row.

11th row P1[1:7], K1 tbl, * P5, K2, P5, MB, K1, rep from * to last 17[19:15] sts, P5, K2, P5, K1 tbl, P4[6:2].

13th row P1[1:7], K1 tbl, * P5, K2, P4, MB, K1, MB, rep from * to 1dst 17[19:15] sts, P5, K2, P5, K1 tbl, P4 [6:2].

15th row P1[1:7], K1 tbl, P1, * P4, K2, P3, MB, P1, MB, K1, MB, rep from * to last 16[18:14] sts, P4, K2, P5, K1 tbl, P4[6:2].

16th row As 2nd row.

These 16 rows form the bobble pat. Complete to match left front, reversing all shapings.

Sleeves

Using smaller needles, cast on 30[34:34] sts. Work 2½ in., K2, P2 ribbing as given for back, ending with a first row.

Next row Rib 1, * M1, rib 1, rep from * to end. 59[67:67] sts.

Next row K3[6:4], M1, * K3[4:3], M1, rep from * to last 2[5:3] sts, K to end. 78[82:88] sts.

Change to larger needles and begin pat as given for back beg with a 13th pat row. Work 13th–24th rows once, then work 1st–24th rows again. Now work 1st–16th rows of bobble pat as given for back.

Shape top

Keeping continuity of pat, bind off 3 sts at beg of next 2 rows. Dec 1 st at each end of next and every other row until 30[36:44] sts rem. Work 1 row.

2nd and 3rd sizes only

Dec 1st at each end of every row until 30 sts rem. Work 1 row.

All sizes

Bind off.

Pockets (make 2)
Using larger needles, cast on 37 sts
and work in pat as foll:
1st row (RS) K2, * P5, K2, rep from *
to end.
2nd and every other row P2, * K5,
P2, rep from * to end.
3rd row K2, (P5, MB, K1, P5, K2)
twice, P5, K2.
5th row K2, (P4, MB, K1, MB, P5,
K2) twice, P5, K2.
7th row K2, (P3, MB, P1, MB, K1,
MB, P4, K2) twice, P5, K2.
9th row As 1st row.
11th row K2, (P5, K2, P5, MB, K1)
twice, P5, K2.
13th row K2, (P5, K2, P4, MB, K1,
MB) twice, P5, K2.
15th row K2, P1, (P4, K2, P3, MB,
P1, MB, K1, MB) twice, P4, K2.
16th row As 2nd row.
Rep these 16 rows once more, dec 3
sts evenly across last row. Change to
smaller needles and work 2½ in. K2,
P2 ribbing as given for back.
Bind off in ribbing.

To finish
Join shoulders.
Button band
With RS of work facing, using circular
needle, pick up and K 9[11:12] sts
from center back neck to shoulder
seam, 35[37:40] sts from shoulder
seam to beg of neck shaping, then
114 sts from beg of neck shaping to
cast-on edge. 158[162:166] sts. Work
in rows. Beg with a 2nd row work 15
rows K2, P2 ribbing as given for back.
Bind off in ribbing.
Buttonhole band
With RS of work facing, using smaller
needles, pick up and K 114 sts from
cast-on edge to beg of neck shaping,
35[37:40] sts from beg of neck
shaping to shoulder and 9[11:12] sts
from shoulder to center back neck.
158[162:166] sts.
Beg with a 2nd row work 7 rows K2,
P2 ribbing as given for back.
1st buttonhole row Rib 6, bind off 2
sts, * rib 8, (including st used in
binding off), bind off 2, rep from * 9
times more, rib to end.
2nd buttonhole row Rib to end,
casting on 2 sts over those bound off
in previous row.
Rib a further 6 rows. Bind off in
ribbing. Join center back neck seam
of bands. Join side and sleeve seams.
Set in sleeves, easing fullness at top.
Sew on pockets. (See Special
technique page 97.) Sew on buttons.
100

David Barnes

Hat
Using smaller needles, cast on 74 sts.
1st row K2, * P2, K2, rep from *.
2nd row P2, * K2, P2, rep from *.
Rep last 2 rows for 8 in., ending with a
first row.
Next row Rib 19, (M1, rib 18) twice,
M1, rib 19. 77 sts.
Change to larger needles and begin
pat.
1st row (RS) K1, * P3, K1, rep from *
to end.
2nd row P1, * K3, P1, rep from *.
Rep these 2 rows until work measures
13¾ in. from cast-on edge, ending
with a WS row.
Shape crown
1st row K1, * P2 tog, P1, K1, rep
from * to end. 58 sts.
2nd row P1, * K2, P1, rep from *.
3rd row K1, * P2, K1, rep from *.
4th row As 2nd row.
5th row K1, * P2 tog, K1, rep from *
to end. 39 sts.
6th row P1, * K1, P1, rep from *.
7th row K1, * P1, K1, rep from *.
8th row As 6th row.
9th row K1, * K2 tog, rep from * to
end. 20 sts.
10th row (P2 tog) 10 times. 10 sts.
Break yarn, thread through rem sts,
draw up and fasten off.

To finish
Join seam, reversing K2, P2 ribbing
section to roll back. Roll brim to RS
and catch-stitch in position.

Adapting the coat

**Try adding color to the tweedy
coat to give it a completely
different look.**

The basic coat is worked in a worsted-
weight yarn that knits up into a rich
tweedy fabric with a very countrified
look. The subdued coloring is extremely elegant but if more color is
required try adding some embroidering in vivid tapestry wools. You can
choose completely different contrasts
or reflect some of the flecks in the
tweedy yarn. Some of the ribs of the
lattice of traveling stitches could be followed with chain-stitched lines, or
some of the windows of the lattice
could be filled in with satin stitch. If
you prefer to knit in colors rather than
embroider them, work the bobbles on
the yoke, pockets and sleeve tops in
one or more contrasting shades.

Sanquhar patterns

The small Scottish town of Sanquhar in Dumfriesshire is the home of some very distinctive checked patterns. They were traditionally worked in natural undyed yarn in combinations of brown, dark gray or black with white, pale gray or cream, and are commonly found on hats, socks and gloves.

Simon Butcher / Victor Yuan

Skills you need

* **Working with color**
* **Circular knitting**

If you do not know these skills refer to pages 174 and 186.

Materials

Sanquhar patterns, like most traditional Scottish patterns, look best worked in smooth, pure wool yarns like the Shetland wool used in the basic accessories. They look especially authentic in the traditional colors but brighter shades can also be used to great effect as is seen in many of the Pattern Library samples on pages 105-107.

Special technique – working a thumb

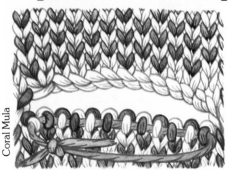

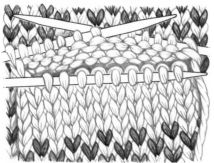

Coral Mula

1 Work as given in the pattern to the thumb position. Slip a given number of stitches onto a spare thread. Cast on the same number of stitches in their place. Work to the end of the round then continue working the main part of the glove.

2 When the main part is finished knit the stitches from the spare yarn, then pick up and K the same number of stitches from the cast-on edge. Distribute these stitches among three needles and with the fourth needle work in rounds until the thumb is the correct length.

3 Shape the top of the thumb by knitting two stitches together across the next round. Work one round. Break yarn and thread it through the remaining stitches. Pull them tightly together and fasten off the yarn on the wrong side.

The basic Sanquhar accessories

Round off your wardrobe with this classic collection of accessories all knitted on four needles and worked in beautiful traditional Scottish patterns.

Sizes
Gloves 7½ in. around hand above thumb
Fingerless gloves 7½ in. around hand above thumb
Beret to fit an average head
Ankle socks length of foot 8¾ in. (adjustable)
Long socks length of foot 9¾ in. (adjustable)
Length of leg to heel (top turned down) 19 in.
Scarf length excluding fringe 60½ in.

Gauge
28 sts and 28 rows to 4 in. over pat on size 5 needles
32 sts and 40 rows to 4 in. over stockinette st on size 2 needles

Materials
Gloves 1 oz fingering-weight Shetland-type yarn in main color (A)
1 oz in contrasting color (B)

Fingerless gloves 1 oz in main color (C)
1 oz in contrasting color (D)
Beret 2 oz in main color (A)
1 oz in contrasting color (B)
Ankle socks 2 oz in main color (A)
1 oz in contrasting color (B)
Long socks 4 oz in main color (C)
1 oz in contrasting color (D)
Scarf 10 oz in main color (C)
5 oz in contrasting color (D)
1 set each size 2, 3 and 4 knitting needles pointed at both ends

Gloves
Right glove
*** Using size 2 needles and A, cast on 44 sts and divide onto 3 needles. (Mark next st as first st of round). Using 4th needle work in rounds of K1, P1 ribbing for 2¼ in.
Next round Rib 2, pick up loop between last st and next st on LH needle and work into the back of it – called M1, (rib 6, M1) 7 times. 52 sts.

Change to size 4 needles and cont in stockinette st, begin pat from chart 1 as foll (read every round from right to left):
1st round K1A, * K1B, K1A, rep from * to last 27 sts, work in pat first round from chart 1.
2nd round K1B, * K1A, K1B, rep from * to last 27 sts, work in pat 2nd round from chart 2.
These 2 rows establish the pat for the palm and the back of the hand worked from chart.
Keeping chart correct, work a further 13 rounds. **
Place thumb
Next round K1, sl next 11 sts onto a safety pin, cast on 11 sts, work in pat to end. Work 11 rounds.
First finger
Change to size 3 needles and A.
Next round K8, sl next 37 sts onto a length of yarn, cast on 2 sts, K7. 17 sts. ***
K 30 rounds.
Shape top
Next round K1, * K2 tog, rep from * to end.
K one round.

Break off yarn and thread it through rem sts, draw up tightly and fasten off.

2nd finger

Join in yarn to next st of round.

Next round K6, cast on 2 sts, K last 7 sts of round, pick up and K 2 sts from base of first finger. 17 sts.

K 36 rounds.

Complete as given for first finger.

**** 3rd finger

Join in yarn to next st of round.

Next round K6, cast on 2 sts, K last 6 sts of round, pick up and K 2 sts from base of 2nd finger. 16 sts.****

K 30 rounds.

Shape top

Next round * K2 tog, rep from * to end.

K one round.

Thread yarn through rem sts, draw up and fasten off.

4th finger

Join in yarn to rem sts.

Next round K12, pick up and K 2 sts from base of 3rd finger. 14 sts.

K 26 rounds.

Complete as given for 3rd finger.

Thumb

With RS of work facing, using size 3 needles and A, K 11 sts from safety pin, then pick up and K 11 sts from cast-on sts. 22 sts.

K 26 rounds.

Complete as 3rd finger.

Left glove

Work as given for right glove from *** to **.

Place thumb

Next round Work in pat on 13 sts, sl next 11 sts onto a safety pin, cast on 11 sts, work in pat to end.

Work 11 rounds.

First finger

Change to size 3 needles and A.

Next round K17, sl these sts onto a length of yarn, K15, cast on 2 sts, leave rem sts on a length of yarn.

Complete as given for first finger of right glove.

2nd finger

Next round Sl last 6 sts from first length of yarn onto needle, join in A, pick up and K 2 sts from base of first finger, K7 sts from second length of yarn, cast on 2 sts. 17 sts.

Complete as given for 2nd finger of right glove.

3rd finger

Next round Sl last 6 sts from first length of yarn onto needle, join in A. Pick up and K 2 sts from base of 2nd finger, K 6 sts from second length of yarn, cast on 2 sts. 16 sts.

Complete as given for 3rd finger of right glove.

4th finger

Next round Sl last 5 sts on first length of yarn onto needle, join in A, pick up and K 2 sts from base of 3rd finger, K7 sts rem on second length of yarn. 14 sts. Complete as 4th finger of right glove.

Thumb

Work as given for right glove.

Fingerless gloves
Right fingerless glove

Work as given for right glove from *** to ***, working from chart 2.

Next round K7, K2 tog, K8. 16 sts.

K 4 rounds. Work 3 rounds K1, P1 ribbing. Bind off loosely in ribbing.

2nd finger

Join in yarn to next st of round.

Next round K6, cast on 2 sts, K last 7 sts of round, pick up and K 2 sts from base of first finger. 17 sts.

Next round K15, K2 tog, 16 sts.

Complete as first finger.

3rd finger

Work as 3rd finger of right glove from **** to ****.

K 4 rounds. Complete as first finger.

4th finger

Join in yarn to rem sts.

Next round K12, pick up and K 2 sts from base of 3rd finger. 14 sts.

K 3 rounds. Complete as first finger.

Thumb

Using size 3 needles and A, with RS of work facing K 11 sts from safety pin,

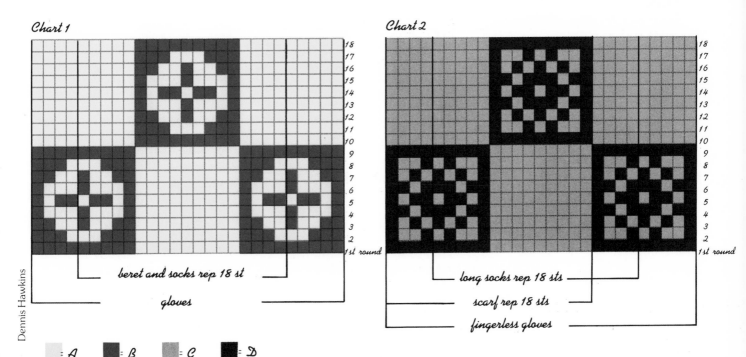

Chart 1

beret and socks rep 18 st

gloves

Chart 2

long socks rep 18 sts

scarf rep 18 sts

fingerless gloves

1st round

: A   : B   : C   : D

Dennis Hawkins

then pick up and K 11 sts from cast-on sts. 22 sts.
Complete as first finger.

Left fingerless glove

Work as given for left glove working from chart 2, completing fingers as given for right fingerless glove.

Beret

Using size 2 needles and A, cast on 126 sts and divide onto three needles. (Mark next st as first of round).
Work 11 rounds K1, P1 ribbing.
Next round * (K2, M1) 27 times, (K1, M1) 9 times, rep from * once more. 198 sts.
Change to size 4 needles and begin pat from chart 1.
Work 27 rounds.

Shape crown

Cont in A only.
Next round * K2 tog, K2, rep from * to last 2 sts, K2 tog. 148 sts.
Next round K to end.
Next round (K12, sl 1, K2 tog, psso) 9 times, K13. 130 sts.
Next round Sl first st onto end of last needle, K to end.
Next round (K10, sl 1, K2 tog, psso) 10 times. 110 sts.
Next round (K8, sl 1, K2 tog, psso) 10 times. 90 sts.
Cont to dec in this way until the round (sl 1, K2 tog, psso) 10 times has been worked. 10 sts.
Next round K to end.
Next round (K2 tog) to end. 5 sts.
Thread yarn through the rem sts, draw up and fasten off.

Ankle socks

Using size 2 needles and A, cast on 72 sts and divide onto 3 needles. (Mark next st as first of round). Work 4 rounds K1, P1 ribbing.
Change to size 4 needles and begin pat from chart 1.
Work 18 rounds.
Change to size 2 needles and cont in A only.
Next round (K3, K2 tog) 4 times, (K2, K2 tog) 8 times, (K3, K2 tog) 4 times. 56 sts.
Work in K1, P1 ribbing for 2 in. Turn work inside out, so reversing fabric.
K 12 rounds.

Divide for heel

Next round K13, sl last 14 sts of round to other end of same needle. 27 sts.
Divide rem sts onto 2 needles and leave for instep.
Cont on 27 sts for heel in rows as foll:
1st row (WS) Sl 1, P to end.
104

2nd row Sl 1, K to end.
Rep these 2 rows 15 times more, then the first row again.

Turn heel

1st row K19, K2 tog tbl, turn.
2nd row P12, P2 tog, turn.
3rd row K12, K2 tog tbl, turn.
Rep 2nd and 3rd rows 5 times more, then the 2nd row again.
Next row K7 to complete heel (6 sts rem on LH needle).
Sl all instep sts onto one needle. With spare needle, K6 sts rem for heel, pick

up and K 16 sts along side of heel, with 2nd needle K29 instep sts, with 3rd needle pick up and K 16 sts along side of heel, K7 heel sts. 74 sts.
Shape instep in rounds as foll:
1st round K to end.
2nd round First needle – K to last 3 sts, K2 tog, K1, 2nd needle – K to end, 3rd needle – K1, K2 tog tbl, K to end.
Rep these 2 rounds until 56 sts rem. Cont without shaping. Work 48 rounds.
(Length of foot may be adjusted here if necessary.)
Next round First needle – K to end, 2nd needle – K1, K2 tog tbl, K to last 3 sts, K2 tog, K1, 3rd needle – K to end.

Shape toe

1st round First needle – K to last 3 sts, K2 tog, K1, 2nd needle – K1, K2 tog tbl, K to last 3 sts, K2 tog, K1, 3rd needle – K1, K2 tog tbl, K to end.
2nd round K to end.
Rep last 2 rounds until 30 sts rem. K sts from first needle onto end of 3rd needle. Graft or bind off sts tog from 2 needles.

Long socks

Using size 2 needles and C, cast on 72 sts and divide onto 3 needles. (Mark next st as first of round). Work 4

rounds K1, P1 ribbing.
Change to size 4 needles and begin pat from chart 2. Work 18 rounds.
Change to size 2 needles and cont in A only.
Next round K to end.
Next round (K6, M1) 12 times. 84 sts.
Work in K1, P1 ribbing for 2¼ in. Turn work inside out so reversing fabric.
K 40 rounds.

Shape leg

1st round K2 tog, K to last 3 sts, K2 tog tbl, K1.
K 5 rounds.
Rep the last 6 rounds until 60 sts rem. Cont without shaping until work measures 13¾ in. from reversing of fabric.

Divide for heel

Next round K14, sl last 15 sts of round to other end of same needle. 29 sts.
Divide rem sts onto 2 needles and leave for instep.
Cont on 29 sts for heel in rows as foll:
1st row (WS) Sl 1 P-wise, P to end.
2nd row Sl 1 K-wise, * K1, ybk, sl 1 P-wise, rep from * to last 2 sts, K2.
Rep these 2 rows 16 times more, then the first row again.

Turn heel

1st row K17, sl 1, K1, psso, turn.
2nd row P6, P2 tog, turn.
3rd row K7, sl 1, K1, psso, turn.
4th row P8, P2 tog, turn.
Cont in this way until all sts are worked onto one needle ending with a P row. 17 sts.
Next row K9 to complete heel (8 sts rem on LH needle).
Sl all instep sts onto one needle. With spare needle, K8 sts rem for heel, pick up and K 18 sts along side of heel, with 2nd needle K31 instep sts, with 3rd needle pick up and K 18 sts along side of heel, K9 heel sts. 84 sts.
Shape instep in rounds as foll:
1st round K to end.
2nd round First needle – K to last 3 sts, K2 tog, K1, 2nd needle – K, 3rd needle – K1, K2 tog tbl, K to end. Rep these 2 rounds until 58 sts rem. Cont without shaping. Work 56 rounds. (Length may be adjusted here.) Sl first st of 2nd needle onto end of first needle and last st of 2nd needle onto 3rd needle.

Shape toe

1st round First needle – K to last 3 sts, K2 tog, K1, 2nd needle – K1, K2 tog tbl, K to last 3 sts, K2 tog, K1, 3rd needle – K1, K2 tog tbl, K to end.
2nd round K to end.

Rep these 2 rounds until 26 sts rem, ending with a 2nd round.
K sts from first needle onto end of 3rd needle. Graft or bind off sts tog from 2 needles.

Scarf

Using size 4 needles and C, cast on 144 sts and divide onto 3 needles. (Mark next st as first round). K one round.
Cont in stockinette st, begin pat from chart 2 until work measures approx 60½ in. from cast-on edge ending

Simon Butcher

with a 9th pat row.
Bind off

To finish

Press scarf flat and join ends. Cut rem yarn into 14¼ in. lengths. Using 3 strands of C and 3 strands of D tog make a fringe to run along the short ends.

Adapting the Sanquhar accessories

The basic patterns are ideal for making up in many different versions to team with anything in your wardrobe.

All the charts in the Pattern Library can be used in one way or another for the gloves, scarf, beret or socks. The chessboard patterns will repeat one

and a half times across the back of the gloves. The seed pattern can be used on the palm of the gloves, or less conventionally, as an all-over pattern on any of the garments. Either of the plaid patterns can be used on the scarf. The basic accessories have all been worked in traditional colors but these patterns look just as good in brighter shades.

Reading the charts

All the charts should be worked in stockinette stitch. When working in the round knit every round and read all the rows on the charts from right to left. When working on two needles read odd-numbered (knit) rows from right to left and even-numbered (purl) rows from left to right.

Sanquhar patterns

1 Sanquhar cross

Many Sanquhar patterns follow this "chessboard" format. Sometimes, as in the patterns on the basic socks, gloves, beret and scarf, only the dark squares are decorated with a motif. In other cases the motif is reversed on the light squares as here.

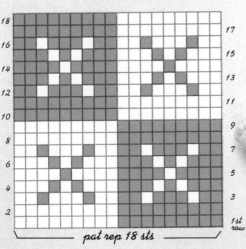

pat rep 18 sts

2 Shepherd's plaid

This pattern repeats over 12 stitches, plus 1 extra if worked on two needles. In the round work the basic pattern repeat only. It can be used on the scarf.

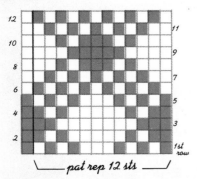

pat rep 12 sts

3 Sanquhar seed

Sanquhar check patterns are often combined with a simple all-over seed pattern in the same color combination as the main pattern. The pattern might be used on the palms, fingers and thumbs of gloves, for example, or on the feet and legs of socks. This pattern repeats over 6 stitches. It can be used on all the basic accessories.

rep 6 sts

4 Fleur de lis plaid

This pattern can be used on the basic scarf. It repeats over 12 stitches in the round, or 12 stitches, plus 1 extra if worked on two needles.

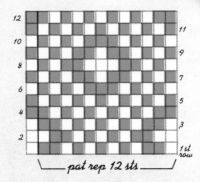

pat rep 12 sts

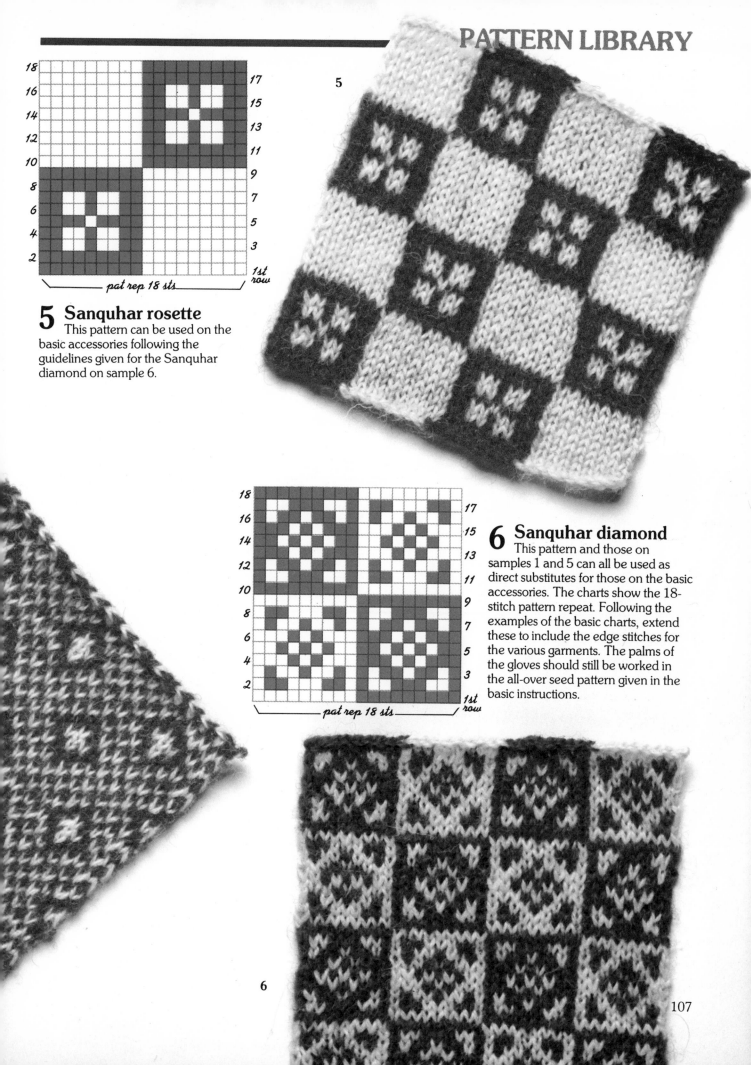

5 Sanquhar rosette

This pattern can be used on the basic accessories following the guidelines given for the Sanquhar diamond on sample 6.

6 Sanquhar diamond

This pattern and those on samples 1 and 5 can all be used as direct substitutes for those on the basic accessories. The charts show the 18-stitch pattern repeat. Following the examples of the basic charts, extend these to include the edge stitches for the various garments. The palms of the gloves should still be worked in the all-over seed pattern given in the basic instructions.

107

KNITWEAR FOR MEN
Aran

Skills you need

* **Decreasing**
* **Using a cable needle**

If you do not know these skills refer to pages 175 and 178.

Materials

The intricate textures of Aran patterns work best in the natural homespun yarn traditionally used by Aran knitters and known as "bainin". The original yarns were dyed locally to soft subtle creams and browns, using vegetable dyes, but they are now available in many colors. Aran stitches can work well in finer yarns, though to some extent the strong three-dimensional effect will be lost. The sweater is knitted in 100% wool knitting worsted.

Special technique – flat seam

1 Use a flat seam when seaming heavily textured fabrics. Place the two edges together RS facing, and secure the end of the yarn with a double stitch.

2 Continue along the seam as shown taking care to match rows or stitches on the two pieces of knitting.

Coral Mula

The basic Aran sweater

This classic creamy sweater encrusted with traditional Aran textures looks good and is warm enough to withstand the cruelest winter weather.

Sizes
To fit 32-34[36-38:40-42]in. bust/chest
Length 24[26½:27½]in.
Sleeve length 17[18:18½]in.
Note: Instructions for larger sizes are in square brackets []; where there is only one set of figures it applies to all sizes.

Gauge
22 sts and 28 rows to 4 in. over Irish moss st (see page 113) on size 6 needles

Materials
30[33:37]oz knitting worsted or fisherman yarn
1 pair each size 4 and 6 knitting needles
1 cable needle

Back
** Using smaller needles, cast on 113[123:131] sts. Work in K1, P1 ribbing for 2 in.
Change to larger needles and work in pat as follows:
1st row K1, (P1, K1) 4[6:8] times, P2, K4, * P2, C3B, K3, P5, Tw3B, K1, Tw3F, P5, C3B, K3, P2, * K1, (P1, K1) 8[9:9] times, rep from * to * once,

Aran abbreviations

CN – cable needle.
C4F – **cable 4 front** (sl next 2 sts onto CN and leave at front of work, K2, then K2 from CN).
C4B – **cable 4 back** (sl next 2 sts onto CN and leave at back of work, K2, then K2 from CN).
C3F – **cable 3 front** (sl next st onto CN and leave at front of work, K2, then K1 from CN).
C3B – **cable 3 back** (sl next 2 sts onto CN and leave at back of work, K1, then K2 from CN).
Tw3F – **twist 3 front** (sl next 2 sts onto CN and leave at front of work, P1, then K2 from CN).
Tw3B – **twist 3 back** (sl next st onto CN and leave at back of work, K2, then P1 from CN).
Tw5B – **twist 5 back** (sl next 3 sts onto cable needle and leave at back of work, K2, then P1, K2 from CN).
Cr3B – **cross 3 back** (sl next st onto

CN and leave at back of work, K2, then K1 from CN).
Tw2B – **twist 2 back** (sl next st onto CN and leave at back of work, K1 tbl, then P1 from CN).
Tw2F – **twist 2 front** (sl next st onto CN and leave at front of work, P1, then K1 tbl from CN).
C2Ftbl – **cable 2 front through back of loop** (sl next st onto CN and leave at front of work, K1 tbl, then K1 tbl from CN).
C2Btbl – **cable 2 back through back of loop** (sl next st onto CN and hold at back of work, K1 tbl then K1 tbl from CN).
C2F P-wise – **cable 2 front purlwise** (sl next st onto CN and leave at front of work, P1, then P1 from CN).
C2Ftbl P-wise – **cable 2 front through back of loop purlwise** (sl next st onto CN and leave at front of work, P1 tbl, then P1 tbl from CN).

108

Tom Leighton

K4, P2, K1, (P1, K1) 4[6:8] times.
2nd row P1, (K1, P1) 4[6:8] times,
K2, P4, * K2, P6, K5, P2, K1, P1, K1,
P2, K5, P6, K2, * P1, (K1, P1) 8[9:9]
times, rep from * to * once, P4, K2,
P1, (K1, P1) 4[6:8] times.
3rd row P1, (K1, P1) 4[6:8] times,
P2, C4B, * P2, K3, C3F, P4, Tw3B,
K1, P1, K1, Tw3F, P4, K3, C3F, P2, *
P1, (K1, P1) 8[9:9] times, rep from *
to * once, C4B, P3, (K1, P1) 4[6:8]
times.
4th row K1, (P1, K1) 4[6:8] times,
K2, P4, * K2, P6, K4, P2, (K1, P1)
twice, K1, P2, K4, P6, K2, * K1, (P1,
K1) 8[9:9] times, rep from * to * once,

P4, K3, (P1, K1) 4[6:8] times.
5th row K1, (P1, K1) 4[6:8] times,
P2, K4, * P2, C3B, K3, P3, Tw3B,
(K1, P1) twice, K1, Tw3F, P3, C3B,
K3, P2, * K1, (P1, K1) 8[9:9] times,
rep from * to * once, K4, P2, K1 (P1,
K1) 4[6:8] times.
6th row P1, (K1, P1) 4[6:8] times,
K2, P4, * K2, P6, K3, P2, (K1, P1) 3
times, K1, P2, K3, P6, K2, * P1 (K1,
P1) 8[9:9] times, rep from * to * once,
P4, K2, P1, (K1, P1) 4[6:8] times.
7th row P1, (K1, P1) 4[6:8] times,
P2, C4B, * P2, K3, C3F, P2, Tw3B,
(K1, P1) 3 times, K1, Tw3F, P2, K3,
C3F, P2, * P1, (K1, P1) 8[9:9] times,

rep from * to * once, C4B, P3, (K1,
P1) 4[6:8] times.
8th row K1, (P1, K1) 4[6:8] times,
K2, P4, * K2, P6, K2, P2, (K1, P1) 4
times, K1, P2, K2, P6, K2, * K1, (P1,
K1) 8[9:9] times, rep from * to * once,
P4, K3, (P1, K1) 4[6:8] times.
9th row K1, (P1, K1) 4[6:8] times,
P2, K4, * P2, C3B, K3, P2, K3, (P1,
K1) 4 times, K2, P2, C3B, K3, P2,
* K1, (P1, K1) 8[9:9] times, rep from
* to * once, K4, P2, K1, (P1, K1)
4[6:8] times.
10th row P1, (K1, P1) 4[6:8] times,
K2, P4, * K2, P6, K2, P3, (K1, P1) 4
times, P2, K2, P6, K2, * P1, (K1, P1)

109

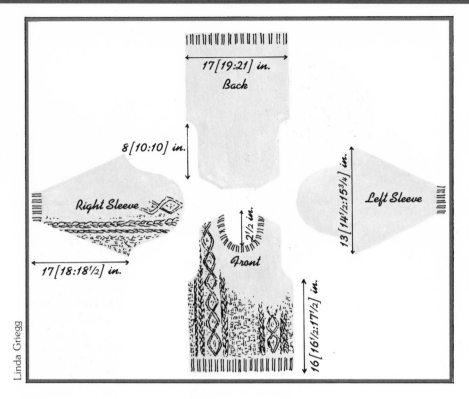

Back

17[19:21] in.

8[10:10] in.

Right Sleeve

17[18:18½] in.

13[14½:15¾] in.

Left Sleeve

2½ in.

Front

16[16½:17½] in.

Linda Griegg

8[9:9] times, rep from * to * once, P4, K2, P1, (K1, P1) 4[6:8] times.

11th row P1, (K1, P1) 4[6:8] times, P2, C4B, * P2, K3, C3F, P2, Tw3F, (K1, P1) 3 times, K1, Tw3B, P2, K3, C3F, P2, * P1, (K1, P1) 8[9:9] times, rep from * to * once, C4B, P3, (K1, P1) 4[6:8] times.

12th row K1, (P1, K1) 4[6:8] times, K2, P4, * K2, P6, K3, P3, (K1, P1) 3 times, P2, K3, P6, K2, * K1, (P1, K1) 8[9:9] times, rep from * to * once, P4, K3, (P1, K1) 4[6:8] times.

13th row K1, (P1, K1) 4[6:8] times, P2, K4, * P2, C3B, K3, P3, Tw3F, (K1, P1) twice, K1, Tw3B, P3, C3B, K3, P2, * K1, (P1, K1) 8[9:9] times, rep from * to * once, K4, P2, K1, (P1, K1) 4[6:8] times.

14th row P1, (K1, P1) 4[6:8] times, K2, P4, * K2, P6, K4, P3, (K1, P1) twice, P2, K4, P6, K2, * P1, (K1, P1) 8[9:9] times, rep from * to * once, P4, K2, P1, (K1, P1) 4[6:8] times.

15th row P1, (K1, P1) 4[6:8] times, P2, C4B, * P2, K3, C3F, P4, Tw3F, K1, P1, K1, Tw3B, P4, K3, C3F, P2, * P1, (K1, P1) 8[9:9] times, rep from * to * once, C4B, P3, (K1, P1) 4[6:8] times.

16th row K1, (P1, K1) 4[6:8] times, K2, P4, * K2, P6, K5, P3, K1, P3, K5, P6, K2, * K1, (P1, K1) 8[9:9] times, rep from * to * once, P4, K3, (P1, K1) 4[6:8] times.

17th row K1, (P1, K1) 4[6:8] times, P2, K4, * P2, C3B, K3, P5, Tw3F,

K1, Tw3B, P5, C3B, K3, P2, * K1, (P1, K1) 8[9:9] times, rep from * to * once, K4, P2, K1, (P1, K1) 4[6:8] times.

18th row P1, (K1, P1) 4[6:8] times, K2, P4, * K2, P6, K6, P5, K6, P6, K2, * P1, (K1, P1) 8[9:9] times, rep from * to * once, P4, K2, P1, (K1, P1) 4[6:8] times.

19th row P1, (K1, P1) 4[6:8] times, P2, C4B, * P2, K3, C3F, P6, Tw5B, P6, K3, C3F, P2, * P1, (K1, P1) 8[9:9] times, rep from * to * once, C4B, P3, (K1, P1) 4[6:8] times.

20th row K1, (P1, K1) 4[6:8] times, K2, P4, * K2, P6, K6, P2, K1, P2, K6, P6, K2, * K1, (P1, K1) 8[9:9] times, rep from * to * once, P4, K2, K1, (P1, K1) 4[6:8] times.

These 20 rows form pat. Cont in pat until work measures 16[16½:17½] in. from beg, ending with a WS row.
Shape armholes
Keeping pat correct, bind off 6[7:8] sts at beg of next 2 rows.
Dec 1 st at each end of next 5 rows.
Dec 1 st at each end of foll 4[2:3] alt rows. 83[95:99] sts. **
Cont in pat without further shaping until work measures 8[10:10] in. from beg of armhole shaping, ending with a WS row.
Shape shoulders
Keeping pat correct, bind off 7 sts at beg of next 6 rows. Bind off 4[7:8] sts at beg of next 2 rows. Leave rem 33[39:41] sts on a stitch holder.

Front

Work as given for back from ** to **. Cont in pat without further shaping until work measures 5¾[6½:7¾]in. from beg of armhole shaping, ending with a WS row.
Shape left front neck
Next row Work in pat on 34[37:38] sts, turn, leaving rem sts on a spare needle. *** Dec 1 st at neck edge on next and 8 foll alt rows. 25[28:29] sts.
Shape left shoulder
Bind off 7 sts at beg of next and foll 2 alt rows.
Work 1 row.
Bind off rem 4[7:8] sts. ***
Shape right front neck and shoulder
Return to sts on spare needle, sl next 15[21:23] sts on a stitch holder. On rem 34[37:38] sts work in pat to end of row. Complete to match left front and shoulder from *** to ***, reversing all shapings.

Sleeves (alike)

Using smaller needles, cast on 43[49:53] sts. Work in K1, P1 ribbing for 3 in, inc 1 st at each end of last row 45[51:55] sts.
Change to larger needles and work in pat as follows:
1st row (P1, K1) 0[1:2] times, K0[1:1], P2, K4, P2, C3B, K3, P5, Tw3B, K1, Tw3F, P5, C3B, K3, P2, K4, P2, K0[1:1], (P1, K1) 0[1:2] times.
2nd row (P1, K1) 0[1:2] times, P0[1:1], K2, P4, K2, P6, K5, P2, K1, P1, K1, P2, K5, P6, K2, P4, K2, P0[1:1], (K1, P1) 0[1:2] times.
3rd row (P1, K1) 0[1:2] times, P2[3:3], C4B, P2, K3, C3F, P4, Tw3B, K1, P1, K1, Tw3F, P4, K3, C3F, P2, C4B, P2[3:3], (K1, P1) 0[1:2] times.
4th row (K1, P1) 0[1:2] times, K2[3:3], P4, K2, P6, K4, P2, (K1, P1) twice, K1, P2, K4, P6, K2, P4, K2[3:3] (P1, K1) 0[1:2] times.
5th row (K1, P1) 0[1:2] times, K0[1:1], P2, K4, P2, C3B, K3, P3, Tw3B, (K1, P1) twice, K1, Tw3F, P3, C3B, K3, P2, K4, P2, K0[1:1], (P1, K1) 0[1:2] times.
6th row (P1, K1) 0[1:2] times, P0[1:1], K2, P4, K2, P6, K3, P2, (K1, P1) 3 times, K1, P2, K3, P6, K2, P4, K2, P0[1:1], (K1, P1) 0[1:2] times.
7th row (P1, K1) 0[1:2] times, P2[3:3], C4B, P2, K3, C3F, P2, Tw3B, (K1, P1) 3 times, K1, Tw3F, P2, K3, C3F, P2, C4B, P2[3:3], (K1, P1) 0[1:2] times.

110

8th row (K1, P1) 0[1:2] times, K2[3:3], P4, K2, P6, K2, P2, (K1, P1) 4 times, K1, P2, K2, P6, K2, P4, K2[3:3], (P1, K1) 0[1:2] times.

9th row (K1, P1) 0[1:2] times, K0[1:1], P2, K4, P2, C3B, K3, P2, K3, (P1, K1) 4 times, K2, P2, C3B, K3, P2, K4, P2, K0[1:1], (P1, K1) 0[1:2] times.

10th row (P1, K1) 0[1:2] times, P0[1:1], K2, P4, K2, P6, K2, P3, (K1, P1) 4 times, P2, K2, P6, K2, P4, K2, P0[1:1], (K1, P1) 0[1:2] times.

11th row (P1, K1) 0[1:2] times, P2[3:3], C4B, P2, K3, C3F, P2, Tw3F, (K1, P1) 3 times, K1, Tw3B, P2, K3, C3F, P2, C4B, P2[3:3], (K1, P1) 0[1:2] times.

12th row (K1, P1) 0[1:2] times, K2[3:3], P4, K2, P6, K3, P3, (K1, P1) 3 times, P2, K3, P6, K2, P4, K2[3:3], (P1, K1) 0[1:2] times.

13th row (K1, P1) 0[1:2] times, K0[1:1], P2, K4, P2, C3B, K3, P3, Tw3F, (K1, P1) twice, K1, Tw3B, P3, C3B, K3, P2, K4, P2, K0[1:1], (P1, K1) 0[1:2] times.

14th row (P1, K1) 0[1:2] times, P0[1:1], K2, P4, K2, P6, K4, P3, (K1, P1) twice, P2, K4, P6, K2, P4, K2, P0[1:1], (K1, P1) 0[1:2] times.

15th row (P1, K1) 0[1:2] times, P2[3:3], C4B, P2, K3, C3F, P4, Tw3F, K1, P1, K1, Tw3B, P4, K3, C3F, P2, C4B, P2[3:3], (K1, P1) 0[1:2] times.

16th row (K1, P1) 0[1:2] times, K2[3:3], P4, K2, P6, K5, P3, K1, P3, K5, P6, K2, P4, K2[3:3], (P1, K1) 0[1:2] times.

17th row (K1, P1) 0[1:2] times, K0[1:1], P2, K4, P2, C3B, K3, P5, Tw3F, K1, Tw3B, P5, C3B, K3, P2, K4, P2, K0[1:1], (P1, K1) 0[1:2] times.

18th row (P1, K1) 0[1:2] times, P0[1:1], K2, P4, K2, P6, K6, P5, K6, P6, K2, P4, K2, (K1, P1) 0[1:2] times.

19th row (P1, K1) 0[1:2] times, P2[3:3], C4B, P2, K3, C3F, P6, Tw5B, P6, K3, C3F, P2, C4B, P2[3:3], (K1, P1) 0[1:2] times.

20th row (K1, P1) 0[1:2] times, K2[3:3], P4, K2, P6, K6, P2, K1, P2, K6, P6, K2, P4, K2[3:3], (P1, K1) 0[1:2] times.

These 20 rows form pat. Cont in pat for 4 rows.

Keeping pat correct, working extra sts into pat, inc 1 st at each end of next and every foll 4th row until there are 73[79:79] sts then inc 1 st at each end of every foll 5th row until there are 77[87:93] sts. Work straight until sleeve measures 17[18:18½] in. from cast-on edge.

Shape sleeve top
Bind off 6[7:8] sts at beg of next 2 rows. Dec 1st at each end of next 5 rows. Dec 1st at each end of every other row until 29[33:33] sts rem. Work 1 row. Bind off 3 sts at beg of next 6 rows. Bind off rem 11[15:15] sts.

To finish
Join left shoulder seam.

Neckband
With RS facing, using smaller needles, pick up and K 33[39:41] sts from back neck, 26 sts from left side neck, 15[21:23] sts from center front, 26 sts from right side neck. 100[112:116]sts. Work in K1, P1 ribbing for 2½ in. Bind off. Join right shoulder seam. Fold neckband in half to WS and slipstitch in position. Set in sleeves. Join side and sleeve seams.

Adapting the Aran Sweater

Substitute any of the Aran patterns on the following pages for those on the basic sweater.

Planning the design
Aran stitch patterns are traditionally arranged in vertical panels on a background of reverse-stockinette stitch. All-over patterns, for example, Irish moss stitch or honeycomb, can be varied in width according to the number of repeats used. Others, like lozenge, occupy a fixed number of stitches. Generally there will be a central panel running down the front of the garment with a number of other panels arranged in reverse order on either side. This is usually repeated on the back with a variation on the sleeves.

Charting the pattern
Before beginning make a chart showing your chosen arrangement of panels for the back and sleeves. The example here is for the back of the first size basic Aran sweater. The number of stitches must add up to the number of cast-on stitches, in this case 113 stitches. Any odd stitches should be incorporated into an all-over pattern or the reverse-stockinette stitch that divides the vertical panels.

Gauge
Match your gauge to that of the basic sweater by knitting up a sample in Irish moss stitch (see page 113) and adjusting the needle size if necessary.

Chart for Aran Sweater (back)

9 sts	2	4	2	6	2	13	2	6	2	17	2	6	2	13	2	6	2	4	2	9
Irish moss	rev.st.st.	cable	rev.st.st.	wheatear	rev.st.st.	diamond	rev.st.st.	wheatear	rev.st.st.	Irish moss	rev.st.st.	wheatear	rev.st.st.	diamond	rev.st.st.	wheatear	rev.st.st.	cable	rev.st.st.	Irish moss

Coral Mula

Aran patterns

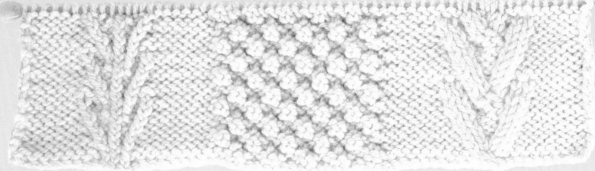

1 Tree of life
This pattern is worked over 9 sts.
1st row (RS) P3, K3tbl, P3.
2nd row K3, P3tbl, K3.
3rd row P2, Tw2B, K1tbl, Tw2F, P2.
4th row K2, (P1tbl, K1) twice, P1tbl, K2.
5th row P1, Tw2B, P1, K1tbl, P1, Tw2F, P1.
6th row K1, P1tbl, (K2, P1tbl) twice, K1.
7th row Tw2B, P1, K3tbl, P1, Tw2F.
8th row P1tbl, K2, P3tbl, K2, P1tbl.

9th row P2, Tw2B, K1tbl, Tw2F, P2.
4th–9th rows form pat repeat.

2 Trinity stitch
This all-over pattern is worked over a multiple of 4 sts.
1st and 3rd rows (RS) P across row.
2nd row * (K1, P1, K1) all into next st (called 3 from 1), P3tog, rep from *.
4th row * P3tog, 3 from 1, rep from *.
These 4 rows form pat repeat.

3 "V" stitch
This stitch works over 12 sts.
1st row (RS) P4, C4F, P4.
2nd and every other row K the P sts of previous row and P the K sts.
3rd row P3, Tw3B, Tw3F, P3.
5th row P2, Tw3B, P2, Tw3F, P2.
7th row P1, Tw3B, P4, Tw3F, P1.
9th row Tw3B, P1, C4F, P1, Tw3F.
The 2nd–9th rows form pat repeat.

4 Interlace
This stitch is worked over 12 sts, plus 4 edge sts.
1st row (RS) P3, C4B, P2, C4B, P3.
2nd row K3, P4, K2, P4, K3.
3rd row P2, (Tw3B, Tw3F) twice, P2.
4th row (K2, P2) twice, (P2, K2) twice.
5th row P2, K2, P2, C4F, P2, K2, P2.
6th row As 4th row.
7th row P2, (Tw3F, Tw3B) twice, P2.
8th row K3, P4, K2, P4, K3.
These 8 rows form the pat repeat.

5 Ladder of life
This all-over pattern is worked over a multiple of 6 sts, plus 1 extra.
1st row (RS) P1, * K5, P1, rep from *.
2nd row K1, * P5, K1, rep from *.
3rd row P across row.
4th row K1, * P5, K1, rep from *.
These 4 rows form pat repeat.

6 Zigzag and bobble
This pattern works over 14 sts.
1st row (RS) P3, K2, P9.
2nd and every other row P all the K sts of previous row and K all the P sts.
3rd row P3, Tw3F, P8.
5th row P4, Tw3F, P7.

7th row P5, Tw3F, P6.
9th row P6, Tw3F, P5.
11th row P7, Tw3F, P4.
13th row P5, (K1, yfwd, K1, yfwd, K1) all into next st, (turn, K5, turn, P5) twice, lift 2nd, 3rd, 4th and 5th sts over first st and off needle (called make bobble), P2, Tw3F, P3.
15th row P8, Tw3B, P3.
17th row P7, Tw3B, P4.
19th row P6, Tw3B, P5.
21st row P5, Tw3B, P6.
23rd row P3, Tw3B, P7.
25th row P3, Tw3B, P2, make bobble, P5.
27th row P3, Tw3F, P8.
28th row As 2nd row.
The 5th–28th rows form pat repeat.

7 Irish moss stitch

This all-over pattern is used on the basic Aran sweater. It is worked over an even number of sts.

1st and 2nd rows (RS) * K1, P1, rep from *.
3rd and 4th rows * P1, K1, rep from *.
These 4 rows form pat repeat.

8 Two by two cable

This pattern is used on the basic Aran sweater. It is worked over 4 sts.
1st row (RS) K across row.
2nd and 4th rows P across row.

3rd row C4B.
These 4 rows form pat repeat.

9 Wheatear cable

This pattern is used on the basic Aran sweater. It is worked over 6 sts.
1st row (RS) C3B, K3.
2nd and 4th rows P across row.
3rd row K3, C3F.
These 4 rows form pat repeat.

10 Diamond

This stitch works over 14 sts.
1st row (RS) P5, C4F, P5.
2nd and every other row K all P sts of

previous row and P all K sts.
3rd row P4, Cr3B, Tw3F, P4.
5th row P3, Cr3B, P1, K1, Tw3F, P3.
7th row P2, Cr3B, (P1, K1) twice, Tw3F, P2.
9th row P1, Cr3B, (P1, K1) 3 times, Tw3F, P1.
11th row P1, Tw3F, (K1, P1) 3 times, Tw3B, P1.
13th row P2, Tw3F, (K1, P1) twice, Tw3B, P2.
15th row P3, Tw3F, K1, P1, Tw3B, P3.
17th row P4, Tw3F, Tw3B, P4.
18th row As 2nd row.
These 18 rows form pat repeat.

11 Mock cable

This pattern works over 4 sts.
1st row (RS) P2, K 2nd st on LH needle tbl, then K first st, discarding both sts at same time.
2nd, 3rd and 4th rows P2, K2.
These 4 rows form pat repeat.

12 Trellis

This stitch works over 24 sts.
1st row (RS) P1, K1tbl, P3, K2, (P4, K2) twice, P3, K1tbl, P1.
2nd row K1, P1tbl, K3, C2F P-wise, (K4, C2F P-wise) twice, K3, P1tbl, K1.
3rd row P1, K1tbl, P2, (Tw2B, Tw2F, P2) 3 times, K1tbl, P1.
4th row K1, P1tbl, (K2, P1) 6 times, K2, P1tbl, K1.

5th row P1, K1tbl, P1, (Tw2B, P2, Tw2F) 3 times, P1, K1tbl, P1.
6th row K1, P1tbl, K1, P1, (K4, C2F P-wise) twice, K4, P1, K1, P1tbl, K1.
7th row P1, K1tbl, P1, Tw2F, (P2, Tw2B, Tw2F) twice, P2, Tw2B, P1, K1tbl, P1.
8th row K1, P1tbl, (K2, P1) 6 times, K2, P1tbl, K1.
9th row P1, K1tbl, (P2, Tw2F, Tw2B) 3 times, P2, K1tbl, P1.
The 2nd-9th rows form pat repeat.

13 Marriage lines

This stitch works over 15 sts.
1st row (RS) K1tbl, P5, (K1tbl, P1) twice, (P1, K1tbl) twice, K1tbl.
2nd and every other row Ptbl

the Ktbl sts of the previous row, and K the P sts.
3rd row K1tbl, P4, Tw2B twice, P1, Tw2B twice, K1tbl.
5th row K1tbl, P3, Tw2B twice, P1, Tw2B twice, P1, K1tbl.
7th row K1tbl, P2, Tw2B twice, P1, Tw2B twice, P2, K1tbl.
9th row K1tbl, P1, Tw2B twice, P1, Tw2B twice, P3, K1tbl.
11th row K1tbl, P1, Tw2F twice, P1, Tw2F twice, P3, K1tbl.
13th row K1tbl, P2, Tw2F twice, P1, Tw2F twice, P2, K1tbl.
15th row K1tbl, P3, Tw2F twice, P1, Tw2F twice, P1, K1tbl.
17th row K1tbl, P4, Tw2F twice, P1, Tw2F twice, K1tbl.
The 2nd-17th rows form pat repeat.

Slip-stitch color patterns

Deceptively intricate color patterns can be produced quite easily with slipstitch techniques. In general only one color is used during any single row.

Skills you need

* **Simple increasing**
* **Slipping stitches**

If you do not know these skills refer to pages 174 and 181.

Materials

Slip-stitch color patterns, or "color-slip" patterns as they are sometimes called, are usually worked in plain smooth yarns whether wool, cotton, silk or synthetic. Where the stitch pattern is composed of knit stitches only on the right side the effect is flat and smooth. Where there are purl stitches on the right side there is much more texture to the stitch and this is emphasized by heavier, chunky yarns. The basic sweater is made in a plain soft worsted-weight yarn composed of wool, acrylic and mohair fibers.

Special technique – fitting a shawl collar

1 Join the shoulder seams. Mark the center of the back neck with a colored thread.

2 Match the center of the cast-on on edge of the collar to the center back neck. Join the collar to the back and sides of the neck edge.

3 Join the row-end edges of the collar to the front neck, lapping the right edge over the left edge (or the left edge over the right edge).

Coral Mula

The basic slip-stitch sweater

The light crunchy textures of a three-color slip-stitch pattern and warm autumnal colors make this shawl-collared sweater an all-weather favorite for men or women.

Sizes
To fit 38 [40:42] in. chest
Length 23¾ [25¼:25½] in.
Sleeve seam 19 [19:19½] in.

Note: Instructions for larger sizes are in square brackets []; where there is only one set of figures it applies to all sizes.

Gauge
22 sts and 31 rows to 4 in. over pat on size 5 needles

Materials
15 [17:19] oz knitting worsted in main color (A)
8 [9:11] oz in contrasting color (B)
6 [8:8] oz in contrasting color (C)
1 pair each size 3 and 5 knitting needles

Back
** Using smaller needles and A, cast on 104 [112:116] sts.
Work in K2, P2 ribbing for 2¾ in.
Next row Rib 12 [16:18], * work twice into next st, rib 7, rep from * to last 4 [8:10] sts, K to end. 115 [123:127] sts.
Change to larger needles and begin pat.
Sl all sl sts with yarn on WS of work.
1st row (RS) With A, K across row.
2nd row With A, P across row.
3rd row With B, K3, * sl 1, K3, rep from * to end.
4th row With B, P3, * sl 1, P3, rep from * to end.
5th row With C, K1, * sl 1, K3, rep from * ending last rep K1.
6th row With C, K1, * sl 1, K3, rep from * ending last rep K1.
7th and 8th rows As 3rd and 4th rows.
9th row As 5th row with A instead of C.
10th row With A, P1, * sl 1, P3, rep from * ending last rep P1.
11th-12th rows As 1st-2nd rows.
13th row With B, K1, * sl 1, K3, rep from * ending last rep K1.
14th row With B, P1, * sl 1, P3, rep from * ending last rep P1.
15th row With C, K3, * sl 1, K3, rep from * to end.

16th row With C, K3, * sl 1, K3, rep from * to end.
17th and 18th rows As 13th and 14th rows.
19th row As 15th row with A instead of C.
20th row With A, P3, * sl 1, P3, rep from * to end.
These 20 rows form the pat.**
Cont in pat until work measures 24¾ [25¼:25½] in. from cast-on edge, ending with a WS row.
Shape shoulders
Keeping pat correct, bind off 13 [14:15] sts at beg of next 4 rows, then 14 [15:14] sts at beg of foll 2 rows. Bind off rem 35 [37:39] sts.

Front
Work as given for back from ** to **.
Cont in pat until work measures 17 [17¼:17¼] in. ending with a WS row.
Shape neck
Next row Work in pat on 40 [43:44] sts, bind off 35 [37:39], work in pat to end.
Work right side of neck first.
Cont without shaping until work matches back to shoulder shaping, ending at armhole edge.

Shape shoulder
Bind off 13 [14:15] sts at beg of next and foll alt row.
Work 1 row.
Bind off rem 14 [15:14] sts.
With WS of work facing, return to sts for left side of neck. Join in yarn and complete to match first side, reversing shaping.

Sleeves
Using smaller needles and A, cast on 56 sts. Work 2¾ in. K2, P2 ribbing.
Next row Rib 5 [5:1], * work twice into next st, rib 1, rep from * to last 5 [5:1] sts, rib to end. 79 [79:83] sts.
Change to larger needles.
Cont in pat as given for back, inc 1 st at each end of the next and every foll 12th row until there are 97 [97:101] sts.
Cont without shaping until work measures 19 [19:19½] in. from cast-on edge, ending with a WS row.
Bind off loosely.

Collar
Using smaller needles and A, cast on 172 [176:192] sts. Work in K2, P2 ribbing for 6¼ [6¾:7] in.
Bind off loosely in ribbing.

To finish
Join shoulder seams. Mark 8½ [8½:9] in. down from shoulders on back and front. Set in sleeves. Join side and sleeve seams.
Sew on collar (see Special Technique on page 115).

Adapting the slip-stitch sweater

Two of the Pattern Library stitches can be used on the basic sweater.

The slip-stitch pattern on the basic sweater is worked over a multiple of four stitches, plus three extra. Two of the stitch patterns are worked over the same number of stitches and can therefore be substituted for the basic stitch. Work the ribbing as instructed in the basic pattern then work your chosen stitch instead of the 20-stitch pattern repeat given. Remember that the yarn quantities will have to be adjusted if the number of colors differs from that of the basic pattern.

116

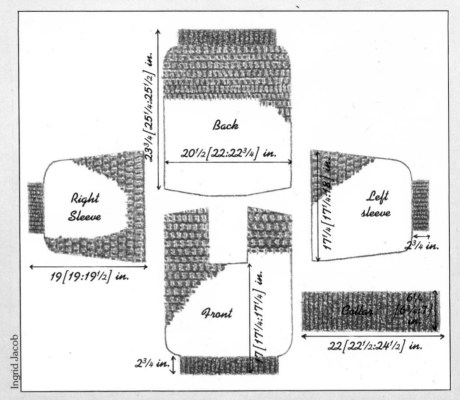

Ingrid Jacob

Slip-stitch color patterns

1 Waffle slip-stitch
This pattern is worked over a multiple of 10 stitches, plus 5 extra, and in 3 colors (A, B and C). Slip all slip stitches with yarn on wrong side.
1st row (RS) With A, K across row.
2nd row With A, (P1, K1) twice, * P2, K1, P1, K1, rep from * to last 6 sts, P2, (K1, P1) twice.
3rd row With B, K5, * (sl 1, K1) twice, sl 1, K5, rep from * to end.
4th row With B, K5, * (sl 1, K1) twice, sl 1, K5, rep from * to end.
5th row A, K across row.
6th row With A, K5, * (P1, K1) twice, P1, K5, rep from * to end.
7th–10th rows As 3rd–6th rows.
11th–12th rows As 3rd–4th rows.

13th–14th rows As 1st–2nd rows.
15th row With C, (sl 1, K1) twice, sl 1, * K5, (sl 1, K1) twice, sl 1, rep from * to end.
16th row With C, (sl 1, K1) twice, sl 1, *K5, (sl 1, K1) twice, sl 1, rep from * to end.
17th row As 5th row.
18th row With A, (P1, K1) twice, P1, *K5, (P1, K1) twice, P1, rep from * to end.
19th–20th rows As 15th–16th rows.
21st row As 5th row.
22nd row As 18th row.
23rd row As 15th row.
24th row As 16th row.
These 24 rows form the pattern repeat.

1

2 Surprise pattern

This pattern is worked over a multiple of 4 stitches, plus 1 extra, and in 5 colors (A, B, C, D, and E). Slip all slip stitches with yarn on wrong side of work.

1st row (WS) With A, P across row.
2nd row With B, K2, * sl 1, K3, rep from * to last 3 sts, sl 1, K2.
3rd row With B, P2, * sl 1, P3, rep from * to last 3 sts, sl 1, P2.
4th row With C, K4, * sl 1, K3, rep from * to last st, K1.
5th row With C, P4, * sl 1, P3, rep from * to last st, P1.
6th row With A, K1, * sl 1, K1, rep from * to end.
7th row With A, P across row.
8th row With D, K2, * sl 1, K1, rep from * to last st, K1.
9th row With D, P4, * sl 1, P3, rep from * to last st, P1.
10th row With E, K2, * sl 1, K3, rep from * to last 3 sts, sl 1, K2.
11th row With E, P across row.
12th row With A, K1, * sl 1, K1, rep from * to end.
These 12 rows form the pattern repeat.

Simon Wheeler

3 Shadow box

This stitch is worked over a multiple of 4 stitches, plus 3 extra, and in 3 colors (A, B and C). Slip all slip stitches with yarn on wrong side of work.

1st row (RS) With A, K across row.
2nd row With A, K1, * K1 winding yarn twice around needle, K3, rep from * ending last rep K1 instead of K3.
3rd row With B, K1, * sl 1 dropping extra loops, K3, rep from * ending last rep K1 instead of K3.
4th row With B, K1, * sl 1, K3, rep from * to last 2 sts, sl 1, K1.
5th row With C, K1, * sl 2, K2, rep from * to last 2 sts, sl 1, K1.
6th row With C, K1, sl 1, * P2, sl 2, rep from * to last st, K1.
These 6 rows form the pattern repeat.

4 Striped check

This pattern is worked over a multiple of 4 stitches, plus 3 extra, and in 4 colors (A, B, C and D). Slip all slip stitches with yarn on wrong side of the work. Cast on with color D.

1st row (RS) With A, K1, * sl 1, K3, rep from * to last 2 sts, sl 1, K1.
2nd row With A, P1, * sl 1, P3, rep from * to last 2 sts, sl 1, K1.
3rd row With B, * K3, sl 1, rep from * to last 3 sts, K3.
4th row With B, * P3, sl 1, rep from * to last 3 sts, P3.
5th-6th rows With C, as 1st-2nd rows.
7th-8th rows With D, as 3rd-4th rows.
These 8 rows form the pattern repeat.

117

C Cables

Traditionally cables symbolize the twisted ropes used on ships' rigging and they are still a prominent feature of many types of nautical knitting. But they can also be combined with other stitches to make elegant garments for landlubbers too.

Spike Powell

Skills you need

* **Decreasing**
* **Using a cable needle**
* **Simple increasing**

If you do not know these skills refer to pages 174, 175 and 178.

Materials

Cables are best knitted in smooth untextured yarns that emphasize the twists and turns of the stitches. Thick chunky yarns produce the traditional fisherman-knit effects. Fine yarns, such as sport-weight or Shetland, are also suitable and produce an elegant rather than rugged effect. Avoid bouclés and other heavily textured novelty yarns. The sweater is knitted in a smooth yarn of mixed woolen and synthetic fibers.

Special technique – working a polo neck

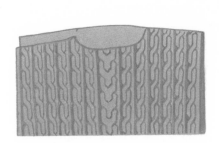

1 *Join the left shoulder seam. Pick up and knit the number of stitches specified in the pattern along the back neck, down the left side of the neck, along the front neck and up the right side of the neck.*

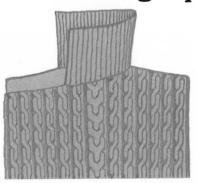

2 *Work in ribbing for twice the required depth of the polo neck or as specified in the pattern. Bind off loosely in ribbing.*

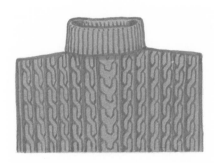

3 *Join the right shoulder seam and the collar seam reversing the collar seam to fold to the right side.*

Coral Mula

The basic cable sweater

Coiling cables are worked all over a snug polo sweater that's warm in all kinds of weather.

Sizes
To fit 35¾ [38¼:40¼:42¼] in. chest
Length 26½ [26¾:27¼:27½] in.
Sleeve seam 21¾ in.

Note: Instructions for larger sizes are in square brackets []; where there is only one set of figures it applies to all sizes.

Gauge
19 sts and 25 rows to 4 in. over stockinette stitch on size 6 needles
26 sts and 27 rows to 4 in. over cable pat on size 6 needles

Materials
30 [32:32:34] oz of knitting worsted
1 pair each size 5 and 6 knitting needles
A cable needle

Cable Panel A — worked over 6 sts.
1st row (RS) K across row.
2nd, 4th and 6th rows P across row.

3rd and 5th rows K across row.
7th row Sl next 3 sts onto cable needle and hold at back of work, K3, then K3 from cable needle, (called C6B).
8th row P across row.
These 8 rows form cable panel A.

Cable Panel B — worked over 12 sts.
1st row (RS) K across row.
2nd, 4th and 6th rows P across row.
3rd and 5th rows K across row.
7th row C6B, sl next 3 sts onto cable needle and hold in front of work, K3 then K3 from cable needle, (called C6F).
8th row P across row.
These 8 rows form cable panel B.

Cable Panel C — worked over 6 sts.
1st row (RS) K across row.
2nd, 4th and 6th rows P across row.
3rd and 5th rows K across row.
7th row C6F across row.
8th row P across row.

These 8 rows form cable panel C.

Back
***Using smaller needles cast on 91 [95:99:107] sts.
Next row K1, * P1, K1, rep from * to end.
Next row P1, * K1, P1, rep from * to end.
Rep the last 2 rows for 2¼ in., ending with a RS row.
Next row Rib 3 [6:6:5], pick up loop lying between needles and rib tbl — called make one, or M1, (rib 2, M1) 12 [12:11:6] times, (rib 3, M1) 12 [12:14:24] times, (rib 2, M1) 12 [12:11:6] times, rib 4 [5:7:6]. 128 [132:136:144] sts.
Change to larger needles.
1st row (RS) P2 [4:6:2],* work first row of cable panel A, P2, rep from * 6 [6:6:7] times more, work first row of cable panel B, ** P2, work first row of cable panel C, rep from ** to last 2 [4:6:2] sts, P to end.
2nd row K2 [4:6:2], ** work 2nd row of cable panel C, K2, rep from ** 6 [6:6:7] times more, work 2nd row of cable panel B, * K2, work 2nd row of cable panel A, rep from * to last 2

[4:6:2] sts, K to end.
These 2 rows establish the pattern.
Cont in this way until work measures
17¼ in. from beg, ending with a WS
row.

Shape armholes

Keeping pat correct, bind off 8 sts at
beg of next 2 rows.
112 [116:120:128] sts.
Next row P0 [2:4:0], work in pat as
set to last 0 [2:4:0] sts, P0 [2:4:0].
Next row K0 [2:4:0], work in pat as
set to last 0 [2:4:0] sts, K0 [2:4:0]. ***
Cont in this way until work measures
9 [9½:9¾:10¼] in. from beg of
armholes ending with a RS row.

Shape shoulders

Next row K2 [4:6:2], * P2 tog, P2,
P2 tog, K2, rep from * 3 [3:3:4] times
more, work in pat to last 38 [38:38:42]
sts, ** K2, P2 tog, P2, P2 tog, rep
from ** to last 2 [4:6:2] sts, K to end.
96 [100:104:108] sts.
Bind off 28 [29:30:32] sts at beg of
next 2 rows. Leave rem
40 [42:44:44] sts on a spare needle.

Front

Work as given for back from *** to
***.

Cont in this way until work measures
6 [6¼:6¼:6¾] in. from beg of
armholes, ending with a WS row.

Divide for neck

Next row Work in pat on 46 [48:50:54]
sts, turn and leave rem sts on a spare
needle, work 2 tog, work in pat to end.
Keeping pat correct, dec 1 st at neck
edge on foll 5 [7:7:7] rows. Now dec
1 st at neck edge on every other row
until 36 [37:38:42] sts rem. Cont
without shaping until work matches
back exactly to shoulder shaping,
ending with a RS row.

Shape shoulder

Next row K2 [4:6:2], * P2 tog, P2,
P2 tog, K2, rep from * to last 2 [1:0:0]
sts, P to end. 28 [29:30:32] sts.
Bind off.
Return to sts on spare needle. With
RS of work facing, sl the center 20 sts
onto a stitch holder, rejoin yarn to
next st, work in pat to end. Complete
to match first side of neck, reversing
shapings.

Sleeves

Using smaller needles, cast on 47
[47:49:49] sts and work 2¼ in. in K1,
P1 ribbing as given for back, ending
with a RS row.
120

Next row Rib 3 [3:2:2], (M1, rib 2) 5
[5:6:6] times, (M1, rib 3) 7 times, (M1,
rib 2) 5 [5:6:6] times, rib 3 [3:2:2]. 64
[64:68:68] sts.
Change to larger needles.
1st row (RS) P0 [0:2:2], * P2, work
first row of cable panel A, rep from *
twice more, P2, work first row from
cable panel B, ** P2, work first row
from cable panel C, rep from ** to last
2 [2:4:4] sts, P to end.
2nd row K2 [2:4:4], ** work 2nd row
of cable panel C, K2, rep from **
twice more, work 2nd row of cable
panel B, K2, * work 2nd row of cable
panel A, K2, rep from * to last 0
[0:2:2] sts, K to end.
Cont in this way, inc 1 st at each end
of every 3rd row until there are 120
[124:130:136] sts. Cont without
shaping until work measures 21¾ in.
from beg, ending with a WS row. Bind
off.

To finish

Do not press.
Join left shoulder seam.

Polo neck

Using smaller needles and with RS of
work facing, K sts on back neck to last
2 sts, dec 1 st, pick up and K 16
[16:18:18] sts down left side of neck,
K across the sts on stitch holder, pick
up and K 16 [16:18:18] sts up right
side of neck. 91 [93:99:99] sts.
Next row K to end.
Work in K1, P1 ribbing as given for
back for 3¼ in.
Change to larger needles and work a
further 3¼ in. Bind off loosely in
ribbing. Join right shoulder and collar,

reversing seam to fold onto RS. Mark
center of bound-off edge of sleeves
with a pin, match pin to shoulder
seam, then sew sleeves to back and
front, matching the last rows of sleeve
to bound-off sts at underarm. Join side
and sleeve seams.

Adapting the cable sweater

**Many of the cables can be
adapted to the basic sweater.**

Choosing a cable

The central cable (Panel B) on the
basic sweater works over 12 stitches.
Those on either side (Panels A and C)
work over 6 stitches — those on the
left twisting to the left and those on the
right twisting to the right. Both the
wide cable and the irregular cable
work over 12 sts and can be used
instead of the central cable on the
sweater. The simple cables either side
can be twisted more tightly or loosely
to suit your pattern tension. To use
other cables, chart the pattern for the
back and sleeve, allowing at least two
stitches in reverse stockinette stitch
between each cable. The stitches used
in the cable panels and the reverse
stockinette stitches dividing them must
add up to the number of stitches at the
end of the increase row after the ribbing. The gauge on different cable patterns varies considerably. Check any
substitute patterns carefully.

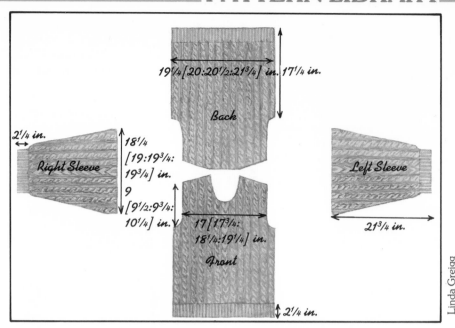

19¼ [20:20½:21¾] in. 17¼ in.

Back

2¼ in.

Right Sleeve

18¼ [19:19¾: 19¾] in.

9 [9½:9¾: 10¼] in.

17 [17¾: 18¼:19¼] in.

Front

2¼ in.

Left Sleeve

21¾ in.

Linda Greigg

Cable patterns

1 Crossed cable
This cable works over 10 sts.
1st, 3rd and 5th rows P2, K6, P2.
2nd, 4th and 6th rows K2, P6, K2.
7th row P2, sl next 3 sts onto cable needle and hold at back of work, K3, then K3 from cable needle, P2.
8th, 10th and 12th rows As 2nd row.
9th and 11th rows As first row.
13th, 15th, 17th and 19th rows P4, K2, P4.
14th, 16th, 18th and 20th rows K4, P2, K4.
These 20 rows form the pat repeat.

2 Chain cable
This cable works over 14 sts.
1st, 5th and 7th rows P4, K6, P4.
2nd, 4th, 6th, 8th and 10th rows K4, P6, K4.
3rd and 9th rows P4, sl next 3 sts onto cable needle and hold at back of work, K3, then K3 from cable needle, P4.
11th row P3, sl next st onto cable needle and hold at back of work, K3, then P1 from cable needle, sl next 3 sts onto cable needle, and hold at front of work, P1, then K3 from cable needle, P3.
12th, 14th, 16th, 18th, 20th, 22nd and 24th rows K3, P3, K2, P3, K3.
13th, 15th, 17th, 19th, 21st and 23rd rows P3, K3, P2, K3, P3.
25th row P3, sl next 3 sts onto cable needle and hold at front of work, P1, then K3 from cable needle, sl next st onto cable needle and hold at back of work, K3, then P1 from cable needle, P3.
26th row As 2nd row.
The 3rd-26th rows form the pat repeat.

3 Wide cable
This cable works over 12 sts.
1st and 5th rows K across row.
2nd and every other row P across row.
3rd row * Sl next 3 sts onto cable needle and hold at front of work, K3, then K3 from cable needle (called C6F), rep from * once more.
7th row K3, C6F, K3.
8th row P across row.
These 8 rows form the pat repeat.

4 Irregular cable
This pattern works over 12 sts.
1st and every other row (WS) K2, P8, K2.
2nd row P2, K4, sl next 2 sts onto cable needle and hold at front of work, K2, then K2 from cable needle, P2.
4th row P2, K8, P2.
6th row As 2nd row.
8th row P2, sl next 2 sts onto cable needle and hold at back of work, K2, then K2 from cable needle, K4, P2.
10th row As 4th row.
12th row As 8th row.
These 12 rows form the pat repeat.

Fair Isle

These beautifully intricate patterns originated on the island of the same name between the Shetland and Orkney Isles off the north-east coast of Scotland. They combine subtle colors with wonderfully imaginative variations on a basic library of motifs of religious and folkloric symbolism.

Spike Powell

Skills you need

* **Decreasing**
* **Working with color**
* **Picking up stitches**

If you do not know these skills refer to pages 174, 175 and 177.

Materials

The yarn used in the basic pullover is a natural wool Shetland two-ply fingering-weight yarn — the authentic yarn used in Fair Isle knitting. A similar yarn is obtainable from Jamieson and Smith,.90 North Road, Lerwick, Shetland. It is approximately equivalent to a standard fingering yarn.

Special technique – grafting stockinette stitch

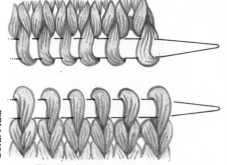

1 *This technique is used to join the shoulder seams of the basic pullover. Place the edges to be joined on a flat surface with the stitches facing each other. Thread a tapestry needle with a length of yarn at least four times the width of edge.*

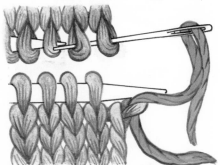

2 *Insert the needle through the first stitch on the lower edge from the back, then through the first stitch on the upper edge through the front then through the second stitch on the upper edge from the back, with-drawing the knitting needle from each stitch as you work.*

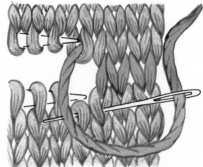

3 *Insert the needle through the first stitch on the lower edge from the front, then the second stitch on the lower edge from the back, then the second stitch on the upper edge from the front, then the third stitch on the upper edge from the back. Carry on across the row.*

Coral Mula

The basic Fair Isle pullover

Knitted in marvelous muted earth colors, this neat pullover looks good on men and women, and with clever accessorizing the mood can be towny or countrified.

Sizes
To fit 32-34 [36-38] in. chest/bust
Length 23½ [25½] in.

Note: Instructions for the larger size are in square brackets []; where there is one set of figures it applies to both sizes.

Gauge
32 sts and 28 rows to 4 in. over Fair Isle pat on size 4 needles

Materials
12 oz Shetland fingering yarn in main color (A)
1 oz in each of 5 contrasting colors
1 pair each sizes 2 and 4 knitting needles
Size 2 circular needle

Back
* Using smaller needles and A, cast on 144 [168] sts. Work in K1, P1 ribbing for 2¾ [3] in., ending with a WS row. Change to larger needles and beg with a K row cont in stockinette st working 45 rows in Fair Isle pat from chart. Read odd-numbered rows as K rows and even-numbered rows as P rows. Now repeat chart reading odd-numbered rows as P rows and even-numbered rows as K rows.
These 90 rows form the pat.
Work in pat until work measures 14½ [15] in. from cast-on edge, ending with a WS row.*
Shape armholes
Bind off 7 [8] sts at beg of next 2 rows. Dec 1 st at each end of the foll 9 [10] rows, then at each end of the 3 foll other rows. 106 [126] sts.
Cont without shaping until work measures 23½ [25½] in. from cast-on edge, ending with a WS row.

Leave these sts on a spare needle.

Front
Work as given for back from * to *.
Shape armhole and neck
Next row Bind off 7 [8] sts, work in pat on 63 [74] sts, K2 tog, turn, leaving rem sts on a spare needle, work in pat to end.
Complete left side of neck first. ** Dec 1 st at armhole edge on the foll 9 rows and then on the 3 foll other rows, *at the same time,* dec 1 st at neck edge on the next and every other row until 24 [26] sts rem. Cont without shaping until work measures 23¾ [26] in. from cast-on edge, ending with a WS row. Leave these sts on spare needle.
** Return to sts for right side of neck. With RS of work facing, join in yarn to next st, K2 tog, work in pat to end.
Next row Bind off 7 [8] sts, work in pat to end. Complete as given for left side of neck from ** to **.

To finish

With RS of work facing, beg at armhole edge, graft 24 [26] sts from front shoulders to back.

Neck border

With RS of work facing, using circular needle and A, beg at center front, pick up and K 60 [72] sts up right side of neck, K across the 58 [74] sts on back neck, pick up and K 60 [72] sts down the left side of neck. 178 [218] sts. Work backwards and forwards.

1st row (WS) P2 tog, * K2, P2, rep from * to last 4 sts, K2, P2 tog.

2nd row P2 tog, P1, * K2, P2, rep from * to last 5 sts, K2, P1, P2 tog.

Cont in this way, keeping K2, P2 ribbing correct and dec 1 st at each end of every row. Work a further 11 [13] rows. Bind off in ribbing dec on this row as before.

Arm borders

With RS facing, using smaller needles and A, pick up and K 120 [144] sts around armhole edge. Work 11 rows K2, P2 ribbing. Bind off in ribbing. Press with a warm iron over a damp cloth.

Join side seams and front neckband.

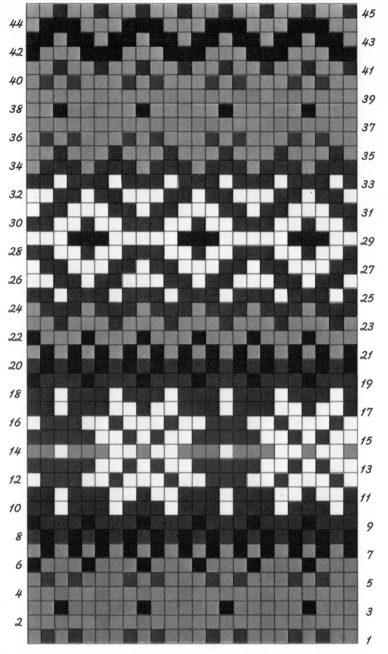

Dennis Hawkins

Main color

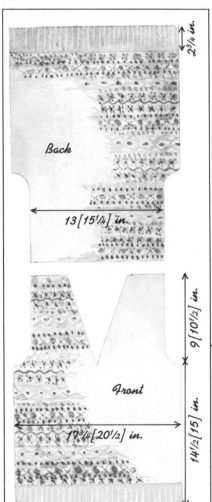

Linda Greigg

124

Adapting the Fair Isle pullover

Using the pattern library

All the charts show the basic pattern repeat used in the samples, plus a centralizing stitch (to the left of the pattern repeat), plus edge stitches. Strictly speaking, traditional Fair Isle patterns are always worked over an odd number of stitches consisting of the pattern repeat, the centralizing stitch that balances the pattern and, if necessary, an equal number of edge stitches on either side. However, the basic pullover has been worked over an even number of stitches. To adapt the pattern library charts to the pullover, therefore, you must bend the rules a little. Choose a chart with the same pattern repeat as the pullover (24 stitches) and work the basic repeat only, ignoring the centralizing stitch. This means your pattern will be slightly unbalanced at the left-hand side by one stitch and the side seams will not, therefore, show a perfect match. However, this is unlikely to be noticeable in the finished garment.

Fair Isle patterns

The motifs and patterns found in Fair Isle knitting are of diverse origin. Like all seafaring communities the islanders have always enjoyed extensive contact with foreigners. A fruitful exchange of knitting patterns has taken place ever since the Vikings colonized the northern islands and is still going on today. This accounts for the similarity between many Fair Isle motifs and those found in other countries. The Maltese cross, for example (seen in samples 1, 2, 4, 5, 8 and 9) occurs in knitting patterns from Scandinavia to the Mediterranean. The Seeds of Life (sample 4), the Crown of Glory, Hearts (both sample 3) and the Rose of Sharon (samples 6 and 7) are also widespread. The islanders responded to outside influences in different ways and, just as there are clear distinctions between the patterns of Fair Isle, the Shetlands and the Scottish Hebrides, even on Fair Isle itself certain patterns and styles can be traced to particular

families, something that is echoed in Scottish clan tartans. Traditionally a sweater would also incorporate motifs reflecting the occupation or social position of its owner.

Many types of color patterned knitting are often wrongly described as "Fair Isle". Authentic Fair Isle is always worked in stockinette stitch in a natural loosely-woven yarn. In the old days the yarn, spun locally from native sheep, was used in its natural color or dyed with natural dyestuffs obtained from mosses, seaweeds, lichen, heather, bracken and so on. The colors range from muted to glowing but are always soft, never harsh. The distinctive characteristic of the patterning is the marked horizontal banding effect with different motifs being used in each band. Traditionally bands were repeated only when the knitter had exhausted her inspiration. In spite of the apparent intricacy of the designs, no more than two colors are used in

each row. The subtle shading effects are achieved by changing the ground color on one row of a band and the contrasting color on the next. The infinite variety of Fair Isle patterns is, to a great extent, the result of a richly imaginative use of color so that the same sequence of motifs can take on a completely original appearance. This is seen in samples 1 and 2, 6 and 7, 8 and 9, 10 and 11, 12 and 13, 14 and 15. In each pair of samples the arrangement of Fair Isle motifs and bands is exactly the same, only the colors are different.

Reading Fair Isle charts

Read all knit rows (odd-numbered) from right to left, and all purl rows (even-numbered) from left to right. The edge stitches are worked at the beginnings and ends of rows only. The centralizing stitch, marked C on the charts, is worked after the last repeat of the pattern only.

1

2

Steve Tanner

Dennis Hawkins

40 **39**
38 **37**
36 **35**
34 **33**
32 **31**
30 **29**
28 **27**
26 **25**
24 **23**
22 **21**
20 **19**
18 **17**
16 **15**
14 **13**
12 **11**
10 **9**
8 **7**
6 **5**
4 **3**
2 **1**

rep = 24 sts

100 %
Black

3

38 **37**
36 **35**
34 **33**
32 **31**
30 **29**
28 **27**
26 **25**
24 **23**
22 **21**
20 **19**
18 **17**
16 **15**
14 **13**
12 **11**
10 **9**
8 **7**
6 **5**
4 **3**
2 **1**

rep = 24 sts

4

34 **33**
32 **31**
30 **29**
28 **27**
26 **25**
24 **23**
22 **21**
20 **19**
18 **17**
16 **15**
14 **13**
12 **11**
10 **9**
8 **7**
6 **5**
4 **3**
2 **1**

rep = 24 sts

John Hutchinson

5

6

7

10

8

9

11

rep = 32 sts

rep = 32 sts

rep = 12 sts

13

12

rep = 24 sts

15

14

rep = 8 sts

More design ideas

Fair Isle designs are traditionally to be found on thick, wooly clothes, for both indoor and outdoor wear. This tam o' shanter and gloves pick out the subtle country colors of autumn and winter and look most at home in a chilly landscape.

128

Seed stitch variations

Seed stitch and its variations produce firm close fabrics with a light crunchy surface texture. They are ideal all-over stitches and seed stitch itself makes an excellent edging.

Ray Moller

Skills you need

* **Decreasing**
* **Using a cable needle**

If you do not know these skills refer to pages 175 and 178.

Materials

Where the stitch detail is important use only plain smooth yarns as the textures of seed stitches are so subtle that they are easily obscured by fancy yarns. They work well in worsted-weight or chunky yarns like the pure wool used in the basic sweater but are also effective in a fine sport-weight or cotton. Contrast colors can sometimes be introduced as shown in the Pattern Library.

Special technique – setting in raglan sleeves

1 Work the neck ribbing as instructed by picking up the required number of stitches along the back neck, left sleeve top, front neck and right sleeve top and working in single ribbing to the required depth. Bind off.

2 Join each raglan seam in turn, placing right sides together and using a back-stitch seam. Join the neck ribbing neatly.

3 Finally join the side and underarm seams. If preferred the back left, front left and front right raglan seams may be joined before working the neck ribbing. Finish by joining the back right raglan seam then the side and underarm seams.

John Hutchinson

The basic seed-rib sweater

Subtle earth colors and a clever mix of textures make this beautiful pure-wool sweater practically perfect for town or country wear.

Sizes
To fit 38 [40:42] in. chest
Length 26¾ [27¼:27½] in.
Sleeve seam 19¼ in.

Note: Instructions for larger sizes are in square brackets []; where there is only one set of figures it applies to all sizes.

Gauge
16 sts and 22 rows to 4 in. over seed rib pat (see page 133) on size 8 needles

Materials
23 [25:27] oz semi-bulky wool yarn in main color (X)
4 oz in contrasting color (Y)
2 oz in contrasting color (Z)
1 pair each size 7 and 8 knitting needles
Cable needle
130

Back
** Using smaller needles and X cast on 72 [74:78] sts.
Work 3 in. K1, P1 ribbing ending with a RS row.
Next row Rib 7 [4:7], * work twice into next st, rib 3, rep from * ending last rep rib 8 [5:6]. 87 [91:95] sts.
Change to larger needles and begin pat.
1st row P1, (K1 tbl, P1) 4 [5:6] times, * K6, P1, (K1 tbl, P1) 7 times, rep from * to last 15 [17:19] sts, K6, P1, (K1 tbl, P1) 4 [5:6] times.
2nd row K9 [11:13], * P6, K15, rep from * ending last rep K9 [11:13].
3rd-4th rows As 1st-2nd rows.
5th row P1, (K1 tbl, P1) 4 [5:6] times, * sl next 3 sts onto cable needle and leave at front of work, K3, then K3 from cable needle (called C6F), P1, (K1 tbl, P1) 7 times, rep from * to last 15 [17:19] sts, C6F, P1, (K1 tbl, P1) 4 [5:6] times.
6th row As 2nd row.
These 6 rows form the pat.
Rep these 6 rows 12 times more.

Shape raglan armholes
*** Keeping pat correct, bind off 5 [6:7] sts at beg of next 2 rows.
2nd and 3rd sizes only
Next row K1, sl 1, K1, psso, work in pat to last 3 sts, K2 tog, K1.
Next row P2, work in pat to last 2 sts, P2.
3rd size only
Rep last 2 rows once more. *** 77 sts.
All sizes: begin yoke pat
1st row K1, sl 1, K1, psso, P5, sl next st onto cable needle and leave at back of work, K1, then P1 from cable needle, (called Cr2B), P3, * sl next st onto cable needle and leave at front of work, P1 then K1 from cable needle, (called Cr2F), P4, Cr2B, P3, rep from * to last 9 sts, Cr2F, P4, K2 tog, K1.
2nd row P2, K3, Cr2F, K5, * Cr2B, K2, Cr2F, K5, rep from * to last 8 sts, Cr2B, K2, Cr2F, P2.
3rd row K1, sl 1, K1, psso, * Cr2F, Cr2B, P7, rep from * to last 6 sts, Cr2F, K1, K2 tog, K1.
4th row P2, * sl next st onto cable needle and leave at back of work,

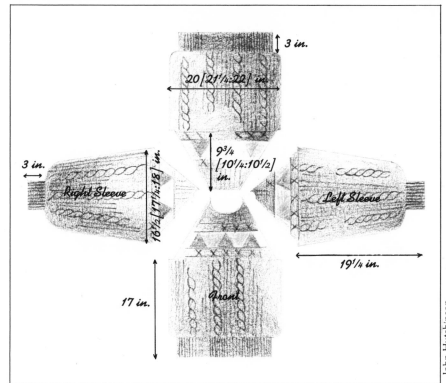

John Hutchinson

P1, then P1 from cable needle, (called C2F P-wise), K9, rep from * to last 5 sts, C2F P-wise, K1, P2.

5th row K1, sl 1, K1, psso, P1, Cr2F, P7, * Cr2B, Cr2F, P7, rep from * to last 5 sts, Cr2B, K2 tog, K1.

6th row P2, K1, Cr2B, K5, * Cr2F, K2, Cr2B, K5, rep from * to last 6 sts, Cr2F, K2, P2.

Change to color pat.

7th row With Y, K1, sl 1, K1, psso K to last 3 sts, K2 tog, K1.

8th row With Y, P across row.

9th row With Y, K1, sl 1, K1, psso, K2, * sl next st onto cable needle and leave at front of work, K1, then K1 from cable needle, (called C2F), K12, with Y, sl next st onto cable needle and leave at back of work, K1, then K1 from cable needle, (called C2B), K6, rep from * ending last rep K1, K2 tog, K1 instead of K6.

10th row P5Y, * P12Z, P10Y, rep from * ending last rep P6Y.

11th row With Y, K1, sl 1, K1, psso, K2, * C2F, K10Z, with Y, C2B, K8, rep from * ending last rep K1, K2 tog, K1 instead of K8.

12th row P5Y, * P10Z, P12Y, rep from * ending last rep P6Y.

13th row With Y, K1, sl 1, K1, psso, K2, * C2F, K8Z, with Y, C2B, K10, rep from * ending last rep K1, K2 tog, K1, instead of K10.

14th row P5Y, * P8Z, P14Y, rep from * ending last rep P6Y.

15th row With Y, K1, sl 1, K1, psso,

K2, * C2F, K6Z, with Y, C2B, K12, rep from * ending last rep K1, K2 tog, K1, instead of K12.

16th row P5Y, * P6Z, P16Y, rep from * ending last rep P6Y.

17th row With Y, K1, sl 1, K1, psso, K2, * C2F, K4Z, with Y, C2B, K14, rep from * ending last rep K1, K2 tog, K1.

18th row P5Y, * P4Z, P18Y, rep from * ending last rep P6Y.

19th row With Y, K1, sl 1, K1, psso, K2, * C2F, K2Z, with Y, C2F, K16, rep from * ending last rep K1, K2 tog, K1.

20th row P5Y, * P2Z, P20Y, rep from * ending last rep P6Y.

21st row With Y, K1, sl 1, K1, psso, K2, * C2F, C2B, K18, rep from * ending last rep K1, K2 tog, K1.

22nd row With Y, P across row.

23rd row With Y, K1, sl 1, K1, psso, K2, * C2F, K20, rep from * ending last rep K1, K2 tog, K1.

Cont in X only.

24th row P across row.

25th row K1, sl 1, K1, psso, P4, Cr2B, P3, * Cr2F, P4, Cr2B, P3, rep from * to last 8 sts, Cr2F, P3, K2 tog, K1.

26th row P2, K2, Cr2F, K5, * Cr2B, K2, Cr2F, K5, rep from * to last 7 sts, Cr2B, K3, P2.

27th row K1, sl 1, K1, psso, K1, Cr2B, P7, * Cr2F, Cr2B, P7, rep from * to last 5 sts, Cr2F, K2 tog, K1.

28th row P2, K10, * C2F P-wise,

K9, rep from * to last 4 sts, C2F P-wise, P2.

29th row K1, sl 1, K1, psso, Cr2F, P7, * Cr2B, Cr2F, P7, rep from * to last 4 sts, P1, K2 tog, K1.

30th row P2, Cr2B, K5, * Cr2F, K2, Cr2B, K5, rep from * to last 5 sts, Cr2F, K1, P2.

Next row K1, sl 1, K1, psso, work in P1, K1 ribbing to last 3 sts, K2 tog, K1.

Next row P2, rib to last 2 sts, P2. ** Rep the last 2 rows until 23 sts rem. Leave these sts on a st holder.

Front

Work as given for back from ** to **. Rep the last 2 rows until 41 sts rem, ending with a WS row.

Shape neck

Next row K1, sl 1, K1, rib 14, bind off 7 sts, rib to last 3 sts, K2 tog, K1. Complete right side of neck first. Cont shaping raglan edge as before, *at the same time*, dec 1 st at neck edge on every row until 3 sts rem. Keeping neck edge straight, cont to dec at armhole edge as before until 2 sts rem.

Next row K2 tog and fasten off. With WS of work facing, rejoin yarn to sts for left side of neck. Complete to match first side reversing all shapings.

Right sleeve

**** Using smaller needles and X, cast on 38 [38:40] sts and work in K1, P1 ribbing for 3 in.

Next row Rib 4 [1:2], * rib 2, work twice into next st, rep from * to last 4 [1:2] sts, rib to end. 48 [50:52] sts. Change to larger needles and work in pat.

1st row K6 [P1, K6: K1 tbl, P1, K6], P1, (K1 tbl, P1) 7 times, K6, P1, (K1 tbl, P1) 7 times, K6 [K6, P1: K6, P1, K1 tbl].

2nd row P6 [K1, P6: K2, P6], K15, P6, K15, P6 [P1, K1: P6, K2].

3rd-4th rows As 1st-2nd rows.

5th row C6F [P1, C6F: K1 tbl, P1, C6F], P1, (K1 tbl, P1) 7 times, C6F, P1, (K1 tbl, P1) 7 times, C6F [C6F, P1:C6F, P1, K1 tbl].

6th row As 2nd row.

These 6 rows form the pat. Inc and work into pat 1 st at each end of the next and every foll 6th row until there are 70 [74:78] sts.

Cont without shaping until the pat has been worked 15 times in all, ending with a 6th row.

Shape raglan top

Work as given for back from *** to ***

131

All sizes

Begin yoke pat

1st row K1, sl 1, K1, psso, P1, * Cr2F, P4, Cr2B, P3, rep from * ending last rep P1, K2 tog, K1, instead of P3.

2nd row P2, K2, * Cr2B, K2, Cr2F, K5, rep from * ending last rep K2, P2, instead of K5.

3rd row K1, sl 1, K1, psso, P2, * Cr2F, Cr2B, P7, rep from * ending last rep P2, K2 tog, K1.

4th row P2, K3, * C2F P-wise, K9, rep from * ending last rep K3, P2.

5th row K1, sl 1, K1, psso, P1, * Cr2B, Cr2F, P7, rep from * ending last rep P1, K2 tog, K1.

6th row P2, * Cr2F, K2, Cr2B, K5, rep from * ending last rep P2. Change to color pat.

7th row With Y, K1, sl 1, K1, psso, K to last 3 sts, K2 tog, K1.

8th row With Y, P across row.

9th row With Y, K1, sl 1, K1, psso, K4, * C2F, K12Z, C2B, K6, rep from * ending last rep, K4, K2 tog, K1.

10th row P8Y, * P12Z, P10Y, rep from * to last 8 sts, P8Y.

11th row With Y, K1, sl 1, K1, psso, K4, * C2F, K10Z, with Y, C2B, K8, rep from * ending last rep K4, K2 tog, K1.

12th row P8Y, * P10Z, P12Y, rep from * ending last rep P8Y.

13th row With Y, K1, sl 1, K1, psso, K4, * C2F, K8Z, with Y, C2B, K10, rep from * ending last rep K4, K2 tog, K1.

14th row P8Y, * P8Z, P14Y, rep from * ending last rep P8Y.

15th row With Y, K1, sl 1, K1, psso, K4, * C2F, K6Z, with Y, C2B, K12,

rep from * ending last rep K4, K2 tog, K1.

16th row P8Y, * P6Z, P16Y, rep from * ending last rep P8Y.

17th row With Y, K1, sl 1, K1, psso, K4, *C2F, K4Z, with Y, C2B, K14, rep from * ending last rep K4, K2 tog, K1.

18th row P8Y , * P4Z, P18Y, rep from * ending last rep P8Y.

19th row With Y, K1, sl 1, K1, psso, K4, * C2F, K2Z, with Y, C2B, K16, rep from * ending last rep K4, K2 tog, K1.

20th row P8Y, * P2Z, P20Y, rep from * ending last rep P8Y. Cont in Y only.

21st row K1, sl 1, K1, psso, K4, * C2F, C2B, K18, rep from * ending last rep K4, K2 tog, K1.

22nd row P across row.

23rd row K1, sl 1, K1, psso, K4, * C2F, K20, rep from * ending last rep K4, K2 tog, K1.
Change to X.

24th row P across row.

25th row K1, sl 1, K1, psso, * Cr2F, P4, Cr2B, P3, rep from * ending last rep K2 tog, K1.

26th row P2, K1, * Cr2B, K2, Cr2F, K5, rep from * ending last rep K1, P2.

27th row K1, sl 1, K1, psso, P1, * Cr2F, Cr2B, P7, rep from * ending last rep P1, K2 tog, K1.

28th row P2, K2, * C2F P-wise, K9, rep from * ending last rep K2, P2.

29th row K1, sl 1, K1, psso, * Cr2B, Cr2F, P7, rep from * ending last rep K2 tog, K1.

30th row P2, K3, Cr2B, K5, * Cr2F, K2, Cr2B, K5, rep from * to last 7 sts,

Cr2F, K3, P2.

Next row K1, sl 1, K1, psso, work in P1, K1 ribbing to last 3 sts, K2 tog, K1.

Next row P2, rib to last 2 sts, P2. ****
Rep the last 2 rows until 12 sts rem, ending with a WS row.

Shape top

Next row Bind off 5 sts, rib to last 3 sts, K2 tog, K1.

Next row P2, rib 2, work 2 tog.

Next row Work 2 tog, K2 tog, K1.

Next row P1, P2 tog.

Next row K2 tog. Fasten off.

Left sleeve

Work as given for right sleeve from **** to ****.
Rep the last 2 rows until 12 sts rem, ending with a RS row.
Complete to match right sleeve, reversing shaping.

Neckband

Using smaller needles and X, with RS of work facing, rib across 23 sts on back neck, pick up and K 7 sts from left sleeve top, pick up and K 33 sts from front neck edge, and 7 sts from right sleeve top. 70 sts.
Work 7 rows K1, P1 ribbing.
Bind off in ribbing.

To finish

Join raglan seams and neckband. Join side and sleeve seams.

Adapting the seed-rib sweater

Paneled sweaters like this are not easy to adapt but there a few ways to give it a slightly different look.

Adding color

The body of the basic sweater is constructed of panels of seed rib divided by simple three by three cables. T e seed rib pattern can itself be varied by adding two contrasting colors as shown in sample 5. Alternatively the cable could be worked in two colors either by striping it horizontally or by working each side of the cable in a different color.

Seed stitch variations

1 **Seed stitch**

This pattern can be worked over any number of stitches. Over an even number work as folls:

1st row * K1, P1, rep from * to end.

2nd row * P1, K1, rep from * to end.

These 2 rows form the pattern repeat. Over an odd number of stitches work as folls:

1st row K1, * P1, K1, rep from * to end.

This row forms the pattern repeat.

1

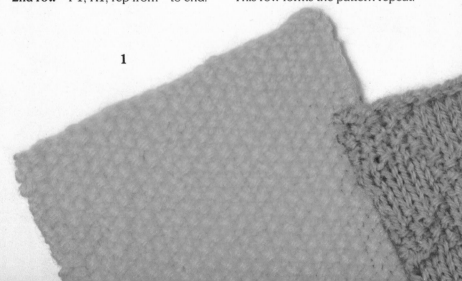

2 Seed lattice

This pattern is worked over a multiple of 14 stitches, plus 2 extra.

1st row (RS) K across row.
2nd, 4th and 6th rows P2, * (K1, P1) twice, K1, P2, rep from * to end.
3rd, 5th and 7th rows K3, *P1, K1, P1, K4, rep from * ending last repeat K3.
8th row P2, * K12, P2, rep from * to end.
9th row K2, * P12, K2, rep from * to end.
10th row P across row
11th, 13th and 15th rows K2, * (P1, K1) twice, P1, K2, rep from * to end.
12th, 14th and 16th rows P3, * K1, P1, K1, P4, rep from * ending last repeat P3.
17th row P7, * K2, P12, rep from * to last 9 sts, K2, P7.
18th row K7, * P2, K12, rep from * to last 9 sts, P2, K7.
These 18 rows form pattern repeat.

2

3 Bicolor seed stitch

This pattern is worked over an odd number of stitches in two colors (A, B). Strand contrast yarn on WS of work.

1st row (RS) With A, * P1, K1, rep from * to last st, P1.
2nd and 3rd rows * P1B, K1A, rep from * to last st, P1B.
4th row As 1st row.
5th and 6th rows * P1A, K1B, rep from * to last st, P1A.
These 6 rows form pattern repeat.

4 Zigzag seed stitch

This pattern is worked over a multiple of 10 stitches.

1st row * K5, (P1, K1) twice, P1, rep from * to end.
2nd row * (P1, K1) 3 times, P4, rep from * to end.
3rd row * K3, (P1, K1) twice, P1, K2, rep from * to end.
4th row * P3, (K1, P1) twice, K1, P2, rep from * to end.
5th row * (K1, P1) 3 times, K4, rep from * to end.
6th row * P5, (K1, P1) twice, K1, rep from * to end.
7th row As 5th row.
8th row As 4th row.
9th row As 3rd row.
10th row As 2nd row.
These 10 rows form the pattern repeat.

3

5 Three-color seed rib

This is an adaptation of the stitch used on the basic sweater in three colors (A, B, C). Strand contrasting yarns on WS of work.

1st row (WS) With A, K across row.
2nd row P1A, * with B, K1 tbl, P1A, rep from * to end.
3rd row K1A, * K1B, K1A, rep from * to end.
4th row With A, P1, * K1 tbl, P1, rep from * to end.
5th-8th rows As 1st-4th rows using C instead of B.
These 8 rows form the pattern repeat.

4

6 Seed checks

This pattern is worked over a multiple of 10 stitches, plus 5 extra.

1st, 3rd and 5th rows (WS) P5, * (K1, P1) twice, K1, P5, rep from * to end.
2nd and 4th rows K5, * (K1, P1) twice, K6, rep from * to end.
6th, 8th and 10th rows (P1, K1) twice, P1, * K5, (P1, K1) twice, P1, rep from * to end.
7th and 9th rows (P1, K1) twice, P1, * P5, (P1, K1) twice, P1, rep from * to end.
These 10 rows form pattern repeat.

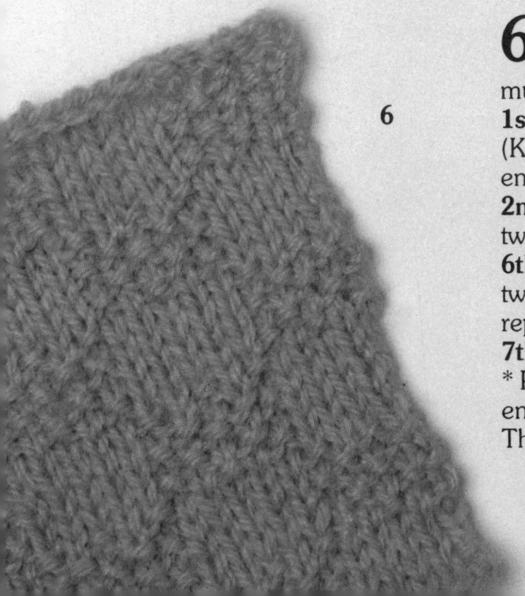

6

5

Simon Butcher

Maxi knitting

Extra-large needles are used not only for knitting super-chunky yarns but also for creating interesting fabrics from a number of fine yarns twisted together.

134

Skills you need

* **Decreasing**
* **Increasing**

If you do not know these skills refer to pages 175 and 176.

Materials

Maxi knitting offers endless opportunities for experimenting with the many novelty yarns that are available. In addition, other materials that would normally be too bulky to knit can be incorporated, for example, fabric strips and rug wool. Make sure that the materials used are compatible as far as cleaning methods are concerned. The basic jacket uses combined strands of chenille, fine bouclé in three colors, a heavy bouclé slub and a mohair bouclé producing a richly textured fabric in a subtle mixture of tones.

Special technique – working the pocket edging

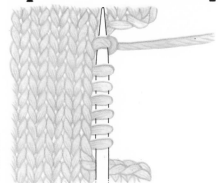 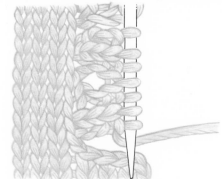 

Coral Mula

1 *Pick up and knit the required number of stitches along the pocket opening on the jacket front.*

2 *Work in single ribbing for the given number of rows making an eyelet buttonhole as instructed.*

3 *Bind off in ribbing and sew the row ends of the edging in position on the jacket front.*

The basic maxi jacket

Knit this tweedy looking jacket in double-quick time using six strands of multi-textured yarn in simple stockinette stitch on giant needles.

Sizes
To fit 38 [42] in. chest
Length 31 [33] in.
Sleeve seam 19 [20] in.

Note: Instructions for the larger size are in square brackets []; where there is only one set of figures it applies to both sizes.

Gauge
5½ sts and 8 rows to 4 in. over stockinette st on size 19 needles

Materials
13 oz chenille yarn
13 oz fine bouclé yarn in each of two colors
14 oz fine bouclé yarn in a third color
21 [23] oz bulky slubbed bouclé yarn
16 [18] oz mohair bouclé
9 buttons
1 pair each size 19, 17 and 5 knitting needles

Special note: Use one strand of each yarn together throughout.

Back
Using size 17 needles, cast on 33 [37] sts.
Work in K1, P1 ribbing as foll:
1st row K1, * P1, K1, rep from * to end.
2nd row P1, * K1, P1, rep from * to end.
Rep the last 2 rows twice more.
Change to size 19 needles and beg with a K row cont in stockinette st.
Work 8 [10] rows.
Shape pockets
Cast on 3 sts at beg of next 2 rows. 39 [43] sts.
Work 8 rows.
Bind off 3 sts at beg of next 2 rows. 33 [37] sts.
Work 16 [18] rows.
Shape armholes
Bind off 2 [3] sts at beg of next 2 rows.
Dec 1 st at beg of next 2 rows. 27 [29] sts.
Work 18 rows.
Shape shoulders
Bind off 8 [9] sts at beg of next 2 rows.
Bind off rem 11 sts.

Left front
Using size 17 needles, cast on 15 [17] sts. Work 6 rows K1, P1 ribbing as given for back.
Change to size 19 needles and beg with a K row cont in stockinette st.
Work 8 [10] rows.
Shape pocket
Next row Bind off 3 sts, K to end.
Work 9 rows.
Next row Cast on 3 sts, K to end.
Work 17 [19] rows.
Shape armhole
Next row Bind off 2 [3] sts, K to end.
Next row P across row.
Next row K2 tog, K to end. 12 [13] sts.
Work 12 rows.
Shape neck
Next row Bind off 2 sts, P to end.
Next row K across row.
Next row P2 tog, P to end.
Rep the last 2 rows once more. 8 [9] sts.
Work 2 rows.
Shape shoulder
Bind off rem sts.

Right front
Using size 17 needles, cast on 15 [17] sts. Work 6 rows K1, P1 ribbing as

135

given for back.
Change to size 19 needles and beg with a K row cont in stockinette st. Work 9 [11] rows.

Shape pocket
Next row Bind off 3 sts, P to end.
Work 9 rows.
Next row Cast on 3 sts, P to end.
Work 17 [19] rows.

Shape armhole
Next row Bind off 2 [3] sts, P to end.
Next row K across row.
Next row P2 tog, P to end. 12 [13] sts. Work 12 rows.

Shape neck
Next row Bind off 2 sts, K to end.
Next row P across row.
Next row K2 tog, K to end.
Rep the last 2 rows once more. 8 [9] sts.
Work 2 rows.

Shape shoulder
Bind off rem sts.

Sleeves

Using size 17 needles, cast on 13 [15] sts. Work 6 rows K1, P1 ribbing as given for back.
Change to size 19 needles.
Next row K0 [1], * K1, pick up loop between last st knitted and next st on LH needle and K it tbl (called M1), K2, M1, rep from * to last 1 [2] sts, K1 [2], 21 [23] sts.
Beg with a P row work 7 rows stockinette st. Inc and work into stockinette st 1 st at each end of the next and every foll 8th row until there are 27 [29] sts.
Work 9 [11] rows.

Shape top
Bind off 2 [3] sts at beg of next 2 rows.
Dec 1 st at beg of next and every row until 11 sts rem.
Bind off.

Collar

Using size 19 needles, cast on 6 sts.
Cont in g st (every row K).
Work 62 rows. Bind off.

Armbands

Using size 19 needles, cast on 2 sts.
Cont in g st.
Work 4 rows.
Inc 1 st at beg of next 2 rows.
Rep the last 6 rows once more. 6 sts.
Work 24 rows.
Dec 1 st at beg of next 2 rows.
Work 4 rows.
Rep the last 6 rows once more. 2 sts.
Bind off.
136

Pocket edgings

Using size 17 needles, with RS of work facing, pick up and K 7 sts along front pocket opening edge.
1st row K1, P1, K1, yfwd, K2 tog, P1, K1.
2nd row (P1, K1) 3 times, P1.
3rd row (K1, P1) 3 times, K1.
Bind off loosely in ribbing.

Button band

Using size 19 needles, cast on 4 sts.
Cont in g st.
Work 86 [90] rows.
Bind off.

Buttonhole band

Using size 19 needles, cast on 4 sts.
Cont in g st.
Work 2 [4] rows.
Buttonhole row K1, yfwd, K2 tog, K1.
Work 13 rows.
Rep the last 14 rows 4 times more, then the buttonhole row again.
Work 9 [11] rows, then the buttonhole row again.
Work 3 rows.
Bind off.

Pocket linings

Using size 5 needles and one strand of

fine bouclé only, cast on 7 sts.
Beg with a K row cont in stockinette st.
Work 2 rows.
Next row Cast on 8 sts, K to end.
Next row P across row.
Rep the last 2 rows once more. 23 sts.
Work 18 rows.
Dec 1 st at beg of next 8 rows.
Inc 1 st at beg of next 8 rows.
Work 20 rows.
Next row Bind off 8 sts, K to end.
Next row P across row
Rep the last 2 rows once more.
Bind off.

To finish

Join shoulder, sleeve and side seams, leaving pockets open.
Sew down the ends of the pocket edgings.
Fold pocket linings in half to form bags, join sides and sew top edges to inside the pocket opening.
Set in sleeves.
Fold collar in half lengthwise and sew to neck edge. Sew on button and buttonhole bands.
Fold armbands in half lengthwise and sew in position over shoulders and armhole seam.
Sew on buttons.

Collar — 4³/4 in. — 18¹/2 in.

Back — 23³/4 [26¹/2] in. — 20¹/2 [22¹/2] in. — 19¹/4 [21] in. — 10¹/2 in.

3 in. 3 in. — 26 [27¹/4] in. — Button & Buttonhole Bands

Right Sleeve — 15 [16¹/2] in. — 2³/4 in.

Left Sleeve

Right Front — 8³/4 [9¹/2] in.

Left Front — 10¹/2 [12¹/4] in. — 2³/4 in.

Pocket Linings — 5 in. — 4¹/4 in.

Arm Bands — 14¹/2 in. — 4³/4 in.

Adapting the maxi jacket

By using different yarn mixtures you can revolutionize the look of the basic jacket.

Creating original fabrics

The basic jacket is worked in a mix of one strand of each of six different types or colors of yarn knitted together to produce a highly textured tweedy fabric. Some of the Pattern Library samples show how different combinations of yarn result in completely original fabrics.

The most unusual results are often created with novelty yarns but plain yarns in a variety of thicknesses and colors wound together can also be effective. Experiment with odd balls of leftover yarn adding and subtracting strands until you achieve an attractive mixture.

If you intend to use a substitute for the basic jacket yarn make sure that the gauge matches that given in the pattern. This is particularly important in maxi knitting because of the exaggerated size of the individual stitches.

Maxi patterns

1 Maxi mesh

Simple eyelets become giant eyelets when this fine mohair is knitted on size 17 needles.

1st row K1, * yfwd, K2 tog, rep from * to end.
2nd row P across row.
These 2 rows form the pattern repeat.

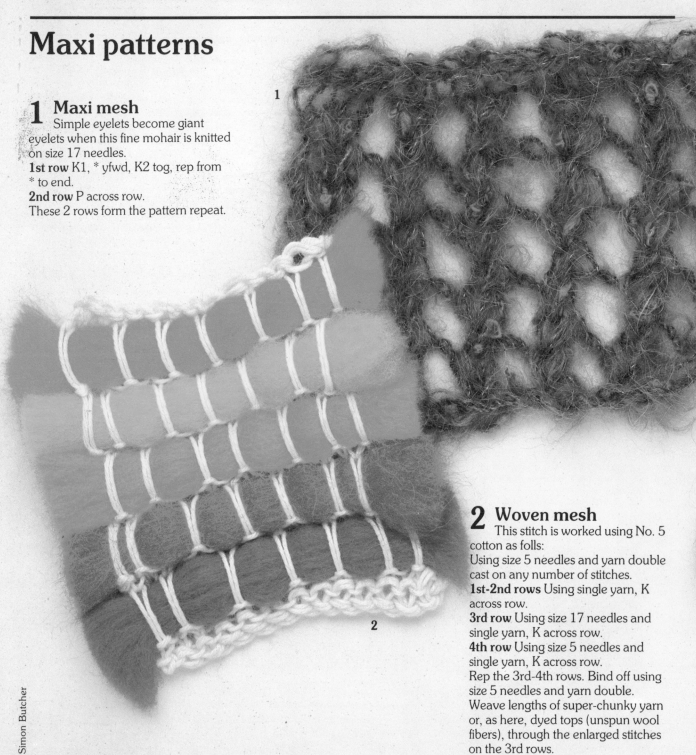

1

2

2 Woven mesh

This stitch is worked using No. 5 cotton as folls:
Using size 5 needles and yarn double cast on any number of stitches.
1st-2nd rows Using single yarn, K across row.
3rd row Using size 17 needles and single yarn, K across row.
4th row Using size 5 needles and single yarn, K across row.
Rep the 3rd-4th rows. Bind off using size 5 needles and yarn double.
Weave lengths of super-chunky yarn or, as here, dyed tops (unspun wool fibers), through the enlarged stitches on the 3rd rows.

137

3 Golden tweed

Six widely differing yarns have been used in this sample knitted in garter stitch on size 15 needles. Two are a fine cotton and linen mixture. The others are a slub cotton and glitter mixture, a fine glitter thread, a random-dyed bouclé and an interesting multi-colored, multi-ply wool and mohair mixture.

5 Chunky honeycomb

Even subtle textures are exaggerated to dramatic effect when they are knitted in thick yarn. This stitch, knitted in super-chunky yarn on size 15 needles, is worked over an even number of stitches.

1st-2nd rows K across row.
3rd row (RS) * K1, K st in row below next st on LH needle (called K1 below), rep from * to end.
4th row * K the unworked strand of previous row with st above it (called K1 above), K1, rep from * to end.
5th row * K1 below, K1, rep from * to end.
6th row * K1, K1 above, rep from * to end.
The 3rd-6th rows form the pattern repeat.

4 Slub

This sample was knitted in stockinette stitch on size 15 needles. Only two strands of yarn are used — a chunky and random-dyed slub.

Twisted stitches

Twisted-stitch patterns feature lines of knit stitches moving diagonally across the fabric. These, unlike traveling stitches, are worked without the aid of a cable needle and produce firm close textures ideal for all types of garment.

Eamonn McCabe

Skills you need

If you do not know these skills refer to pages 175 and 180.

Materials

Twisted stitches work well in any type of plain yarn. The textures will not show up in textured yarns like mohairs, bouclés and slubs. Tightly twisted yarns like crêpe and Guernsey yarns are particularly suitable and it is especially important to use a needle size that is not too large for the thickness of the yarn in order to maintain the "twist". The basic sweater, jerkin and leg warmers are worked in a knitting worsted to produce practical all-weather garments.

Special technique – twisting stitches

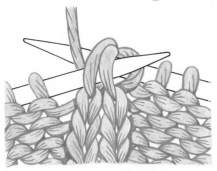

1 *To work a twist to the right, knit the next two stitches together but do not slip them off the left-hand needle. Knit the first of the stitches again, and now slip both stitches off the needle.*

2 *To work a twist to the left, knit the second stitch on the left-hand needle through the back of the loop, then knit the first and second stitches together through the back of the loop and slip both stitches off the needle.*

3 *On the twisted-stitch panels on the basic garments these two actions are worked consecutively with a knit stitch between them to produce a fern-like motif as shown.*

The basic twisted-stitch garments

A highly textured twisted fern stitch is worked all over this loose easy-to-wear jerkin and echoed in panels on a matching turtleneck pullover and leg warmers.

Sizes
To fit 38 [40:42] in. chest
Pullover length 26½ [27:28] in.
Pullover sleeve seam 22½ [23¼:24] in.
Jerkin length 31 [32:32¾] in.
Leg warmers length 24 in.

Note: Instructions for the larger sizes are in square brackets []; where there is only one set of figures it applies to all three sizes.

Gauge
20 sts and 24 rows to 4 in. over reverse stockinette st on size 6 needles
24 sts and 28 rows to 4 in. over twisted-stitch pat on size 6 needles

Materials
Pullover
38 [40:42] oz knitting worsted
Jerkin
40 [42:44] oz knitting worsted
Leg warmers
15 oz knitting worsted
140

1 pair each sizes 4 and 5 knitting needles

Pullover
Back
** Using smaller needles, cast on 100 [106:112] sts. Work in twisted ribbing as foll:
1st row * K1 tbl, P1, rep from * to end.
This row forms twisted ribbing. Cont in ribbing for 3 in.**
Change to larger needles.
Next row (WS) K across row.
Next row P across row.
These 2 rows form reverse stockinette st.
Rep these 2 rows until work measures 16¼ [16½:17] in. from cast-on edge, ending with a K row.
Shape armholes
Bind off 3 sts at beg of next 2 rows. 94 [100:106] sts.
Cont without shaping until work measures 9 [9½:10] in. from beg of armholes, ending with a K row.
Change to twisted ribbing.

Work a further 1¼ in.
Shape shoulders
Bind off 28 [30:32] sts in ribbing at beg of next 2 rows. Bind off in ribbing rem 38 [40:42] sts.

Front
Work as given for back from ** to ** inc 6 sts evenly across last row. 106 [112:118] sts.
Change to larger needles and begin working in reverse stockinette st with twisted-stitch panels as foll:
1st, 3rd, 5th, 7th and 9th rows (WS) K9 [11:13], * P1, (K2, P5, K2, P1) twice *, K46 [48:50], rep from * to * again, K to end.
2nd, 4th, 6th, 8th and 10th rows P9 [11:13], * K1 tbl, (P2, K2 tog but do not sl sts of LH needle, K first st again, then sl both sts from needle (called RT), K1, K tbl 2nd st on LH needle but do not sl sts off needle, K2 tog tbl first and 2nd sts and sl both sts from needle (called LT), P2, K1 tbl) twice *, P46 [48:50], rep from * to * again, P to end.
11th, 13th, 15th, 17th and 19th rows K9 [11:13], * P3, (K2, P1, K2, P5) twice ending last rep P3*, K46

[48:50], rep from * to * again, K to end.

12th, 14th, 16th, 18th and 20th rows P9 [11:13], * K1, (LT, P2, K1 tbl, P2, RT, K1) twice, * P46 [48:50], rep from * to * again, P to end. These 20 rows form the pat. Cont in pat until work measures 16¼ [16½:17] in. from cast-on edge, ending with a WS row.

Shape armholes
Bind off 3 sts at beg of next 2 rows. 100 [106:112] sts.
Cont without shaping until work measures 6¼ [6¾:7] in. from beg of armholes, ending with a WS row.

Shape neck
Next row Work in pat on 39 [41:43] sts and turn, leave rem sts on a spare needle. Dec 1 st at neck edge of next and every other row until 31 [33:35] sts rem. Cont without shaping until work measures 9 [9½:10] in. from beg of armholes, ending with a WS row. Change to twisted ribbing.
Next row K1 tbl, * P1, K1 tbl, rep from * to end.
Next row P1, * K1 tbl, P1, rep from * to end.
Rep last 2 rows for 1¼ in., ending at armhole edge.

Shape shoulder
Bind off rem sts in ribbing. With RS of work facing, return to sts on spare needle, cast off center 22 [24:26] sts, work in pat to end. Complete to match first side of neck, reversing shapings.

Sleeves
Using smaller needles, cast on 50 [52:54] sts. Work 3 in. twisted ribbing as given for back.
Change to larger needles. Beg with a P row cont in reverse stockinette st, inc 1 st at each end of every foll 4th row until there are 104 [108:112] sts.
Cont without shaping until work measures 22 [22¾:23¾] in. from cast-on edge, ending with a K row. Change to twisted ribbing as given for back. Work a further 1¼ in. Bind off in ribbing.

To finish
Join right shoulder seam.
Turtleneck collar
With RS of work facing, using larger needles, pick up and K 18 sts down left side of neck, pick up and K 22 [24:26] sts from center front, pick up and K 18 sts up right side of neck and 38 [40:42] sts across back neck. 96 [100:104] sts. Work in twisted ribbing as given for back for 8 in. Bind off in

ribbing. Join left shoulder and neckband, reversing seam to roll to RS. Set in sleeves flat joining bound off sts at underarms to final rows on sleeve. Join side and sleeve seams.

Jerkin
Back
Using larger needles, cast on 131 [141:151] sts. Work twisted ribbing as foll:
1st row (RS) K1 tbl, * P1, K1 tbl, rep from * to end.
2nd row P1, * K1 tbl, P1, rep from * to end.
Rep last 2 rows for 2 in. ending with a RS row.
Begin twisted-stitch pat.
1st, 3rd, 5th, 7th and 9th rows (WS) P1, (K2, P5, K2, P1) to end.
2nd, 4th, 6th, 8th and 10th rows K1 tbl, (P2, RT, K1, LT, P2, K1 tbl) to end.
11th, 13th, 15th, 17th and 19th rows P3, (K2, P1, K2, P5) to last 8 sts, K2, P1, K2, P3.
12th, 14th, 16th, 18th and 20th rows K1, (LT, P2, K1 tbl, P2, RT, K1) to end.
These 20 rows form the pat.
Cont in pat until work measures 20 [20½:21] in. from cast-on edge, ending with a WS row.

Shape armholes
Bind off 5 sts at beg of next 2 rows. 121 [131:141] sts.
Cont without shaping until work measures 9¾ [10¼:10½] in. from beg of armholes, ending with a WS row. Change to twisted ribbing as for back. Work 1¼ in., ending with a WS row.

Shape shoulders
Bind off in ribbing 40 [44:48] sts at beg of next 2 rows. Bind off in ribbing rem 41 [43:45] sts.

Pocket linings (make 2)
Using larger needles, cast on 26 sts. Work 6 in. stockinette st, ending with a P row. Leave sts on a holder.

Right front
Using larger needles, cast on 75 [79:85] sts. Work 2 in. twisted ribbing

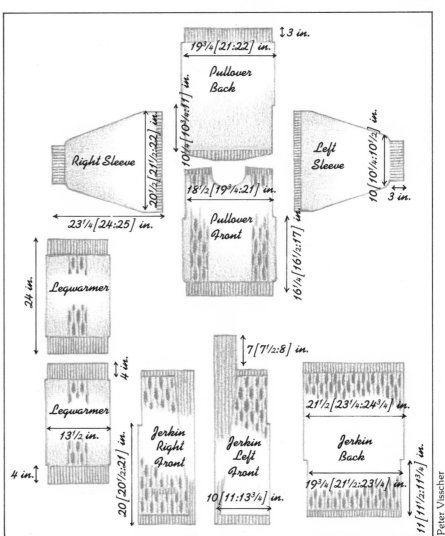

Peter Visscher

as given for back. Inc 1 st at end of last row on 2nd size only 75 [80:85] sts. Begin twisted-stitch pat with ribbed border as foll:

1st, 3rd, 5th, 7th and 9th rows (WS) P1, (K2, P5, K2, P1) to last 14 [19:14] sts, K0 [5:0], rib to end.

2nd, 4th, 6th, 8th and 10th rows Rib 14, P0 [5:0], K1 tbl, (P2, RT, K1, LT, P2, K1 tbl) to end.

11th, 13th, 15th, 17th and 19th rows P3, (K2, P1, K2, P5) to last 22 [27:22] sts, K2, P1, K2, P3, K0 [5:0], rib to end.

12th, 14th, 16th, 18th and 20th rows Rib 14, P0 [5:0], K1, (LT, P2, K1 tbl, P2, RT, K1) to end.

These 20 rows form twisted-stitch pat. *** Cont in pat, taking 1 more st into rib at inner border edge on the 8th and every foll 10th row, *at the same time*, place pocket when work measures 8 in. from cast-on edge, ending at side edge, as foll:

Next row Work in pat on 15 sts, bind off 26 sts, work in pat across sts of pocket lining, pat to end. Cont as set, taking sts into rib as before until work measures 20 [20½:21] in. ending at side edge.

Shape armhole
Bind off 5 sts at beg of next row. 70 [75:80] sts.

Cont without further shaping until there are 30 [31:32] sts in ribbing and 40 [44:48] sts in pat.

Cont as set until work measures 9¾ [10¼:10½] in. from beg of armhole shaping, ending with a WS row. Cont in twisted ribbing only. Work 1¼ in., ending at armhole edge. ***

Shape shoulder
Bind off these sts in ribbing.

Left front

Using larger needles, cast on 75 [79:85] sts. Work 2 in. twisted ribbing as given for back. Inc 1 st at beg of last row on 2nd size only.
Commence twisted-stitch pat with ribbing border as foll:

1st, 3rd, 5th, 7th and 9th rows (WS) Rib 14, K0 [5:0], P1, (K2, P5, K2, P1) to end.

2nd, 4th, 6th, 8th and 10th rows K1 tbl, (P2, RT, K1, LT, P2, K1 tbl) to last 14 [19:14] sts, P0 [5:0], rib to end.

11th, 13th, 15th, 17th and 19th rows Rib 14, K0 [5:0], P3, (K2, P1, K2, P5) to last 8 sts, K2, P1, K2, P3.

12th, 14th, 16th, 18th and 20th rows K1, (LT, P2, K1 tbl, P2, RT, K1) to last 14 [19:14] sts, P0 [5:0], rib to end.

These 20 rows form the pat. Complete to match right front working from *** to ***.

Shape shoulder
Bind off in ribbing 40 [44:48] sts, rib to end. Cont in ribbing on rem sts for a further 7 [7½:8] in. Bind off in ribbing.

To finish
Join shoulder seams and sew collar to back of neck. Join collar edges.

Armbands
With RS of work facing, using larger needles, pick up and K 157 [167:173] sts evenly around armhole edge. Work 2 in. in twisted ribbing as given for back. Bind off in ribbing. Fold ribbing in half to WS and catch down.

Pocket edgings
With RS facing, using larger needles, pick up and K 26 sts along pocket edge. Work 1¼ in. twisted ribbing. Bind off in ribbing. Sew down pocket linings and edges.

Leg warmers
Using smaller needles, cast on 71 sts. Work 4 in. in twisted ribbing as given for jerkin back. Change to larger needles and work as foll:

1st row K25, work from * to * as given for 1st row of pullover front, K25.

2nd row P25, work from * to * as given for 2nd row of pullover front, P25.

Cont in this way until work measures 20 in. from cast-on edge, ending with a WS row. Change to smaller needles and work 4 in. in twisted ribbing as given for jerkin back. Bind off in ribbing.

To finish
Join back seam.

Adapting the twisted-stitch garments

Take extra-special care with gauge when adapting twisted-stitch patterns.

Twisted stitches can be used either as all-over patterns or in panels. Both these uses are employed on the basic garments. In theory there is no reason why you could not knit all the garments in a plain stitch only. However, since the gauge of the twisted-stitch panels is tighter than that of the reverse stockinette stitch this would result in the garments being a little wider than the basic garments. In the case of the pullover and leg warmers the difference would be negligible but the chest measurement of the jerkin would be 8¾ [9½:10¼] in. larger. When substituting twisted-stitch patterns for plain patterns the effect reverses and the garments are narrower.

142

1 Twisted-stitch diamond
This pattern is worked over a multiple of 16 stitches, plus 1 extra.

1st and every other row (WS) P across row.

2nd row K1, * (LT) 3 times, K3, (RT) 3 times, K1, rep from * to end.

4th row K2, * (LT) 3 times, K1, (RT) 3 times, K3, rep from * ending last rep K2 instead of K3.

6th and 8th rows As 2nd and 4th rows.

10th row K across row.

12th row K2, * (RT) 3 times, K1, (LT) 3 times, K3, rep from * ending last rep K2 instead of K3.

14th row K1, * (RT) 3 times, K3, (LT) 3 times, K1, rep from * to end.

16th and 18th rows As 12th and 14th rows.

20th row K across row.
These 20 rows form the pat rep.

1

Twisted-stitch patterns

Note: Special twisted-stitch abbreviations are given in the basic pattern.

2 Twisted wave stitch

This pattern is worked over a multiple of 6 stitches, plus 1 extra.

1st row (RS) K across row.
2nd row P2, * K2, P4, rep from * to last 5 sts, K2, P3.
3rd row K2, * LT, K4, rep from * to last 5 sts, LT, K3.
4th row P2, * K1, P1, K1, P3, rep from * ending last rep P2.
5th row K3, * LT, K4, rep from * to last 4 sts, LT, K2.
6th row P3, * K2, P4, rep from * to last 4 sts, K2, P2.
7th row K across row.
8th row As 6th row.
9th row K3, * RT, K4, rep from * to last 4 sts, RT, K2.
10th row As 4th row.
11th row K2, * RT, K4, rep from * to last 5 sts, RT, K3.
12th row As 2nd row.
These 12 rows form the pattern repeat.

3 Broken lattice

This pattern is worked over a multiple of 8 stitches, plus 4 extra.

1st and every other row (WS) P across row.
2nd row K1, RT, * LT, K2, LT, RT, rep from * to last st, K1.
4th row RT, K2, * LT, K2, RT, K2, rep from * to end.
6th row K3, * RT, LT, RT, K2, rep from * to last st, K1.
8th row * K2, RT, K2, LT, rep from * to last 4 sts, K2, RT.
These 8 rows form the pattern repeat.

4 Twisted waffle stitch

This pattern is worked over a multiple of 4 stitches, plus 2 extra.

1st row (RS) P2, * RT, P2, rep from * to end.
2nd row K2, * P2, K2, rep from * to end.
3rd row P1, * K2 tog, (yo) twice, sl 1, K1, psso, rep from * to last st, P1.
4th row P2, * (K1, P1) into yo twice of previous row, P2, rep from * to end.
5th row K2, * P2, LT, rep from * to last 4 sts, P2, K2.
6th row P2, * K2, P2, rep from * to end.
7th row P1, yo, * sl 1, K1, psso, K2 tog, (yo) twice, rep from * to last 5 sts, sl 1, K1, psso, K2 tog, yo, P1.
8th row K2, * P2, (K1, P1) into yo twice of previous row, rep from * to last 4 sts, P2, K2.
These 8 rows form the pattern repeat.

143

BABIES AND CHILDREN
Cumbrian knitting

Skills you need

* **Decreasing**
* **Decorative increasing**

If you do not know these skills refer to page 175.

Materials

Traditionally Cumbrian knitting is worked in soft cotton yarn equivalent to baby yarn in either white or cream. These authentic materials produce a delightful play of light and shade over the surface of the fabric.

However, the textures of Cumbrian knitting can work equally well when updated with modern yarns in a variety of colors. The crib quilt is knitted in a baby yarn made of a mixture of wool and acrylic fibers.

Special technique – the thumb method of casting on

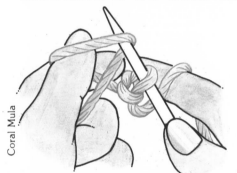
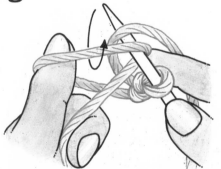
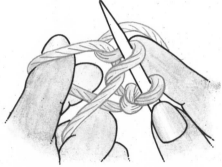

Coral Mula

1 *Make a slip knot 24 in. from the end of the yarn. Place it on the needle. Hold the yarn from the ball in your right hand and wrap the long end around the left thumb. Insert the needle under the loop on the thumb.*

2 *Take the yarn from the ball under and over the point of the needle and bring it through the loop on the thumb to make a new stitch.*

3 *Slip the loop off the thumb. Pull the yarn to tighten the stitch. Wrap the yarn around the thumb as before and repeat these steps for the required number of stitches. A 24 inch end is enough for about 60 stitches.*

The basic Cumbrian quilt

Brighten up baby's room with a beautiful Cumbrian crib quilt in delicate pastel shades.

Size
Width approx 20½ in.
Length approx 32¼ in.

Gauge
16 sts and 22 rows to 2 in. over stockinette stitch on size 0 needles.

Materials
6 oz baby yarn in main color (A)
2 oz in each of 5 contrasting colors (B,

C, D, E, F)
1 pair size 0 knitting needles

Full-size patch
Using A, cast on 60 sts by the thumb method.
1st row (WS) K across row.
2nd row * K2 tog, yfwd, rep from * to last 2 sts, K2.
3rd row K across row.
4th row With A, K3, K2 tog, K to last 5 sts, K2 tog, K3.
5th row K3, P to last 3 sts, K3.
6th row As 4th row.
7th row As 5th row.

8th row K3A, with B K2 tog, K to last 3 sts, K2 tog, K3A.
9th row K3A, with B K to last 3 sts, K3A.
10th row K3A, with B P2 tog, P to last 5 sts, P2 tog, K3A.
11th row As 9th row.
12th row As 10th row.
13th row With A, as 5th row.
14th row With A, as 4th row.
15th row With A, as 5th row.
16th row With A, as 4th row.
17th row K3A, with C P to last 3 sts, K3A.
18th row K3A, with C P2 tog, P to

144

last 5 sts, P2 tog, K3A.
19th row K3A, with C K to last 3 sts, K3A.
20th row As 18th row.
21st row As 19th row.
Rep 4th-21st rows once more using D instead of B and E instead of C. Then work 4th-12th rows using F instead of B. 14 sts.
Using A, cont in garter st (K every row), dec 1 st in center of each row until 1 st rem.
Fasten off.
Make 42 more pieces the same way.

Left-hand side border patch
Using A, cast on 30 sts by the thumb method.
1st-3rd rows Work as given for full-size patch.
4th row K3, K2 tog, K to end of row.

5th row K1, P to last 3 sts, K3.
6th row As 4th row.
7th row As 5th row.
8th row K3A, with B K2 tog, K to end of row.
9th row With B K to last 3 sts, K3A.
10th row K3A, with B P2 tog, P to last st, K1.
11th row As 9th row.
12th row As 10th row.
Carry on in this way, following the color sequence given for full-size patch, and working the garter st border at the beg of RS rows only and dec as before inside this edge only. K the last st on RS rows and the first st on WS rows throughout.
Cont until 3 sts rem.
Next row With A, K2 tog, K1.
Next row K across row.
Next row K2 tog.

Fasten off.
Work 7 more pieces in the same way.

Right-hand side border patch
Work as given for left-hand side border patch, reversing the garter st border and shaping to the other side. Work 7 more pieces in the same way.

To finish
Do not press.
Join patches together as shown in photograph on page 146, reversing three patches to fit top edge.

Adapting the Cumbrian crib quilt

Although the basic triangular patch shape cannot be varied, try using different yarns and color combinations to ring the changes on the basic pattern.

Substituting yarns

Cumbrian knitting is a form of patchwork that uses a number of triangular shapes pieced together, so you can make the quilt any size you like simply by making more triangles and more side pieces. Since the exact size of the quilt can be varied in this way there should be no problems about using different yarns. A crib quilt should be made in a soft washable yarn like the one used in the basic pattern, but a rug or cushion or bed-spread, for example, could well be made in a thicker wool or cotton. If a thicker yarn is used the size of the patch will of course, be larger.

Fringing

Many traditional Cumbrian quilts have a fringe at the top and bottom edges. Cut lengths of yarn just over twice the desired length of fringe and knot them in groups through the eyelets in the edges of the top and bottom patches.

Flower stitches

Knitting techniques are particularly suitable for creating flower-like shapes. The combination of lace, embossed and bobble stitches provides a versatile collection of textures with which to plant your own botanical garden.

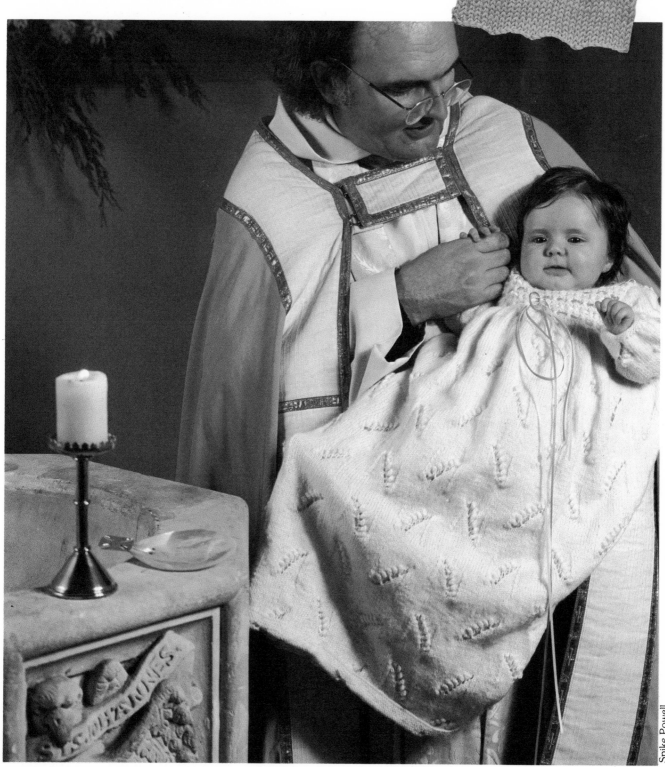

Skills you need

* **Decorative increasing**
* **Decreasing**
* **Eyelets**

If you do not know these skills refer to pages 175 and 182.

Materials

The christening robe is knitted in a soft baby yarn composed of woolen and synthetic fibers. It could also be worked in a cotton yarn of similar weight. Excessively fluffy or textured yarns are not suitable for baby clothes but the lacy flower stitches would look pretty in mohair, for example, if used for other garments. The embossed stitches are best worked in smooth yarns.

Special technique – gathering

1 Fullness in, for example, a skirt can be gathered by decreasing rapidly across one row. For medium fullness the gathering row should contain twice the number of stitches required for the bodice or waistband. Knit two stitches together across row.

2 For extra fullness the gathering row should contain three times the number of stitches required for the bodice. Knit three stitches together across the row.

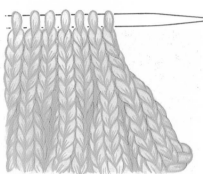

3 Work the bodice or waistband straight up from the gathering row.

The basic christening gown

Fine satin ribbon threaded through the eyelets of a delicate lily pattern adds a touch of color to this beautiful christening gown.

Size
To fit 18-20 in. chest
Length 28 in.
Sleeve seam 6¾ in.

Gauge
20 sts and 40 rows to 4 in. over bodice pat on size 3 needles

Materials
11 oz baby yarn
1 pair each size 2 and 3 knitting needles
Size E crochet hook
3 small buttons
6¾ yd. of ⅛ in. wide satin ribbon in dark shade
6 yd. ribbon in pale shade

Front
** Using smaller needles, cast on 165 sts and K 7 rows.
Change to larger needles and begin lily pat.
1st row K4, * sl 1, K1, psso, K6, (yfwd, K1) twice, sl 1, K1, psso, K24, rep from * ending last rep K5.

2nd and other rows P across row.
3rd row K4, * sl 1, K1, psso, K5, yfwd, K1, yfwd, K2, sl 1, K1, psso, K24, rep from * ending last rep K5.
5th row K4, * sl 1, K1, psso, K4, yfwd, K1, yfwd, (K1, P1, K1, P1, K1) all into next st, pass the 4th, 3rd, 2nd and first sts over last st (called MB), K2, sl 1, K1, psso, K24, rep from * ending last rep K5.
7th row K4, * sl 1, K1, psso, K3, yfwd, K1, yfwd, MB, K3, sl 1, K1, psso, K24, rep from * ending last rep K5.
9th row K4, * sl 1, K1, psso, K2, yfwd, K1, yfwd, MB, K4, sl 1, K1, psso, K24, rep from * ending last rep, K5.
11th row K4, * sl 1, K1, psso, (K1, yfwd) twice, MB, K5, sl 1, K1, psso, K24, rep from * ending last rep K5.
13th row K4, * sl 1, K1, psso, yfwd, K1, yfwd, MB, K6, sl 1, K1, psso, K24, rep from * ending last rep K5.
15th row K22, * sl 1, K1, psso, (K1, yfwd) twice, K6, K2 tog, K24, rep from * ending last rep K23.
17th row K22, * sl 1, K1, psso, K2, yfwd, K1, yfwd, K5, K2 tog, K24, rep from * ending last rep K23.
19th row K22, * sl 1, K1, psso, K2, MB, yfwd, K1, yfwd, K4, K2 tog, K24, rep from * ending last rep K23.
21st row K22, * sl 1, K1, psso, K3, MB, yfwd, K3, K2 tog, K24, rep from * ending last rep K23.
23rd row K22, * sl 1, K1, psso, K4, MB, yfwd, K1, yfwd, K2, K2 tog, K24 rep from * ending last rep K23.
25th row K22, * sl 1, K1, psso, K5, MB, (yfwd, K1) twice, K2 tog, K24, rep from * ending last rep K23.
27th row K22, * sl 1, K1, psso, K6, MB, yfwd, K1, yfwd, K2 tog, K24, rep from * ending last rep K23.
28th row P across row.
These 28 rows form the pat. Cont in pat until work measures approx 23¾ in. from beg, ending with a 14th or 28th row.
Next row (K2 tog) 6 times, (K3 tog) 47 times, (K2 tog) 6 times. 59 sts.
Change to bodice pat.
1st row (WS) P across row.
2nd and 3rd rows P across row.
4th row K1, * yfwd, sl 1, K1, psso, rep from * to end.
These 4 rows form the bodice pat.
Shape armholes
Keeping pat correct, bind off 4 sts at beg of next 2 rows, dec 1 st at each

148

end of next and every other row until 45 sts rem. ** Cont without shaping until work measures 2¼ in. from beg of armholes, ending with a RS row.

Shape neck
Next row Work in pat on 19 sts, bind off 7 sts loosely, work in pat to end. Work left side of neck first. Dec 1 st at neck edge on the next and every other row until 14 sts rem. Cont without shaping until armhole measures 4 in., ending at armhole edge.

Shape shoulder
Bind off 4 sts at beg of next row and 5 sts at beg of foll alt row. Work 1 row. Bind off rem 5 sts. With WS facing return to sts on right side of neck. Rejoin yarn. Complete to match left side of neck reversing shaping.

Back
Work as given for front from ** to **. Work 1 row.

Divide for back opening
Next row Work in pat on 20 sts, K5, turn, and leave rem sts on a spare needle.
Next row K5, work in pat to end.
Next row Work in pat to last 5 sts, K5. Rep the last 2 rows until work matches front to shoulder shaping, ending at armhole edge.

Shape shoulder
Bind off 4 sts at beg of next row and 5 sts at beg of 2 foll alt rows. Work 1 row. Bind off rem 11 sts. Return to sts on spare needle. With RS facing rejoin yarn to next st, cast on 5 sts, K across these 5 sts, work in pat to end.
Next row Work in pat to last 5 sts, K5. Complete to match first side of neck reversing shaping.

Sleeves
Using smaller needles, cast on 37 sts and K 4 rows.
Next row K4, * K into front and back of next st, rep from * to last 5 sts, K5. 65 sts.
Change to larger needles and begin lily pat.
1st row K8, * sl, K1, psso, K6, (yfwd, K1) twice, sl 1, K1, psso, K24, rep from * ending last rep K9.
2nd and every other row P across row.
3rd row K8, * sl 1, K1, psso, K5, yfwd, K1, yfwd, K2, sl 1, K1, psso, K24, rep from * ending last rep K9.
5th row K8, * sl 1, K1, psso, K4, yfwd, K1, yfwd, MB, K2, sl 1, K1, psso, K24, rep from * ending last rep K9.
7th row K8, * sl 1, K1, psso, K3, yfwd, K1, yfwd, MB, K3, sl 1, K1, psso, K24, rep from * ending last rep K9.
9th row K8, * sl 1, K1, psso, K2, yfwd,

K1, yfwd, MB, K4, sl 1, K1, psso, K24, rep from * ending last rep K9.
11th row K8, * sl 1, K1, psso, (K1, yfwd) twice, MB, K5, sl 1, K1, psso, K24, rep from * ending last rep K9.
13th row K8, * sl 1, K1, psso, yfwd, K1, yfwd, MB, K6, sl 1, K1, psso, K24, rep from * ending last rep K9.
15th row K26, * sl 1, K1, psso, (K1, yfwd) twice, K6, K2 tog, K24, rep from * ending last rep K27.
17th row K26, * sl 1, K1, psso, K2, yfwd, K1, yfwd, K5, K2 tog, K24, rep from * ending last rep K27.
19th row K26, * sl 1, K1, psso, K2, MB, yfwd, K1, yfwd, K4, K2 tog, K24, rep from * ending last rep K27.
21st row K26, * sl 1, K1, psso, K3, MB, yfwd, K1, yfwd, K3, K2 tog, K24, rep from * ending last rep K27.
23rd row K26, * sl 1, K1, psso, K4, MB, yfwd, K1, yfwd, K2, K2 tog, K24, rep from * ending last rep K27.
25th row K26, * sl 1, K1, psso, K5, MB, (yfwd, K1) twice, K2 tog, K24, rep from * ending last rep K27.
27th row K26, * sl 1, K1, psso, K6, MB, yfwd, K1, yfwd, K2 tog, K24, rep from * ending last rep K27.
28th row P across row.
These 28 rows form the pat. Cont in pat until work measures 6¾ in. from cast-on edge, ending with a WS row.

Shape top
Bind off 4 sts at beg of next 2 rows, and 2 sts at beg of foll 6 rows.
Dec 1 st at each end of the next and ever other row until 35 sts rem, ending with a WS row.
Bind off 2 sts at beg of next 6 rows.
Bind off rem 23 sts.

To finish
Using a back-stitch seam, join shoulders.

Neckband
With RS of work facing, using smaller needles, pick up and K 61 sts evenly around neck edge. K 5 rows. Bind off. Thread ribbon through holes on bodice, alternating shades, and tack down ends. Set in sleeves. Cut short lengths of ribbon, thread at random through the holes in lily pattern on skirt and sleeves, sew down row ends on WS. Join side and sleeve seams. Tack down the underlap on back neck opening. Crochet 3 button loops on right back and sew on buttons to correspond. Cut a length of ribbon approx 71 in. long in each shade, and thread both through eyelet holes at waist, bringing ends out at center front to tie.

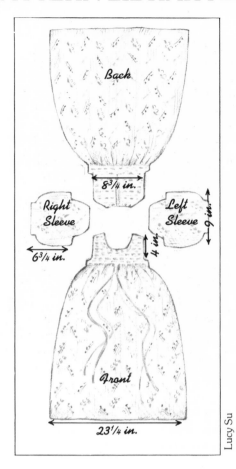

Lucy Su

Adapting the christening gown

Pick a pretty flower stitch to make an extra-special dress for an extra-special baby.

Choosing the stitch
There are several stitches in the Pattern Library that can be used instead of the lily pattern on the skirt of the christening gown. Work the bodice in the same eyelet stitch and the sleeves in a plain stitch like stockinette stitch. The sleeves could also be worked in the eyelet stitch used on the bodice. Many of the substitute stitches also have holes that can be used as a channel for ribbon weaving. If you intend to use a substitute stitch remember to knit a gauge sample in the new pattern and check it against the gauge measurement in the basic pattern.

1

Flower stitches

2 Canterbury bells
This pattern works over a multiple of 8 stitches, plus 1 extra.
1st and every other row (WS) P across row.
2nd row K1, * yfwd, sl 1, K1, psso, K3, K2 tog, yfwd, K1, rep from * to end.
4th row K2, * yfwd, sl 1, K1, psso, K1, K2 tog, yfwd, K3, rep from * ending last rep K2.
6th row P1, * K2, yfwd, sl 1, K2 tog, psso, yfwd, K2, P1, rep from * to end.
8th, 10th, 12th, 14th and 16th rows P1, * sl 1, K1, psso, (K1, yfwd) twice, K1, K2 tog, P1, rep from * to end.
These 16 rows form the pattern repeat.

2

3 Laburnum stitch
This pattern works over a multiple of 5 stitches, plus 2 extra.
1st row (RS) P2, * sl 1 with yarn in front, ybk, K2 tog, psso, yo twice, P2, rep from * to end.
2nd row K2, * P into back of 1st yo then into front of 2nd yo, P1, K2, rep from * to end.
3rd row P2, * K3, P2, rep from * to end.
4th row K2, * P3, K2, rep from * to end.
These 4 rows form the pattern repeat.

3

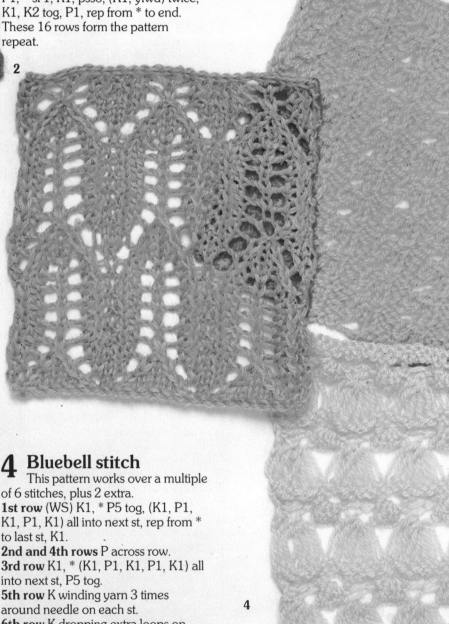

1 Cottonseed stitch
This pattern works over a multiple of 11 stitches. It can be substituted for the lily pattern on the skirt of the basic dress.
1st row (RS) * K1, (K1, yfwd, K1, yfwd, K1) all into next st, turn, K5, turn, P5, turn, K1, sl 1, K2 tog, psso, K1, turn, P3 tog — called MB (make bobble) — K2, yfwd, K1, yfwd, K4, K2 tog, rep from * to end.
2nd, 4th, 6th, 8th and 10th rows * P2 tog, P10, rep from * to end.
3rd row * K5, yfwd, K1, yfwd, K3, K2 tog, rep from * to end.
5th row * K6, yfwd, K1, yfwd, K2, K2 tog, rep from * to end.
7th row * K7, (yfwd, K1) twice, K2 tog, rep from * to end.
9th row * K8, yfwd, K1, yfwd, K2 tog, rep from * to end.
11th row * Sl 1, K1, psso, K4, yfwd, K1, yfwd, K2, MB, K1, rep from * to end.
12th, 14th, 16th, 18th and 20th rows * P10, P2 tog tbl, rep from * to end.
13th row * Sl 1, K1, psso, K3, yfwd, K1, yfwd, K5, rep from * to end.
15th row * Sl 1, K1, psso, K2, yfwd, K1, yfwd, K6, rep from * to end.
17th row * Sl 1, K1, psso, (K1, yfwd) twice, K7, rep from * to end.
19th row * Sl 1, K1, psso, yfwd, K1, yfwd, K8, rep from * to end.
These 20 rows form the pattern repeat.

4 Bluebell stitch
This pattern works over a multiple of 6 stitches, plus 2 extra.
1st row (WS) K1, * P5 tog, (K1, P1, K1, P1, K1) all into next st, rep from * to last st, K1.
2nd and 4th rows P across row.
3rd row K1, * (K1, P1, K1, P1, K1) all into next st, P5 tog.
5th row K winding yarn 3 times around needle on each st.
6th row K dropping extra loops on each st.
These 6 rows form the pattern repeat.

4

5 Rosebud mesh

This pattern repeats over a multiple of 10 stitches, plus 1 extra.

1st and every other row (WS) P across row.

2nd row K2 tog, * yfwd, K3, yfwd, K into front and back of next st, yfwd, K3, yfwd, sl 1, K2 tog, psso, rep from * ending last rep sl 1, K1, psso.

4th row Sl 1, K1, psso, * yfwd, sl 2, K1, p2sso, yfwd, K2 tog, yfwd, sl 1, K1, psso, (yfwd, sl 2, K1, p2sso) twice, rep from * ending last rep K2 tog.

6th row K2, * K2 tog, yfwd, K3, yfwd, sl 1, K1, psso, K3, rep from * ending last rep K2.

8th row K1, * K2 tog, yfwd, K1 tbl, yfwd, sl 1, K2 tog, psso, yfwd, K1 tbl, yfwd, sl 1, K1, psso, K1, rep from * to end. These 8 rows form the pattern repeat.

6 Dahlia stitch

This pattern works over a multiple of 12 stitches, plus 4 extra.

1st row K2, * yfwd, K2 tog, rep from * to last 2 sts, K2.

2nd and 4th rows K2, P to last 2 sts, K2.

3rd row K across row.

5th and 8th rows K2, * sl 1, K2 tog, psso, K4, yfwd, K1, yfwd, K4, rep from * to last 2 sts, K2.

6th, 7th and 9th rows K2, * P3 tog, P4, yo, P1, yo, P4, rep from * to last 2 sts, K2.

These 9 rows form the pattern repeat.

7 Garland stitch

This pattern usually repeats over 7 stitches. By adding 2 edge stitches on either side it can be substituted for the lily pattern on the skirt of the basic dress as follows.

1st row (WS) P across row.

2nd-5th rows K across row.

6th row K2, * K1, K2 tog, yfwd, K1, yfwd, sl 1, K1, psso, K1, rep from * to last 2 sts, K2.

7th row P2, * P2 tog tbl, yo, P3, yo, P2 tog, rep from * to last 2 sts, P2.

8th row K2, * K1, yfwd, K2 tog, yfwd, sl 1, K2 tog, psso, yfwd, K1, rep from * to last 2 sts, K2.

9th row P2, * P1, yo, P2 tog, P1, P2 tog tbl, yo, P1, rep from * to last 2 sts, P2.

10th row K2, * K2, yfwd, sl 1, K2 tog, psso, yfwd, K2, rep from * to last 2 sts, K2.

11th-14th rows K across row.

15th row P across row.

16th row K across row.

These 16 rows form the pattern repeat.

Looped stitches

Many original stitch patterns can be created by elongating stitches and then crossing or twisting the loops to form raised diagonal lines on the surface of the background stitch. They are most interesting when worked in several colors but can be used solely for texture.

Skills you need

* Decreasing
* Using a cable needle
* Simple increasing

If you do not know these skills refer to pages 174, 175 and 178.

Materials

Using several contrasting colors in stitch patterns such as looped stitches provides an ideal opportunity for mixing plain and textured yarns. Many beautiful fabrics can be created by using, for example, a mohair yarn with one or two plain contrasts. Where plain yarns only are used the effect of looped stitches is severely geometric. This is shown in the basic sweater which is knitted in an all-synthetic smooth fingering-weight yarn.

Special technique – cross two over four

1 *This technique is used on the 5th and 11th pattern rows. Slip the next five stitches onto a cable needle and hold it at the back of the work. Knit one stitch from the left-hand needle as usual.*

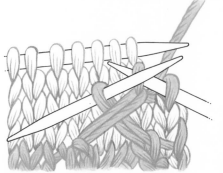

2 *Slip the last four stitches from the cable needle back onto the left-hand needle. Bring the remaining stitch on the cable needle to the front of the work.*

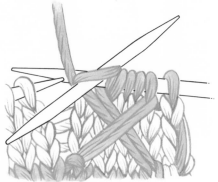

3 *Knit four from the left-hand needle then knit the stitch on the cable needle.*

The basic looped-stitch sweater

Knit a loopy sweater in bright buttery yellow with fresh white contrast. This one has an interesting stepped collar and two matching patch pockets on the front.

Sizes
To fit 26 [28:30] in. chest
Length 21 in.
Sleeve seam 19 in. including cuff
Note: Instructions for the larger sizes are in square brackets []; where there is only one set of figures it applies to all sizes.

Gauge
36 sts and 38 rows to 4 in. over looped pat on size 4 needles

Materials
7 [8:9]oz fingering yarn in each of two colors (A and B)
1 pair each size 1 and 4 knitting needles
Cable needle

Back
** Using smaller needles and A, cast on 116 [126:136] sts. Work in K1, P1 ribbing for 39 rows.
Next row P8 [13:7], P into the front and back of next st (called inc 1), * P8 [8:10], inc 1, rep from * to last 8 [13:7] sts, P8 [13:7]. 128 [138:148] sts.
Change to larger needles and begin looped pat.
1st and 3rd rows With B, K1, sl 1, * K4, sl 1, rep from * to last st, K1.
2nd and 4th rows P1, sl 1, * P4, sl 1, rep from * to last st, P1.
3rd-4th rows Rep 1st-2nd rows once.
5th row With A, K1, * sl next 5 sts onto cable needle and hold at back of work, K1, sl last 4 sts from cable needle onto LH needle, bring the rem st on cable needle to front of work,

Ray Moller

K4, then K1 from cable needle (called cross 2 over 4), K4, rep from * ending last rep K1.

6th row With A, K to end.
7th-10th rows Rep 1st-2nd rows twice.
11th row With A, K6, * cross 2 over 4, K4, rep from * to last 2 sts, K2.
12th row With A, K to end.
These 12 rows form the pat. Rep these 12 rows 7 times more.
Shape armholes
1st row With B, bind off 7 sts, K4 (including st used in binding off),

* sl 1, K4, rep from * to last 2 sts, K2.
2nd row Bind off 7 sts, P4 (including st used in binding off), * sl 1, P4, rep from * to end.
3rd row K2 tog, K2, * sl 1, K4, rep from * to last 5 sts, sl 1, K2, K2 tog.
4th row P2 tog, P1, * sl 1, P4, rep from * to last 4 sts, sl 1, P1, P2 tog.
5th row With A, K2 tog, * cross 2 over 4, K4, rep from * to last 8 sts, cross 2 over 4, K2 tog.
6th row With A, K2 tog, K to last 2 sts, K2 tog.
7th row With B, K2 tog, K3, * sl 1,

K4, rep from * to last 6 sts, sl 1, K3, K2 tog.
8th row P2 tog, P2, * sl 1, P4, rep from * to last 5 sts, sl 1, P2, P2 tog.
9th row K2 tog, K1, * sl 1, K4, rep from * to last 4 sts, sl 1, K1, K2 tog.
10th row P2 tog, * sl 1, P4, rep from * to last 3 sts, sl 1, P2 tog.
98 [108:118] sts. **
Cont without shaping.
Work the 11th-12th pat rows once, then work the 1st-12th pat rows 5 times and the 1st-6th rows once more.

153

Shape shoulders

Bind off 8 [9:10] sts at beg of next 8 rows. Leave the rem 34 [36:38] sts on a spare needle.

Front

Work as given for back from ** to **. Cont without shaping. Work 11th-12th pat rows once, then 1st-12th pat rows twice.

Divide for neck

1st row With B, K1, (sl 1, K4) 7 [8:9] times, K1, turn leaving rem 61 [66:71] sts on a spare needle. Complete left side of neck first.

2nd row P2 tog, P3, (sl 1, P4) 6 [7:8] times, sl 1, P1.

3rd row K1, (sl 1, K4) 6 [7:8] times, sl 1, K2, K2 tog.

4th row P2 tog, P1, (sl 1, P4) 6 [7:8] times, sl 1, P1.

5th row With A, K1, (cross 2 over 4) 3 [3:4] times, K1 [6:1], K2 tog. 33 [38:43] sts.

6th row With A, K to end.

Cont without shaping until work matches back to shoulder shaping, ending at armhole edge.

Shape shoulder

Bind off 8 [9:10] sts at beg of next and foll 2 alt rows. Work 1 row. Bind off rem 9 [11:13] sts.

Return to sts on spare needle, sl the center 24 sts onto a stitch holder, join in yarn to neck edge.

1st row With B, K1, (K4, sl 1), 7 [8:9] times, K1.

2nd row P1, (sl 1, P4) 6 [7:8] times, sl 1, P3, P2 tog.

3rd row K2 tog, K2, (sl 1, K4) 6 [7:8] times, sl 1, K1.

4th row P1, (sl 1, P4) 6 [7:8] times, sl 1, P1, P2 tog.

5th row With A, K2 tog, sl 1, (K4, cross 2 over 4) 3 [3:4] times, K1 [6:1]. 33 [38:43] sts.

6th row With A, K to end.

Complete to match first side of neck, reversing shapings.

Sleeves

Using smaller needles and A, cast on 58 [68:68] sts.

Work in K1, P1 ribbing for 40 rows. Change to larger needles and work 1st-12th pat rows as given for back. Cont in pat inc 1 st at each end of the next and every foll 6th row until there are 98 [108:108] sts. Cont without shaping until work measures approx 19 in. from cast-on edge, ending with a WS row.

Shape top

Work 1st-4th [1st-10th:1st-10th] rows of armhole shaping as given for back. Keeping pat correct, dec 1 st at each end of the next and every other row until 30 [34:34] sts rem. Bind off.

Collar

Using smaller needles and A, cast on 171 sts. Work in ribbing as foll:

1st row Sl 1 P-wise, * K1, P1, rep from * to end.

2nd row Sl 1 K-wise, * P1, K1, rep from * to end.

Rep the last 2 rows 10 times more.

Next row Sl 1 P-wise, rib 26, leave these sts on a spare needle, bind off 117, rib 27.

Work first collar point. Rib 9 rows.

Next row Bind off 12, rib to end. Rib 9 rows. Bind off in ribbing. Rejoin to sts on spare needle. Rib 10 rows.

Next row Bind off 12, rib to end. Rib 9 rows. Bind off in ribbing.

Pockets (make 2)

Using smaller needles and A, cast on 33 sts. Work 13 rows in ribbing as given for collar.

Next row Bind off 10sts, rib to end. Rib 9 rows.

Next rows Bind off 10 sts, rib to end. Rib 9 rows. Bind off in ribbing.

To finish

Join shoulder, side and sleeve seams. Set in sleeves. Position pockets on front and sew in place. Sew on collar. Fold back cuffs.

Adapting the looped-stitch sweater

Several versions of this sweater will take your children right through the winter.

Varying the basic stitch

Two of the samples in the Pattern Library show how the looped stitch pattern on the basic sweater can be varied by adding, in the one case, bobbles, and, in the other, a small square motif. Using these as examples it is possible to invent other adaptations. A third color could be introduced on, for example, the 6th and 11th rows thus striping the criss-cross loops, or on the 7th-10th rows to stripe the background fabric.

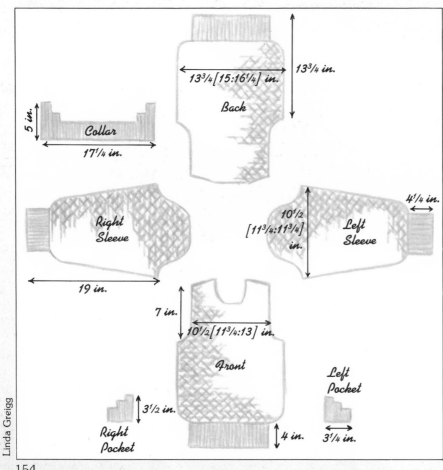

Linda Greigg

Looped stitches

1 Cross-stitched stripe

This stitch works over a multiple of 10 stitches, plus 1 extra, and uses three colors (A, B, C).

1st row (WS) With A, P across row.
2nd row With A, K across row.
3rd row With A, P6, * P1 winding yarn twice around needle, P2, P1 winding yarn twice around needle, P6, rep from * ending last rep P1.
4th row With B, K1, * sl 1 allowing extra loop to fall, K2, sl 1 allowing extra loop to fall, K6, rep from * to end.
5th row With B, K6, * yfwd, sl 1 P-wise, ybk, K2, yfwd, sl 1 P-wise, ybk, K6, rep from * ending last rep K1.
6th row With B, K1, * sl 1 P-wise, K2, sl 1 P-wise, K6, rep from *.
7th-9th rows Rep 5th-6th rows once, then 5th row again.
10th row With A, K1, * sl next st off LH needle and hold at front of work, K 3rd st on LH needle then the first

then the 2nd st and discard all sts at the same time, return sl st onto LH needle and K (called cross 4), K6, rep from * to end.
11th row With A, P across row.
12th row With A, K across row.
13th row With A, P1, * P1 winding yarn twice around needle, P2, P1 winding yarn twice around needle, P6, rep from * to end.
14th row With C, K6, * sl 1 allowing extra loop to fall K2, sl 1 allowing extra loop to fall, K6, rep from * ending last rep K1.
15th row With C, K1, * yfwd, sl 1 P-wise, ybk, K2, yfwd, sl 1 P-wise, ybk, K6, rep from * to end.
16th row With C, K6, * sl 1 P-wise, K2, sl 1 P-wise, K6, rep from * ending last rep K1.
17th-19th rows Rep 15th-16th rows once, then 15th row again.
20th row With A, K6, * cross 4, K6, rep from * ending last rep K1.
These 20 rows form the pattern repeat.

2 Popcorn loop stitch

This stitch works over a multiple of 5 stitches, plus 1 extra, and uses three colors (A, B, C).

1st row (WS) With A, P across row.
2nd row K across row.
3rd row P1, * P1 winding yarn twice around needle, P2, P1 winding yarn twice around needle, P1, rep from * to end.
4th row With B, K1, sl 1 allowing extra loop to fall, K2, sl 1 allowing extra loop to fall, (K1, yfwd, K1, yfwd, K1) all into next st, rep from * ending last rep K1.
5th row With B, K1, * yfwd, sl 1, P2, sl 1, ybk, K5, rep from * to last 5 sts, sl 1, P2, sl 1, ybk, K1.
6th row With B, K1 * ybk, sl 1, K2, sl 1, P5, rep from * to last 5 sts, ybk, sl 1, K2, sl 1, K1.
7th row With B, K1, * yfwd, sl 1, P2, sl 1, K2 tog, K3 tog, pass the 2nd st on RH needle over the last st, rep from * to last 5 sts, yfwd, sl 1, P2, sl 1, ybk, K1.
8th row With A, K1, * sl next st off LH needle and hold at front of work, sl 2, sl next st off needle and hold at front of work, return first st held back onto LH needle, sl 2 sts on RH needle back onto LH needle, return 2nd st held back onto LH needle, K5, rep from * to end.
These 8 rows form the pattern repeat. Cont using contrast colors as required.

1

2

Simon Butcher

3 Checked loop stitch

This is a variation of the loop stitch on the basic sweater. It includes color (C) and is worked over a multiple of 5 stitches, plus 3 extra. Work basic loop stitch as given with 2nd, 3rd and 4th rows as foll:

2nd row With B, P1, sl 1 * P1, with C, P2, with B, P1, sl 1, rep from * to last st, P1.

3rd row With B, K1, sl 1, * K1, with C, K2, with B, K1, sl 1, rep from * to last st, K1.

4th row As 1st row.

3

4 Bobble loop stitch

This stitch is worked over a multiple of 10 stitches, plus 3 extra. It is a variation of the loop stitch on the basic sweater and introduces contrasting color (C).

Work basic loop stitch as given with 3rd, 4th, 9th and 10th rows as foll:

3rd row With C, K1, sl 1, * K4, sl 1, cast on 2 sts, bind off 2 sts, K2, cast on 2 sts, bind off 2 sts, sl 1, rep from * to last st, K1.

4th row With C, K across row.

9th row With C, K1, sl 1, * cast on 2 sts, bind off 2 sts, K2, cast on 2 sts, bind off 2 sts, sl 1, K4, sl 1, rep from * to last st, K1.

10th row With C, K across row.

5 Flower loop stitch

This stitch works over a multiple of 10 stitches, plus 3 extra, and uses three colors (A, B, C).

1st row (RS) With B, K across row.

2nd row With B, K1, * yfwd, sl 1, ybk, K1, rep from * to end.

3rd row With C, K1, * sl 1, K1, rep from * to end.

4th row With C, P1, * sl 1, P1, rep from * to end.

5th-6th rows With B, K across row.

7th row With A, K across row.

8th row With A, P across row.

9th row With B, K across row.

10th row With B, K5, * K3 winding yarn 3 times around needle, K7, rep from * ending last rep K5.

11th row With A, K1, * sl 1, K3, sl 3 allowing extra loops to fall, K3, rep from * ending last rep, sl 1, K1.

12th row With A, P1, * sl 1, P3, sl 3, P3, rep from * ending last rep sl 1, P1.

13th row With A, K5, * sl 3, K7, rep from * ending last rep K5.

14th row With A, P5, * sl 3, P7, rep from * ending last rep P5.

15th row With A, K3, * sl 2, sl next st off needle and hold at front of work, sl 2 sts from RH needle onto LH needle, pick up and K held st, K3, sl next st off needle and hold at front of work, K2, pick up and K held st, K3, rep from * to end.

16th row With C, P1, sl 2, * [(P1, K1, P1) all into next st, sl 2] twice, (P1, K1, P1) all into next st, sl 3, rep from * to last 10 sts, [(P1, K1, P1) all into next st, sl 2] 3 times, P1.

17th row With C, K1, sl 2, * P3, turn, K3, turn, sl 1, K2 tog, psso, — called make bobble (MB) —, (sl 2, MB) twice, sl 3, rep from * to last 16 sts, (MB, sl 2) 3 times, K1.

18th row With A, P to end.

19th-20th rows As 7th-8th rows. These 20 rows form the pattern repeat.

Picot point knitting

Pretty edgings for baby and children's clothes can be made with picot point techniques. They can also be used for creating lace or mesh fabrics and for delicate flower motifs that can be appliquéd onto plainer fabrics.

Skills you need

*Decreasing
*Simple increasing
*Picot point knitting

If you do not know these skills refer to pages 174, 175 and 183.

Materials

Where picot point knitting is used to add decorative edgings it is usually worked in the same yarn as the basic garment. In fine cottons and silks the overall effect is rather delicate and fragile but heavier chunky yarns can also be used and in such cases the picot edge assumes a bolder, more three-dimensional appearance.

The edge can be worked in the same color as the garment or in a contrasting color, as is shown in the basic child's bathrobe, which is knitted in a warm chunky yarn.

Special technique – picot point flowers

1 The bathrobe is appliquéd with flowers made by picot point techniques as follows. Make a slip knot on left-hand needle. Cast on 3 stitches. Bind off 3 stitches. Place remaining loop on left-hand needle.

2 Make another petal into the remaining loop. Make 4 more petals in the same way.

3 Join the petals into a circle by picking up and knitting a stitch into the original slip knot. Bind off 1 stitch and fasten off. Use the end of the yarn to sew the flower to the background fabric.

Coral Mula

The basic picot-trimmed bathrobe

Make this cozy bathrobe in very little time with soft chunky yarn. To make it cheerful and fun add pretty picot edgings and appliqué bright picot flowers to the front.

Sizes
To fit 24[26:28] in. chest
Length 20½[21¼:22] in.
Sleeve seam 10½[12½:13¾] in.

Note: Instructions for larger sizes are in square brackets []; where there is only one set of figures it applies to all sizes.

Gauge
14 sts and 18 rows to 4 in. over stockinette st on size 10 needles.

Materials
16 oz bulky yarn in main color (A)
2 oz in each of contrasting colors (B) and (C)
1 pair each size 9 and 10 knitting needles

Back
Beg at neck edge, using larger needles and A, cast on 18[20:22] sts.

Beg with a K row cont in stockinette st. Work 2 rows.
Shape shoulders
Cast on 7[7:8] sts at beg of next 2 rows and 7[8:8] sts at beg of foll 2 rows. 46[50:54] sts.
Cont in stockinette st until work measures 20½[21¼:22] in. from cast-on edge, edging with a WS row.
**Change to B.
Knit 1 row.
Change to smaller needles. Purl 1 row.

157

Work picot binding-off

Next row *Cast on 2 sts, bind off 3 sts, return st used in binding off back onto LH needle, rep from * to end. **

Right front

Beg at shoulder, using larger needles and A, cast on 7[7:8] sts. Beg with a K row cont in stockinette st. Work 2 rows.

Next row Cast on 7[8:8] sts, work to end.

Work 1 row.

Shape neck

Next row K to last 2 sts, work twice into next st, K1.

Work 3 rows.

Rep the last 4 rows 3 times more.

Work 1 row.

Next row Cast on 4[5:6] sts, work to end. 22[24:26] sts.

Cont in stockinette st until work measures 20½[21¼:22] in. from cast-on edge, ending with a WS row.

Complete as given for back from ** to **.

Left front

Beg at shoulder, using larger needles and A, cast on 7[7:8] sts.

Beg with a K row cont in stockinette st. Work 3 rows.

Next row Cast on 7[8:8] sts, work to end.

Shape neck

Next row K1, work twice into next st, K to end.

Work 3 rows.

Rep the last 4 rows 3 times more.

Next row Cast on 4[5:6] sts, work to end. 22[24:26] sts.

Complete as given for right front.

Sleeves

Using larger needles and A, cast on 48[50:52] sts.

Beg with a K row cont in stockinette st, dec 1 st at each end of every foll 3rd [4th:5th] row until 28[30:32] sts rem. Cont without shaping until work measures 9¾[11¾:13¾] in. from cast-on edge, ending with a WS row.

Complete as given for back from ** to **.

Front edgings (alike)

With RS of work facing, using larger needles and C, pick up and K 46[50:54] sts evenly along front edge.

Beg with a P row work 2 rows stockinette st.

Change to smaller needles. Purl 1 row.

Work picot binding-off

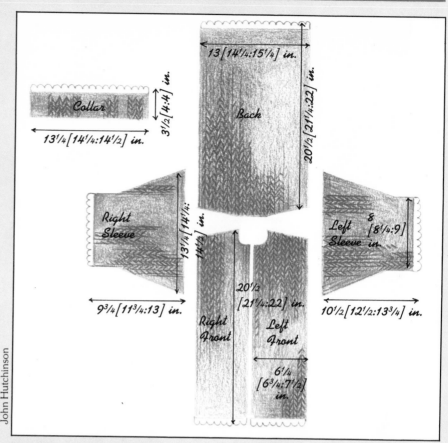

John Hutchinson

Next row *Cast on 2 sts, bind off 3 sts, return st used in binding off back onto LH needle, rep from * to end.

Collar

Using larger needles and A, cast on 48[50:52] sts.

Beg with a K row work in stockinette st for 2¾[3¼:3¼]in. from cast-on edge, ending with a P row.

Complete as given for back from ** to **.

To finish

Join shoulder seams.

Shoulder edgings (alike)

Mark 6¼[6¼:6¾] in. down from shoulder on back and fronts at armhole edge.

With RS of work facing, using larger needles and C, pick up and K 32[32:34] sts between markers.

Complete as given for front edgings.

Front collar edges (both alike)

Using larger needles and B, pick up and K 8 sts from front collar edge.

Purl 1 row. Change to smaller needles.

Work picot binding-off as given for front edgings.

Make 3 picot point flowers (see Special Technique page 157) using smaller needles and oddments. Sew onto garment as shown. Place center of cast-on edge of sleeves to shoulder and set in sleeves.

Sew collar to neck edge joining picot edge at front corners. Join side and sleeve seams.

With C make two twisted cords and sew these to the next edge.

Adapting the bath robe

Plain stockinette stitch fabrics, like that on the bathrobe, can be dressed up in various ways with picot point patterns.

The picot point techniques in the Pattern Library (see page 183 for further information) are most suitable for adding decorative edgings and motifs to existing garments. Try picking up stitches in rows on the plain parts of the fabric and knitting on picot ridges in matching or contrasting colors. The ridges can be worked horizontally across the fabric, or vertically or diagonally. It is also possible to add beads to the edgings, threading on the beads when the contrasting yarn is joined in and placing them at the points of the picots.

Picot point patterns

1 Vertical picot ridges
Picot bound-off ridges can be worked vertically as well as horizontally. Pick up and knit a row of stitches and work the picot row as given for sample 3.

1

2

2 Picot point lattice
This produces a fine mesh fabric. Cast on a multiple of 5 sts, plus 1 extra.
1st row K across row.
2nd row *(Cast on 2 sts, bind off 2 sts, transfer rem st to LH needle) 4 times (called make 4-point chain), bind off 5, transfer rem st on RH needle to LH needle, rep from * to end of row.
3rd row *Make 4-point chain, pick up and K 1 st between 2nd and 3rd points of last 4-point chain of previous row, bind off 1 st, transfer rem st on RH needle onto LH needle, rep from * to end of row.
Rep 3rd row until lattice is required depth. Fasten off.

3 Picot ridges
The picot binding-off method can be used to make decorative ridges on the right side of the work. This technique is best worked on a plain background stitch like the stockinette stitch of the bathrobe. Work a row of purl stitches on the right side of the work at the points on the fabric where the ridges are to be worked. When the garment is completed pick up and knit a row along the purl stitches then work a row of picot points as follows:
Picot row *Cast on 2 sts, bind off 4 sts, return remaining loop on RH needle to LH needle, rep from * to last st, cast on 2 sts, bind off 2 sts. Fasten off.
By binding off varying numbers of stitches between the picot points this ridge can be worked on any number of stitches.

3

Simon Wheeler

Edgings

Edgings can be made separately and sewn onto garments or
knitted in. Either way they give them that extra-special finish.
They range from the simply stylish to extravagant and decorative.

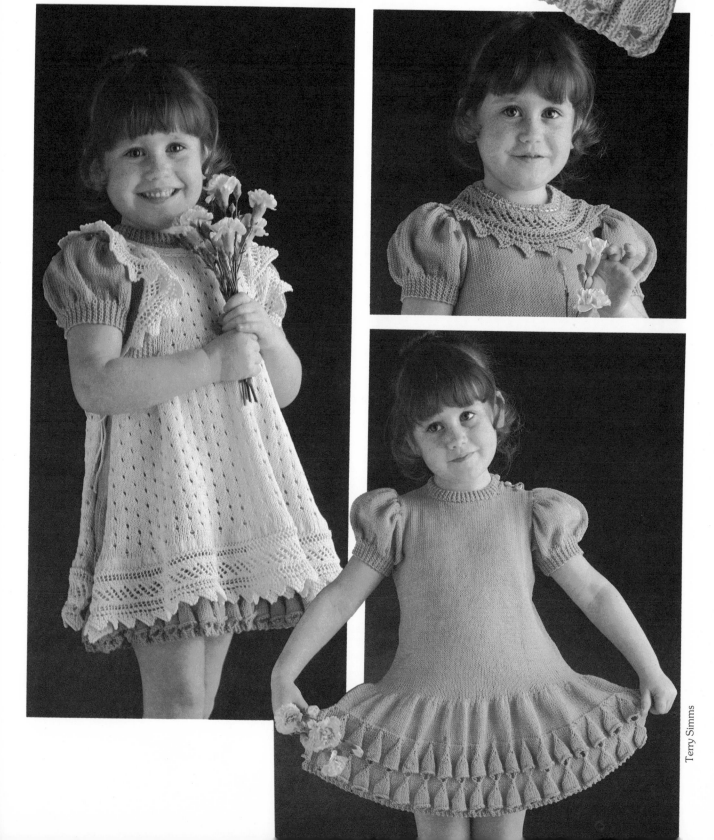

Terry Simms

Skills you need

*Decorative increasing
*Decreasing

If you do not know these skills refer to page 175.

Materials

Edging should be made in a yarn that will complement the main part of the garment. They look especially beautiful worked in fine cottons or light fluffy yarns like mohair and angora. Many of them have eyelet holes that can be used for threading ribbon and they can often be further decorated with small beads or sequins. The basic dress and pinafore are knitted in a fine cotton yarn. The collar can be worn with the tie at the back or front.

Special technique – making buttonholes

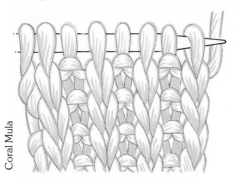 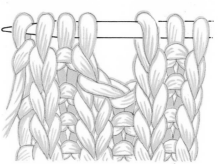 

1 *The back straps of the pinafore dress are fastened with a small buttonhole on the end of each one, buttoning two buttons on the back waistband. Work in twisted ribbing to the buttonhole row.*

2 *On the next row work to the buttonhole position. Bind off 2 stitches (more stitches can be bound off for a larger buttonhole). Work to the next buttonhole position or to end of row.*

3 *On the next row work to the buttonhole position. Cast onto the right-hand needle the same number of stitches as were bound off on the previous row. Work to the next buttonhole position or to end of row.*

The basic party dress and pinafore

This gorgeous party dress, straight from the pages of a fairy tale, will delight any little girl. The dress is trimmed with two layers of bell-like frills. The matching over-pinafore is knitted in a delicate eyelet pattern with lacy edging around the hem and yoke.

Sizes
Dress
To fit 23[24:25] in. chest
Length 18[19¼:20] in.
Sleeve seam 2½ in.
Pinafore
To fit 23-25 in. chest
Length 18 in.

Note: Instructions for larger sizes are in brackets []; where there is only one set of figures it applies to all sizes.

Gauge
Dress
28 sts and 32 rows to 4 in. over stockinette st on size 2 needles
Pinafore
32 sts and 40 rows to 4 in. over stockinette st on size 1 needles

Materials
Dress
13[13:15] oz size 5 silky cotton yarn, 162

such as Pingouin Fil d'Ecosse No. 5
1 pair each sizes 1 and 2 knitting needles
3 buttons
Ribbon (optional)

Pinafore
13 oz size 5 silky cotton yarn
1 pair size 1 knitting needles
2 buttons
Ribbon (optional)

Dress
Back
Using larger needles cast on 160[168:176] sts.
Next row *K1 tbl, P1, rep from * to end.
Rep the last row until work measures ½ in. from the beg. Begin pat.
1st row P4, *cast on 10 sts onto RH needle, P8, rep from * ending last rep P4.
2nd row K4, *P10, K8, rep from *

ending last rep K4.
3rd row P4, *K10, P8, rep from * ending last rep P4.
4th row As 2nd row.
5th row As 3rd row
6th row As 2nd row.
7th row P4, *sl 1, K1, psso, K6, K2 tog, P8, rep from * ending last rep P4.
8th row K4, *P8, K8, rep from * ending last rep K4.
9th row P4, *sl 1, K1, psso, K4, K2 tog, P8, rep from * ending last rep P4.
10th row K4, *P6, K8, rep from * ending last rep K4.
11th row P4, *sl 1, K1, psso, K2, K2 tog, P8, rep from * ending last rep P4.
12th row K4, *P4, K8, rep from * ending last rep K4.
13th row P4, *sl 1, K1, psso, K2 tog, P8, rep from * ending last rep P4.
14th row K4, *P2, K8, rep from * ending last rep K4.
15th row P4, *K2 tog, P8, rep from * ending last rep P4.
16th row K4, *P1, K8, rep from * ending last rep K4.
17th row P3, *K2 tog, P7, rep from * ending last rep P4.
18th row K to end.

These 18 rows form the pat. Work a further 18 rows.

Change to stockinette st. Beg with a K row work a further 1½[2:2½] in. ending with a P row. This point marks "hipline" — skirt length may be adjusted here.

Next row K2[0:1], *K1, K2 tog, rep from * to last 2[0:1] sts, K2[0:1]. 108 [112:118] sts.

Next row P across row.

Next row K10[1:4], *K2[3:3], K2 tog, rep from * to last 10[1:4] sts, K10[1:4]. 86[90:96] sts.

Beg with a P row cont in stockinette st until work measures 14[15¼:16] in. from the beg, ending with a P row. Length to armhole may be adjusted here.

Shape armholes

Bind off 6[8:11] sts at beg of next 2 rows and 2 sts at beg of foll 4 rows. 66 sts.**

Cont in stockinette st until work measures 18[19¼:20] in. from the beg, ending with a P row.

Shape shoulders

Bind off 4 sts at beg of next 4 rows and 10 sts at beg of foll 2 rows. Bind off the rem sts.

Front

Work as given for back to **. Cont in stockinette st until work measures 16[17¼:18] in. from the beg, ending with a P row.

Shape neck

Next row K22, bind off 22 sts, K to end.

Work right side of neck first.

Next row P to last 2 sts, P2 tog.

Next row K2 tog, K to end.

Rep the last 2 rows once more. 18 sts. Beg with a P row cont in stockinette st until work matches back to shoulder shaping ending at armhole edge.

Shape shoulder

Bind off 4 sts at beg of the next and foll alt row. Work 1 row. Bind off rem sts. Return to sts on left side of neck. With WS facing, rejoin yarn to next st.

Next row P2 tog, P to end.

Next row K to last 2 sts, K2 tog.

Rep the last 2 rows once more. Complete to match first side of neck, reversing shaping.

Sleeves

Using smaller needles cast on 60 sts.

Next row *K1 tbl, P1, rep from *.

Rep the last row until work measures 1¼ in. from the beg.

Change to larger needles.

Next row *K twice into next st, rep from * to end. 120 sts.

Beg with a P row, cont in stockinette st until work measures 2½ in. from beg, ending with a P row. Sleeve length may be adjusted here.

Shape sleeve top

Bind off 8 sts at beg of next 2 rows and 2 sts at beg of foll 4 rows. 96 sts. Dec 1 st at each end of every row until 48 sts rem. Bind off 6 sts at beg of next 4 rows. Bind off the rem 24 sts.

Detachable collar

Using larger needles cast on 18 sts.

Next row (WS) K6, P7, K5.

Begin pat.

1st row Sl 1, K2, yfwd, K2 tog, K2, K2 tog, yfwd, K5, yfwd, K2 tog, (yfwd, K1) twice.

2nd row K6, yfwd, K2 tog, P7, K2, yfwd, K2 tog, K1.

3rd row Sl 1, K2, yfwd, K2 tog, K1, (K2 tog, yfwd) twice, K4, yfwd, K2 tog, (yfwd, K1) twice, K2.

4th row K8, yfwd, K2 tog, P7, K2, yfwd, K2 tog, K1.

5th row Sl 1, K2, yfwd, K2 tog, (K2 tog, yfwd) 3 times, K3, yfwd, K2 tog, (yfwd, K1) twice, K4.

6th row K10, yfwd, K2 tog, P7, K2, yfwd, K2 tog, K1.

7th row Sl 1, K2, yfwd, K2 tog, K1, (K2 tog, yfwd) twice, K4, yfwd, K2 tog, (yfwd, K1) twice, K6.

8th row Bind off 8 sts, K4 including st used in binding off, yfwd, K2 tog, P7, K2, yfwd, K2 tog, K1.

These 8 rows form the pat.

Rep these 8 rows 14 times more.

*** Cont in garter st (every row K).

Bind off 4 sts at beg of next 2 rows.

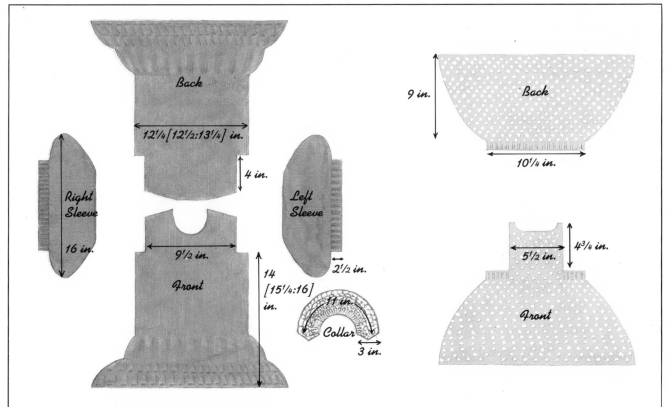

Dec 1 st at each end of the next and every other row until 2 sts rem.
Next row K2 tog and fasten off.
With RS of work facing, pick up and K 10 sts from cast-on edge.
Work from *** to end.

To finish
Join right shoulder seam.
Neckband
With RS of work facing, using smaller needles pick up and K 84 sts evenly around neck edge.
Work in ribbing as given for back for ½ in., ending with a WS row. Bind off in ribbing. Press lightly as instructed on yarn label, taking care not to flatten pat. Join side seams, matching pat. Sew together ½ in. at armhole edge of left shoulder seam. Join sleeve seams, set in sleeves gathering sleeve head to fit. Sew buttons to front shoulder and make button loops to correspond.
Pin collar to a curve to fit neck edge and press firmly. Either thread ribbon through eyelet holes on collar or make plaited cord.

Pinafore
Back
Using smaller needles cast on 336 sts.
Beg with a K row work 5 rows in stockinette st.
Next row *P2 tog, rep from * to end. 168 sts.
Begin pat.
1st row K across row.
2nd and every other row P across row.
3rd row *K6, yfwd, K2 tog, rep from * to end.
5th row K across row.
7th row K2, *yfwd, K2 tog, K6, rep from * ending last rep K4.
8th row P across row.
These 8 rows form the pat. Cont in pat until work measures 9 in. from the beg, ending with an 8th pat row.
Pinafore length may be adjusted here.
Next row (RS) *K2 tog, rep from * to end. 84 sts.
Next row P across row. **
Next row *K1 tbl, P1, rep from * to

Simon Butcher

end.
Rep the last row 5 times more.
Bind off in ribbing.

Front
Work as given for back to **.
1st row (K1 tbl, P1) 10 times, K7, (yfwd, K2 tog, K6) 4 times, yfwd, K2 tog, K3, (P1, K1 tbl) 10 times.
2nd row (P1, K1 tbl) 10 times, P44, (K1 tbl, P1) 10 times.
3rd row (K1 tbl, P1) 10 times, K44, (P1, K1 tbl) 10 times.
4th row As 2nd row.
5th row (K1 tbl, P1) 10 times, K3 (yfwd, K2 tog, K6) 5 times, K1, (P1, K1 tbl) 10 times.
6th row As 2nd row
7th row Bind off 20 sts in ribbing. K to last 20 sts, (P1, K1 tbl) 10 times.
8th row Bind off 20 sts in ribbing, P to end. 44 sts.
Cont in pat.
1st row (RS) K1, *K6, yfwd, K2 tog, rep from * to last 3 sts, K3.
2nd and every other row P across row.
3rd row K across row.
5th row K3, yfwd, K2 tog, *K6, yfwd, K2 tog, rep from * to last 7 sts, K7.
7th row K across row.
8th row P across row.
These 8 rows form the pat. Rep these 8 rows 4 times more, ending with an 8th pat row. Length of pinafore may be adjusted here.
Shape neck
Next row K8, bind off 28 sts, K to end.
Complete right side of neck first.
Next row P to last 2 sts, P2 tog.
Next row K2 tog, K to end.
Rep the last 2 rows twice. Bind off rem 2 sts.
Return to sts at left side of neck. With WS of work facing, rejoin yarn to next st.
Next row P2 tog, P to end.
Next row K to last 2 sts, K2 tog.
Rep the last 2 rows twice. Bind off rem 2 sts.

Hem edging (make 2 pieces)
The pieces are worked sideways.
Using smaller needles cast on 18 sts.
Next row (WS) K6, P7, K5.

Begin pat.
1st row Sl 1, K2, yfwd, K2 tog, K2, K2 tog, yfwd, K5, yfwd, K2 tog, (yfwd, K1) twice.
2nd row K6, yfwd, K2 tog, P7, K2, yfwd, K2 tog, K1.
3rd row Sl 1, K2, yfwd, K2 tog, K1, (K2 tog, yfwd) twice, K4, yfwd, K2 tog, (yfwd, K1) twice, K2.
4th row K8, yfwd, K2 tog, P7, K2, yfwd, K2 tog, Kl.
5th row Sl 1, K2, yfwd, K2 tog, (K2 tog, yfwd) 3 times, K3, yfwd, K2 tog, (yfwd, K1) twice, K4.
6th row K10, yfwd, K2 tog, P7, K2, yfwd, K2 tog, K1.
7th row Sl 1, K2, yfwd, K2 tog, K1, (K2 tog, yfwd) twice, K4, yfwd, K2 tog, (yfwd, K1) twice, K6.
8th row Bind off 8 sts, K3, yfwd, K2 tog, P7, K2, yfwd, K2 tog, K1.
These 8 rows form the pat. Rep rows 1-8 inclusive 41 times more. Bind off.

Yoke edging (make 2 pieces)
Work as given for hem edging for 16 in. ending with an 8th pat row. Bind off.

Neckband and straps
Using smaller needles cast on 8 sts.
Next row *K1 tbl, P1, rep from *.
Rep the last row until work measures ½ in. from the beg.
1st buttonhole row Rib 3, bind off 2, rib to end.
2nd buttonhole row Rib, casting on over those sts bound off in previous row. Cont in ribbing until work measures 19½ in. from the beg, ending with a WS row.
Length may be adjusted here.
Now work the 2 buttonhole rows again. Work a further ½ in. in ribbing. Bind off in ribbing.

To finish
Join hem edging pieces and sew to hem. Sew neckband to yoke. Sew edging to yoke and band, gathering slightly. Cut ribbon into 4, or make 4 simple plaited cords and sew under arms. Sew buttons on waistband at center back.

1

Adapting the party dress and pinafore

The edgings shown in the Pattern Library can be used instead of those on the pinafore.

Altering the length

At various points in the pattern — at the hipline, before the armhole shaping and before the sleeve head shaping on the dress and before the waist shaping on the pinafore — the length of the garments may be adjusted to suit your child's height. At these points work more or fewer rows in pattern to make the garments longer or shorter.

Edging patterns

1 Basic bell edging

The bell edging on the child's dress is worked from the bottom up. This one is worked from the top down. It can be made separately and sewn onto the finished garment. It works over a multiple of 6 stitches, plus 1 extra.

1st-5th rows K across row.
6th row K3, *P1, K5, rep from * ending last rep K3.
7th row P3, *yo, K1, yo, P5, rep from * ending last rep P3.
8th row K3, *P3, K5, rep from * ending last rep K3.
9th row P3, *yo, K3, yo, P5, rep from * ending last rep P3.
10th row K3, *P5, K5, rep from * ending last rep K3.
11th row P3, *yo, K5, yo, P5, rep from * ending last rep P3.
12th row K3, *P7, K5, rep from * ending last rep K3.
13th row P3, *yo, K7, yo, P5, rep from * ending last rep P3.
14th row K3, *P9, K5, rep from * ending last rep K3.
15th row P3, *yo, K9, yo, P5, rep from * ending last rep P3.
16th row K3, *P11, K5, rep from * ending last rep K3.
Bind off in pattern. This ruffle can be made longer and fuller by continuing to increase as set each side of the "bells".

Substituting edgings

Either of the edgings in the pattern library that are worked sideways can be used instead of the lacy edging on the pinafore dress. Simply cast on the given number of stitches and work the edging until it is long enough to fit the front of the pinafore. Make a piece the same length for the back. Make two more pieces to fit either side of the yoke and down the neckband to make the back straps.

2 Saw-toothed edging

This edging is worked from side to side. Cast on 9 stitches.
1st row K across row.
2nd row P across row.
3rd row Sl 1, K2, yfwd, K2 tog tbl, K2 tbl, make 1 by knitting up loop between last st worked and next st from front (called M1), K2 tbl.
4th row K2 tbl, P1, P2 tbl, K2, yfwd, K2 tog tbl, P1.
5th row Sl 1, K2, yfwd, K2 tog tbl, K3 tbl, M1, K2 tbl.
6th row K2 tbl, P1, P3 tbl, K2, yfwd, K2 tog tbl, P1.
7th row Sl 1, K2, yfwd, K2 tog tbl, K4 tbl, M1, K2 tbl.
8th row K2 tbl, P1, P4 tbl, K2, yfwd, K2 tog tbl, P1.
9th row Sl 1, K2, yfwd, K2 tog tbl, K5 tbl, M1, K2 tbl.
10th row K2 tbl, P1, P5 tbl, K2, yfwd, K2 tog tbl, P1.
11th row Sl 1, K2, yfwd, K2 tog tbl, K6 tbl, M1, K2 tbl.
12th row K2 tbl, P1, P6 tbl, K2, yfwd, K2 tog tbl, P1.
13th row Sl 1, K2, yfwd, K2 tog tbl, K7 tbl, M1, K2 tbl.
14th row K2 tbl, P1, P7 tbl, K2, yfwd, K2 tog tbl, P1.
15th and 17th rows Sl 1, K2, yfwd, K2 tog tbl, K10 tbl.
16th row K10 tbl, K2, yfwd, K2 tog tbl, P1.
18th row Bind off 6 sts, K1 tbl, P1, P1 tbl, K2, yfwd, K2 tog tbl, P1.
The 3rd-18th rows form the pattern repeat.

3

3 Leaf edging

This edging if worked sideways. Cast on 8 stitches.
1st row (RS) K5, yfwd, K1, yfwd, K2.
2nd row P6, inc 1 by knitting into the front and back of next st, K3.
3rd row K4, P1, K2, yfwd, K1, yfwd, K3.
4th row P8, inc 1, K4.
5th row K4, P2, K3, yfwd, K1, yfwd, K4.
6th row P10, inc 1, K5.
7th row K4, P3, K4, yfwd, K1, yfwd, K5.
8th row P12, inc 1, K6.
9th row K4, P4, sl 1, K1, psso, K7, K2 tog, K1.
10th row P10, inc 1, K7.
11th row K4, P5, sl 1, K1, psso, K5, K2 tog, K1.
12th row P8, inc 1, K2, P1, K5.
13th row K4, P1, K1, P4, sl 1, K1, psso, K3, K2 tog, K1.
14th row P6, inc 1, K3, P1, K5.
15th row K4, P1, K1, P5, sl 1, K1, psso, K1, K2 tog, K1.
16th row P4, inc 1, K4, P1, K5.
17th row K4, P1, K1, P6, sl 1, K2 tog, psso, K1.
18th row P2 tog, bind off next 5 sts using P2 tog to bind off first st, P3, K4.
These 18 rows form the pattern repeat.

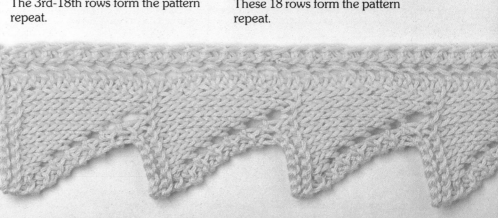

Entrelacs

Entrelacs (from the French for "interlacing") produce fascinating woven fabrics. They can be worked in one or more colors and the method used is surprisingly simple to work.

Skills you need

*Picking up stitches
*Decreasing

If you do not know these skills refer to pages 175 and 177.

Materials

Entrelacs can be worked in one or two colors to produce a simple woven look. When more than two colors are used interesting woven color effects can be achieved. Any type of yarn can be used — combinations of two textures can form very interesting effects. When using only one color try adding bobbles, beads or small stitch patterns. These can be used in a regular pattern or dotted over the work at random. Combinations of yarns, patterns and trimmings that can be used are endless and it is worth experimenting with small samples to produce a design that you will enjoy knitting.

Special technique – working triangles and rectangles

Coral Mula

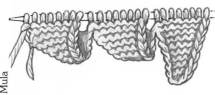

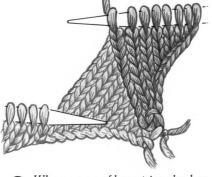

1 Stitches are cast on for the width of the fabric, then each base triangle is worked separately by working turning rows — beginning with two stitches and working one more stitch on every other row until the correct number of stitches is on the right-hand needle. For this sample eight stitches are used for each triangle.

2 When a row of base triangles has been worked turn the work and work a selvege triangle — see sweater pattern for full instructions. The eight stitches of the selvege triangle are left on the right-hand needle.

3 To work the rectangle, pick up eight stitches along the side of the first base triangle, then work on these stitches only. Form subsequent rectangles by picking up stitches along the side of base triangles. Form subsequent rows of rectangles by picking up stitches from rectangles and selvege triangles.

The basic entrelacs sweater

This military-style sweater knitted in bicolor entrelacs has practical shoulder buttoning and would look good on any active youngster.

Sizes
To fit 24-27 [28-31] in. chest.
Length 19 [21] in.
Sleeve seam 13 [15¼] in.

Note: Instructions for larger size are in square brackets []; where there is only one set of figures it applies to both sizes.
166

Gauge
28 sts and 36 rows to 4 in. over stockinette st on size 3 needles.

Materials
14[16] oz sport-weight yarn in main color (A)
6 oz in contrasting color (B)

1 pair each size 2 and 3 knitting needles
6 buttons

Back
Using larger needles and A, cast on 64[72] sts loosely. Form base triangles by working turning rows.

Ray Moller

1st row (WS) P2, turn.
2nd row K2.
3rd row P3, turn.
4th row K3.
5th row P4, turn.
6th row K4.
7th row P5, turn.
8th row K5.
9th row P6, turn.
10th row K6.
11th row P7, turn.
12th row K7.
13th row P8, do not turn.
First triangle completed. Leave these 8 sts on right-hand needle and rep last

13 rows 7[8] times more, so forming 8[9] triangles.
Cut off A.
*Join in B and work across first 8 sts for selvege triangle.
1st row K2, turn.
2nd row P2.
3rd row Inc in first st by working into front and back of st, sl 1, K1, psso, turn.
4th row P3.
5th row Inc in first st, K1, sl 1, K1, psso, turn.
6th row P4.
7th row Inc in first st, K2, sl 1, K1,

psso, turn.
8th row P5.
9th row Inc in first st, K3, sl 1, K1, psso, turn.
10th row P6.
11th row Inc in first st, K4, sl 1, K1, psso, turn.
12th row P7.
13th row Inc in first st, K5, sl 1, K1, psso, do not turn.
Selvege triangle completed. Leave these 8 sts on right-hand needle and work first rectangle.
****1st row** Pick up and K 8 sts along side of base triangle, turn.

167

2nd row P8.
3rd row K7, sl 1, K1, psso, turn —
two sections joined.
Rep 2nd and 3rd rows until all 8 sts
from base triangle have been dec,
ending with a 3rd row.**
Rep from ** to ** 6[7] times more.
Work selvege triangle.
1st row Pick up and K 8 sts along side
of last triangle worked, turn.
2nd row P2 tog, P6, turn.
3rd and every other row K across
row.
4th row P2 tog, P5, turn.
6th row P2 tog, P4, turn.
8th row P2 tog, P3, turn.
10th row P2 tog, P2, turn.
12th row P2 tog, P1, turn.
14th row P2 tog.
Cut off B.
Join in A and work rectangles.
1st row Pick up and P 7 sts along side
of triangle just worked. 8 sts.
2nd row K8.
3rd row P7, P2 tog, turn.
Rep 2nd and 3rd rows until all 8 sts
from next rectangle have been dec,
ending with a 3rd row.
Do not turn after last row.
Leave these 8 sts on right-hand
needle.
***Pick up and P 8 sts alongside of
next rectangle.
Rep 2nd and 3rd rows until all 8 sts
from next rectangle have been dec,
ending with a 3rd row.
Do not turn after last row. ***
Rep from *** to *** 6[7] times more.
Cut off A.*
Rep from * to * until work measures
approx 11½[13] in. from beg, ending
with a row of rectangles and two
selvege triangles worked in B.
Cut off B.
Join in A and work a row of triangles
to complete pat.
1st row Pick up and P 8 sts along side
of last triangle worked, turn. 9 sts.
2nd row K9.
3rd row P2 tog, P6, P2 tog, turn.
4th row K8.
5th row P2 tog, P5, P2 tog, turn.
6th row K7.
7th row P2 tog, P4, P2 tog, turn.
8th row K6.
9th row P2 tog, P3, P2 tog, turn.
10th row K5.
11th row P2 tog, P2, P2 tog, turn.
12th row K4.
13th row P2 tog, P1, P2 tog, turn.
14th row K3.
15th row (P2 tog) twice, turn.
16th row K2.
17th row P3 tog, do not turn.
168

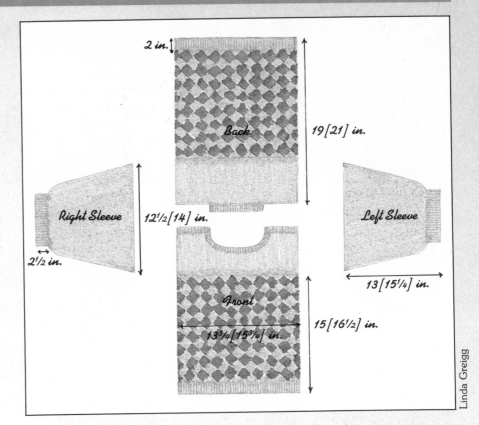

2 in.

19[21] in.

Back

12½[14] in.

Right Sleeve

2½ in.

Left Sleeve

Front

13[15¼] in.

13¾[15¾] in.

15[16½] in.

Linda Greigg

Rep first to 17th rows until 8[9]
triangles have been worked and 1 st
remains. Do not cut off yarn, turn.
Begin yoke
With RS facing using larger needles
and A, pick up and K 98[110] sts
across top of triangles just worked.
99[111] sts.
Beg with a P row, work 4[4½] in.
stockinette st, ending with a K row.
Shape shoulders
1st row P to last 8[9] sts, turn.
2nd row Sl 1, K to last 8[9] sts, turn.
3rd row Sl 1, P to last 16[18] sts, turn.
4th row Sl 1, K to last 16[18] sts, turn.
5th row Sl 1, P to last 24[26] sts, turn.
6th row Sl 1, K to last 24[26] sts, turn.
7th row Sl 1, P to last 31[34] sts, turn.
8th row Sl 1, K to last 31[34] sts, turn.
9th row P across all 99[111] sts.
Cut off A.

Back neck border
Sl 31[34] sts from each side onto a
holder.
With RS facing, using smaller needles
and A, K across center 37[43] sts inc
2 sts evenly across the row. 39[45] sts.
Next row P1, *K1, P1, rep from * to
end.
Next row K1, *P1, K1, rep from * to
end.
Rep the last 2 rows 3 times more.
Bind off in ribbing.

Front
Work as for back until 11[13] rows
fewer have been worked to beg of
shoulder shaping, ending with a P
row.
Divide for neck
Next row K37[42], K2 tog, turn and
leave rem sts on a spare needle.
Complete left side of neck first. Dec 1
st at neck edge on next 6[8] rows.
Work 1 row.
Dec 1 st at neck edge on next row.
31[34] sts.
Work 2 rows.

Shape shoulder
1st row (WS) P23[25], turn.
2nd and every other row Sl 1, K to
end.
3rd row P15[16], turn.
5th row P7[8] turn.
6th row K across row.
Leave all 31[34] sts on a holder.
With RS facing place center 21[23] sts
from spare needle onto a holder, join
A to next st, K2 tog, K to end. 38[43]
sts.
Work to match first side, reversing
shaping.

Sleeves
Using smaller needles and A, cast on
46[50] sts.
Work 2½ in. in K1, P1 ribbing.
Next row (WS) Rib 1[5], pick up and

K the loop between last st worked and next st on left-hand needle (called M1), (rib 4[3], M1) 11[13] times, rib 1[6]. 58[64] sts.
Change to larger needles and beg with a K row, work in stockinette st inc 1 st each end of every foll 5th row until there are 90[102] sts. Cont without shaping until work measures 13[15¼] in. from cast-on edge ending with a P row. Bind off.

To finish
Press sleeves and yoke only on WS.

Front neck border
With RS facing, using smaller needles and A, pick up and K 14[16] sts down left side of neck, K the sts from the holder, then pick up and K 14[16] sts up right side of neck. 49[55] sts.
Work 8 rows in K1, P1 ribbing as given for back neck border.
Bind off in ribbing.

Shoulder borders
Right back
With RS facing, using smaller needles and A, K31[34] sts from shoulder inc 2 sts evenly, then pick up and K 6 sts from back neck border. 39[42] sts.
Work 8 rows in K1, P1 ribbing as for back neck border. Bind off in ribbing.

Left back
Start at top of back neck border and work as for right back border.

Left front
With RS facing, using smaller needles and A, K31[34] sts from shoulder inc 2[3] sts evenly, then pick up and K 6 sts up front neck border. 39[43] sts.
Work 3 rows K1, P1 ribbing as for back neck border.
1st buttonhole row (Rib 10[11], bind off 2) 3 times, rib 3[4].
2nd buttonhole row Rib to end, casting on 2 sts over those bound off in previous row.
Work 3 rows in ribbing.
Bind off in ribbing.

Right front
Work as for left front, starting at top neck border and working first buttonhole row as foll:
Buttonhole row Rib 3[4], (bind off 2, rib 10[11] sts) 3 times.
Waistbands (back and front alike)
With RS facing, using smaller needles and A, pick up and K 96[102] sts evenly along lower edge.
Work 2 in. K1, P1 ribbing. Bind off in ribbing. Lap front over back to depth of ribbing. Mark 6¼[7] in. down from shoulders on back and front. Sew sleeves between markers. Join side and sleeve seams. Sew on buttons.

Adapting the entrelacs sweater

Many of the entrelacs patterns on the following pages can be easily adapted to the basic sweater pattern. Try working with one color only and adding texture by working bobbles into the knitting or adding studs or beads when the fabric is finished.

Choosing yarn
Always choose two yarns of the same thickness. If you use yarns of different thicknesses you will find that your work will be distorted and unbalanced. Also remember to take the stitch pattern into account — do not use a textured yarn with a textured stitch because you will lose any detail.

Gauge
Always knit a test sample before you begin your garment because your gauge may change if you are working a detailed pattern. This applies especially where cables are to be worked. If you are simply adding beads or studs your gauge should not alter.

Entrelacs patterns

1 Mohair entrelacs
Work entrelacs as given in the basic sweater pattern using two contrasting fluffy yarns.

2 Glitter entrelacs
Work entrelacs as given in the basic sweater pattern using a glitter mixture for A and a plain yarn for B.

1

2

3 Reverse entrelacs

With A, cast on a multiple of 8 sts. Form base triangles by working turning rows.

1st row (WS) K2, turn.
2nd row P2.
3rd row K3, turn.
4th row P3.
5th row K4, turn.
6th row P4.
7th row K5, turn.
8th row P5.
9th row K6, turn.
10th row P6.
11th row K7, turn.
12th row P7.
13th row K8, do not turn.

First triangle completed. Leave these 8 sts on right-hand needle and rep last 13 rows to end. Cut off A.
*Join in B and work across first 8 sts for selvege triangle.

1st row P2, turn.
2nd row K2.
3rd row Inc in first st, P2 tog, turn.
4th row K3.
5th row Inc in first st, P1, P2 tog, turn.
6th row K4.
7th row Inc in first st, P2, P2 tog, turn.
8th row K5.
9th row Inc in first st, P3, P2 tog, turn.
10th row K6.
11th row Inc in first st, P4, P2 tog, turn.
12th row K7.
13th row Inc in first st, P5, P2 tog, do not turn.

Selvege triangle completed. Leave these 8 sts on right-hand needle and work first rectangle.

**1st row Pick up and P 8 sts along side of next section, turn.
2nd row K8.
3rd row P7, P2 tog, turn — two sections joined.
Rep 2nd and 3rd rows until all 8 sts from section have been dec, ending with a 3rd row.**
Rep from ** to ** to end.
Work selvege triangle.
1st row Pick up and P 8 sts along side of last section, turn.
2nd row Sl 1, K1, psso, K6, turn.
3rd and every other row P across row.
4th row Sl 1, K1, psso K5, turn.
6th row Sl 1, K1, psso, K4, turn.
8th row Sl 1, K1, psso, K3, turn.
10th row Sl 1, K1, psso, K2, turn.
12th row Sl 1, K1, psso, K1, turn.
14th row Sl 1, K1, psso, do not turn.
Cut off B. Join in A and work rectangles.
1st row Pick up and K 7 sts along side of triangle just worked, turn. 8 sts.
2nd row P8.
3rd row K7, sl 1, K1, psso, turn.
Rep 2nd and 3rd rows until all 8 sts from next rectangle have been dec, ending with a 3rd row. Do not turn after last row. Leave these 8 sts on right-hand needle.
***Pick up and K 8 sts along side of next rectangle. Rep 2nd and 3rd rows until all 8 sts from next rectangle have been dec, ending with a 3rd row. Do not turn after last row. ***
Rep from *** to *** to end. Cut off A.*
Rep from * to * for depth required,

ending with a row of rectangles and 2 selvege triangles worked in B. Cut off B.
Join in A and work a row of triangles to complete pat.
1st row Pick up and K 8 sts along side of last triangles worked, turn. 9 sts.
2nd row P9.
3rd row Sl 1, K1, psso, K6, sl 1, K1, psso, turn.
4th row P8.
5th row Sl 1, K1, psso, K5, sl 1, K1, psso, turn.
6th row P7.
7th row Sl 1, K1, psso, K4, sl 1, K1, psso, turn.
8th row P6.
9th row Sl 1, K1, psso, K3, sl 1, K1, psso, turn.
10th row P5.
11th row Sl 1, K1, psso, K2, sl 1, K1, psso, turn.
12th row P4.
13th row Sl 1, K1, psso, K1, sl 1, K1, psso, turn.
14th row P3.
15th row (Sl 1, K1, psso) twice.
16th row P2.
17th row Sl 1, K2 tog, psso, do not turn.
Rep first to 17th rows to end.
Fasten off.

4 Bobble entrelacs

Work entrelacs as given in basic sweater pattern, working a large purl bobble (see page 179) in the center of each rectangle. The sample is worked in one color only but it could equally well be knitted in two colors.

3

4

5 Four-color entrelacs

Using A, cast on a multiple of 6 sts. Form base triangles by working turning rows.

1st row (WS) With A, P2, turn.
2nd row K2.
3rd row P3, turn.
4th row K3.
5th row P4, turn.
6th row K4.
7th row P5, turn.
8th row K5.
9th row P6, do not turn.
First triangle completed. Leave these 6 sts on right-hand needle. With B, rep last 9 rows. Alternating A and B rep last 9 rows to end. Cut off A and B. Join in C and work across first 6 sts for selvege triangle.

1st row K2, turn.
2nd row P2.
3rd row Inc in first st, sl 1, K1, psso, turn.
4th row P3.
5th row Inc in first st, K1, sl 1, K1, psso, turn.
6th row P4.
7th row Inc in first st, K2, sl 1, K1, psso, turn.
8th row P5.
9th row Inc in first st, K3, sl 1, K1, psso, do not turn.
Selvege triangle completed. Leave these 6 sts on right-hand needle. Join in D and work first rectangle.
*__1st row__ Pick up and K 6 sts along side of base triangle, turn.
2nd row P6.
3rd row K5, sl 1, K1, psso, turn — two sections joined.

Rep 2nd and 3rd rows until all 6 sts from base triangle have been dec, ending with a 3rd row, do not turn.* Alternating C and D, rep from * to * to end. Work selvege triangle.

1st row Pick up and K 6 sts along side of last triangle, turn.
2nd row P2 tog, P4, turn.
3rd and every other row K across row.
4th row P2 tog, P3, turn.
6th row P2 tog, P2, turn.
8th row P2 tog, P1, turn.
10th row P2 tog, do not turn.
Cut off C and D. Join in B and work rectangles.

1st row Pick up and P 5 sts along side of triangle just worked. 6 sts.
2nd row K6
3rd row P5, P2 tog, turn.
Rep 2nd and 3rd rows until all 6 sts from next rectangle have been dec, ending with a 3rd row. Do not turn after last row. Leave these 6 sts on right-hand needle. Join in A.
Pick up and P 6 sts along side of next rectangle. Rep 2nd and 3rd rows until all 6 sts from next rectangle have been dec, ending with a 3rd row. Do not turn after last row.
Alternating B and A rep from ** to ** to end. Cut off A and B. Join in D and work across first 6 sts for selvege triangle as before. Join in C.
Alternating C and D, work rectangles to end. With D, pick up and K 6 sts along side of last rectangle and work a selvege triangle as before. Cut off C and D. Join in A.
Pick up and P 6 sts along side of

triangle just worked. 6 sts.
Work rectangle as before. Join in B. Alternating B and A work rectangles, as before, to end. Cut off A and B. Continue in this way, alternating C and D, B and A, D and C and A and B for depth required, ending with selvege triangles worked at each end in D.
Join in A and work a row of triangles to complete pat.
1st row Pick up and P 6 sts along side of next triangle, turn, 7 sts.
2nd row K7.
3rd row P2 tog, P4, P2 tog, turn.
4th row K6.
5th row P2 tog, P3, P2 tog, turn.
6th row K5.
7th row P2 tog, P2, P2 tog, turn.
8th row K4.
9th row P2 tog, P1, P2 tog, turn.
10th row K3.
11th row (P2 tog) twice, turn.
12th row K2.
13th row P3 tog, do not turn.
Rep first to 13th rows to end. Fasten off.

More design ideas

Complex shaping should be avoided when knitting entrelacs. As a square or rectangle incorporated into a coat or dress, or as paneling around the bottom of a skirt, entrelacs looks most effective. This dog's coat has been knitted as a basic rectangle with increases and decreases in plain stockinette stitch. For an article such as this to remember to use a machine-washable, hardwearing yarn.

5

Learning to knit is easy but to knit well needs practice. Start getting the feel of using needles to make stitches by using up odd scraps of yarn before attempting your first pattern. Choose a pair of needles that are comfortable to hold – neither too short nor too long. Try to work to a regular rhythm – this will keep your stitches even, creating a good tension and a neat finish.

Holding the yarn and the needles

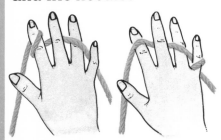

1 The working yarn can be held in either the left or right hand. Threading the yarn between the fingers helps control both the speed and evenness of the knitting. The two methods shown are right-hand methods — usually easier for beginners — where the yarn is looped either around the index finger or around the little finger.

2 There are several ways of holding the needles. Most people experiment until they find a method that suits them and is both comfortable and efficient. The method shown is popular since it provides a firm, but not rigid, hold in which the needles can be easily used. The needle in the left hand is referred to as the left-hand needle, the needle held in the right hand as the right-hand needle.

Casting on

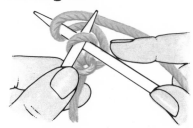

1 The cable method produces a firm, elastic edge suitable for most purposes. Make a slip knot and place it on the left-hand needle. Insert the right-hand needle through the front of the loop as shown. Take the yarn under and over the point of the right-hand needle.

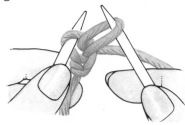

2 Draw the yarn through the loop on the left-hand needle, thus making a new loop on the right-hand needle. Transfer the loop on the right-hand needle to the left-hand needle.

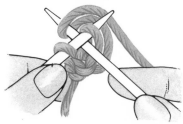

3 Insert the right-hand needle between the loops on the left-hand needle. Take the yarn under and over the point of the right-hand needle.

4 Draw the yarn between the loops on the left-hand needle. Place the new loop on the left-hand needle. Repeat stages 3 and 4 until the required number of stitches has been cast on.

The knit stitch (K)

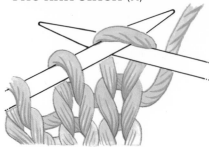

1 Take the needle holding the stitches in your left hand. With the yarn at the back of the work insert the right-hand needle through the front of the first stitch.

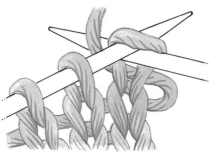

2 Take the yarn under and over the point of the right-hand needle.

3 Draw the yarn on the right-hand needle through the stitch on the left-hand needle.

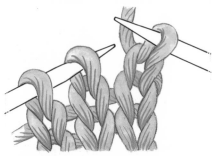

4 Slip the left-hand stitch off the needle, so completing the knit stitch. Knitting every row forms a garter stitch (g st) fabric.

Together with the knit stitch and casting on, the following skills are the bare bones of the craft of knitting. All the other skills are based on these.

The purl stitch (P)

1 Hold the needle with the cast-on stitches in your left hand. With the yarn at the front of the work insert the right-hand needle through the front of the first stitch from right to left.

2 Take the yarn over and under the point of the right-hand needle.

3 Draw the yarn on the right-hand needle through the stitch on the left-hand needle. Slip the left-hand stitch off the needle, so completing the purl stitch.

Joining in new yarn

Ideally new yarn should be joined in at the beginning of a row. It takes a length of yarn roughly four times the width of the knitting to complete a row. If the yarn is too short, let it hang at the edge of the work. Take a new ball and start the new row. Knot and darn both ends in at the wrong side when finishing.

Splicing yarn

Occasionally new yarn must be joined in the middle of a row; for example, to avoid excessive wastage of expensive yarn or when knitting a scarf where yarn joins at the edge would show. In such cases the best method is to splice the ends of the old and new balls. Unravel both ends for about 3 in. Twist the ends together to make a single thread. Work the next stitches very carefully.

Binding off knitwise

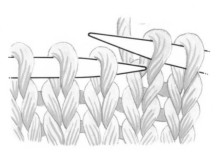

1 With the yarn at the back of the work, knit the first two stitches on the left-hand needle as usual.

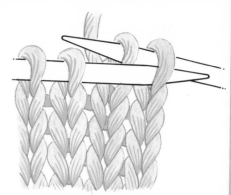

2 With the tip of the left-hand needle lift the first stitch knitted over the second stitch knitted and off the needle. One stitch has been bound off.

3 Work the next stitch on the left-hand needle as usual. Lift the second stitch knitted over it and off the needle. Two stitches have been bound off.

4 Repeat step 3 across the row. Break off the yarn, thread it through the last stitch and tighten.

Simple increasing
Increase one stitch (inc 1)

1 This method is used most often to make increases at the beginnings and ends of rows. Insert the right-hand needle knitwise into the front of the stitch on the left-hand needle.

2 Knit the stitch on the left-hand needle as usual but without slipping it off the needle.

3 Insert the right-hand needle into the back of the same stitch knitwise. Take the yarn under and over the point of the right-hand needle.

4 Draw the loop through, discarding the stitch on the left-hand needle, thus making two stitches out of one. This method is also called "knitting into the front and back of the same stitch".

Working with color
Weaving yarns

1 Hold the yarn in use in your right hand and the yarn not in use in your left hand. Knit the first stitch as usual. On the next and every other stitch, insert the right-hand needle knitwise. Take the yarn in the left hand over the right-hand needle, then knit with the yarn in the right hand as usual.

2 On purl rows, work in exactly the same way. Bring the yarn not in use over the top of the right-hand needle on every other stitch, but the weaving takes place at the front of the work and the stitches are purled. This method is used where the yarn is carried over more than five stitches.

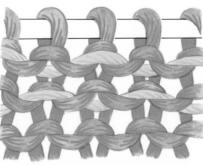

3 Weaving yarns avoids untidy long strands at the back of the work.

Stranding yarns

1 On right-side rows, knit the required number of stitches with the first color. Drop the yarn. Pick up the second color and knit the required numbers of stitches with that. Pick up the first color again and carry it loosely across the back of the work before knitting the next stitches.

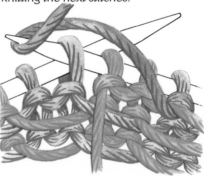

2 On wrong-side rows, work in exactly the same way as for right-side rows but purl the stitches and carry the yarn loosely across the front of the work. This method is used where the yarn is carried over no more than three or four stitches.

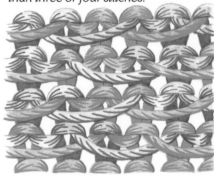

3 The back of the work will be neat provided the yarns are carried evenly and at the same tension as the knitting. If the yarns are carried too tightly the right side of the work will pucker.

All lace stitch patterns involve increasing and decreasing techniques. Extra stitches are "made" during a row and taken off during the same or subsequent rows. The combination of made stitches and decreases creates the holes that form the lacy effects.

Decorative increasing
Yarn forward (yfwd)

This method is used to make a stitch between two knit stitches. After the first knit stitch the yarn is at the back of the work. Bring the yarn forward between the needles. Knit the next stitch as usual.

Yarn over needle (yo)

1 This method is used to make a stitch between two stitches. Between two purl stitches, the yarn is at the front of the work. Take the yarn over then under the right-hand needle. Purl the next stitch as usual.

2 The same method is used to make a stitch between a knit and a purl stitch. After the knit stitch take the yarn under, over, then under the right-hand needle. Purl the next stitch as usual.

3 This method is used to make a stitch between a purl and a knit stitch. After the purl stitch the yarn is at the front of the work. Take yarn over the right-hand needle. Knit the next stitch as usual.

Decreasing
Knit two stitches together (K2 tog)

1 Insert the right-hand needle knitwise into the second then the first stitch on the left-hand needle. Take the yarn under and over the point of the right hand needle.

2 Draw the yarn through the first and second stitches on the left-hand needle, discarding both stitches at the same time, thus making one stitch.

Purl two stitches together (P2 tog)

1 Insert the right-hand needle purlwise into the first then the second stitch on the left-hand needle. Take the yarn over and under the point of the right-hand needle.

2 Draw the yarn through the first and second stitches on left-hand needle, thus making one stitch out of two.

Slip one, knit one, pass slipped stitch over (sl 1, K1, psso)

1 Insert the right-hand needle into the next stitch on the left-hand needle as if to knit it. Slip the stitch off the needle onto the right-hand needle.

2 Knit the next stitch on the left-hand needle as usual. With the point of the left-hand needle, lift up the slipped stitch and pass it over the stitch just knitted and off the needle.

Twisting stitches
Knit through back of loop (K tbl)

Insert the right-hand needle from right to left through the back of the next stitch on the left-hand needle. Knit the stitch as usual.

Increasing

There are many different methods of increasing stitches in knitting. Some are virtually invisible in the completed fabric, others are more visible. Some are intended to create specific decorative effects.

Lifted increase (knitwise)

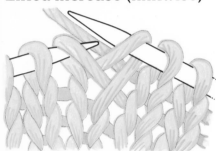

1 This is one of the least visible forms of increasing. Insert the right-hand needle into the stitch below the next stitch on the left-hand needle from front to back.

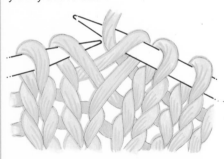

2 Lift the stitch and knit it in the usual way by taking the yarn under and over the point of the right-hand needle and drawing it through the stitch.

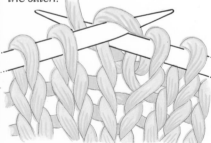

3 Knit the stitch above the lifted stitch as usual. This method is often referred to as "knit one below".

Lifted increase (purlwise)

1 On purl rows, insert the right-hand needle into the stitch below the next stitch on the left-hand needle from back to front. Lift and purl it.

2 Insert the needle into the stitch above the lifted stitch and purl it as usual. This method is often referred to as "purl one below".

Make one knitwise

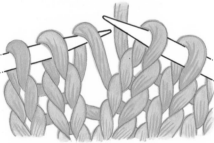

1 With the left-hand needle pick up the loop between the stitch just worked and the next stitch on the left-hand needle from front to back.

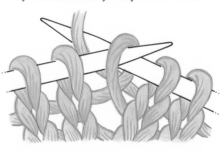

2 Knit as usual into the back of the raised loop on the left-hand needle. This makes an almost invisible increase.

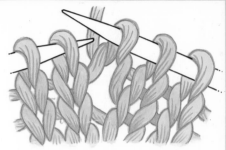

3 A visible hole that can be used for decorative purposes is formed by knitting the raised loop through the front rather than the back.

Make one purlwise

1 On purl rows, with the left-hand needle pick up the loop between the stitch just worked and the next stitch on the left-hand needle from front to back.

2 Purl into the back of the raised loop on the left-hand needle. This makes an almost invisible increase.

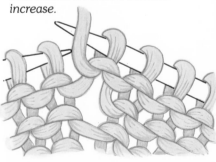

3 This method can also be varied to make a visible hole in the fabric by purling the raised loop through the front rather than the back.

There are several "tricks of the trade" in knitting, which experienced knitters know and which patterns rarely explain in detail. For beginners here are a few of the most useful ones.

Holding stitches

1 Inserting pockets or working neckbands and neck edges usually requires that a number of stitches be held without being bound off until later in the pattern. If the number of stitches is very small they can be held on a safety pin.

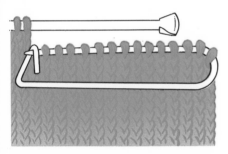

2 More than ten stitches should be held on a special stitch holder with the end closed to secure them.

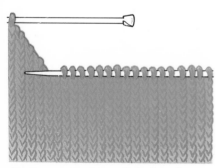

3 Large numbers of stitches, for example, on the front of a V-necked sweater, can be held on a spare needle.

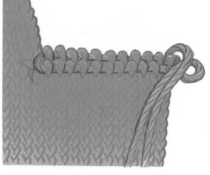

4 In intricate patterns where a spare needle or stitch holder would be awkward to handle (for example, on gloves) the stitches can be held on a piece of spare yarn.

Picking up stitches

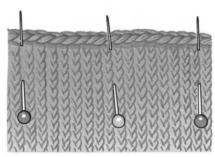

1 Stitches often need to be picked up around neck edges and armholes so that a neckband and armhole band can be knitted. To ensure they are picked up evenly, divide the edge into equal sections and mark them with pins.

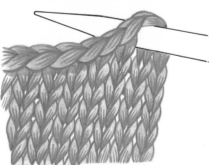

2 Divide the number of sections into the number of stitches specified in the pattern and start picking up an equal number of stitches per section. Insert the tip of the needle into a row end on vertical edges or a stitch on horizontal edges.

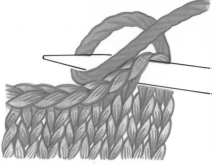

3 With the yarn at the back of the work, take it under and over the point of the needle, and draw a loop through.

4 Insert the tip of the needle into the next stitch or row end. Take the yarn under and over the point of the needle and draw a loop through. Carry on in this way until the correct number of stitches has been picked up.

Picking up a dropped stitch ladder

Dropping stitches, even several rows down, is not necessarily a disaster. If the stitch is a simple one like stockinette stitch the stitch can be picked up easily with a crochet hook. With the right side of work facing, insert the hook from the front into the dropped stitch, then under the horizontal thread just above it. Pull the thread through the dropped stitch. Continue upwards until all the threads of the ladder have been picked up.

Using a cable needle

The use of a cable needle is the basis of many knitting techniques including cable stitch patterns, Aran and traveling stitches. Cable needles are short double-pointed needles. They are used to move stitches from one position to another in the same row and so change the order in which they are worked. On knit rows, cabling to the front twists the stitches to the left on the right side of the work; cabling to the back twists them to the right on the right side. On purl rows cabling front twists the stitches to the right and cabling back to the left.

Cable four front (C4F)

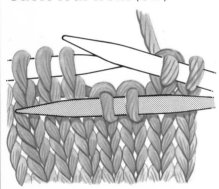

1 *Slip the next two stitches onto the cable needle and leave it at the front of the work.*

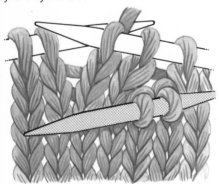

2 *Knit the next two stitches on the left-hand needle in the usual way.*

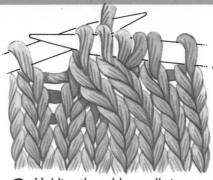

3 *Holding the cable needle in your left hand, knit off the two stitches on the cable needle.*

Cable four back (C4B)

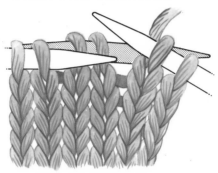

1 *Slip the next two stitches onto the cable needle and leave it at the back of the work.*

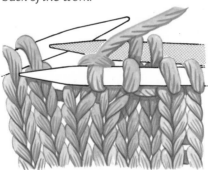

2 *Knit the next two stitches on the left-hand needle in the usual way.*

3 *Holding the cable needle in your left hand, knit off the two stitches on the cable needle.*

Cable 4 front purlwise (C4F P-wise)

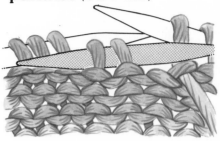

1 *Slip the next two stitches onto the cable needle and leave it at the front of the work.*

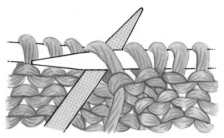

2 *Purl the next two stitches on the left-hand needle in the usual way, then purl the two stitches on the cable needle.*

Cable 4 back purlwise (C4B P-wise)

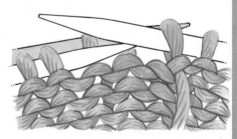

1 *Slip the next two stitches onto the cable needle and leave it at the back of the work.*

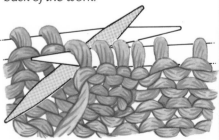

2 *Purl the next two stitches on the left-hand needle in the usual way, then purl the two stitches on the cable needle.*

Coral Mula

Making bobbles

Bobbles are made in various ways depending on whether they are large or small, and knit or purl, but the basic principle remains the same: several increases are made into one stitch; these stitches are worked on in various ways to form a small piece of knitting attached to the main work by one stitch, then decreased until only one stitch is left. The bobble "sits" on top of the background fabric.

Large knit bobble

1 Work to the bobble position. Knit into the next stitch without slipping it off the needle, bring the yarn forward, knit again into the same stitch, bring the yarn forward, knit again into the same stitch and slip it off the left-hand needle.

2 Turn the work. Purl across the five "made" stitches. Turn the work and knit across the five stitches.

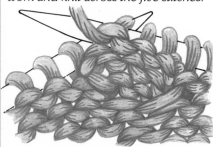

3 Turn the work and purl two stitches together, purl one stitch, purl two stitches together across the five stitches.

4 Turn the work. Slip one stitch, knit two stitches together. Pass the slipped stitch over the decrease to complete the bobble.

Large purl bobble

1 Work as for step one of the large knit bobble. Turn the work and knit across the five made stitches. Turn the work and purl across the five made stitches.

2 Turn the work and knit two stitches together, knit one stitch, knit two stitches together across the five stitches.

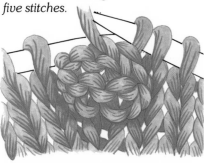

3 Turn the work. Slip one stitch, purl two stitches together. Pass the slipped stitch over the decrease to complete the bobble.

Small knit bobble

1 To make a knit bobble, work to the bobble position. Knit into the next stitch without slipping it off the needle, bring the yarn forward, knit again into the same stitch and slip it off the needle.

2 Turn the work. Purl the three "made" stitches. Turn the work and knit the three made stitches. Turn the work, purl two stitches together, purl one stitch. Turn the work, slip one stitch, knit one stitch, pass the slipped stitch over the knit stitch to complete the bobble.

Small purl bobble

1 Work to the bobble position. Knit into the next stitch without slipping it off the needle, bring the yarn forward, knit again into the same stitch and slip it off the needle. Turn the work. Knit the three "made" stitches.

2 Turn the work. Purl the three made stitches. Turn the work, knit two stitches together, knit one stitch. Turn the work, slip one stitch, purl one stitch, pass the slipped stitch over the purl stitch and off the needle.

179

Working into the back of the loop

Stitches are usually knitted or purled through the front of the loops. For some stitch patterns, however, they must be worked through the back of the loops thus twisting or crossing them. This technique is characteristic of early Arabic knitting and is similar to the cross-knit looping of early Peruvian textiles. Sometimes the entire fabric is composed of twisted knit and purl stitches. They can also be used singly to emphasize the lines of a textured pattern, as twisted stitches are more prominent than ordinary stitches.

Twisting knitwise

1 Insert the right-hand needle through the back of the next stitch on the left-hand needle as shown. Take the yarn under and over the point of the right-hand needle.

2 Draw a loop through the stitch and drop the stitch off the left-hand needle to complete it.

Twisting purlwise

1 Insert the right-hand needle through the back of the next stitch on the left-hand needle as shown. Take the yarn over and under the point of the right-hand needle.

2 Draw a loop through the stitch and drop the stitch off the left-hand needle to complete it.

Twisted decreasing (knitwise)

1 Insert the right-hand needle through the backs of the next two stitches on the left-hand needle as shown. Take the yarn under and over the point of the right-hand needle.

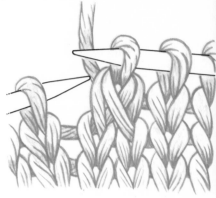

2 Draw a loop through both stitches and drop them off the left-hand needle at the same time to complete the decrease.

Twisted decreasing (purlwise)

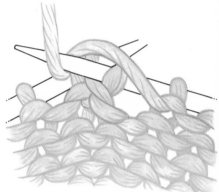

1 Insert the right-hand needle through the backs of the next two stitches on the left-hand needle as shown. Take the yarn over and under the point of the right-hand needle.

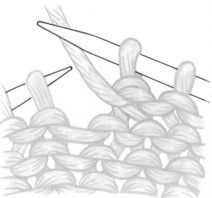

2 Draw a loop through both stitches and drop them off the left-hand needle, so completing the decrease.

Slipping stitches

Stitches are "slipped", that is, passed from one needle to another without being worked, for a variety of reasons. They can be slipped knitwise or purlwise and with the yarn at the front or back. Stitches may be slipped singly or several stitches may be slipped at a time.

Slipping knitwise

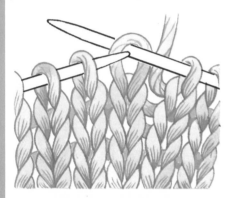

1 *Stitches are always slipped knitwise when they form part of a slip stitch decrease on a knit row. Insert the right-hand needle into the front of the next stitch on the left-hand needle as if to knit it but transfer the stitch onto the right-hand needle without knitting it. Work the next stitch as usual.*

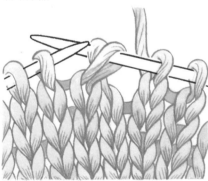

2 *On some double decreases two stitches must be slipped at once. In such cases insert the right-hand needle into the fronts of the next two stitches on the left-hand needle as if to knit them together and transfer them to the left-hand needle without knitting them.*

Slipping purlwise

1 *Stitches are slipped purlwise when they form part of a decrease on a purl row or of any fancy pattern that requires the same stitch to be worked on the next or subsequent rows, for example, mosaic stitches and slip stitch textured patterns. Insert the right-hand needle into the next stitch on the left-hand needle as if to purl it but pass it to the right-hand needle without purling it.*

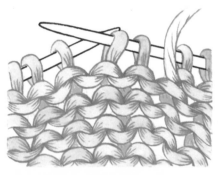

2 *To slip more than one stitch purlwise simply insert the right-hand needle into the required number of stitches as if to purl them and transfer them straight onto the right-hand needle without purling them.*

Yarn front

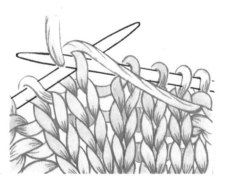

1 *The front of the work refers to the side facing the knitter regardless*

of whether it is the right or wrong side of the fabric. When slipping after purl stitches the yarn is already in front. Slip the required number of stitches and knit or purl the next stitch as instructed.

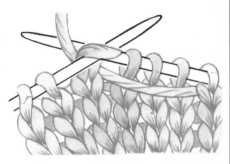

2 *After knit stitches bring the yarn to the front between the needles, slip the required number of stitches and purl or knit the next stitch as instructed in the pattern.*

Yarn back

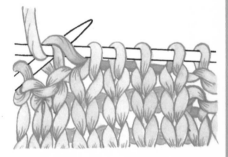

1 *The back of the work refers to the side facing away from the knitter regardless of whether it is the right or wrong side of the fabric. When slipping after knit stitches the yarn is already at the back. Slip the required number of stitches and knit or purl the next stitch as instructed.*

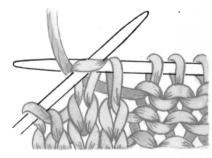

2 *After purl stitches take the yarn back between the needles, slip the required number of stitches and knit or purl the next stitch.*

Making eyelets

Eyelets are small holes arranged decoratively on a knitted background. They are formed in many different ways but the basic principle is the same: each eyelet is composed of a decorative increase and a compensating decrease.

Chain eyelet

1 *This is the most popular single eyelet method. Work to the position of the eyelet. Bring the yarn forward between the needles and take it over the needle to knit the next two stitches together.*

2 *Purl the next row including the yarn taken over the needle.*

Open eyelet

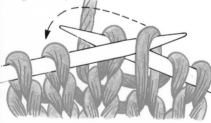

1 *This is rounder and more clearly defined than the chain eyelet. Work to the eyelet position. Bring the yarn forward between the needles. Slip the next stitch knitwise. Take the yarn over the needle to knit the following stitch. Pass the slipped stitch over the knit stitch.*

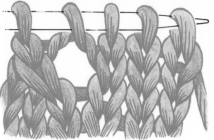

2 *Purl the next row including the yarn taken over the needle.*

Double eyelet

1 *This makes a large round eyelet. Work to the eyelet position. Knit the next two stitches together. Bring the yarn forward.*

2 *Slip the next stitch knitwise. Take the yarn over the needle to knit the following stitch. Pass the slipped stitch over the knit stitch.*

3 *On the next row, purl every stitch but purl and knit into the yarn taken over the needle.*

Picot eyelet

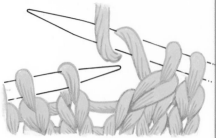

1 *Work to the eyelet position. Knit the next two stitches together. Take the yarn twice around the needle.*

2 *Slip the next stitch knitwise. Knit the following stitch. Pass the slipped stitch over the knit stitch.*

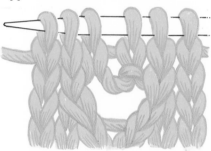

3 *On the next row, purl every stitch but purl the first loop taken over the needle and knit the second.*

Picot hem

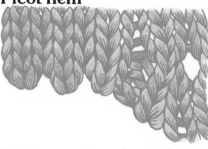

Eyelets are used to make picot hems. Work a row of chain eyelets along the fold line of the hem as close together as possible. When the garment is completed, fold the hem along the picot row and slip stitch the edge in place.

Picot point knitting

This is an unusual form of decorative knitting. It can be used on its own to make small flower motifs, medallions and a kind of mesh or lace similar to Irish crochet. Alternatively use it to make edgings and borders for garments knitted in a variety of plainer stitches.

The basic picot point

1 Picot point knitting is all based on a simple point motif made as follows. Begin by making a slip knot and place it on the left-hand needle. Cast on 2 stitches.

2 Now bind off the same 2 stitches, leaving one loop on the right-hand needle. Transfer this loop onto the left-hand needle, thus completing a single point.

3 Make a chain of points by continuing to make single points. Cast on 2 more stitches, then bind them off and return the remaining loop to the left-hand needle. Continue making loops until the chain is the required length.

4 The points can be made larger by casting more stitches on and binding them off. For example, make a slip knot then cast on 4 stitches. Now bind off the same 4 stitches and transfer the remaining loop to the left-hand needle.

Picot point cast-on

This makes a pretty edge for plain stockinette stitch. Simply make a chain of picot points the length of the edge, pick up the number of cast-on stitches along the plain edge of the chain and knit upwards from them.

Picot point binding off

1 This is another decorative edge for binding off plain stitches but it is also much used when making lace mats and edgings. Push the needle knitwise through the first stitch in the edge to be bound off. Cast on 2 stitches.

2 Bind off 3 stitches leaving 1 loop on the right-hand needle.

Transfer this loop on to the left-hand needle ready for the next stage.

3 Cast on 2 stitches, then bind off 3 and return the remaining loop to left-hand needle as before. Carry on across the bound-off row. This edge can be worked in the same color as the main fabric or in a contrast as here.

4 Work more space between the points by binding off an extra stitch between them as follows. Cast on 2 stitches, bind off 4 stitches. Return remaining loop to left-hand needle and repeat this across the row.

Crown picot edging

1 This can be used as a decorative cast-on or bound-off edge or made separately as follows. Cast on a multiple of 4 plus 2 stitches. Knit 1 row. Make a chain of 4 picot points into the first stitch.

2 Bind off 4 stitches. Transfer remaining stitch onto left-hand needle. Make another chain of 4 picot points. Repeat to end, ending last repeat bind off 1. Fasten off.

Mary Tomlin

Smocking

Smocking can be worked after the knitting is complete or it can be knitted in as the work progresses. Both techniques can be applied to produce decorative fabrics or, as in dressmaking, to control fullness in, for example, the sleeves or bodice of a garment. In addition there are some stitch patterns (*see* pages 26-27) that would look like conventional smocked fabrics.

Applied smocking

1 *Ribbed fabrics provide the most suitable backgrounds, especially a three-by-one rib. Cast on a multiple of 8 stitches, plus 3 extra and work as follows:* **1st row** *(RS) P3, (K1, P3) to end.* **2nd row** *K3, (P1, K3) to end. Repeat these two rows. Work the fabric one and a half times the required width after smocking.*

2 *Work the first smocking row beginning at the right-hand side on fourth row. Thread a needle with matching or contrasting yarn and secure the end of the yarn at the back. Bring it to the front at the left of the second rib, then to the back to the right of the first rib to make a stitch. Make two more stitches in the same way, pulling the smocking thread tightly to draw the ribs together and ending with the thread at the back.*

3 *Bring the needle to the front to the left of the fourth rib, then to the back to the right of the third rib. Make two stitches drawing the ribs together. Continue across the row.*

4 *Work the second row of smocking on the ninth row. Gather together pairs of ribs as before, working from right to left, beginning with the second and third ribs, then the fourth and fifth ribs, and so on, staggering the pairs between those on the first smocking row.*

5 *Continue in this way, smocking alternate pairs of ribs on successive smocking rows and leaving four knitting rows between them.*

Knitted-in smocking

1 *Work four rows of a background fabric as given for applied*

smocking (step 1). On the next row rib 8 stitches then slip the last 5 of these onto a cable needle at the front.

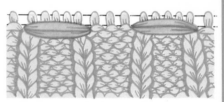

2 *Take a smocking thread, leave a long end at the back of the work and wrap the thread clockwise twice around the stitches on the cable needle ending with the thread at the back.*

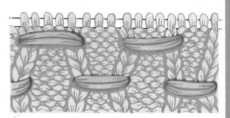

3 *Slip the five stitches back onto the right-hand needle, rib 8 stitches then slip the last 5 of these onto the cable needle at the front and wrap the smocking thread around them as before. Continue in this way carrying the thread across the back.*

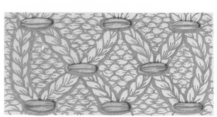

4 *Rib three more rows. On the next row rib 12 stitches, slip the last 5 of these onto a cable needle at the front and wrap the smocking thread around them as before. Rib 8 stitches then smock the last 5 of them. Continue in this way across the row.*

5 *Smock on every fourth row as set until the fabric is the required depth. Work three more rows before binding off, then draw up the smocking threads on each row.*

Traveling stitches

The techniques necessary for traveling stitches are worked with a cable needle. The object is to "move" the knit stitches over the background (usually reverse stockinette stitch). The many permutations involve from two to eight stitches.

Crossing two stitches right

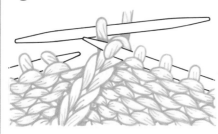

1 *Slip the next (purl) stitch onto a cable needle and hold it at the back of the work. Knit the next stitch on the left-hand needle.*

2 *Now purl the stitch held on the cable needle, thus moving the knit stitch over the purl background one stitch to the right.*

Crossing two stitches left

1 *Slip the next (knit) stitch onto a cable needle and hold it at the*

front of the work. Purl the next stitch on the left-hand needle.

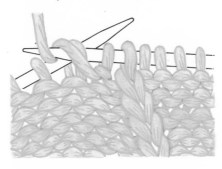

2 *Now knit the stitch held on the cable needle, thus moving the knit stitch to the left over the purl background.*

Crossing three stitches right

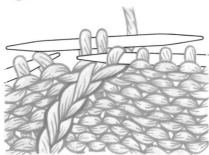

1 *Work to the point two stitches before the knit stitch that is to "travel". Slip the next two (purl) stitches onto a cable needle and hold it at the back of the work. Knit the next stitch on the left-hand needle.*

2 *Now purl the two stitches on the cable needle, thus moving the knit stitch two stitches to the right over the reverse stockinette stitch background.*

Crossing three stitches left

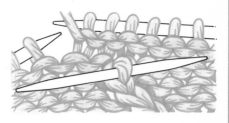

1 *Slip the next (knit) stitch onto a cable needle and hold it at the front of the work. Purl the next two stitches on the left-hand needle.*

2 *Now knit the stitch on the cable needle, thus moving it two stitches to the left.*

Crossing four stitches

1 *Slip the next three stitches onto a cable needle and hold it at the back of the work. Knit the next stitch on the left-hand needle, then bring the yarn to the front of the work. Slip two stitches from the cable needle back onto the left-hand needle.*

2 *Purl two from the left-hand needle then knit one from the cable needle.*

Coral Mula

Circular knitting

Circular knitting is carried out using a set of four or more double-pointed needles or a circular needle. It produces a tubular seamless fabric, ideal for items such as socks and gloves. Many traditional types of sweater such as Aran, Fair Isle and especially Guernsey were also worked in the round. Since circular knitting is worked with the right side facing on every round, the construction of stitch patterns is different from that which obtains in flat knitting. Stockinette stitch, for example, is worked by knitting every round, and garter stitch by alternately knitting and purling rounds. Circular needles can also be used for flat knitting when the number of stitches is too great for ordinary needles.

Casting onto four needles

1 Using any of the usual methods, cast on the required number of stitches onto one of the needles.

2 Distribute these stitches among three of the set of four needles. Form the needles into a triangle making sure that the stitches are not twisted as you do so.

3 Place a marker loop to mark the beginning of rounds. Join the stitches into a round by using the fourth needle and the working yarn from the last stitch on the third needle to knit first stitch on first needle.

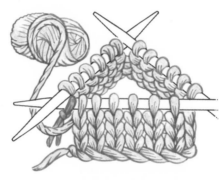

4 Continue knitting off the stitches on the first needle, then use the first needle to knit off the stitches on the second needle and so on until the round is completed. Slip the marker loop at the beginning of each round. Alternatively the end of yarn left after casting on can be used as a marker.

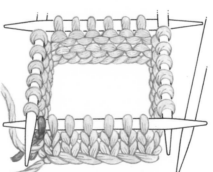

5 When using a set of five needles, cast on the stitches onto four needles and use the fifth needle to work off the stitches. The same principle holds for working with larger sets of needles — cast onto one less than the total number of needles and use the spare needle as the actual working needle.

Using a circular needle

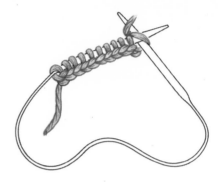

1 Circular needles come in lengths varying from 16 to 40 in. They can only be used where the number of cast-on stitches is sufficient to reach from one point to the other. Use one point to cast on stitches onto the other point in the usual way.

2 When the stitches have been cast on, join them into a round by transferring the left-hand point to the right hand and vice versa, then knit first cast-on stitch using the working yarn from the right-hand point.

3 Continue using the right-hand point to knit off the stitches until the round is completed. Mark the beginning of rounds using a marker loop or the cast-on end of yarn.

Gauge

Gauge is the most important single factor in the success of any piece of knitting. However imaginative the design, or beautiful the yarn, the final result will inevitably be disappointing if the gauge has not been carefully checked at the start.

What is gauge?

At its simplest, the gauge of knitting is a measurement of its tightness or looseness. It describes the number of stitches and rows it takes to achieve a given width and length. Gauge is affected by four factors: type of yarn, needle size, stitch pattern and the individual knitter.

Yarn

Yarns come in a wide range of thicknesses and finishes. The labels of many yarns nowadays recommend a gauge measurement. This is the gauge which, in the manufacturer's opinion, will produce the most suitable finish for that particular yarn, and is especially useful when designing your own garments or when substituting a new yarn for the one specified in the pattern. Often pattern designers use the "wrong" gauge deliberately, to achieve special effects — a floppier or more rigid fabric, for example — so whatever the label says always match your gauge to the one given in the pattern. In general, however, thicker, chunkier yarns must be knitted on larger needles than fine yarns, and produce a gauge of fewer rows and stitches to the square inch. Even yarns apparently of the same weight and thickness can display variations in gauge. All sport-weight yarns, for example, do not knit up to the same gauge.

Needle size

This has an obvious effect on knitting gauge. The larger the needles, the looser the fabric and the fewer the rows and stitches to the square inch. This is clearly demonstrated by casting on a given number of stitches and knitting in stockinette stitch for, say 8 in., using the same yarn throughout but changing to smaller needles every few rows. Work a purl row on the right side between each needle size. The width of the knitting and the distance between the rows will gradually decrease.

Stitch pattern

Different stitch patterns are designed to produce fabrics with widely varying surface textures and properties. Some, like seed stitch, are tight firm fabrics that hold their shape well. Lacy patterns are, by definition, loose and open. Ribs are stretchy, tending to pull inwards across their width. All these properties affect gauge measurement. The same yarn and needle size will result in widely differing gauge over different stitch patterns. For this reason you cannot substitute a new stitch pattern for the one specified and assume that the resulting garment will be the correct measurements. The gauge of the new stitch pattern must be carefully checked against the original one. Often it is not possible to match both row and stitch gauge simultaneously. In such cases you should use a needle size that will achieve the correct stitch tension and follow the measurement diagram for length.

The knitter

Gauge is almost as personal a thing as handwriting or fingerprints. It is rarely possible to find two people who knit to the same gauge. It is therefore never advisable to allow anyone else to finish a piece of knitting that you have started. It is also the reason why you must adjust your personal gauge to that of any pattern before beginning work on it. The gauge of the pattern is that of the designer of the pattern and the chances are that his or her gauge will be different from yours. You cannot adjust your gauge successfully by trying to knit more loosely or tightly that you usually do. This will simply interrupt the natural rhythm of your knitting. It will be uncomfortable to work and, as you relax into your normal style it will almost certainly produce an unevenness of gauge over the whole garment. If your gauge needs adjusting it must be done by changing the needle size.

Checking gauge

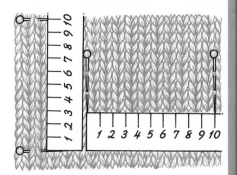

1 Knit a gauge sample using the same yarn, needle size and stitch pattern specified in the gauge measurement (in this case 10 stitches and 14 rows to 4 in.), casting on a few more stitches and working more rows than given. Place a ruler along the width of the sample and mark off the measurement with pins at right angles to the ruler. Place the ruler vertically on the sample and mark off the measurement with pins. Count the stitches and rows between pins.

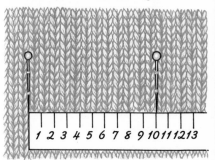

2 If there are too many stitches or rows your gauge is tighter than that of the designer. Knit another sample using larger needles and check it again.

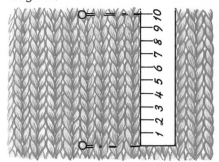

3 If there are too few stitches and rows between the pins your gauge is looser than that of the designer. Knit another sample on smaller needles and check it again.

Coral Mula

187

Crochet

The attractive and highly wearable crochet patterns in this chapter encompass a wide variety of stitches and techniques, with plenty of designs that can be worked by virtual beginners as well as some more complex items using a mixture of stitches, yarns and colors to achieve a high-fashion effect.

As with the knitting patterns, there is a wide-ranging collection of clothes for women, as well as sweaters, a vest, T-shirt, pullover and jacket for men, and some delightful clothes and accessories for babies and children. In addition, there are some lovely things to make for your home, since the versatility of crochet lends itself to a range of lace edgings and cloths; there is even a group of charming and unusual crocheted flowers.

As with knitting patterns, it is advisable to make a gauge sample before you start the main work, especially if you are using a different yarn from the one originally specified. Do not be put off if you are a comparative beginner and the pattern seems too complicated; in most cases you will find that the Pattern Library and Adaptations suggest ways in which the basic pattern can be simplified.

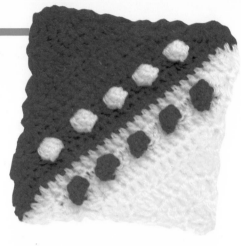

CROCHET FOR WOMEN
Bobbles

Skills you need

*Increasing
*Decreasing
*Using two colors
*Bobbles

If you do not know these basic skills, refer to pages 295 and 298.

Materials

Bobbles look good worked in most colors and yarns. However, it is helpful to work a small test sample to make certain that the bobbles can be seen. Very dark or light colors may make small bobbles invisible, whereas a medium shade or contrast color will ensure that all bobbles stand out.

Similarly, mohair and bouclé are best used to make large bobbles, since small bobbles may appear buried in a textured fabric. For these reasons, the sweater on page 191 — made in a wool-mohair yarn, roughly equivalent to a double knitting — has large bobbles worked in a contrasting color.

Special technique – crochet ribbing

Coral Mula

1 *A crochet rib with "knit" and "purl" stitches can be formed by working around the stems of the stitches on the previous row. Work the turning chain. Take the yarn over the hook and insert it from front to back between the stems of the first and second doubles. Bring the hook to the front between the second and third doubles. Complete the double as usual.*

2 *To form the "purl" stitches of the rib, take the yarn around the hook and insert the hook from back to front between the stems of the second and third doubles. Then bring the hook from front to back between the stems of the third and fourth doubles. Complete the double in the usual way.*

3 *Continue in this way along the row, working the last stitch around the stem of the turning chain. On following rows, keep the ribbing correct by working from front to back around the stems of the doubles that form the "knit" ribs and from back to front around the stems of the "purl" doubles.*

The basic bobble pattern

Crochet yourself a cheerful sweater in a warm, lightweight yarn. Use two strongly contrasting shades as we have done, or choose toning colors for a softly subtle look.

Sizes
Misses' sizes 10 [12:14:16]
Length 22½ [23¼:24:24¾] in.
Sleeve seam 18½ [19¼:19¾:20½] in.

Note: Instructions for larger sizes are in square brackets []; where there is only one set of figures it applies to all sizes.

Gauge
7dc and 3 rows to 2 in. on Size 1 hook

Materials
7 [9:9:11] oz sport-weight wool-mohair blend yarn in main color (A)
7[7:9:9] oz in contrasting color (B).
Size G and I crochet hooks

Back and front (alike)
Note: Work the 2 sts at each end of every row at a slightly looser tension to keep work flat.
Using Size I hook and A, ch 4.
Base row Work 4dc into 4th ch from hook. Turn.
1st inc row Ch 3, work 2dc into first dc, 1dc into each of next 3dc, work 3dc into top of turning ch. Turn. 9sts.
2nd inc row Ch 3, 2dc into first dc, 1 dc into each st to last st, 3dc into top of turning ch. Turn. 4sts inc.
Rep last row 17 [18:19:20] times. 81 [85:89:93] sts.

Steve Campbell

Next row (RS) Ch 3, 2dc into first dc, 1dc into next dc, change to B, 5dc into next dc, remove loop from hook, insert hook from front to back in top of first dc, replace loop on hook and draw through the dc(1 bobble formed on RS of work), *change to A, 1dc into each of next 3dc, change to B, 1 bobble into next dc, rep from * to last 2 sts, 1dc into next dc, 3dc into top of turning ch. Turn. Fasten off B. Rep 2nd inc row once. 89 [93:97:101] sts.

Fasten off A. Attach B.
1st dec row Ch 3, skip first dc. Leaving last loop of each st on hook, work 1dc into each of next 3 sts, yo and draw through all 4 loops (2 dc dec). Work 1dc into each st to within

191

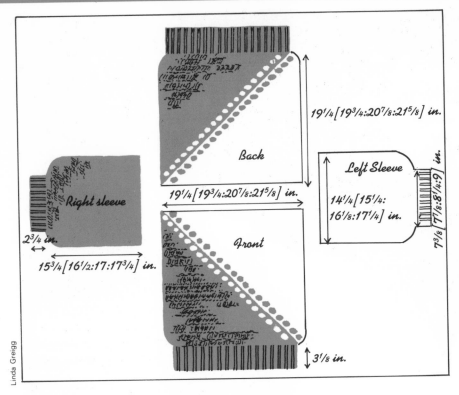

Right sleeve

Back

Front

Left Sleeve

19¼[19¾:20⅞:21⅝] in.

19¼[19¾:20⅞:21⅝] in.

14¼[15¼:16⅛:17¼] in.

2¾ in.

15¾[16½:17:17¾] in.

7⅜[7⅞:8¼:9] in.

3⅛ in.

Linda Greigg

last 4 sts, dec 2dc over next 3 sts, 1dc into top of turning ch. Turn. 4 sts dec.
2nd dec row (WS) Ch 3, skip first dc, dec 2dc over next 3 sts, *change to A, work 1 bobble in next dc but insert hook from back to front in top of first of 5dc to make the bobble at the back (RS) of work. Change to B, 1dc into each of next 3dc, rep from * to last 5 sts, 1 bobble in next dc, dec 2dc over next 3 sts, 1dc into top of turning ch. Turn. Fasten off A.
Rep 1st dec row until 5 sts rem.
Next row Ch 3, skip first dc. Leaving last loop of each st on hook, work 1dc into each of next 3dc, 1dc into top of turning ch, yo and draw through all 5 loops. Fasten off.

Sleeves
Make one sleeve in A and one sleeve in B.
With size I hook, ch 52 [56:60:64]
Base row Work 1dc into 4th ch from hook, 1dc into each ch to end. Turn. 50 [54:58:62] sts.
1st row Ch 3, skip first dc, work 1dc into each st, ending with 1dc in top of turning ch. Turn.
Rep 1st row 20 [21:22:23] times.
Dec row Ch 3, skip first dc, * leaving last loop of each st on hook, work 1dc into each of next 2dc, yo and draw through all 3 loops. Rep from * to last st, 1dc into top of turning ch. Turn. 26 [28:30:32] sts.
Rep 1st row once more.
192

Cuff
Change to size G hook.
Next row Ch 2, skip first dc, *work 1dc around stem of next dc, inserting hook from front from right to left (1dc front worked), work 1dc around stem of next dc, inserting hook from back, from right to left (1dc back worked), rep from * to end, ending 1dc front around stem of turning ch. Turn. Rep last row 6 times. Fasten off.

Waistband
With wrong sides tog place back and front tog with A sections tog and with B sections tog. Join side seams for 13 rows and shoulder seams for 7 rows. With smaller hook join A to side seam, work 104 [108:112:116]sc evenly around lower edge, sl st to first sc.
Next round Ch 3, skip first sc, 1dc into each sc to end, sl st to top of 3ch.
Next round Ch 2, *1dc front around next dc, 1dc back around next dc, rep from * ending 1dc front around last dc, sl st to top of 2 ch.
Rep last round 6 times. Fasten off.

To finish
Join sleeve seams. Matching colors, set in sleeves. Using smaller hook and B, work 1 round of sc evenly around neck, sl st to first sc. Fasten off.

Adapting the basic sweater pattern

Vary the basic sweater or add bobbles to your favorite simple crochet pattern.

The front and back of the sweater on page 191 are worked diagonally beginning and ending at a corner, with the colors changing at the widest point. The bobbles are in contrasting colors to emphasize the diagonal styling.

Varying the pattern
The basic sweater could easily be crocheted in one background color, with bobbles worked every few rows, either in the same or in a contrasting color and placed on the sleeves, as well as on the front and back, to produce a highly textured fabric. Randomly scattered bobbles, crocheted along with the main fabric or added to the background after it has been completed, could be worked in contrasting colors or the main fabric could be striped in narrow or broad bands.
More experienced workers could, after working a gauge swatch, use the measurement diagram as a guide to the basic shape and work the back and front vertically, in the usual way, beginning at the lower edge and including bands of horizontally placed bobbles.

Adding bobbles
It is easy to add bobbles to a pattern worked in double, or single crochet. Use the smaller, triple bobbles with a single crochet fabric and the larger, double crochet bobbles with doubles. Large bobbles, like those in the basic sweater pattern, can be added to other stitch patterns after the main fabric is completed by working into the free loops at the top of the stitches on the right side of the fabric.

Buying yarn
Bobbled fabrics need more yarn than plain fabrics, so if you add more bobbles to the basic sweater or to any other pattern, buy more yarn than quoted so that you have enough and remember to check your gauge.

Mosaic patterns

Mosaics are repeating color patterns that are very easy to work since, unlike jacquard patterns, the kaleidoscopic effects are achieved by using only one color on each row.

Chris Dawes

193

Skills you need

*Single crochet
*Picking up stitches

If you do not know these basic skills refer to pages 177 and 295.

Materials

Colorful mosaic patterns are very versatile, being suitable for anything from cheerful and practical children's clothes to fashionable garments for men and women. When working these patterns, choose plain yarns like the acrylic/wool knitting worsted used to make the sweater on page 193.

Consider the effect you want to create when choosing colors. The basic sweater has been worked in soft pastel shades of the same tone – bright contrasting colors would make the garment look completely different. Work the ribbed band in one of the colors you have used in the sweater.

Special technique – basic three-color mosaic

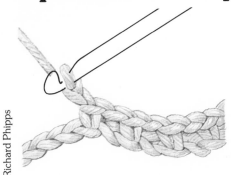

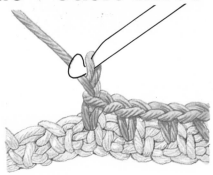

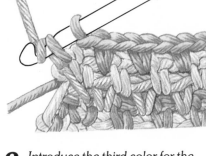

1 *The sweater on page 193 is worked in a three-color single crochet and chain mosaic. Work the base row in the main color as instructed, forming a row of alternating chain spaces and single crochet.*

2 *Join in the second color on the last stitch of the base row. On the following row work a single crochet into each chain space and a chain above each single crochet.*

3 *Introduce the third color for the next row and work as in step 2. Continue in this way using the three different colors in sequence. Do not cut the ends of old yarn when changing color, but leave it at the edge of the work ready for the next row in that color.*

The basic mosaic sweater

This pretty sweater is designed on classic lines with raglan sleeves and a V-neckline. Make it in soft pastel shades using one of them for the knitted waistband and borders.

Sizes
Misses' size 10 [12:14:16]
Length from back neck 24 [24½:24¾:25] in.
Sleeve seam 17¼ in.
Note: Instructions for the larger sizes are given in square brackets []; where there is only one set of figures it applies to all sizes.

Gauge
20 sts and 19½ rows to 4 in. worked on size F hook
(1sc, 1ch = 2 sts)

Materials
11 [11:13:13] oz of knitting worsted in main color (A)
7 [7:9:9] oz each of contrasting colors, (B) and (C)

Size F crochet hook
Pair of size 2 knitting needles

Note: Carry yarns not in use loosely up side of work. Join in new color by drawing it through last two loops on hook in old color.

Back
Using A, ch 93 [99:105:111]
Base row (RS) Using A, work 1sc into 3rd ch from hook, *ch 1, skip next ch, 1sc into next ch, rep from * to end. Turn. 92 [98:104:110] sts. Working in color sequence of 1 row B, 1 row C, 1 row A, cont in pat as follows:
Pat row Ch 1 to count as first sc, skip first st, *1sc into next ch 1 sp, ch 1, skip next sc, rep from * ending last rep with 1sc into last st. Turn.

Cont in pat until work measures 12 in. from beg, ending with a row in A.

Shape raglan armholes
Keeping pat and color sequence correct:
1st row Sl st across first 3 sts, work in pat to last 2 sts, turn. 88 [94:100:106]sts.
2nd row Work in pat.
3rd row Dec 1 st at each end of the row.
Rep last 2 rows 16 more times. 54 [60:66:72] sts.
Rep 3rd row only 11 [13:15:17] more times. 32 [34:36:38] sts. Fasten off.

Front
Work as for back until, 2 [4:4:4] rows fewer have been worked to beg of raglan, thus ending with a row in B [C:C:C].
Divide for neck
Keeping pat and color sequence correct:
Next row Work in pat first 43 [46:49:52] sts, turn and cont on these sts for first side of neck.

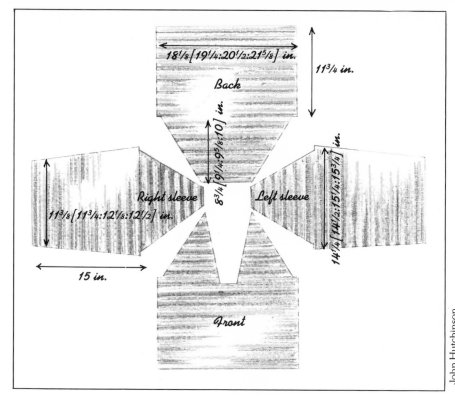

Back

18⅛ [19¼:20½:21⅝] in.

11¾ in.

8¾ [9¼:9⅝:10] in.

Right sleeve

Left sleeve

11⅜ [11¾:12⅛:12½] in.

14¼ [14½:15¼:15¾] in.

14¼ [14½:15¼:15¾] in.

15 in.

Front

John Hutchinson

slightly stretched, fits raglan from beg of dec at underarm to neck edge. Bind off in ribbing.

Sew borders to raglans on front and back. Sew raglan edges of sleeves to borders.

Neck border
Using knitting needles and A, cast on 7 sts and work in ribbing as for raglan borders until border, when slightly stretched, fits around neck opening, beg and ending at center front. Bind off in ribbing.

Sew border to neck edge, lapping the right end over the left at the center front.

To finish
Do not press. Join side and sleeve seams, joining ends of raglan borders at underarm. Press seams very lightly.

Adapting the basic mosaic sweater

Vary the color sequence of the basic sweater to produce many simple variations.

Many instructions for garments worked in basic single crochet, half double or double can be adapted to mosaic patterns. Check that the number of stitches given for the base row of the instructions can be divided by the number of stitches in the mosaic pattern repeat, leaving enough for the edge stitches.

Because most mosaic patterns have short stitch repeats, quite complicated shaping is possible when designing your own garments. However, if you prefer to avoid shaping, mosaic patterns are interesting enough to use on, for example, T-shaped sweaters or tops with little or no shaping.

Seaming
Any garment worked in a mosaic pattern looks more professional if you take extra care when seaming to ensure that the rows of color match exactly at the side seams. Sew seams in the main color when using toning colors as in the basic sweater. If the colors contrast strongly, use fine, synthetic "invisible" sewing thread.

Next row Work in pat.
2nd, 3rd and 4th sizes only
Next row Dec 1 st at neck edge. Work 1 row in pat.
All sizes
Shape raglan armhole
Next row Sl st over first 3 sts, pat to end.
Dec 1 st at armhole edge on next 17 alt rows and then on the foll 8[8:12:16] rows *and at the same time* shape neck edge by dec 1 st at neck edge on 2nd row and every foll 4th row until 11 [12:13:14] sts in all have been decreased at neck edge. 5 [7:5:3] sts. Dec 1 st at armhole edge on the next 3 [5:3:1] rows.
Fasten off rem 2 sts.
Return to sts left at beg of neck shaping. With RS facing, skip next 6 sts and rejoin appropriate color to next st, work in pat to end. 43 [46:49:52] sts.
Complete to match first side of neck, reversing all shaping.

Sleeves
Using A, ch 59 [61:63:65].
Base row Using A, work as for back. 58 [60:62:64] sts.
Work 8 [8:7:7] rows in pat as for back.
Next row Inc 1 st at each end of row. Inc 1 st at each end of every foll 9th [9th:8th:8th] row 6 [6:7:7] more times. 72 [74:78:80] sts.
Work even in pat until work measures 15 in. from beg, ending with a row

in A.
Shape raglan top
Keeping pat and color sequence correct:
1st row Sl st over first 3 sts, work in pat to last 2 sts turn.
68 [70:74:76] sts.
2nd row Work in pat.
3rd row Dec 1 st at each end of row.
Rep 2nd and 3rd rows 13 [14:14:15] more times, ending with a 3rd row. 40 [40:44:44] sts.
Rep 3rd row only 17 [17:19:19] more times. 6 sts. Fasten off.

Waistbands
With RS facing, using knitting needles and A, pick up and K 79 [83:89:93] sts along lower edge of front and back. Work 3⅛ in. in K1, P1 ribbing. Bind off in ribbing.

Cuffs
With RS facing, using knitting needles and A, pick up and K 49[51:53:55] sts along lower edge of sleeve. Work 2¼ in. in K1, P1 ribbing. Bind off in ribbing.

Raglan borders (make 4)
Using knitting needles and A, cast on 9 sts.
1st row (RS) K2, *P1,K1, rep from * to last st, K1.
2nd row P2, *K1, P1, rep from * to last st, P1.
Rep these 2 rows until strip, when

Mosaic patterns

1 Cluster mosaic

Use 5 colors, A,B,C,D and E. Using A, make a multiple of 2ch plus 4 extra.

Base row Using A, leaving last loop of st on hook work 1dc into 4th ch from hook (called short double or short dc), skip next ch, 1 short dc into next ch, yo and draw through all 3 loops on hook, *ch 1, 1 short dc into same ch, miss next ch, 1 short dc into next ch, yo and draw through all 3 loops on hook, rep from * to end. 1dc into last ch. Turn.

1st row (RS) Using B, ch 1, 1sc into first dc, *leaving last loop of each st on hook work 2dc into sp formed between next 2 short dc, yo and draw through all 3 loops on hook (cluster formed), 1sc into next ch 1 sp, rep from * ending with 1sc into top of turning ch. Turn.

2nd row Using A, ch 3, skip first sc, 1 short dc into each of first 2sc, yo and draw through all 3 loops on hook, * ch 1, 1 short dc into same sc, 1 short dc into next sc, yo and draw through all 3 loops on hook, rep from * to last sc, 1dc into last sc. Turn.

1st and 2nd rows form pat. Rep them throughout, working foll 1st rows in sequence C,D,E and B.

1

2

2 Open mosaic

Use 2 colors, A and B. Using A, make a multiple of 2ch plus 4 extra.

Base row Using A, 1dc into 6th ch from hook, *ch 1, skip next ch, 1dc into next ch, rep from * to end. Turn.

1st row (RS) Using B, ch 1 to count as first sc, skip first st, *1sc into next ch 1 sp, ch 1, skip next dc, rep from * to turning ch, 1sc into sp formed by turning ch, 1sc into next turning ch. Turn.

2nd row Using A, ch 4, skip first 2sc, *1 dc into next ch 1 sp, ch 1, skip next sc, rep from * to turning ch, 1dc into turning ch. Turn.

1st and 2nd rows form pat. Rep them throughout.

3

3 Simple mosaic

Work pat row as for back of sweater on page 194, using A and B alternately.

Horizontal patterns

Horizontal patterns are highly versatile, being suitable for anything from fashionable garments to the simplest baby clothes. Choose beautiful yarns and colors to display the strong crosswise lines of these useful patterns.

Skills you need

*Working into the back loop
*Horizontal buttonholes

If you do not know these skills refer to pages 297 and 299.

Materials

Horizontal patterns can be worked in most yarns, though fancy yarns are best used for simple, striped patterns. The cardigan opposite has been worked in an acrylic-wool, Shetland-type knitting worsted. However, most plain worsted-weight yarns could be substituted and the narrow stripes of the cardigan provide the ideal method of using up small amounts of yarn. (Of course, if you are substituting yarn — whether left over or new — remember to check your gauge carefully.) The cardigan has been worked in autumnal shades, but bright colors would be just as attractive.

Special technique – whirl pattern

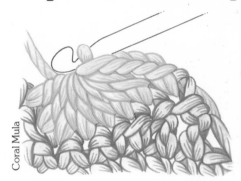

1 *Pattern band B on the basic cardigan is a two-color whirl pattern. Using the first color, work the first, graduated-stitch row as instructed in the pattern. Change to the second color. After working the edge stitch, work seven doubles together into the next seven stitches to form the first half whirl.*

2 *Continue in this way to the end of the row. Complete the whirl on the third row by working six doubles and one triple into the space formed at the top of each group of seven doubles. Work one single crochet into each single crochet between half whirls to anchor the whirl.*

3 *Return to the first color and for the last pattern row follow the instructions given for the first pattern row. This straightens the top edge to allow you to work the next row of the basic cardigan instructions.*

Coral Mula

The basic striped cardigan

Horizontal becomes vertical in this casual, comfortable cardigan that is surprisingly easy to make.
Size
Misses' size 34-38 in. bust
Length including waistband 21¼ in.
Sleeve seam 19¼ in.
Gauge
15 sts and 14 rows to 4 in. worked on size G hook

Materials
6 oz knitting worsted in main color (A)
6 oz in contrasting color (B)
4 oz in contrasting color (C)
2 oz in each of contrasting colors (D) and (E)
Sizes G and H crochet hooks
5 buttons

Note: The cardigan is worked in two sections, each beginning at the cuff,

which are then joined at the center back.

Left side
Cuff Using size G, crochet hook and A, ch 21.
Base row Work 1 sc into 2nd ch from hook, 1sc into each ch to end. Turn. 20 sts.
Next row Ch 1, skip first st, 1 sc into *back* loop only of each st to end.

Turn.
Rep last row 34 more times.
Change to size H hook, and use loop on hook to beg to work into one edge of cuff:
Next row (RS) Ch 3, skip first row end, 1dc into each row end to end. Turn. 36 sts.
Next row Ch 1, skip first st, 1 sc into next st, (2sc into next st, 1sc into each of next 7 sts) 4 times, 2sc into next st, 1sc into last st. Turn. 41 sts.
Pattern band A
Change to B.
1st row (RS) Working in sc, inc one st at each end of the row. 43 sts.
2nd row (RS) Work in dc.
198

Change to A.
3rd row Working in sc, inc one st at each end of the row. 45 sts.
4th row Work in sc.
Change to B.
5th row Ch 1, skip first st, *inserting hook from front to back work 1dc around stem of next st on last dc row (1dc front below worked) 1sc into each of next 2sc, rep from * to last 2 sts, 1dc front below, 1sc into last st. Turn.
6th row Work in dc.
Rep 3rd-6th rows once more, inc one st at each end of 7th row, and working each dc front below on 9th row into corresponding dc on 4th row. 47 sts.

Next row Change to D and work in sc working into back loops only and inc one st at each end of row. 49 sts.
Next row Change to A and work in sc.
Pattern band B
Change to C.
1st row (RS) Ch 4, skip first st, *1dc into next st, 1hdc into next st, 1sc into each of next 3 sts, 1hdc into next st, 1dc into next st, 1tr into next st, rep from * to end. Turn.
Change to D.
2nd row Ch 1, 1sc into first tr, *ch3, leaving last loop of each st on hook work 1dc into each of next 7 sts, yo and draw through all 8 loops on hook (half whirl formed), ch 3, 1sc into next

tr, rep from * to end, working last sc into top of turning ch. Turn.
3rd row Ch 1, 1sc into first sc, *(6dc, 1tr) into sp at top of half whirl, 1sc into next sc, rep from * to end. Turn. Change to C.
4th row As for 1st row.
Next row Change to A and work in sc.
Next row Change to D and work in sc.
Next row Change to E and work in sc working into front loops only.
Cont in dc, working in stripe sequence as follows: 1 row in E, 2 rows in B, 3 rows in C, 2 rows in D, 2 rows in E, 3 rows in B, 3 rows in C.
At the same time shape sleeve as follows:
Next row Work in dc.
Next 2 rows Work in dc, inc one st at each end of row.
Working in stripe sequence as above, rep last 3 rows 5 times in all. 69 sts.
Next row Work in dc. Do not turn.
Shape Bodice
Using C, at the end of last row of stripe sequence, ch 27. Turn and remove hook from loop. Using spare length of C, ch 26 and fasten off. Return to loop just left.
Next row (WS) Work 1sc into 2nd ch from hook, 1sc into each of next 25 ch, 1sc into each of 69 sts on top of sleeve, 1sc into each of 26ch just worked. Turn. 121 sts.
Next row Change to B and work in dc.
Next 3 rows Work in sc, working one row each in E, D and A.
Change to C and work the 4 rows of pattern band B, omitting all incs.
Next 4 rows Work in sc, working one row each in A, D, E and B.
Cont with B and work the 10 rows of pattern band A, working one more sc at end of 5th row and omitting all incs.
Next row Change to E and work in sc.
Next row Change to C and work in dc.**
Back bodice extension
Next row With RS facing and using C, ch 1, skip first st, 1sc into each of next 49 sts, turn. 50 sts.
Shape back neck
Next row Sl st over first 3 sts, ch 1, skip first st, 1sc into each st to end. Turn. 48 sts.
Next row Ch 1, skip first st, 1sc into each st to last 3 sts, work 2sc tog, 1sc into last st. Turn.
Next row Ch 3, work 2dc tog, 1dc into each st to end. Turn. 46 sts.
Change to B and work 2 rows in dc.
Change to C and work 1 row in dc and 1 row in sc. Fasten off.

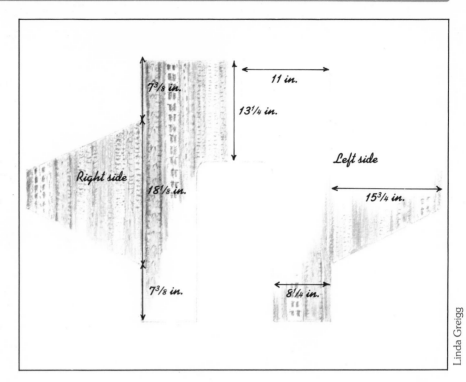

Right side
Work as for left side to **.
Fasten off.
Back bodice extension
Next row With RS facing and using C, rejoin yarn to 72nd st of row, ch 1, skip first st, 1sc into each st to end. 50 sts.
Complete to match left back neck, reversing all shaping.
Fasten off, but do not cut yarn.

To finish
With RS tog, join center-back seam with crochet sl st. Fasten off.
Press center-back seam lightly. Join underarm and side seams, carefully matching stripes at underarm.
Striped border
1st row With RS facing, join C to first st on lower edge, ch 1, skip first st, 1sc into each st up right front, 1sc into each row end on back neck (*at the same time* place colored markers at beg of RH back bodice extension, center-back seam and beg of LH back bodice extension), and 1 sc into each st down left front. Turn.
Next 7 rows Work in sc, working 2sc tog at each of the markers on the back neck and working in stripe sequence as follows: 2 rows in B, 1 row in E, 1 row in D, 1 row in A, 1 row in B and 1 row in A. Fasten off.

Waistband
Using size G hook and A, ch 21.
Work in single crochet ribbing as for cuff until work measures 26¾ in, or your waist measurement, when slightly stretched.
Fasten off.
Using size G hook and A, work 1 row of sc into row ends on lower edge to neaten edge and ease in fullness.
Sew waistband to lower edge of bodice from RS, easing in fullness. Do not press seam.

Buttonhole band
Mark position of 5 buttonholes on lower right front.
1st row Using size G hook and with RS facing, join A to first st on lower edge, ch 1, skip first st, 1sc into each st up right front, 1sc into each sc across back neck, working 2sc tog at markers, and 1sc into each st down left front. Turn.
2nd row Ch 1, skip first st, *work in sc to position of buttonhole, ch 2, skip next 2 sts, 1sc into next st, rep from * 4 more times, 1sc into each st to end. Turn.
3rd row Work in sc
4th row Work in crab st (see page 262). Fasten off.
Sew buttons to left front to correspond with buttonholes.

199

Adapting the basic striped cardigan

Use the Pattern Library to make several versions of the basic, simply-shaped cardigan.

Simple substitutions

The basic cardigan is worked from cuff to cuff in horizontal bands of pattern and simple stripes to produce a vertically-striped garment.

Any of the samples in the Pattern Library could be substituted, the easiest method being to make the cardigan in a combination of the simple, striped patterns.

Enlarging the cardigan

The cardigan will fit Misses' sizes 34 to 38 in., but it can easily be made larger by working more rows on the sleeves and on the back bodice extension.

Make enough waistband to fit, when slightly stretched, around your waist and sew it to the lower edge, easing any fullness to fit.

Horizontal patterns

1 Fancy clusters

Make a multiple of 9ch plus 2 extra.

Base row (RS) 1sc into 2nd ch from hook, *1sc into each of next 3ch, (ch 7, 1sc into next ch) 3 times, 1sc into each of next 3ch, rep from * to end. Turn.

1st row Ch 7, *(leaving last loop of each st on hook work 4dc into next 7ch loop, yo and draw through all 5 loops on hook — cluster formed —, 2ch) twice, cluster into next 7ch loop, ch 6, rep from * to end, omitting ch 6 at end of last rep and working ch 2, 1dtr into last sc. Turn.

2nd row Ch 1, skip first dtr, *(2sc into next ch 2 loop) 3 times, 6sc into next ch 6 loop, rep from * to end, omitting 6sc at end of last rep and working 2sc into sp formed by turning ch. Turn.

3rd row Ch 3, skip first st, 1dc into each st to end. Turn.

4th row Ch 1, skip first st, *1sc into each of next 3 sts, (ch7, 1sc into next st) 3 times, 1sc into each of next 3 sts, rep from * to end. Turn.

Rep 1st-4th rows throughout, ending with a 2nd row.

Note: This pattern can be worked in one or two colors as shown.

2 Narrow stripes

Use 2 colors, A and B, and work alternate rows of hdc and sc, changing color after every row or every other row.

3 Simple clusters

Make a multiple of 2ch plus 2 extra.

Base row (RS) 1sc into 2nd ch from hook, 1sc into each ch to end. Turn.

1st row Ch 3, leaving last loop of each dc on hook work 2dc into first st, yo and draw through all 3 loops on hook (cluster worked), *miss next st, (1dc, 1 cluster) into next st, rep from * to last 2 sts, miss next st, 1dc into last st. Turn.

2nd row Ch 1, skip first st, *1sc into top of next cluster, 1sc into next dc, rep from * to end, ending with 1sc into top of turning ch.

Rep 1st and 2nd rows throughout.

Irish lace

Elaborate Irish crochet fabrics, formed from a rich combination of flowers, leaves and shamrocks combined with picot mesh, all worked in fine cotton, are among the most beautiful and most elaborate of crochet laces.

Terry Simms

201

Skills you need

*Irish crochet

If you do not know these skills refer to page 305.

Materials

Although other, thicker yarns are sometimes used, Irish crochet looks best when worked in fine cotton like the number 5 cotton used to make the T-shirt and vest on page 201. If you have never worked with fine cotton before, you may meet gauge problems. In this case, you may find the suggestions given on page 308 helpful. Traditional Irish crochet as used for the basic vest, is in the heirloom class — similar pieces made in the last century are now much sought after — so look after it carefully. Wash gently with mild soapflakes, shape it on a towel and allow it to dry naturally.

Special technique – working raised motifs

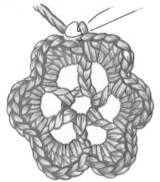

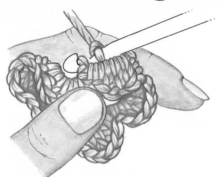

1 *The outer petals of the flowers on the T-shirt and vest on page 201 are worked behind the previous rounds to give a three-dimensional appearance. Work the first two rounds as given in the pattern to form a small flower.*

2 *Holding the work as shown and inserting the hook from back to front, work one single crochet around the stem of the next double on the first round. Chain five. Continue in this way, ending with a slipstitch to the first single crochet. On the next round work in the chain loops to form the petals.*

3 *To form a many-layered motif like the rose on the vest, repeat step 2, working the single crochet around the corresponding single crochet on the last-but-one round. The petals are made larger by working more chain and then more graduated stitches on the following round.*

The basic Irish crochet patterns

For those who love Irish crochet: a pretty T-shirt for a small girl and, for you, an heirloom vest.

Child's T-shirt
Sizes
To fit 23 [24:25½] in. chest
Length 13¾ [15:16⅛] in.
Sleeve seam 3½ in.

Note: Instructions for larger sizes are given in square brackets []; where there is only one set of figures it applies to all sizes.

Gauge
8 loops and 17 rows to 4 in. over mesh pattern

Materials
4 [4:5] oz No 5 crochet cotton
Size B crochet hook
1 small button

Back
Using size B hook, ch 79 [82:85].
Base row 1sc into 7th ch from hook, *ch 4, skip next 2ch, 1sc into next ch, rep from * to end. Turn. 25 [26:27] ch 4 loops.
Pat row Ch 6, *1sc into next ch 4 loop, ch 4, rep from * to last loop, 1sc into last loop. Turn.
Rep pat row until work measures 8¼ [9:9¾]in. from beg.
Shape armholes
Next row Sl st across first ch 4 loop and to center of next loop, 1sc into center of same loop, work 22 [23:24] loops. Turn.
Rep last row once more, working 20 [21:22] loops. Turn.**
Next row Sl st across first ch 4 loop and to center of next loop, 1sc into center of same loop, work 19 [20:21] loops. Turn.
Cont without further shaping until work measures 13 [14¼:15¼] in.

from beg.
Shape shoulders
Next row Sl st across first 2 ch 4 loops and to center of next loop, 1sc into same loop, work 14 [15:16] loops. Turn.
Rep last row once more, working 10 [11:12] loops. Turn.
Next row Sl st across first ch 4 loop and to center of next loop, 1sc into center of same loop, work 8 [9:10] loops. Turn.
Next row Sl st to center of first ch 4 loop, 1sc into same loop, work 7 [8:9] loops. Fasten off.

Front
Work as given for back to **.
Divide for neck
Next row Sl st across first ch 4 loop and to center of next loop, 1sc into center of same loop, work 9[10:10] loops, turn.
Cont on these loops only without

202

further shaping until work measures 12⅛ [12½:13¾] in. from beg, ending at neck edge.

Shape neck
Next row Sl st across next 2 ch 4 loops, 1sc into next sc, ch 6, 1sc into first ch 4 loop, pat to end. Turn 7 [8:8] loops. Work one pattern row without shaping.
Next row Sl st to center of first ch 4 loop, 1sc into same loop, rep pat to end. Turn. 6 [7:7] loops.
Work one pattern row without shaping.
Rep last shaping row once more. 5[6:6] loops.

Shape shoulder
Next row Sl st across first 2 ch 4 loops and to center of next loop, 1sc into same loop, rep pat to end. Turn. 2 [3:3] loops.
Next row Ch 6, 1sc into first loop, ch 4, 1sc into next loop.
Fasten off.
Rejoin yarn to next ch 4 loop at beg of neck division and work 2nd side of neck to correspond with first, reversing all shaping.

Sleeves (both alike)
Using size B hook, make 52 [55:58] ch.
Base row As for Back. 16 [17:18] loops.
Cont in pat as for Back until work measures 3½ in. from beg.

Shape top
Next row Sl st across first ch 4 loop and to center of next loop, 1sc into same loop, rep pat across 13 [14:15] loops. Turn.
Next row Sl st to center of first ch 4 loop, 1sc into same loop, rep pat across 12 [13:14] loops. Turn.
Rep pat row twice without shaping.
Next row Sl st to center of first ch 4 loop, 1sc into same loop, rep pat across 11 [12:13] loops. Turn.
Next row Sl st to center of first ch 4 loop, 1sc into same loop, rep pat across 10 [11:12] loops. Turn.
Rep last 4 rows, work one loop less on each dec row until 8 [9:10] loops rem.
Rep last 2 rows only until 4 [5:6] loops rem. Fasten off.

To finish
Join shoulder seams. Set in sleeves. Join side and sleeve seams, using an invisible seam.

Lower edging
Using size B hook and with RS facing, join yarn to a side seam, ch 1, *2sc

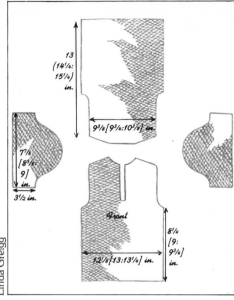

into first loop, ch 3, sl st to first of ch 3 (picot formed), 3sc into next loop, picot, rep from * all around lower edge, ending with sl st to first ch. Fasten off.

Neck edging
With RS facing, join yarn to a shoulder seam and work as for Lower edging.

Sleeve edgings
With RS facing, join yarn to sleeve seam and work as for Lower edging.

Rosebud
Ch 6, join with a sl st to form a circle.
1st round Ch 6, (1dc, 3ch) 5 times into circle, sl st into 3rd of ch 6.
2nd round (1sc,1hdc, 3dc,1hdc, 1sc) into each ch 3 loop.
3rd round Working behind last round, 1sc around first dc on 1st round, *ch 5, 1sc around next dc on 1st round, rep from * ending with sl st into first sc.
4th round (1sc, 1hdc, 5dc, 1hdc, 1sc) into each ch 5 loop, sl st to first sc. Fasten off. Work 3 more rosebuds in the same way.

Leaf
Ch 16.
Base row 1sc into 3rd ch from hook, 1sc into each ch to last ch, 3sc into last ch, 1sc into each ch along opposite side of foundation ch, 1sc into turning ch.
On foll rows work into *back* loop only of each st:
1st row 1sc into each of next 11sc. Turn.
2nd row Ch 1, skip first st, 1 sc into each of next 10sc (1sc,1ch,1sc) into center sc, 1sc into each sc to within

4sc of tip of leaf, turn.
3rd row Ch 1, skip first sc, 1sc into each sc to ch1 at base of leaf, (1sc, 1ch, 1sc) into ch 1 sp, 1sc into each sc to within 3sc of previous row.
4th and 5th rows As 3rd.
6th row As 3rd, working 3sc into ch 1 sp at base of leaf.
Fasten off. Work 5 more leaves in the same way.

To finish
Sew motifs around neck as shown. Sew on button. Ch 6. Fasten off. Sew to neck to correspond with button.

Traditional Irish vest
Note: Before beginning, see Know-How 12, page 305. Because of the method of working, it is not possible to give exact yarn quantity, size and gauge.

Materials
Twilley's Lyscordet as required (vest shown was made from 8 x 25g balls)
Size B crochet hook
Paper dressmaking pattern for simple vest
Medium-weight interfacing as required

Rose
Using size B hook, ch 8, join with a sl st to form a circle.
1st round Ch 6, (1dc, 3ch) 7 times into circle, sl st to 3rd of ch 6.
2nd round (1sc, 1hdc, 3dc, 1hdc, 1sc) into each ch 3 loop.
3rd round Working behind last round, 1sc around first dc on 1st round, (5ch, 1sc around next dc) 7 times, ch 5, sl st to first sc.
4th round (1sc, 1hdc, 5dc, 1hdc, 1sc) into each ch 5 loop.
5th round Working behind last round, 1sc around first sc of 3rd round, (ch 7, 1sc around next sc) 7 times, ch 7, sl st to first sc.
6th round (1sc, 1hdc, 7dc, 1hdc, 1sc) into each ch 7 loop.
7th round Working behind last round, 1sc around first sc of 5th round, (ch 9, 1sc around next sc) 7 times, ch 9, sl st to first sc.
8th round (1sc, 1hdc, 9dc, 1hdc, 1sc) into each ch 9 loop, sl st to first sc.
Fasten off. Make one more rose in the same way.

Rosebud
Work as for child's T-shirt. Make 21.

Leaf
Work as for child's T-shirt. Make 22.

To finish
Cut out back and fronts of vest from interfacing, omitting seam allowances around neck, armholes and front and lower edges. Join side seams.
Tack motifs into position on interfacing as shown.
Using size B hook, join yarn to first motif and work picot mesh as follows:
Base row *Ch 2, 1 picot (ch 3, sl st into first of ch 3), ch 3, 1 picot, ch 2, sl st into next motif or same motif, rep from * to end. Turn.

Pat row Ch 2 or sl st along a motif as necessary, *1 picot, ch 3, rep from * to end.
Cont filling in between motifs, working straight rows of picot mesh across back. When all motifs are joined and interfacing covered with picot mesh, remove all tacking. Join shoulder seams.
Edging
Working over a cord of 3 strands of crochet cotton, *(3sc, 1 picot) into each ch loop all around neck, front

and lower edges and around armholes.

Adapting the basic Irish patterns

Use the rich motifs and meshes of Irish crochet to create modern or traditional lace.

Adapting the T-shirt
The child's T-shirt is adapted simply by substituting motifs from the Pattern Library for those given in the basic

pattern. Sew the smaller motifs around the neckline as shown on page 201, or arrange larger motifs over the body of the T-shirt. Use matching cotton sewing thread to sew the motifs invisibly to the mesh. If you do not want to substitute motifs, vary the T-shirt by making a motif in a contrasting color.

Adapting the vest
The basic vest could be made using any of the motifs or the mesh in the Pattern Library, though a picot mesh is traditional. The vest has motifs around the edges only, but using motifs all over the vest would create a beautifully ornate fabric.

Irish crochet patterns

1 Fancy clover
Ch 7, join with a sl st to form a circle.
1st round Ch 1, 15sc into circle, sl st to first sc.
2nd round *Ch 4, skip next sc, (1 dc, ch 2, 1dc) into next sc, ch 4, skip next sc, sl st into each of next 2sc, rep from *, ending with sl st into last sc.
3rd round *(3sc, ch 4, 3sc) into next ch 4 loop, (2sc, ch 4, 2sc) into next ch 2 loop, (3sc, ch 4, 3sc) into next ch 4 loop, sl st between 2 sl st of 2nd round, rep from * to end.
Stem Ch 16, 1sc into 2nd ch from hook, 1sc into each ch to end, sl st to base of clover. Fasten off.

2 Bluebell
Ch 10. From now on, work over a cord.
Base row 1sc into 2nd ch from hook, 1sc into each of next 7 ch, 5sc into last ch, 1sc into each of next 8 ch along opposite side of foundation, 3sc over cord only, 1sc into each of next 7 sc, 3 sc over cord only. Turn. From now on work into back loop only of each st.
1st row Ch 1, skip first sc, 1sc into each of next 10sc, 3sc into end sc, 1sc into each of next 8sc, 3sc over cord only. Turn.
2nd row Ch 1, skip first sc, 1sc into each of next 13sc, work 20sc over cord for stem. Fasten off.

3 Honeycomb mesh
Make a multiple of 4 ch plus 10.
Base row 1dc into 10th ch from hook, *ch 4, skip next 3 ch, 1dc into next ch, rep from * to end. Turn.
Pat row Ch 8, 1dc into first ch 4 loop, *ch 4, 1dc into next ch 4 loop, rep from * to end. Turn.
Rep pat row for length required.

4 Triple leaf
Ch 15. From now on, work each st over a cord.
1st row 1sc into 2nd ch from hook, 1sc into each of next 12 ch, 5sc into last ch, 1sc into each ch along opposite side of foundation ch, work 3sc over cord only, working into back loop of each st, work 1sc into each of next 11sc. Turn.
From now on work into back loop only of each st.
2nd row Ch 1, skip first sc, 1sc into each of next 11sc, 3sc into center of 3sc of previous row, 1sc into each of next 12 sc. Turn.
3rd row Ch 1, skip first st, 1sc into each of next 12 sc, 3sc into center sc of 3sc of previous row, 1sc into each of next 10 sc. Turn.
4th row Ch 1, skip first st, 1sc into each of next 10 sc, 3sc into center sc of 3sc of previous row, 1sc into each of next 11sc. Turn.
5th row Ch 1, skip first st, 1sc into each of next 11 sc, 3 sc into center sc of 3sc of previous row, 1sc into each of next 9 sc. Turn.
6th row Ch 1, skip first st, 1sc into each of next 9sc, 3sc into center sc of 3 sc of previous row, 1sc into each of next 9 sc. Fasten off.
Make 2 more leaves in the same way and sew together as shown.

2

1

5 Picot flower

Ch8, join with a sl st to form a circle.

1st round Ch 1, 20sc into circle, sl st to first ch.

2nd round 1sc into same place as sl st, *ch 10, skip 3sc, 1sc into next sc, rep from *, ending with sl st into first sc.

3rd round (Ch 1, 1hdc, 2dc, 1 picot — ch 3, sl st into first of 3 ch —, 3tr, 1 picot, 3tr, 1 picot, 2dc, 1hdc, 1sc) into each ch 10 loop, sl st to first ch. Fasten off.

6 Wheel

Ch 6, join with a sl st to form a circle.

1st round Ch 1, 12sc into circle, sl st to first sc.

2nd round Ch 4, (1dc, ch 1) into each sc, sl st to 3rd of ch 4.

3rd round Ch 1, 3sc into each ch 1 sp, sl st to first sc.

4th round *Ch 4, sl st to first ch to form a picot, 1sc into each of next 3sc, rep from * to end, sl st to base of first picot. Fasten off.

7 Four-leaf clover

Stem Working over a triple cord, work 24 sc.

Flower center Work 21sc over cord, join with a sl st to first of these 21sc. Pull the cord to form a circle.

Petal Leave the cord and work into the sc of the circle thus:

1st row (Ch 1, 1sc into next st) 4 times. Turn.

2nd row Ch 1, 1sc into first sc, (ch 1, 1sc under next ch 1 of 1st row) 4 times, ch 1, 1sc into same place as last sc. Turn.

3rd row (Ch 1, 1sc under ch 1) 6 times, ch 1, 1sc into same place as last sc. Turn. Work 2 more rows without shaping, then one more row, missing one st at each end. Fasten off. Work 3 more petals in the same way, missing 1sc of ring between 2 petals.

From now on work over cord:

Edging Work a row of sc all round outer edges of petals, working (1sc into same place as last st at beg of petal, 1sc into missed sc on circle, 1sc into same place as first st of next petal) between 2 petals. At end of last petal cont working sc into sts of stem. Fasten off.

Chain effects

Beautiful chain-effect patterns can be produced surprisingly easily by working surface slip stitch on a plain or filet mesh crochet background.

Skills you need

*Decreasing
*Triple crochet

If you do not know the basic skills, refer to pages 295 and 296.

Materials

Most yarns are suitable for surface chain effects, and extremely attractive results can be achieved by using a textured yarn such as a thick bouclé to work the chains. However, it is usually better if the background is worked in a plain yarn to avoid the chain effect being overwhelmed by a highly textured surface. For summer tops like the one on page 207, a four-ply cotton as we have used is ideal, though the garment would look equally pretty with longer sleeves and worked in a wool yarn.

Special technique – surface slip stitch

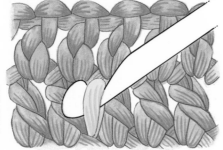

1 To work surface slip stitch into a solid background, begin at the lower edge and, with the yarn at the back of the work, insert the hook into the space between two stitches. Take the yarn over the hook and draw through a loop.

2 Insert the hook into the next space between two stitches. Take the yarn over the hook and draw through a loop. The first surface slip stitch has been anchored to the background fabric. Continue in this way to form the surface chain effects.

3 Work surface slip stitch on a filet mesh background fabric in the same way, but insert the hook from front to back into the chain space between two doubles.

Basic chain-effect sweater

Mouth-watering ice-cream colors are used for this cool cotton sweater decorated with horizontal and vertical stripes.

Sizes
Misses' sizes 10 [12:14]
Length from shoulder 22½ in.
Sleeve seam 5 in.
Note: Instructions for larger sizes are in brackets []; where there is one set of figures it applies to all sizes.

Materials
6 oz of a sport-weight smooth cotton yarn in each of two colors (A and B)
1 oz in contrasting color (C)

Size H crochet hook
Pair of size 5 knitting needles

Gauge
11 tr and 5 rows to 4¼ in. worked on size H hook

Note: When shaping, work edge sts at a slightly looser tension to keep work flat.

Back
**Using crochet hook and A, ch 47 [49:51] loosely.
Base row 1tr into 5th ch from hook, 1tr into each ch to end. Turn. 44[46:48] sts.

Pat row Ch 4, skip first tr, 1tr into each tr, 1tr into top of turning ch. Turn.
Work 12 more rows in pat.

Shape armholes
1st row Sl st into each of first 4tr, ch 4, 1tr into each tr to last 3 sts, turn. 38 [40:42] sts.**
2nd row Ch 4, skip first tr, leaving last loop of each st on hook, work 1tr into each of next 3 sts, yo and draw through all 4 loops (2tr dec), 1tr into each tr to last 4 sts, dec 2tr over next 3 sts, 1tr into top of turning ch. Turn. 34 [36:38] sts. Work 8 rows in pat. Fasten off.

Coral Mula

Front
Work as for back from ** to **
Shape left neck
1st row Ch 4, skip first tr, dec 2tr over next 3 sts, 1tr into each of next 7 [8:9] tr, dec 2tr over next 3 sts, 1tr into next tr, turn. Cont on these 11 [12:13] sts for first side of neck.
2nd row Ch 4, skip first tr, dec 2tr over next 3 sts, 1tr into each of next 6 [7:8] sts, 1tr into top of turning ch. Turn.
3rd row Ch 4, skip first tr, 1tr into each of next 4 [5:6] tr, dec 2tr over next 3 sts, 1tr into top of turning ch.

Turn. 7 [8:9] sts.
Work in pat for 7 rows. Fasten off.
Note: There is one more row on front than on back, making the shoulder seams fall slightly toward the back.
Shape right neck
1st row Skip center 8tr after right neck and join A to next tr, ch 4, dec 2tr over next 3 sts, 1 tr into each of next 7 [8:9] tr, dec 2tr over next 3 sts, 1tr into top of turning ch. Turn.
2nd row Ch 4, skip first tr, 1tr into each of next 6 [7:8] sts, dec 2tr over next 3 sts, 1tr into top of turning ch. Turn.

3rd row Ch 4, skip first tr, dec 2tr over next 3 sts, 1tr into each of next 4 [5:6] tr, 1tr into top of turning ch. Turn.
Work in pat for 7 rows. Fasten off.

Sleeves (alike)
Using crochet hook and A, ch 39.
Work base row as for back. 36 sts.
Work in pat for 4 rows.
Shape top
1st row As first row of armhole shaping of back. 30 sts.
2nd row As 2nd row of armhole shaping of back.
3rd row Ch 4, skip first tr, leaving last

loop of each st on hook, work 1 tr into each of next 2 sts, yo and draw through all 3 loops (1tr dec), 1tr into each tr to last 3 sts, dec 1tr over next 2 sts, 1tr into top of turning ch. Turn. Rep 2nd and 3rd rows twice. 12 sts. Fasten off.

Waistbands

With RS facing and using knitting needles, join A to first ch of base row of back. Pick up and knit 60 [62:64] sts evenly along base edge. Work 1½ in. in K1,P1 ribbing. Bind off *very loosely* in ribbing.
Work other waistband to match.

Horizontal stripes

With RS of back facing and using crochet hook, join B to the top of first st of base row.
Stripe row Ch 4, 1tr into top of each st of base row. Fasten off.
Skip the next 2 rows. Rep stripe row into the top of next row.
Cont in this way to shoulders.
Work front and sleeves to match.

Vertical stripes

Note: When working vertical stripes, work through the corresponding sps of horizontal stripe and background tog where appropriate. Work the vertical stripes at a slightly tighter tension than the background to draw the work up and reduce the length slightly.

1st stripe With RS of back facing and using crochet hook, join C to the sp between the center 2 sts of base row. Keep yarn at back of work. Fold each horizontal stripe downward toward the waistband. Yo, (insert hook into same sp as joining, yo and draw through loop on hook) twice, *insert hook into corresponding sp of next row, yo and draw through loop on hook, insert hook into same sp, yo and draw through loop on hook, rep from * to top. Fasten off.
2nd stripe Skip the next 3 sps to the right and join C to the next sp between sts. Fold each horizontal stripe upward toward the top of the work. Work as for first stripe.
Cont in this way over all the back, skipping 3 sps between each stripe and folding horizontal stripes alternately downward and upward as shown in the photograph.
Work front and sleeves to match.

To finish

Join shoulders. Join side and sleeve seams. Set in sleeves.
Neck edging
1st round With RS facing and using crochet hook, join A to neck edge at shoulder. Work sc evenly around neck, working a multiple of 5sc plus 1 extra, sl st into first sc.
2nd round 1sc into first sc, *1hdc into each sc, 1dc into each of next 2sc, 1hdc into next sc, 1sc into next sc, rep from * to end, sl st into first sc. Fasten off.
Sleeve edging
Work as for neck edging.

Adapting the chain-effect sweater

Use our surface slip stitch patterns to make beautiful chain-effect fabrics.

Surface chain stitch is extremely easy to work on to a plain crochet or filet mesh background fabric to form raised chain effects.

Gauge

However, gauge is very important since the slip stitches can easily pucker the background fabric in the direction of working.
Before beginning to work the chain effects on the main fabric, experiment on a small sample of the background. If the fabric puckers badly, try using a larger hook; if the puckering is slight, it is usually sufficient to work at a slightly looser tension.
The puckering effect can, however, sometimes be turned to advantage, as in the sweater on page 207, in which the surface slip stitches are deliberately worked tightly to draw up the fabric, giving a gathered effect.

Designing chain effects

Draw your design roughly on paper before beginning and use as a guide when working the chain effects.
The pattern samples show geometric variations of surface slip stitch patterns, but you can also work horizontal or diagonal lines, or zigzags. Alternatively, work spirals, circles or other shapes.
Use surface slip stitch to outline raised stitches like bobbles, or to emphasize embroidery.
If you want a particularly raised effect, work the slip stitches with a thicker yarn than that used for the background fabric, or use the yarn doubled.

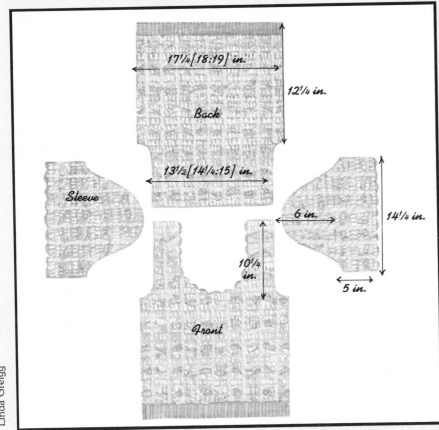

17¼[18:19] in.

12¼ in.

Back

13½[14¼:15] in.

Sleeve

6 in.

14¼ in.

10¼ in.

5 in.

Front

Linda Greigg

Chain-effect patterns

1 Fine stripe pattern

Use two colors: A and B.
Background Using A, make a 1dc, ch 1 filet mesh of any number of sps.
Chains With RS facing, join B to first sp of base row. Keep yarn at back of work. Yo, (insert hook into same sp as join, yo and draw through loop on hook) twice, *insert hook into corresponding sp of row above, yo and draw through loop on hook, insert hook into same sp, yo and draw through loop on hook, rep from * to end, turn, ch 1, work up next row of sps in the same way. Continue in this way over entire background. Fasten off.

2 Vertical chains on stripes

This pattern could be used to make the sweater on page 207.
Use two colors: A and B.
Background Work in tr in stripes of 1 row each of A and B with an even number of sts.
1st row With RS facing, join B to the sp between the center 2tr of the base row. Keep yarn at back of work. Yo, (insert hook into same sp as join, yo and draw through loop on hook) 3 times, *insert hook into corresponding sp of row above, yo and draw through loop on hook, (insert hook into same sp, yo and draw through loop on hook) twice, rep from * to end. Fasten off.
2nd row Working to the right, skip the next two sps between tr and with RS facing, join A to the next sp between tr. Work as for 1st row. Skipping two sps between each row, and alternating A and B, continue in this way over entire background.

1

2

3

3 Vertical chain pattern

This pattern could be used to make the sweater on page 207. Use three colors: A, B and C.
Background Using A, work in tr with an even number of sts.
1st row With RS facing, join B to the sp between the center 2tr of the base row. Keep yarn at back of work. Yo, (insert hook into same sp as join, yo and draw through loop on hook) 3 times, *insert hook into corresponding sp of row above, yo and draw through loop on hook, (insert hook into same sp, yo and draw through loop on hook) twice, rep from * to end. Fasten off.

2nd row Working to the right, skip the next two sps between tr and with RS facing, join C to the next sp between tr. Work as for 1st row. Skipping two sps between each row, and alternating B and C, continue in this way over entire background.

Fine edgings

You can change the look of your entire wardrobe by the clever way in which you apply fine crochet edgings to your clothes. With an eye for color and strategic positioning, you can use these edgings to bring about startling transformations.

Mike Goodall

Skills you need

*Crochet with fine cotton

If you do not know the basic skills, refer to page 308.

Materials

For best results, fine edgings should be worked in thin thread. We have used a fine lurex yarn, roughly equivalent to a No 20 cotton, but the same edging could be worked in the equivalent cotton to edge a summer top or dress. The edgings on pages 211-212 could be worked in even finer cotton, though obviously, the finer the cotton, the narrower the edging that will be produced. When crocheting with fine cotton, always use a thin steel hook. You may find this difficult at first, but the results are stunning.

Special technique – sewing an edging to ribbing

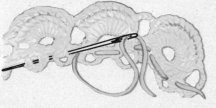

Coral Mula

1 The edging on page 210 curves naturally, giving a ruffled look when it is sewn to a straight edge. To achieve the same look with a straight edging, use matching yarn to run a few gathering stitches through the edging. Draw up to the length required.

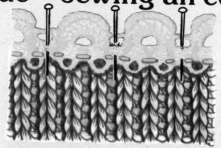

2 Pin the right side of the edging to the wrong side of the ribbing as shown. Place the pins vertically and stretch the edging slightly as you do so.

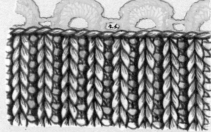

3 Using yarn to match the sweater and a fine sewing needle, sew the edging to the ribbing using stab stitch, so that the small stitches are on the right side of the ribbing. Remove the edging when laundering the sweater and wash separately.

The basic fine edging

The edging on this classic jersey adds a dash of sparkle and glamour.

Size
The edging measures approx. 1½ in. deep at the widest point.

Gauge
Three 7dc groups measure 1½ in. across

Materials
To edge the cuffs and the V-neck of a woman's sweater:
2×350 yd. spools of fine lurex yarn
No. 1 steel crochet hook

Note: This edging is naturally curved to form a frill when attached to a straight edge. If a frill is not required, stretch the edging by pinning it out straight and lightly spraying with water. Allow to dry naturally.

Edging
Using steel crochet hook, ch 20.
Base row 1dc into 10th ch from hook, ch 2, skip next 4 ch, (1dc, ch 2, 1dc) into next ch, ch 2, skip next 4 ch, (1dc, ch 2, 1dc) into last ch. Turn.
1st row Ch 3, 6dc into first ch 2 sp, skip next ch 2, 7dc into next ch 2 sp, skip next ch 2, 11dc into last loop. Turn.
2nd row Ch 9, 1dc into first dc, ch 2, skip next 6dc, (1dc, ch 2, 1dc) into next dc, ch 2, (1dc, ch 2, 1dc) into 4th dc of next group, ch 2, (1dc, ch 2, 1dc) into 4th dc of last group. Turn.
3rd row Ch 3, 6dc into first ch 2 sp, (skip next ch 2, 7dc into next ch 2 sp) twice, skip next ch 2, 11dc into last loop. Turn.
4th row Ch 9, 1dc into first dc, ch 2, skip next 6dc, (1dc, ch 2, 1dc) into next dc, ch 2, (1dc, ch 2, 1dc) into 4th dc of next group. Turn.
Rep 1st-4th rows for length required. Fasten off.

To finish
Sew edgings to neck and wrists as shown above.

Adapting the fine edging

Using any of these fine edgings to add delicate beauty to your most precious clothes.

Fine edgings should be used to decorate lightweight garments. Turn baby's christening gown into a family heirloom with fine edging, or edge the collar and cuffs of a delicate blouse or dress. Edging a favorite sweater, as shown here, will transform a simple garment into something special.
Choose a finely knitted plain sweater to set off the edging to best effect.

Caring for fine edgings
Never iron fine cotton edgings; this will simply flatten them. Instead, pin out the edging to the correct size and spray lightly with water. (A spray mister, sold by florists for plants, is ideal.) Then allow the edging to dry naturally.
When the garment is washed, always remove the edging and wash it separately. Dark colors could run and ruin your hard work.

211

Fine edging patterns

1

1 Coronet edging
Ch 4.
Base 1dc into 4th ch from hook, turn, *ch 3, 1 dc into sp between last dc and ch 3, turn. Rep from * for length required so that the number of spaces is divisible by 4 plus 2.

Work foll rows into one long edge of base:
1st row (WS) *Ch 4, skip next sp, 1sc into next sp, ch 8, skip next sp, 1sc into next sp, rep from * to end, ending with ch 4, skip next sp, 1sc into last sp. Turn.

2nd row Ch 2, 1sc into first ch 4 sp, *11dc into next ch 8 sp, 1sc into next ch 4 sp, rep from * to end. Turn.
3rd row Ch 2, 1sc into first sc, *ch 6, (1sc, ch 3, 1sc) into center dc of next 11dc group, ch 6, 1sc into sc between groups, rep from * to end. Fasten off.

2

2 Petal edging
Use two colors: A and B.
Using A, ch 6.
Base Work so that the number of ch 5 loops on each long edge is divisible by 4 plus 1. Work foll rows into one long edge of base:

1st row (RS) Ch 5, 1sc into first ch 5 loop, *ch 4 (leaving last loop of each tr on hook work 4tr, yo and draw through all loops on hook (cluster worked), ch 3, cluster, ch 3, cluster) into next ch 5 loop, ch 4, 1sc into next ch 5 loop, rep from * to end, ending

with ch 4, 1sc into last ch 5 loop. Fasten off.
2nd row With RS facing, join B to first sc, ch 4, cluster into same sc, *ch 4, skip ch 4 loop, 2sc into next ch 3 loop, ch 6, 2sc into next ch 3 loop, ch 4, cluster into next sc, rep from * to end. Fasten off.

Ray Duns

3

3 Irish picot edging
Ch 16.
Base row 1sc into 10th ch from hook, ch 6, sl st into 4th ch from hook (picot formed), ch 7, sl st into 4th ch from hook (picot formed), ch 2, 1sc into last ch. Turn.
1st row (RS) Ch 11, sl st to 4th ch from hook, ch 2, 1sc into next loop

between picots, ch 6, sl st into 4th ch from hook, ch 7, sl st to 4th ch from hook, ch 2, 8dc into next ch 10 loop. Turn.
2nd row Ch 4, skip first dc, (1dc into next dc, ch 1, skip next dc) 3 times, 1dc into last dc, ch 5, 1sc into next loop between picots, ch 6, sl st into 4th ch from hook, ch 7, sl st into 4th

ch from hook, ch 2, 1sc into center of last loop. Turn.
3rd row Ch 11, sl st to 4th ch from hook, ch 2, 1sc into next loop between picots, ch 6, sl st into 4th ch from hook, ch 7, sl st into 4th ch from hook, ch 2, 8dc into ch 5 loop. Turn. 2nd and 3rd rows form pat. Rep them for length required. Fasten off.

Filet motifs

Filet crochet is derived from two basic stitches — double crochet and chain stitch. Motifs are created against a trellis of these two stitches by building up blocks of double crochet. Fine yarns, particularly cotton, are best suited to this work.

Skills you need

*Filet crochet

If you do not know the basic skills, refer to page 304.

Materials

Cottons of varying thicknesses are most frequently used for filet crochet. Very fine, lightweight cottons worked on a fine hook can be used to make lacy edgings and insertions that can be added to household linens such as tablecloths, handkerchiefs, napkins etc., whereas thicker crochet cottons are more suitable for making summer tops and shawls. Traditionally filet crochet was worked in white or écru cotton, but these cottons are now available in many different colors to make interesting fabrics. Thicker knitting yarns are sometimes used when making a garment in filet crochet, but, on the whole, the most effective results are achieved by using crisp cottons so that the motifs stand out clearly against the background net.

Special technique – making a crochet cord

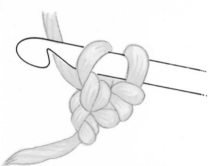

1 Ch 2 to start. Hold the chain between finger and thumb of left hand and work 1sc into 2nd ch from hook. Turn the work so that foundation ch is at top. Insert hook into back loop and work 1sc into foundation loop of 2nd ch made at beginning.

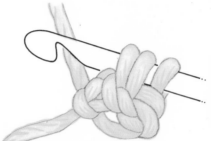

2 Turn chain so that bottom is now at top next to hook and insert hook into 2 loops at side of chain.

3 Take yarn over and through 2 loops on hook. Yarn over hook and through rem 2 loops to make a twisted stitch. By turning stitches in this way you achieve a twisted cord.

The basic filet sun top

Fine cotton has been used to make a pretty filet crochet summer top, patterned with roses and bordered with simple filet lace.

Sizes
Misses' sizes 12-14 [14-16]
Length 13¾ in. excluding straps

Note: Instructions for larger sizes are in square brackets []; where there is one set of figures it applies to both sizes.

Gauge
20 spaces and 20 rows to 4 in. on No. 3 steel crochet hook

Materials
5 oz No. 20 crochet cotton
No. 3 steel crochet hook
5 buttons
214

Top (both sizes)
Using crochet hook ch 207.
1st row 1dc into 4th ch from hook, 1dc into each of next 2 ch, (ch 2, skip 2 ch, 1dc into next ch) twice, (2 sps made), 1dc into each of next 3 ch (block made), now work 60 sps, 1 block, 2 sps, 1 block. Turn.
2nd row Ch 3, skip first dc, 1dc into each of next 3dc (block made over block at beg of row), ch 2, 1dc into next dc) twice, (2 sps made over 2 sps), 1dc into each of next 3dc (block made over block) now work 47 sps, (2dc into next sp, 1dc into next dc) twice, (2 blocks made over 2 spaces) now work 11 sps, 1 block, 2 sps, 1dc into each of next 2dc, 1dc into next ch (block made over block at end of row). Turn.
3rd row 1 sl st into each of first 4dc (1 block dec) ch 3, (2dc into next sp, 1dc into next dc) twice, ch 2, skip 2dc,

1dc into next dc (sp made over block), now work 10 sps, 1 block, 2 sps, 1 block, 23 sps, 2 blocks, 22 sps, 2 blocks. Turn.
4th row Ch 5, 1dc into 4th ch from hook, 1dc into next ch, 1dc into next dc, (block inc at beg of row) 2 sps, 1 block, 20 sps, 1 block, 2 sps, 2 block, 22 sps, 1 block, 2 sps, 1 block, 10 sps, 1 block, 1 sp, ch 2, skip 2dc, insert hook into next ch and draw yarn through, yo and draw through one loop on hook (a foundation ch made), complete as a dc, *yo, insert hook into foundation ch and draw yarn through, yo and draw through one loop on hook (another foundation ch made) complete as a dc, rep from * twice more (a block inc at end of row), ch 3. Turn.
Smaller size only
5th-88th rows Work from chart.
88th row is marked by arrow.

Turn chart and work from 88th row marked by arrow back to first row. Fasten off.

Larger size only
5th-94th rows Work from chart, noting that 94th row is marked by an asterisk.

Turn chart and work from 94th row marked by * back to first row. Fasten off.

Buttonhole band (both sizes)
1st row Join yarn to 3rd dc made on last row, 1sc into same place as join, (2sc into next sp, 1sc into next dc) twice, 1sc into each of next 3dc, (2sc into next sp, 1sc into next dc) 60 times, 1sc into each of next 3dc (2sc into next sp, 1sc into next dc) twice, ch 1. Turn.
2nd row 1sc into each of first 58 sc, (ch 5, skip 5sc, 1sc into each of next 28sc) 4 times, ch 5, skip 5 ch, 1sc into each of next 4sc, ch 1. Turn.
3rd row (1sc into each sc, 5sc into next ch 5 sp) 5 times, 1sc into each sc, ch 5. Turn.
4th row Skip first 3sc, 1dc into next sc, (ch 2, skip 2sc, 1dc into next sc) 65 times. Fasten off.

Button band (both sizes)
1st row Join yarn to 3rd dc made on first row, 1sc into same place as join, (2sc into next sp, 1sc into base of next dc) twice, 1sc into base of each of next 3dc, (2sc into next sp, 1sc into base of next dc) 60 times, 1sc into base of each of next 3dc, (2sc into next sp, 1sc into base of next dc) twice, ch 1. Turn.
2nd row 1sc into each sc, ch 1. Turn.
3rd row 1sc into each sc, ch 5. Turn.
4th row As 4th row of buttonhole band.

Shoulder straps (make 2)
Ch 9.
1st row 2 blocks. Turn.
2nd row Ch 5, inc 1 block, 2 sps, inc 1 block. Turn.
3rd row Ch 3, 1 block, 2 sps, 1 block. Turn.
4th row Dec 1 block, ch 3, 2 blocks. Turn.
Rep 2nd to 4th rows until work measure 14½ in. from beg, or length required. Fasten off.

To finish
Sew shoulder straps in place. Sew on buttons to correspond with buttonholes.

Cord (make 2)
Ch 2 to start and holding this between finger and thumb of left hand, work 1sc into 2nd ch from hook, turn, inserting hook into back of loop, work 1sc into foundation loop of 2nd ch made , *turn, insert hook into 2 loops at side, yarn over and draw through 2 loops on hook, yarn over and draw through rem 2 loops, rep from * until work measures 47½ in. from beg, or length required. Fasten off. Slot cords through at waistline and top.
Damp and pin out to measurements. Allow to dry.

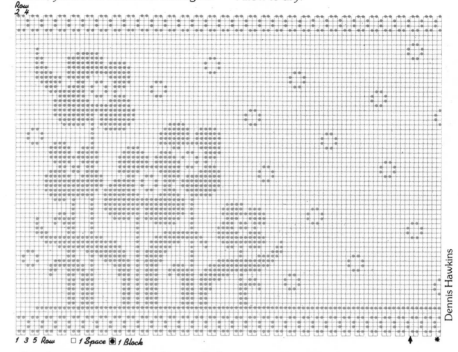

1 3 5 Row   □ *1 Space* ● *1 Block*

Dennis Hawkins

Adapting the filet sun top

Substitute another filet pattern by working from one of the following charts, placing the motifs on a plain fillet net background.

Filet crochet, traditionally worked in fine cottons, is really a simple form of lace inspired by filet guipure lace. It had its heyday at the end of the 19th century when filet crochet could be seen decorating almost any piece of household linen, baby clothing or underwear. The motifs are worked on a basic net background with spaces filled in with blocks of crochet to create the motifs. The motifs can either be small and scattered all over the fabric, or quite large and used either individually or to create denser patterns over the basic net.

The basic patterns
The basic net is made by working individual double crochets with either one or two chain stitches between, with the blocks formed by working one or two double crochets into these spaces. The size of the net must be determined before creating a filet design, and when working from a printed pattern, this will be specified.

Using a filet chart
Since many filet operations are fairly complicated and intricate, the pattern is set out in the form of a chart, as row-by-row instructions for the motifs would be far too complicated and lengthy. Each blank square on the chart represents a space, not one stitch, and each block is indicated by a symbol — for example — a ●, as here, or an X — so that you can see how many blocks to work in one row to form the pattern.

Right side rows are usually worked by reading the chart from right to left, and wrong side rows from left to right. When designing your own filet chart, remember that although spaces, and blocks are represented by squares on the graph paper, these do not represent the actual size of the space or block, it is important to make a sample gauge square in the yarn and pattern of your choice so that you can judge the size of the completed motif.

Filet patterns

1 Cupid's bow

Worked over a basic net of 1dc and 1 ch with 1dc worked into each ch 1 space to form blocks.

1st motif row Ch 4, 1dc into next dc, (ch 1, 1dc into next dc) 29 times, 1dc into ch 1 space, 1dc into next dc (ch 1, 1dc into next dc) to end of row, working last dc into 3rd ch of turning chain.

Following chart, work rem 32 rows of motif.

Heart

Worked over a basic net of 1dc and 1 ch with 1dc worked into each ch 1 space to form blocks.

1st motif row Ch 4, 1dc into next dc, (ch 1, 1dc into next dc) 4 times, 1dc into next ch 1 space, 1dc into next dc, (ch 1, 1dc into next dc) to end of row working last dc into 3rd ch of turning chain.

Following chart work rem 9 rows of motif.

First motif row

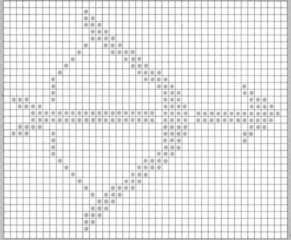

First motif row 1

2 Swans

Worked over a basic net of 1dc and 1 ch with 1dc worked into each ch 1 space to form blocks.

1st motif row Ch 4, 1dc into next dc, (ch 1, 1dc into next dc) 4 times, (1dc into ch 1 space, 1 dc into next dc) 17 times, (ch 1, 1dc into next dc) to end of row working last dc into 3rd ch of turning chain.

Following chart, work rem 28 rows of motif.

Small swan

Worked over a basic net of 1dc and 1 ch with 1dc worked into each ch 1 space to form blocks.

1st motif row Ch 4, 1dc into next dc (ch 1, 1dc into next dc) 3 times, 1dc into ch 1 space, 1dc into next dc) 9 times, (ch 1, 1dc into next dc) to end of row, working last dc into 3rd ch of turning chain.

Following chart work rem 12 rows of motif.

First motif row

2

First motif row

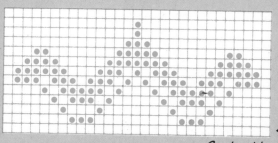

First motif row

First motif row

3 Large butterfly

Worked over a basic net of 1dc and 2 ch with 2dc worked into each ch 2 space to form blocks.

1st motif row Ch 5, 1dc into next dc, (ch 2, 1dc into next dc) 14 times, (2dc into next ch 2 space, 1 dc into next dc) 4 times, (ch 2, 1dc into next dc) to end of row working last dc into 3rd ch of turning chain.

Small butterfly

Worked over a basic net of 1dc and 2 ch with 2dc worked into each ch 2 space to form blocks.

1st motif row Ch 5 to count as first dc and ch 2 space, 1dc into next dc, (ch 2, 1dc into next dc) 3 times, 2dc into

next ch 2 space, 1dc into next dc, (ch 2, 1dc into next dc) 7 times, 2dc into ch 2 space, 1dc into next dc, (ch 2, 1dc into next dc) 3 times working last dc into 3rd ch of turning chain.
Following chart, work rem 12 rows.

First motif row

First motif row

4 Birds

Worked over a basic net of 1dc and 1 ch with 1dc worked into each ch 1 space to form blocks.

1st motif row Ch 4, 1dc into next dc, ch 1, 1dc into next dc, 1dc into ch 1 space, 1dc into next dc, (ch 1, 1dc into next dc) to end of row, working last dc into 3rd ch of turning chain.
Following chart, work rem 38 rows of motif.

Flying bird

Worked over a basic net of 1dc and 1 ch with 1dc worked into each ch 1 space to form blocks.

1st motif row Ch 4, 1dc into next dc, (ch 1, 1dc into next dc) 13 times, 1 dc into next ch 1 space, 1dc into next dc, (ch 1, 1dc into next dc) 14 times working last dc into 3rd ch of turning chain.
Following chart work rem 10 rows.

217

Chevrons

Both plain and fancy chevron or zigzag patterns are created by simply alternating groups of increased and decreased stitches along the row.

Skills you need

* Double Crochet
* Shaping
* Horizontal buttonholes

If you do not know the basic skills, refer to pages 294, 295 and 299.

Materials

Fancy chevrons look best worked in a plain yarn to show off the lacy or bobbly fabric. However, simple chevrons can be made in fancy yarns as long as you work contrasting colored stripes so that the zigzag pattern is not hidden by the hairs or loops of the yarn. If the cardigan and scarf on page 218 — worked in a thin glitter yarn — were crocheted in one color, the shiny yarn could easily detract from the chevron pattern; worked in stripes of black and copper, the zigzag pattern is obvious.

Special technique – working chevrons

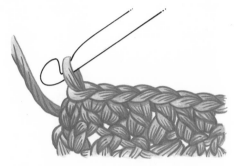

Coral Mula

1 *The zigzag effect of chevrons is produced by alternately increasing and decreasing stitches at intervals along a row. The zigzags point up where stitches have been increased and down where stitches have been decreased.*

2 *When working some chevron patterns, it can be difficult to keep the edges straight. Patterns will therefore suggest that you increase one stitch where the zigzag points down at the end of a row and decrease one stitch at the side edge where the zigzag points up.*

3 *To straighten top edges, work gradually longer stitches to the lowest point of the zigzag, working the longest stitch into the center stitch of the decreasing, and then work shorter stitches to the highest point, working the shortest stitch into the center stitch of the increasing.*

The basic chevron cardigan and scarf

For your most glamorous nights — an elegant cardigan and scarf in a glittery yarn.

Sizes
Cardigan: Misses' sizes 12 [14:16]
Length from shoulder approx 25in.
Sleeve seam 19in.
Scarf measures approx 60in. by 8in.

Note: Instructions for larger sizes are in brackets []; where there is only one set of figures it applies to all sizes.

Gauge
26dc and 13 rows to 4 in. in pat worked on size C hook

Materials
Cardigan 11 [13:15] oz of a fingering-weight glitter yarn in main color (A)
10 [12:14] oz in contrasting color (B)
Scarf 4 oz of a fingering-weight glitter yarn in main color (A)
4 oz in contrasting color (B)

Size C crochet hook
6 buttons

Note: To keep the edges of the work straight, one stitch has been increased at the end of a row where the zigzag points down at the edge, and one stitch has been decreased where the zigzag points up. When shaping the fronts or sleeves, count the stitches carefully, so that the correct number is increased or decreased. Count the 3 double crochets worked into one stitch as 3, and the 3 double crochets worked together as 1.

Note: When measuring the work, measure between its farthest points — that is, between a downward-pointing zigzag on the lower edge and an upward-pointing zigzag on the top edge.

Scarf
Using A, ch 55.
Base row 1dc into 4th ch from hook, 1dc into each of next 3 ch. *3dc into

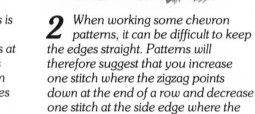

next ch, 1dc into each of next 5 ch, (yo, insert hook into next ch, yo, draw through a loop, yo, draw through 2 loops on hook) 3 times, yo, draw through all 4 loops on hook (called work 3dc tog), 1 dc into each of next 5 ch*, rep from * to * twice more, 3dc into next ch, 1 dc into each of last 5 ch. Turn. 55 sts.

Pat row Ch 3, skip first 2dc, 1dc into each of next 4dc, **3dc into center dc of 3dc group, 1dc into each of next 5dc, work 3dc tog, 1dc into each of next 5dc**, rep from ** to ** twice more, 3dc into next dc, 1dc into each of next 4dc, skip next dc, 1dc into top of turning ch. Turn.
Rep pat row throughout, working 1 more row in A and cont in stripe sequence as follows: 2 rows B, 2 rows A, 1 row B, 1 row A, 3 rows B, 2 rows A, 2 rows B, 1 row A, 1 row B, 3 rows A. Cont in pat, working stripe sequence, until work measures approx 60 in. ending with 3 rows in A. Fasten off.

Cardigan
Back
Using A, ch 123 [127:137].

Base row 1dc into 4th ch from hook, 1dc into each of next 2 [4:2]ch, work from * to * as for base row of Scarf 8 [8:9] times, 3dc into next ch, 1dc into each of last 4 [6:4]ch. Turn. 123 [127:137] sts.

Pat row Ch 3, skip first 2dc, 1dc into each of next 3 [5:3]dc, **3dc into center dc of 3dc group, 1dc into each of next 5dc, work 3dc tog, 1dc into each of next 5dc**, rep from ** to ** 7 [7:8] more times, 3dc into next dc, 1dc into each of next 3 [5:3]dc, skip next dc, 1dc into top of turning ch. Turn. Rep pat row throughout, working 1 more row in A, and working stripe sequence as set for Scarf until work measures 17 in. Mark both ends of the last row with contrasting threads. Cont in pat in stripe sequence until work measures 25 in. ending with a row in A.

Straighten top edge
Using A, ch 3, 1dc into each of next 1 [3:1]dc, 1hdc into each of next 2dc, *1sc into next dc, sl st into center dc of 3dc group, 1sc into next dc, 1hdc into each of next 2dc, 1dc into each of next 2dc, 1tr into each of next 3dc, 1dc into each of next 2dc, 1hdc into each of next 2dc, rep from *7 [7:8] more times, 1sc into next dc, sl st into center dc of 3dc group, 1sc into next dc, 1hdc into each of next 2dc, 1dc into each of next 1 [3:1] dc, 1dc into top of turning ch. Fasten off.

220

Left front
Using A, ch 67 [70:73].

Base row 1dc into 4th ch from hook, 1dc into each of next 2 [4:4]ch, work from * to * as for base row of Scarf 4 times, 3dc into next dc, 1dc into each of last 4 [5:8] dc. Turn. 67 [70:73] sts.

Working in pat and stripe sequence as for back, cont until work measures 17 in.

Mark beg of last row for armhole.

Shape neck edge
Keeping armhole edge straight, dec 1 st at neck edge on every row until 40 [42:44] dc rem.

Work even in pat until work measures same as back, ending with a row in A.

Straighten top edge
Using A, straighten edge as for back, working sl st into center of 3dc group and working 3tr over 3dc worked tog. Fasten off.

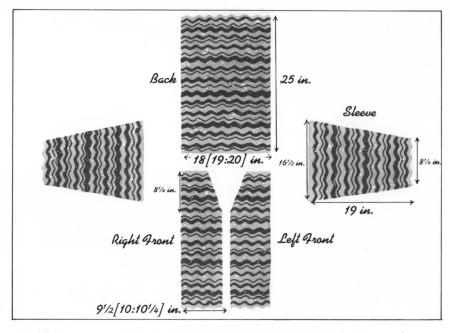

Right front
Work as for left front, reversing shaping.

Sleeves (alike)
Using A, ch 55.

Work base row and pat row as for Scarf. 55 sts.

Cont in pat and stripe sequence as for Scarf, inc 1dc at each end of every alternate row until there are 111 sts.

Work even until work measures 19 in., ending with a row in A.

Straighten top edge as for back.

Fasten off.

Front band
Join shoulder seams.

With RS facing, join A to right front at the inner corner of the lower edge. Work 2 sc into each row end up right front, across back neck and down left front. Work 5 more rows of sc, ending at lower right front. Turn.

Buttonhole row Ch 1, skip first sc, 1 sc into each of next 3sc,* ch 3, skip next 3sc, 1sc into each of next 16sc, rep from * 4 more times, ch 3, skip next 3sc, 1sc into each sc to end. Turn.

Next row Ch 1, skip first sc, 1sc into each st to end, working 3sc into ch 3 sp of previous row.

Work 5 more rows in sc.

Fasten off.

To finish
Set in sleeves. Sew side and sleeve seams. Sew on buttons.

Adapting the chevron pattern

Create dazzling zigzag fabrics by using simple or fancy chevron patterns.

Simple chevrons can be adapted easily by working the stitches slightly differently. For example, the double crochet chevron used to make the cardigan and scarf on page 218 would look very different if the double crochets were worked into the backs of the stitches of the previous row or if chain-one spaces were substituted for double crochet.

More complicated chevron patterns are difficult to substitute because of their varying gauges and frequently large stitch multiples. If you do decide to use a fancy chevron, perhaps basing the pattern on a measurement diagram or a paper pattern, check your gauge very carefully.

Fancy — and to a lesser extent, simple — chevrons may cause difficulties when counting stitches because of the number of increased and decreased stitches. Always count every stitch of an increased group and count each decreased group as one stitch.

The finished result will look more professional if you pay special attention to finishing. If the yarn allows, press the work carefully. Use an invisible seam, which will help you to match striped patterns exactly.

Fashion yarns

The wide range of exciting fashion yarns available today naturally leads to more adventurous and inventive designs, so be daring and take this opportunity of working with unusual textures.

Skills you need

* Elongated stitches
* Crochet with fashion yarns

If you do not know the basic skills, refer to pages 300 and 309.

Materials

Fashion yarns, now available in a wide range of colors and textures, tend to be more expensive than basic double knitting or four ply, so choose patterns that display their luxurious beauty to best effect. In this way, the extra cost will be an investment rather than an extravagance. When using fashion yarns, it is possible, as we have done in the jacket on page 221, to combine yarns from different manufacturers; the basic jacket is worked in a pure alpaca, used double throughout, a mohair/synthetic yarn that is roughly equivalent to a double knitting and a wool/synthetic bouclé.

Special technique – make the epaulettes

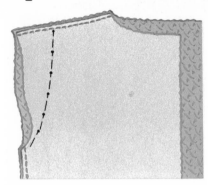
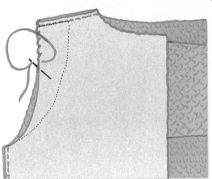
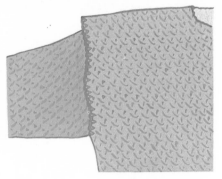

Coral Mula

1 *Join the shoulder and side seams, leaving the armhole open. Join the sleeve seams, sewing on the cuffs. Pin the shoulder seam 2 in. in from the armhole edge. Then pin a sloping line between the first pin at the shoulder and the underarm seam point.*

2 *Set in the sleeves, pinning carefully so that the top of the sleeve matches the sloping line of pins. Leave the armhole edge free to form the epaulette and, with wrong sides facing, oversew the top of the sleeve to the front and back.*

3 *Set in the other sleeve in the same way. Complete the epaulettes by working one round of single crochet around the edges, working one stitch into each row end.*

The basic fashion jacket

This beautiful jacket has a designer look with its clever shaping and rich texture. Wear it with a soft leather belt for extra style.

Sizes
Misses' sizes 10-12 [14-16]
Length approx 27½ in.
Sleeve seam approx 19 in.

Note: Instructions for larger sizes are in square brackets []; where there is only one set of figures it applies to both sizes.

Gauge
7 sc to 2in. and 16 rows to 3in.

Materials
19 [21]oz semi-bulky mohair yarn (A)
18 [21]oz fingering-weight alpaca yarn (B)
23 [25]oz bulky-weight yarn (C)
Size C and H crochet hooks
3 toggle fasteners
Note Use B double throughout.

Pattern
1st-5th rows Using A, ch 1, 1 sc into first sc, 1sc into each sc to end. Turn.
6th row (RS) Using B, ch 1, 1 sc into first sc of last row, *skip next sc of last row and work 1sc into corresponding sc 1 row below, skip next sc of last row and work 1 sc into corresponding sc 2 rows below, cont in this way working next sc 3 rows below, next sc 4 rows below, next sc 3 rows below, next sc 2 rows below and next sc 1 row below, 1sc into next sc of last row*, rep from * to * to end. Turn.
7th-11th rows Using B, ch 1, 1sc into first sc, 1sc into each sc to end. Turn.
12th row Using C, work as for 6th row.
13th-15th rows Using C, ch 1, 1sc into first sc, 1sc into each sc to end. Turn.
16th row Using A, ch 1, 1 sc into first sc of last row, * (skip next sc of last row and work 1sc into corresponding sc 1 row below) twice, skip next sc of last row and work 1sc into corresponding sc 2 rows below, cont in this way working next sc 3 rows below, next sc 2 rows below and (next sc 1 row below) twice, 1sc into next sc of last row*, rep from * to * to end. Turn.
These 16 rows form pat.

Note: The 1st color band ends after the 5th row, the 2nd color band after the 11th row and the 3rd color band after the 15th row.

Back
Using A and size H hook, ch 74 [82].
Base row 1sc into 2nd ch from hook, 1sc into each ch to end. Turn. 73 [81] sc. Beg with the 2nd pat row, cont in pat until 3 bands of color have been worked.

222

Shape sides

Keeping pat correct, dec 1 st at each end of last row of each band of color until 55[61] sc rem. Work 4 bands of color without shaping. Inc 1 st at each end of last row of next and every alt band of color until there are 65 [71] sc. Work even until work measures approx 26⅜in. from beg, ending with a 7th row.

Shape shoulders

Next row Keeping pat correct, work in pat to last 4 [5] sts, turn. Rep last row 3 times. Work even in pat 1 row.
Next row Sl st into 4 sc, work in pat to last 4 sc, turn.
Next row Sl st into 3 sc, work in pat to last 3 sc, turn.
Rep last row once. Fasten off.

Left front

Using A and size H hook, ch 34 [38]. Work base row as for back. 33 [37] sc. **Beg with the 2nd pat row, cont in pat until 3 bands of color have been worked, noting that for the larger size the 6th and 12th pat rows will end with 1sc 4 rows below and the 16th pat row will end with 1sc 3 rows below.**

Shape sides

Keeping pat correct, dec 1 sc at the end — side edge — of last row of each band of color until 24 [27] sc rem. Work 4 bands of color without shaping. Inc 1 sc at the end — side edge — of last row of next and every alt band of color until there are 29 [32]sc. Work even until 2 fewer rows have been worked than on back to shoulder, thus ending with a 5th pat row.

Shape neck

1st row Work as 6th pat row to last 7 [8] sc, turn.
2nd row Sl st into 2 sc, pat to end. Turn.
3rd row Work in pat to last 2 sc, turn.

Shape shoulder

1st row Work in pat to last 4 [5] sc, turn.
Work in pat 1 row.
Rep last 2 rows once.
Next row Work in pat to last 4 sc, turn.
Next row Sl st into 3 sc, pat to end. Fasten off.

Right front

Using A and size H hook, ch 46 [50]. Work base row as for back. 45 [49] sc. Beg with the 2nd pat row cont in pat until 3 bands of color have been worked, noting that for the **smaller size** the 6th and 12th pat rows should

be worked thus: ch 1, 1 sc into first sc, next sc 3 rows below, next sc 2 rows below, next sc 1 row below, next sc into next sc of last row, then rep from * to * of 6th pat row to end. The 16th pat row should be worked thus: ch 1, 1 sc into first sc, next sc 2 rows below, (next sc 1 row below) twice, next sc into next sc of last row, then rep from * to * of 16th pat row to end.

Shape work

Keeping pat correct, dec 1 st at beg — side edge — of last row of each band of color until 36 [39] sc rem. Work 4 bands of color without shaping. Inc 1 sc at beg — side edge — of the last row of next and every alt band of color until there are 41 [44] sc. Cont straight until 2 fewer rows have been worked than on back to shoulder, ending with a 5th pat row.

Shape neck and shoulders

1st row Join B to 17th sc of row, work in pat to end. Turn.
2nd row Work in pat to last 3 [4] sc, turn.
3rd row Sl st into 2 sc, work in pat to last 4 [5] sc, turn.
4th row Work in pat to last 2 sc, turn.

5th row Work in pat to last 4 [5] sc, turn. Work in pat 2 rows straight.
8th row Sl st into 4 sc, work in pat to end.
9th row Work in pat to last 3sc, turn. Fasten off.

Sleeves

Using A and size H hook, ch 42 [46]. Work base row as for back. 41 [45] sc. Work as left front from ** to **. Work 3 more bands of color as set.

Shape sleeve

Keeping pat correct, inc 1 st at each end of the 4th and 6th rows of next band of color. Inc 1 st at each end of last row of 8th and 9th bands of color. 49 [53] sc.
With pat as set, cont until work measures approx 19 in. from beg, ending with a 5th or 15th pat row.

Shape top

1st row Sl st into 3 sc, pat to last 3 sc, turn.
Keeping pat correct, dec 1 sc at each end of the 2nd, 4th and 6th rows of each A band and each B band and at each end of the 2nd, 3rd and 4th rows of each C band until 7 [11] sc rem. Fasten off.

Collar

With A and size H hook, ch 82. Work base row as for back. 81 sc. Beg with 2nd pat row, cont in pat until work measures approx 7 in. from beg, ending with a 6th pat row.

Shape collar

1st row Keeping pat correct, sl st into 2 sc, pat to last 2 sc, turn. Work in pat 1 row. Rep 1st row. Work in pat 3 rows. Rep 1st row. Work in pat 1 row. **Next row** Sl st in first sc, pat to last sc, turn. Work in pat 1 row. Rep last 2 rows twice. Fasten off.

Cuffs

Using A and size H hook, ch 18. Work base row as for back. 17 sc. Beg with 2nd pat row, cont in pat until work measures approx 13 [14] in. ending with a complete band of color. Fasten off.

Toggle loops (make 3)

With C and size H hook, ch 10. Work 2 rows sc. Fasten off.

To finish

Do not press. Pin out each piece to correct shape, spray lightly with water and allow to dry naturally. Use one strand of B to join all seams. Join shoulders. Join sleeve seams. Join short ends of cuffs. With RS of cuffs to WS of sleeve, sew on cuffs. Turn up cuff to RS. Using A and size C hook, work 1 round of sc around edge of cuffs. Join side seams, leaving top 9¾ in. open for armholes. Place a pin on each shoulder seam, 2 in. from armhole edge. With pins mark a sloping line between first pin and top of side seam. Placing edge of sleeve top to line of pins, sew sleeve neatly on WS leaving the crochet free at armhole edge to form an epaulette. Using A and size C hook, work 1 round of sc around edge of epaulettes. With RS of collar to WS of jacket, sew last row of collar to neck edge. Fold collar in half onto RS of jacket, with base row overlapping the first collar seam. Catch stitch neatly at shoulders and at center back neck. Finish row-ends at front edges. With RS facing, using C and size H hook, work 2 rows of sc up right front edge, ending at fold in collar. Fasten off. Work 1 row down left front edge in the same way. Sew toggle loops to right front edge and toggles to left front.

224

Adapting the fashion jacket

Experiment with luxurious fashion yarns to create your own original designer jacket.

The basic jacket is worked in an elongated stitch pattern (see page 226) and is elevated to designer class by the carefully shaped waist, the epaulettes and the deep collar and cuffs.

Simple variations

Beginners, who might find the basic jacket a little daunting, could follow the instructions using one fashion yarn, rather than three. Use simple single crochet instead of elongated stitches and emphasize the lines of the jacket by using a contrasting yarn to edge the cuffs, collar and front edges. Other patterns, using two or more yarns, could be substituted, but because the basic jacket has been carefully designed so that the pattern matches at the seams, you should only substitute a pattern that repeats over exactly the same number of rows as the basic jacket pattern — that is, sixteen. Otherwise, the patterns will not match at the seams and will detract from the appearance of the garment.

Choose yarns with contrasting color and textures — fluffy, smooth and bouclé — for best results.

Other variations

More experienced workers could of course substitute another elongated-stitch pattern.

Using colored pens, draw the pattern's stitch and row repeat on graph paper so that one square represents one stitch. Draw your substitute pattern in the same way, making sure that it has exactly the same stitch and row repeat as the original.

Gauge

Of course, whatever your substitute pattern, you should make sure that the gauge matches that of the basic jacket. Using the yarn and stitch pattern of your choice, make a square. Pattern yarns can be difficult to check for gauge because of their texture and because they often cannot be pressed. Pin out the square, taking care not to over-stretch the sample, and spray lightly with water. Allow to dry naturally, and then hold up to the light and count the number of stitches and rows to four inches.

Fashion-yarn patterns

1 Single crochet stripes

This pattern could be used to make the jacket on page 221.
Use 3 colors: A, B and C.
Can be worked over any number of sts.
Work throughout in sc stripes pat.
1st to 5th rows Color A.

6th row (WS) Color B.
7th to 11th rows Color C.
12th row Color A.
13th to 15th rows Color B.
16th row Color C.
1st–16th rows form pat. Rep them throughout.

1

2 Cat's claw stitch

This pattern could be used to make the jacket on page 221. Use 2 colors, A and B. Using A, make a multiple of 4 ch plus 2 extra.

Base row Using A, 1sc into 2nd ch from hook, 1sc into each ch to end. Turn.

Note On first rep of pat only, the base row stands for the 1st pat row and therefore the 1st pat row should not be worked.

1st row Using A, ch 1, 1sc into first sc, 1sc into each sc to end. Turn.

2nd-11th rows Rep 1st row 10 times.

12th row (RS) Using B, ch 1, 1sc into first sc, (skip next sc of last row, insert hook through the corresponding sc 2 rows below, yo and draw loop through and up to height of first sc of row, yo and draw through 2 loops — elongated sc worked in, skip next sc of last row and work 1 elongated sc into corresponding sc 4 rows below, skip next sc of last row and work 1 elongated sc into corresponding sc 2 rows below, 1 sc into next sc of last row) to end. Turn.

13th-15th rows Using B, ch 1, 1sc into first sc, 1sc into each sc to end. Turn.

16th row As 1st row.

1st-16th rows form pat. Rep them throughout.

Note: The sample ends with the 15th row.

3 V-stitch

Make a multiple of 3 ch plus 1 extra.

Base row 1dc, ch 1, 1dc all into 5th ch from hook, (skip next 2ch, 1dc, ch 1, 1dc all into next ch) to last 2 ch, skip next ch, 1dc into last ch. Turn.

1st row Ch 3, (1dc, ch 1, 1dc all into next ch 1 sp) to end, ending 1dc into top of turning ch. Turn.

Rep 1st row for pat.

4 Crossed doubles worked in spaces

Make an odd number of ch.

Base row 1dc into 4th ch from hook, 1dc into ch before ch into which last dc was worked, (skip next ch, 1dc into next ch, 1dc into skipped ch — pair of Xdc worked) to last ch, 1hdc into last ch. Turn.

1st row Ch 2, (1dc into sp after next pair of Xdc, 1dc into sp before same pair of Xdc — pair of Xdc worked) to end, ending 1hdc into top of turning ch. Turn.

Rep 1st row for pat.

5 Fur stitch

Make an even number of ch.

Base row 1sc into 2nd ch from hook, (ch 1, skip next ch, 1sc into next ch) to end. Turn.

1st row Ch 1, 1sc into first sc, (1sc into next ch 1 sp, ch 1) to end, omitting ch 1 at end of last rep and ending with 1sc into last sc. Turn.

2nd row Ch 1, 1sc into first sc, (ch 1, 1sc into next ch 1 sp) to end, working 1sc at end of last rep into last sc of 1st row. Turn.

1st-2nd rows form pat. Rep them throughout.

Simon Butcher

MEN'S WEAR

Elongated stitches

Martin Palmer

Skills you need

* **Single crochet**
* **Crab stitch**
* **Elongated stitches**

If you do not know the basic skills, refer to pages 262, 295 and 300.
226

Materials

Elongated-stitch patterns can be worked in both plain and fancy yarns. If you decide to use the latter, remember that the patterns look best if the basic stripes are worked in a fancy yarn and the elongated stitches themselves are worked in a plain yarn. This combination of textures produces beautiful fabrics, but beginners may find these yarns difficult to work with as it is not easy to see where the hook should be inserted when working the elongated-stitch patterns. However, plain yarns used by themselves, either in toning or contrasting combinations, will produce very attractive fabrics.

Special technique – working a pointed lower edge

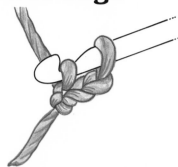

1 *The pointed lower edges of the fronts of the basic vest are worked by increasing from a small number of chain stitches while at the same time keeping the elongated-stitch pattern correct. Begin with three chain stitches and work one single crochet into the third chain from the hook. Turn.*

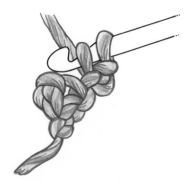

2 *On the next row begin with two chains and increase by working one single crochet into the second chain from the hook. Work one single crochet into the next single crochet and finish the row with one single crochet into the turning chain. Turn.*

3 *The third row begins as before with two chains. Work one single crochet into the second chain from the hook, one single crochet into each of the next two single crochet and two single crochet into the last single crochet. Turn. Continue increasing in this way for the width required.*

The basic elongated-stitch vest

The keynote of this short vest is stylish warmth.

Sizes
Men's sizes 38-40 [40-42] in. chest
Length (from back neck) 19½in.

Note: Instructions for the larger size are in square brackets []; where there is only one set of figures it applies to both sizes.

Gauge
15sc and 22 rows to 4 in. worked on size F hook. Gauge for knit ribbing: 27 sts and 30 rows to 4 in. worked on size 4 needles.

Materials
8 [9]oz of a knitting worsted in main color (A)
4 [6]oz in contrasting color (B)
Sizes C and F crochet hooks
Pair of size 4 knitting needles
Note: Strand yarn not in use loosely up side of work. Change colors by using new color to complete last st worked in old color.

Left front (both sizes worked alike)
Using size F hook and A, ch 3.
Base row 1sc into 3rd ch from hook. Turn.
1st row Ch 2, 1sc into 2nd ch from hook, 1sc into next sc, 1sc into turning ch. Turn.

2nd row Ch 2, 1sc into 2nd ch from hook, (1sc into each of next 2sc, 2sc into last sc). Turn.
3rd row Ch 2, 1sc into 2nd ch from hook, 1sc into each sc to last sc, 2sc into last sc. Turn.
Rep last row 3 times more. 13sc.
Change to B.
7th row Ch 2, 1sc into 2nd ch from hook, (1sc into each of next 2sc, 1sc into next st one row below, 1sc into next st 2 rows below, 1sc into next st 3 rows below, 1sc into next st 4 rows below, 1sc into next st 5 rows below, 1sc into next st 4 rows below, 1sc into next st 3 rows below, 1sc into next st 2 rows below, 1sc into next st one row below, 1sc into next of previous row, 2sc into last st. Turn.
Rep 3rd row 5 times. 25sc.
Change to A.
13th row Ch 2, 1sc into 2nd ch from hook, 1sc into each of next 3sc, *1sc into next st one row below, 1sc into next st 2 rows below, 1sc into next st 3 rows below, 1sc into next st 4 rows below, 1sc into next st 5 rows below, 1sc into next st 4 rows below, 1sc into next st 3 rows below, 1sc into next st 2 rows below, 1sc into next st one row below, 1sc into next st of previous row, rep from * once more, 1sc into next sc, 2sc into last st. Turn.
Rep 3rd row 3 times. 33sc.
17th and 18th rows Ch 1, skip first sc, 1sc into each st to end. Turn.

Change to B.
19th row Ch 1, skip first sc, 1sc into next sc, *1sc into next st one row below, 1sc into next st 2 rows below, 1sc into next st 3 rows below, 1sc into next st 4 rows below, 1sc into next st 5 rows below, 1sc into next st 4 rows below, 1sc into next st 3 rows below, 1sc into next st 2 rows below, 1sc into next st one row below, 1sc into next st of previous row, rep from * twice more, 1sc into turning ch. Turn.
20th-24th rows As 17th row.
Change to A.
25th row Ch 1, skip first sc, 1sc into next st 5 rows below, *1sc into next st 4 rows below, 1sc into next st 3 rows below, 1sc into next st 2 rows below, 1sc into next st one row below, 1sc into next st of previous row, 1sc into next st one row below, 1sc into next st 2 rows below, 1sc into next st 3 rows below, 1sc into next st 4 rows below, 1sc into next st 5 rows below, rep from * twice more, 1sc into turning ch. Turn.
26th-30th rows As 17th row.
Keeping color sequence correct, work 19th-30th rows twice more, then work 19th to 25th rows once more.
Shape front
Keeping pat correct, begin front shaping:
62nd row Ch 1, skip first sc, 1sc into each st to end. Turn
63rd row Ch 1, skip first sc, 1sc into

227

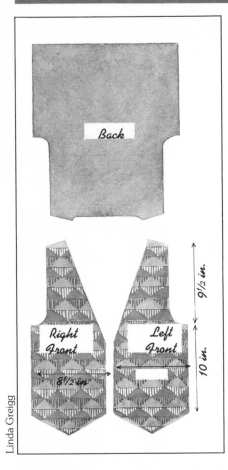

Linda Greigg

(diagram labels: Back, Right Front, Left Front, 9½ in., 10 in., 8½ in.)

each sc to end, dec 1 st at inner edge by omitting 1sc into turning ch. Turn.
64th-66th rows As 62nd row.
67th row As 63rd row.
68th row As 62nd row.
Shape armhole
Cont to dec 1 st at inner edge on every 4th row, *at the same time* begin armhole shaping:
69th row Sl st into each of first 3sc, 1sc into each st to end. Turn.
70th row Ch 1, skip first sc, 1sc into each of next 25sc. Turn.
71st row As 63rd row.
72nd row Ch 1, skip first sc, 1sc into each of next 22sc, turn.
73rd row As 62nd row.
74th row Ch 1, skip first sc, 1sc into each of next 21sc, turn.
75th row As 63rd row.
76th row Ch 1, skip first sc, 1sc into each of next 19sc, turn.
77th row As 62nd row.
78th row Ch 1, skip first sc, 1sc into each of next 18sc, turn.
79th row As 63rd row.
Keeping armhole edge straight, cont in pat, dec 1 st at inner edge on every foll 4th row, until 10sc rem and work measures 9½ in. from beg of armhole.
Next row Sl st into each of first 3sc, 1sc into each st to end. Turn.
Next row Ch 1, skip first sc, 1sc into
228

each of next 5sc. Turn.
Next row Sl st into each of first 3sc, 1sc into each st to end. Turn.
Fasten off.

Right front (both sizes worked alike)
Work as for Left front, reversing all shaping.

Front border
Mark positions of 4 buttonholes on Left front.
1st row With RS facing and using size C hook, join A to lower side edge of Right front, and work 1sc into each row end or st to top of shoulder, ch 40 for back neck border, cont down left front and lower edge, working 1sc into each row end and st as before. Turn.
2nd row Ch 1, skip first sc, *1sc into each sc to sc at point, 3sc into next sc, 1sc into each sc to corner, 2sc into next sc, (1sc into each sc to buttonhole marker, ch 3, skip next 3sc) 4 times, 1sc into each sc to beg of front shaping, 2sc into next sc, 1sc into each sc to ch 40 at back neck*, 1sc into each of 40 ch, rep from * to *, omitting buttonholes and reversing order of working.
3rd row Ch 1, skip first sc, 1sc into each sc to end, inc at points and corners as on last row and omitting 1sc into turning ch. Turn.
4th row As 3rd row, but do not turn.
5th row Ch 1, skip first sc, *working from left to right*, 1sc into each sc to end (see page 262).
Fasten off.

Buttons (make 4 alike)
Using size C hook and A, leave an end of 19¾ in. and ch 3, 9dc into 3rd ch from hook, sl st to top of ch 3, 1sc into each dc.
Break yarn and thread into yarn needle.
Wind 19¾ in. length of yarn into tight little ball and insert into button. Thread the yarn in the needle through the button and draw up tightly to form a round button.
Sew buttons to Right front to match buttonholes.

Back
Using knitting needles and A, cast on 122 [134] sts.
Work in K1, P1 ribbing until work measures same as side Fronts to armholes including band at lower edge.

Shape armholes
Keeping pat correct, bind off 7[13] sts at beg of next 2 rows.
Dec 1 st at both ends of every foll row until 80 sts rem.
Cont without further shaping until work measures 9¾ in. from beg of armhole shaping.
Shape shoulders
Bind off 3 sts at beg of next 4 rows.
Next row Bind off 3 sts, work in pat 44 sts, turn, bind off 24 sts, work in pat to end.
Cont on rem sts, bind off 3 sts at beg of every row until no more sts rem.
Fasten off.
Work other shoulder to match.

To finish
Press crochet only.
Seam shoulders and back neck.
Join side seams.

Armhole borders (both alike)
1st round Using size C hook and A, beg at underarm seam and work in sc around armhole edge. Join with a sl st to first st. Turn.
2nd round Ch 1, skip first sc, 1sc into each sc to end, join with a sl st to first ch. Turn.
3rd and 4th rounds As 2nd round, but do not turn at end of 4th round.
5th round Work one round of sc from left to right as for Front border.
Fasten off.

The vest on page 226 has a knitted back, worked in knit one, purl one ribbing to ensure a neat fit.

Simon Butcher

Triangles

Crochet triangles can be worked either in rounds like other polygons or in rows. They can be used by themselves or in combination with squares and hexagons to form dazzling afghan rugs and blankets or very individual patchwork clothes.

Belinda

Skills you need

* **Shaping**

If you do not know this basic skill, refer to page 295.

Materials

Like other polygonal motifs, triangles can be worked in most yarns, though very hairy or looped yarns can be difficult to crochet with and so should be avoided by beginners. Small, multicolored triangles can easily be joined to make attractive and useful afghan rugs or blankets and this is the ideal opportunity for using small amounts of yarn left over from other projects. However, when constructing a garment from large one-color triangles it is wiser to buy yarn so that you are sure of matching dye lots. The basic sweater on page 229 uses this method and is made in a pure wool Aran yarn.

Special technique – right-side seaming

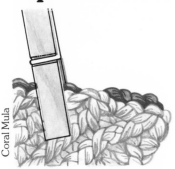

Coral Mula

1 *Right-side seaming is an easy method of achieving an exact match on seams when joining a complex garment like the sweater shown here. Hold the edges of the two triangles together with wrong sides facing — clothespins are better than dressmaker's pins on thick crochet. Use a tapestry needle and two strands of spliced yarn matching one of the triangles.*

2 *Join the yarn to the wrong side of the corner of the triangle nearer to you. Insert the needle from back to front into the edge of the farther triangle, catching one strand only of the edge stitch. Then insert the needle from front to back slightly farther along the edge of the same triangle. Draw up the yarn tightly.*

3 *Insert the needle from front to back into the edge of the nearer triangle. Insert the needle from back to front slightly farther along the same edge. Draw up the yarn tightly. Continue in the same way to the end. This method produces a flat, invisible seam which is very strong.*

The basic triangle sweater

This rugged sweater, worked in an Aran yarn with an interesting tweedy fleck, is great for the outdoor life. Because the triangles are worked separately and then joined together, it is possible to make this chunky sweater without straining your arms.

Size
Men's sizes 38-40 in. chest
Length from shoulder 27 in.
Sleeve seam 19 in.

Materials
24 oz of a knitting worsted-weight tweed yarn in main color A (dark brown)
13 oz in contrasting color B (medium brown)
18 oz in contrasting color C (beige)
Size H crochet hook
Pair of size 4 knitting needles

Gauge
14 sts and 10 rows to 4 in. over pat worked on size H hook

Note: Turning chain counts as one stitch throughout.
Note: Back and front are made from triangular motifs that are worked separately and sewn together.

Large triangles
Make 2 in C.
Ch 97.
Base row 1dc into 4th ch from hook, 1dc into each ch to end. Turn. 95 sts.
1st row (RS) Ch 2, skip first 2 sts, inserting hook from right to left and from front to back work 1dc around stem of next dc – 1dc front worked –, *inserting hook from right to left and from back to front work 1dc around stem of next dc – 1dc back worked –,

1dc front, rep from * to last 2 sts, skip next st, 1dc into top of turning ch. Turn. 93 sts.
2nd row Ch 2, skip first 2 sts, 1dc front, *1dc back, 1dc front, rep from * to last 2 sts, 1 dc into next st, turn. 91 sts.
3rd row As 2nd row. 89 sts.
4th row Ch 2, skip first 2 sts, work next 2dc tog, 1dc front, * 1dc back, 1dc front, rep from * to last 4 sts, work next 2dc tog, 1dc into next st, turn. 85 sts.
5th row Ch 2, skip first 2 sts, 1dc back, * 1dc front, 1dc back, rep from * to last 2 sts, 1dc into next st, turn. 83 sts.
6th-8th rows As 5th row. 77 sts.
9th row Ch 2, skip first 2 sts, work next 2dc tog, 1dc back, * 1dc front, 1dc back, rep from * to last 4 sts, work next 2dc tog, 1dc into next st, turn. 73 sts.
10th-13th rows As 2nd row. 65 sts.

230

Rep 4th-13th rows once more, then rep 4th-12th rows once more. 19 sts.
33rd row As 4th row. 15 sts.
34th-36th rows As 5th row. 9 sts.
37th row Ch 2, skip first 2 sts, work next 2dc tog, 1dc back, work next 2dc tog, 1dc into next st, turn. 5 sts.
38th row Ch 2, skip first 2 sts, 1dc front leaving last loop on hook, 1dc into next st leaving last loop on hook, yo and draw through all 3 loops on hook.
Fasten off.

Medium triangles
Make 4 in B.
Ch 53. Work base row as for large triangle. 51 sts.
Work first-17th rows as for large triangle. 11 sts.
18th row As 9th row of large triangle. 7 sts.
19th row As first row of large triangle. 5 sts.
20th row At 38th row of large triangle.
Fasten off.

Small triangles
Make 6 in A, 4 in B and 6 in C.
Ch 39. Work base row as for large triangle. 37 sts.
Work first-12th rows as for large triangle. 9 sts.
13th row Ch 2, skip first 2 sts, work next 2dc tog, 1dc front, work next 2dc tog, 1dc into next st, turn. 5 sts.
14th row As 38th row of large triangle, work 1dc back instead of 1dc front.
Fasten off.

Sleeves (alike)
Using A, ch 47
Base row 1dc into 4th ch from hook, 1dc into each ch to end. Turn. 45 sts.
Beg pat
1st row (RS) Ch 2, skip first st, 1dc front. * 1dc back, 1dc front, rep from * to last st, 1dc into top of turning ch. Turn.
2nd row Ch 2, skip first st, 1dc back, * 1dc front, 1dc back, rep from * to last st, 1dc into top of turning ch. Turn.
First and 2nd rows form pat.
Shape sleeve
Keeping pat correct, inc one st at each end of next and every following 5th row until there are 59 sts.
Work even in pat until work measures 13½ in., ending with a WS row.
Divide for top
Next row Work in pat first 29 sts, turn.
Next row Ch 2, skip first 2 sts, work in pat to end. 28 sts.
Next row Work in pat to last 2 sts, 1dc

John Hutchinson

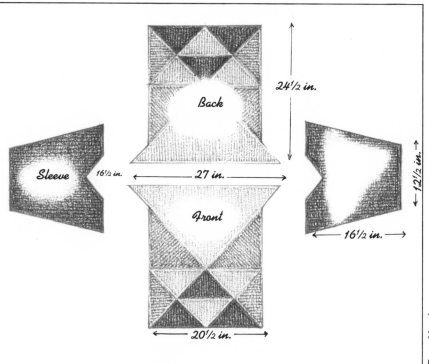

Peter Visscher

231

into next sts, turn. 27 sts.
Rep last 2 rows 3 more times. 21 sts.
Fasten off.
With RS facing, return to sts skipped
at beg of top, skip next st and rejoin A
to next st.
Next row Ch 2, skip st at base of joining.
work in pat to end. 29 sts.
Complete to correspond with first side
of sleeve top, reversing all shaping.

To finish
Block if necessary.

Cuffs (alike)
With RS facing, using knitting needles
and A, pick up and K 44 sts along
lower edge of sleeve.
Work 2½ in. of K2, P2 ribbing.
Fasten off.
Place a contrasting marker 8 in. from
each end of longest side of large
triangles.
Join triangles as shown in diagram on
page 231 to form back and front. Join
long edges of large triangles between
corners and markers, leaving edges

between markers open for neck.
Back waistband
With RS facing, using knitting needles
and A, pick up and K 92 sts along
lower edge of back.
Work 2½ in. of K2, P2 ribbing.
Bind off in ribbing.
Front waistband
Work as for back waistband.
Set in sleeves.
Join side and sleeve seams.
Press seams very lightly.

Adapting the basic triangle sweater

**Make lots of triangles from the
selection in the Pattern Library
and join them together to make
a dazzling and colorful, highly
individual afghan.**

Because it is essential that the triangles
should fit together exactly, it is difficult
to substitute another stitch unless it
works to exactly the same gauge as the

single ribbing used in the basic sweater. However, different color combinations could make the sweater look
completely different. For example,
while three colors have been used to
make the triangles on the basic sweater, there is no reason why a fourth or
even fifth color could not be used.
Similarly, each individual triangle
could be worked in more than one

color — the possible combinations of
stripes are numerous. Bear in mind
that diamond patterns can easily be
adapted when you are working
triangles.
Finally, all the pieces of the sweater
could be worked in one color to
produce a patchwork sweater that
depends for its impact on texture
rather than color.

Triangular motifs

1 **Simple, striped triangle**
You could vary these further, by
working some as diamonds instead of
triangles.

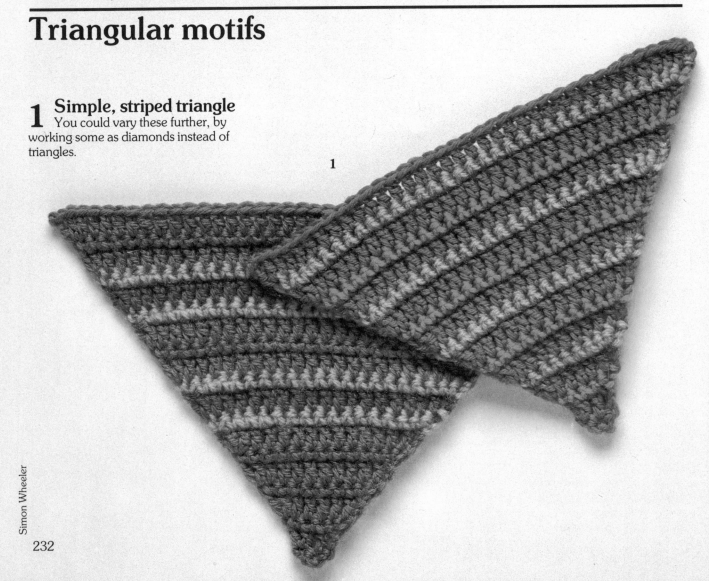

1

2

3

2 Spoked triangle

Ch 12, sl st to first ch to form a circle.

1st row Ch 5, (1tr into circle, ch 1) 5 times, 1tr into circle. Turn.

2nd row Ch 5, *leaving last loop of each st on hook work 4dc into next ch 1 sp, yo and draw through all 5 loops on hook (cluster made), ch 2, rep from * into each sp all around, ending with cluster into sp formed by turning ch, ch 2, 1dc into 3rd turning ch. Turn.

3rd row Ch 5, 4dc into first ch 2 sp, * (ch 3, 1sc into next ch 1 sp) twice, ch 3*, (4dc, ch 2, 4dc) into next ch 2 sp, rep from * to * once more, ch 3, 4dc into sp formed by turning ch, ch 2, 1dc into 3rd turning ch. Turn.

4th row Ch 5, 4dc into first ch 2 sp, *ch 1, skip first ch 3 sp, * (4dc into next ch 3 sp, ch 1) twice *, (4dc, ch 2, 4dc) into next ch 2 sp, ch 1, rep from * to * once more, 4dc into sp formed by turning ch, ch 2, 1dc into 3rd turning ch. Turn.

5th row Ch 4, *4dc into first ch 2 sp, * (4dc into next ch 1 sp) 3 times *, (4dc, ch 2, 4dc) into next ch 2 sp, rep from * to * once more, 4dc into sp formed by turning ch, ch 1, 1dc into 3rd turning ch. Turn.

Cont in this way until triangle is the required size.

3 Shamrock triangle

Use 2 colors, A and B.

Using A, ch 5, sl st to first ch to form a circle.

1st round Ch 1 to count as first sc, 5sc into circle, sl st to first ch.

2nd round Ch 1, 1sc into first sc, *ch 3, 5dc into next sc, remove hook from loop and insert hook into first of 5dc just worked, insert hook into loop just dropped, yo and draw through all loops on hook (popcorn formed), ch 3, 1sc into next sc, rep from * twice more, ending last rep with sl st into first ch.

3rd round Ch 1, 1sc into first sc, * ch 4, 2dc into next ch 3 sp, leaving last loop of each st on hook, work 1dc into same ch 3 sp and 1dc into next ch 3 sp, yo and draw through all 3 loops on hook (2dc tog made), 2dc into next loop, ch 3, 1sc into next sc, rep from * twice more, ending last rep with sl st into first ch.

Fasten off.

4th round Join B to any 2dc tog, ch 1, 1sc into same place as join, * ch 2, 3dc into each of next 2 ch 3 sps formed on 2nd round, ch 2, 1sc into next 2dc tog, rep from * twice more, ending last rep with sl st to first ch. Turn.

5th round Sl st across last ch 2 sp of 4th round, turn, ch 1 * (1sc, 1hdc, 1dc) into ch 2 sp, ch 1, 1dc into next dc, ch 1, (1dc, 1hdc, 1sc) into next ch 2 sp, 1sc into each of next 6dc, rep from * twice more, ending last rep with sl st into first ch.

6th round Ch 1, 1sc into first st, * 1sc into each of next 2 sts, 2sc into next ch 1 sp, (1sc, ch 1, 1sc) into next dc, 2sc into next ch 1 sp, 1sc into each of next 10 sts, rep from * twice more, omitting 1 sc from end of last rep and ending with sl st into first ch.

Fasten off.

Vertical patterns

Vertical patterns are usually worked either by stranding the yarn across the back of the work or by using separate balls of yarn in the jacquard method. These versatile stitches can be worked in a wide variety of yarns and used for most projects.

Skills you need

* **Double crochet**
* **Picking up stitches**

If you do not know these skills, refer to pages 177 and 294.

Materials

Most types of yarn from fine cotton to chunky wool can be used for vertical patterns. Relief patterns should always be worked in plain yarns so that the stitches will be visible, but simple vertical stripes can be worked in any type of yarn, mixtures of plain and fancy yarn being especially effective.

The basic pullover on page 234 has been worked in a double-knitting yarn made from a combination of lamb's and Shetland wool. This yarn, available in soft, misty colors, should be hand-washed according to instructions on the label. Do not press or the pattern will be flattened.

Special technique – economical one-row stripes

1 When changing color at the end of each row in a two-color pattern, you can avoid breaking — and so wasting — yarn by turning only after every alternate row as in the Front pattern on page 236. Work the base row. Remove the hook from the loop and leave the first color at the side of the work. The loop can be held with a safety pin.

2 Do not turn, but return to the beginning of the row. Join the second color to the top of the first stitch with slip stitch. Work in pattern to the loop left in step 1. Insert the hook first into the top of the last stitch and then into the loop. Remove the safety pin, wind the second color around the hook and draw through all loops on the hook. Turn.

3 Drop the second color and draw the first through the loop on the hook. Pull both ends of yarn firmly but not so tightly that the fabric puckers. Work in pattern to the end, leaving a loop as in step 1. Return to the beginning of the row, rejoin the first color as in step 2 and pattern to the end, working into the last stitch and loop as before.

Coral Mula

The basic vertical-patterned pullover

Don't be deterred by the fine verticals on the front of this casual sweater, worked in a soft mixture of Shetland and lamb's wool. The "vertical" pattern is in reality horizontal, formed from cleverly designed single-row stripes.

Sizes
Men's sizes 38 [40:42] in. chest
Length from shoulder 24 in.

Note: Instructions for larger sizes are in square brackets []; where there is only one set of figures it applies to all sizes.

Materials
11 [12:13]oz of knitting worsted-weight yarn in main color (A)
4 [6:6]oz in contrasting color (B)
Size F crochet hook
Pair of size 3 knitting needles

Gauge
4 pat reps and 12 rows to 4 in. over back pat worked on size F hook

5 pat reps and 14 rows to 4 in. over front pat worked on size F hook

Back
Using crochet hook and A, ch 84 [88:92].
Base row 1dc into 4th ch from hook, * skip next ch, 1sc into next ch, skip next ch, 3dc into next ch, rep from * to end, ending last rep with 2dc into last ch. Turn. 81 [85:89] sts.
Begin pat
1st row Ch 1, 1sc into first dc, * 3dc into next sc, 1sc into 2nd of next 3dc, rep from * to end, working last sc into top of turning ch. Turn.
2nd row Ch 3, 1dc into first sc, * 1sc into 2nd of next 3dc, 3dc into next sc, rep from * to end, ending last rep with

2dc into last sc.
1st and 2nd rows form back pat.
Cont in back pat until work measures 12⅛ in. from beg, ending with a 2nd row.
Shape armholes
Next row Sl st across first 5 sts, ch 1, 1sc into sl st at base of ch 1, work in pat to last 4 sts, turn. 73 [77:81] sts.
Next row Sl st across first 5 sts, ch 3, 1dc into sl st at base of ch 3, work in pat to last 4 sts, turn. 65 [69:73] sts.
Beg with a 1st row, cont in pat without further shaping until work measures 21¼ in. from beg.
Fasten off.

Note: Strand yarn not in use *loosely* up side of work.

Front
Using crochet hook and A, ch 104 [108:112].
Base row (RS) Using A, 1dc into 4th

235

ch from hook, * skip next 3 ch, 3dc into next ch, rep from * to end, ending last rep with 2dc into last ch. Do not turn, but return to beg of row.
Next row (RS) Join B with a sl st to top of first ch 3, *3 dc into center ch of next 3 ch missed on Base row, rep from * to end, sl st into last dc of Base row. Turn.

Begin pat
1st row Using A, ch 3, 1dc into first sl st, *3dc into center dc of next 3dc worked on previous row in A, rep from * to last sl st, 2dc into last sl st. Do not turn, but return to beg of row.
2nd row Using B, sl st into top of first 3 ch, *3dc into center tr of next 3dc worked on previous row in B, rep from * to last dc, sl st into last dc.
1st and 2nd rows form Front pat.
Cont in Front pat until work measures 12⅛ in. from beg, ending with a 2nd row.

Shape armholes
Next row Sl st across first pat rep, pat to last pat rep, turn.
Rep last row twice more. 19 [20:21] pat reps.

Divide for neck
Next row Work 9 [10:10] pat reps, turn.

Shape left neck
Cont on these sts only, work in pat 3 rows without shaping.
Next row Work in pat to last pat rep, turn. Rep last 4 rows 3 times more. 5 [6:6] pat reps.
Cont in pat without further shaping until work measures 21¼ in. from beg. Fasten off.

1st and 3rd sizes only
Return to beg of neck shaping, skip center pat rep and keeping pat correct, rejoin yarn to next pat rep.

2nd size only
Return to beg of neck shaping and keeping pat correct, rejoin yarn to next pat rep.

All sizes
Next row Work to end. Turn.
9 [10:10] pat reps.

Shape right neck
Cont on these sts only, work in pat 3 rows without shaping.
Next row Work to last pat rep, turn. Rep last 4 rows 3 times more. 5 [6:6] pat reps.
Cont in pat without further shaping until work matches left side of neck. Fasten off.

Back waistband
With RS facing, using knitting needles and A, pick up and K 104 [110:114]
236

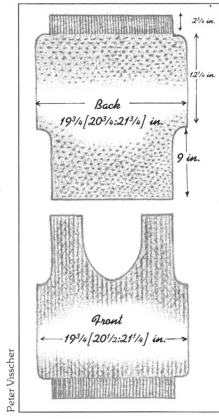

Peter Visscher

Back
19¾[20¾:21¾] in.

2¾ in.

12¼ in.

9 in.

Front
19¾[20½:21¼] in.

sts evenly along lower edge.
Work 2¾ in. in K1, P1 ribbing.
Bind off loosely in ribbing.

Front waistband
With RS facing, using knitting needles and A, pick up and K 102 [106:110] sts evenly along lower edge.
Work 2¾ in. in K1, P1 ribbing.
Bind off loosely in ribbing.

Front neckband
Fold corners of front decs to WS and slip stitch in place.
With RS facing, using knitting needles and A, pick up and K 68 sts down left front neck, one st from center V and 68 sts up right front neck.
1st row (P1, K1) to within 2 sts of center st, K2 tog, P1, K2 tog, (K1, P1) to end.
2nd row K1, (P1, K1) to within 2 sts of center st, P2 tog, K1, P2 tog, (P1, K1) to end.
Rep last 2 rows twice more.
Bind off loosely in ribbing *at the same time* dec one st at each side of center st as before.

Back neckband
Place a contrasting marker on last row of back 5 [6:6] pat reps from each armhole edge.
With RS facing, using knitting needles and A, pick up and K 45 sts between

markers.
Work 6 rows in K1, P1 ribbing.
Bind off loosely in ribbing.

Armbands (both alike)
Join shoulder seams.
With RS facing, using knitting needles and A, pick up and K 130 sts evenly along armhole edge.
Work 6 rows in K1, P1 ribbing.
Bind off loosely in ribbing.

To finish
Do not press.
Join side and armband seams.
Press seams lightly.

Adapting the basic pullover

Vertical patterns range from complex ribbed patterns to simple vertical stripes, but all are versatile enough to be used both for clothes and household furnishings.

Although another pattern cannot be substituted, the basic pullover would look very different if other colors were used. For example, two strong contrasting colors could be used to work the front and would produce a bold, dramatic appearance instead of the subtle look on page 234.
It would be possible — as long as you do not want to retain the vertical features of the pattern — to introduce a third or even a fourth color when working the front of the basic pullover. This would transform the front pattern from a vertical into a mosaic pattern.

The back of the basic pullover is worked in a simple shell pattern using the main color.

Simon Butcher

Ridged patterns

Three-dimensional ridges form beautifully tactile fabrics, especially when alternated with plain crochet stitches. Use these extremely versatile stitches as all-over patterns or to highlight particular features of a garment.

Ray Moller

237

Skills you need

* **Working into a single loop**

If you do not know this basic skill, refer to page 297.

Materials

Ridged patterns are best worked in two or more contrasting colors so that the ridges stand out more clearly from the main fabric. The jacket on page 237 has been worked in a pale and dark shade of one color, using a pure-wool, Shetland-type yarn that is equivalent to double knitting. However, it would look equally good if two completely different colors were used. Textured yarn could be used for the ridges or the background fabric, though both yarns should work to roughly the same gauge. Bouclé ridges on a plain fabric would look very interesting, while glitter ridges on mohair would be ideal for a glamorous evening outfit.

Special technique – three-dimensional ridges

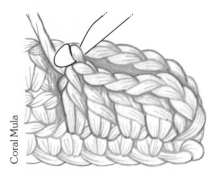

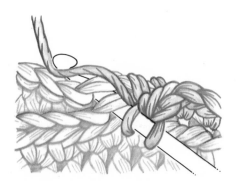

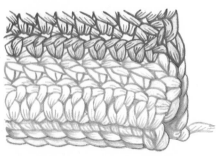

1 Begin with a row of single crochet worked in the first color. On the next row work in half-double crochet, inserting the hook into the front loop only of each stitch. Work a row of half doubles as usual and fasten off, leaving a fairly long end. Return to the skipped loops and rejoin the yarn to the first free loop. Work a row of doubles into the skipped loops.

2 Work two more rows of doubles, inserting the hook under the two top loops of each stitch. Fasten off, leaving a long end. With wrong side facing, insert the hook into the first half double and double at the side edge. Join in the second color and work a row of half doubles, inserting the hook through corresponding half double and double of the two layers.

3 Work three more rows of half doubles as usual. Change back to the first color and work a row of single crochet. Finish the side edges by working a row of single crochet into the row ends. Use the long ends left in steps 1 and 2 so that the colors match the pattern and leave the double rows free on each individual ridge.

The basic ridged jacket

Here's the rugged, ridged jacket that combines style and comfort in just the right proportions. Worked in toning shades of a warm, pure-wool yarn, it's perfect for leisure wear.

Sizes
Men's sizes 38 [40:42] in. chest
Length 27½ in
Sleeve seam 19 in.
Note: Instructions for larger sizes are in brackets []; where there is only one set of figures it applies to all sizes.

Materials
30 [32:34] oz of a Shetland-type knitting worsted in main color (A)
11 [13:15] oz in contrasting color (B)
Sizes C and E crochet hooks
8 buttons

Gauge
16dc to 4 in. worked on size E crochet hook

Back and fronts (worked in one piece to armholes)
Using size C hook and A, ch 48.
Base row 1sc into 2nd ch from hook, 1sc into each ch to end. Turn. 47sc.
Waistband ribbing row Ch 1 to count as first sc, skip first st, 1sc into back loop only of each st to end. Turn.
Rep waistband ribbing row until 160 [168:176] rows have been worked from beg.
Fasten off.

Change to size E hook.
Fold waistband in half lengthwise so that row ends meet.
Next row Using A, work a row of sc through both thickness of waistband row ends. Turn.
160 [168:176] sts.
Inc row Work in sc and inc 8 sts evenly across row. 168 [176:184] sts.
Beg pat
**Next row (WS) Using A, ch 2, skip first st, 1hdc into front loop only of each st to turning ch, 1hdc into top of turning ch. Turn.
Next row Ch 2, skip first st, 1hdc into each st to end, inserting hook under both loops of each st as usual.
Fasten off and do not turn.
Return to loops unworked 2 rows previously and join A to free loop of first st.

Next row (RS) Ch 3, skip first st, 1dc into each free loop to end. Turn.

Next row Ch 3, skip first st, 1dc into each st to end. Turn.

Next row As last row. Turn. Fasten off. With WS facing, insert hook into first hdc and dc of the 2 layers. Join in B.

Next row Using B, ch 2, skip first st, inserting hook into corresponding hdc and dc work in hdc to end. Turn.

Next row Ch 2, skip first st, 1hdc into each st to end. Turn.

Rep last row 3 more times. Change to A.

Next row Using A, ch 1 to count as first sc, skip first st, 1sc into each st to end. Turn.**

Rep from ** to ** until 8th ridge in A has been completed and work measures approx 20½ in. ending with a WS row.

Divide for back and fronts

Next row Work in pat 37 [39:41] sts, sl st across next 10 sts, work in pat 74 [78:82] sts, sl st across next 10 sts, work in pat last 37 [39:41] sts. Turn.

Left front

Working on last set of sts, work even in pat until work measures 26 in., ending at front edge.

Shape neck

Next row Sl st across first 5 sts, work in pat to end. Turn. 33 [35:37] sts. Dec one st at neck edge on next 2 rows and every following alternate row until 18 [18:20] sts rem. Work even until work measures 27 in., ending at armhole edge.

Shape shoulder

Next row Sl st across first 9 [9:10] sts, work in pat to end. Turn.

Next row Work in pat to end. Fasten off.

Back

With WS facing, return to sts left at armholes, skip 10 slipped sts and keeping pat correct, join yarn to next st.

Next row Work in pat to end. Turn. 74 [78:82] sts.

Work even in pat until work measures same as back to beg of shoulder shaping.

Shape shoulders

Next row Sl st across first 9 [9:10] sts, work in pat to last 9 [9:10] sts, turn.

Next row As last row. Fasten off.

Right front

With WS facing, return to sts left at armholes, skip 10 sl sts and keeping pat correct, join yarn to next st.

Next row Work in pat to end. Turn.

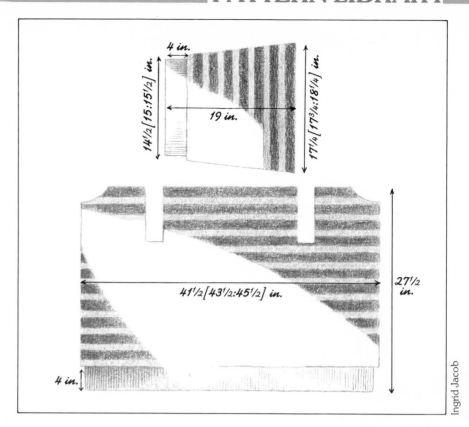

Ingrid Jacob

37 [39:41] sts. Complete to match left front, reversing all shaping.

Sleeves (alike)

Using size C hook and A, ch 30. Work base row and waistband ribbing row as for waistband until 51 [53:55] rows have been worked from beg. Work next row and inc row as for waistband. 59 [61:63] sts.

Using larger hook, rep from ** to ** as for back and fronts until work measures 4¼ in. ending with a WS row.

Shape sleeve

Inc one st at each end of next and every following 6th row until there are 71 [73:75] sts.

Work even until work measures 19 in. Fasten off.

Right front band

Using size C hook and A, ch 19.

Base row 1sc into 2nd ch from hook, 1sc into each ch to end. Turn. 18sc.

Next row Ch 1 to count as first sc, skip first st, 1sc into each st to end. Turn.

Rep last row until band, when slightly stretched, fits up right front from lower edge of waistband to beg of neck shaping. Fasten off.

Left front band

Mark position of 7 buttonholes on left front, the first 1½ in. from lower edge, the last 1¼ in. from neck shaping and the rem 5 evenly spaced in between.

Work left front band as for right front band, working buttonholes as follows:

Next row Ch 1 to count as first sc, skip first st, 1sc into next st, ch 3, skip next 3 sts, 1sc into each of next 8 sts, ch 3, skip next 3 sts, 1sc into each of last 2 sts. Turn.

Next row Ch 1 to count as first sc, skip first st, 1sc into next st, 3sc into next ch 3 sp, 1sc into each of next 8 sts, 3sc into next ch 3 sp, 1sc into each of last 2 sts. Turn.

To finish

Finish all side edges with a row of sc, using colors to match ridge pat (see Special technique, page 26). Fold right front band in half lengthwise so that row ends meet and sew neatly to right front.

Using size C hook and A, work a row of sc through both thicknesses at lower edge.

Attach left front band in the same way and work buttonhole stitch over edges of buttonholes.

Join shoulder seams.

Neckband

Using size C hook and A and with RS facing, join A to first st on right-front band and work 87 [89:91] sc evenly all around neck edge, ending at front edge of left-front band. Turn.

Work in sc as for right-front band for 2 in., ending at right-front edge.

Buttonhole row Work in sc to last 6 sts, ch 3, skip next 3 sts, 1sc into each of last 3 sts. Turn.
Next row Ch 1 to count as first sc, skip first st, 1sc into each st to ch 3 sp, 3sc into next ch 3 sp, 1sc into each st to end. Turn.
Work in sc for 2 in. more and then

make a second buttonhole in the same way.
Work in sc for 2 in. more.
Fasten off.
Fold neckband in half so that first and last rows meet and sew neatly into position on WS using matching yarn and an oversewn seam.

Finish neckband buttonhole. Work a row of sc through both thicknesses to close row ends of neckband.
Set in sleeves, matching center of sleeve top to shoulder seam.
Join side and underarm seams. Sew on buttons to correspond with buttonholes.

Adapting the basic ridged jacket

Experience the ups and downs of ridges by using the Pattern Library to work several versions of the basic jacket. Whatever your variation, it's sure to please.

On the jacket, the ridges are separated by four rows of half double crochet, worked in a contrasting color. The ridges could easily be spaced differently by working more or fewer rows in between.
An interesting, and more difficult, variation could be to work broken ridges.

These could be undecorated or contrasting yarn could be threaded through the tubes. Weaving tops could equally be threaded through fat ridges.

Altering the jacket
The basic jacket could easily be worked as a vest. Work the back and

fronts as given on page 238-9.
Omit the sleeves and substitute armbands, worked in the same way as the right-front band.
The jacket can easily be made longer by working more ridged patterns on the back and fronts before dividing the stitches at the armholes. Sleeves could also be lengthened by working more rows in pattern. Remember always to end on a right or wrong-side row as instructed.

Ridged patterns

1

1 Crab-stitch ridges
Make any number of ch.
Base row Ch 1 into 2nd ch from hook, 1sc into each ch to end. Do not turn.
1st row (RS) Ch 1, working into front loop only and working from left to right, work 1sc into each st to end. Do not turn.
2nd row Ch 1, 1sc into each unworked loop on 1st row. Turn.
3rd row Ch 1 to count as first sc, skip first st, 1sc into each st to end. Turn.
4th row As 3rd row. Do not turn.
First-4th rows form pat. Rep them throughout.

2 Cabled ridges
Make a multiple of 3 ch plus 3 extra.
Base row 1sc into 2nd ch from hook 1sc into each ch to end. Turn.
1st row Ch 1 to count as first sc, skip first st, 1sc into each st to end. Turn.
2nd row (RS) Ch 1, 1sc into first st,* ch 3, skip next 2 sts, 1sc into next st, turn, 1sc into each of 3 ch just worked, turn, inserting hook behind ch 3, work 1sc into each of 2 missed sts, rep from * to last st, 1sc into last st.
3rd row Ch 1, 1sc into first st, * 2sc into next st behind cable, 1sc into next st behind cable, skip sc where ch 3 was attached on last row, rep from * to last st 1sc into last st.
4th row As 1st row.
First-4th rows form pat. Rep them throughout.

2

3 Single crochet ridges

Make any number of ch.
Base row 1sc into 2nd ch from hook, 1sc into each ch to end. Turn.
1st row (RS) Ch 1 to count as first sc, skip first st, 1sc into front loop only of each st to end. Turn.
2nd row Ch 1 to count as first sc, skip first st, 1sc into each unworked loop of 2nd row to end. Turn.
3rd row Ch 1 to count as first sc, skip first st, 1sc into each st to end. Turn.
4th row As 3rd row.
Rep first–4th rows throughout.

4 Popcorn ridges

Make a multiple of 6 ch plus 3.
Base row (RS) 1dc into 4th ch from hook, 1dc into each ch to end. Turn.
1st row Ch 1, 1sc into first st, * ch 1, skip next st, 1sc into next st, rep from * to end. Turn.
2nd row Ch 3, skip first st, * skip next ch 1 sp, (5dc into next ch 1 sp, remove hook from loop, insert into top of first of 5dc just worked and into loop just left, yo and draw through all loops on hook (popcorn formed), ch 1, 1dc, ch 1, popcorn) into next ch 1 sp, skip next ch 1 sp, 1dc into next sc, rep from * to end. Turn.
3rd row Ch 1, 1sc into first st, * (ch 1, 1sc into next ch 1 sp) twice, ch 1, 1sc into next dc, rep from * to end, ending with 1sc into top of turning ch. Turn.
4th row Ch 3, skip first st, * 1dc into next ch 1 sp, 1dc into next sc, rep from * to end. Turn.
Rep first–4th rows throughout.

5 Multicolor ridges

Work as for the basic jacket, omitting two of the half-double rows worked between the ridges and using a different color for edge ridge.

6 Puff stitch ridges

Make a multiple of 2 ch plus 3 extra. Use 2 colors alternately.
Base row 1dc into 4th ch from hook, 1dc into each ch to end. Turn.
1st row (WS) Ch 3, skip first st, * (yo, insert hook into next st, draw through a loop) 4 times, yo and draw through all 9 loops on hook (puff st formed), 1dc into next st, rep from * to end. Turn.
2nd row Ch 3, skip first st, 1dc into each unworked loop of first row to end. Turn.
Rep first and 2nd rows throughout.

Simon Butcher

Jacquard patterns

Jacquard patterns can easily be crocheted using bright colors and simple stitches. Work either small, repeating patterns for a "Fair Isle" or scatter individual motifs as your fancy takes you.

Skills you need

* **Double crochet**
* **Picking up stitches**
* **Jacquard crochet**

If you do not know the basic skills, refer to pages 177, 295 and 303.

Materials

Jacquard patterns are best worked in basic stitches (single crochet, half double and sometimes double) and plain four-ply worsted-weight yarns so that the patterns can be clearly seen. Alternative four plys — one a mixture of cotton and acrylic, the other a pure wool — have been recommended for the teenager's sweater on page 243.

This is possible because not only are both yarns of the same weight, but also there is the same yardage in each. However if you wish to substitute any other four ply, remember that you may need more or fewer skeins than stated in the pattern since the yardage will almost certainly be different.

Special technique – working into knitted ribbing

Coral Mula

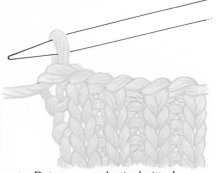

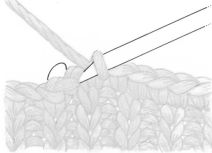

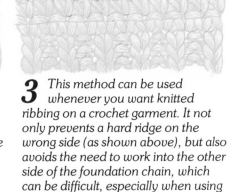

1 *Being more elastic, knitted is often preferable to crocheted ribbing, especially if the garment will receive hard wear. The knitting can be worked after the crochet is completed, or, it can be worked into the top of the knitting. Bind off in ribbing until only one loop remains on the needle.*

2 *Transfer the loop to a crochet hook. Work one chain to count as the first single crochet and skip the first stitch. Inserting the hook under both horizontal loops, work one single crochet into each bound-off stitch to the end of the row. Work following rows in single crochet as usual.*

3 *This method can be used whenever you want knitted ribbing on a crochet garment. It not only prevents a hard ridge on the wrong side (as shown above), but also avoids the need to work into the other side of the foundation chain, which can be difficult, especially when using textured yarns.*

The basic jacquard pattern

Jacquard patterns and smart knitted bands make this sweater irresistible to the fashion-conscious teenager.

Sizes
To fit 28 [30:32½:34½] in. chest
Length 22½ [23:24:24½] in.
Sleeve seam 16 [16:17:17] in.

Note: Instructions for larger sizes are in square brackets []; where there is

only one set of figures it applies to all sizes.

Gauge
24 sts and 30 rows to 4 in. in jacquard pat worked on size C hook

Materials
6 [6:8:8] oz of a sport yarn in main color (A)
4 oz in each of contrasting colors (B, C and D)

2 oz in each of contrasting colors (E and F)
Size C crochet hook
Pair of size 2 knitting needles
Set of 4 size 2 double-pointed knitting needles

Note: Strand yarn not in use loosely on the wrong side of the work.

Back
Using pair of knitting needles and A,

Terry Sims

cast on 99 [103:107:111] sts.
Work in K1, P1 ribbing beg alternate
rows P1, K1, until work measures 2
in. from beg. Bind off in ribbing until
one loop rem.
Transfer loop to crochet hook.
Next row (RS) Ch 1 to count as first
sc, skip first st, 1sc into top of each
bound-off st to end. Turn.
99 [103:107:111] sts.
Next row Ch 1 to count as first sc,
skip first st, 1sc into each st to end.
Cont to work in sc, beg jacquard pat
from chart.
Work 36 rows of jacquard pat 3 times

in all.
3rd and 4th sizes only
Work 5 more rows in jacquard pat.
All sizes
Fasten off at end of last row.
Shape armholes
Keeping jacquad pat correct, skip first
7 sts and rejoin yarn to next st.
Next row Ch 1 to count as first sc,
skip first st work in pat to last 7 sts,
turn. 85 [89:93:97] sts.
Next row Ch 1 to count as first sc,
skip first st, work next 2sc tog, work in
pat to last 3 sts, work 2sc tog, 1sc into
last st. Turn.

Next row Ch 1 to count as first sc,
skip first sc, 1sc into each st to end.
Turn.
Rep last 2 rows until 75 [79:83:87] sts
rem.
Work even until 18th [18th:24th:24th]
row of jacquard pat is complete.
Break off yarn. Join in B.
Next 2 rows Using B, ch 1 to count as
first sc, skip first st, 1sc into each st to
end. Turn.
Break off B. Join in A.
Yoke
Using A only, work in sc for 29
[32:29:32] rows.

243

Shape neck and shoulders

Next row Ch 1 to count as first sc, skip sc, 1sc into each of next 17 [19:20:22] sts, turn.

Next row Ch 1 to count as first sc, skip first sc, work next 2sc tog, 1sc into each st to end. Turn.

Next row Sl st over first 5 [6:6:7] sts, ch 1 to count as first sc, skip first st, 1sc into each st to end. Turn.

Next row Ch 1 to count as first sc, skip first st, 1sc into each of next 5 [6:6:6] sts.
Fasten off.

Skip next 39 [39:41:41] sts on back neck and rejoin A to next st.

Next row Ch 1 to count as first sc, skip first st, 1sc into each st to end. Turn.

Next row Ch 1 to count as first sc, skip first st, 1sc into each st to last 3 sts, work next 2sc tog, 1sc into last. Turn.

Next row Ch 1 to count as first sc, skip first st, 1sc into each of next 11 [12:13:13] sts, turn.

Next row Sl st across first 5 [6:7:7] sts, ch 1 to count as first sc, skip first st, 1sc into each st to end. Fasten off.

Front

Work as for back until 21 [24:21:24] rows of yoke have been completed.

Shape left neck

Next row Ch 1 to count as first sc, skip first st, 1sc into each of next 22 [24:25:27] sts, turn.

Next row Sl st across first 4 sts, ch 1 to count as first sc, skip first st, 1sc into each st to end. Turn.

Next row Ch 1 to count as first sc, skip first st, 1sc into each of next 16 [18:19:20] sts, turn.

Work 7 more rows without further shaping.

Shape left shoulder

Next row Sl st across first 5 [6:6:7] sts, ch 1 to count as first sc, skip first st, 1sc into each st to end. Turn.

Next row Ch 1 to count as first sc, skip first st, 1sc into each of next 5 [6:6:7] sts. Fasten off.

Skip next 29 [29:31:31] sts on front neck and rejoin A to next st.

Complete right neck and shoulder to match left side, reversing all shaping.

Sleeves (both alike)

Using knitting needles and A, cast on 67 [67:75:75] sts.

Work in K1, P1 ribbing as given for back until work measures 2 in. from

244

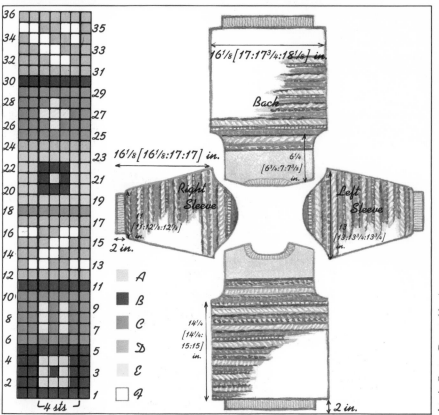

Linda Greigg/Dennis Hawkins

beg. Bind off in ribbing until one loop rem. Transfer loop to size C crochet hook.

Next row (RS) Ch 1 to count as first sc, skip first st, 1sc into top of each bound-off st to end. Turn. 67 [67:75:75] sts.

Next row Ch 1 to count as first sc, skip first st, 1sc into each st to end. Turn.

Cont to work in sc, work first 9 rows of jacquard pat from chart.

Next row Ch 1 to count as first sc, skip first st, 2sc into next st, 1sc into each st to last 2 sts. 2sc into next st, 1sc into last st. Turn.

Keeping jacquard pat correct, cont to inc one st at each end of every foll 10th row 6 [6:4:4] times in all. 79 [79:83:83] sts.

Cont in pat without further shaping until 3 reps of jacquard pat have been worked. Work 1 [1:5:5] more rows in pat. Fasten off.

Shape top

Keeping jacquard pat correct, skip first 6 sts and rejoin yarn to next st.

Next row Ch 1 to count as first sc, skip first st, work in pat to last 6 sts, turn.

Next row Ch 1 to count as first sc, skip first st, work next 2sc tog, work in pat to last 3 sts, work next 2sc tog, 1sc into last st. Turn.

Keeping jacquard pat correct, cont to

dec one st at each end of every foll alt row until 43 [43:47:47] sts rem.

Cont to dec one st at each end of next 12 rows. 19 [19:23:23] sts.

Break off yarn. Join in B.

Next row Using B only, sl st across first 4 [4:5:5] sts, ch 1 to count as first sc, skip first st, 1sc into each of next 10 [10:12:12] sts, turn.

Next row Sl st across first 4 sts, ch 1 to count as first sc, skip first st, 1sc into each of next 3 [3:5:5] sts.
Fasten off.

To finish

Press each piece as recommended on label. Join shoulder seams. Join side and sleeve seams.

Armhole borders (both alike)
Using size C crochet hook and with RS facing, join B to underarm seam. Work 80 [84:86:90] sts evenly around armhole, joining last st to first st with a sl st. Work one more round. Fasten off. Set in sleeves

Neckband
Using A and set of 4 double-pointed knitting needles, pick up and K 112 [112:120:120] sts evenly around neck. Work in rounds of K1, P1 ribbing for 2 in. Bind off.
Turn ribbing to WS and sew to base of ribbing to form a crew neck (see Special technique, page 10).
Press all seams.

Lacets

Lacets are V-shaped stitches, which can either be used by themselves to create a variety of openwork patterns or be combined with blocks and spaces to form lacy filet fabrics.

Skills you need

* **Lacets**

If you do not know this basic skill, refer to page 302.

Materials

Lacet patterns, whether combined with filet crochet or used by themselves, generally look best when worked in plain yarns. Though they can be worked in thicker yarns, fine yarns such as cotton, three ply and four ply are traditionally used. The man's T-shirt on page 245 has been worked in an acrylic-wool yarn, equivalent to four ply. Because of their openwork quality, lacet patterns are ideal for making light weight summer clothes or, combined with filet crochet, traditional household linen.

Special technique – finishing a front opening

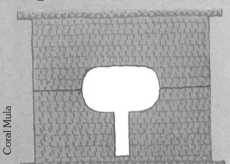

1 The front opening usually begins just above the start of the armhole shaping. Work each side separately, reversing shaping on the second side. Press the front and back as instructed in the pattern. Join the shoulder seams.

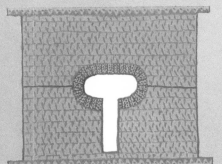

2 With right side facing, pick up stitches evenly around the neck and work in ribbing as required. Bind off loosely in ribbing.

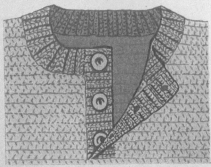

3 Pick up stitches on each side of the neck including the row ends of the neckband. Remember to work buttonholes in the ribbing. Lap the buttonhole band over the button band and sew both neatly to the beginning of the front opening.

Coral Mula

The basic lacet T-shirt

With knitted ribbing bands, neat neckline and contrasting yoke, this cool T-shirt is smart gear for a hot, summer day.

Men's sizes 38 [40:42] in. chest
Length 25 [25½:26] in.
Sleeve seam 8¼ in.

Note: Instructions for larger sizes are in square brackets []; where there is only one set of figures it applies to all sizes.

Materials
13 [15:16] oz. of a sport yarn
Size B crochet hook
Pair of size 2 knitting needles
3 small buttons

Gauge
7 pat reps and 20 rows to 4 in. worked on size B hook

Back
Using knitting needles, cast on 145 [149:157] sts. Work in K1, P1 ribbing until work measures 2½ in. Bind off loosely in ribbing until one loop rem.

Transfer loop to crochet hook.
1st row (RS) Ch 5, * skip next bound-off st, 1sc into next bound-off st, ch 2, skip next bound-off st, 1dc into next bound-off st, ch 2, rep from * to end, omitting last 2ch and working 1dc into last bound-off st. 36 [37:39] pat reps.
2nd row Ch 1, 1sc into first dc, * ch 3, 1sc into next dc, rep from * to end, working last sc into 3rd turning ch. Turn.
3rd row Ch 5, * 1sc into next ch 3 sp, ch 2, 1dc into next sc, ch 2, rep from * to end, omitting last 2 ch and working 1dc into last sc. Turn.
2nd and 3rd rows form the pat.
Cont in pat until work measures 16½ in., ending with a 2nd pat row.

Yoke
Next row Ch 3, skip first st, * 2dc into next ch 3 sp, 1dc into next sc, rep from * to end. Turn.
109 [112:118] sts.

Shape armholes
Next row Sl st over first 9dc, ch 3, 1dc into each of next 92 [95:101] dc, turn leaving 8dc unworked. 93 [96:102] sts. **

Work even in dc until work measures 25 [25½:26] in. Fasten off.

Front
Work as for back to **.
Divide for front opening
Next row Ch 3, skip first st, 1dc into each of next 42 [44:47] sts, turn. 43 [45:48] sts.
Cont in dc on these sts only until work measures 22 [22½:23]in., ending at neck edge.
Shape neck
Next row Sl st over first 8dc, ch 3, work in dc to end. Turn.
Dec 1dc at neck edge on every row until 31 [32:33] dc rem.
Work even until work measures same as back.
Fasten off.
Return to beg of front opening, skip next 7 [6:6]dc and rejoin yarn to next

st. Complete second side to match.

Sleeve (both alike)
Using knitting needles, cast on 93 [101:109] sts. Work in K1, P1 ribbing until work measures 1½in. from beg. Bind off in ribbing until one loop rem. Transfer loop to crochet hook. Work 1st-3rd rows as for back then 2nd row once more. 23 [25:27] pat reps.

Shape sleeve
Next row Ch 4, 1dc into sc at base of ch 4, work in pat to last sc, (1dc, ch 1, 1dc) into last sc. Turn.

Next row Ch 1, 1sc into first dc, ch 1, 1sc into next dc, work in pat to last 2 sts, 1sc into last dc, ch 1, 1sc into 3rd ch of 4 turning ch. Turn.

Next row Ch 5, 1sc into next ch 1 sp, ch 2, 1dc into next sc, work in pat to end, ending with ch 2, 1sc into next ch 1 sp, ch 2, 1dc into last sc. Turn. Work in pat 7 rows without shaping. Rep last 10 rows twice more. 29 [31:33] pat reps. Cont in pat without further shaping until sleeve measures 9⅜in. from beg. Fasten off.

Neckband
Join shoulder seams. With RS facing and using knitting needles, pick up and K 110 [116:122] sts around neck edge. Work in K1, P1 ribbing for 10 rows. Bind off in ribbing.

Buttonband
With RS facing and using knitting needles, pick up and K 50 [54:58] sts down right side of neck. Work in K1, P1 ribbing for 10 rows. Bind off in ribbing.

Buttonhole band
Pick up and K sts down left side of neck as for buttonband. Work 5 rows in K1, P1 ribbing ending at top of neck.

Buttonhole row Rib 6, * bind off 3 sts, rib 12 [13:14]*, rep from * to * once, bind off 3 sts, rib to end.

Next row Rib to first buttonhole, * cast on 3 sts, rib 12 [13:14], rep from * once, cast on 3 sts, rib to end. Work 13 more rows in ribbing. Bind off.

To finish
Join side seams. Join sleeve seams, leaving top 7 rows open. Set in sleeves, sewing 7 rows at sleeve top to sts of armhole shaping. Overlap buttonhole band over buttonband and sew ends to dc at base of neck opening. Sew on buttons.

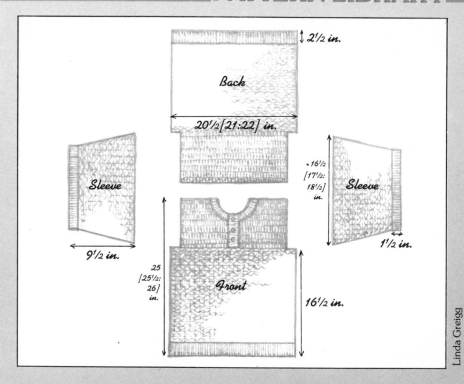

Linda Greigg

Adapting the basic lacet T-shirt

Use lacet patterns to make the basic T-shirt or to use traditional filet crochet designs to make elegant edgings for household linens.

Lacet edgings
Many lacet patterns can be adapted to produce pretty edgings, ideal for trimming lacy garments or filet-crochet household linens. You should experiment before you begin the edging to ensure that your chosen pattern can be used but the following method can be applied to most simple lacet patterns. Work a chain the same length as the required edging plus about 20 extra. Work the base row of your chosen lacet pattern into the chain.

When the edging is the required length, turn, and work the first pattern row. Fasten off. If you want a deeper edging, work more pattern rows before fastening off.

Do not worry about the few chains left unworked after the base row. After fastening off, cut the beginning slip knot and undo the chains.

Lacet patterns

1 Vertical lacets
Make a multiple of 8 ch plus 7.

Base row (RS) 1dc into 4th ch from hook, 1 dc into each of next 3 ch, *ch 2, skip next ch, 1sc into next ch, ch 2, skip next ch, 1dc into each of next 5 ch, rep from * to end. Turn.

1st row Ch 3, skip first dc, 1dc into each of next 4dc, * ch 3, skip next (ch 2, 1sc, ch 2), 1dc into each of next 5dc, rep from * to end. Turn.

2nd row Ch 3, skip first dc, 1dc into each of next 4dc, * ch 2, 1sc into next ch 3 sp, ch 2, 1dc into each of next 5dc, rep from * to end, working last dc into top of turning ch. Turn.

First and 2nd rows form pat.

1

2 Crossed lacets

This could be used in the T-shirt on page 245.

Make multiple of 8 ch plus 2 extra.

Base row 1sc into 2nd ch from hook, *ch 4, skip next 3 ch, 1sc into next ch, rep from * to end. Turn.

1st row (RS) Ch 3, skip first st, *3dc into next ch 4 sp, 1dc into next sc, ch 2, 1sc into next ch 4 sp, ch 2, 1dc into next sc, rep from * to end. Turn.

2nd row Ch 5, *1sc into first of next 5dc, ch 4, 1sc into last of same 5dc, ch 4, rep from * omitting ch 4 at end of last rep and working last sc into top of turning ch. Turn.

3rd row Ch 5, * 1sc into first ch 4 sp, ch 2, 1dc into next sc, 3dc into next ch 4 sp, 1dc into next sc, ch 2, rep from * omitting ch 2 at end of last rep and working last dc into 3rd of 5 turning ch. Turn.

4th row Ch 1, 1sc into first dc, * ch 4, 1sc into last of next 5dc, ch 4, 1sc into first of next 5dc, rep from * to end working last sc into 3rd turning ch. Turn.

First–4th rows form pat. Rep them throughout.

3 Cluster lacet

This could be used in the T-shirt on page 245.

Make a multiple of 6 ch plus 3 extra.

Base row 1dc into 4th ch from hook, * ch 2, skip next ch, 1sc into next ch, ch 2, skip next ch, 1dc into each of next 3ch, rep from *, ending last rep with 1dc into each of last 2ch. Turn.

1st row (RS) Ch 3, skip first dc, 1dc into next dc, * ch 3, 1dc into first of next 3dc, leaving last loop of each st on hook work 5dc into next dc, yo and draw through all 6 loops on hook (cluster formed), 1dc into next dc, rep from * omitting cluster in last rep and working last dc into top of turning ch. Turn.

2nd row Ch 3, skip first dc, 1dc into next dc, * ch 2, 1sc into next ch 3 sp, ch 2, 1dc into next dc, 1dc into top of cluster, 1dc into next dc, rep from * ending last rep with 1dc into last dc, 1dc into top of turning ch. Turn.

Rep first and 2nd rows throughout.

4 Alternating lacets

Make a multiple of 8 ch plus 9.

Base row (RS) 1sc into 7th ch from hook, ch 2, skip next ch, 1dc into next ch, * ch 3, skip next 3ch, 1dc into next ch, ch 2, skip next ch, 1sc into next ch, ch 2, skip next ch, 1dc into next ch, rep from * to end. Turn.

1st row Ch 6, skip first dc, * 1dc into next dc, ch 2, 1sc into next sp, ch 2, 1dc into next dc, ch 3, 1dc into next dc, rep from * to end. Turn.

2nd row Ch 5, 1sc into first sp, ch 2, * 1dc into next dc, ch 3, 1dc into next dc, ch 2, 1sc into next sp, ch 2, rep from * to end, ending skip first 3 turning ch, 1dc into next ch. Turn.

Rep first and 2nd rows throughout.

2

3

4

248

5

7 Lacets and shells
This could be used in the T-shirt on page 245.
Make a multiple of 4 ch plus 2 extra.
Base row 1sc into 2nd ch from hook, * ch 3, skip next 3ch, 1sc into next ch, rep from * to end. Turn.
1st row Ch 3, skip first st, *3dc into next ch 3 sp, ch 1, rep from *, omitting ch 1 at end of last rep and ending with 1dc into last st.
2nd row Ch 1, 1sc into first dc, *ch 2, 1dc into 2nd of 3dc, ch 2, 1sc into next ch 1 sp, rep from * to end, working last sc into top of turning ch. Turn.
3rd row Ch 5, 1sc into first dc, *ch 3, 1sc into next dc, rep from *, ending with ch 2, 1dc into last sc. Turn.
4th row Ch 3, skip first st, 1dc into first ch 2 sp, ch 1, *3dc into next ch 3 sp, ch 1, rep from *, ending with 2dc into last sp. Turn.
5th row Ch 5, 1sc into first ch 1 sp, *ch 2, 1dc into 2nd of next 3dc, ch 2, 1sc into next ch 1 sp, rep from * ending with ch 2, 1dc into top of turning ch. Turn.
6th row Ch 1, 1sc into first dc, *ch 3, 1sc into next dc, rep from * to end working last sc into 3rd ch of turning ch. Turn.
First-6th rows form pat. Rep them throughout. The pat is reversible.

Simon Wheeler

6

5 Horizontal lacets
This could be used in the T-shirt on page 245.
Make a multiple of 4 ch plus 3 extra.
Base row (RS) 1dc into 4th ch from hook, 1dc into each ch to end. Turn.
1st row Ch 1, 1sc into first dc, * ch 3, skip next 3dc, 1sc into next dc, rep from * to end working last sc into top of turning ch. Turn.
2nd row Ch 5, 1sc into first ch 3 sp, ch 2, 1dc into next sc, * ch 2, 1sc into next ch 3 sp, ch 2, 1dc into next sc, rep from * to end. Turn.
3rd row Ch 1, 1sc into first dc, * ch 3, 1sc into next dc, rep from * to end working last sc into 3rd of 5 turning ch. Turn.
4th row Ch 3, skip first st, * 3dc into next ch 3 sp, 1dc into next sc, rep from * to end. Turn.
First-4th rows form pat. Rep them throughout.

6 Lacet mesh
This could be used in the T-shirt on page 245.
Make a multiple of 4 ch plus 9 extra.
Base row 1sc into 7th ch from hook, * ch 2, skip next ch, 1dc into next ch, ch 2, skip next ch, 1sc into next ch, rep from * ending with ch 2, 1dc into last ch. Turn.
1st row Ch 1, 1sc into first dc. * ch 2, 1dc into next sc, ch 2, 1sc into next dc rep from * to end working last sc into 3rd turning ch. Turn.
2nd row Ch 5, * 1sc into next dc, ch 2, 1dc into next sc, ch 2, rep from * to end, omitting ch 2 at end of last rep. Turn.
First and 2nd rows form pat. Rep them throughout. The pat is reversible.

8

8 Simple lacet and bar
Make a multiple of 4 ch plus 6.
Base row 1dc into 10th ch from hook, * ch 3, skip next ch 3, 1dc into next ch, rep from * to end. Turn.
1st row (RS) Ch 5, * 1sc into next ch 3 loop, ch 2, 1dc into next dc, ch 2, rep from * ending with 1sc into turning ch loop, ch 2, skip first 3 turning ch and work 1dc into next ch. Turn.
2nd row Ch 6, skip first dc, * 1dc into next dc, ch 3, skip next sc, rep from * ending with 1dc into 3rd ch of turning ch. Turn.
First and 2nd rows form pat. Rep them throughout.

7

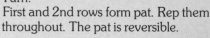

BABIES AND CHILDREN

Random jacquard

Skills you need

*Single crochet
*Half double crochet

If you do not know these basic skills, refer to pages 295 and 296.

Materials

Multi-coloured random jacquard provides an ideal opportunity to use up leftover yarn, but make sure that all yarns are of the same weight and thickness before you begin. Adult garments can be worked in all types of yarn, but baby clothes should be worked in a special baby yarn that will not irritate delicate skin. A synthetic four-ply yarn, designed for baby clothes and made extra soft by the addition of lamb's wool, has been used for the jacket and dungarees on the facing page. The matching blanket has been worked in a thick, pure wool rug yarn.

Special technique – increasing for the sleeves

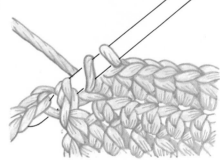

Coral Mula

1 *The basic jacket is worked in one piece beginning at the lower back edge and so stitches must be increased to form the sleeves. Work as given until the back is the required length to the underarms, ending with a wrong-side row. Remove the hook from the loop on the back. Using the second ball of main color. Chain 41 and fasten off.*

2 *Return to the loop on the back left in step 1. Join in the main color at the beginning of the row and chain 41. Work in pat across these in single crochet — 40 sleeve stitches. Work in pat across the first 61 stitches of the back.*

3 *To join the 41 chain worked separately (which will form the left-sleeve stitches), wind the yarn around the hook and insert the hook into the last stitch on the back and into the first of the 41 chain. Wind the yarn around the hook and draw a loop through the chain and last stitch. Wind the yarn around the hook and draw through the remaining three loops on the hook. Work in pat the next 40 stitches — 142 stitches have been worked.*

The basic random jacquard outfit

Use the softest baby yarn to make a jacket and matching overalls. The blanket is worked in the same jacquard pattern as the jacket.

Note: When working jacquard pattern on the jacket and blanket, use a small ball of yarn for each area of color.

Jacket and overalls

Size
To fit 20 in chest (9-12 months)
Jacket length 9⅜ in.
Sleeve seam 7 in.
Overalls length from waist to ankle 17¼ in.
Inside leg to ankle 8¼ in.

Gauge
22 hdc and 18 rows to 4 in. using size C hook
Materials
Jacket 3 oz of a baby yarn in main color (A)
1 oz in each of 3 contrasting colors (B, C and D)
3 small toggles

Ron Kelly

Overalls 5 oz in main color (A)
2 small buttons
Size C crochet hook

Jacket

Note: Jacket is worked in one piece, beg at lower back edge.
Using A, ch 63.
Base row (WS) Using A, 1hdc into 3rd ch from hook, 1hdc into each ch to end. Turn. 62sts.
1st row Using A, ch 2 to count as first hdc, skip first st, following chart on page 253, work 1hdc into each st to end. Turn. Cont in hdc, working jacquard pat from chart until work measures approx 5½ in. and 12th row of chart has been completed.
Shape sleeve
Using 2nd ball of A, ch 41. Fasten off. Return to main piece, join in A at beg of next row and ch 41.
Next row Using D, 1 hdc into 3rd ch

from hook, skip first st, 1hdc into each of next 5 sts, using B 1hdc into each of next 3 sts, work 13th row of chart across next 30 sts and across first 41 sts of back, using B, yo, insert hook into last st of back and into first of separate 41 ch, yo and draw through first ch and last st of back, yo and draw through 3 loops on hook (left-sleeve sts joined to back) work in pat across rem 40ch. Turn. 142 sts. Cont in jacquard pat until work measures 9½ in. ending with a WS row.

Shape right neck
Next row Ch 2, skip first st, work in pat across next 60 sts, turn. 61 sts. Work even in pat for 2 more rows. Keeping jacquard pat correct, inc one st at neck edge on following 4 rows, ending at neck edge. 65 sts.
Next row Using A, ch 5, keeping jacquard pat correct work 1hdc into 3rd ch from hook, 1hdc into each of

next 2 ch, pat to end. 69 sts.

Shape right front
Work even in jacquard pat until sleeve measure 8 in. from underarm, ending at center-front edge.
Next row Ch 2, skip first st, work in pat across next 28 sts, turn. 29sts. Cont in jacquard pat on these sts until work measures 19 in.
Using A, work one row of hdc. Fasten off.
Shape left neck and front
With RS facing, return to back neck sts, skip next 20 sts, keeping jacquard pat correct rejoin yarn to next st.
Next row Ch 2, skip first st, work in pat to end. 61 sts. Complete to match other side of neck and front, reversing all shaping.

To finish
Do not press. Join underarm and side seams.

251

Outer edging

With RS facing and using crochet hook, join A to lower edge at right side seam. Work a round of sc along right front up right-front edge, around neck, down left-front edge, along left front and back, working 1 sc into each st and row end and 3 sc into corners. Work 3 more rounds of sc. Fasten off.

Sleeve edging (both alike)

With RS facing and using crochet hook, join A to sleeve seam. Work a round of sc, working sc into each st. Work 3 more rounds of sc. Fasten off.

Buttonloops (make 3)

Sew toggles into position on left front (for girls) or right front (for boys) placing one toggle ½ in. from neck edge, one 4¾ in. from lower edge and one evenly spaced in between. Make buttonloop on opposite front edge as foll:

With RS facing and using crochet hook, join A to edge st directly opposite toggle, sl st into same place as join, ch 8, sl st into same place as join.

Fasten off.

Overalls

Front

Beg at waist and using crochet hook, ch 62.

Base row (RS) 1hdc into 3rd ch from hook, 1hdc into each ch to end. Turn. 61sts.

Next row Ch 2 to count as first hdc, skip first st, 1hdc into each st to end. Turn.

Cont in hdc until work measures 7⅞ in. from beg, ending with a WS row.

Shape crotch

1st row Ch 2, skip first st, 1hdc into each of next 28 sts, 2hdc into next st, 1hdc into next st, 2hdc into next st, 1hdc into each of last 29 sts. Turn. 63 sts.

2nd, 4th and 6th rows Work in hdc.
3rd row Ch 2, skip first st, 1hdc into each of next 28 sts, 2hdc into next st, 1hdc into each of next 3 sts, 2hdc into each of last 29 sts. Turn. 65 sts.

5th row Ch 2, skip first st, 1hdc into each of next 28 hdc, 2hdc into next st, 1hdc into each of next 5 sts, 2hdc into next st, 1hdc into each of last 29 hdc. Turn. 67 sts.

**Divide for legs

Next row Ch 2, skip first st, 1hdc into each of next 28 sts, turn. 29 sts. Work in hdc on these sts for 3 more rows. Dec one st at inside-leg edge on next and every foll 6th row until 23 sts rem.

252

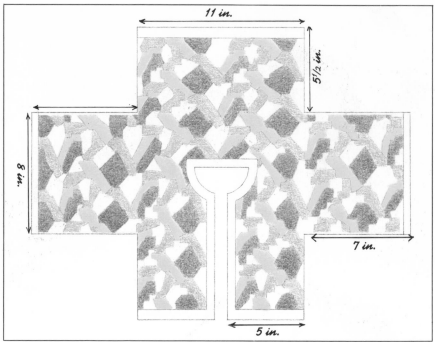

Ingrid Jacob

Cont in hdc without further shaping until work measures 17¼ in. from beg. Fasten off.

With RS facing, return to skipped sts on front, skip next 9 sts, rejoin yarn to next st.

Next row Ch 2, skip first st, 1 hdc into each st to end. 29 sts.

Complete as for first leg, reversing all shaping. **

Back

Work base row and 9 rows of hdc as given for back, ending with a WS row.
Shape back

Next row Ch 2, skip first st, 1hdc into each of next 53 sts, turn.

Next row Ch 2, skip first st, 1 hdc into each of next 46 sts, turn.

Next row Ch 2, skip first st, 1hdc into each of next 39 sts, turn.

Next row Ch 2, skip first st, 1hdc into each of next 32 sts, Turn.

Next row Ch 2, skip first st, 1hdc into each of next 32 sts just worked, 1hdc into 14 sts missed at side edge. Turn.

Next row Ch 2, skip first st, 1hdc into each of next 46 sts, 1hdc into 14 sts missed at side edge. Turn. 61 sts.

Cont in hdc without further shaping until back measures same as front at side edges.

Work from ** to ** as for front.

Feet

Do not press.
Join outside-leg seams.
With RS facing, rejoin yarn to first st on left leg.

Next row Ch 1 to count as first sc, skip first st, * 1sc into each of next 2

sts, work next 2sc tog, rep from * to last st, 1sc into last st. 35 sts.

Work 3 more rows in sc without further shaping.

Next row Sl st across first 4sc, ch 2, skip sl st at base of ch 2, 1hdc into each of next 11 sts, turn. 12 sts.

Work 10 more rows in hdc on these sts without further shaping.
Fasten off.

With RS facing, rejoin yarn to first sl st.

Next row Ch 2, skip first st, 1hdc into each of next 2 sl sts, 1hdc into each of next 10 row ends, 1hdc into each of next 12 sts, 1hdc into each of next 10 row ends, 1hdc into each of next 20 sts. Turn. 55sts.

Next row Ch 2, skip first st, 1hdc into each of next 29 sts, (work next 2hdc tog) 4 times, 1hdc into each of next 15 sts. Turn. 51 sts.

Work 4 more rows of hdc without further shaping.

Next row Ch 2, skip first st, 1hdc into each of next 15 sts, (work next 2hdc tog) twice, 1hdc into each of next 21 sts, (work next 2hdc tog) twice, 1hdc into each of next 6 sts. Turn. 47sts.

Next row Ch 2, skip first st, 1hdc into each of next 5 sts, (work next 2hdc tog) twice, 1hdc into each of next 19sts, (work next 2hdc tog) twice, 1hdc into each of next 14sts. 43 sts.
Fasten off.

Work 2nd foot in the same way, reversing all shaping.

Front bib

**With RS facing and using crochet hook, rejoin yarn to first st on front.

Next row Ch 1 to count as first sc,

skip first 2 sts, 1 sc into each st to last 2 sts, work last 2sc tog. Turn. 59 sts.
Work 4 more rows of sc without further shaping.

Next row Ch 3, skip first st, 1dc into each of next 2 sts, * ch 1, skip next st, 1dc into each of next 3 sts, rep from * to end. Turn.

Next row Ch 1 to count as first sc, skip first st, 1sc into each of next 2 sts, *1sc into next ch 1 sp, 1sc into each of next 3 sts, rep from * to end.

Work one more row in sc. Fasten off. **

With RS facing, skip first 12 sts on bib and rejoin yarn to next st.

Next row Ch 2, skip first st, 1dc into each of next 34 sts, turn. 35 sts.
Work one more row of hdc.
Cont in hdc, dec one st at each end of next on every foll 3rd row until 25 sts rem.
Work one more row in hdc.
Work 2 rows of sc.

Buttonhole row Ch 1 to count as first sc, skip first st, 1sc into next st, ch 3, skip next 3 sts, 1sc into each of next 15 sts, ch 3, skip next 3 sts, 1sc into each of last 2 sts. Turn.

Next row Ch 1 to count as first sc, skip first st, 1 sc into next st, 3sc into next ch 3 sp, 1 sc into each of next 15 sts, 3sc into next ch 3 sp, 1sc into each of last 2 sts. Turn. Fasten off.

With RS facing and using crochet hook, rejoin yarn to first row end of bib and work 1sc into each row end up left side, into each st across top and into each row end down right side. Fasten off.

Back bib
Work from ** to ** as for front bib.

Straps (make 2)
Using crochet hook, ch 61.
Base row 1hdc into 3rd ch from hook, 1hdc into each ch to end. Turn. 60 sts.
Work 3 more rows of hdc.
Fasten off.

To finish
Do not press.
Join inside-leg and foot seams.
Stitch straps into place at back and sew buttons on to straps as required to correspond with buttonholes.
Make a twisted cord 39½ in. long and thread it through the eyelet holes.

Blanket
Size
Blanket measures approx 35¾ in. x 24 in.

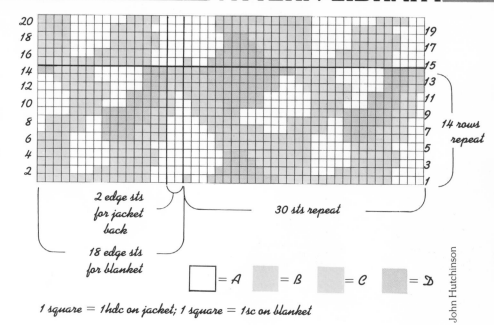

2 edge sts for jacket back

18 edge sts for blanket

30 sts repeat

14 rows repeat

☐ = A   = B   = C   = D

1 square = 1hdc on jacket; 1 square = 1sc on blanket

John Hutchinson

Gauge
9sc and 9 rows to 4 in. using size K crochet hook

Materials
23 oz of a bulky yarn in main color (A)
9 oz in each of 3 contrasting colors (B, C and D)
Size K crochet hook

To make
Using crochet hook and A, ch 49.
Base row (WS) 1sc into 2nd ch from hook, 1sc into each ch to end. Turn. 48 sts.
1st row Using A, ch 1 to count as first sc, skip first st, foll chart shown above work 1sc into each st to end.
Turn.
Cont in sc, working jacquard pat from chart until work measures 32⅝ in. from beg. Using A, work one row of hdc. Fasten off.

Edging
Do not press.
With RS facing and using size K hook, rejoin A to first st on foundation ch.
1st round Ch 1 to count as first sc, skip first st, (1sc into each st to corner st, 3sc into corner st, 1sc into each row end to corner st, 3sc into corner st) twice, ending last rep with 2sc, sl st to first ch. Work 2 rounds of sc. Fasten off.

Adapting the jacquard outfit

Use the Pattern Library to make an original outfit for a baby.

Many of the Pattern Library samples can be used to make the basic jacket and blanket since, unlike conventional jacquard patterns, random jacquard does not have obvious pattern repeats. There is therefore no need to worry about balancing the pattern at the side edges. You can either work a totally random pattern, inventing the design as you go, or work a random-style repeating pattern as on the basic jacket and blanket.

Work the stitch repeat as often as possible within the stitches for the garment. Then work as much of the repeat as required for the remaining stitches. For example, on the chart shown above the 18 edge stitches on the rug are the first 18 stitches of the stitch repeat while the jacket has only two edge stitches.

Random jacquard patterns

1 **Random doubles**
In this sample, which could be used on the baby's jacket and blanket on page 251, blocks of three double crochets have been placed at random. The blocks have been worked in a combination of five colors, introduced at random to give a pleasing effect.

2 **Stairways**
In this sample, which could be used to make the basic jacket and blanket, stairs of double crochet were worked in four separate colors.

3 **Triangles**
A number of different-sized triangles have been worked on this single crochet sample.

4 **Morse**
In this half-double crochet sample, which could be used to make the basic jacket and blanket, colorful dots and dashes have been placed at random on every alternate row on a dark background to striking effect.

Simon Wheeler

Embroidery

Firm crochet fabrics, especially when worked in single crochet, are ideal bases for embroidery and, with a little practice, you will find it remarkably easy to beautify anything from a special outfit for baby to your own favorite sweater.

Skills you need

*Single crochet
* Embroidery on crochet

If you do not know the basic skills, refer to pages 295 and 301.

Materials

We have used sport-weight yarn to work the basic single crochet fabric in the baby's outfit on page 256, since this combination produces a firm fabric that can be embroidered relatively easily, but most weights of plain yarn produce satisfactory results. When choosing embroidery threads there is no need to confine yourself to conventional silks or wools; scraps of glitter, bouclé or random yarn can all be used successfully. Use beads, ribbon or braid to add the finishing touch, or use them alone as short-cuts to an embroidered effect. Whatever you use, always make sure it is easily washed.

Special technique – crochet seaming

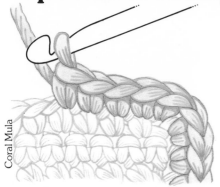

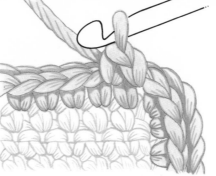

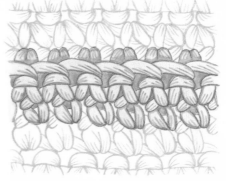

Coral Mula

1 First edge the garment pieces with one row of single crochet, working one stitch into each row end at the side edges and into each stitch at the top and lower edges. Turn corners either by working one chain at each corner, as on the baby's outfit on page 256, or by working three single crochet into each of the corner stitches.

2 To join the pieces, place the edged pieces together **with wrong sides facing**. Using the same yarn as that used for edging, join the yarn to the end of the seam. Work one chain and skip the first stitch on the edging. Insert the hook through both edgings under all four loops. Work one single crochet.

3 Continue in this way, joining the edgings by working one single crochet into each pair of stitches on the edging. Seaming a garment in this way produces a raised decorative seam, which looks particularly attractive when worked in a color to contrast with the main fabric.

The basic embroidered set

The perfect gift for a young baby – a coat, hat and blanket, worked in single crochet and then embroidered with sprigs of pink flowers.

Size
Coat to fit 0-6 months (17¾ in. chest)
Length 9¾ in.
Sleeve seam 5½ in.
Blanket 30 in. long by 24¾ in. wide.

Gauge
18 sts and 19 rows to 4 in. over single crochet worked on size G hook

Materials
Coat and hat 6 oz of a sport-weight yarn in main color (A)
2 oz in contrasting color (B)
Blanket 9 oz in main color (A)
4 oz in contrasting color (B)

Size G crochet hook
Small amounts of embroidery floss in green and two shades of pink

Coat Back
Using crochet hook and A ch 43.
Base row (RS) 1sc into 2nd ch from hook, 1sc into each sc to end. Turn. 42 sc.
Pat row Ch 1, skip first sc, 1sc into each sc to end. Turn.

255

Cont in pat without shaping on these 42 sc until work measures 9⅜ in. from beg. Fasten off.

Edging

Using crochet hook and with RS facing, skip the turning ch, and join B to first sc at beg of last row worked, ch 1, 1sc into each sc to end of row, * ch 1 to form corner, skip first row end of side edge, 1sc into each row end to next corner, ch 1 to form corner *, 1sc into each ch on lower edge, rep from * to * once more, 1sc into turning ch at beg of last row working in A. Fasten off.

Fronts (alike)

Using A, ch 22.

Base row (RS) 1sc into 2nd ch from hook, 1sc into each ch to end. Turn. 21sc.

Cont in pat as given for back on these 21 sc until work measures 9⅜ in. from beg.

Fasten off.

Edging

Work as for back.

Sleeves (alike)

Using A, ch 33.

256

Base row (RS) 1sc into 2nd ch from hook, 1sc into each ch to end. Turn. 32sc.

Cont in pat as given for back on these 32 sc until work measures 5 in. from beg. Fasten off.

Edging

Work as for back.

To finish

Using crochet hook and B, crochet pieces together with WS facing and working through both loops of edging of each piece.

Left shoulder

With back behind left front, join B to ch 1 at top corner, ch 1, skip first sc, 1sc into each of next 12sc.

Fasten off.

Right shoulder

With back behind right front, join B to 13th st from top corner, ch 1, skip first sc, 1sc into each of next 11sc, 1sc into ch 1 at corner. Fasten off.

Left armhole

With sleeve behind front and back, join B to left side at 16th row end from outer edge of shoulder seam and to ch 1 at top corner of sleeve, ch 1, skip first sc, 1sc into each of next 15sc, 1sc into ch 1 at top corner of front, 1sc

into ch 1 at top corner of back, 1sc into each of next 15sc, 1sc into next sc on back and ch 1 at top corner of sleeve. Fasten off.

Right armhole

With sleeve behind front and back, join B to back at 16th row end from outer edge of shoulder seam and to ch 1 at top corner of sleeve, ch 1, skip first sc, 1sc into each of next 15 sc, 1sc into ch 1 at top corner of back, 1sc into ch 1 at top corner of front, 1sc into each of next 15sc, 1sc into next sc on front and ch 1 at top corner of sleeve. Fasten off.

Left side and sleeve seams

With back behind front, join B to ch 1 at lower edge of left front and back, ch 1, skip first sc, 1sc into each sc to sleeve, 1sc into each sc on sleeve, ending with 1sc into ch 1 at lower corners. Fasten off.

Right side and sleeve seams

With back behind front, join B to ch 1 at lower edge of right sleeve, ch 1, 1sc into each sc to front, 1 sc into each sc of front and back, ending with 1sc into ch 1 at lower corners. Fasten off.

Ties (make 2)

Using size G hook and B, make a ch 7

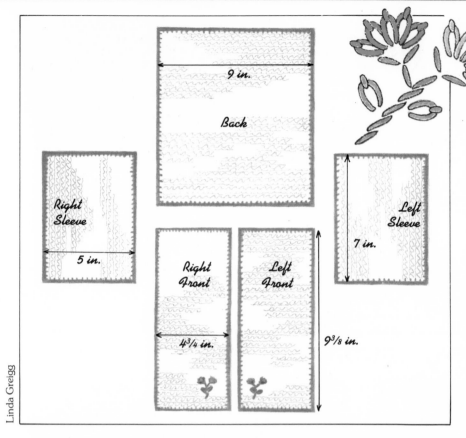

Left Sleeve

7 in.

Back

9 in.

Right Sleeve

5 in.

Right Front

4¾ in.

Left Front

9⅜ in.

in. long. Fasten off.
Sew one end of each tie to front edge 3½ in. from top corner.
Fold back lapels as shown and catch-stitch corners neatly in place.

Hat
Sides (make 2)
Using size G hook and A, ch 27.
Base row (RS) 1sc into 2nd ch from hook, 1sc into each ch to end. 26sc.
Cont in pat as given for coat on these 26sc until work measures 5½ in. from beg. Fasten off.
Edging
Work as given for coat back.
To finish
Using crochet hook with WS tog and working through both loops of the edge of each piece, join B to ch 1 at top right-hand corner, ch 1, 1sc into each sc to corner, 2sc into ch 1 at corner, 1 sc into each sc at row ends of sides to corner, 1sc into ch 1 at corner. Fasten off.
Ties (make 2)
Using B, make a ch 9¾ in. long. Fasten off.
Fold corners of hat onto RS as shown and sew corners neatly in place.
Sew ties to hat.

Blanket
To make a square
Using size G hook and A, ch 22.

Base row (RS) 1sc into 2nd ch from hook, 1sc into each ch to end. Turn. 21sc.
Work pat row as for coat back on these 21sc 21 times.
Fasten off.
Make a total of 30 squares in the same way.
Edging
Work as for coat back.

Make a total of 30 squares in the same way.
Edging
Work as for coat back.

To finish
Note: Squares are arranged so that blanket is 6 squares long by 5 squares wide. Place alternate squares tog horizontally and vertically, and using B oversew together neatly at the edges.
Edging
Using crochet hook and with RS facing, join B to ch 1 at any corner, ch 1, 1sc into each sc to next corner of first square, 1sc into ch 1 at corner, * 1sc into ch 1 at corner of next square, 1sc into each sc to ch 1 at next corner of same square, rep from * round outer edge of blanket, working 2sc into ch 1 at corners of blanket and ending with 1sc into first corner of blanket, join with a sl st to first ch. Fasten off.

Embroidery
The motif above has been embroidered on the coat and blanket, with a slightly smaller version on the hat.
Position the motif at the center of alternate squares on the blanket, reversing the light and dark flowers on alternate rows. Reverse the motif completely for the left-hand corner of the coat and hat. Using embroidery floss, work the stem in stem stitch, the upper stem and sepals in straight stitch, and the leaves and petals in lazy-daisy stitch.

Adapting the baby's embroidered set

Any simple crochet fabric can be enhanced by adding embroidery.

Embroidery on single crochet
Most of the simpler embroidery stitches can be worked on a firm single crochet fabric in much the same way as when using linen or canvas.
Easy designs can be worked freehand on the fabric, but other, more complicated motifs are best planned first on paper. Draw the motif on graph paper so that each square on the paper represents one single crochet stitch. Use different symbols or colors to represent the stitches you intend to use.
There is no need to confine yourself to embroidery on a simple single crochet fabric. Introduce bobbles or holes into

the fabric and outline them with simple embroidery stitches. Or you could work a simple embroidery motif and then outline it with surface crochet or contrasting ribbon.

Other variations
Embroidery on other fabrics is less easy since other crochet stitches do not provide such a firm base.
However, such fabrics can still be decorated to obtain an "embroidered" appearance.
Surface slip stitch produces much the same effect as embroidered chain stitch, while embroidered braid or velvet ribbon can be woven through a double crochet or double-crochet mesh fabric.

Linda Greigg

Checkered patterns

Checkered patterns are remarkably varied, ranging from multi-colored patterns to simple two-color checks, and turn simply shaped garments into designer productions.

Skills you need

* **Double crochet around stem**
* **Using two colors**
* **Horizontal buttonholes**

If you do not know the basic skills, refer to pages 190, 298 and 299.

Materials

In most cases use plain yarns to work checkered patterns; textured yarns will obscure the stitches. When working a multi-colored checkered pattern bear in mind the effect you want to achieve. Choose bright, contrasting colors to catch the eye, or toning shades for a more subtle look. Baby clothes look especially good when worked in checkered patterns, but remember to use a special acrylic/wool baby yarn — as we have done for the blanket and sweater on page 259 — for frequent washing.

Special technique – working an invisible seam

1 *This flat seam is used on the side and underarm seams of the baby's sweater since it enables patterns to be matched easily and does not produce a hard ridge. With right sides up, place the pieces edge to edge, matching patterns.*

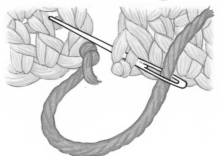

2 *Using a matching yarn — shown above in a contrast color for clarity — and a blunt-ended tapestry needle, secure the yarn to one lower edge. Take the needle over to the other side edge and pass it under one stitch.*

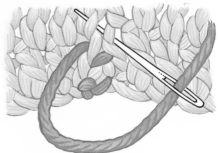

3 *Take the needle back to the first side edge and under the next stitch. Pull the yarn through firmly to make the stitch invisible, but not so tightly that the fabric puckers. Continue catching one stitch on each edge, until the seam is complete.*

The basic blanket and sweater

Check out our sweater and blanket, worked in bold navy and white check, to dress the smartest baby in town.

Sizes
Blanket 30 in. long × 25½ in. wide
Sweater To fit 6-9 months (17-17¾ in. chest)
Length 11 in.
Sleeve seam 8 in.

Gauge
Blanket 16 sts and 20 rows to 4½ in. over pat on size H hook.
Sweater 16 sts and 20 rows to 3¾ in. over pat on size G hook

Materials
Blanket 11oz of a sport-weight yarn

258

in main color (A)
11 oz in contrasting color (B)
Size H crochet hook
Sweater 4 oz of a sport-weight yarn in main color (A)
2 oz in contrasting color (B)
Size F and G crochet hooks
6 buttons

Note: When changing color complete last sc of every WS row with the new color. Carry color not in use loosely up side edge of work.

Blanket
Using size H hook and A, ch 90.
Base row (WS) 1sc into 2nd ch from hook, 1sc into each ch to end. Turn. 89sc.
1st row Using B, ch 1, 1sc into first sc, *(yo, insert hook from front of work, from right to left around stem of next sc and work 1dc, (1dc front worked, 1sc into next sc) 4 times, 1sc into each of next 8sc, rep from * to end, omitting 8sc at end of last rep. Turn.
2nd row Using B, ch 1, 1sc into first sc, 1sc into each dc and sc to end. Turn.
3rd row Using A, ch 1, 1sc into first sc, * (skip next sc of last row, 1dc front around stem of next dc of row before

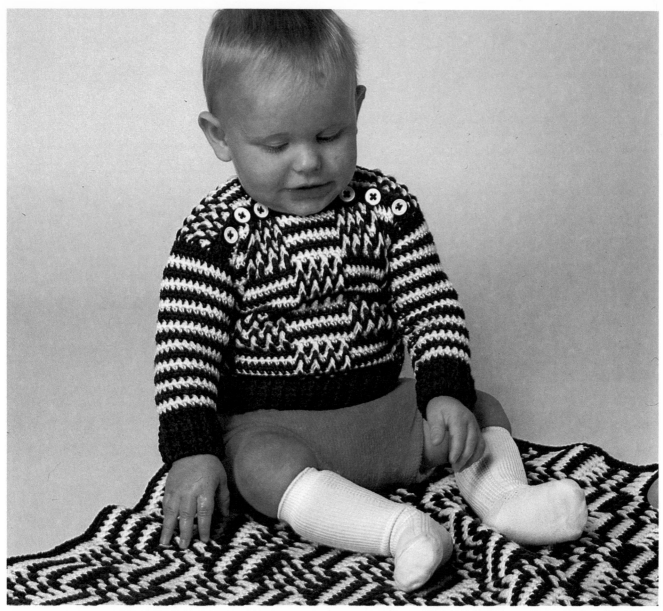

Terry Sims

last, 1sc into next sc of last row) 4 times, 1sc into each of next 8sc, rep from * to end, omitting 8sc at end of last rep. Turn.
4th row Using A, as 2nd row.
5th row Using B, as 3rd row.
6th-10th rows Rep 2nd-5th rows once, then 2nd row again.
11th row Using A, ch 1, 1sc into first sc, 1sc into each of next 8sc, *(skip next sc to last row and work 1dc front around stem of corresponding sc of last A row, 1sc into next sc of last row) 4 times, 1sc into each of next 8sc, rep from * to end. Turn.
12th row Using A, as 2nd row.
13th row Using B, ch1, 1sc into first sc, 1sc into each of next 8sc, * (skip next sc of last row and work 1dc front around stem of next dc of row before last, 1sc into next sc of last row) 4 times, 1sc into each of next 8sc, rep

from * to end. Turn.
14th row As 2nd row.
15th row Using A, as 13th row.
16th-20th rows Rep 12th – 15th rows once, then 12th row again.
21st row Using B, ch 1, 1sc into first sc, * (skip next sc of last row, 1dc front around stem of corresponding sc of last B row, 1sc into next sc of last row) 4 times, 1sc into each of next 8sc, rep from * to end, omitting 8sc at end of last rep. Turn. Rep 2nd-21st rows 5 times, then 2nd-10th rows again. Fasten off.
Edging
1st round With RS facing, join A to corner of long side at end of base row, work sc evenly into row-ends to next corner, 1sc into each st to next corner, work sc evenly into row-ends to next corner.
2nd round Working into other side of

foundation ch, work 2sc into first ch, 1sc into each ch to last ch, 2sc into last ch, (2sc into first sc of next side, 1sc into each sc to last sc before corner, 2sc into next sc) 3 times, sl st to first sc. Fasten off.

Sweater
Front
Using size F hook and A, ch 43.
Base row 1dc into 4th ch from hook, 1dc into each ch to end. Turn. 41 sts.
1st row (RS) Ch 2, skip first dc, (yo, insert hook from front of work, from right to left around stem of next dc and work 1dc – 1dc front worked –, yo, insert hook from back of work, from right to left around stem of next dc and work 1dc – 1dc back worked –) to end, working last dc around stem of turning ch. Turn.
2nd row Ch 2, skip first dc, (1dc back

around stem of next dc, 1dc front around stem of next dc) to end, working last dc round stem of turning ch. Turn.

Rep first and 2nd rows once more, then first row again. Change to size G hook.

Next row Ch 1, 1sc into first st, 1sc into each st to end, working last sc into top of turning ch. Turn.** Work first-21st rows of blanket, then 2nd-19th rows again. Cont with A only. Change to size F hook.

Buttonhole row Ch 1, 1sc into first sc, 1sc into each of next 2sc, (ch 1, skip next sc, 1sc ino each of next 4sc) twice, ch 1, skip next sc, 1sc into each of next 13sc, (ch 1, skip next sc, 1sc into each of next 4sc) twice, ch 1, skip next sc, 1sc into each of last 3sc. Turn.

Next row Ch 1, 1sc into first sc, 1sc into each st to end.
Fasten off.

Back

Work as for front to **. Cont in pat:
1st row Using B, ch 1, 1sc into first sc, 1sc into each of next 8sc, (1dc front around stem of next sc, 1sc into next sc) 4 times, 1sc into each of next 8sc) twice. Turn.
2nd row As 2nd row of blanket.
3rd row As 15th row of blanket.
4th row As 4th row of blanket.
5th row As 13th row of blanket.
6th-10th rows Rep 2nd-5th rows once, then 2nd row again.
11th row Using A, ch 1, 1sc into first sc, * (skip next sc of last row, 1dc front around stem of corresponding sc of

last A row, 1sc into next sc of last row) 4 times, 1sc into each of next 8sc, rep from * twice, omitting 8sc at end of last rep. Turn.
12th row As 4th row of blanket.
13th row As 5th row of blanket.
14th row As 2nd row of blanket.
15th row As 3rd row of blanket.
16th-20th rows Rep 12th-15th rows once, then 12th row again.
21st row Using B, ch 1, 1sc into first sc, 1sc into each of next 8sc, * (skip next sc of last row and work 1dc front around stem of corresponding sc of last B row, 1sc into next sc of last row) 4 times, 1sc into each of next 8sc, rep from * to end. Turn. Rep 2nd-21st rows once, then 2nd-10th rows again.

Front extensions

Next row Work in pat across 13 sts, turn. Keeping pat correct, work 9 more rows on these 13 sts.
Change to size F hook and using A work 2 rows of sc.
Fasten off.

2nd side

Next row With RS facing and using size G hook, skip center 15 sts for back neck and rejoin A to next st. Keeping pat correct, work 10 rows on these 13 sts.
Change to size F hook and using A work 2 rows of sc.
Fasten off.

Sleeves

Using size F hook and A, ch 25. Work as for front to ** on 23 sts. Cont in sc in stripes of 2 rows B and 2 rows A, inc 1 sc at each end of 4th row and

every following 6th row until there are 31sc. Work even until sleeve measures 8 in., ending after a 2-row stripe. Fasten off.

Neck edging

1st row With RS of back facing, using size F hook and A, work 9sc evenly down row-ends of inner edge of first front extension, work 1sc into each sc across back neck and 9sc evenly up row-ends of second front extension. Turn.

2nd row Ch 1, 1sc into first sc, 1sc into each of next 7sc, skip next 2sc, 1sc into each of next 13sc, skip next 2sc, 1sc into each of last 8sc. Fasten off.

To finish

With side edges even, lap last 2 rows of front over last 2 rows of front extensions on back. Catch-stitch row-ends neatly at side edges. Sew buttons to front extensions to correspond with buttonholes. With center of sleeve top even with first row of front extensions, sew in sleeves. Join side and sleeve seams with invisible seams.

Adapting the blanket and sweater

Subtle or bold, our samples are dazzlingly beautiful.

Coloured checkered patterns.

When working jacquard patterns, strand the yarn not in use at the base of the stitches on the wrong side of the work, crocheting over it with the working color. Introduce a new color neatly by using it to complete the last stitch in the old color.

In small, striped checkered patterns take the yarn loosely up the side of the work, but take care not to pull too tightly or the work will pucker at the edges. Enclose the smaller loops in the seam during making up.

Break off the yarn at the end of the row when the color changes in large checkered patterns. Knot the ends and darn in securely after seaming.

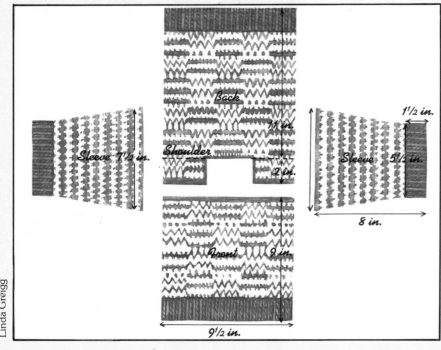

Linda Greigg

260

Using the samples

Experienced workers can use any of the samples to make the sweater. Make a gauge swatch to find the number of stitches over 4 in. of the chosen sample. Calculate the stitches needed to form the lower-edge widths on the measurement diagram. Add or subtract stitches as needed to obtain a multiple of the pattern repeat (shown in the samples' instructions).

The blanket is much easier to adapt. Use your gauge sample to calculate the width and work the length required.

Checkered patterns

1 Crazy stitch

Use six colors, A, B, C, D, E and F.

Use A, make a multiple of 4 ch.

Base row (RS) 3dc into 4th ch from hook, (skip next 3 ch, sl st into next ch, ch 3, 3dc into same ch as sl st) to last 4 sts, skip next 3 ch, 1sc into last ch. Turn.

1st row Using B, ch 3, 3dc into first sc, (skip next 3dc, sl st into top of ch 3 of previous row, ch 3, insert hook in sp between last of the 3dc just missed and the ch 3 of the previous row and work 3dc around stem of the ch 3) to end, ending skip last 3dc, 1sc into top of ch 3 of last row. Turn.

2nd and every other row Using A, work as 1st row.

3rd row Using C, work as 1st row.
5th row Using D, work as 1st row.
7th row Using E, work as 1st row.
9th row Using F, work as 1st row.
10th row Using A, work as 1st row.
1st-10th rows form pat. Rep them throughout.

2 Brick pattern

Use two colors, A and B. Using A, make a multiple of 4 ch.

Base row 1sc into 2nd ch from hook, 1sc into each ch to end.

1st row (RS) Using B, ch 3, skip first sc, 1dc into each of next 2 sts, (ch 1, skip next sc, 1dc into each of next 3 sts) to end. Turn.

2nd row Using A, ch 1, 1sc into first dc, 1sc into each of next 2dc, (working over the top of the ch 1 sp of last row and enclosing it within the st, work 1dc into the skipped sc of the last A row, 1sc into each of next 3dc) to end, working last sc into top of turning ch. Turn.

3rd row Using B, ch 4, skip first 2sc, (1dc into each of next 3 sts, ch 1, skip next sc) to last sc, 1dc into last sc. Turn.

4th row Using A, ch 1, 1sc into first dc, rep bracketed instructions of 2nd row to within turning ch, 1dc into first of skipped sc of last A row, 1sc into 3rd of ch 4. Turn.
1st-4th rows form pat. Rep them throughout.

3 Overlaid check pattern

Use two colors, A and B.
Using A, make a multiple of 4 ch plus 3 extra.

Base row Using A, 1sc into 2nd ch from hook, 1sc into each ch to end. Turn.

1st row Using B, ch 1, 1sc into first sc, 1sc into each sc to end. Turn.
2nd row As 1st row.
3rd row (RS) Using A, ch 1, 1sc into first sc, 1sc into next sc, * (skip next sc of last row and work 1dc around stem of corresponding sc of base row)

twice, 1sc into each of next 2sc of last row, rep from * to end. Turn.
4th row Using A, ch 1, 1sc into first sc, 1sc into each sc and dc to end. Turn.
5th row Using B, ch 1, 1sc into first sc, 1sc into next sc, * (skip next sc of last row and work 1dc around stem of corresponding dc of row before last) twice, 1sc into each of next 2sc of last row, rep from * to end. Turn.
6th row Using B, as 4th row.
7th row Using A, as 5th row.
Rep 4th-7th rows throughout.

Simon Butcher

261

Single crochet variations

Basic single crochet can be simply varied to make firm, textured fabrics that are ideal for hard-wearing garments.

Skills you need

* **Single crochet**
* **Working into one loop**

If you do not know the basic skills, refer to pages 295 and 297

Materials

Almost any yarns can be used for single crochet patterns to achieve an enormous variety of textured fabrics. Where a very textured yarn is to be used, simple single crochet produces a firm fabric where the yarn itself creates the interest. For a straight-forward knitting worsted or even finer yarn, stitch variations can be used to create textured effects, using color rather than yarn to emphasize the pattern. Our vest has been made in a synthetic/wool chunky yarn and combined with a ridged crochet stitch to create a chunky, warm fabric, but the same stitch worked in a finer or more textured yarn would create a different fabric, and you should experiment with a variety of yarns to see the results that can be achieved.

Special technique—working a crab stitch edging

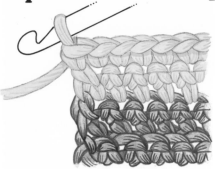

1 Crab stitch is achieved by working single crochet from left to right instead of from right to left, usually on one or more foundation rows of single crochet, depending on how deep you would like the edging to be. End with the right side of the work facing.

2 Do not turn the work once the foundation rows have been completed. Keeping the yarn at left of work, work from left to right. Make one chain, then insert the hook from front to back into the next stitch. Hold the hook over the yarn before drawing yarn through from back to front.

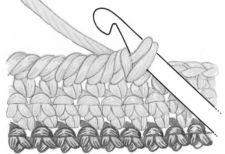

3 Complete the single crochet in the usual way. Continue to work each stitch in the same way, working from left to right instead of from right to left to the end of the row.

The basic single crochet vest

This simple vest is worked in single crochet ridge stitch, and then edged in crab stitch for an unusual finish.

Sizes
To fit 26 [28:30:32] in. chest
Length 17 [19:21:22] in. including border
Note: Length is adjustable.

Note: Instructions for larger sizes are 262

in square brackets []; where there is only one set of figures it applies to all sizes.

Gauge
10sc and 14 rows to 4 in. in pattern using A, worked on size K hook

Materials
9 [11:14:16] oz of a bulky yarn, (A)
2 [2:4:4] oz of a knitting worsted, (B)
Size F crochet hook
Size K crochet hook

Terry Sims

Body (worked in one piece to armholes)
Using larger hook and A, ch 65 [71:77:83].

Base row 1sc into 3rd ch from hook, 1sc into each ch to end. Turn.

Pattern row Ch 2, working into back loop only of each st, work 1sc into each sc to end. Turn.
64 [70:76:82] sts.

Rep pat row until work measures 10½ [11½:12½:13½] in., ending with a WS row.

Divide for armholes
Next row Work in pat across first 13 [14:15:16] sts, turn.
Cont in pat for 10 [12:14:15] more rows on these sts (until armhole measures 4½ [5½:6¾:7½] in.), ending at armhole edge.
Next row Work in pat across first 6 [7:7:8] sts, turn.

Leave 6 [7:7:8] sts unworked for neck. Work 6 [6:7:7] more rows on these 6 [7:7:8] sts. Fasten off.

Back
Return to rem sts at armhole. With RS of work facing, leave 6 [7:8:9] sts unworked at armhole. Rejoin yarn to 7th [8th:9th:10th]st, ch 2, work in pat across first 25 [27:29:31] sts, turn and leave rem sts unworked. Work 16

263

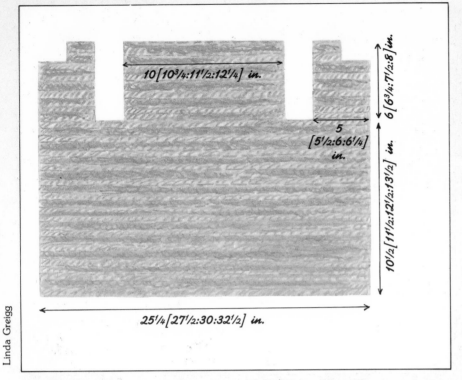

10[10¾:11½:12¼] in.

6[6¾:7½:8] in.

5
[5½:6:6¼]
in.

10½[11½:12½:13½] in.

25¼[27½:30:32½] in.

Linda Greigg

To finish
Join shoulder seams.
Front, neck and lower borders
With RS of work facing and using smaller hook and B, rejoin yarn to center back neck. Work all around edge in sc, working 4sc for every 3 sts on main body at back neck, 1sc into each row end down front edges, 1sc into each st at front neck, 6sc for every 5 foundation sts along lower edge, and 3sc into each right-angled corner. Join with a sl st to center back. Work 4 more rounds sc on these sts, working 1 turning ch at beg of each round and remembering to work 3sc into each corner sc and dec 1sc at inner front neck corner shaping.
Next round Work in crab st (see Special technique page 262) so that sc is worked from left to right rather than right to left. Join with sl st. Fasten off.

Armhole borders
Work as for front, neck and lower edging, working 1sc into each sc at underarm and dec one st at underarm corners on each row. Work 1 round in crab st as before. Fasten off.

[18:21:22] more rows on these sts. Fasten off.

Front
Return to rem sts at armhole. With RS of work facing, leave next 6 [7:8:9] sts unworked, rejoin yarn to 7th [8th:9th:10th] st, ch 2, work in pat across next 12 [13:14:15] sts. Turn.

Work a further 10 [12:14:15] rows in pat on these sts so that armhole measures 4¼ [5½:6¾:7½] in., ending at neck edge.
Shape neck
Next row Sl st over first 8 [8:8:9] sts, ch 2 work pat to end.
Work in pat on rem 6 [7:7:8] sts for 6 [6:7:7] more rows. Fasten off.

Adapting the vest

The stitches on the following pages could be substituted for the ridge stitch used in the vest to create different textures.

Substituting a pattern
In order to substitute one of the alternative patterns you must make a gauge square in the pattern and yarn of your choice. If the gauge obtained is the same as that given in the instructions you can proceed to make the garment from the original instructions immediately. If, however, the gauge is not the same, a certain amount of calculation will be needed before you can start.

Calculating from a gauge square
In order to decide the number of stitches you will need to start your pattern, you must make a gauge square approximately 4 in. square in the yarn and stitch pattern of your choice, and then measure the number of stitches and rows obtained in your sample. You will see from the pattern diagram
264

given with the instructions the width needed for your garment, and from your gauge square can calculate the number of stitches needed to obtain this measurement. For example, if the total width is 28 in. and you obtain 12 stitches to 4 in. you will need 84 stitches to obtain the correct width. Row gauge is not so important on a simple pattern, since fewer or more rows can be worked to achieve the correct length.

Fitting in a pattern
Remember that when you calculate the number of stitches needed for the width of your garment, you must make allowances for the number of stitches needed to accommodate your pattern. If for example your pattern is divisible by four, the number of stitches worked must either also be

divisible by four, or edge stitches must be worked to keep the pattern correct.

Shaping
Where the shape of the garment is quite straightforward and very little shaping occurs at the armhole or neck as in the vest, it should be quite easy to calculate how many stitches need to be decreased, increased or left unworked, using your gauge square and outline diagram once more. By working from the original instructions and gauge you will see how many inches must be decreased to shape the armhole and can then calculate from your own sample the number of stitches you will need to decrease for your particular pattern. For a garment where more complicated shaping or patterns are involved more detailed calculations would have to be made, using graph paper to work out the shape more precisely.

Single crochet variations

1 Albania stitch

Make any number of ch.

Base row 1sc into 3rd ch from hook, 1sc into each ch to end. Turn.

Pattern row Ch 1 to count as first st, inserting hook into front loop only of each st work 1sc into each sc to end, 1sc into turning ch. Turn.

Rep pat row throughout.

2 Double grain stitch

Make a multiple of 2 plus 1 ch with 3 extra ch.

Base row Insert hook into 4th ch from hook, yo and draw through a loop, yo and draw through 2 loops on hook (called 1 exsc), *ch 1, skip ch 1, 1exsc into next ch, rep from * to end. Turn.

Pattern row Ch 2, *1exsc into next ch 1 sp of previous row, ch 1, rep from * to end, 1 exsc into turning ch. Turn.

Rep pat row throughout.

3 Crochet bobble stitch

Make a multiple of 4 ch plus 3 extra.

Base row 1sc into 3rd ch from hook, 1sc into each ch to end. Turn.

1st row (RS) Ch 1 to count as first sc, *ch 4, 1sc into each of next 4sc, rep from *ending ch 4, 1sc into turning ch. Turn.

2nd row Holding 4ch at back (RS) of work, work ch 1 to count as first sc, 1sc into each sc to end, 1sc into turning ch. Turn.

3rd row Ch 1 to count as first sc, 1sc into each of next 2sc, *ch 4, 1sc into each of next 4sc, rep from * to end, ending with ch 4, 1sc into each of last 2sc, 1sc into turning ch. Turn.

4th row As 2nd.

Rep first-4th rows throughout.

4 Daisy stitch

Make an even number of ch plus 1.

Base row 1sc into 3rd ch from hook (1sc, ch 1, 1sc) into next ch (called 1sc group), *skip 1ch, 1sc group into next ch, rep from * to last ch, 1sc into last ch. Turn.

Pattern row Ch 2, *1sc group into center ch 1 sp of next 1sc group worked in previous row, rep from * to end, 1sc into top of turning ch. Turn.

Rep pat row throughout.

5

7 Granite stitch

Make a multiple of 2 plus 1 chain with 3 extra chain.

Base row 1sc into 4th ch from hook to count as first sc and ch 1 space, ch 1, skip 1 ch, 1sc into next ch, rep from * to end. Turn.

Pat row Ch 2 to count as first sc and ch 1 space, 1sc into first ch 1 space of previous row, *ch 1, 1 sc into next ch 1 space of previous row, rep from * to end, working last sc into first turning ch. Turn.

Rep pat row throughout.

8 Flat rib stitch

Make an even number of chain plus 1 extra chain.

Base row 1sc into 3rd ch from hook, 1sc into each ch to end. Turn.

1st row (RS) Ch 1 to count as first sc, working into back loop only of each st, work 1sc into each sc to end, 1sc into turning ch. Turn.

2nd row Ch 1 to count as first sc, working into front loop only of each st, work 1sc into each sc to end, 1sc into turning ch. Turn.

First and 2nd rows form pat and are rep throughout.

5 Two-color cluster stitch

Worked in 2 colors coded as A and B.

Using A make a multiple of 5 chain plus 1 extra chain.

Base row 1sc into 3rd ch from hook, 1sc into each ch to end. Turn.

1st-3rd rows Ch 1 to count as first sc, 1sc into each sc to end, 1sc into turning chain. Turn. Join in B at end of 3rd row.

4th row Ch 1 to count as first sc, 1sc into each of next 4sc, * working in row below draw up a loop below sc just worked and in each of next 2sc, insert hook into next st after st just worked in 4th row, draw yarn through this st and first 3 loops on hook, yo and draw through rem 2 loops on hook (called 1 cluster), 1sc into each of next 4sc in 4th row, rep from * to end, 1sc into turning ch. Turn.

5th row Ch 1 to count as first sc, 1sc into each sc to end, 1sc into turning ch. Turn.

2nd-5th rows form pat and are rep throughout, changing colors at end of 3rd row each time.

8

6

6 Bouclé stitch

Make an even number of chain plus 1 extra.

Base row 1sc into 3rd ch from hook, 1sc into each ch to end. Turn.

Pat row Ch 1, skip first st, * 1sc into front loop only of next st, 1sc into back loop only of next st, rep from * to end, 1sc into turning ch. Turn.

Rep pat row throughout.

Spirals

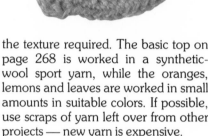

Spirals – also known as continuous rounds – are the ideal method of working small motifs that can be appliquéd onto most fabrics. This technique is not only great fun, but is also a very practical way of adding individuality to clothes.

Skills you need

* **Double crochet**
* **Continuous rounds**

If you do not know the basic skills, refer to pages 273 and 294.

Materials

Spirals can be worked in either sport- or worsted-weight yarn. When working fruit as on the basic sweater, shape and texture are suggested by the use of color and so plain yarn should be used. However, it would be quite possible when working other spirals to use fluffy or bouclé yarns, depending on the texture required. The basic top on page 268 is worked in a synthetic-wool sport yarn, while the oranges, lemons and leaves are worked in small amounts in suitable colors. If possible, use scraps of yarn left over from other projects — new yarn is expensive.

Special technique – 'doughboy' pockets

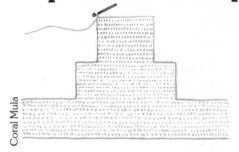

Coral Mula

1 After shaping the armholes at the front, work in double crochet for the length given in the pattern, ending with a wrong side row. Fasten off and turn. Skip stitches as instructed at the beginning of the next row and join in yarn to the next stitch. Pattern the center stitches as instructed. End with a wrong side row and fasten off.

2 Make a length of chain and fasten off. With right side facing, return to the stitches skipped in step 1 and rejoin the yarn to the beginning of the row. Work in pattern across the skipped stitches, place the length of chain behind the pocket and work one double crochet into each chain. Pattern across the stitches skipped at the other edge.

3 Continue in double crochet on these stitches for the stated length, ending with a wrong side row. On the next row join the top of the pocket to the main fabric by working into both the pocket and pocket lining stitches. When the garment is completed, sew the top edge of the pocket lining to the wrong side of the front.

The basic appliquéd top

Sew luscious oranges and lemons on a good-looking top. If citrus fruits are not her favorite, choose from the alternatives in the Pattern Library.

Sizes
To fit 22 [24:26:28] in. chest
Length 14½ [15¾:16¼:17¼] in.
Sleeve seam 9 [10½:12¼:13¾] in.
Note: Instructions for larger sizes are in square brackets []; where there is only one set of figures it applies to all sizes.

Gauge
20dc and 10 rows to 4 in. worked on size C hook

Materials
8 [8:9:9] oz of a sport yarn in main color
Small amounts of sport yarn in yellow, orange green and white
Size C crochet hook.

Note: The top is worked in one piece, beginning at the lower edge of the back.

Main piece
Back
Make 62 [67:72:77] ch.
Base row (RS) 1sc into 2nd ch from

hook, 1sc into each ch to end. Turn. 61 [66:71:76] sts.

1st-6th rows Ch 1 to count as first sc, skip first st, 1sc into each st to end. Turn.

7th row Ch 3, skip first st, 1dc into each st to end. Turn. Rep last row until back measures 9½ [10¼:10¾:11½] in. ending with a WS row.

Shape sleeve

Using a separate length of yarn, make 45 [53:61:69] ch. Fasten off and return to main piece.

Next row Make 47 [55:63:71] ch, 1dc into 4th ch from hook, 1dc into each of next 43 [51:59:67] ch, 1dc into each of next 61 [66:71:76] sts across back, 1dc into first of separate length of ch, 1dc into each ch to end. Turn. 151 [172:193:214] sts.

Work even in dc on these sts until sleeve measures 5 [5½:5½:6] in., ending with a WS row.

Shape neck

Using a separate length of yarn, ch 39 [40:45:48]. Fasten off and return to main piece.,

Next row Ch 3, skip first st, 1dc into each of next 55 [65:73:82] sts, 1dc into first of separate length of ch, 1 dc into each ch to end, skip next 39 [40:45:48] sts on main piece, 1dc into each st to end. Turn. 151 [172:193:214] sts.

Front and sleeve

Work even in dc on these sts until sleeve measures 10¼ [11:11:11¼] in., ending with a WS row.

Fasten off and turn.

Shape front

With RS facing, skip first 45 [53:61:69] sts; rejoin yarn to next st.

Next row Ch 3, skip first st at base of ch 3, 1dc into each of next 60 [65:70:75] sts, turn. 61 [66:71:76] sts.

Work even in dc on these sts until front measures 3¼ [3½:4:4½] in. from armhole, ending with a WS row. Fasten off and turn.

Pocket

With RS facing, skip first 13 [14:15:16] sts; rejoin yarn to next st.

Next row Ch 3, skip first st at base of ch 3, 1dc into each of next 34 [37:40:43] sts. Turn. 35 [38:41:44] sts.

Work even in dc on these sts until pocket measures 5 [5½:5½:6] in, ending with a WS row. Fasten off.

Pocket lining

Using a separate length of yarn, ch 35 [38:41:44]. Fasten off and return to main piece. With RS facing, return to sts skipped at beg of pocket and rejoin yarn of beg of row.

Next row Ch 3, skip first st at base of ch 3, 1dc into each of next 12 [13:14:15] sts, place separate length of ch behind pocket, 1dc into first of separate length of ch, 1dc into each ch to end, skip pocket, 1dc into each of last 13 [14:15:16] sts on main piece. Turn. 61 [66:71:76] sts.

Work even in dc on these sts until pocket lining measures 5 [5½:5½:6] in., ending with a WS row.

Join pocket

Next row Ch1 to count as first sc, skip first st, 1sc into each of next 12 [13:14:15] sts, bring last row of pocket up in front of last row of pocket lining, 1sc into first st on pocket and next st on pocket lining, 1sc into each of next 34 [37:40:43] sts on pocket and pocket lining, 1sc into each of last 13 [14:15:16] sts on pocket lining, working through 2 sts tog. Turn. 61 [66:71:76] sts.

Cont in sc on these sts for 6 more rows.
Fasten off.

To finish

Press or block the work, according to yarn used.

Pocket edgings (both alike)

With RS facing work a row of sc into side edge of pocket, working 2sc into each dc row end.
Work 4 more rows of sc.

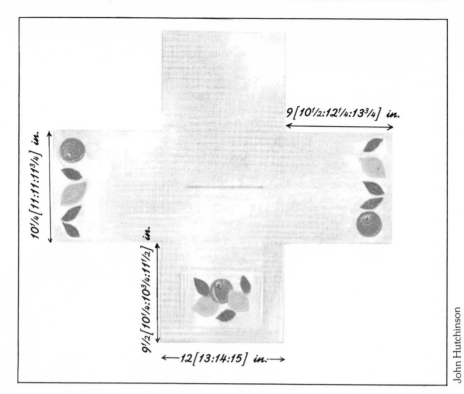

9 [10½:12¼:13¾] in.

10¼ [11:11:11¾] in.

9½ [10¼:10¾:11½] in.

←12 [13:14:15] in.→

John Hutchinson

Fasten off.
Sew sc row ends neatly to RS of front. Sew top of pocket lining to WS of front.

Join sleeve and side seams, leaving 2¼ [2¾:2¾:3] in. open at bottom of each side seam to form slits.

Neck edging

With RS facing work one round of sc into neck edge, working 1sc into each st and joining last to first st with a sl st. Fasten off.

Cuff edgings (both alike)

With RS facing work one round of sc into cuff edge, working 2sc into each dc row end and joining last to first st with a sl st. Fasten off.

Lower edging

With RS facing join yarn to top of RH slit.

Next row Ch 1, 2sc into each row end to corner, 3sc into corner, 1sc into each st on last row of front, 3sc into corner, 2sc into each row end to top of LH slit, 2sc into each row end to corner, 3sc into corner, 1sc into each st on base row of back, 3sc into corner, 2sc into each row end to top of RH slit, sl st to first ch. Fasten off.

Note: Fruit and leaves are worked in continuous rounds (see page 273).

Oranges (make 3)

Using orange, ch 4, sl st to first ch to from a ring.

1st round 8sc into ring.

2nd round 2sc into each of next 8sc. 16sc.

3rd round (2sc into next sc, 1sc into next sc) 8 times. 24sc.

4th round (2sc into next sc, 1sc into each of next 2sc) 8 times. 32sc.

5th round (2sc into next sc, 1sc into each of next 3sc) 8 times. 40sc.

Cont to inc 8sc on each round in this way until orange measures 2¼ in. in diameter, sl st to next sc. Fasten off.

Make two more oranges in the same way, working a "highlight" of 18sc in yellow on the 5th round of one orange.

Lemons (make 4)

Using yellow work as for oranges until work measures 1¾ in. in diameter.

Next round * 1sc into next st, 1dc into next st, 2tr into next st, 1dc into next st *, 1sc into each st to opposite side of circle, rep from * to * once more, 1sc into each st to end. Fasten off.

Make three more lemons in the same way, working a "highlight" of 10sc in white on the 5th round of one lemon.

Leaves (make 9)

Using green, ch 8.

1st round 1sc into 2nd ch from hook, 1sc into each of next 5ch, 3sc into last ch, 1sc into rem loop of each of next 6ch.

2nd round Ch 3, skip next ch, *1sc into next sc, 1hdc into next sc, 1dc into each of next 3sc, 1hdc into next sc, 1sc, into next sc *, 1sc into next sc, rep from * to * once more, sl st to first ch.
Fasten off.
Make eight more leaves in same way.
To apply motifs
Using green, embroider one cross stitch on each orange to represent the stalk.
Press or block each motif.
Sew three leaves, two lemons (including lemon with a white highlight) and highlighted orange to the front pocket. Sew one orange, one lemon and three leaves to each sleeve.

Adapting the basic appliquéd top

Use up your old scraps of yarn and at the same time transform a plain garment into a mouth-watering treat by sewing on realistic fruits and vegetables worked in spirals.

Any of the spiral fruits and vegetables in the Pattern Library could be sewn onto the basic top. Use nature's colors for authenticity, choosing different shades to suggest, for example, the bloom on fruit or natural highlights and shadows. When sewing on the spirals, use matching yarn — split if necessary — and slip-stitches, worked just under the edge.
Spiral shapes can be worked quite freely in single crochet, with other stitches introduced to alter the shape; for example, the lemons on the basic top are formed by working doubles and triples at opposite points on the spiral. You may need to experiment to obtain a convincing shape. Having a picture or the object itself in front of you while you work is a great help, especially when matching colors.

Spiral patterns

1 Apple

Use red or green as the main color, introducing brown, yellow, white or pink as desired.
Work as for Orange on page 269 until work measures approx 2 in. in diameter.
Next 2 rounds 1sc into each sc to opposite side of circle, sl st into next st, 1sc into each sc to end.
Next round 1sc into each sc to opposite side of circle, sl st into next sl st. Fasten off.
Stalk Either embroider the stalk in stem stitch or join brown yarn to indentation on apple, work 4ch, sl st into each ch, sl st into joining on apple. Fasten off.
Calyx Using brown, work a cross stitch on the opposite indentation to the stalk.
Leaf Work as given for leaf of Orange on p.269 using one or two shades of green as desired.

1

2 Lime

Use green as the main color, introducing yellow and white as desired. Work as for Lemon as instructed overleaf.

2

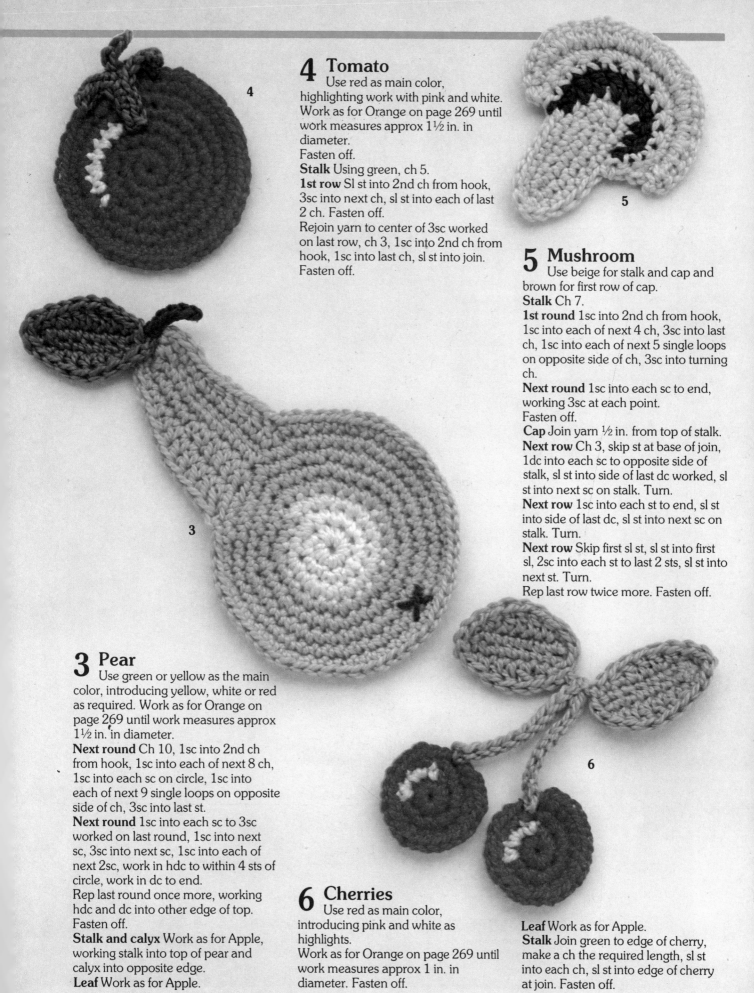

4 Tomato

Use red as main color, highlighting work with pink and white. Work as for Orange on page 269 until work measures approx 1½ in. in diameter.

Fasten off.

Stalk Using green, ch 5.

1st row Sl st into 2nd ch from hook, 3sc into next ch, sl st into each of last 2 ch. Fasten off.

Rejoin yarn to center of 3sc worked on last row, ch 3, 1sc into 2nd ch from hook, 1sc into last ch, sl st into join. Fasten off.

5 Mushroom

Use beige for stalk and cap and brown for first row of cap.

Stalk Ch 7.

1st round 1sc into 2nd ch from hook, 1sc into each of next 4 ch, 3sc into last ch, 1sc into each of next 5 single loops on opposite side of ch, 3sc into turning ch.

Next round 1sc into each sc to end, working 3sc at each point.

Fasten off.

Cap Join yarn ½ in. from top of stalk.

Next row Ch 3, skip st at base of join, 1dc into each sc to opposite side of stalk, sl st into side of last dc worked, sl st into next sc on stalk. Turn.

Next row 1sc into each st to end, sl st into side of last dc, sl st into next sc on stalk. Turn.

Next row Skip first sl st, sl st into first sl, 2sc into each st to last 2 sts, sl st into next st. Turn.

Rep last row twice more. Fasten off.

3 Pear

Use green or yellow as the main color, introducing yellow, white or red as required. Work as for Orange on page 269 until work measures approx 1½ in. in diameter.

Next round Ch 10, 1sc into 2nd ch from hook, 1sc into each of next 8 ch, 1sc into each sc on circle, 1sc into each of next 9 single loops on opposite side of ch, 3sc into last st.

Next round 1sc into each sc to 3sc worked on last round, 1sc into next sc, 3sc into next sc, 1sc into each of next 2sc, work in hdc to within 4 sts of circle, work in dc to end.

Rep last round once more, working hdc and dc into other edge of top. Fasten off.

Stalk and calyx Work as for Apple, working stalk into top of pear and calyx into opposite edge.

Leaf Work as for Apple.

6 Cherries

Use red as main color, introducing pink and white as highlights.

Work as for Orange on page 269 until work measures approx 1 in. in diameter. Fasten off.

Leaf Work as for Apple.

Stalk Join green to edge of cherry, make a ch the required length, sl st into each ch, sl st into edge of cherry at join. Fasten off.

HOME CRAFTS

Fabric work

Belinda

Skills you need

*Single crochet
*Fabric work

If you do not know the basic skills, refer to pages 295 and 306.

Materials

Most types of woven fabric can be used for crochet — we used cotton and synthetic mixtures for the rug on page 272 — but knitted fabrics that stretch should be avoided. If you must buy fabric specially, look for cheap remnants. Otherwise, buying fabric would be extremely expensive — it may take as much as 5 inches of fabric strip to work one single crochet stitch. Instead, cut up your own old clothes or use secondhand shops and jumble sales as a cheap source of suitable fabrics.

Special technique – continuous rounds

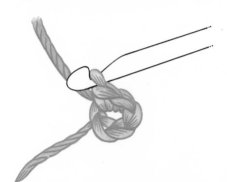

1 *The rug on page 272 is worked in continuous rounds of crochet. At the beginning of the first and following round, omit the one chain that is normal when working rounds of single crochet.*

2 *To end a round, work one single crochet into the last stitch. Do not join the first and last stitch as usual, but simply begin the next round by working one single crochet into the first stitch of the round.*

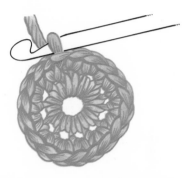

3 *To change color when working continuous rounds, work the last single crochet in the old color. Insert hook into first stitch of round and draw through new color. Continue in pattern, working into same place as join, using the new color and working over the end of old color.*

Coral Mula

The basic fabric rug

This rug looks equally at home in the bathroom or by the fireside. Choose the coloring to blend with your room.

Size
The rug measures 37 in. in diameter.

Gauge
First 4 rounds measure approx 3½ in. in diameter

Materials
Approx. 22 yds. of cotton or cotton-polyester in assorted patterns
Size K crochet hook
Note: Quantity of fabric depends on weight of fabric and width of strips, and is therefore only approximate.
Note: To avoid an ugly "stepped" appearance, introduce new fabric as follows: after working last sc in old fabric, insert hook into first sc of round and draw through new fabric. Using new fabric, 1sc into same place as join and cont in pat.

To make
Cut bias strips approx 1¼ in. wide from fabric. Join strips with machine stitching as shown on page 306, and wind into balls.
Using crochet hook and fabric strip, ch 6, form circle with a sl st.
1st round 12sc into circle. Do not join this or any foll round with a sl st.
2nd round (1sc into next sc, 2sc into next sc) to end. 18sc.
3rd round (1sc into each of next 2sc, 2sc into next sc) to end. 24 sc.
4th and every foll other round 1sc into each sc to end.
5th round (1sc into each of next 3sc, 2sc into next sc) to end. 30sc.
7th round (1 sc into each of next 4sc, 2sc into next sc) to end. 36sc.
Cont to inc 6sc in this way on 9th and every other round until 24 rounds have been worked. 84sc.
25th round (1sc into each of next 6sc, 2sc into next sc) to end. 96 sc.
26th round (1sc into each of next 7sc, 2sc into next sc) to end. 108sc.

Cont to inc 12sc in this way on 29th and every other round until rug measures approx. 37 in.
Next round 1sc into each sc to end.
Next round 1sc into each sc to end, join with a sl st to first sc. Fasten off.

Adapting the fabric rug

The possibilities of creativity are endless when you crochet with fabric.

Most types of fabric can be used to make rugs, including nylon net, lurex, satin and pure wool, as well as the cotton used for our samples.
However, before you make your rug, decide where you will be using it. Lightweight cottons and novelty fabrics are fine for bedrooms, while kitchens need rugs made in heavier fabrics.

273

This rule applies to whatever you decide to make. In addition, remember that though cutting the strips on the bias will make them less likely to fray it is wise not to use fabrics that fray heavily to make articles that require a great deal of laundering.

Estimating quantities
It is particularly difficult to calculate how much fabric you will need when working fabric crochet. The least approximate method is to work one row with the strip and to then undo it. By noting the length of strip required to work one row, you should be able to estimate roughly the amount needed to work the entire article.

Appearance
Working a row of crochet, together with the usual gauge square, will also help you to see what kind of pattern the fabric will produce, though the final appearance of fabric work is often unpredictable.

There are, however, some general guidelines. Plain fabrics will of course produce plain-colored crochet. Small prints will, except from nearby, look like a plain version of the dominant color. Stripes and large prints look random-dyed when they are crocheted.

Fabric work samples

1 Picot
This sample was crocheted in two printed and one plain cotton fabric. The picots on the last round are formed from three chain.

Ray Duns

2 Print and plain
Two polyester-cotton fabrics, one printed and one plain, were used to make this sample. The fabrics were used alternately to work two rounds each.

Monogram filet

Filet crochet, with its square blocks and spaces, lends itself particularly well to monograms. Two alphabets in contrasting styles are given here, but it is easy to graph your own.

Belinda

Skills you need

*Filet crochet

If you do not know the basic skills, refer to page 304.

Materials

Monograms or complete words and phrases worked in filet crochet take some time to make, so take care that the letters can be clearly seen. Use a fairly fine, untextured yarn like the number 20 cotton used to make the sheet trims shown here. Make sure that the color of the trim contrasts strongly with that of the sheets — similar colors would make the monograms illegible. Always remove the trim before washing the sheet.

Special technique – graphing filet letters

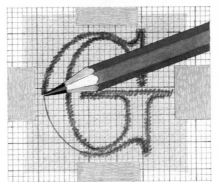

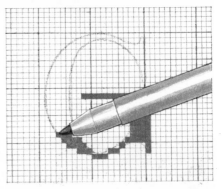

1 *Using tracing paper and a soft pencil, trace the outline of the letter — it could be taken from a book, magazine or your own design. Turn over to the other side of the paper and carefully trace the outline of the letter as shown.*

2 *Turn back to the first side of the paper and stick the tracing to graph paper with masking tape to prevent slipping. Using a soft pencil, shade over the outline of the letter. The shape of the letter should appear on the graph paper.*

3 *Remove the masking tape and tracing paper. Shade the squares of graph paper within the outline of the letter, shading squares that are partly outside the outline to obtain a good shape. When working the filet, the shaded areas will be blocks and the clear areas will be mesh.*

Richard Phipps

The basic sheet trims

Sew a long strip of white filet, which says "Sleep well" in three languages, onto a sheet.

Sizes
To fit single [double] sheet
Width 5½ in.
Total length 72 [92] in.
Length of lettered panel 36 [50½] in.
Note: Instructions for the larger size are in square brackets []; where there is only one set of figures, it applies to both sizes.

Materials
4 [5] oz of No.20 crochet cotton
No. 3 steel crochet hook

Gauge
10½ spaces and 11 rows to 2½ in. worked over plain filet mesh

Single-sheet trim
Ch 83.
Base row 1dc into 8th ch from hook,
(ch2, skip next 2 ch, 1dc into next ch) 4 times, 1dc into each of next 6 ch, (ch2, skip next 2 ch, 1dc into next ch) 19 times. Turn.
1st row (WS) Ch 5, skip first dc, (1dc into next dc, ch 2) 17 times, 1dc into next dc, 2dc into next sp, 1dc into next dc, (ch2, skip next 2dc, 1dc into next dc) twice, 2dc into next sp, 1dc into next dc, (ch2, 1dc into next dc) 3 times, ch 2, 1dc into last sp. Turn.
Last row forms 18 sps, 1 block, 2 sps, 1 block, 4 sps.
2nd row 5 sps, 2 blocks, 19 sps. Turn.
3rd row 18 sps, 1 block, 2 sps, 1 block, 4 sps. Turn.
Rep 1st and 2nd rows until a total of 90 rows have been worked from beg. Then work 180 rows of chart, beg 1st row at edge marked with an arrow. Work 90 rows to match those worked at beg of trim, ending with a WS row. Turn and do not fasten off.

Picot edging
(3sc, ch 3, sl st to top of last sc — picot formed) into each sp to end. Fasten off.

Single-crochet edging
With RS facing, rejoin yarn to first sp on opposite edge of trim, work 3sc into each sp to end. Fasten off.

Double-sheet trim
Work base and 1st-2nd rows as for single-sheet trim. Then rep 1st and 2nd rows until 104 rows have been worked from beg.
Work 252 rows of the chart, beg 1st row at the edge marked with an arrow. Work 104 rows to match those worked at beg of trim, ending with a WS row. Complete as for single.

To finish
Press work under a damp cloth. Sew trim to sheet turn-back as shown.

Adapting the basic sheet trims

Use these Roman and Victorian alphabets to add the personal touch to your home.

The charts on page 277 for the basic sheet trim contain the alphabet in Roman capital letters. The Pattern Library chart on page 278 shows a Victorian alphabet. Either chart can be used to work monogram filet.
Using the yarn of your choice, work a tension sample to check the number of spaces in a 4 in. square of filet mesh. Measure the length and width of the proposed filet fabric — for example, a pillow trim or curtain.
Divide the length of the filet by 4 in. and multiply by the number of spaces to 4 in. on the length of the gauge sample. Calculate the number of spaces in the width in the same way.

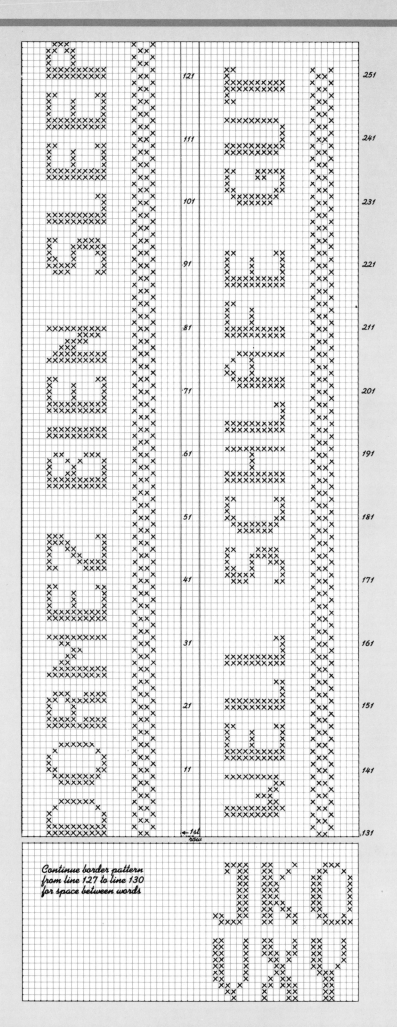

Continue border pattern
from line 127 to line 130
for space between words

Dennis Hawkins

277

Dennis Hawkins

Wired flowers

Life-like crocheted flowers, made in fine cotton yarn, are interesting to crochet and can be used in the same way as their natural originals — as bouquets, boutonnieres, garlands and trimmings.

Belinda

279

Skills you need

*Wired flowers
*Double triple and triple triple crochet

If you do not know these skills, refer to pages 307 and 297.

Materials

Number 20 cotton, like that used for the basic flowers, is available in a wide range of colors. This makes it possible to reproduce almost exactly the shadings of the natural flower to astonishingly realistic effect. The petals retain their shape best if they are wired (see page 307) with fine, flexible wire, available from craft shops. Stems are

formed from thicker wire, cut to the required length and bound tightly with green tape. Both the wire and tape can be bought from florists. Some flowers have prominent stamens and sepals. Artificial stamens in various sizes can be bought from craft shops, while sepals can be made from either green felt or thick crêpe paper.

Special technique – large, separate leaves

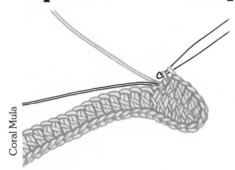

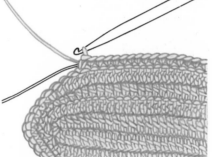

Coral Mula

1 A few large leaves add realism to a flower arrangement. Those on page 282 are worked in much the same way as the flowers. Ch 80 and work the base row over thin craft wire, leaving two 2 in.-long ends extending from the leaf base.

2 Work the next three rows as instructed in the pattern. Cut a piece of thin craft wire to fit all around the leaf plus approximately 4 in. Work a row of sc into the edges of the leaf, at the same time working over the wire so that two 2 in.-long ends extend from the lower edge.

3 If you are using a short vase, cut off about 1½ in. from each wire and bend back the remainder to secure (above left). If a stem is needed, twist the leaf wires around a length of thick wire cut to the length required. Bind the leaf to the stem with green tape (above right).

The basic wired flowers

Preserve the freshness of springtime by making these flowers. Use them in pretty nosegays or for dramatic effect, arrange a mass of the same flowers in an elegant vase.

Sizes
One tulip petal measures approx 2¼ in. in height
One daffodil petal measures approx 1½ in. in height
One small iris petal measures approx 2 in. in height

Gauge
12 sts to 1⅛ in. over dc using No. 3 steel crochet hook

Materials
No. 20 crochet cotton, in small amounts of each of the foll colors:
Tulip Pink and green
Daffodil Yellow and gold
Iris Purple, gold and green
Large leaves Green
No. 3 steel crochet hook
Fine, soft craft wire for flowers
280

Florist's thick wire in lengths required for stems
Florist's green tape
Artificial stamens to suit flower

Note: When wiring flowers, see page 307, Know-How.

Tulip

Petals (make 6)
Using crochet hook and pink, ch 5.
Base row (RS) 2dc into 4th ch from hook, 3dc into last ch. Turn. 6 sts.
1st row Ch 3, 1dc into dc at base of first ch 3, 2dc into next dc, 1dc into each of next 2dc, 2dc into each of last 2 sts. Turn. 10 sts.
2nd and 3rd rows As 1st row. 18 sts.
4th row Ch 3, skip first st, 1dc into each st to end. Turn.

5th-8th rows As 4th row.
9th row Ch 3, skip first st, (work next 2dc tog) 8 times, 1dc into last st. Turn. 10 sts.
10th row Ch 1 to count as first sc, skip first st, 1sc into next dc, 1dc into each of next 6dc, 1sc into next dc. Fasten off.
Cut a piece of craft wire to fit all around petal plus approx 4 in. Arrange wire around petal so that 2 lengths, each approx. 2 in., extend below base of petal.
With RS facing, rejoin pink to base of petal and, covering wire at the same time, work a row of sc into all edges of petal, working 1sc into each st and 2sc into each dc row end.
Fasten off.

Leaf (make 1)
Using crochet hook and green, ch 50.
Base row (WS) 1dc into 4th ch from hook, 1dc into each ch to last ch, 5dc into last ch, working into other edge of

chain, 1dc into each ch to first ch 4. Turn.

Next row Ch 1, *1sc into each of next 10 sts, 1hdc into each of next 8 sts, 1dc into each of next 10 sts, 1tr into each of next 10 sts, 1dc into each of next 4 sts, 1hdc into each of next 4sts, 1sc into each st to 3rd of 5dc at end of leaf, 3sc into 3rd dc, now work in reverse ending at *, ending at base of leaf.
Fasten off.
Wire Leaf as for Tulip petal, working 1sc into each st.

To finish
Holding stamens in the center, overlap petals for form Tulip and tape on to thick wire to form stem. Tape Leaf into position and then tape rest of stem.

Daffodil

Trumpet
Using crochet hook and gold, ch 4, sl st to first ch to form a circle.
1st round Ch 3, 9dc into circle, sl st to top of first ch 3. 10 sts.
2nd round Ch 2, skip first st, 1sc into each st to end, sl st to top of first ch 2.
3rd round Ch 3, skip first st, *2dc into next st, 1dc into each of next 2 sts, rep from * twice more, sl st to top of first ch 3. 13 sts.

4th round As 2nd round.
5th round Working into front loops only of each st, ch 3, skip first st, 2dc into each st to end, sl st to top of first ch 3. 25 sts.
6th round As 2nd round.
7th round Ch 3, skip first st, 1dc into each dc, sl st to top of first ch 3.
8th-11th rounds Rep 6th and 7th rounds twice more.
12th round As 6th round
13th round Ch 3, skip first st, 2dc into each st to end. 49 sts.
14th round Ch 1, 1hdc into same place as ch 1, *3dc into next st, (1hdc, 1sc) into next st, (1sc, 1hdc) into next st, rep from * to end.
Fasten off.

Petals (make 6)
Join yellow to free loop of first st on 5th round of Trumpet.
1st row Working into free loops of 5th round, ch 3, 1dc into same place as ch 3, 2dc into next st, 2dc into next st. Turn. 6 sts.
2nd row Ch 3, skip first st, 2dc into each of next 4dc 1dc into last st. Turn. 10 sts.
3rd row Ch 3, skip first st, 2dc into next dc, 1dc into each of next 6dc, 2dc into next dc, 1dc into last st. Turn. 12 sts.
4th row Ch 3, skip first st, 1dc into each st to end. Turn.
5th and 6th rows As 4th row.

7th row Ch 3, skip first st, *work next 2dc tog, rep from * 4 times more, 1dc into last st. Turn. 8 sts.
8th row Ch 3, skip first st, *work next 2dc tog, rep from * twice more, 1dc into last st.
9th row Ch 3, skip first st, work next 3dc tog, 1dc into last st. Fasten off.**
Join yellow to same loop as last 2dc worked on first row of previous petal. Rep from ** to **.
Work 4 more petals in this way. Cut a piece of craft wire to fit all around petals plus approx 4 in.
Arrange wire around petals so that 2 lengths, each approx 2 in. extend below base of one petal.
Working over wire, edge petals with sc as for Tulip petals.
Fasten off.

To finish
Twist petal wire around thick wire to form stem. Bind stem and petal wire with tape.

Iris

Two-color petal (make 3)
Using gold, ch 20.
Base row Working over wire throughout, work 1sc into 2nd ch from hook, 1sc into each of next 10 ch, 1hdc into each of next 6 ch, 2dc into next ch, (3dc, 1tr, 3dc) into last ch, working into other side of ch, work 2dc into next ch, 1 hdc into each of next 6 ch, 1sc into each ch to end. Turn.
Break off gold and wire leaving 2 ends of wire, each 2 in. at base of petal.
Join in purple.
Next row *Ch1, 1sc into each of first 3 sts, 1hdc into each of next 6 sts, 1dc into each of next 7 sts, 1tr into next st**, 2tr into each of next 10 sts, 1tr into next st, 1dc into each of next 7 sts, 1hdc into each of next 6 sts, 1sc into each st to end.
Fasten off.

Large purple petal (make 3)
Using purple, ch 20.
Using purple, and wire work base row as for two-color petal.
Next row Using purple, work from * to ** as for two-color petal, 2tr into each of next 2 sts, (1tr, 1dtr) into next st, 2dtr into next st, (1dtr, 1tr tr) into next st, ch 5, sl st into same st, sl st into next st, ch 5, (1tr tr, 1dtr) into same st, 2dtr into next st, (1dtr, 1tr) into next st, 2tr into each of next 2 sts, now work from ** to * in reverse.
Fasten off.

Small purple petal (make 3)
Using purple, and wire work ch, and work base row as for two-color petal. Fasten off.

Leaf (make 2)
Using green ch 30.
Base row 1sc into 2nd ch from hook, 1sc into each of next 5 ch, 1hdc into each of next 5 ch, 1dc into each of next 17 ch, 5dc into last ch, working into other edge of foundation ch, work 1dc into each of next 17ch, 1hdc into each of next 5 ch, 1sc into each ch to end. Turn.
Wire and edge Leaf as for Tulip Leaf.

To finish
Place petals together as shown on page 307, bending petals as required. Tape flower wires to thick wire to form stem and tape to position of leaf. Bind leaf to stem and tape rem stem.

Large leaves
Using green, ch 80.
Base row Working over craft wire throughout, work 1dc into 4th ch from hook, 1dc into each ch to last ch, 5dc into last ch, working into other side of ch work 1dc into each ch to last 3 ch.
282

Turn. Cut wire leaving two 2 in.-long ends.
Next row Ch 1 to count as first sc, skip first st, 1sc into each of next 50 sts, 1hdc into each of next 10 sts, 1dc into each of next 16 sts, 1hdc into each of next 2 sts, 1sc into next st, 3 sl st into st at tip of leaf, 1sc into next st, 1hdc into each of next 2 sts, 1dc into each of next 16 sts, 1hdc into each of next 10 sts, 1sc into each of next 10 sts, sl st into next dc, turn.
Next round 1sc into each of next 5 sts, 1hdc into each of next 10 sts, 1dc into each of next 20 sts, 1hdc into each of next 3 sts, 1sc into each of next 2 sts, 3sc into st at tip of leaf, 1sc into each of next 2 sts, 1hdc into each of next 3 sts, 1dc into each of next 20 sts, 1hdc into each of next 10 sts, 1sc into each of next 10 sts, sl st into next st, turn.
Next row 1sc into each of next 5 sts, 1hdc into each of next 10 sts, 1dc into each of next 26 sts, 1hdc into each of next 3 sts, 1sc into each of next 2 sts, 3sc into st at tip of leaf, 1sc into each of next 2 sts, 1hdc into each of next 3 sts, 1dc into each of next 26 sts, 1hdc into each of next 10 sts, 1sc into each st to end. Turn.
Next row Working over craft wire, work a row of sc all around leaf. Fasten off.
Tape leaf to wire as required.

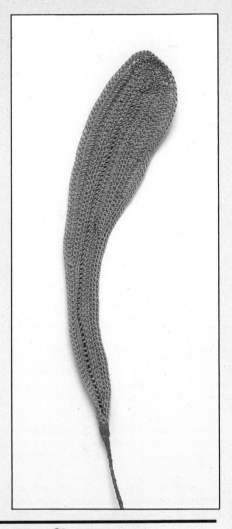

Adapting the basic flowers

You can create anything from a small nosegay to an enormous bouquet by adapting the Pattern Library flowers by using different colors and yarns.

Using other colors to work the basic flowers would alter their appearance considerably. For example, by using golden orange for the Daffodil trumpet and white for the petals, you could create a Narcissus. Both the Tulip and Iris could be worked in other colors to make different varieties of flower.

Working green plants
Realistic green plants can also be crocheted if you choose colors to match the leaves. Plants like *Adiantum* which have small leaves, can be worked in the No. 20 cotton used for the flowers, while larger-leafed plants like *Philodendron* should be worked in No. 5 cotton.

Thick stems can be made from French knitting or alternatively from narrow single crochet tubes, wired with florist's thick wire. Use bouclé yarn to represent soil and work the pot in plain brown yarn or use a real pot. Crochet plants are usually lighter than their natural equivalents and so can easily over balance. This problem can be avoided if you weight the bottom of the pot with sand or a quick-setting heavy-weight filler.

Wired flowers

1 Freesia

Using random cotton, ch 4, sl st to first ch to form a circle.

1st round Ch 3, working over approx 6 in. of wire, work 8dc into circle, sl st to top of first ch 3, 9 sts.

2nd round Ch 3, skip first st, 1dc into each st to end, sl st to top of first ch 3.

3rd round Ch 3, skip first st, 2dc into next st, (1dc into each of next 2 sts, 2dc into next st) twice, 1dc into next st, sl st to top of first ch 3, 12 sts.

4th round Ch 3, skip first st, (2dc into next st, 1dc into each of next 2 sts) 3 times, 2dc into next st, 1dc into next st, sl st to top of first ch 3. 16 sts.

5th round Ch 3, skip first st, (2dc into next st, 1dc into next st) 7 times, 2dc into last st, sl st to top of first ch 3. 24 sts.

6th round As 2nd round.

7th round Ch 3, 1dc into base of ch 3, (3tr into next st, 2dc into next st, sl st into next st, 2dc into next st) 5 times, 3tr into next st, 2dc into next st, sl st into next st.

Fasten off.

Make 3 more flowers in the same way. Cut length of thick wire and bend over for approx ½ in. at one end. Bind with tape to form bud at top of stem. Tape stem to position of first flower. Insert stamens into first flower and wire securely to stem approx ½ in. below bud.

Attach rem 3 flowers to stem in the same way, spacing them approx ½ in. apart.

Bind rem stem with tape.

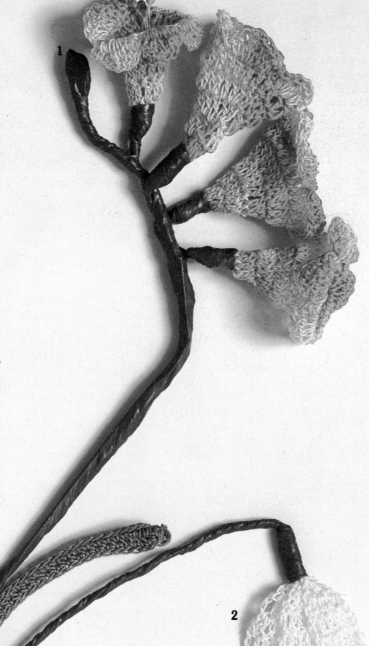

Steve Tanner

2 Snowdrop

Use white for flower and green for leaf.

Flower Using white, ch 4.

Base row 2dc into 4th ch from hook. Turn. 3 sts.

1st row Ch 3, skip first st, 2dc into each of next 2 sts. Turn. 5 sts.

2nd and 3rd rows Ch 3, skip first st, 1dc into each st to end. Turn.

4th row Ch 3, skip first st, work next 4dc tog.

Fasten off.

Make 3 more petals in the same way.

Leaf Using green, ch 50.

Base row 1sc into 2nd ch from hook, 1sc into each ch to last ch, 3sc into last ch. Turn.

Next row Working over craft wire, work 1sc into each ch on other side of foundation to end.

Fasten off. Cut craft wire, leaving a 2 in.-long end.

Place 4 petals together as shown. Bind lower edges of petals tog with tape.

Bind and attach flower to stem. Bind stem to position of leaf. Attach leaf to stem and bind rem stem.

283

3

3 Bluebell

Bud Using blue, ch 6, leaving a 2¼ in.-long end of yarn.

Base row 1sc into 2nd ch from hook, 1dc into each of next 3 ch, 1sc into last ch. Turn.

1st-4th rows Ch 1, 1sc into first sc, 1dc into each of next 3dc, 1sc into last sc. Turn.

Fasten off, leaving a 2¼ in.-long end of yarn.

Roll work into a tight bud over end of thick wire. Bind tape around bottom of bud and around ends and onto wire to form stem.

Flowers Using blue, ch 4, sl st to first ch to form a circle. Leave a 2¼ in.-long end of yarn.

1st round Ch 1, 8sc into circle, sl st to first sc. 9 sts.

2nd-4th rounds Ch 1, 1sc into each sc to end, sl st to first sc.

5th round Ch 1, 2sc into each sc to end, sl st to first sc. 16 sts.

6th round Ch 1, * 1sc into next st, 1dc into next st, 3tr into next st, 1 dc into next st, rep from * to end, sl st to first sc.

Fasten off, leaving a 2½ in. long end of yarn. Thread ends of yarn through ch 4 circle.

Make 3 more flowers in the same way. Use ends of yarn to attach flowers to stem. Attach flowers at approx ½ in. intervals and bind stem with tape.

4 Primula

Use 2 colors, yellow and purple. Using yellow, ch 5, sl st to first ch to form a circle.

1st round Working over approx 6 in. of craft wire work (1sc, 2dc) 5 times into circle, sl st to first sc. 15 sts. Break off yellow and change to purple.

2nd round Ch 1, * 1sc into next sc, (2dc, 1tr) into next dc, (1tr,2dc) into next dc, rep from * 4 times more, sl st to first sc. 35 sts.

3rd round *1sc into next sc, 2dc into next st, (1dc, 1sc) into next st, (1sc, 1dc) into next st, sl st into next st, rep from * ending with sl st into first sc.

Fasten off.

Insert one stamen into center of flower. Bind stamen and wire under flower.

Tape flower onto thick wire. Tape wire to form stem.

4

5 Lily

Using orange, ch 6.

Base row 1dc into 4th ch from hook, 2dc into each of last 2 ch. Turn. 6 sts

1st row Ch 3, 1dc into base of ch 3, 2dc into next st, 1dc into each st to last 2 sts, 2dc into each of last 2 sts. Turn. 10 sts.

2nd and 3rd rows As 1st row. 18 sts.

4th row Ch 3, skip first st, 1dc into each st to end. Turn.

5th row As 4th row.

6th row Ch 3, skip first st, (work next 2dc tog) twice, 1dc into each st to last 5 sts, (work next 2dc tog) twice, 1dc into last st. Turn. 14 sts.

7th row Ch 3, skip first st, work next 2dc tog, 1dc into each st to last 3 sts, work next 2dc tog, 1dc into last st. Turn. 12 sts

8th-11th rows As 7th row. 4 sts.

12th row Ch 3, skip first st, work next 2dc tog, 1dc into last st.

Fasten off.

Make 5 more petals in the same way. Bend craft wire to shape of petal, leaving 2 ends, each approx 2 in. Working over wire, work one row of sc all around each petal. Place several large stamens in center of 3 petals. Arrange rem petals around first petals as shown. Twist petal wire and stamens together.

Tape flower onto thick wire.
Tape wire to form stem.

5

Steve Tanner

284

Stars

Star-shaped motifs are formed by working in the round in much the same way as when making hexagons and other polygons. Most stars have either six or eight sides, but all can be sewn or crocheted together to make delicate household linen.

Belinda

Skills you need

* **Triple crochet**
* **Working with fine cotton**

If you do not know these skills, refer to pages 296 and 308.

Materials

Stars, like many motifs, are best worked in a smooth, crisp yarn so that the crochet retains its shape. Cotton is ideal, though synthetic yarns of the same texture are also suitable. The thickness of the yarn of course governs the eventual size of the motif — the thicker the yarn, the larger the motif. The tablecloth on page 285 is formed from motifs worked in number 20 mercerized cotton, but as can be seen in the Pattern Library on page 288, slightly thicker cotton could be used for a chunkier look.

Special technique – working an open center

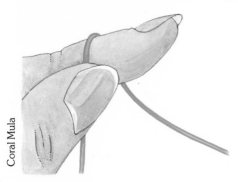

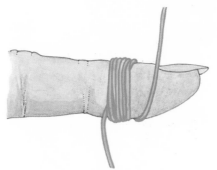

Coral Mula

1 *Some motifs worked in the round have a large, open center. This is sometimes formed from a circle of chain, but a neater method has been used for the motifs in the basic tablecloth. Hold the yarn over the little finger of your left hand about 4 in. from the cut end. Hold the ball of yarn in your right hand.*

2 *Wind the yarn from the ball 20 times around the tip of your little finger. Cover the short end as you wind to secure it and wind firmly but not too tightly so that the resulting circle can be removed easily from your finger.*

3 *Carefully remove the yarn circle from your finger. Then, holding circle and working yarn in your left hand, use a hook of the required size to work a slip stitch into the circle to prevent it from unwinding.*
Continue the motif as given in the pattern. Then join motifs while working the last rounds.
Note When using thicker yarn, wind the yarn fewer times around your little finger.

The basic star-motif tablecloth

A fine lacy tablecloth that can be made to any size.

Size
Large star motif measures 4¼ in. between widest points

Gauge
Small filling motif measures approx 1¼ in. between widest points

Materials
No. 20 crochet cotton
No. 3 steel crochet hook

First star motif
** Using crochet hook, wind yarn 20 times around tip of little finger to form a circle, sl st into circle.
1st round Ch 4, 3tr into circle, (ch 3, 4tr into circle) 7 times, ch 3, sl st to top of first ch 4.
286

2nd round Ch 1, 1sc into next tr, ch 3, sl st to last sc worked – picot formed –, 1sc into each of next 2tr, * (1sc, ch 3, 1sc) into next ch 3 sp, 1sc into each of next 2tr, picot, 1sc into each of next 2tr, rep from * 7 times more, (1sc, ch 3, 1sc) into next ch 3 sp, sl st to first ch.
3rd round Sl st across first 4sc and into first ch 3 sp, ch 4, 1tr into same ch 3 sp, (ch 10, work 2tr tog into next ch 3 sp) 7 times, ch 10, sl st to top of first ch 4.
4th round Ch 1, (13 sc into next ch 10 sp) 8 times, sl st to first ch.
5th round Ch 4, skip next sc, (1dc into next sc, ch 1, skip next sc) 51 times, sl st to 3rd of ch 4.
6th round Ch 1, (2sc into next ch 1 sp) 52 times, sl st to first ch.
7th round Sl st across first 4sc, (ch 7, skip next 4sc, 1sc into next sc, ch 10,

skip next 7sc, 1sc into next sc) 8 times. **
8th round * (4sc, picot, 4sc) into next ch 7 loop, 9sc into next ch 10 loop, ch 7, sl st into 5th of 9sc just worked, (4sc, picot, 4sc) into next ch 7 loop, 4sc into remainder of ch 10 loop, rep from * to end, ending with sl st to first sc.
Fasten off.

Second star motif
Work from ** to ** of first star motif.
8th round (4sc, picot, 4sc) into next ch 7 loop, 9sc into next ch 10 loop, ch 7, sl st into 5th sc of 9sc just worked, (4sc, ch 1, sl st to corresponding picot on first star motif, ch 1, 4sc) into next ch 7 loop, 4sc into remainder of ch 10 loop, complete round as for 8th round of first star motif.

Continue working second star motifs

in this way until table cloth is the required width.

First filling motif

Begin and work 1st round as for first star motif.

2nd round Ch 1, 1sc into next tr, picot, 1sc into each of next 2tr, 1sc into next ch 3 sp, ch 1, sl st to large picot on inner edge of first star motif, ch 1, 1sc into same ch 3 sp, 1sc into each of next 2tr, picot, 1sc into each of next 2tr, (1sc, ch 3, 1sc) into next ch 3 sp, 1sc into each of next 2tr, picot, 1sc into each of next 2tr, 1sc into ch 3 sp, ch 1, sl st to large picot on inner edge of second star motif, complete round as for 2nd round of first star motif.
Fasten off.
Continue working filling motifs in the same way between large star motifs.

Next star motif row

Work from ** to ** as for first star motif.

8th round * (Ch 4, picot, ch 4) into next ch 7 loop, 9sc into next ch 10 loop, ch 7, sl st into 5th of 9sc just worked, (4sc, ch 1, sl st to corresponding large picot on first motif of previous star motif row, ch 1, 4sc) into next ch 7 loop, 4sc into remainder of ch 10 loop*, rep from * to * once, joining ch 1 to corresponding ch 1 sp on next filling motif, complete round as for 8th round of first star motif.
Work foll large star motifs in the same way, joining each motif to previous large star motif of this row, filling motif of previous row, next large star motif of previous row and next filling motif of previous row. Cont in this way until the tablecloth is required length, omitting filling motifs from last row of large star motifs.

Edging

With RS facing and using crochet hook, join yarn to first picot of corner motif.

1st round Ch 4, 1tr into same picot, ch 10, 1sc into next large picot, (ch 10, 1sc into next picot, ch 10, 1sc into next large picot) 4 times, ch 10, work 2tr tog into last picot of same motif, work 2tr tog into first picot of next motif, (ch 10, 1sc into next large picot, ch 10, 1sc into next picot) 3 times omitting 1sc at end of last rep, work 2tr tog into last large picot, rep from * to end, working extra ch 10 loops on corner motifs as required, sl st to top of first ch 4.

Geoff Dann

2nd round (7sc, picot, 7sc) into first loop, *9sc into next loop, ch 7, sl st into 5th of 9sc just worked, (4sc, picot, 4sc) into next ch 7 loop, 4sc into remainder of ch 10 loop*, rep from * to * 7 times more, ** (7sc, picot, 7sc) into next loop**, rep from ** to ** once more, rep from * to * 4 times

more, cont in this way, working extra picot points at each corner as required, sl st to first sc.
Fasten off.

To finish

Darn in all ends.
Press tablecloth under a damp cloth.

Adapting the basic tablecloth

Put stars in your eyes by working the heavenly motifs in the Pattern Library.

The lace tablecloth can easily be varied by introducing different colors.
The filling motifs could, for example, be worked either in a completely different color or in a lighter shade of the same color. Similarly a contrasting color could be used to emphasize the centers of the large star motifs.

Using stars

Star motifs can either be sewn together to form simple garments like summer tops, scarves and shawls or they can be used individually. Sew them to a knitted or crocheted sweater – worked in white or silver yarn they would resemble snowflakes – or work them in glitter yarn in many colors and use them as soft, washable Christmas decorations. They will not tarnish and will be safe for children.

287

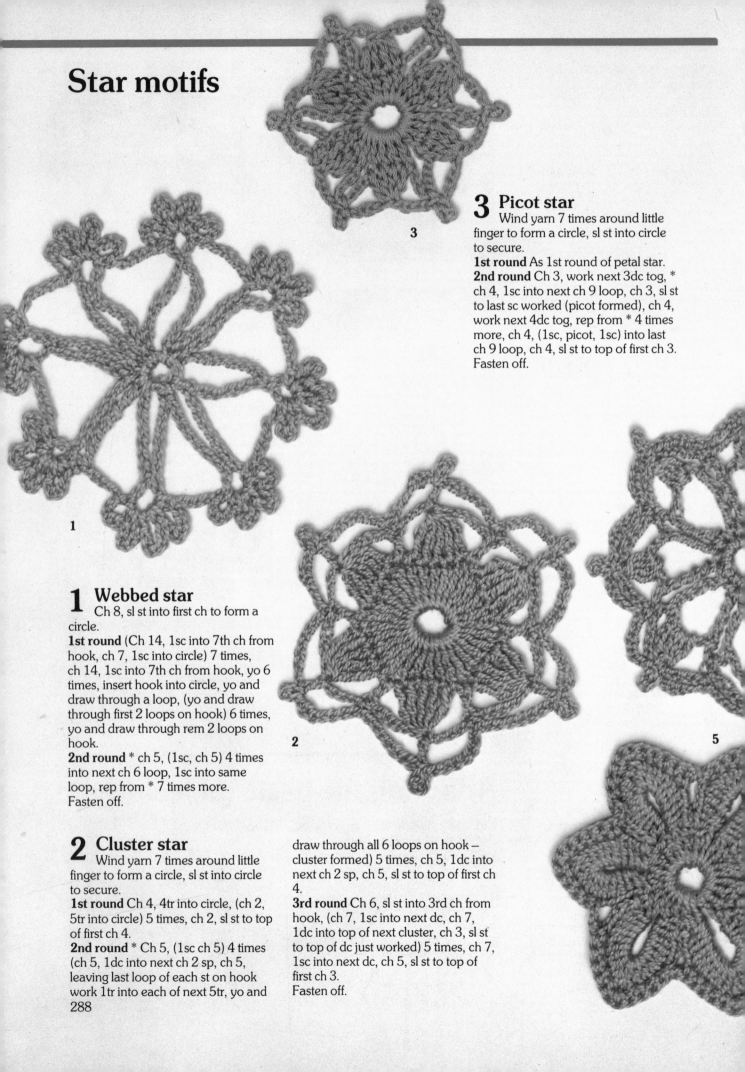

Star motifs

1 Webbed star

Ch 8, sl st into first ch to form a circle.

1st round (Ch 14, 1sc into 7th ch from hook, ch 7, 1sc into circle) 7 times, ch 14, 1sc into 7th ch from hook, yo 6 times, insert hook into circle, yo and draw through a loop, (yo and draw through first 2 loops on hook) 6 times, yo and draw through rem 2 loops on hook.

2nd round * ch 5, (1sc, ch 5) 4 times into next ch 6 loop, 1sc into same loop, rep from * 7 times more. Fasten off.

2 Cluster star

Wind yarn 7 times around little finger to form a circle, sl st into circle to secure.

1st round Ch 4, 4tr into circle, (ch 2, 5tr into circle) 5 times, ch 2, sl st to top of first ch 4.

2nd round * Ch 5, (1sc ch 5) 4 times (ch 5, 1dc into next ch 2 sp, ch 5, leaving last loop of each st on hook work 1tr into each of next 5tr, yo and

288

draw through all 6 loops on hook – cluster formed) 5 times, ch 5, 1dc into next ch 2 sp, ch 5, sl st to top of first ch 4.

3rd round Ch 6, sl st into 3rd ch from hook, (ch 7, 1sc into next dc, ch 7, 1dc into top of next cluster, ch 3, sl st to top of dc just worked) 5 times, ch 7, 1sc into next dc, ch 5, sl st to top of first ch 3. Fasten off.

3 Picot star

Wind yarn 7 times around little finger to form a circle, sl st into circle to secure.

1st round As 1st round of petal star.

2nd round Ch 3, work next 3dc tog, * ch 4, 1sc into next ch 9 loop, ch 3, sl st to last sc worked (picot formed), ch 4, work next 4dc tog, rep from * 4 times more, ch 4, (1sc, picot, 1sc) into last ch 9 loop, ch 4, sl st to top of first ch 3. Fasten off.

4 Openwork star

Ch 8, sl st to first ch to form a circle.

1st round Ch 1, 16sc into circle, sl st to first sc.

2nd round Ch 11, 1dtr into next sc, (ch 3, 1dtr into next sc, ch 6, 1dtr into next sc) 7 times, ch 3, sl st to 5th of first ch 11.

3rd round Sl st into each of first ch 2, ch 3, work 3dc tog into same ch 6 loop of previous round, (ch 5, 1sc into next ch 3 loop, ch 5, work 4dc tog into next ch 6 loop) 7 times, ch 5, 1sc into next ch 3 loop, ch 5, 1sc into top of first ch 3.

4th round Ch 3, sl st to last sc worked (picot formed), ch 6, 1sc into next sc, ch 6, 1sc into top of next cluster) 8 times, omitting last sc and ending with sl st to beg of round. Fasten off.

6

4

6 Large star

Ch 10, sl st to first ch to form a circle.

1st round Ch 4, 3tr into circle, (ch 3, 4tr into circle) 7 times, ch 3, sl st to top of first ch 4.

2nd round Ch 4, work next 3tr tog, (ch 6, 1sc into next ch 3 loop, ch 6, work next 4tr tog) 7 times, ch 6, 1sc into next ch 3 loop, ch 6, sl st to top of first ch 4.

3rd round 8sc into first ch 6 loop, * 8sc into next ch 6 loop, 4sc into next ch 6 loop, ch 5, sl st into 4th of 8sc just worked, (4sc, ch 3, sl st to last sc worked — picot formed —, 4sc) into next ch 5 loop, 4sc into rem of ch 6 loop, rep from * 6 times more, 8sc into next ch 6 loop, sl st into each of next 4sc, ch 5, sl st into 4th sc just worked, (4sc, picot, 4sc) into next ch 5 loop, sl st to next sc. Fasten off.

5 Treble star

Wind yarn 7 times around little finger to form a circle, sl st into circle to secure.

1st round As 1st round of petal star.

2nd round Sl st into first dc, * 1sc into next dc, (9dc, ch 2, 9dc) into next ch 9 loop, skip next 2dc, rep from * 5 times more, sl st into first sc. Turn.

3rd round Sl st into each of first 4dc, * 1sc into each of next 5dc, 2sc into next ch 2 loop, 1sc into each of next 5dc, ch 2, skip next 8dc, rep from * 5 times more, sl st to first sc. Fasten off.

7

7 Chain star

Wind yarn 7 times around little finger to form a circle, sl st into circle to secure.

1st round Ch 3, 2dc into circle, (ch 9, 3dc into circle) 7 times, ch 9, sl st into top of first ch 3.

2nd round (1sc into next dc, ch 4, 1sc into next ch 9 loop, ch 4, skip next dc) 8 times.

3rd round (1sc into next sc, ch 5, 1sc into next ch 4 loop, ch 3, sl st to last sc worked (picot formed), 1sc into next ch 4 loop, ch 5) 8 times, sl st to first sc. Fasten off.

8 Petal star

Wind yarn 7 times around little finger to form a circle, sl st into circle to secure.

1st round Ch 3, 3dc into circle, (ch 9, 4dc into circle) 5 times, ch 9, sl st to top of first ch 3.

2nd round * Ch 3, 9sc into next ch 9 loop, ch 5, sl st into 5th sc worked, 7sc into ch 5 loop just worked, 4sc into same ch 9 loop, rep from * to end. Fasten off.

8

Geoff Dann

Ornate medallions

Whether worked in knitting yarn or crochet cotton, these unusual crochet squares can be used to make beautifully textured fabrics. You can use the medallions to make an entire fabric or they can be combined with plainer squares for an interesting embossed effect, ideal for bedspreads, baby blankets or afghans.

Skills you need

*Double crochet
*Working raised flowers

If you do not know these skills, refer to pages 294 and 202.

Materials

Textured stitches are most effective when worked in a plain knitting or crochet yarn, so that the clusters, popcorn stitches, loops and flowers used to create the ornate medallions stand out clearly against the back-ground fabric.

Plain sport and worsted-weight yarns are all suitable for the technique, as are most crochet cottons.
More ornate yarns, such as a bouclé or textured mohair for example, tend to detract from the heavily patterned effect and should be avoided.

Special technique – making a popcorn

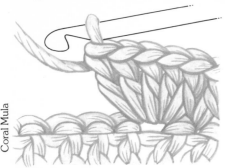

1 With right side of work facing, crochet in pattern to the point where popcorn stitch is to be made. Work five double crochet into the next stitch.

2 Withdraw the hook from the working loop and insert it from front to back through the top of the first of the five doubles just made, while holding the working loop with the left hand.

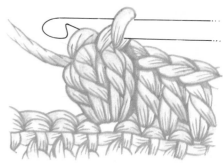

3 Keeping the hook in place, re-insert it into working loop and draw this loop through the first stitch of the five double group to make the popcorn stitch. Make sure that the stitches are drawn together neatly to achieve a good shape.

Coral Mula

Crocheted bedspread

This pretty crocheted bedspread, made from beautifully textured medallions, is worked in a soft sport yarn. It can be made for either a single or a double bed in a color to match the decor of your bedroom.

Sizes
Single bed size measures 72 × 96 in.
Double bed measures 86 × 96 in.

Gauge
One motif measures approx 13¼ in. square

Materials
67 oz of a sport-weight yarn for single bed size
74 oz of same for double bed size
Size C crochet hook

Square
Ch 8. Join with a sl st to form a circle.
1st round Ch 3, 1dc into circle, * (ch 3, 2dc into circle), rep from * 6 times more, ch 3. Join with a sl st to top of first ch 3. Eight 2dc groups.
2nd round Sl st to center of next ch 3 loop, 1sc into same place as sl st, * (ch 4, 1sc) into next ch 3 loop, rep from * 6 times more, ch 4. Join with a sl st to first sc.
3rd round Into each ch 4 loop work (1sc, 1hdc, 5dc, 1 hdc, 1sc).
4th round * Ch 6, inserting hook from back of work, work 1sc around next sc of 2nd round, rep from * to end.
5th round Into each ch 6 loop work

Belinda

291

(1sc, 1hdc, 7dc, 1hdc, 1sc).

6th round As 4th, working 8 ch instead of 6 ch.

7th round As 5th, working 9 dc instead of 7 dc.

8th round As 4th, working 10 ch instead of 6 ch.

9th round Ch 9, 1dtr into st at base of ch 9, * (ch 1, 1dc into ch 10 loop) 3 times into same loop, (ch 1, 1dc into ch 10 loop) 3 times into next loop, ch 1, (1dtr, ch 3, 1dtr) into sc between next 2 loops, rep from * to end omitting (1dtr, ch 3, 1dtr) at end of last rep. Join with a sl st to 6th of first ch 9.

10th round Sl st into first ch 3 loop, ch 3, (1dc, 3 ch, 2dc) into same loop, * 1dc into dtr, (1dc into next ch 1 sp, 1dc into next dc) 6 times, 1dc into next ch 1 sp, 1dc into next dtr, (2dc, ch 3, 2dc) into ch 3 sp, rep from * to end omitting (2dc, ch 3, 2dc) at end of last rep. Join with a sl st to top of first ch 3.

11th round Ch 3, * 1dc into next dc, (2dc, ch 3, 2dc) into next ch 3 sp, 1dc into each of next 18 dc, rep from * to end omitting 1dc at end of last rep. Join with a sl st to top of first ch 3.

12th round Ch 3, * 1dc into each of next 3dc, (2dc, ch 3, 2dc) into next ch 3 sp, 1dc into each of next 20dc, rep from * to end omitting 1dc at end of last rep. Join with a sl st top of first ch 3.

13th round Ch 4, * skip 1dc, 1dc into next dc, ch 1, skip next dc, 1dc into next dc, ch 1, skip next dc, (2dc, ch 3, 2dc) into next ch 3 sp, (ch 1, skip next dc, 1dc into next dc) 11 times, ch 1 rep from * to end omitting 1dc and ch 1 at end of last rep. Join with a sl st to 3rd ch of first ch 4.

14th round Sl st into next ch 1 sp, ch 4, * (1dc into next sp, ch 1) twice, (2dc, ch 3, 2dc) into next ch 3 sp, (ch 1, 1dc into next sp) 12 times, ch 1, rep from * to end omitting 1dc and ch 1 at end of last rep. Join with a sl st to 3rd ch of first ch 4.

15th round Ch 3, * (1dc into next sp, 1dc into next dc) 3 times, 1dc into next dc, (2dc, ch 3, 2dc) into next ch 3 sp, 1dc into each of next 2dc, (1dc into next sp, 1dc into next dc,) 12 times, rep from * to end omitting 1dc at end of last rep. Join with a sl st to top of first ch 3.

16th round Ch 3, * work 5dc into next dc, withdraw hook from working loop, insert hook through top of first of these 5dc then back into working loop and draw working loop through

292

first of 5dc (called 1 popcorn — 1pc), 1dc into each of next 3dc, 1pc into next dc, 1dc into each of next 4dc (2dc, ch 3, 2dc) into ch 3 sp, 1dc into each of next 4dc, (1pc into next dc, 1 dc into each of next 3dc) 6 times, rep from * to end omitting 1dc at end of last rep. Join with a sl st to top of first ch 3.

17th round Ch 3, * (1dc into top of next pc, 1dc into each of next 3dc) twice, 1dc into each of next 3dc, (2dc, ch 3, 2dc) into next ch 3 sp, 1dc into each of next 6dc, (1dc into top of next pc, 1dc into each of next 3dc) 6 times, rep from * to end omitting 1dc at end of last rep. Join with a sl st to top of first ch 3.

18th round Ch 4, * (skip 1dc, 1dc into next dc, ch 1) 6 times, (2dc, ch 3, 2dc) into ch 3 sp, (ch 1, skip 1dc, 1dc into next dc) 16 times, ch 1, rep from * to end omitting 1dc and ch 1 at end of last rep. Join with a sl st to 3rd of first ch 4.

19th round Sl st into next sp, ch 4, * (1dc into next sp, ch 1) 6 times, (2dc, ch 3, 2dc) into next ch 3 sp, ch 1, (1dc into next sp, ch 1) 17 times, rep from * to end omitting 1dc and 1 ch at end of last rep. Join with a sl st to 3rd ch of first ch 4.

20th round Ch 3, * (1dc into next sp, 1dc into next dc) 7 times, 1dc into next dc, (2dc, ch 3, 2dc) into next ch 3 sp, 1dc into next dc, (1dc into next dc, 1dc into next sp) 17 times, rep from * to end. Join with a sl st to top of first ch 3.

21st round Sl st to next dc, 3 ch, * 1dc into each of next 2dc, (1pc into next dc, 1dc into each of next 3dc) 3 times, 1dc into each of next 2dc, (2dc, ch 3, 2dc) into next ch 3 sp, 1dc into

Steve Tanner

each of next 5dc, (1pc into next dc, 1dc into each of next 3dc) 8 times, 1pc into next dc, 1dc into next dc, rep from * to end omitting 1dc at end of last rep. Join with a sl st to top of first ch 3.

22nd round Ch 3, * 1dc into each of next 18 sts, (2dc, ch 3, 2dc) into next ch 3 sp, 1dc into each of next 41 sts, rep from * to end omitting 1dc at end of last rep. Join with a sl st to top of first ch 3.

23rd round Sl st to next dc, ch 4, * (skip next dc, 1dc into next dc, ch 1) 9 times, (2dc, ch 3, 2dc) into next ch 3 sp, ch 1 (skip next dc, 1dc into next dc, ch 1) 22 times, rep from * to end omitting 1dc and ch 1 at end of last rep. Join with a sl st to 3rd ch or first 4 ch. Fasten off.

Make 35 squares in all for single bed size and 42 squares in all for double bed size.

To finish

Block and press each square lightly on WS to correct size. Sew squares into strips of five by seven for single bed size and six by seven for double bed size.

Fringe

Make a fringe along two sides and one end of bedspread by cutting four lengths of yarn 8 in. each in length for each fringe and knotting these four strands into each ch 1 sp along edge. Trim evenly as necessary.

Adapting the basic bedspread

Choose either of the medallions featured on the opposite page to make a beautiful bedspread.

Substituting motifs

Substituting one square for another is quite simple in crochet, since the squares can be sewn or crocheted together to make the complete fabric. The size of the square you choose is not important, since it is quite simple to make fewer or more squares, depending on the size required for the completed fabric. To calculate the number of squares you will need, make a sample square in the hook and yarn of your choice, measure the size of the finished square and calculate the number needed for the bedspread from this measurement.

In some cases the final round of a motif can be repeated, working more stitches on each side of the motif until it is the required size. If you choose one of these squares as an alternative to the bedspread medallion featured on page 291, you can then make your motif exactly the same size, so that no calculations will have to be made regarding the number of squares needed to make the bedspread.

The squares should be blocked and pressed before they are sewn together so that they are all of equal size, thus achieving a perfectly finished fabric.

Ornate medallions

1 Diamond cluster motif

Ch 6. Join with a sl st to form a circle.

1st round Ch 3 to count as first dc, 2dc into circle, (ch 2, 3dc into circle) 3 times, ch 2. Join with a sl st to top of first ch 3. Four blocks of 3dc.

2nd round Ch 3, * leaving last loop of each st on hook, work 5tr into next dc, yo and draw through all loops on hook — called 5tr cluster —, 1dc into next dc, (2dc, ch 2, 2dc) into next ch 2 sp, 1dc into next dc, rep from * to end omitting 1dc at end of last rep. Join with a sl st to top of first ch 3.

3rd round Ch 3, * 1dc into top of cluster, 1dc into next dc, 5tr cluster into next dc, 1dc into next dc, (2dc, ch 2, 2dc) into next ch 2 sp, 1dc into next dc, 5tr cluster into next dc, 1dc into next dc, rep from * to end omitting 1dc at end of last rep. Join with a sl st to top of first ch 3.

4th round Ch 3, * 5tr cluster into next dc, 1dc into next dc, 1dc into top of next cluster, 1dc into next dc, 5tr cluster into next dc, 1dc into next dc (2dc, ch 2, 2dc) into ch 2 sp, 1dc into next dc, 5tr cluster into next dc, 1dc into next dc, 1dc into top of next cluster into next dc, 1dc into next dc, end omitting 1dc at end of last rep. Join with a sl st to top of first ch 3.

5th round Ch 3, * 1dc into top of next cluster, 1dc into next dc, 5tr cluster into next dc, 1dc into each of next 5sts, (2dc, ch 2, 2dc) into next ch 2 sp, 1dc into each of next 5 sts, 5tr cluster into next dc, 1dc into next dc, rep from * to end omitting 1dc at end of last rep. Join with a sl st to top of first ch 3.

6th round Ch 3, * 5tr cluster into next dc, 1dc into each of next 9 sts, (2dc, ch 2, 2dc) into next ch 2 sp, 1dc into each of next 9 sts, rep from * to end omitting 1dc at end of last rep. Join with a sl st to top of first ch 3.

7th round Ch 3, * 1dc into each of next 12 sts, (2dc, ch 2, 2dc) into next ch 2 sp, 1dc into each of next 11 sts, rep from * to end omitting 1dc at end of last rep. Join with a sl st to top of first ch 3.
Fasten off.

2 Shell and popcorn motif

Ch 6. Join with a sl st to form a circle.

1st round Ch 3 to count as first dc, 1dc into circle, (ch 3, 3dc into circle) 3 times, ch 3, 1dc into circle. Join with a sl st to top of first ch 3. Four 3dc blocks.

2nd round Ch 3, * work 5dc into next st, withdraw hook from working loop and insert through top of first of 5dc, insert hook back into working loop and draw through first of 5dc (called 1pc), 5dc into ch 3 sp, 1pc into next dc, 1dc into next dc, rep from * to end omitting 1dc at end of last rep. Join with a sl st to top of first ch 3.

3rd round Ch 5, * skip first pc, 1pc into next dc, 1dc into next dc, 3dc into next dc, 1dc into next dc, 1 pc into next dc, ch 2, skip 1pc, 1dc into next dc, ch 2, rep from * to end omitting 1dc and ch 2 at end of last rep. Join with a sl st to 3rd ch of first ch 5.

4th round Sl st into next ch 2 sp, ch 5, * skip 1pc, 1pc into next dc, 1dc into next dc, 3dc into next dc, 1dc into next dc, 1pc into next dc, ch 2, skip next pc, 1dc into ch 2 sp, ch 2, 1dc into next ch 2 sp, ch 2, rep from * to end omitting 1dc and ch 2 at end of last rep. Join with a sl st to 3rd ch of first 5 ch.

5th round Sl st into next sp, ch 5, * skip 1pc, 1pc into next dc, 1dc into next dc, 3dc into dc, 1dc into next dc, 1pc into next dc, ch 2, (1dc into next ch 2 sp, ch 2) 3 times, rep from * to end omitting 1dc and ch 2 at end of last rep. Join with a sl st to 3rd ch of first ch 5.

6th round Work as 5th, but working section in brackets 4 times instead of 3.

7th round As 5th, but working section in brackets 5 times instead of 3.
Cont working in this way until motif is required size.
Fasten off.

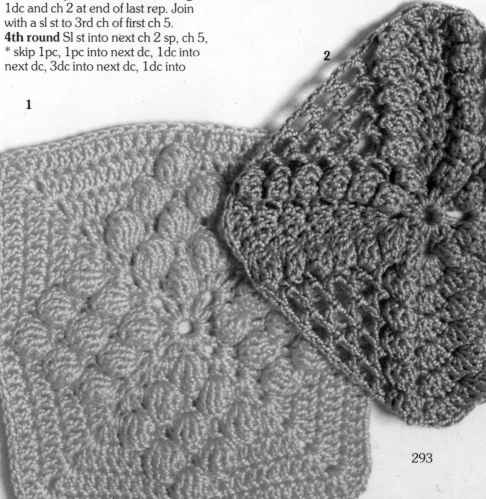

1

2

The crochet Know-How section provides a basic crochet course, progressing step-by-step from the foundation chain to some of the more advanced techniques you need to know. At the same time it gives a step-by step guide to any particular stitches required to make the project given in the Pattern Library section.

Foundation chain (ch)

1 Hold the hook in your right hand as if you were holding a pencil.

2 Thread the yarn as shown between the fingers of the left hand so that it flows freely and evenly.

3 Make a slip loop on the hook. Take the yarn over the hook and draw through the loop to make the first chain. After making a few chains, move up your finger and thumb to just below the hook.

Double crochet (dc)

1 Make a chain the length needed. Take the yarn counter clockwise over the hook. Skip the first three chain and insert the hook from front to back under the top two loops of the fourth chain from the hook. (The three chains missed at the beginning should be counted as the first double crochet.)

2 Take the yarn counter clockwise over the hook and draw yarn through the chain — three loops on the hook.

3 Take the yarn counter clockwise over the hook. Draw the yarn through the first two loops on the hook — two loops remain on the hook.

4 Take the yarn counter clockwise over the hook. Draw the yarn through the remaining two loops on the hook — one double crochet has been worked and one loop only remains on the hook.

Working afghan squares in rounds

Here's how to work simple granny squares, but the basic principle can be applied to all types of afghan square.

1 Make a small number of chains — usually between four and six — and join into a circle with a slip stitch, insert hook in first chain, yarn over hook, and draw through chain and through loop on hook.

2 On the first round, work four groups of double crochet into the circle, spaced by chain stitches. Fasten off.

3 To begin the next round, join the new color to the next chain space and work three chains to count as the first double crochet. On this and following rounds, work two double crochet groups separated by chain spaces at each corner, and one group of doubles into each chain space on the edges.

Coral Mula

Increasing

1 To increase one stitch in a single crochet, half double or double crochet fabric, simply work two stitches into the top of one stitch of the previous row. Although increases are usually worked at the edges of fabric, they can, if necessary, be worked into any stitch of the row.

2 It can sometimes be possible to achieve a neater edge when increasing by working all the extra stitches one stitch in from each edge. At the beginning of the row work the turning chain and skip the first stitch, work two stitches into the next stitch; at the end of the row, work to within the last two stitches (including the turning chain) and work two stitches into the next stitch and one stitch into the top of the turning chain.

3 Occasionally it may be necessary to increase two or more stitches into one stitch of the previous row. To increase two stitches into one stitch, simply work three stitches all into one stitch (i.e. two increased stitches plus the original stitch).

Decreasing

Decreases can be worked into any stitches, but are usually worked near the edges. Like increases, decreases should, if possible, be worked one stitch in from the edge to ensure a neat finish. The principle is the same for single, half double and double crochet – two or more incomplete stitches are linked together into one stitch – but the working methods differ.

1 To decrease one single crochet stitch, insert the hook into the next stitch, yarn over hook and draw through a loop – two loops on the hook; insert the hook into the next stitch, yarn over hook and draw through a loop – three loops on the hook; yarn over hook and draw through all three loops – one single crochet decreased.

2 To decrease one half double stitch, take the yarn over the hook, insert the hook into the next stitch, yarn over hook and draw through a loop – three loops on the hook; yarn over hook, insert the hook into the next stitch and work as before until five loops remain; yarn over hook and draw through all five loops – one half double decreased.

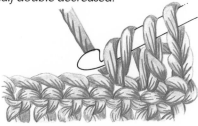

3 To decrease one double crochet take the yarn over the hook, insert the hook into the next stitch,

yarn over hook and draw through a loop – three loops on the hook; yarn over hook and draw through the first two loops – two loops on the hook. Work the next stitch as before until three loops remain, yarn over hook and draw through all three loops – one double crochet decreased.

Single crochet (sc)

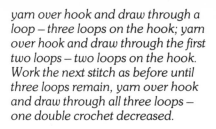

1 To work the base row, skip the first of the foundation chain and insert the hook from front to back under the top two loops of the second chain from the hook. Take the yarn over the hook and draw through a loop — two loops on the hook.

2 Take the yarn over the hook and draw it through the two loops on the hook — one loop remains and one single crochet has been worked. Work one single crochet into the next and every foundation chain, then turn over the work as you would a page in a book.

3 To begin the next row, work one turning chain to count as the first stitch. Skip the last stitch of the previous row and work one single crochet into every following stitch, working the last single crochet into the turning chain of the previous row. Repeat for single crochet fabric.

This Know-How describes how to work more basic crochet stitches — slip stitch, half double, and triple crochet. Half double forms a fine, neat fabric, while slip stitch and triple crochet can be used in combination with other basic stitches to create intricate decorative fabrics.

Slip stitch (sl st)

1 To work slip stich along a foundation chain, insert the hook from front to back under the top two loops of the second chain from the hook. Take the yarn counter clockwise over the hook and draw it through the chain and loop on the hook — one loop remains and one slip stitch has been worked. Continue in this way to the end.

2 Slip stitch is often used when shaping. When the required number of slip stitches has been worked, slip stitch into the next stitch, work the turning chain to count as the first stitch (here we show two for a half double fabric) and continue in pattern.

3 Slip stitch is also used when working in rounds to join the last stitch of the round to the first. After the last stitch has been worked, insert the hook into the top of the turning chain, which counts as the first stitch, and work a slip stitch.

Half double crochet (hdc)

1 To work the base row, take the yarn over the hook and insert the hook from front to back under the top two loops of the third chain from the hook. Take the yarn over the hook and draw through a loop — three loops on the hook.

2 Take the yarn over the hook and draw through all three loops — one loop remains and one half double has been worked. Take the yarn over the hook and work a half double as before into the chain. Continue in this way to the last chain. Turn the work.

3 Work two chains to count as the first half double. Skip the first half double of the previous row and work into the next stitch.

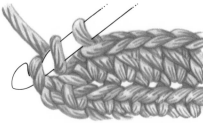

4 Work one half double into each half double to the turning chain. Then work one half double into the top of the turning chain and turn.

Triple crochet (tr)

1 To work the base row, take the yarn counter clockwise over the hook **twice** and insert the hook from front to back under the top two loops of the fifth chain from the hook. Take the yarn once over the hook and draw through the first two loops on the hook — three loops remain on the hook.

2 Take the yarn over the hook and draw it through the first two loops on the hook — two loops remain. Take the yarn over the hook and draw it through the remaining two loops on the hook — one loop remains and one triple crochet has been worked. Continue working triples in this way into the next and each chain to the end. Turn.

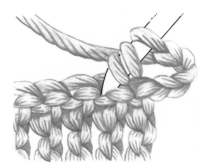

3 At the beginning of the next and every following row, work four turning chains to count as the first triple crochet. At the end of each row work the last triple into the top of the four turning chains.

Interesting effects can be produced quite simply by varying slightly the method of working basic stitches. Double crochet variations are shown here, but these methods could be applied to most of the basic stitches.

Note: Unless the pattern states otherwise, when working these variations always begin a row with a turning chain to count as the first stitch and end a row by working into the top of the turning chain.

Working around the stem

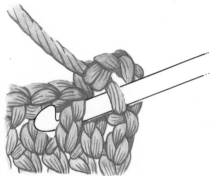

1 To work a double crochet from the front – known as "1dc front" — around the stem of a stitch, yarn over hook, and insert the hook from front to back into the space between two stitches. Bring the hook to the front of the work between the second and next stitch. Complete the stitch in the normal way.

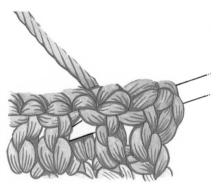

2 Work a double crochet from the back — known as a "1dc back" — around the stem of a stitch in the same way, but insert the hook between stitches from back to front and then from front to back.

3 A neat crochet ribbing pattern can be formed by working double crochet around the stem from the front and back alternately along the row.

Working between stitches

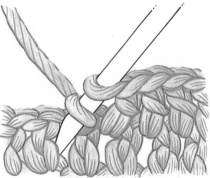

Yarn over hook and insert the hook from front to back into the space between two stitches beneath the small connecting loop at the top of the stitch. Complete the stitch in the usual way.

Working into a single loop

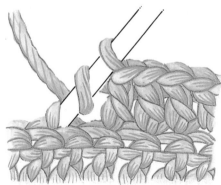

1 To work a double into the back loop of a stitch, yarn over hook and insert the hook into the back loop of the two loops lying at the top of the stitch. Complete the stitch in the usual way.

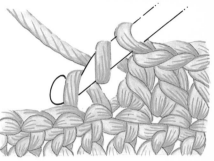

2 A double worked into the front loop of a stitch is formed in the same way, except that the hook is inserted into the front loop of the two loops lying at the top of the stitch.

Double triple and triple triple (dtr and tr tr)

These long stitches are usually worked as a fancy stitch or in one of the variations shown above.

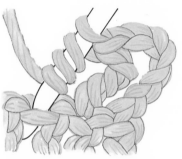

1 Begin a dtr row with five turning chains. Yarn over hook three times and insert the hook into the next stitch. Yarn over hook and draw through a loop — five loops on hook. *Yarn over hook and draw through first two loops on hook*, repeat from * to * three times more until there is one loop left on the hook.

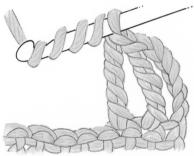

2 Triple treble is worked in the same way except that each row begins with six turning chains and the yarn is wound four times around the hook. Insert the hook into the next stitch and work from * to * five times until one loop remains.

Color bobbles

Even the most colorful bobbled fabrics can be worked in basic stitches, but however elaborate your fabric, it is important to fasten off and join in the new ball of yarn securely. Use the methods shown and your work will never unravel.

Fastening off

Work the last stitch of the last row in the usual way. Cut the yarn to approximately 4 in. Yarn over hook and draw through the loop on the hook to fasten off.

Joining in new yarn

Always join new yarn at the end of a row. Insert hook into turning chain, yarn over hook and draw through a loop — two loops on hook. Cut off old yarn to 4 in. Complete stitch using the new yarn.

Using two colors

1 To change color on any crochet fabric, work the stitch (double crochet shown above) as usual until there are two loops on the hook. Drop the old color and draw the new through two loops on hook.

2 When working in stripes, change color as in step 1 on the last stitch of a row, drawing the new color through the last two loops on the hook. Work the turning chain in the new color.

3 Use separate balls of yarn when working large areas in one color. However, when working only a few stitches in each color, carry the color not in use loosely on the wrong side at the base of the row, working over it with the other color.

Triple crochet bobbles

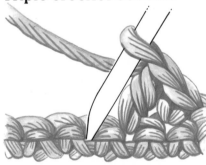

1 Small bobbles can be worked on a single crochet fabric by bending triples in half. With the wrong side facing, work a triple in the usual way. Work a single crochet into the next stitch, bending the triple in half to form a small bobble on the front of the work. If the bobble seems flat after it has been bent in half, push it through to the right side of the work with the fingers.

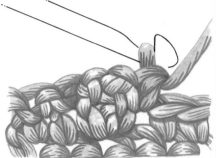

2 Larger bobbles may be formed by working two or more triples into the next stitch, but leaving the last loop of each triple stitch on the hook. Yarn over hook and draw through all loops. Secure the bobbles as in step 1. (Wrong side shown above.)

Double crochet bobbles

1 Large bobbles or popcorn stitches can be worked by drawing double crochets together. Work five doubles as usual into the next stitch. Remove the loop from the hook and insert the hook into the top of the first of the five doubles. Put the loop back onto the hook and draw it through the first double to form the bobble.

2 To work large bobbles in another color or yarn after the main fabric has been completed, with right side facing, insert the hook into the free loop at the top of a stitch. Work three chains and four double crochet into the free loop. Complete the bobble as in step 1 and fasten off.

Buttonholes

Buttonholes keep their shape best when worked in areas of firm, closely textured stitches like single crochet. They can be either worked as part of the main fabric or in a separate band.

1 *Before beginning, place the button on the crochet. Count the number of rows or stitches covered by the diameter of the button, then subtract one. This will give a rough idea of the number of chains or rows needed to form the buttonhole, but check as you work.*

2 *Crocheted buttonholes should look very neat, but they will keep their shape better if reinforced with buttonhole stitch. Use a tapestry needle and matching yarn, following the instructions for buttonhole stitch on page 397.*

Vertical buttonholes

1 *Beginning at the edge nearest the buttonhole, work to the position of the buttonhole. Turn, leaving the remaining stitches unworked. Work the number of rows needed for the buttonhole, ending at the buttonhole edge.*

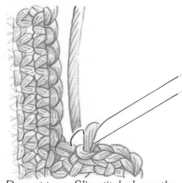

2 *Do not turn. Slip stitch down the edge of the buttonhole, working the last stitch into the same place as the first stitch on the side of the buttonhole.*

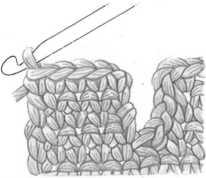

3 *Skip one stitch and work into each of the stitches left unworked in step 1. Work in pattern on these stitches until the second edge of the buttonhole is the same number of rows as the first, ending at the side edge.*

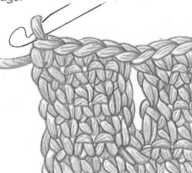

4 *Turn and work to the buttonhole. Work one stitch into the edge stitch on the other side of the buttonhole to join the two sides together. Work in pattern to the end of the row. Count the stitches to make sure none have been accidentally missed. Turn and continue in pattern working over the top stitches of the buttonhole very carefully. Repeat steps 1 to 4 for each buttonhole.*

Horizontal buttonholes

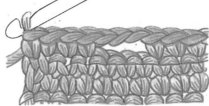

1 *Beginning at the edge nearest to the buttonhole, work to the position of the buttonhole. Make the chain needed to form the buttonhole. Skip the same number of stitches and work into the next stitch.*

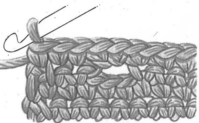

2 *On the return row, work one stitch into each chain of the previous row. Work to the end of the row. One horizontal buttonhole has been formed.*

Button loops

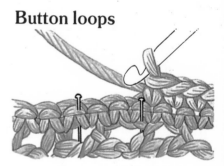

1 *With the wrong side facing, work one row of single crochet into the side edge of the work. Mark the position of the loops with pins. Turn and work to the first pin.*

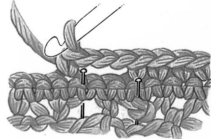

2 *Make enough chains to slip easily, but not loosely, over the button. Skip the same number of stitches. Work a single crochet into the next stitch. Continue in this way until all loops have been worked.*

Coral Mula

Varying stitches

As shown on page 297, relatively simple variations of basic stitches can produce interesting patterns.

Elongated stitches

Zigzag effects can be created very easily by working single crochet stitches of varying lengths into contrasting colored rows below.

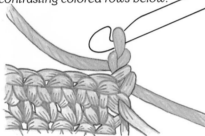

1 Work the number of single crochet rows required in the first color. Drop this color and join in a contrasting color. Make one chain and skip the first stitch.

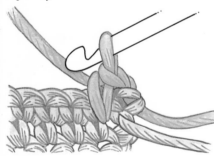

2 Skip the last row in the first color and insert the hook into the preceeding row one stitch to the left. Work a single crochet as normal, extending the yarn so that the fabric is not pulled out of shape.

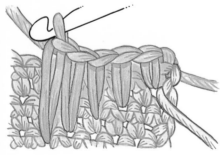

3 Insert the hook one row below and one stitch to the left of the

last point. Work a single crochet as normal. Continue in this way until the slope is the length required.

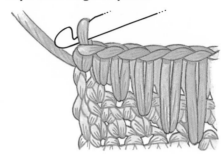

4 Work the second side of the zigzag in the same way, but work one row higher and one stitch to the left each time. Complete the pattern by working one single crochet into the last row in the first color. End each row by working one into the turning chain.

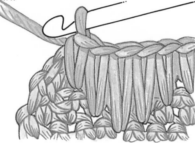

5 When shaping elongated-stitch fabric, work the decreasing or increasing in the single crochet rows. Then adjust the zigzag pattern to fit.

Equal weaving

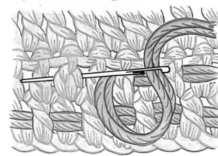

1 A firm fabric can be produced by weaving yarn through a double crochet fabric. Work the fabric as normal on any number of chains. To weave horizontally thread the yarn into a tapestry needle and secure at the right-hand edge. Weave alternately over and under the double crochets.

2 Weaving through a filet mesh produces a less closely textured fabric. Make an even number of chains. Work one double crochet into the sixth chain from the hook. *Work one chain, skip the next chain and work one double crochet into the next chain. Repeat from * to end and turn.

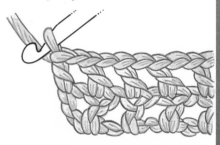

3 On following rows begin with four turning chains. * Work one double crochet into the next double and work one chain. Repeat from * to the turning chain. Work the last double into the third turning chain.

4 To weave horizontally use a tapestry needle and secure yarn as in step 1. Weave the yarn alternately over and under doubles.

5 Weave vertically by threading the yarn vertically between doubles, so that it lies alternately over and under each row.

On pages 297 and 300 we showed how to vary basic crochet stitches, either by working the stitches slightly differently or by weaving contrasting yarn through the fabric. A third way of varying simple crochet fabrics is by embroidery. For beginners a single crochet fabric, worked with a firm gauge in sport weight yarn on a size F hook is the ideal fabric. Other stitches, such as double crochet, can be decorated, but working the embroidery is more difficult.

Embroidery on single crochet

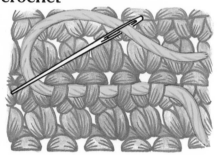

1 Thread the embroidery yarn — sport weight is probably easiest for beginners — into a large-eyed tapestry needle. When working embroidery to cover an area — for example, in satin stitch — secure the yarn by threading it through the center of a few stitches on the right side of fabric. Work over the end of the yarn when embroidering.

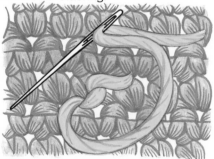

2 To secure the yarn when working running stitch or stem stitch, work a small backstitch on the wrong side of the crochet fabric, making sure not to pull the fabric out of shape and that the backstitch is invisible on the right side.

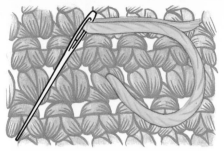

3 When working embroidery, try to insert the needle through the center of the stitches. Working between rows or stitches could easily pull the crochet out of shape, thus forming a hole.

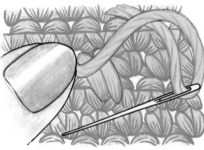

4 Never pull the embroidery yarn too tightly through the crochet as this could pucker the fabric. Holding the yarn with the thumb and forefinger of the left hand while you draw it through the fabric should help you to keep the tension loose.

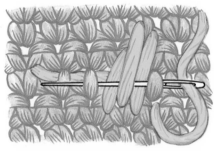

5 To fasten off the embroidery yarn, take it to the back of the work and run it through the embroidery stitches. Cut off the end close to the stitches.

Embroidery on double crochet

Double crochet forms a less firm fabric than that produced by single crochet, so if you embroider on doubles, use a crochet cotton to form a strong fabric. Use lightweight silks to avoid stretching the crochet. Secure and fasten off the yarn as when embroidering on single crochet.

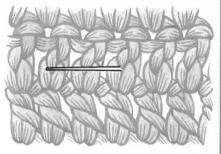

1 When working an all-over or free-hand embroidery design on double crochet or mesh fabrics, insert the needle through the center of the stitches as for single crochet.

2 Outline filet motifs with satin stitch. Work the embroidery stitches very loosely holding the yarn as in step 4 above to avoid puckering the filet and inserting the needle into top of each double.

3 Decorate a double crochet and chain space fabric by working buttonhole stitch loosely around the doubles.

4 Use a woolly yarn to work back stitch very loosely around doubles for a "darned" look.

Lacets

Lacets are two-row patterns, formed from a combination of V-shaped *lacets* and chain *bars*.

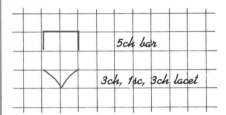

5ch bar

3ch, 1sc, 3ch lacet

1 Patterns may be formed entirely from lacets, but often they are combined with filet spaces and blocks; in this case filet charts are used. The symbols are given in the diagram above, showing the number of chains in the lacet and bar.

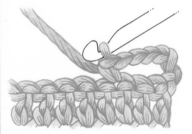

2 Begin with the lacet row. Ch 6 to count as the first dc and ch 3. Skip the first 3 sts and work 1sc into the next st. Ch 3, skip the next 2 sts and work 1dc into next st.

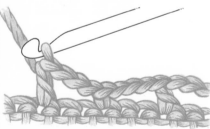

3 Ch 3, skip the next 2 sts and work 1sc into the next st. Ch 3, skip the next 2 sts and work 1dc into the next st. This step forms the lacet and is repeated to the end.

4 Work the bar on the next row. Begin with eight chains to count as the first double crochet and five chains. Skip the first double and work one double into the next double. * Work five chains to form the next bar and work one double into the next double. Repeat from *.

5 To work a lacet over a bar, work the doubles into the doubles of the bar row and work the single crochet into third of chain five of each bar.

Tubular crochet

When rounds of crochet are worked without shaping, tubular fabrics are formed, thus avoiding the need for much tedious seaming and forming a neat fabric.

1 Begin with a length of chain equal to the circumference of the circle. Join the chain with a slip stitch.

2 The first round begins with the correct number of turning chains — in this case three for a double crochet fabric.

3 Working in a clockwise direction, work as normal into each chain. Join the last stitch to the top of the turning chain with a slip stitch.

4 Begin the following rounds with the turning chain to count as the first stitch. To keep the number of stitches correct, skip the first stitch at the base of the turning ch. Rep step 3.

Note that when working in rounds, the RS is always facing, so most patterns differ from when they are worked in rows. To make a tube look the same as a row section, work thus:

5 Work steps 1 to 3. At the end of the round, turn so that the WS is facing. *Work the turning ch, skip the first st and work to the end. Join to the turning ch with a sl st.

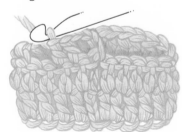

6 At the end of this round, turn* so that the right side, or outside, of the tube is facing. Repeat from * to * for the length required.

Jacquard
Working from charts

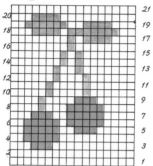

1 Odd-numbered rows are shown on the right-hand side of the chart and even-numbered rows on the left. Read odd-numbered rows from the right to left and even-numbered rows from left to right.

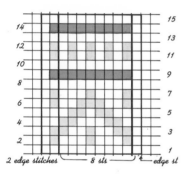

2 On "Fair Isle" charts the stitches shown within the bold lines are repeated across the row, while those outside the lines are worked at the beginning and end of the rows only.

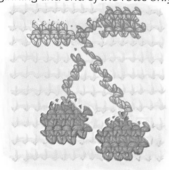

3 Patterns may sometimes instruct you to "reverse the chart" to produce a mirror-image as above. This is simply done by reading the odd-numbered rows from left to right and the even-numbered rows from right to left.

Stranding yarn

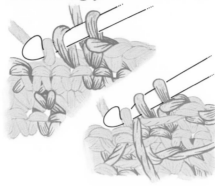

1 When working jacquard patterns, change colors as shown on page 298. In repeating patterns as in step 2, strand the yarn not in use loosely at the back of the work on the right-side rows (above left). On wrong-side rows strand the yarn at the front of work (above right).

2 It is possible to work over the yarn not in use (see page 298) to produce a double fabric. This technique can also be used when introducing a new ball of yarn. Work over the ends as shown to avoid darning in ends when the work is completed.

Working large motifs

1 When working motifs like the cherries in step 1 (top left) do not waste yarn by stranding. Instead use separate balls of yarn for each section of color. To prevent tangles, you can either use bobbins or yard lengths of yarn. The latter will tangle, but because they are fairly short, it is easy to pull each length free as required.

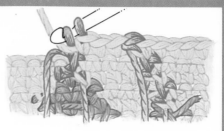

2 Change colors as normal, but leave the old color hanging on the wrong side of the work ready for the return row. If necessary, however, strand across a few stitches, for example, across the cherry stems.

Charting motifs

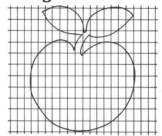

1 Work a gauge sample in your yarn; for best results work in single crochet. Draw up a graph of the gauge; squares across represent stitches, squares down represent rows. Sketch the motif onto the graph.

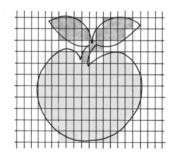

2 Using suitable colors, block in the shape within the outline, shading whole stitches.

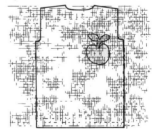

3 To position a motif, draw the outline of the garment onto graph paper. Place the motif as required on the graph and use as a chart when working the garment.

Filet crochet
Filet charts

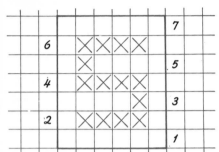

1 *Filet crochet is usually worked by following graphed charts, in which **blocks** of double crochet and chain **spaces** are shown as crosses and blank squares respectively. In the chart above, each blank square represents a two-chain space plus a connecting double, while each cross represents two doubles plus a connecting double.*

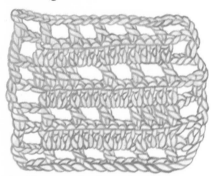

2 *The sample above has been worked following the chart in step 1. Read the odd-numbered rows from right to left and the even-numbered rows from left to right.*

3 *Sometimes filet patterns are worked so that each space is formed from one chain plus a connecting double and each block is*

formed from one double plus one connecting double. The same filet charts can be followed to form a narrower fabric. The sample above has been worked from the chart in step 1.

Mesh background

1 *Make a multiple of three chains plus two extra. Work one double crochet into the eighth chain from the hook. * Chain two. Skip the next two foundation chains and work one double into the next foundation chain. Continue from * to the last foundation chain.*

2 *On the following rows begin by working five chains to count as the first double and two-chain space. Work one double into the next double. * Work two chains and then one double into the next double. Continue from * to the end, working the last double into the turning chain.*

Beginning with a block

1 *To begin a piece of filet with a block of double crochet, make*

enough foundation chain for the spaces and blocks of the first row. Work two more chains and then work one double into the fourth chain from the hook; the first three chains count as the first double. Complete the first block by working one double into each of the next two foundation chains.

2 *On following rows, to begin with a block work three chains to count as the first double. Skip the first double and work one double into each of the next three doubles.*

Working a block above a space

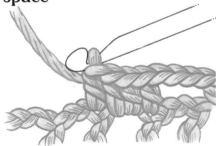

Work one double into the next connecting double. Then work two doubles into the space, followed by one double into the next connecting double.

Working a space above a block

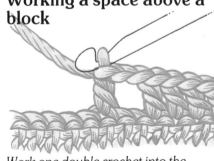

Work one double crochet into the next connecting double. Work two chains, skip the next two doubles and work one double into the next double.

Irish crochet

Formed by combining simple or picot mesh with elaborate motifs, Irish crochet is generally worked in fine cotton. Today, motifs are usually sewn onto the mesh, but the traditional method produces beautifully irregular lace fabrics.

Working over a cord

To give a raised effect, Irish motifs — which are usually worked in single crochet — may be worked over a cord. Use a cord either three or four strands of cotton twisted together or a thicker cotton in the same color. When the motif is completed, cut off the cord close to the stitches.

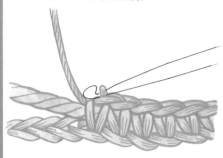

1 Having worked the foundation chain, hold the cord at the back of the work in the left hand. Work into the chain and over the cord at the same time.

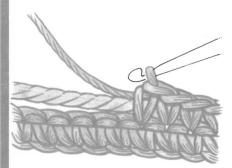

2 At the end of the row, turn and work the next row over the cord, holding the cord at the back of the work.

3 To work over the cord alone, hold it away from the main body of the crochet, and work along the cord, pushing the stitches together to cover the cord.

Traditional Irish crochet

As the basic outline, choose a fairly simple dressmaking pattern without elaborate shaping. Make up the pattern using a medium-weight interfacing (you could use the traditional muslin or linen), omitting shoulder seams and cutting away seam or hem allowances on the front, neck and lower edges. Ignore facings and do not seam or set in sleeves.

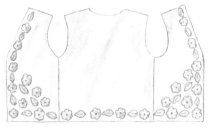

1 Lay the seamed pattern pieces out flat and arrange the motifs on the interfacing as you wish. Pin and tack the motifs firmly to the interfacing.

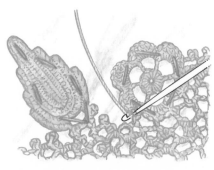

2 Using a matching yarn, fill in the spaces between the pattern motifs with picot mesh. Join the mesh to the edge of the motifs as you work using

single crochet or slip stitch. Do not worry if the mesh seems irregular. This is unavoidable and adds to the beauty of the lace.

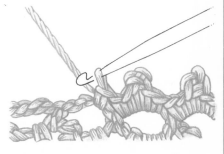

3 Remove the work from the interfacing and, after blocking (see below), seam shoulder and sleeve seams and set in sleeves. Work a narrow picot edging into the neck, front and lower edges, or work a separate edging and sew it to the mesh.

Seaming lace fabrics

Do not press Irish or any other crochet lace, but pin out the work to the correct size and lightly damp it. Allow it to dry naturally.

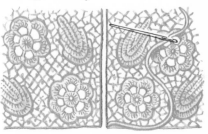

1 With right sides upwards, place the pieces edge to edge as shown. Secure a matching thread to the lower corner of the RH piece.

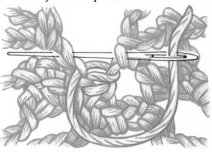

2 Insert the needle under one thread on the left-hand edge, insert the needle under one thread on the right-hand edge. Continue in this way, pulling the thread tightly so that the seam is invisible, but not so tightly that the work puckers.

Coral Mula

Fabric work

Crochet with fabric strips is an ideal method of using up remnants or old clothes. Before beginning, sort the fabric according to the tones — it is quite possible to mix weights and types of fabric — dividing the fabric into dark-, light- and medium-colored groups.

Preparing the strips

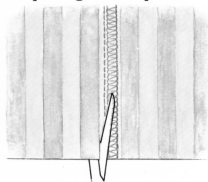

1 *If you are using old clothes, wash and iron them thoroughly. Cut the garment into its pattern pieces close to the seams. Don't waste time trying to rip out the seams since the fabric there is likely to be heavily creased and weakened by stitching.*

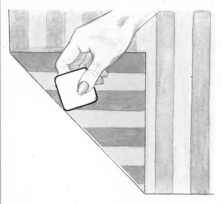

2 *The strips are generally cut on the bias since this provides strong strips that are less likely to fray. The extra strength gained by cutting strips on the bias is necessary for articles likely to receive hard wear. To find the true bias, fold the fabric so that the horizontal grain is parallel to the vertical grain. Mark the bias using tailor's chalk.*

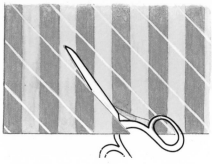

3 *Open out the fabric and, using a ruler and tailor's chalk, mark the bias strips onto the fabric, each ½ in. wide. Then, using sharp dressmaking scissors, cut the strips. There is no need to oversew or finish the edges since the bias strips fray only slightly, giving an interesting "furry" appearance.*

Joining the strips

After cutting out, choose one of the methods below to join the strips. As the strips are joined, wind the fabric into a ball.

1 *Make the joins a feature of the garment — this method is not suitable for household furnishings — by knotting the strips together with a reef knot. As you crochet, push the knots through to the right side.*

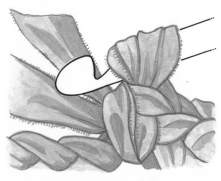

2 *If you prefer an invisible join and if the crochet will not receive*

hard wear, join the strips by clipping the ends of the old and new strips diagonally. Overlap the strips by about 2¾ in. and work with the double thickness until the new strip is joined in.

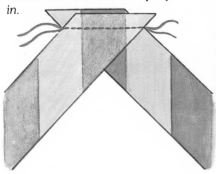

3 *For a strong join, overlap the strips, cut the edges to an angle and place them together as shown. Then machine stitch the two strips together approximately ¼ in. from the edges. Machining makes the strongest possible join.*

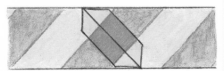

4 *Trim the loose threads. Press open the seam and clip the corners as shown to make a neat join. Each join should be treated similarly throughout the work.*

Working with fabric

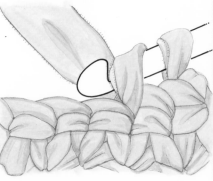

In general, crochet with fabric as you would with yarn, beginning and fastening off in the usual way. The fabric strips will naturally fold as you crochet. Don't try to open them out — the folds add to the texture and strength of the finished crochet as well as to its visual effect.

Coral Mula

Wired flowers

Working crocheted flowers can be time-consuming, but very few special materials are needed (see page 280).

Petals

Before you begin, examine an actual specimen. Work the petals as required, copying the natural flower by decreasing or increasing as necessary. The flowers on pages 280-84 should give some guidance.

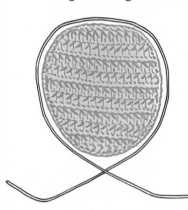

1 *Unless the flowers are fairly small, they will retain their shape better if the petals are wired. Cut a piece of craft wire approximately 4 in. longer than the circumference of the petal. Bend the wire so that is surrounds the petal and two ends, each about 2 in., extend at the bottom.*

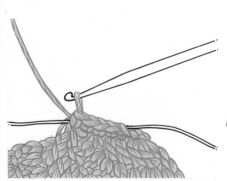

2 *Rejoin the yarn to the lower edge of the petal and work a row of single crochet into the edge, enclosing the wire. Work the stitches closely together so that the wire is covered. Wire each petal in exactly the same way.*

3 *When all the petals have been wired, assemble the flower. Place the second petal next to the first, overlapping the edges as necessary. Bend the petals into the required shape — the wire makes them very pliable. Twist together the lengths of wire extending below the petals. Continue adding petals in this way, always twisting together the wire to hold the petals in position.*

Stems

1 *Cut a length of thick wire as required for the stem. Wind the twisted lengths of petal wire firmly around the top of the stem.*

2 *Wind florist's green tape tightly around the stem, beginning where the petals meet on the underside of the flower. Overlap the tape as you wind so that the stem wire is completely hidden.*

Leaves

Large, unattached leaves — as on tulips – can be worked in much the same way as petals (see page 280). Other flowers, however, have leaves that are attached to the stem.

1 *When working a single attached leaf, make and wire it in the same way as a petal, twisting together the short lengths of uncovered wire. Unstemmed leaves can be attached as for the Iris leaf on page 282. For a stemmed leaf, work a few single crochet over the twisted wires to form the leaf stem. Twist the remaining wire around the main stem and bind the stem as above.*

2 *When working a leaf spray, work the individual leaves, each having a short stem, as above. Make a short stem from several lengths of craft wire twisted together. Twist the wires from the first leaf around the top of the leaf stem. Work single crochet very tightly over the wire to the position of the second leaf. Attach the second leaf as before. Continue in this way, leaving a length of uncovered wire. Use this to attach the spray to the main stem.*

Needlewoman's Notebook
Crochet with fine cotton

To produce delicate crochet mats and doilies, all you need is some fine cotton, a steel hook and, for perfect results, a little know-how and a few hours' practice.

Fine crochet cotton can be bought in sizes 10, 20, 30, 40, 50, 60 and 80, the last being the thinnest.

A wide range of solid and random-dyed colors is available in 10, 20 and 40 cottons. Shades in other sizes are limited, though cotton can be dyed with cold-water dyes.

Although cotton sewing threads cannot be used for crochet, good results can be obtained by using polyester sewing thread, which is sold in many shades.

Fine cottons are worked with steel hooks, ranging from the largest size, No. 2, to the smallest, No. 6.

Gauge When working with cotton, keep it taut by threading it between the fingers of the left hand. The crochet should be firm with no loose stitches and it should be difficult to insert the hook into the top of a stitch. Keep the working loops well down the neck or narrow part of the hook. After completing a stitch, tighten the top by pulling back the cotton with the fingers of the left hand.

Beginning When working a number of motifs, all the centers should be the same size.

Leave at least 6 in. of yarn before the beginning slip knot. After completing the motif, thread the tail through a fine sewing needle and weave through the stitches of the first round. Put a thin knitting needle through the center of the circle, pull up the tail tightly and secure. Slide out the knitting needle.

Work a foundation chain fairly loosely. If it is too tight, undo and start again, or the lower edge will pucker. If it is too loose, run through a thread and tighten.

Joining thread Cotton up to size 20 can usually be spliced together.

Finer cottons should be joined in a piece of solid pattern. Thread the new end into a fine sewing needle and work through the old yarn for about 4 in., leaving loose ends of the same length.

With both methods, leave surplus ends at the back of the work and darn in separately after finishing.

Finishing Work the last stitch of the final row very carefully, and after cutting the yarn do not pull too tightly. Thread the yarn into a sewing needle and work over the top of the adjacent stitches.

Pressing should be avoided as it will flatten the work. Instead, damp or wash the work, pin it out with rustless pins and leave to dry. Starch any ruffled edges and support with wedges of tissue paper during drying.

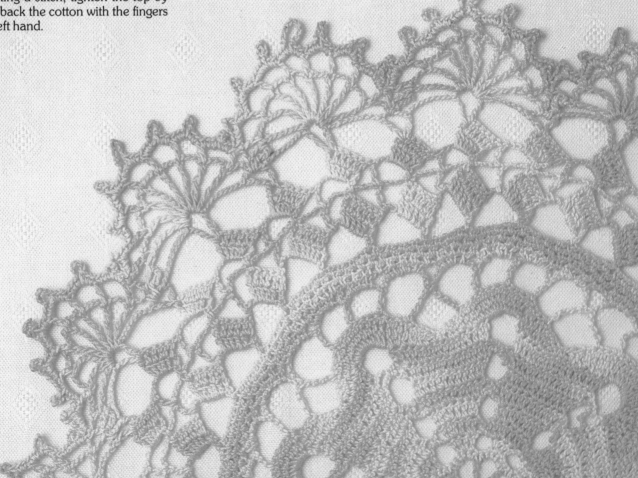

Needlewoman's Notebook

Crochet with fashion yarns

Crochet is one of the most rewarding and creative of the traditional crafts. Worked in modern yarns using the correct methods, crochet takes on a different contemporary look.

Choosing a pattern Avoid designs with fussy shaping. Not only will a textured yarn hide shaping details, but you may also find it difficult to keep track of the progress of the increasing or decreasing.

Simple stitches like half double or double crochet are best. A bouclé or glitter would hide complex stitch patterns, while a fluffy yarn looks matted if worked in a firm fabric stitch.

Foundation chain It may be difficult when working the base row to insert the hook correctly under two loops of each chain when the foundation chain is worked in a textured yarn.

Avoid this problem by working the chain in a matching plain yarn — many manufacturers now produce coordinated ranges of plain and fashion yarns — and then working the base and following rows in the fashion yarn.

Gauge Try not to work fashion yarns too tightly, but don't consciously try to work loosely. You are likely to forget and the gauge will alter. Instead, obtain the correct gauge by using a larger-size hook.

Checking gauge on a textured yarn can be difficult. Stitches and rows will be clearer if you hold the work up to a strong light source, such as a reading lamp.

Matching Aran wool and bouclé

Matching acrylic and wool mix and bouclé

Mohair and glitter

Acrylic and wool chunky and novelty yarn

Pure glitter and wool and glitter mix

Working with fashion yarns Similarly, it may be difficult to keep track of your progress, so each time you finish work, mark clearly on the pattern where you have reached. Always insert any contrasting color markers in the work as suggested in the pattern, and insert any extra markers that you find helpful.

You may find it easier to insert the hook between the stitches (see page 297), instead of under the top two loops as usual. This will slightly alter stitch and row gauge, so allowances should be made.

Fashion yarns cannot usually be spliced, so always join in a new ball at the edge of the work. Darn any ends into the seams when making up.

Finishing Always follow the instructions on the label when pressing. Some yarns, especially those containing metallic thread cannot be ironed, so flatten seams by leaving them under a heavy weight overnight.

Work edgings in a matching plain yarn, using a firm single crochet or ribbing for a neat hard-wearing finish.

It is unlikely that a fashion yarn can be used for finishing, so use a matching plain yarn to sew a conventional seam, to work a decorative crochet join or to sew on buttons.

Decorative Sewing

Decorative sewing crafts, including embroidery, needlepoint, patchwork, appliqué and quilting, offer innumerable ways of adding the stamp of homemade exclusivity to your clothes and surroundings. This chapter opens with a selection of hand-embroidered clothes, among them some charming smocked sunsuits for children and overalls decorated with Dorset feather stitching. For the advanced embroidress, there is a beautiful broderie anglaise blouse or a cut-work skirt.

The section entitled Home Embroidery contains examples of needlepoint, cross-stitch and blackwork, and includes a sampler, cushions, a footstool, a runner, a tablecloth, a breakfast set and a rug. Once again, the additional samples give further design ideas, and many of the patterns can be put to other uses: the Danish cross-stitch design for the tablecloth could, for example, be used on bed-linen or curtains.

The patchwork, appliqué and quilting designs offer both old and new interpretations of these traditional crafts, including a fun laundry bag that just might persuade children to put their dirty clothes in the bag instead of waiting for an adult to do it!

As with the Knitting and Crochet chapters, the final section gives reference pictures demonstrating all the stitches used, plus some alternatives with which you might like to experiment.

FASHION EMBROIDERY

Broderie anglaise

Skills you need

* **Buttonhole stitch**
* **Raised satin stitch**
* **Overcast stitch**
* **Eyelet chain**

If you do not know these skills, refer to pages 397 and 409.

Materials

Broderie anglaise is most successful worked on a closely woven fabric such as cambric, cotton, lawn, very fine linen, sheer wool or crêpe-de-chine. Fine textured fabrics are less likely to fray around eyelets and edges when the garment is worn and laundered.

Choose an embroidery floss to match the color and weight of your fabric. Work cotton fabrics with cotton or mercerized thread and sheer wools or crêpe-de-chine with a fine twisted silk. Pastel colors are particularly effective.

Special technique – making eyelets

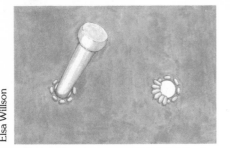

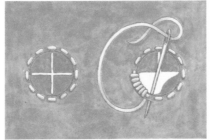

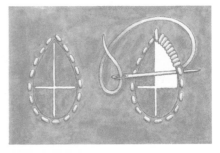

Elsa Willson

1 *For eyelets smaller than ¼ in., first work running stitch around the traced outline. With a knitting needle pierce the center, using the running stitches as a guide to size. Then work close overcast stitching neatly around the edge.*

2 *For eyelets larger than ¼in., outline in running stitch and cut a small cross in the center fabric. Begin to overcast the eyelet, turning the fabric to the back as you overcast the folded edge. Trim excess fabric from the wrong side.*

3 *Oval eyelets are worked in a similar way to large eyelets; outlining, cutting the center fabric and overcasting around the edge. This time, begin the outlining by making a vertical stitch at the top, to give a sharp point to the oval.*

The basic broderie anglaise blouse

This pretty summer blouse is cut from a simple all-in-one pattern, with hand-decorated neck and sleeve edges embroidered in softly shaded blue.

Size
To fit 34-38 in. bust

Materials
1½ yd. of 36 in.-wide fine cream or white cotton lawn
5 skeins of stranded embroidery floss in variegated blue
Matching sewing thread
Dressmaker's graph paper
Knitting needle
Small sharp-pointed scissors

Instructions
Working on a clean, smooth surface, copy the blouse pattern to scale on tissue paper. Fold the lawn in half, placing the cut edges together. Crease along the fold as a guide for the shoulder line. Unfold the fabric and matching the crease with the shoulder line of the pattern, pin the two together. Enlarge embroidery design to scale on graph paper. Using a hard pencil, lightly trace around the pattern and

the embroidery motifs, remembering to extend the design onto the back section. Do not turn the fabric close to the neck and sleeve edges until you have completed the embroidery.

The embroidery can be worked freely by hand, or with an embroidery hoop. The neck and sleeve edges can be worked by hand, or machine stitched for speed. Using two strands of embroidery thread throughout, work the embroidery following the stitch diagrams. Work buttonhole stitch around the neck and sleeve edge scallops and the lily petals.

Use raised satin stitch on the small

Victor Yuan

bows and oval leaves. Work overcast stitch on all the flower and leaf stems. Pierce small eyelets for the tiny flower sprigs and cut larger ovals for the leaves as shown. To complete the embroidery, work eyelet chain on the large ribbon bow at the neck.

Press the finished embroidery on the wrong side under a damp cloth on a well-padded ironing board.
Trim away the excess fabric around the neck and sleeve edges, using the sharp points of the scissors to cut closely between the scallops.

With wrong sides together fold the blouse along the shoulder line. Match the scallops under the sleeve and trim the remaining fabric to the cutting line. Stitch the side seams with a tiny French seam. Slip stitch a narrow rolled hem and side opening to finish.

313

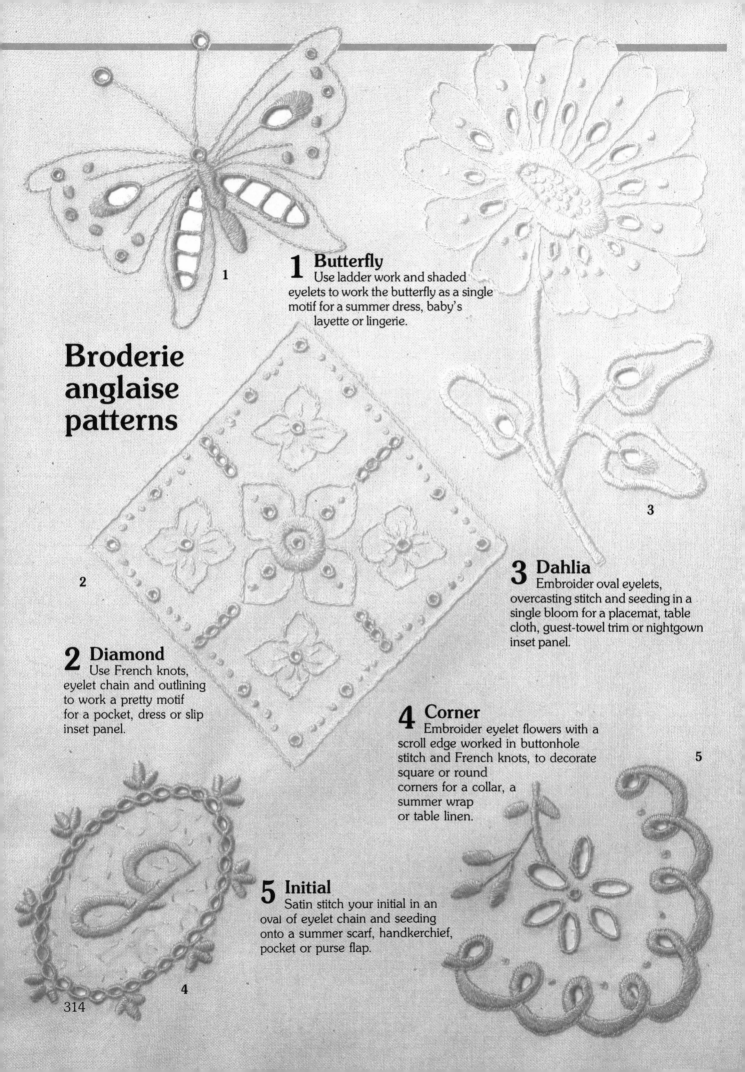

Broderie anglaise patterns

1 Butterfly
Use ladder work and shaded eyelets to work the butterfly as a single motif for a summer dress, baby's layette or lingerie.

2 Diamond
Use French knots, eyelet chain and outlining to work a pretty motif for a pocket, dress or slip inset panel.

3 Dahlia
Embroider oval eyelets, overcasting stitch and seeding in a single bloom for a placemat, table cloth, guest-towel trim or nightgown inset panel.

4 Corner
Embroider eyelet flowers with a scroll edge worked in buttonhole stitch and French knots, to decorate square or round corners for a collar, a summer wrap or table linen.

5 Initial
Satin stitch your initial in an oval of eyelet chain and seeding onto a summer scarf, handkerchief, pocket or purse flap.

7 Spray
Work eyelet flowers and leaves with an outline-stitch stem into a single spray for a dress shoulder or chemise top, or as a border repeat for a skirt hem or pillow cover.

8 Heart
Tiny eyelets, embroidered flowers and French knots describe the heart motif. Use singly on a shirt front or back, on baby's clothes or combine it with the spray as an alternative blouse design.

6 Ladybug
Use a simple outline stitch, eyelets and French knots to work a fun insect on children's clothes.

9 Flower basket
Use simple surface stitches and eyelets to give a very feminine look to a summer dress, negligee or pillow set.

Simon Butcher

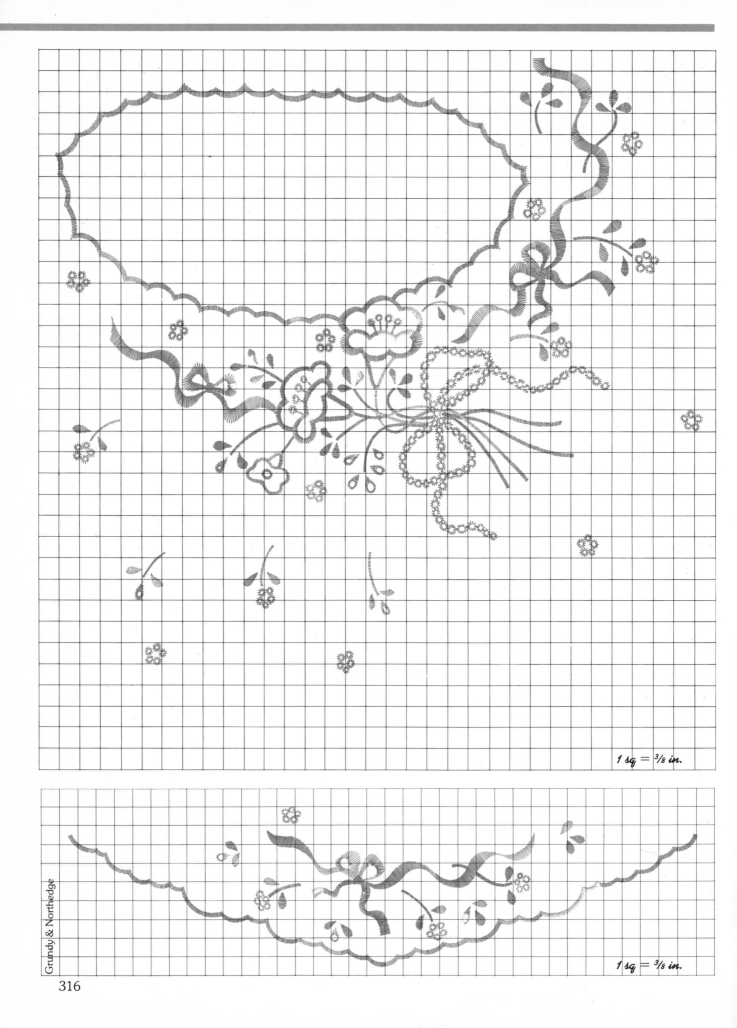

1 sq = ³⁄₈ in.

1 sq = ³⁄₈ in.

Adapting the broderie anglaise blouse

A simple motif will personalize the plainest of garments. Isolate a motif from the basic broderie anglaise design, choose one from the selection, or combine several to make your own design.

If you are a beginner, choose something simple to work first, such as the heart or the ladybug, before moving on to more complex designs, such as the butterfly and flower basket. A single motif can look very effective worked on the front or pocket of a blouse or on the turnings of short sleeves. Adapt motifs to suit the shape of the article you are embroidering. Necklines and collars can also be tailored to some extent to suit the motif.

Work these motifs in white on white for a traditional look, or vary the color of the embroidery or the fabric for a more modern effect. Pastel shades compliment the delicate embroidery particularly well and variegated thread can be used to add interest to the basic design. Large motifs can benefit from subtle changes in color, and small motifs can be worked in paler or darker shades of the same color. Richer colors can also look attractive embroidered with toning thread.

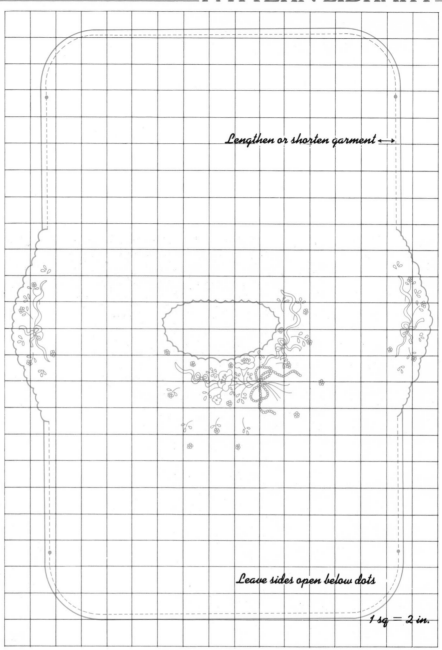

Lengthen or shorten garment →

Leave sides open below dots

1 sq = 2 in.

More design ideas

Choose a simple flower motif or garlanded initial to decorate the front of a pretty scalloped collar on a summer dress or cotton blouse. Float sprigs of flowers around the neckline of a cotton nightgown or set a beautifully embroidered diamond panel into gathers at the center of a bodice.

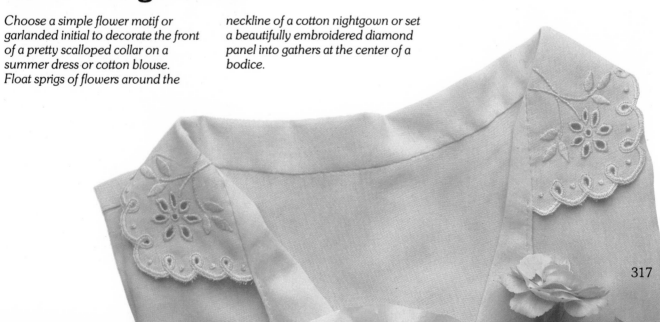

317

Cutwork

This delicate and lacy form of embroidery consists of a combination of "cut away" areas, simple buttonhole stitching, bars and picots. Successful cutwork depends on a well-planned design. It is essential to have all the main points attached and bars well-laced to avoid loose sections occurring when the background fabric is cut away.

318

Skills you need

* **Running stitch**
* **Buttonhole stitch**
* **French knots**
* **Stem stitch**
* **Raised satin stitch**
* **Ladder work**
* **Buttonholed branched bars**

If you do not know these skills, refer to pages 397, 398, 408 and 409.

Materials

In choosing fabric for cutwork, the first consideration should be that it is closely woven with an even texture. Natural fibers such as cottons and linens are well-tried favorites since they keep their shape when the background areas are cut away, showing the cut design to its best advantage. However, softer fabrics such as a wool and cotton blend, brushed cotton or T-shirt knits can be used to great effect, especially where there are few areas to be cut away, emphasizing perhaps a prettily cut edge, as in the skirt border.

For the embroidery, use a crewel needle and stranded cotton in two or three strands, depending on the weight of your foundation fabric.

Special technique – buttonholing and cutting

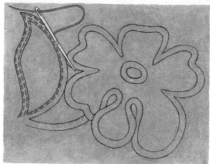

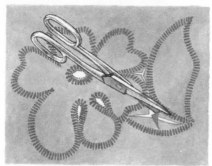

Elsa Willson

1 *After transferring your design onto the fabric you are ready to begin outlining. Work two rows of running stitch just inside the double lines of the design. Follow the natural flow of each line, stitching with a relaxed even tension. Take care not to pull these running stitches, or the finished cutwork will be uneven.*

2 *Complete the running stitching and then work buttonhole stitch over the double lines. Place the stitches close together and always with the looped edge facing toward the areas that will later be cut away. Start and finish a thread neatly within the lines, avoiding stranding across the back, which might otherwise be cut.*

3 *To cut away background fabric, first make initial cuts from the right side, cutting across the center of the area into any points. Turn work to wrong side and carefully cut away fabric, as near to the buttonhole edge as possible. Stroke any remaining threads of fabric up and away from the edge before trimming.*

The basic cutwork skirt

Capture the height of summer by embroidering this simple wrap-around skirt with a border of clematis flowers. Cleverly designed petals, butterfly wings, leaves and tendrils are combined into the prettiest of cutwork edges.

Size

To fit a 26½ in. waist and 36 in. hip (size 12).

For slightly larger or smaller sizes, make the appropriate enlargements or reductions to each pattern piece.

Materials

2¾ yd. of 45 in.-wide wool/cotton blend fabric in medium blue
4 skeins of stranded cotton to match fabric
Matching sewing thread
¼ yd. of 36 in.-wide interfacing
Large sheet of tracing paper
Dressmaker's carbon paper
Dressmaker's graph paper

Instructions

Enlarge the skirt pattern onto dressmaker's graph paper, marking notches and the straight grain of the fabric. Cut out. Press the fabric on the wrong side. Pin the pattern pieces in position and cut out. Work the embroidery before making up the skirt.

Working the embroidery

Enlarge the border design to scale on tracing paper. Place the right side front skirt panel on a flat surface, right side facing, and pin the tracing in position, matching the right angles at the hem and waist and aligning the trailing bor-

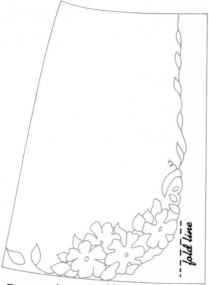

John Hutchinson

Position the vertical border of the enlarged design along the fold line and the base on the hemline.

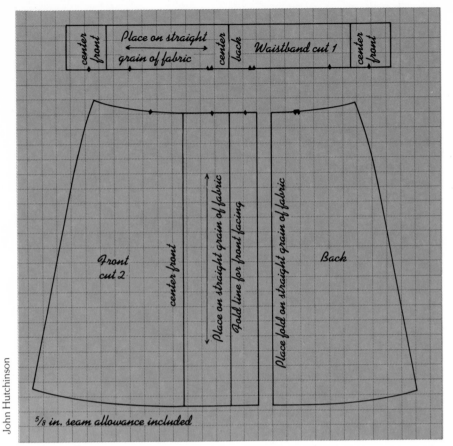

center front

Place on straight grain of fabric

center back

Waistband cut 1

center front

Front cut 2

center front

Place on straight grain of fabric

Fold line for front facing

Place fold on straight grain of fabric

Back

5/8 in. seam allowance included

John Hutchinson

1 square = 1½ in

Adapting the cutwork skirt

In cutwork it is those areas that are designed to be cut away that give it much of its charm and generally a design requires little or no other decoration by way of mixed colors. Here we give a series of motifs for alternative decorative edges worked both in the traditional white thread on white fabric and a fruit border in naturalistic colors while other motifs are worked in single colors throughout.

As an alternative to embroidering the wrap-around skirt, a very pretty effect could be made by working the garland motif around the bottom edge of an A-line skirt for instance, with matching jacket fronts. You may, however, prefer simply to work a small area of a dress hem line, at the center front and back, or perhaps to give an interesting shape to the overall outline, you could work the two side panels, instead.

Set a completely different mood with the cherry and strawberry border by working it around the bottom edge of a colored linen jacket and skirt.

Use stem stitch and French knots to decorate the flower centers, and position overcast bars carefully to strengthen cut areas.

der with the fold line on the skirt front. Transfer the design using carbon paper. Outline the design first in running stitch as shown opposite, using one strand of thread. Work the bars as they occur by laying three threads across the areas that will be cut away, and overcasting or buttonholing. Buttonhole around the edge of the design using two strands. Stem stich leaf veins in two strands and the lines at flower centers and butterfly antennae in one strand. Work French knots in two strands and the larger spots around the edge of the design in raised satin stitch, using one strand. Press the finished embroidery on the wrong side.

Finishing the skirt

Machine stitch side seams together, press flat and machine stitch the edges to finish. Take care in fitting the lower embroidered edge neatly into the side seam where it joins the hem of the back panel. Cut away fabric along edge of vertical border on right front. Stitch under ¼ in. on left front edge and turn in to form facing as shown. Machine stitch along the waistline edge ¼ in. inside the seam line using a long stitch. Tack interfacing to wrong side of waistband and pin to right side of skirt. Pull up gathers to fit, turn

under seam allowance and slip stitch in place. Attach hooks and bars to fasten. Try on the skirt and adjust if necessary before finally cutting away the background fabric around the cutwork border and hemming back and left side. Cut two strips 2¾ in. × 26 in. on straight grain for waist ties.

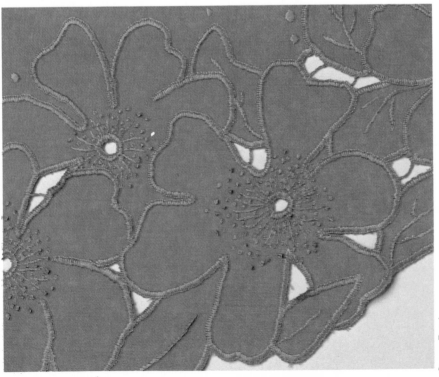

Simon Butcher

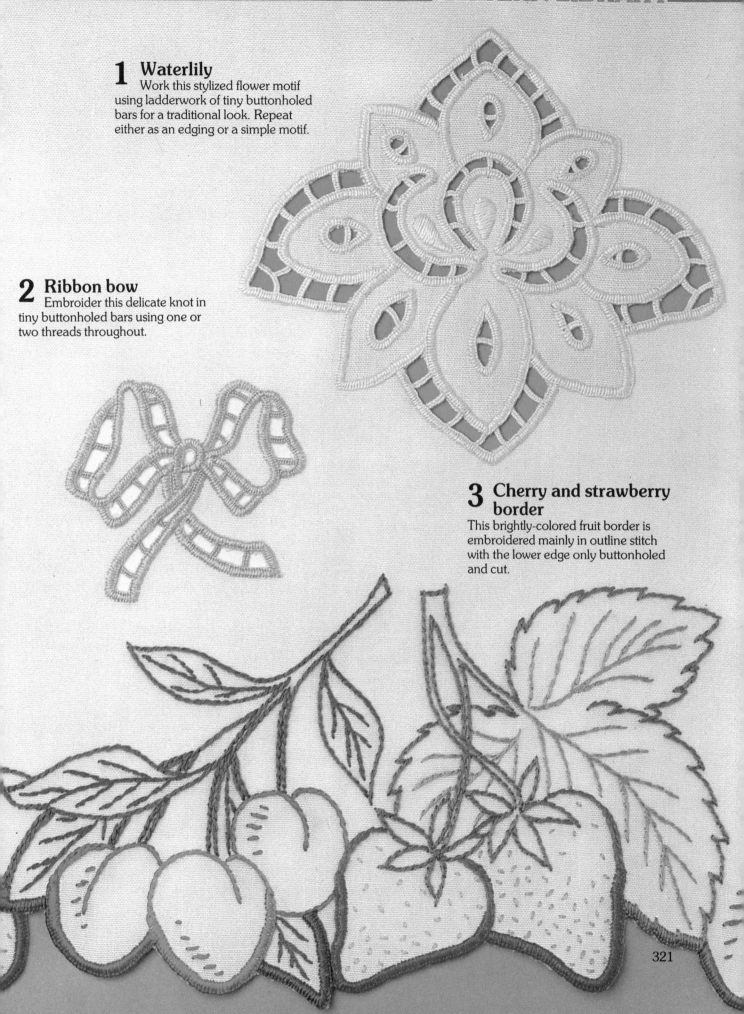

1 Waterlily
Work this stylized flower motif using ladderwork of tiny buttonholed bars for a traditional look. Repeat either as an edging or a simple motif.

2 Ribbon bow
Embroider this delicate knot in tiny buttonholed bars using one or two threads throughout.

3 Cherry and strawberry border
This brightly-colored fruit border is embroidered mainly in outline stitch with the lower edge only buttonholed and cut.

More design ideas

Take a single flower motif and repeat it to make this charming border pattern for a hand towel, nightgown, sachet, sheet or pillow corner.

Chart for cutwork skirt
1 square = 5/8 in.

Ingrid Jacob

322

White embroidery

The decorative craft of embroidering white thread on white fabric is as ancient as the development of linen cloth. Highly suitable for many domestic and fashion items, it is as rewarding and effective today as it was in the past.

Ray Moller

Skills you need

* **French knots**
* **Stem stitch**
* **Voiding**
* **Trailing stitch**

If you do not know these skills, refer to pages 396, 397, 398 and 401.

Materials

White embroidery thread relies entirely on the contrast between the embroidery stitch, thread and ground fabric. It can be applied to many different fabrics, each with their own distinctive textures. Fabrics such as polished linen, matte cotton, transparent muslin and organdy or crinkly crêpe, shiny satin and smooth silk may all be used equally successfully.

Depending on the required effect, and for what purpose you intend the finished article, both decorative and diaphanous effects can be created. When designing your own embroidery, first choose the appropriate fabric, then a suitable motif and embroidery threads to match.

For linen fabrics, choose strong linen threads, stranded cottons, or pearl embroidery threads; for muslin and organdy, choose fine silk, rayon or mercerized cotton threads; for crêpe, satin and silk fabrics, use smooth or twisted silk threads, stranded cotton or rayon floss.

Special technique – working padded satin stitch

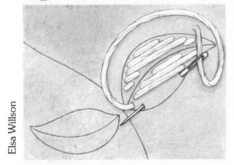

1 With six strands of embroidery thread in the needle, work a series of straight stitches to cover the area to be padded. Keep the stitches within the trace line.

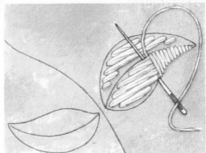

2 With three strands of embroidery thread in the needle, work satin stitch at right angles over the padding threads. Keep the stitches together, inserting the needle on the outside line.

3 Work satin stitch on the opposite side of the leaf in the same way as previously described, leaving a space in the middle to suggest the vein, see voiding, page 396.

Elsa Willson

The basic white-embroidered nightgown

This Victorian-style nightgown is made from off-white polyester crêpe with a satin yoke that is beautifully embroidered with sprays of wild honeysuckle.

Size
To fit 36 in. bust
Length of underarm seam 20 in.

Materials
4½ yd. of 45 in.-wide off-white polyester crêpe
⅜ yd. of 36 in.-wide off-white satin
3 skeins of white stranded embroidery thread
No. 7 crewel embroidery needle
⅝ yd. of matching rayon bias binding
Matching polyester sewing thread
Three ⅜ in.-wide white pearl buttons, with shank
Narrow elastic to fit wrists
Dressmaker's carbon paper (yellow)
Dressmaker's graph paper
Embroidery hoop
⅜ yd. of light-weight interlining

Instructions
Following the cutting layout given opposite, enlarge the pattern pieces onto dressmaker's graph paper. Mark pieces, straight grain lines, and notches where necessary. Note that ⅝ in. seam allowances are included throughout. Cut out. Press the satin fabric to remove all creases. Place the front yoke pattern piece in position on satin fabric and tack around the edge. Do not cut out. It is better to work the embroidery before cutting out to prevent fraying.

Place remaining nightgown pattern pieces onto crêpe fabric, including back yoke, and cut out as instructed.

The embroidery
Enlarge the embroidery motif given on page 326 onto tracing paper.

Place the tracing on the straight grain of the satin yoke and using carbon paper, transfer the motif to the right side of the two yoke fronts. Reverse the tracing for the right and left sides. Stretch the fabric in the embroidery hoop. Following the Special Technique, work padded satin stitch on the leaves, honeysuckle flowers, berries and honey bees. Couching over six strands of thread with three strands of thread in the needle, work the stems in trailing stitch. Fill the centers of the flowers with French knots, also with three strands of thread in the needle. Remove the embroidery from the frame and carefully press on the wrong side. Cut out. Work the second yoke section in the same way.

324

Making up the nightgown

Machine stitch a gathering thread between notches on upper edges of both front and back sections. Pull up to fit yoke. With wrong sides together, and with yoke edges matching, join front and back shoulder seams using a ¼ in. French seam. Stay stitch the neck edge.

For the front and back ruffle, place right sides together and stitch center front and center back seams. Press open and trim points. Join front and back ruffle at shoulder seams. Machine stitch a narrow hem along unnotched edge. Gather notched edges.

Pin ruffle in place, with wrong side of ruffle to right side of garment, matching centers and shoulder seams. Regulate gathers and tack in place.

For the front opening, fold binding in half lengthwise with wrong sides together. With right sides together, pin binding to front edges. Tack and stitch ⅜ in. from edge. Press seam toward binding. Fold binding over edge, turn under a small hem and slip stitch to seam. Press. On wrong side, slip stitch opening together below notch.

With right sides together, centers and shoulder seams matching, pin yoke to front and back sections. Stitch and trim the seam.

Using the collar pattern piece, cut out the interfacing and tack to collar facing. Press turning on long side of facing and trim ¼ in. Clip neck edge of yoke to stay stitching. With right sides together, pin and tack main collar piece to neck edge, matching shoulder seams. The collar should extend ⅝ in. at front opening edges. Stitch neck edge, trim and clip curves. Press seam towards collar.

For the neck ruffle, make a narrow hem on unnotched edge and gather notched edge. With right sides together, pin ruffle to collar, tapering ends at center front.

With right sides together, pin collar facing to top edge of collar, matching

Ray Moller

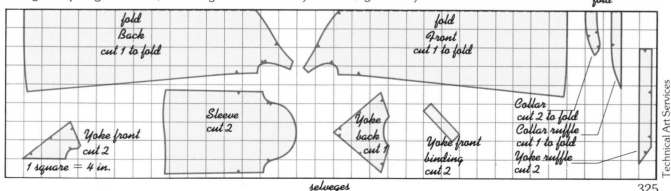

As an alternative to the plain hemline shown, decorate the hem with either one or two rows of tucks or a gathered frill.

Technical Art Services

notches. Stitch, trim seam and clip curves. Turn facing to right side, press and slip stitch to neck seam.

For the sleeves, make a narrow hem on wrist edge. Pin and stitch bias binding to wrong side 2½ in. from hem. Cut elastic to required length and insert through casing. Stitch across ends of casing and through elastic. Gather sleeves at top edge between notches. With right sides together, pin sleeves to armholes matching the shoulder seams. Pull up gathers to fit. Tack, stitch and stitch again ⅛ in. in from first seam. Trim.

Using a ¼ in. French seam, stitch each underarm and side seam in one continuous movement. Pay particular attention to the stitching, especially where the elastic casings meet, and feed it carefully through the machine. Try on, turn hem to required length, and slip stitch.

Sew on the three buttons to left front opening and make buttonhole-stitched loops to correspond. Remove all tacks and press.

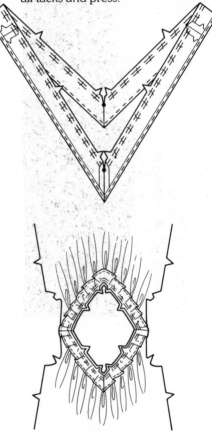

The ruffle (above) shows narrow hem on unnotched edge with double line of gathering threads around edge to be attached. Ruffle (below) is tacked to garment with gathers evenly spaced away from the shoulders.

326

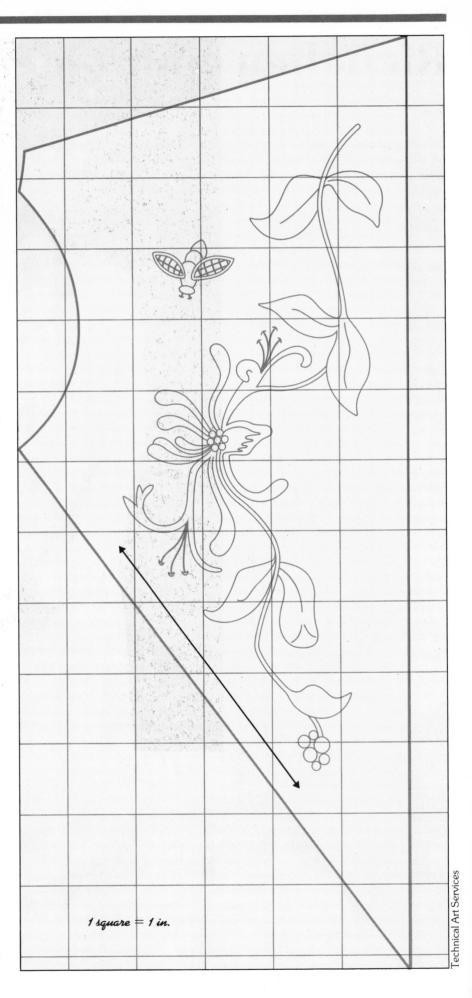

1 square = 1 in.

Richelieu embroidery

This is a very decorative form of cutwork where spider rings and bars are worked to fill the "cut away" areas and where tiny looped picots are added to the buttonholed edges, giving a beautiful lacy effect that's perfect for the christening gown shown here.

Ray Moller

Skills you need

* **Buttonhole stitch**
* **Buttonholing and cutting**
* **Buttonhole bars**

If you do not know these skills, refer to pages 319, 397 and 408.

Materials

Cutwork of all kinds requires a fairly smooth, closely-woven fabric such as those woven from natural linen or cotton fibers. Fine lawn, batiste, chambray or handkerchief linen would be an excellent choice for baby wear. A fine polyester and cotton blend fabric will also give quite good results, but pure polyester, acrylic and other synthetic fabrics should be avoided.

These fabrics are springy and tend to fray easily, making them difficult to control. Silks can also be difficult to cut and stitch with perhaps the exception of good crêpe de chine fabrics.

The embroidery thread should match the type and weight of fabric used. Similarly, the buttonholing, bars and picots should be neither too fine nor too heavy for the piece of embroidery.

Special technique – working looped picots on a spider web

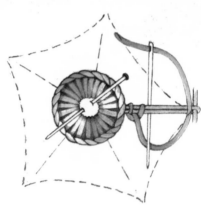

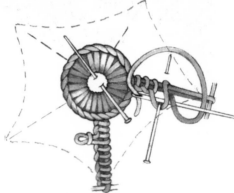

Mary Tomlin

1 Make the foundation ring by first widing the embroidery thread two or three times around a stiletto or knitting needle to the required size. Continuing with the same thread, buttonhole around and join the stitches to complete the ring. Keep the thread attached.

2 Pin the ring in place and make the first bar by picking up a small stitch on the outside edge of the web. Take the needle back to the starting point, pick up a stitch from the edge of the ring and continue to buttonhole the bar to the center without piercing the fabric underneath.

3 For the picot, pin through the fabric as shown. Take the thread under the pin head from left to right and up over the bar. Pass the needle downward behind the bar and pull through. Take through the loop on the pin and twist the thread once around the needle before pulling through. Pull the thread tight, remove the pin and finish the bar. Complete the spider web.

The basic christening gown

This delightful winter christening gown, made from snowy white lawn and with a green contrasting lining, is embroidered with colorful sprigs of holly on the yoke and sleeves.

Size
To fit age 12 months
Finished length 34⅝ in.

Materials
36 in.-wide cotton lawn in the following amounts and colors: 2¾ yd. white and 2¼ yd. green
One skein stranded embroidery floss in each of the following colors: white, variegated green and variegated red
10 yd. of 1½ in.wide white lace edging

1⅜ yd. of ¼ in.-wide white satin ribbon
Dressmaker's graph paper
10 in. embroidery hoop
Hard or dressmaker's tracing pencil

Instructions
Using dressmaker's graph paper, copy the pattern pieces to scale from the chart given opposite where one square equals 2 in. Cut out.
Press the fabric to remove all creases. Place the pattern pieces in position

and with pins or tacks, mark out the gown sections following the instructions given. Work the embroidery on the yoke and sleeves before cutting out and making up.
To transfer the motifs, place the lawn over the holly-leaf trace patterns matching the straight grain to the center line, and using a hard or dressmaker's tracing pencil, trace the motifs through. Stretch the fabric in the embroidery hoop.
Work the embroidery in one strand of thread throughout. Following the colors given, first work the spider webs and all the connecting bars in buttonhole stitch. Then, buttonhole the

holly motifs and finally, the outline, re-membering to keep the twisted edge of the stitch facing the area that will later be cut away. Using small, sharp-pointed embroidery scissors, carefully cut away the areas of background fabric. Press the embroidery on the wrong side.

Finishing the christening robe

Replace the pattern pieces on the fabric and cut out each section, allowing for folds and seams as instructed. Cut out the appropriate lining sections from the contrasting fabric.

Cut a bias strip of white lawn 1 in. × 7 in. for the neck binding.

Yoke

With the straight grain and notches matching, place the right side of the green fabric under the front and back yoke sections. Pin and tack around the edges. Attach the two side sections to the yoke front taking ¼ in. seams. Stay stitch ¼ in. away from the neck edge on all three pieces. Finish the un-notched edges of the yoke backs, then turn in on the fold line and press to the inside to form facings. Tack at the neck edges to hold layers.

Front and back

Working on the wrong side, face the front with the green panel placed bet-ween the notches. Turn under ¼ in. on the long sides and tack in place. Working on the right side, apply lace trim to the seam lines. Make gathering stitches along the upper edge between the armhole seams. Repeat for the two back sections. Turn under and stitch ¼ in. on the back opening to finish.

Attaching yoke

Working on the wrong side, pin the front to the yoke front matching center notches. Pull up the gathers to fit, tack and stitch, avoiding the point of the yoke. Press the seams toward yoke. On the right side, tack the point of the yoke neatly in position, over the gathers, and cover the seam with lace. Trim away the excess fabric under the point. Before repeating for the two back sections, open out the yoke fac-ings. Finally, press up the lower edge, turn facing to seam line and slip stitch.

Neck binding

With right sides together stitch the shoulder seams. Tack and stitch the bias strip to the neck edge, making a ¼ in. seam and leaving the short ends extending. Turn in the ends and ¼ in. on the bias strip and slip stitch.

Sleeves

For each sleeve, turn ¾ in. to the wrong side on the wrist edge of both fabrics. Place the green fabric behind and tack as before. Make gathering stitches between notches on each sleeve top. Apply lace to the outer edge and a second row 1 in. above. With right sides together, pin the sleeves in place matching the dots at the shoulder seams. Pull up the gathers to fit. Tack and stitch between the side seams, easing the fullness. Stitch a second time, trim and press seam toward sleeve. Stitch the side

and sleeve seams in one. Stitch center back seam to point marked.

Frill

For the contrasting frill, stitch the seams to form a circle. Turn a ⅛ in. hem to the right side and cover with lace. Gather the top edge into four manageable sections, and set aside.

On the main garment, turn under and tack a 2 in. hem. Press fold and attach lace to the lower edge. On the wrong side, pin and tack the frill in place over the pressed edge, pulling up gathering to fit. Apply lace to the right side, using the tacks as a guideline. Finally, re-move all tacks and press.

To finish, attach three sets of ribbon ties, each one measuring 8 in. long, to the back opening. Tie into bows.

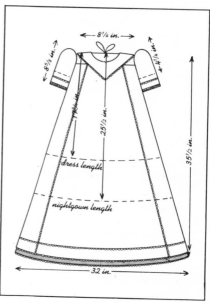

Berry/Fallon

³⁄₈ in. seams included on skirt, sleeve and frill
¼ in. seams included on bias and all yoke sections

contrasting fabric

Yoke front
cut 1 main fabric
cut 1 contrasting fabric

Yoke side
cut 2 in main fabric

Yoke back
cut 2 main fabric
cut 2 contrasting fabric fold

fold

Front
cut 1 contrasting fabric

Bias
cut 1
main fabric

center back

Back
cut 2 main fabric

Frill
cut 3
contrasting fabric

cut 1 main fabric

cut 2 contrasting fabric

Embroidery position

Sleeve
cut 2 main fabric
cut 2 contrasting fabric

selveges

Each square = 2 in.

John Hutchinson

329

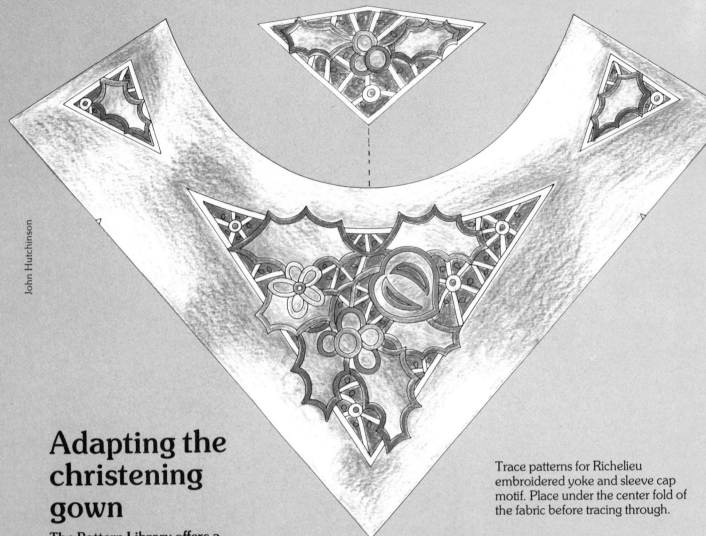

Adapting the christening gown

The Pattern Library offers a selection of seasonal motifs that can be embroidered especially to suit the time of a new baby's christening.

Use the basic christening gown pattern and embroider either spring, summer or autumn motifs on the yoke, sleeves or belt. Pick up the color for the contrasting fabric from the embroidery threads suggested for each season. As an alternative to a full-length gown the skirt could be shortened and the sleeve embroidery omitted for a special nightgown or shorten the sleeves and skirt to make a very pretty dress for summer in plain or printed fabrics.

1 Winter roses

Red, white and yellow are perfect colors for embroidering this tiny crescent of wintry Christmas roses on the dress yoke. Use a cheerful, bright red silk for the lining.

Trace patterns for Richelieu embroidered yoke and sleeve cap motif. Place under the center fold of the fabric before tracing through.

Richelieu embroidery designs

1

330

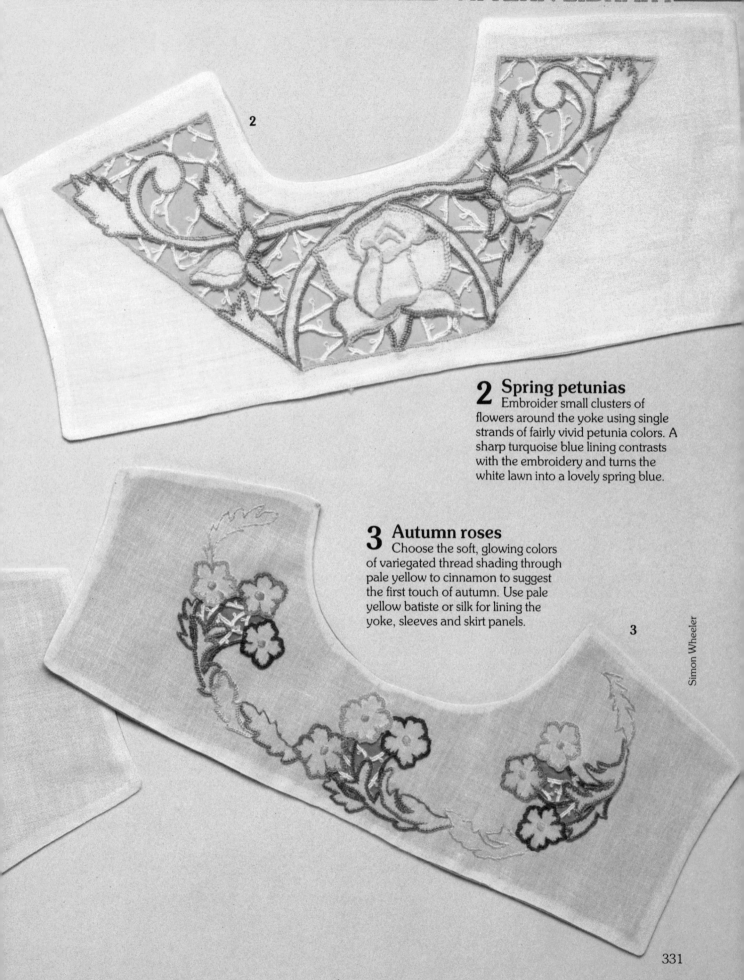

2 Spring petunias
Embroider small clusters of flowers around the yoke using single strands of fairly vivid petunia colors. A sharp turquoise blue lining contrasts with the embroidery and turns the white lawn into a lovely spring blue.

3 Autumn roses
Choose the soft, glowing colors of variegated thread shading through pale yellow to cinnamon to suggest the first touch of autumn. Use pale yellow batiste or silk for lining the yoke, sleeves and skirt panels.

Simon Wheeler

Dorset feather stitching

Give a modern look to a traditional technique by embroidering a colorful feather stitch border on a child's overalls or trousers. To complete the outfit, make Dorset crosswheel buttons in the same bright colors.

Skills you need

* French knots
* Buttonhole stitch
* Feather-stitch

If you do not know these skills, refer to pages 397 and 400.

Materials

Feather stitch designs look most effective worked in light-colored thread on a dark background. Use a firm, plain fabric, such as a heavyweight cotton or a fine wool. Felt is also suitable. For the embroidery, a twisted thread is best. If stranded floss is used, work with four strands or the stitches will not look heavy enough. Feather stitch is very extravagant on thread, so you will need a longer length of thread than usual. Mixing matte and shiny threads together in the same design can be very effective.

Special technique – Dorset crosswheel buttons

1 The button base is a metal curtain ring. Prepare a long length of thread, about two yards, to cover the ring and make the spokes of the wheel. Tie the thread to the top of the ring and buttonhole stitch all around in a clockwise direction. Conceal the loose end of the knot under the first few stitches.

2 Turn the outer edge of the buttonhole stitches to the inside of the ring. To make the spokes, take the thread from the bottom of the ring to the top. Carry the thread around from southeast to northwest, then from east to west and so on around the ring. Finish with a cross in the center as shown.

3 Working from the center with the same thread, backstitch over each spoke as shown. Continue around the spokes, turning the ring counter-clockwise with each stitch. To make a multi-colored wheel, change to another color, fastening off the thread at the back. Continue until the wheel is filled.

The basic Dorset feather-stitched overalls and trousers

Contrast bands of feather stitching with plain colors to add interest to clothes.

Size
Overalls to fit 20½ in. waist, age 3
Trousers to fit 21¾ in. waist, age 5

Materials
Overalls
1½ yd. of 36 in.-wide or 1¼ yd. of
45 in.-wide red-and-white striped heavyweight cotton
4 in. of 36 in.-wide white heavyweight cotton
1 skein each of red, blue, yellow and green twisted embroidery floss
11¾ in. of ¾ in.-wide elastic
Four ¾ in. diameter curtain rings
Matching sewing thread
Dressmaker's graph paper
Tracing paper

Trousers
1½ yd. of 36 in.-wide or 1¼ yd. of
45 in.-wide pale blue heavyweight cotton poplin
1 skein each of scarlet, dark blue, yellow, green and white twisted embroidery floss
11¾ in. of ¾ in.-wide elastic
24 in. of 1 in.-wide elastic
2¼ yd. of dark blue rick-rack braid
Two ¾ in. metal cover buttons
Small piece of dark blue cotton
Matching sewing thread
Dressmaker's graph paper

Terry Sims

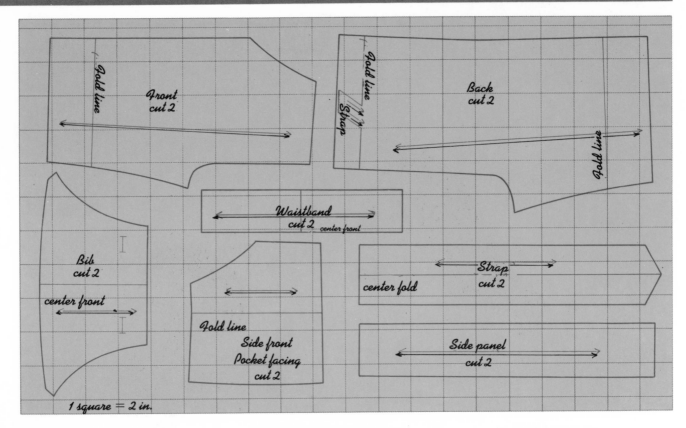

Front cut 2
Fold line

Back cut 2
Fold line

Fold line
Strap

Waistband
cut 2 center front

Bib
cut 2
center front

center fold

Strap
cut 2

Fold line
Side front
Pocket facing
cut 2

Side panel
cut 2

1 square = 2 in.

Instructions

Transfer the Dorset feather stitch patterns using dressmaker's carbon paper or the template method. Trace actual-size section of border on page 335 to use as a pattern or position guide. To make a template of the pine cone motif, trace the motif from the page and paste the tracing onto cardboard. Allow to dry and cut carefully along the outline. Rule straight lines on the fabric panel to denote the feather stitching or buttonhole stitching at the edge of the border, as appropriate.

Take care to position them at an equal distance from the center of the panel. Position the template at the center of the border, following the details on page 335 for arrangement, and using the tracing of the border as a guide. Draw around the template with tailor's chalk or pencil. Repeat the pattern along the length of the panel.

Work the embroidery over the lines of the design, following the details for stitch and color reference. Work the feather stitch motifs at the center of the border first, and then the outer lines of the design. Keep the tension of the stitch even, and work fairly loosely. It will help to hold one stitch in place with the thumb before working the next.

Enlarge the pattern pieces to size on dressmaker's graph paper. Cut out

and position on the fabric, taking care to align pieces on the straight grain of the fabric where necessary. Pin and cut out.

To make up the overalls, first stitch the bib and bib facing right sides together. Clip curves, turn right side out and press. With right sides together, stitch the pocket facings to the front and press to the inside. Fold the facing along the fold line, right sides together. Stitch along lower edge to make the pocket. Tack pocket top to front, and straight side edges together.

To make the straps, fold pieces right sides together lengthwise. Stitch, leaving diagonal end open. Clip corners. Turn right side out and press. Tack diagonal end in position on right side of back as indicated on pattern piece so that it will be turned to the inside when the top of the back is hemmed.

Stitch front to back at inner leg seams, right sides together, then pin, tack and stitch seam at crotch. Clip curves. With right sides together pin and tack waistband to front. Stitch. Trim seams and press toward waistband. With right sides together, pin, tack and stitch bottom of bib to waistband. Face with second waistband piece.

Stitch embroidered side panels to back and front pieces. Turn under a ¾ in. hem at the top of the back. Insert elastic and adjust to fit before securing ends at side seams and cutting. Shape

top of panel to fit, and hem.

Turn a small hem at the bottom of the legs and stitch. Fold leg to inside along fold line and then turn 1½ in. to outside to form cuff. Pin and attach in place by stitching a crosswheel button on the cuff at the center of the border. Make buttonholes on the bib as indicated and stitch crosswheel buttons to straps to fit.

To make up the trousers, finish the pockets as for overalls. Stitch the inside leg and crotch seam before inserting the Dorset feather stitch panels at the sides. Join waistband to front, right sides together. Turn under a hem on free edge and turn to inside, then slip stitch in place. Turn the back section to the inside along fold line. Slip stitch in place and thread elastic through casing as before. Fold leg bands in half, right sides together and stitch across end to join. Attach bands to bottom of legs right sides together. Turn back a hem on free edge and turn to inside. Slip stitch to wrong side. Tack rick-rack braid over the seam at each side of the embroidered panel and couch in place with overcast stitch.

Cover the metal cover buttons with fabric to match the rick-rack braid or pick out one of the colors used in the embroidery. Stitch in place on the waistband at top of pockets.

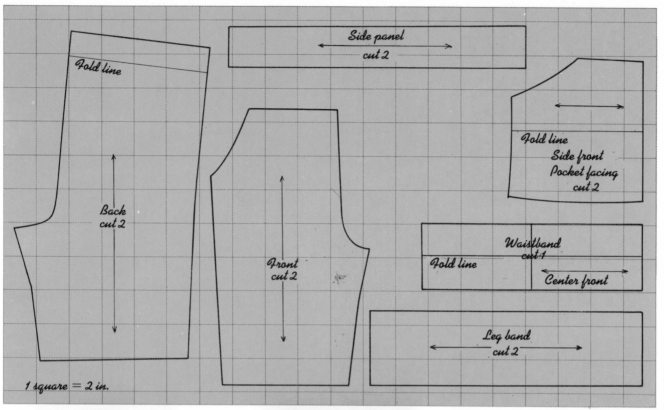

Side panel
cut 2

Fold line

Back
cut 2

Front
cut 2

Fold line
Side front
Pocket facing
cut 2

Fold line

Waistband
cut 1

Center front

Leg band
cut 2

1 square = 2 in.

Berry/Fallon

More design ideas

Work a simple border around a vest or a wide border around the hem of a skirt for a casual or ethnic look. Choose a single motif for matching hat and gloves, or embroider a fine design on silk to make a diary or address book something special.

Adapting the overalls and trousers

Make your own design by mixing and matching brightly-colored Dorset feather stitch patterns with rick-rack braid and interesting stitches.

Either of the two borders given on page 336 can be worked on a panel and set in overalls or trousers. Straight borders also lend themselves to belts and suspenders. Try embroidering the waistband or straps on overalls or a

pinafore for a different effect. The patterns themselves can also be adapted. Remove the bib from the overall pattern, shorten the leg and elasticize the waist completely to make a pair of shorts. The cuffs are now ideal for an embroidered border. Plan a design on paper with the article in mind. Use narrow borders or single motifs on small items and combine rows of patterns to make a wide band for use on larger items. Incorporate ribbons and rick-rack braid.

335

Dorset feather stitch patterns

1 Narrow border
Work buttonhole and satin stitch motifs around a chain stitch center, broken by groups of three spine chain stitches for a delicate border.

2 Simple border
This regular border of alternating motifs is quick and effective. Outline motifs in chain stitch and give shape with a single line of feather stitch, between buttonhole edging.

3 Corner design
This corner design is worked almost entirely in buttonhole stitch. Whip with a contrasting color for variety and finish swirls with French knots. Use the design as it stands to add a pretty touch to a corner, or continue the alternating pattern repeat as above for a full border.

4 Tear-drop motif
This elegant motif is worked in a combination of chain, wheatear, buttonhole and fly stitch, with French knots at the center. Use singly, or repeat vertically to make a delicate border.

Smocking

Smocking is one of the prettiest forms of securing gathered fullness on garments where some elasticity is needed. It can be stitched in bands of varying depths across yokes, around waists, wrist and ankle cuffs, as the main feature of the garment.

Skills you need

* **Diamond stitch**
* **Double closed wave stitch**
* **Single cable stitch**
* **Wave stitch**

If you do not know these skills, refer to pages 406 and 407.

Materials

For smocking light summer garments, feather-weight fabrics are essential. There is a tremendous variety available, woven in superb color ranges. To offset colored smocking patterns, it is better to use plain-colored ground fabrics and vice versa. Although many small prints, stripes, checks and spots make excellent ground fabrics, and in some cases can be used to form a grid for the smocking stitches, additional colors should be restricted. In fact it is much better to work the smocking in a single color. While sheer silk, rayon, crêpe and some synthetics are especially suited for smocking adult garments, soft cotton fabrics such as lawn, batiste, and fine synthetics are ideal for smocking children's wear.

Smocking on fine fabrics requires an equally fine embroidery thread such as twisted or stranded cotton floss.

In calculating the amount of fabric required for the fullness of smocking, allow approximately three times the finished measurement.

Special technique – ironing on dots

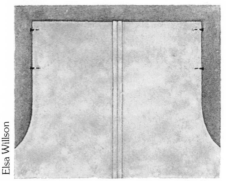
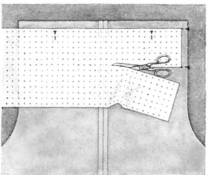
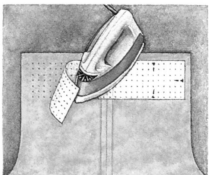

1 First, join any seams to make the required width of fabric to be smocked. Press seam open and place the fabric right side down on an ironing board or flat padded surface. Mark the area to be smocked with fine pins.

2 Since transfer ink cannot be fully guaranteed to wash out from all fabrics, it is important to choose the very palest color, such as silver, especially for fine fabrics. Cut the transfer paper to the exact size and lightly pin in place.

3 With the iron set to maximum heat, pass it quickly and lightly over the dots. To prevent the paper from slipping, and the dots from showing on the right side, work quickly with a lifting movement, removing the paper as you press. For covering very large areas, join the dots evenly.

The basic smocked sunsuits

Make these cool cotton all-in-ones with bands of smocking on the bib and knee cuffs for the beach, a summer birthday party, or just for fun.

Size
Age one year: length from bib to knee cuff 13 in.
Age three years: length from bib to knee cuff 21⅝ in.

Materials
Age one year
1⅛ yd. of blue 36 in.-wide cotton lawn or cambric
19¾ in. of ¼ in.-wide elastic
Matching sewing thread
One skein each stranded embroidery floss in the following colors: pink,
delphinium, buttercup
One sheet (8 in. × 36 in.) of ¼ in.-square smocking dots

Age three years
1¾ yd. of yellow 36 in.-wide cotton lawn or chambray
19¾ in. of ¼ in.-wide elastic
Matching sewing threads
One skein each of stranded embroidery floss in the following colors: pink, delphinium, jade
One sheet (8 in. × 36 in.) of ¼ in.-square smocking dots

Instructions
For age one year, copy the pattern to scale given opposite, where one square equals 2 in., onto dressmaker's drafting paper and cut out.

Press the fabric to remove all creases.

Pin the pattern pieces in place and cut out. Using ⅝ in. seams throughout, unless otherwise stated, join the back and front seams together, finish and press open.

Following the Special Technique, iron on 21 rows of dots for the bib front. Gather the fabric ready for the smocking. Follow the colors given and work rows of diamond stitch to complete the bib. Press on the wrong side and remove the gathering threads.

With right sides together, pin band to bib. Make straps; pin to edge in positions indicated. Turn under a ⅜ in. double hem at top edge of back sec-

338

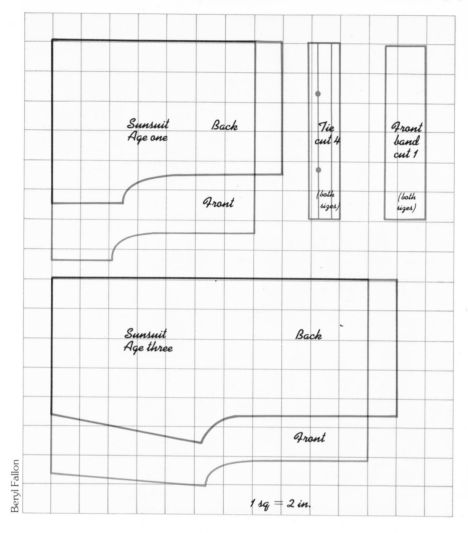

Sunsuit
Age one

Back

Front

Tie
cut 4

(both
sizes)

Front
band
cut 1

(both
sizes)

Sunsuit
Age three

Back

Front

1 sq = 2 in.

Beryl Fallon

John Hutchinson

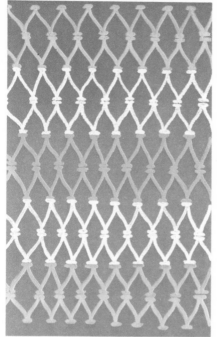

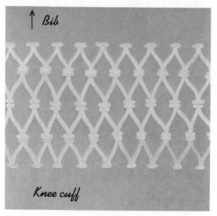

↑ Bib

Knee cuff

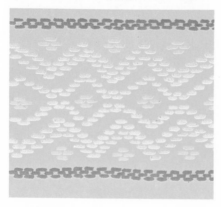

tion. Insert elastic to fit baby's back. Stitch side seams and finish edges together. With right sides together, stitch facing to top band. Turn under and hem stitch to wrong side. Hand stitch straps to inside back in positions indicated.

Turn under a stitch a ¼ in. double hem on both legs. Iron on nine rows of dots ¾ in. away from the edge. Gather fabric as before and work diamond stitch in color sequence. Press on wrong side and remove gathering threads. Stitch the inside leg seam, turn and finish together.

For the age three sunsuit, copy the

pattern to scale and make up as described. Iron on 11 rows of dots on the bib and five on the knee cuff. Using wave stitch outlined with cable stitch, follow color and stitch guide to complete smocking.

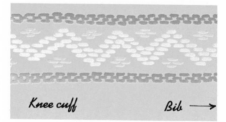

Knee cuff   Bib ➝

Adapting the basic smocked sunsuits

Choose from the selection of alternative smocking patterns given on pages 406 and 407 to decorate your sunsuit.

Quite different effects can be made by changing both the depth of the smocking and the stitches, and by using diffe-

rent colors and threads.

Very elastic stitches should be held firm with one or two rows of rope stitch or cable stitch worked either as a border, or repeated in pattern throughout deeper bands of smocking.

Experiment with fine stripes, checked and dotted fabrics using the pattern as

a grid for the smocking gathers.

In addition to colored smocking, try embroidering with light threads on dark-colored fabrics and vice versa. A further idea is to introduce surface embroidery using feather stitches with French knots and bullion stitches worked in the spaces between.

339

HOME EMBROIDERY
Alphabet Sampler

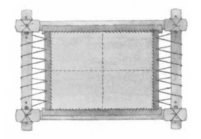

Skills you need

* **Tent stitch**
* **Cross stitch**

If you do not know these skills refer to page 402.

Materials

Samplers were traditionally stitched on linen, fine canvas, cotton or wool, using silk or cotton threads. If the sampler is to be worked in cross stitch, a fairly firm, even-weave fabric should be used, so that the threads can be counted easily. This could be cotton, burlap, fine wool or linen. Most embroidery threads can be used, but stranded thread is best as the number of strands can be varied according to the fabric. Metallic threads can also look very attractive. Needlepoint samplers are usually worked on either single or double thread canvas in tapestry yarn.

Special technique – dressing a slate frame

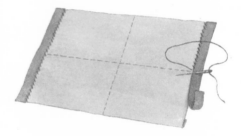

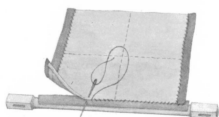

1 Cut the material to size, adding an extra 2 in. all around to the finished dimensions of the sampler. Turn under and tack a ⅜ in. hem at the top and bottom edges and stitch a length of webbing or strong tape 1 in. wide to the other two sides. Mark the center of the top, bottom and each side and run a line of stitches across in contrasting thread.

2 Match the center top of the material to the center of the webbing on one roller and pin, working from the center out. Oversew, using a strong thread, again from the center out. Repeat with the bottom edge. Fit the arms of the frame into the slots at the end of the rollers and roll any surplus material around the rollers until the canvas is stretched taut.

3 Insert the pegs in the arms to secure the frame, making sure the rollers are equally spaced. Thread a tapestry needle with carpet thread or strong string, and secure one end around the point where the arm and roller intersect. Lace the webbing to the arm of the frame at 1 in. intervals to pull the material taut, and tie securely at the other corner.

Elsa Willson

The basic sampler

This sampler is based on traditional designs and has all the charm of times gone by.

Size
10¼ in. × 8 in.

Materials
15¾ in. of single thread canvas, 18 holes to 1 in.

1 skein of each of the following shades of stranded embroidery floss: maroon; dull pink; pale pink; dark green; bright green; pale green; red; brown; gold; orange; yellow; royal blue; pale blue; gray; white.

Instructions
The best way to work a sampler this size is to mount it on a slate frame. This will keep it in good shape. It can be worked in the hand without a frame, but will need to be stretched back into shape when finished.

Work the sampler in tent stitch or cross stitch, using two or three strands of thread. Find the center of the canvas and work from the center out, following the chart on page 345. Each square represents one tent or cross stitch. Work the design as shown, leaving the canvas as background color, or fill in the background with cream or beige thread. If you do this work, do the design first and fill in the ground later.

Work one color or a small area of different colors at a time. Do not carry long threads over the back of the canvas between areas of color.

340

ABCD
JKLM
RSTUV
a b c d e f
m n o p q
w x

John Hutchinson

PATTERN LIBRARY

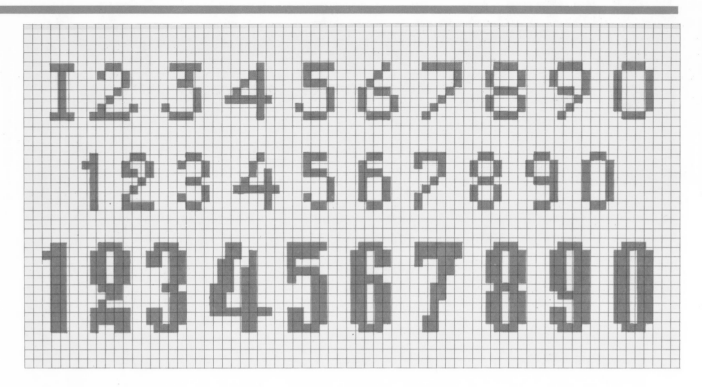

Adapting the sampler

Select a border design to suit the size of your sampler and enhance the alphabet of your choice.

Choose the border design and the letters and numbers you will need for the words and date on your sampler and then work out the complete design roughly by tracing them from the chart. When you have the spacing and proportions correct, transfer the whole design onto graph paper, using colored crayons or different symbols to indicate the colors. This will make it easier to work the design and count the threads on the fabric when you start to stitch. Alternatively, trace out each work or line on separate pieces of paper and move them around until you get the position right before transfering the design to graph paper. Find and mark the central square of your design to help you to position it.

Borders can be difficult, as they usually consist of a repeat pattern and you must be sure that the repeat fits properly into the corner design. It is a good idea to begin with the central repeat and work outward to each corner. It often helps to adjust the distance between the border and the edge of the central design. The spacing and position of the central design can also be altered to fit the border area.

344

More design ideas

Letters and numbers can be embroidered in a variety of styles.

Use the alphabet to personalize fashion items or objects for the home or add a personal touch to a carefully chosen present by embroidering the initials of a friend. The letters could also be used to make a message for a birthday, wedding or christening.

Linda Greigg

Florentine work

The beauty of Florentine work is created by the magnificent use of colors and tonal gradations. The flame-like zigzag lines moving up and down the canvas give it its special character.

Skills you need

* **Dressing a slate frame**
* **Florentine stitch**

If you do not know these skills, refer to pages 340 and 405.

Materials

Florentine work should be stitched on single thread canvas or the canvas threads will show between the vertical stitches. Suitable canvas sizes are 10, 12, 13, 14, 16 and 18 holes to 1 in. Tapestry, crewel and Persian wools can all be used and come in a wide range of colors. The thickness of yarn required depends on the canvas size. Straight stitches will require a thicker thread on any given canvas than diagonal stitches. Persian and crewel yarns are more versatile than tapestry yarn as the number of strands used can be varied to suit the canvas. Use one thickness of tapestry yarn or three strands of crewel yarn on 14 canvas, and four strands of crewel yarn on 12 canvas. Silk and cotton thread add luster and can be used for special effects. Use in combination with wool to achieve the right thickness.

Special technique – establishing the pattern

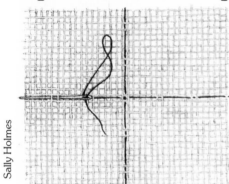

1 Find the center of the canvas by running a horizontal and a vertical line of tacking stitches through the center points of opposite sides of the canvas. Alternatively, rule two lines using a waterproof marker.

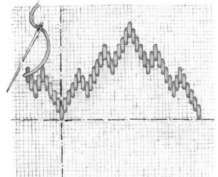

2 Stitch the skeleton line from the center to one side, arranging the pattern so that the basic scallop or zigzag sits centrally on, or to either side of the center lines. Return to the center and stitch to the opposite edge to complete the first row.

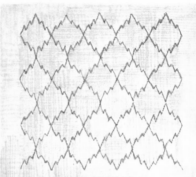

3 Continue working the skeleton rows from the center up, and then from the center to the bottom, until a framework is established over the entire area. Fill in colors, working from top to bottom of each repeat.

Sally Holmes

The basic Florentine pillows

Work these two very different Florentine designs in cool blues or warm pinks to make beautiful patterned pillows.

Size
Approximately 17¾ in. × 17¾ in.

Materials
Blue design
19¾ in. × 19¾ in. of single thread canvas, 16 holes to 1 in.
Three-ply Persian wool in the following shades and amounts:
1 skein of cream
4 skeins of pale blue, silver pink
6 skeins of blue, lt blue
8 skeins of green
19¾ in. of 36 in.-wide velvet
Matching sewing thread
17¾ in. pillow form
11¾ in. zipper

Pink design
19¾ in. × 19¾ in. of single thread canvas, 16 holes to 1 in.
Crewel wool in the following shades and amounts:
1 skein of terra cotta and med. brown, putty
2 skeins of dull rose pink
3 skeins of elephant gray, mid olive green
4 skeins of chocolate brown
19¾ in. of 36 in.-wide velvet
Matching sewing thread
17¾ in. pillow form
11¾ in. zipper

The blue design
The design is worked in two strands of yarn over four threads of canvas, on a slate frame and finished with a velvet edging and backing. Find the center of the canvas as shown above, count nine holes to the left of the vertical center line and two holes down from the horizontal center line. Bring the needle up at this point to work the central scallop in blue. Work four more scallops to the right and four to the left to complete the first row. Complete the framework, stitching five skeleton rows of scallops above the central row and five below.

Once the framework is complete, fill in the colors, following the chart on page 348. Work from the top of each scallop to the central tip.

Make straight edges following the pattern, and compensate with smaller stitches where necessary.

The main Florentine pattern is framed with a border of six rows of counted satin stitch, worked over four threads of canvas. Beginning with the inner row, work along the length of each side to the edge of the embroidery and miter corners by working next stitches

347

over three, two and one thread. Work the inner row in silver pink and continue in green, silver pink, pale blue, lt. blue and green.

Pink design

The design is worked in three strands of crewel yarn over four threads of canvas, on a slate frame.

Find the center of the canvas and bring the needle up at this point to begin the basic pattern. Work two-and-a-half patterns to the right and left of the vertical center line to form the first row. Stitch three skeleton rows above the central row and four below to complete the framework.

Fill in colors, working from the top to the bottom of each repeat. Begin with a row of mid olive green, stitching in-side the framework and omitting the center tip. Continue with colors as shown in chart, and finish with olive in the center tip.

Fill out to a straight edge at the top and bottom of the design in olive, following the pattern and compensating with shorter stitches where necessary.

Work a border in chocolate brown over eight threads of canvas at each vertical side of the design.

Finishing the pillows

Remove work from frame and trim canvas to six threads from the finished embroidery.

Cut two strips of velvet measuring 3⅛ in. wide by the length of the finished Florentine plus 1⅛ in.

Pin the strips to the sides of the em-broidery, right sides together, leaving ⅝ in. seam allowance at each end. Stitch as close to the Florentine as possible. Press seams away from the embroidery.

Cut two more lengths of velvet, measuring 3⅛ in. wide by the length of the Florentine plus 5 in. Pin to top and bottom, across the top and bottom of the side strips. Tack and stitch in place.

Cut a piece of velvet 19 in. square for the back of the pillow. Pin zipper in position at the center of the bottom edge of the pillow front and back. Stitch. With right sides together, pin, tack and stitch from end of zipper around the remaining sides and back to zipper. Fasten off, press seams open, and turn right side out.

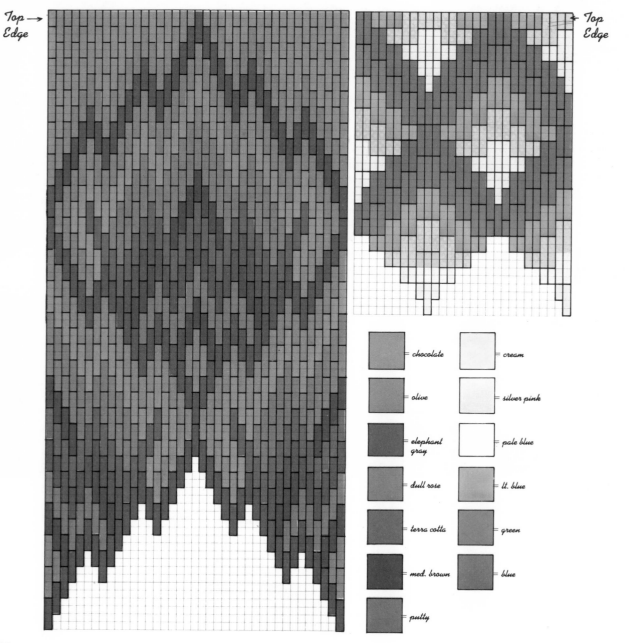

Top → Edge

Top ← Edge

= chocolate
= cream
= olive
= silver pink
= elephant gray
= pale blue
= dull rose
= lt. blue
= terra cotta
= green
= med. brown
= blue
= putty

John Hutchinson

348

Assisi

This attractive embroidery is rich in historic tradition. It is said to have been brought to the Italian town of Assisi by Saint Francis on his return from the Holy Land. Select a traditional design or a modern variation and embroider an attractive table runner.

Julian Nieman

Skills you need

* Cross stitch

If you do not know this skill, refer to page 402.

Materials

Like other counted thread techniques, Assisi work should be done on an even-weave fabric such as linen or cotton. It should be fairly firm to take the weight of solid areas of cross stitch. Traditionally, the cloth was natural, cream or white.

The design can be worked in stranded cotton, pearl cotton or twisted floss, depending on the weight of fabric. Again, the traditional colors of thread were blue, red and green, with black or another dark color for the Holbein stitch outline.

349

Special technique – Italian hemstitch border

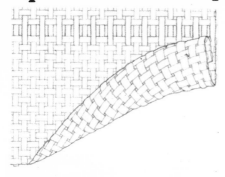

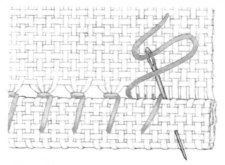

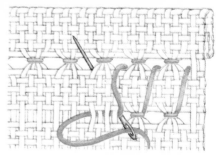

1 *First work Antique hemstitch to hold the hem in place. Withdraw one or two threads 10 to 15 threads from the edge, depending on the weight of your fabric. Roll under the hem to the edge of the drawn threads.*

2 *Work the hemstitch from left to right on the wrong side. Pick up four vertical threads, inserting the needle to the right of the threads, and bringing it through to the left. Reinsert the needle and pass it between the hem bringing it out two threads to the right and four threads down. Pull firmly and repeat.*

3 *Work Italian hemstitch from right to left on the right side. Withdraw a single thread five threads from the hemstitching. Bring the needle out to the right side of a hemstitch. Insert it five threads down and encircle four threads to the left. Reinsert it and pass it diagonally upward, bringing it out to the left of the hemstitch, ready for the next stitch.*

The basic table runner

This attractive table runner is worked in a traditional Assisi color. The design is typical of those found in early sixteenth-century pattern books.

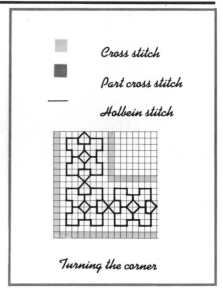

■ *Cross stitch*

■ *Part cross stitch*

— *Holbein stitch*

Turning the corner

Size
Approx. 18 × 42 in.

Materials
⅝ yd. of 60 in.-wide ivory even-weave linen
3 skeins of blue embroidery floss

Instructions
Find the center of the linen at each of the shorter sides and run a line of tacking stitches through these two points in a contrasting color thread. Working from the chart on page 351, center the Assisi design across one end of the table runner, using the tacking as a guide. The base of the main Assisi design should sit approximately 4¾ in. from the cut edge of the linen.
Work the Holbein stitch outline and then fill in the cross stitch background. Both the Holbein and the cross stitch should be worked over three threads of linen.
Once the Assisi border is complete, work the Holbein stitch border along the top and bottom of the design. Continue the border 29 repeats along the length of the table runner and then across the end. Center the Assisi design beneath the border at the other

350

end and work as before.
Assisi embroidery is traditionally finished with Italian hemstitch. Roll a narrow hem and stitch as shown to produce a neat edge.
The corners of the table runner can be decorated with tassels. Pass the thread six or eight times through a gap at the corner of the Italian hemstitch border and around the index finger of the left hand to give a constant length to the tassel. Wind the thread twice around the top of the tassel, between the finger and the edge of the linen, to sec-ure and fasten off with two or three stitches on the wrong side of the linen.

Adapting the design

Most of the alternative designs are taken from early pieces of Assisi and are typical of the early motifs. Stylized animals and birds, and geometric designs inspired by mosaic patterns are particularly common.
Assisi can be worked entirely in simple cross stitch and outlined in Holbein stitch. Italian cross stitch, two sided cross stitch, long-armed cross stitch and punch stitch can all be used for variation.
While the traditional colors for Assisi work are red, green and blue, you can experiment to make a more modern piece of work or to coordinate with a particular color scheme. Whatever color you choose, keep the work simple, with just a few colors on a light background. Use a darker shade of the same color or black for the outline stitch. Alternatively, you could reverse the traditional colors and embroider white or pale blue on blue.

Grundy Northedge

More design ideas

Peasant style clothes look very effective with a border of Assisi embroidery. Work a panel around the hem of a gathered skirt. Use a single motif to decorate a pocket.

351

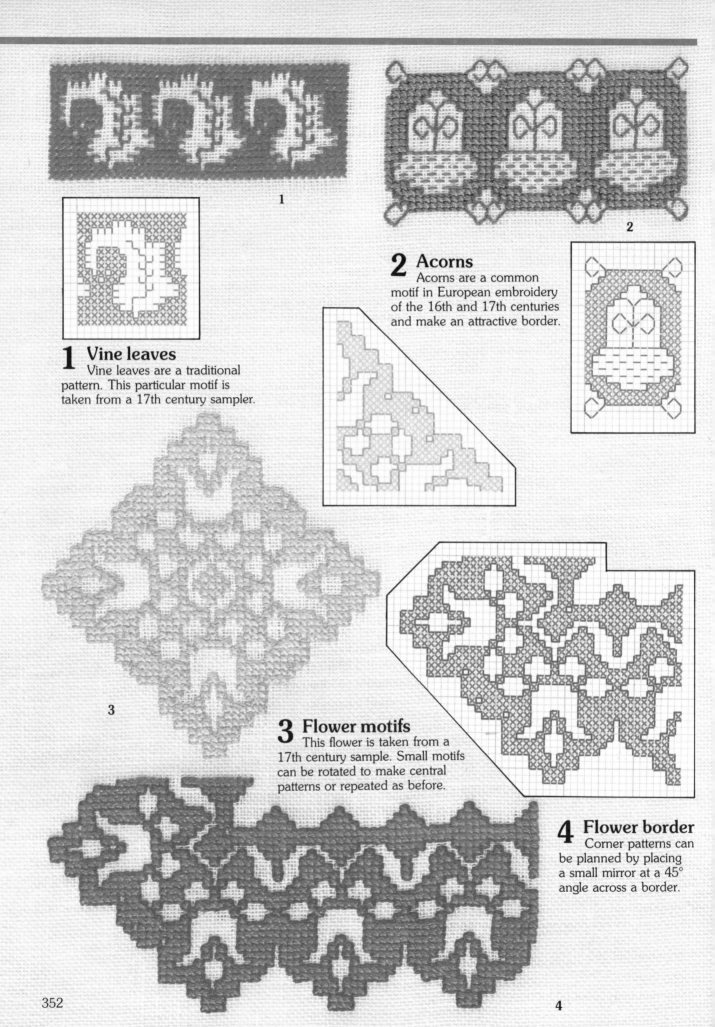

1 **Vine leaves**
Vine leaves are a traditional pattern. This particular motif is taken from a 17th century sampler.

2 **Acorns**
Acorns are a common motif in European embroidery of the 16th and 17th centuries and make an attractive border.

3 **Flower motifs**
This flower is taken from a 17th century sample. Small motifs can be rotated to make central patterns or repeated as before.

4 **Flower border**
Corner patterns can be planned by placing a small mirror at a 45° angle across a border.

Cross stitch

Cross stitch can be used to interpret an infinite number of patterns and motifs. These beautiful naturalistic designs are of Danish origin. Straight from the fields and hedgerows, they will bring charm and style to your dining room.

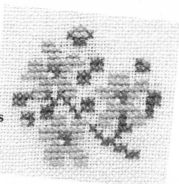

Skills you need

* Cross stitch

If you do not know this skill refer to pages 402.

Materials

Use a fine linen (27 or 30 threads to 1 in.) to retain the delicacy of these designs. Coarser linen and other even-weave fabrics can be used to produce a bolder effect if required.

Work the designs in Danish flower thread, which comes in a range of beautiful colors similar to those produced by natural dyes, or stranded embroidery floss. Use one strand of Danish flower thread or two strands of stranded embroidery floss on fine linen, increasing the number of strands to suit coarser linens.

Use decorative lace and braids to add a pretty touch.

Special technique – lace insertion

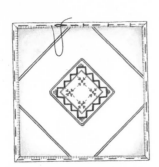

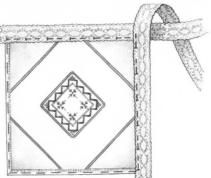

1 Once the embroidery is complete, trim the edges of the linen. Taking each edge in turn, fold ¼ in. of linen to the right side. Finger press along the fold and tack in place, mitering the corners neatly.

2 Take a corner motif and a length of lace. Pin the lace along the top of the square so that it covers the raw edge of the linen. Tack in place. Take a second piece of lace and attach it to the right-hand edge.

3 Pin the horizontal band of lace to the bottom edge of a second motif and the vertical band to the right-hand edge. Continue adding squares and lace, weaving the bands of lace alternately over and under at intersections, until the cloth is complete. Machine stitch.

Ingrid Jacob

The basic cross-stitch tablecloth

This pretty tablecloth is composed of two alternating motifs set on a diamond trellis and finished with lace.

Size
Approximately 33 in. × 33 in.

Materials
⅝ yd. of 60 in.-wide bleached Danish linen, 27 threads to 1 in.
Danish flower thread or stranded embroidery floss in the following shades and amounts:
1 skein of pale pink, soft pink, mid pink, dark pink, yellow, mid green, leaf green, pale green, dark green, brown, light brown
3 skeins of red and green
4½ yd. of straight-edged lace
4½ yd. of lace with a scalloped edge
Matching sewing thread
354

Linda Greigg

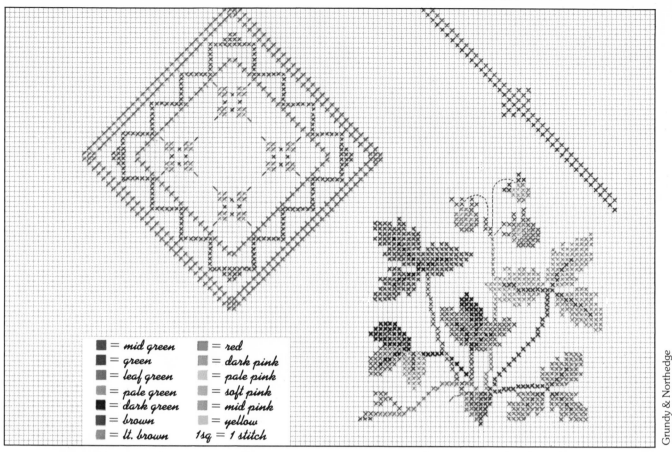

Key:
- ■ = mid green
- ■ = green
- ■ = leaf green
- ■ = pale green
- ■ = dark green
- ■ = brown
- ■ = lt. brown
- ■ = red
- ■ = dark pink
- □ = pale pink
- ■ = soft pink
- ■ = mid pink
- ■ = yellow
- 1 sq = 1 stitch

Grundy & Northedge

Instructions

The tablecloth is made up of nine 9 in. squares. Four of these are embroidered with the wild strawberry plant, and five with the strawberry flower motif. The Danish method of working cross stitch is to work the linen freely in the hand.

Cut a 9¾ in. square, following the weave of the linen, and oversew the edges to prevent fraying. Find the center of the linen by running a vertical and horizontal line of tacking stitches through the square from the center point on two sides. Find the center of the wild strawberry plant motif with the aid of the arrows. Begin the embroidery at the center, working in one strand of embroidery thread over two threads of linen. Work one area of color at a time, following the charts above. Avoid carrying threads across the back of the work.

When the embroidery is complete, trim ¼ in. from each edge of the linen, leaving a 9⅜ in. square. Cut the lace into four equal lengths. Finish the edges and insert the lace as shown on page 354, taking care to arrange the motifs in the correct sequence. When the lace insertion is complete, finish the edge of the tablecloth with scalloped lace.

Adapting the cross-stitch tablecloth

Choose a fruit or a group of fruits and embroider them to your own design.

Decide first on an approximate finished size of tablecloth, and from this measurement work out the number and size of squares needed. Remember to allow for the width of the lace in your calculations. Always work on the basis of an odd number of squares to achieve a balanced repeat, and plan the arrangement of the whole cloth on paper before starting to stitch.

Any of the fruit, berry or flower de-signs given on page 356 can be worked in place of the strawberry plant on a 9 in. square. Draw the motif on graph paper at the center of the square, and work out the positioning of the diamond trellis to balance the motif at the center.

A flower or berry could be worked as a spot motif at the corners of the square in place of the trellis. By repeating the same motif in each corner another diamond pattern will be created.

Choose lace or braid to suit the design.

More design ideas

Embroider placemats or napkin rings with a motif to match your tablecloth, or work a pretty repeat border along a kitchen blind. Enlarge a flower motif by working larger crosses to decorate a needlecase.

Cross-stitch patterns

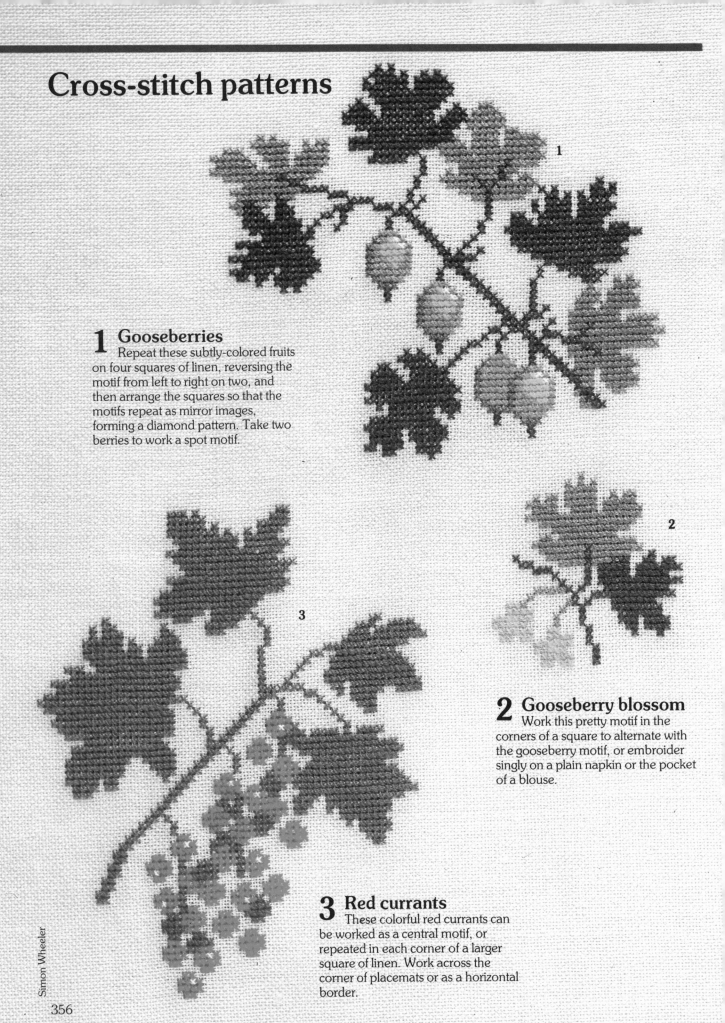

1 Gooseberries
Repeat these subtly-colored fruits on four squares of linen, reversing the motif from left to right on two, and then arrange the squares so that the motifs repeat as mirror images, forming a diamond pattern. Take two berries to work a spot motif.

2 Gooseberry blossom
Work this pretty motif in the corners of a square to alternate with the gooseberry motif, or embroider singly on a plain napkin or the pocket of a blouse.

3 Red currants
These colorful red currants can be worked as a central motif, or repeated in each corner of a larger square of linen. Work across the corner of placemats or as a horizontal border.

Simon Wheeler

356

Blackwork

Blackwork, or Spanish work, dates from the sixteenth century when it was widely used throughout Europe to decorate clothing and household linen. Flowers and leaves have always been a popular subject for blackwork and are an effective decoration.

Frank Herholdt

357

Skills you need

* **Back stitch**
* **Holbein stitch**

If you do not know these skills, refer to pages 397 and 399.

Materials

Blackwork should always be done on an even-weave fabric, preferably closely-woven, such as cotton, linen or fine burlap. To make even and regular stitch patterns, use a blunt-ended tapestry needle. Traditionally, it was worked in black thread on white fabric, but other colors can be used, although dark colors are the most effective. Pearl cotton and stranded embroidery floss are best on a fine fabric, but coarser threads such as crewel wool can be used on heavier material in large pieces of work. If you use stranded floss, it is often enough to use a single strand for the details and two strands for the outline stitches. Never use too thick a thread or the delicacy of the stitches will be lost.

Special technique – transfering a design using tacking stitches

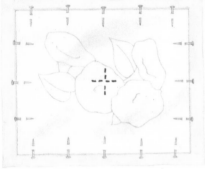

1 *Trace the design you wish to use onto fine tracing paper and mark the center. Mark the center of the fabric with a colored thread. Place the tracing on the fabric and pin, matching the center points.*

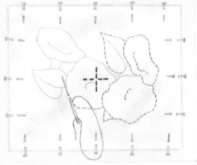

2 *Using a colored sewing thread, work small even running stitches along the lines of the design, sewing through both the paper and the fabric.*

3 *With the work flat, carefully tear away the paper, leaving the outline of the design marked out in tacking stitches on the fabric ready to be embroidered.*

Elsa Willson

The basic tea and egg cozies

These tea and egg cozies use blackwork patterns just as they were worked on household linen as long ago as Elizabethan times.

Size
9¼ in. × 12½ in.

Materials
⅜ yd. of cream even-weave linen, 32 threads to 1 in.
1 skein each of black, green and red stranded embroidery floss
⅜ yd. polyester batting
⅜ yd. dark sateen lining fabric

Instructions
Enlarge the tea cozy pattern to size and cut out. Pin to the linen and tack around the outline of the pattern in colored thread so that the embroidery can be worked in a frame. Transfer the design, positioning the motif so that it will be in the center of the front of the cozy when cut out. Embroider, using

two strands of thread for the outlines and one for the detail stitches.
When the embroidery is finished, cut out the embroidered front along the tacking stitch outline and cut a second piece of linen for the back of the cozy. Cut two pieces of batting and two of linen, using the same pattern. Trim the seam allowance from the bottom straight edge of the batting, and place the two pieces together. Sew along the curved seam line, leaving the bottom edge open. Clip the curves and trim the seam allowance close to the stitching. Turn inside out.
With right sides together, sew the back and front pieces of linen along the seam line as for the batting. Clip the curves and turn right side out.
Fit the batting into the linen cover. Sew the lining pieces, right sides together, as for the linen, clip curves and trim. Fit the lining inside the batting. Turn in the seam allowance on the bottom edge of the linen and the lining, folding the linen under the edge of

the batting to ensure a neat finish on the front. Slip stitch the linen and lining together.
Make up the egg cozy in the same way.

Adapting the blackwork patterns

By mixing stitch patterns with different thicknesses of thread a whole range of tones can be created.

Use varying tones to suggest the subtle shape and form of flowers, fruit and foliage, carefully choosing the stitch pattern to give the required amount of light and shade.
As well as using single colored threads, try experimenting with different color combinations or gold and silver thread for added sparkle.

Tea cozy

Transfer the main plant from the above diagram and use for the tea cozy. Transfer the two flower motifs on to the fabric for each egg cozy.

Copy the chart below to scale, using the outer line for a pattern for the tea cozy and the inner for the egg cozies.

More design ideas

Work a single bloom and frame it under glass, or give it a fabric mounting for a special keepsake present. Use the egg cozy pattern turned upside-down to show off a tiny spray of flowers on a child's zipped purse.

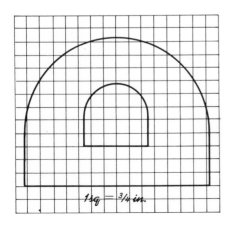

1 sq = ¾ in.

Hexagonal patchwork
FABRIC CRAFT

This is one of the earliest types of English patchwork, best remembered by some of the most beautiful heirlooms left by our great grandmothers. Quilts and coverlets were handstitched with amazing ingenuity, mixing precious oddments of fabric, transforming them into a completely individual textile.

Tom Leighton

360

Skills you need

* Piping
* Making templates

If you do not know these skills, refer to pages 410 and 411.

Materials

As patchwork can involve piecing together many different fabrics, it is essential that the fabrics you choose should be of a similar weight and construction. This will largely guarantee that the finished patchwork will keep its shape and wear evenly. In selecting your fabrics, resist the temptation to include even one or two patches from fabric that is either slightly elastic, too flimsy or partly worn. These patches will stretch and wear disappointingly quickly, spoiling what might otherwise have been a beautiful piece of hand-sewn patchwork.

For best results, choose fabrics that are closely-woven, roughly the same weight, new and color fast. For handling and shaping hexagons of all sizes, the most popular fabrics are light to middle-weight cottons and silks. Stitch the patches together with a matching or neutral-colored thread. Use quilting thread for very strong stitching.

Special technique – covered buttons

Sally Holmes

1 This base used here is a popular two-part button mold made from a light metal alloy. Measure the diameter of the button mold and add ¼ in. all around. Make a paper template to this size and pin it to the wrong side of your fabric. Cut out close to the edge of the template. Run a gathering thread of even-length running stitches around the edge leaving the two ends free.

2 Draw up the two threads together, gathering the fabric to shape. Place the top part of the button mold in the center and pull the threads tight. Knot them firmly and tie off. Press the gathered fabric down towards the center, stretching it firmly over the teeth on the outside edge of the mold.

3 Place the back section of the button over the button shank and press it firmly in position. Dry cleaning is recommended for covered buttons, otherwise they should be removed before hand-washing a garment.

The basic patchwork vest

For sheer style and elegance in hexagonal patchwork, this man's vest combines the sublety of silks and satin with bold vertical stripes.

Size
Chest 38-40 in.
Center back seam 20½ in.

Materials
¾ yd. of 45 in.-wide gray Thai silk, or similar fabric
⅛ yd. each of 36 in.-wide fabric in eight mixed patterns, including plain silks and patterned cottons of the same weight, in coordinated colors
1⅜ yd. of 36 in.-wide gray satin
⅝ yd. of 36 in.-wide lightweight interfacing

4 yd. of narrow piping cord
Four ½ in. two-part button molds
Thin cardboard
Matching sewing threads
24 in. × 18 in. of insulating board, optional (this is useful for arranging the patterns with pins before sewing them together)

Instructions
Make separate tracings of the two hexagons given. From the cardboard, make one large template for cutting out the fabric patches. Using the remaining cardboard or old greeting cards, carefully cut out at least 205 small templates for backing the patches.
Cut out five 1½ in.-wide bias strips

from the gray silk for piping, join into one length and set aside. From the remaining silk, cut 105 patches and from the mixed fabrics cut 100 patches.
For the right front, follow the diagram for placing the patches and join the first row on the straight grain.
When buttons and buttonholes are to be used, it is important that the corresponding first rows on both fronts should be stitched together on the straight grain. Use the board to arrange the next row of mixed patches, pinning them into a pleasant arrangement on the straight grain. If you wish to get the interesting light and dark effect on the next and every alternate row, place the gray silk patches at opposite angles to each other. To complete the right front, continue to arrange each row and join the patches

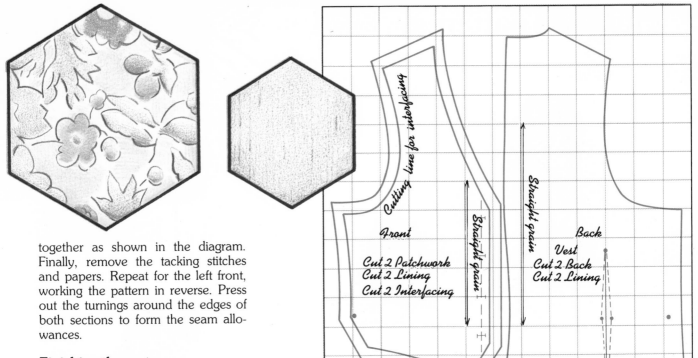

Berry/Fallon

together as shown in the diagram. Finally, remove the tacking stitches and papers. Repeat for the left front, working the pattern in reverse. Press out the turnings around the edges of both sections to form the seam allowances.

Finishing the vest

Using dressmaker's graph paper, copy the pattern pieces to scale and cut out. Cut out the front interfacings and the vest back and the lining from the gray satin.

Carefully place the front interfacing paper pattern on the wrong side of each patchwork section, reversing it to make a left and right and mark the outline with chalk or tacking stitches as

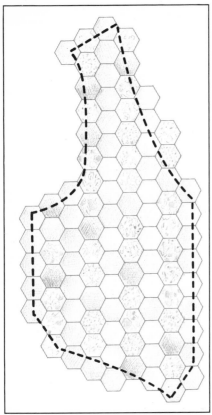

shown below. Make a row of machine stitching close to the line to support the hand stitching of the patchwork. Allow for the seams and trim the edges. Tack the interfacing onto the wrong side of both front sections. Stitch the center back seam of the vest back and press seams open. Stitch and press the darts. Join the back to the fronts at the shoulder seams and press seams open. Stitch lining in the same way.

Prepare the piping and stitch it to the vest on the sewing line starting at one side seam. Continue around both fronts, the neck and armhole edges. Place the lining and vest right sides together. Pin, tack and stitch around the edges enclosing the piping and leaving the side seams open. Trim seams and clip curves. Turn to the right side, pul-

ling the fronts gently through the shoulder seam and out through an unstitched side seam. Press carefully on the wrong side. Splice the piping cord at the underarm point before stitching the side seams together to the point marked. Press the seams open. Turn under the lining seam allowance and slip stitch at the side seams. Mark the positions of the buttonholes on the left front as shown and make hand or machine-stitched buttonholes. If necessary, finish off by hand, working strengthening bars at each end. To mark the position of the buttons, place the vest on a flat surface with the fronts overlapped correctly and pin through the center of each buttonhole. Make four gray silk buttons and stitch them in place.

Adapting the basic patchwork vest

Shown here are some alternative arrangements that can be stitched into the basic patchwork.

By making the individual patches smaller or bigger, longer or shorter, plain-colored or patterned, you can make many interesting permutations. Choose quiet-colored cottons and simple patterns for everyday wear, with rich, shiny silks and bolder colors for special party effects. Follow the same principle of stitching the patchwork pieces into a fabric before cutting out. Instead of piping the edges, you could cover them with a contrasting braid.

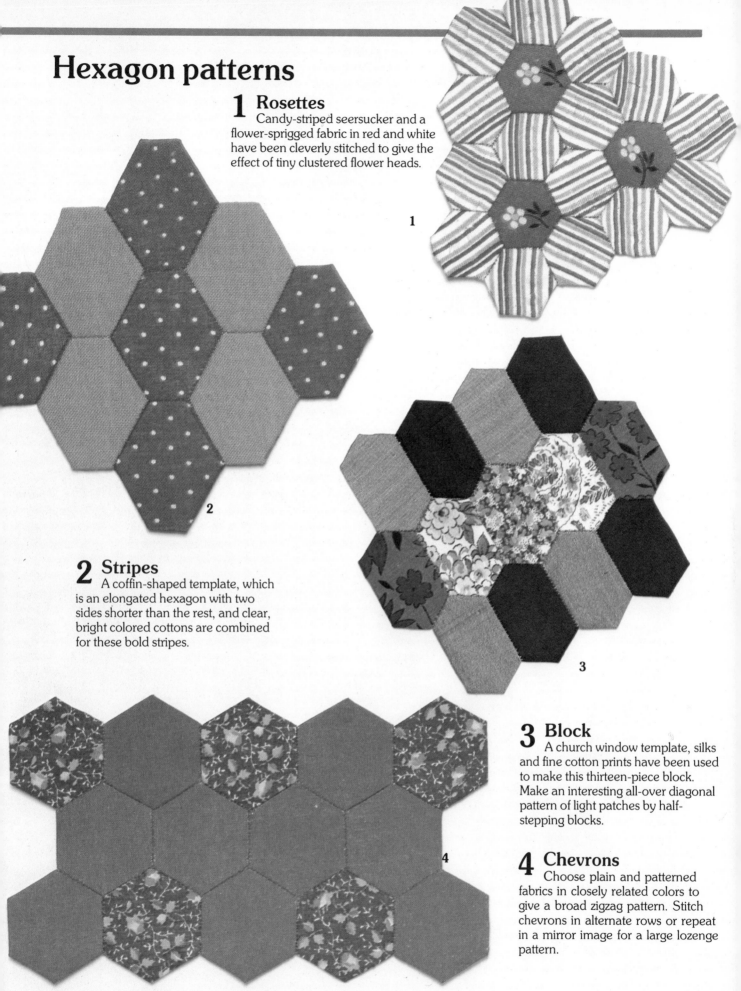

Hexagon patterns

1 Rosettes
Candy-striped seersucker and a flower-sprigged fabric in red and white have been cleverly stitched to give the effect of tiny clustered flower heads.

2 Stripes
A coffin-shaped template, which is an elongated hexagon with two sides shorter than the rest, and clear, bright colored cottons are combined for these bold stripes.

3 Block
A church window template, silks and fine cotton prints have been used to make this thirteen-piece block. Make an interesting all-over diagonal pattern of light patches by half-stepping blocks.

4 Chevrons
Choose plain and patterned fabrics in closely related colors to give a broad zigzag pattern. Stitch chevrons in alternate rows or repeat in a mirror image for a large lozenge pattern.

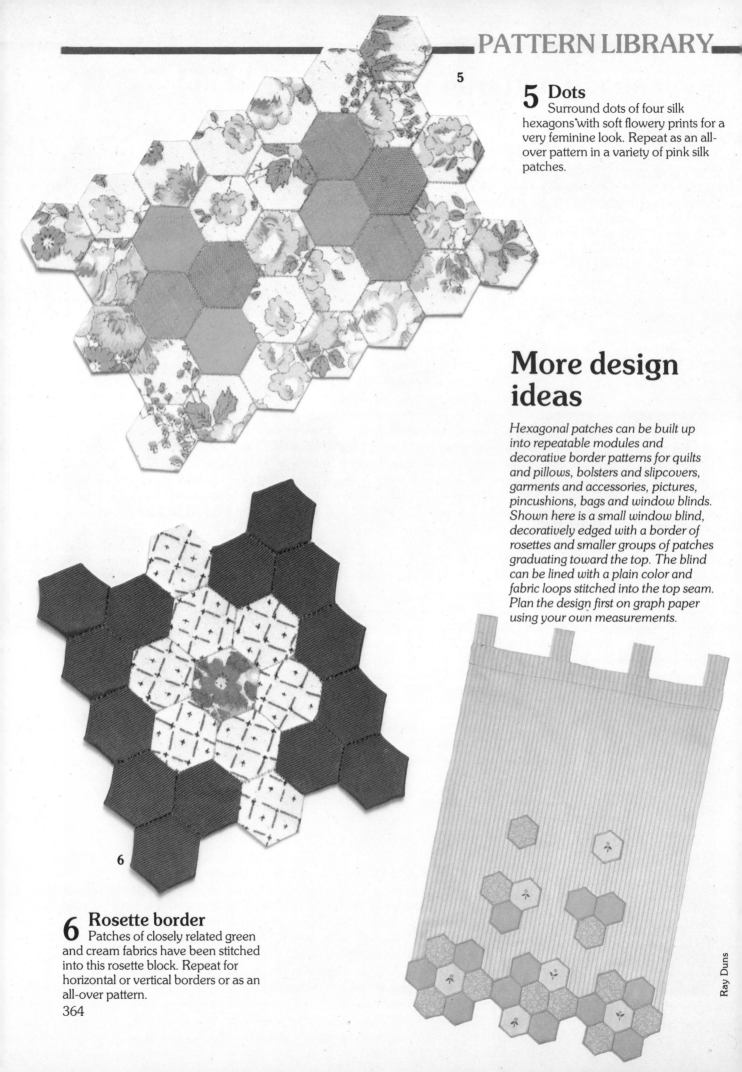

5

5 Dots
Surround dots of four silk hexagons with soft flowery prints for a very feminine look. Repeat as an all-over pattern in a variety of pink silk patches.

More design ideas

Hexagonal patches can be built up into repeatable modules and decorative border patterns for quilts and pillows, bolsters and slipcovers, garments and accessories, pictures, pincushions, bags and window blinds. Shown here is a small window blind, decoratively edged with a border of rosettes and smaller groups of patches graduating toward the top. The blind can be lined with a plain color and fabric loops stitched into the top seam. Plan the design first on graph paper using your own measurements.

6

6 Rosette border
Patches of closely related green and cream fabrics have been stitched into this rosette block. Repeat for horizontal or vertical borders or as an all-over pattern.

364

Ray Duns

American patchwork
FABRIC CRAFT

Patchwork quilts have become collectors' items. Choose one of these traditional American block designs and make your own colorful patchwork quilt. All the blocks can be assembled on a sewing machine.

Skills you need

* Cutting a template
* Tufting or tieing

If you do not know these skills, refer to page 411.

Materials

Patchwork block patterns are most successful when made from closely woven pure cotton dress-weight fabrics. Do not mix fabrics of very different weights, and avoid crease-resistant synthetic materials. Wash and iron all fabrics before use, to test for dye fastness and shrinking. Make sure there is plenty of contrast by mixing not only different colors and tones, but stripes, dots and checks.

Kim Sayer

Special technique – machine-stitching blocks

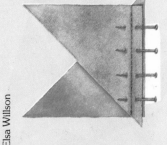

Elsa Willson

1 Position the patches right side together and pin, keeping the pins at right angles to the cut edge. For most shapes match the cut edges. When sewing shapes with diagonal edges such as triangles, it is important to match the seam line, not the cut edges.

2 Align the edges of the pinned patches with the edge of the presser foot to give a ¼ in. seam allowance. Keep this throughout the project. Sew the patches together, beginning and ending with a back stitch. Remove the pins as you stitch.

3 Always press the seams to one side before joining the next patch or row. When joining a lighter patch to a darker one, press the seam to the darker color so that it does not show on the right side. Give a final pressing when the block is completed.

The basic quilt

Follow these instructions to make a Lady of the Lake quilt or adapt them as described below to make a Courthouse Steps quilt.

Size
91½ in. × 79 in.

Materials
Closely woven cottons in the following quantities: 5½ yd. of 36 in.-wide white or light-colored fabric; 2¼ yd. of 36 in.-wide red printed fabric; 3⅝ yd. of 36 in.-wide assorted plain and printed fabric in various colors
5½ yd. of 45 in.-wide cotton for backing
5½ yd. of 45 in.-wide quilt batting

To make the quilt
The quilt is constructed of 42 blocks (6 blocks × 7 blocks). Each block measures 12½ in. square. The backing is brought to the front of the quilt to make a self-binding edge of 1 in. on all sides. The three layers are tufted or tied together.

Trace the two templates from the page and glue onto cardboard. Cut out with a cutting knife. A ¼ in. seam allowance is included.

Lay the templates on the wrong side of the fabric, with the edges parallel to the weave of the fabric so that only the diagonal side of the template is on the bias. Outline each patch with a colored pencil and cut individually. Cut 84 large light-colored triangles, 84 large red triangles, 1,008 small light-colored triangles and 1,008 small assorted fabric triangles.

Assemble the patches for one block. To keep the impression of windmill sails at the corners of the blocks, keep the same color combination at the corner of each block constant throughout. Make up the remaining 41 blocks and sew into 7 rows of 6 blocks, sewing a large red triangle to a large light-colored one each time. Sew the rows together and iron the completed patchwork top. It should measure 90 in. × 77¼ in. including seam allowances.

Cut and join the batting to measure 91½ in. × 79 in. Cut and join the backing fabric to measure 94½ in. × 81⅝ in.

Pin and tack the three layers together, working from the center of the quilt to the center of each side and the four corners. Bring the backing to the front and turn under a hem of ⅜ in. Sew it to the patchwork by hand, using a hem stitch, ¼ in. from the edge. Miter the corners and tuft the three layers together.

Adapting the quilt

Choose one of the American patchwork block designs from the selection given.

Each patchwork block is accompanied by a chart showing the arrangement of patches. The template shapes are shaded in red and numbered to correspond with the patch guide also given.

Pieced blocks are usually square shapes between 8 in. and 16 in. Simple blocks such as Evening Star or Railroad can be smaller and more numerous than a more complicated block such as Devil's Claws. A larger number of smaller blocks gives a more interesting pattern than fewer large blocks with oversized pieces.

Decide on the approximate dimensions of your project. Divide the width of the project by the width of the block to find out how many blocks will fit. Do the same for the length. Multiply the number of blocks in the length by the number in the width to find the total number of blocks. Borders can be added to make up the size if required. Whichever block you choose it is a good idea to make a colored chart of the design beforehand. You can experiment with colors and see how different patterns are formed when blocks are set together. This chart is also useful for estimating the size of blocks, templates and fabric, and is a useful guide when sewing the patches.

American patchwork patterns

1 Square star

A four-patch block that can be colored many ways to give a variety of designs.

Four-patch (16 squares)
1) × 4 blue/white print
2) × 4 blue
   × 4 red/white/blue print
3) × 8 blue
   × 8 red/white stripe
   × 8 red/white/blue print
   × 8 blue/white print
Total 44 pieces each block.

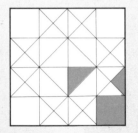

1

2 Cactus basket

There are many different basket patterns. This one is also called Desert or Texas Rose and is an exceptionally interesting one to sew.
1) × 4 pink
   × 4 violet
2) × 2 green
3) × 4 violet/green print
   (reversible shape)
4) × 2 green print
5) × 2 green print
6) × 2 green print
7) × 4 green print
8) × 2 green
Total 26 pieces each block.

2

3 T blocks

A widely used block also known as Capital T. This pattern is suitable when larger size blocks are required.

Nine-patch (36 squares)
1) × 4 yellow stripe
2) × 8 light green
3) × 4 yellow print
   × 4 dark green
4) × 8 dark green
   × 8 yellow print
   × 8 yellow stripe
Total 44 pieces each block.

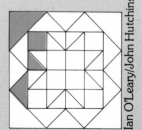

3

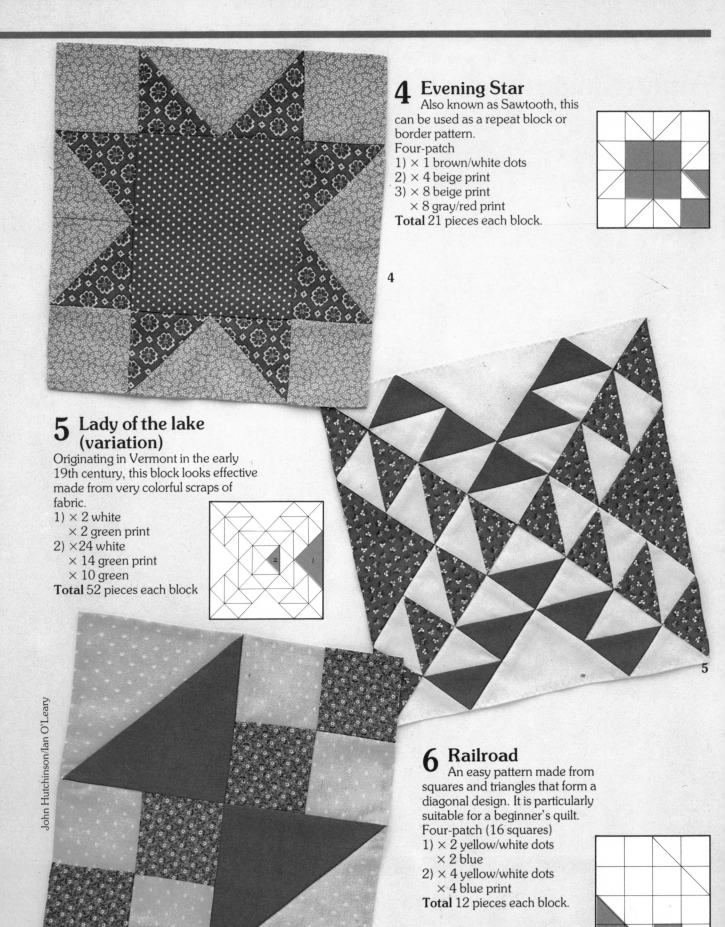

4 Evening Star

Also known as Sawtooth, this can be used as a repeat block or border pattern.

Four-patch
1) × 1 brown/white dots
2) × 4 beige print
3) × 8 beige print
   × 8 gray/red print
Total 21 pieces each block.

4

5 Lady of the lake (variation)

Originating in Vermont in the early 19th century, this block looks effective made from very colorful scraps of fabric.
1) × 2 white
   × 2 green print
2) ×24 white
   × 14 green print
   × 10 green
Total 52 pieces each block

5

6 Railroad

An easy pattern made from squares and triangles that form a diagonal design. It is particularly suitable for a beginner's quilt.

Four-patch (16 squares)
1) × 2 yellow/white dots
   × 2 blue
2) × 4 yellow/white dots
   × 4 blue print
Total 12 pieces each block.

6

John Hutchinson/Ian O'Leary

7

7 Courthouse steps

This block is particularly suitable for using up odd scraps of fabric. Cut fabric into strips of equal width and join together in the sequence below.

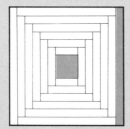

8 Devil's claws

Also known as Bright Stars, Cross Plains or Lily. Use one block for a pillow or repeat for a quilt.
Four-patch (64 squares)
1) × 4 pink print
2) × 24 lilac
   × 16 dark lilac
   × 20 dark violet
   × 24 lilac/cream print
   × 4 pink print
3) × 4 lilac
Total 96 pieces each block.

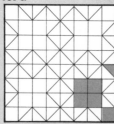

8

9 Indian trail

Also known as Forest Path, Rambling Road or Winding Path, this intricate block poses more of a challenge to the experienced needleworker

Four-patch (64 squares)
1) × 4 red/black print
   × 4 black/white stripe
2) × 4 red
3) × 24 black
   × 20 red print
   × 4 red
Total 60 pieces each block.

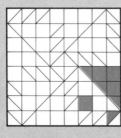

9

PATCHWORK

English patchwork

Skills you need

* Piping

If you do not know this skill, refer to page 410.

Materials

Small interlocking patches are a feature of English patchwork, so the fabric needs to be one that folds well. Firmly-woven pure cotton is the ideal choice. Always wash and iron before using to ensure color-fastness and guard against shrinkage. Delicate floral patterns are normally associated with this type of patchwork. Mix with toning plain cottons of the same weight.

Other fabrics can also be used, although different types of fabric should not be mixed in one article. Silk, needlecord and velvet are all suitable, although velvet and needlecord are more suited to larger patches.

Special technique – preparing clamshell patches

Elsa Willson

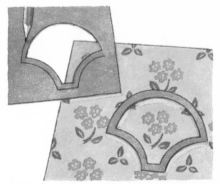

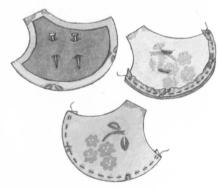

1 To make the main template, trace the template shape from the page and glue tracing to stiff cardboard. Cut out accurately. Place on thin cardboard and draw around edges to make a clamshell guide. Cut several guides as they wear out during the course of the work.

2 To make a window template, take a piece of cardboard that has had a guide cut from it, draw a line ¼ in. all around the outside of the shape and cut out. Place on right side of fabric to select part of the pattern for the patch, positioning on the straight grain whenever possible. Draw around outer edge and cut out.

3 Pin the clamshell guide to right side of fabric with two pins. Fold ¼ in. allowance to wrong side, making small pleats to keep the curve smooth and in line with the guide. Leave ⅜ in. straight at each end of the curve so that patches fit closely together. Secure with tiny running stitches and remove pins.

The basic patchwork tea cozy and cushions

Combine plain and patterned fabrics in colors to suit your living room to make an unusual tea cozy and pretty cushions. Arrange clamshells in stripes or pyramid formation.

Size
Tea cozy 10 in. × 12 in.
Oblong pillow 16½ in. × 8⅝ in.
Square pillow 11¾ in. × 11¾ in.
370

Materials
Tea cozy
½ yd. of 36 in.-wide green cotton
¼ yd. of 36 in.-wide pink cotton
½ yd. of 36 in.-wide patterned cotton
⅛ yd. of 36 in.-wide blue cotton
⅞ yd. of piping cord
¾ yd. of 36 in.-wide lining fabric
2 pieces of polyester batting ⅜ yd. square
2 pieces of non-woven interfacing ⅜ yd. square

Belinda

Oblong pillow

⅛ yd. of 36 in.-wide green cotton
⅜ yd. of 36 in.-wide pink cotton
½ yd. of 36 in.-wide patterned cotton
1¾ yd. of piping cord

Square pillow

⅝ yd. of 36 in.-wide pink cotton
⅛ yd. of 36 in.-wide cotton with large floral print
⅛ yd. of 36 in.-wide cotton with small floral print

1¾ yd. of piping cord
Small piece of thin cardboard

12 in. of elastic
2 drawing pins
Cork mat or soft board slightly larger than the finished size of the item

Tea cozy

Prepare 42 green clams, 22 pink clams, 30 patterned clams and 12 blue clams, as described above.
Assemble the clamshells, following the photographs on page 372 for arrangement. Starting at the top of the tea cozy, place the first two patches side by side on the cork mat or soft board, so that the edges touch.

Place the elastic across the clamshells ¼ in. above the raw edge at the bottom of the curve, stretch slightly to give a straight line and pin at each side. Align the first row of patches with the elastic and pin to the board.
Make the next row by placing the center top of each patch at the join of the patches in the previous row, moving the elastic down to align patches. Pin clams to the board and continue until the design is complete.
The patches must now be securely pinned together and removed from the board. Carefully remove pins and

371

repin through scalloped edge, taking care not to move the patches out of position. Tack and slip stitch patches together. Repeat for second side.

Slip stitch patchwork to the plain green fabric, to give a straight edge above the clamshells for top seams. Pipe and machine stitch the two sides together, attaching loop at the top.

Cut two pieces of non-woven interfacing to shape adding ⅝ in. seam allowances and slip stitch separately to the inside back and front of the cover. Repeat with two pieces of lining, slip stitching to cover along bottom edge.

Cut two pieces of batting and four pieces of lining to shape, adding seam allowances. Take two pieces of lining and place between two pieces of batting. Stitch together. Trim seams close to stitching and turn inside out. Machine stitch remaining pieces of lining together and insert into batting pad. Slip stitch lining together along bottom edge to make a removable pad.

Square pillow
Prepare 12 pink clams, 20 clams in small floral print, and 28 in large floral print. Assemble following the arrangement shown above.

Cut bias strips for piping and two pieces 13 in. × 13 in. in pink. Stitch four clamshell patchworks to front. Pipe and machine stitch front to back.

Oblong pillow
Prepare eight green clams, eight pink clams and 46 patterned clams, and assemble as shown on the left, joining to a strip of green fabric at center and pink fabric at each end.

Cut bias strips for piping and piece for back in pink cotton. Pipe and machine stitch patchwork front to back.

Pieced patchwork

Piecing patchwork into interesting arrangements is a very satisfying pastime. While it provides the opportunity for great individual creativity to both the expert and beginner alike, it also offers scope for making many useful items, and most important of all, real economy.

Ian O'Leary

Skills you need

* **Tufting or tieing**

If you do not know this skill, refer to page 411.

Materials

One of the many pleasures of patchwork is that it can be an excellent way of using up oddments of fabric. These may be left over from other projects or bought as sale purchases. Before selecting fabrics for your patchwork, it is helpful to separate oddments into groups according to their type and weight, for instance, velvet and corduroy, suit-weight linen and cotton, sheer silk, voile and taffeta, dress-weight cotton and silk, and so on. This will make selecting the colors much easier.

It should also be remembered that to give really crisp edges and outlines to your pieced patchwork, it is best to use a variety of closely-woven fabrics such as dress-weight cottons.

Work with matching sewing threads of mercerized cotton, polyester thread or silk according to the type of fabric used.

Special technique – piecing the striped block

1 Begin with a basic square of fabric backed with tissue paper cut to the same size; tack around the edges. (A light paper backing prevents fabric stitched on the bias from stretching out of shape.) From colored fabrics, cut long, straight-grain strips varying in width from ⅝ in. to 1½ in. Taking a ¼ in. seam, pin and stitch the first strip diagonally across.

2 Cut off any excess length and keep the remaining strip ready to repeat the same color later on. Turn the fabric strip to the right side and press flat. Measure the width along the strip for accuracy and trim if necessary. Trim the ends of the strip to the same size as the basic square.

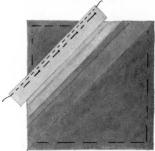

3 With the right sides and raw edges together, pin and stitch the second strip in position. Repeat for the next and subsequent strips varying the width as well as the colors of each one. Continue in this way until the area is filled. Tear away the tissue paper and remove tacks.

Richard Phipps

The basic patchwork quilt

This very elegant quilt has a central panel of pieced blocks showing a Roman stripe pattern. The plain border can be adjusted to fit any size bed.

Size
Approx. 78½ in. square

Materials
From 45 in.-wide dress-weight cotton, the following amounts and colors are required:
4½ yd. light brown for backing and binding the quilt
2¾ yd. dark brown for the border
2 yd. olive green for the basic pieced blocks
Oddments of mixed colors to an approximate total of 2 yd.
¼ yd. of 45 in.-wide golden yellow for
374

the inner border
4½ yd. of 36 in.-wide lightweight polyester batting
One skein of brown soft embroidery thread
Tissue paper

Instructions
From the olive green fabric, cut out 25 pieces each 9⅜ in. square. This includes a ⅜ in. seam allowance all around. Stitch strips of fabric diagonally to each of these squares, mixing the colors and varying the widths as described in the Special Technique.

Place the finished blocks for the central panel into a pleasing arrangement, with the diagonal stripes following the same direction. Arrange five blocks into five rows to measure 44¼ in. square. When diagonally divided

blocks are arranged like this, the basic square is immediately changed and gives instead a rather classical effect of alternating plain and patterned triangles.

Taking ⅜ in. seams and using matching sewing thread, pin and stitch the blocks together. First join the vertical seams between the blocks and make horizontal rows, and then join the rows together. It is important at this stage to keep the points of the triangles and the square blocks accurately matched. Complete the central panel, pressing the seams upward and to one side to reduce very bulky seams.

From the golden yellow fabric, cut out four strips for the inner border. Cut two measuring 1⅛ in. wide by 44¼ in. long and two 1⅛ in. wide by 45 in. long. Taking a ⅜ in. seam, pin and

Alternative pieced patterns

stitch the short border strips to two opposite sides of the central panel. Press the seams outward. Repeat for the other two sides. If necessary, trim the border to ¾ in.

From the dark brown fabric cut out four pieces for the outer border. Cut two pieces 17 in. wide by 45 in. long and two pieces 17 in. by 78½ in. Stitch them to the quilt as before, pressing the seams outward from the center panel. When joining the widths of batting and backing fabric, avoid central seams when possible.

Make the batting and the backing for the quilt 78½ in. square. To do this, begin by cutting the 4½ yd. length of batting in half to make two pieces, each 2¼ yd. long. Then, cut down the middle of one piece to make two pieces each 19¾ in. × 2¼ yd. Working on a large flat surface (a carpeted floor space is ideal), place the two narrow pieces at either side of the wide section, butt the edges together and oversew by hand. Use the same method for the backing fabric, setting aside the trimmed lengths of fabric for the final binding. Machine stitch the seams and press to one side.

Assemble the three layers of the quilt by first placing the backing right side down, and then the batting and the quilt top with the right side uppermost. Pin and tack the three layers together, stitching all over the quilt, in lines 9¾ in. apart, first one way and then the other. Working from the wrong side, and with soft embroidery thread in the needle, knot the quilting ties at each corner of the pieced blocks.

Machine quilt the outer border, beginning by stitching a line ⅜ in. away from the inner border. Extend machine-stitched lines from each of the central squares, across the width of the border. Complete the inner squares to measure 8⅝ in. This leaves an outer border of rectangles 7 in. × 8⅝ in.

Tack around the quilt ¾ in. away from the outer edge. From the remaining backing fabric cut strips 1½ in. wide and join where necessary to give the required length. With right sides together, apply binding to the top and bottom edges of the quilt and then machine stitch, taking in a ⅜ in. seam. Fold to the wrong side, turn in ⅜ in. and slip stitch to the machine line. Repeat on the opposite edges finishing the corners square. Remove all the tacking threads and press the quilt carefully on both sides.

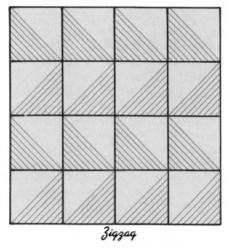

Zigzag

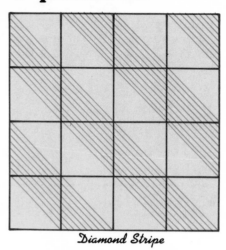

Diamond Stripe

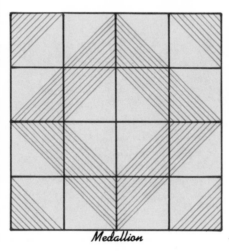

Medallion

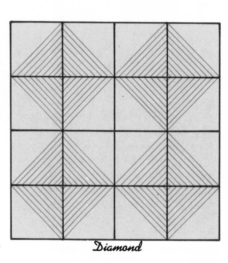

Diamond

Half Border

Counter Point

This selection of arrangements for the center panel of the basic quilt shows zigzag, striped and diamond patterns.

Dennis Hawkins

375

APPLIQUÉ
Appliqué pictures

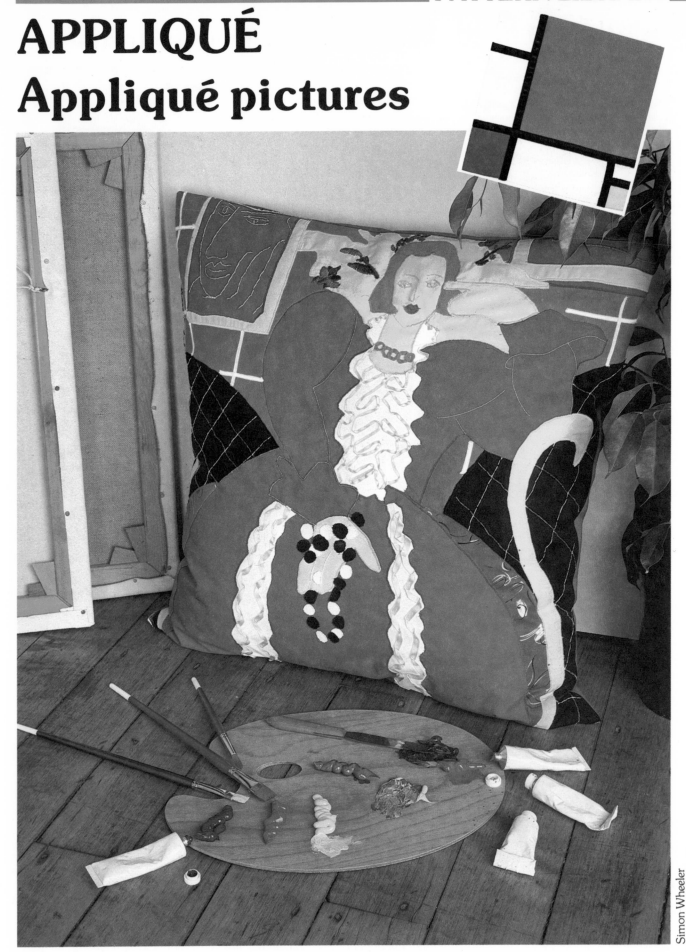

Skills you need

* Machine appliqué
* Back stitch
* Satin stitch
* Running stitch
* Buttonhole stitch

If you do not know these skills, refer to page 397.

Materials

Almost any material is suitable for appliqué, but it is easier to work with fabric that does not fray too much. Felt and cotton are ideal, and both come in a wide range of plain colors. Patterned fabrics, such as floral prints and stripes, can be used for some areas of the picture, and for textural effect use fabrics such as corduroy and satin. Delicate fabrics and pale colors may need interfacing. For the zigzag stitching use sewing threads to match the colors of the fabrics. When the main shapes are sewn in place, the details can be filled in with embroidery threads, ribbon, braid and beads.

Special technique – making an appliqué pattern

1 Enlarge the design by copying it square by square on to ¾ in. squared paper. Draw the straight lines first, then the curved lines and finally fill in the details.

2 Trace the enlarged design onto a large sheet of tracing paper. Keep this drawing on one side to refer to when you come to assemble the appliqué shapes to make up the final picture.

3 Using the enlarged tracing, trace onto a separate piece of tracing paper. Number each pattern piece as on the original chart and mark the color.

Coral Mula

The basic pillow

This appliqué pillow was inspired by the strong and pure colors used by French Fauvist painters. It is made almost entirely in cotton, recreating the fresh, simple character of the movement's style.

Size
Approx. 22½ in. square

Materials
Polyester cotton, 46 in.-wide, in the following colors: ⅞ yd. white; ⅞ yd. blue; ⅝ yd. red; ⅜ yd. black; ⅜ yd. yellow; scraps of brown, pink and red-and-white print
1¾ yd. of light-blue double-face satin ribbon in two widths, ⅛ in. and ¼ in.
24 in. white tape, ¼ in.-wide
Scraps of black and white iron-on interfacing
Sewing threads in colors to match fabrics
Stranded embroidery cotton in light green, dark green, gray, red, black and white
22½ in. square pillow form
22½ in. zipper
¾ in. squared graph paper, 24 in. square
Tracing paper

Pin each of the main pattern pieces onto the correct color cotton, following the straight grain of the fabric. Iron interfacing onto the back of the smaller shapes, the mouth, the black and white beads and the necklace before cutting out. Mark all the lines to be embroidered with tailor's chalk or pencil.
Embroider the face in gray thread, using back stitch worked from the wrong side.
Embroider the white lines on the black fabric, using back stitch worked from the right side. Back stitch is also used for the white lines on the blue picture and the black lines on the yellow pic-ture, and for the white lines separating the fingers. The rest of the embroidery is worked after the appliqué shapes have been assembled.
Cut a 24 in. square from the white cotton, and mark a ¾ in. border all around for the seam allowances. Following the large tracing, lay each of the main appliqué shapes on top of the white background fabric, in numerical order. Pin, then tack each shape in place, overlapping the fabric where necessary.
Using the satin-stitch sewing machine foot and matching thread, zigzag stitch carefully around each shape. Fold the white tape in half lengthwise and zig-zag stitch in place on top of the red fabric, stitching along the center of each strip and across the ends. Machine straight stitch the fine white lines on the dress. The smaller shapes (the mouth, the black and white beads and the necklace) are hand appliquéd, using buttonhole stitch.

377

To make the frills on the dress, hand-stitch the narrower ribbon on the bodice and the wider ribbon on the skirt, using running stitch down the center. Twist the ribbon every ¾-1⅛ in. and keep it loose for a ruffled effect.

Finally embroider the leaves in satin stitch, using the two shades of green. Cut a 24 in. square from the remaining blue fabric for the back of the pillow. With right sides together, machine stitch the front and back cov-

ers together along both sides and the top edge, leaving a ¾ in. seam. Trim the excess seam allowance and cut across the corners. Turn the cover to the right side and press. Set zipper into the bottom opening and insert the pillow foam.

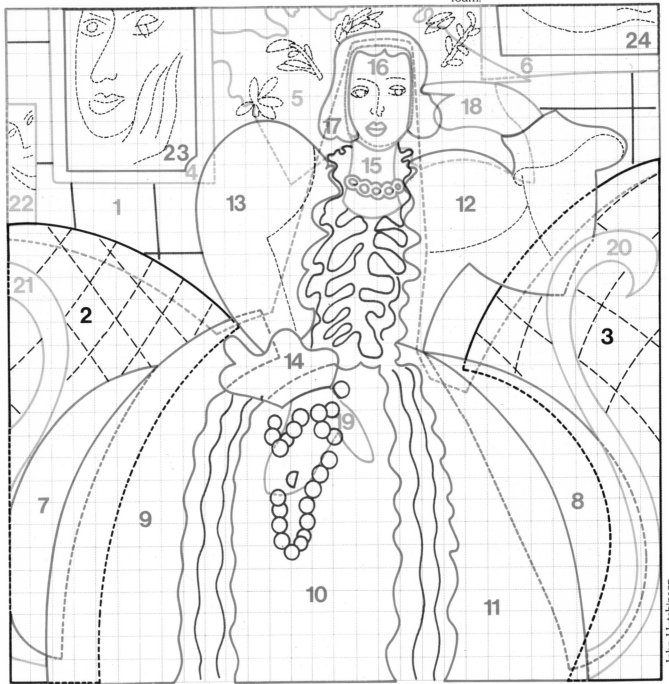

John Hutchinson

Adapting the appliqué pillow

Choose your favourite painting and convert it to appliqué.

Modern paintings with bold, simple shapes are most suitable for appliqué. Abstract paintings with geometric lines

are very straightforward, or you can be more adventurous and choose a figurative painting. Break the painting down into separate areas of color, simplifying where necessary. Trace the shapes from a book illustration or print, and

enlarge to the size required by placing a grid over the original and transfering it square by square onto larger-square paper. Try using different fabrics: a matte fabric for a sombre painting, or a shiny fabric for a vivid painting.

378

Applied motifs

These original padded motifs made in subtly toned satin and silk can be applied to almost any article to give an unusual and stylish finish. Choose any motif from the selection given and make this elegant evening bag to match a favorite dress.

Skills you need

* Piping

If you do not know this skill, refer to page 410.

Materials

Fabrics should be chosen with great care. Many are suitable for these padded motifs, but to be really effective the motifs should complement the garment or article to which they are applied, so compatible fabrics should be chosen. Cotton, silk and satin are ideal and can be used in isolation or mixed to produce a more varied effect. Net and organdy can be appliquéd to any of these to create an impression of fragility or transparency. As these fabrics are fine and rather flimsy, they will benefit from a little stiffening. A layer of lightweight interfacing will give the motif some body.

Stranded cotton or silk thread can be used to embroider details on the finished motif, and beads and sequins also add interest.

Use polyester fiberfill to pad out the motifs. This is an ideal stuffing as it pulls apart easily and can be used in small amounts to give the motifs gentle contours. This shaping is emphasized by fabrics with a shiny surface, such as satin, which creates its own highlights and shadows.

Special technique – making a braided strap

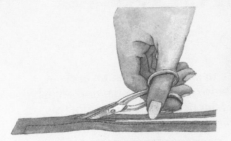

1 *Decide on the finished length of the strap and cut a ¾ in.-wide bias strip to one and a half times this length. Join if necessary as shown. You will need three strips in all to make the strap. Choose a fabric and colors to match or tone with the bag.*

2 *Fold each strip in half lengthwise with right sides together. Tack and stitch along the length ¼ in. from the edge and across one end to close. Trim the seam allowance close to the stitching.*

3 *Turn right side out using a knitting needle as shown. Continue until the entire strip is right side out. Iron and braid the three strips loosely to make a flat braided strap.*

Elsa Willson

The basic evening bag

This evening bag is simple to make, yet the result is highly professional and very unusual.

Size
7¾ in. × 8 in.

Materials
⅝ yd. of 36 in.-wide turquoise satin
¼ yd. of 36 in.-wide pink satin
⅛ yd. of 36 in.-wide blue satin
¼ yd. of 36 in.-wide green satin
⅜ yd. of 36 in.-wide acrylic batting
1⅛ yd. of ⅛ in. piping cord
A small amount of polyester fiberfill
Small piece non-woven interfacing
1 large bead
Small pearl beads
Turquoise and pink sewing thread
1 skein of stranded embroidery floss in turquoise, yellow and pink
Enlarge the pattern on page 382 to size and add ⅜ in. seam allowance. Cut two pieces for the back of the bag and two for the front in turquoise satin. Cut one front and one back in acrylic batting. Take one of the front and back pieces in satin and tack the batting to the wrong side. Quilt the front and lower half of the back, leaving flap unquilted. Cut a bias strip 31½ in. × ¾ in. from the turquoise satin to cover the piping cord. Tack the bias strip in position along the length of the cord and pin it to the right side of the back of the bag, following the seam line. Tack. Snip the seam allowance on the curves so that the piping does not pull the bag out of shape. Place the quilted front right side down on the back of the bag, over the piping. Tack and

stitch around the edge through all the layers. Turn the bag right side out and press it with a cool iron.
Cut three strips 31½ in. × ¾ in. in turquoise, blue and pink for the strap. Make them up into a braid as described above and tack it in position at the sides of the bag.
To line the bag pin and tack the remaining front and back right sides together and stitch. Turn the seam allowance to the wrong side across the front and around the flap and place inside the bag, wrong sides together. Slip stitch to the bag to finish.
To make the motif first make separate tracings of the flower and leaves. Cut two pieces of fabric and a piece of non-woven interfacing approximately 4 in. larger than the tracing for each element of the motif. Transfer each

tracing to the right side of one piece of the relevant fabric. Place the two pieces of fabric wrong sides together with the interfacing between to give the fabric body. Tack all three layers firmly together to prevent them slipping during stitching. Zigzag along the edges of the design and fasten the ends. Make a small slit in the back of the motif and insert sufficient fiberfill to give it some shape. Oversew the slit to close. Stitch the flower and leaves together to form the complete motif.
Embroider the top surface of the flower with French knots and stem stitch and decorate with miniature pearls. Cut around the edge of the motif with a pair of sharp embroidery scissors, taking care not to cut the stitching. Sew in position on the bag.

Adapting the evening bag

Change the mood of the evening bag by making it in a different color and applying a motif of your choice.

Choose a motif you particularly like from the selection given. The flower motifs range from a delicate violet to a rambling rose and the butterfly and dragonfly are also very effective. Each motif is accompanied by a trace pattern.
Color is a very important feature of the bag. Part of its attractiveness lies in the

subtle contrasts of color, so choose colors for the bag and the motif carefully. If the bag is intended as an accessory for a particular garment, remember to bear this in mind.
Once you have chosen the colors trace the motif from the page and follow the instructions for the basic evening bag.

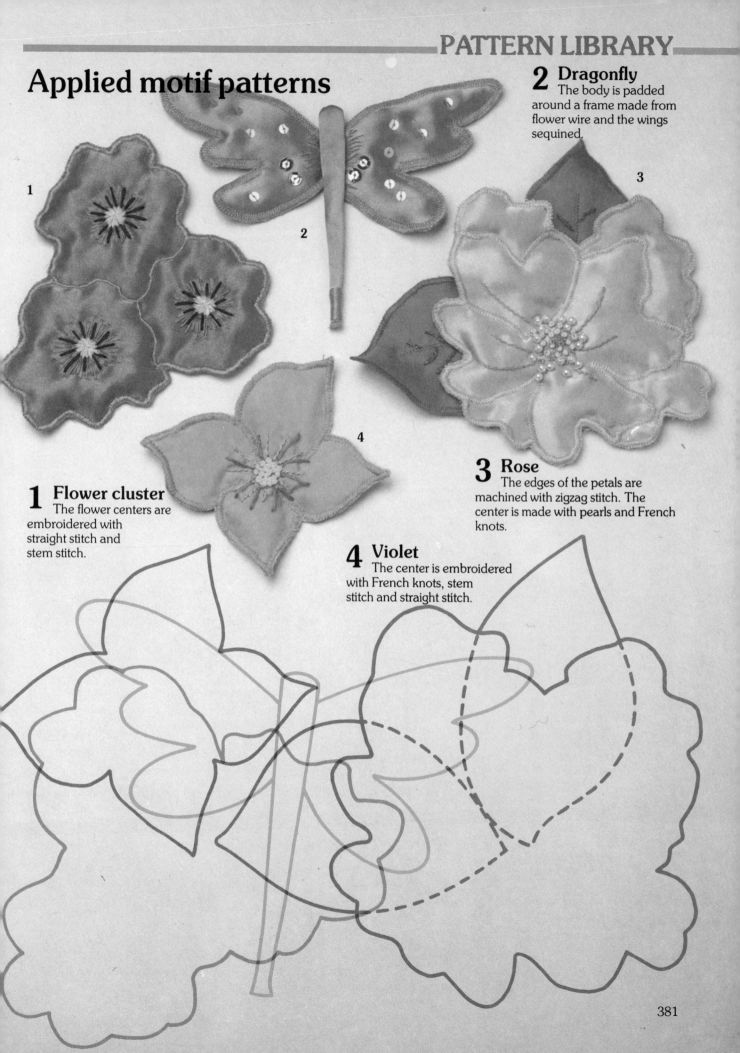

Applied motif patterns

2 Dragonfly
The body is padded around a frame made from flower wire and the wings sequined.

1 Flower cluster
The flower centers are embroidered with straight stitch and stem stitch.

3 Rose
The edges of the petals are machined with zigzag stitch. The center is made with pearls and French knots.

4 Violet
The center is embroidered with French knots, stem stitch and straight stitch.

5 Buttercup
The combination of organdy and silk petals make this an interesting motif.

5

6 Blue flower
This has an interesting center of French knots, straight stitch and stem stitch.

6

More design ideas

Incorporate any one of the motifs as a decorative feature on a neckline. They would look equally effective applied to the pockets of a silky evening jacket.

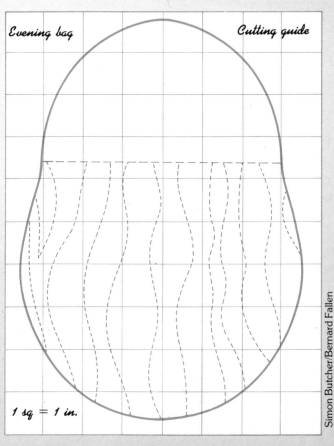

Evening bag   Cutting guide

1 sq = 1 in.

Simon Butcher/Bernard Fallen

382

Lace fabric appliqué

This technique offers some of the daintiest and prettiest effects in embroidery. By using fabrics and trims that are in themselves richly textured, lacy and highly decorative, it is fairly easy for a beginner to appliqué quite large areas with very pleasing results.

Skills you need

* Piping

If you do not know this skill, refer to page 410.

Materials

White, ivory or cream-colored "wedding lace" and lace curtaining can be bought by the yard in a variety of widths. They may be woven from synthetic or natural fibers or from a mixture of both. When buying lace fabric off the bolt make sure you buy enough to include the full repeat. Pieces of antique lace, filet net, doilies and crocheted mats may be used for lace appliqué with great success. There are many varieties of lace trim available in white and neutral colors. They can be bought as single motifs or by the yard. These vary in depth from 3/8 in. to approximately 12 in. The range includes patterns with decorative edges of deep or shallow scallops, points, picots and arches through straight-sided insertions to colored patterns and pretty trims with motifs outlined in gold or silver thread. All cotton, lace fabrics and trims should be pre-shrunk. Light to medium-weight silk, satin, cotton and polyester fabrics are suitable as ground fabrics. For delicate fabrics, a fine polyester or silk thread is best for stitching.

Special technique – appliquéing fine lace fabrics

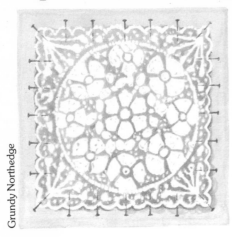
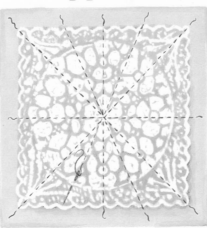
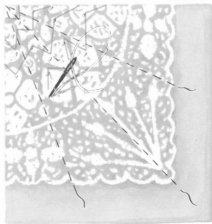

Grundy Northedge

1 To pre-shrink lace, soak new lace overnight in cold water or handwash antique lace in pure soap flakes, rinse and lightly starch. Carefully ease the lace to shape and, if necessary, pin out around the edges. With a clean iron and medium heat, press on the wrong side while still damp. Use a lift and press action to prevent the iron from snagging the open mesh. Cut to size.

2 Place the lace on the ground fabric (if required, cut batting and lining to size) and pin together. Working from the center outward tack through all layers as shown. It is a good idea here to use a contrasting colored tacking thread. It will be much easier to see when it comes to removing it from the finished appliqué.

3 Working from the middle outward and with fine matching sewing thread, stitch the lace in place. Work through all layers making tiny stitches on the right side about 3/4 in. to 2 in. apart. Continue in a zigzag movement carrying the long threads on the back. To give maximum support to very fine lace, stitch through the solid contours of the pattern.

The basic lace appliqué pillow cover

This prettily-frilled pillow cover is made from white cotton lace appliquéd onto a creamy ground fabric. Its classic lines are softened with gold and satin trims and a deep double frill.

Size
31½ in. square, including the frill

Materials
1½ yd. of 91 in.-wide cream cotton

sheeting
27½ in. square of white cotton lawn
27½ in. square of light synthetic batting
1⅛ yd. of 49 in.-wide white lace curtaining fabric
2½ yd. of 2 in.-wide white lace insertion
4⅝ yd. of 2 in.-wide white lace trim with scalloped edge
1¾ yd. of 1⅛ in.-wide white lace trim
5½ yd. of washable gold piping

4⅝ yd. of ⅜ in.-wide cream satin ribbon
Matching sewing thread
One 26 in. square pillow
Brass pins

Instructions
Front

Note that for large pillows intended to stand in an upright position, it is best to support the appliqué with a light interfacing. Use a thin layer of synthetic batting in between the ground fabric and a fine cotton lining.

With the exception of the batting, wash and press all the fabrics and trims before cutting out. This will test for shrinkage and colorfastness.

Following the measurement chart, cut the required lace motifs and trims to size allowing ¾ in. for seams where necessary. Cut out the lining, batting and cream ground fabric, each measuring 27½ in. square. With right sides outside, place the batting between the two fabrics and pin together. Mark the center of the ground fabric both ways with a line of tacking stitches. Pin, tack and stitch the central diamond motif in place.

Tack gold piping to the sides of the insertion for the side sections, leaving the raw edges on the short sides. Stitch in place, overlapping the raw edges of the diamond. Back each small lace square with a piece of ground fabric, turn under the raw edges and press. Pipe around each square. Tack and stitch in place overlapping the raw edges of each side section. Stitch the satin ribbons in place, leaving the ends free for tying into a bow.

Apply the lace corner sections, placing the outside edges into the seam allowance. Cover the raw diagonal edges with lace trim, tack and stitch. Remove the tacking stitches.

Back and pocket

From the main fabric, cut out the back section measuring 30 in. × 27½ in. Make a hem along one short side, first turning over ⅜ in. then 2 in. Cut out the pocket section 27½ in. × 11¾ in. placing one long edge to a selvege.

A detail of the pillow shown in the main picture. The tied bow sits neatly on top of the frill.

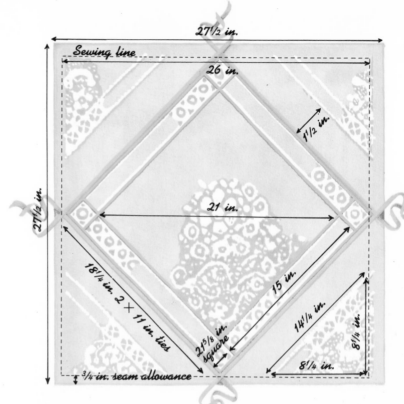

Frill

Allowing roughly 1½ times the measurement of the pillow's perimeter, cut two pieces of main fabric 82½ in. × 10¼ in. Join the two pieces together along the short sides to form a circle and press the seams open. With the right side outside, fold lengthwise in half and press. Machine stitch a row of gathering stitches ⅜ in. from the raw edge through both thicknesses. Cut approximately 165 in. of 2 in-deep lace trim. Join to form a circle and stitch to the frill below the gathering thread.

Finishing

With right sides together, pull up the gathers to fit around the pillow and tack the frill to the top section of the pillow cover, easing around the corners and taking ¾ in. turnings. Place the bottom section and pocket over the frill, neatly folding and pinning the corners of the frill to reduce bulk and stitch, taking ¾ in. turnings. Trim the seams and finish with zigzag stitch. Remove all tacking threads. Turn the pocket underneath, press on the wrong side and turn the pillow cover right side out.

Adapting the lace appliqué pillow cover

Give the pillow a complete different look by changing the appliqué design.

It would be easy to change the pillow simply by incorporating an embroidered design at the center. On the other hand, variations can be made to the basic design itself by, for example, substituting the gold piped border for a gathered trim and piping around the edges. You may, however, prefer to choose either your own colored ground fabric to team with a special color scheme, or use colored laces instead. If these cannot be bought, lace can quite easily be dyed to a number of colors using commercial cold-water dyes.

Appliqué lace fabrics and trims can be complimented with ribbons, tiny artificial flowers, narrow braids and cords; a useful and decorative means of covering raw edges of fabric.

Laundry bag

Teach children to tie bows, loop loops and be tidy with this cheerful laundry bag. It's a fun way of learning new skills.

Finished size 26 in. × 23¾ in.
You will need: Two pieces of denim fabric 25½ in. × 31½ in., one piece of lining fabric 25½ in. × 27½ in. and matching thread. 8 in. of medium-weight batting, 1⅛ yd. of heavy-weight interfacing and 1⅛ yd. of iron-on interfacing. 27½ in. of piping cord, 8 in. of Velcro fastener, small pieces of fabric and scraps of felt. One pair of suspenders or small slide fasteners, eyelets, snaps, one 4 in. zipper, small shoelaces, buttons, ribbons and lace trimmings. One 23¼ in. length of dowel or garden cane.
Copy the pattern to scale from the graph in which one square equals 2 in. and leaving ⅜ in. seam allowances around all unshaded appliqué pieces, cut from suitable fabrics.
Using iron-on interfacing, bond all shaded appliqué pieces to the RS of one piece of denim fabric.
Tack the denim fabric to heavy-weight interfacing.
Thread the piping cord under the posts of the washing line and tuck lace under the hem and into the cuffs of the child's yellow dress. Place "washing" in the top of the basket.

Kinga Phiewska

Simon Wheeler

Using a closely-spaced zigzag stitch and matching threads, appliqué all shaded pieces into place.

Tack the cloud shapes to one layer of polyester batting and two of heavy-weight interfacing.

Using a closely-spaced zigzag stitch and matching colored thread, stitch around the outline and details of the cloud shape.

Place clouds on the denim fabric with the lowest point 10½ in. below the top edge of the denim, and stitch the lower edge of the clouds into place.

Punch eyelet holes and lace the bodice of the flowered dress. Fit buttons, zipper and suspenders to the overalls, sew a button to the back of the blue dress and work a buttonhole to match. Fix a snap to the top of the yellow smock and stitch ribbons to hair. Work a row of machine embroidery along one side and across the bottom of the curtain fabric.

Stitching on the WS so that the seams do not show, stitch the yellow smock, blue dress back and curtain into place.

Cut clothes pins from felt and zigzag stitch small pieces of Velcro fastener to the WS of each one. Sew corresponding pieces of Velcro to the top of each item on the washing line.

Press each "clothes pin" in place.

Tack lining to the WS of appliquéd denim fabric.

Hem the top edge of each denim piece.

Place the denim pieces with RS facing and taking ⅝ in. seams, pin, tack and stitch the lower edges and the side seams.

Fold the top 6 in. to the inside of the bag (with the cloud shape standing above the foldline of the top front edge).

Make two 6 in. loops from denim fabric and fix 2 in. from either end of the length of dowel.

Make two buttonholes along the top folded edge of the bag back.

Place dowel in the pocket along the top edge of the bag back, and thread loops through the buttonholes.

Hang the bag from a length of dowel or from hooks fixed into a wall.

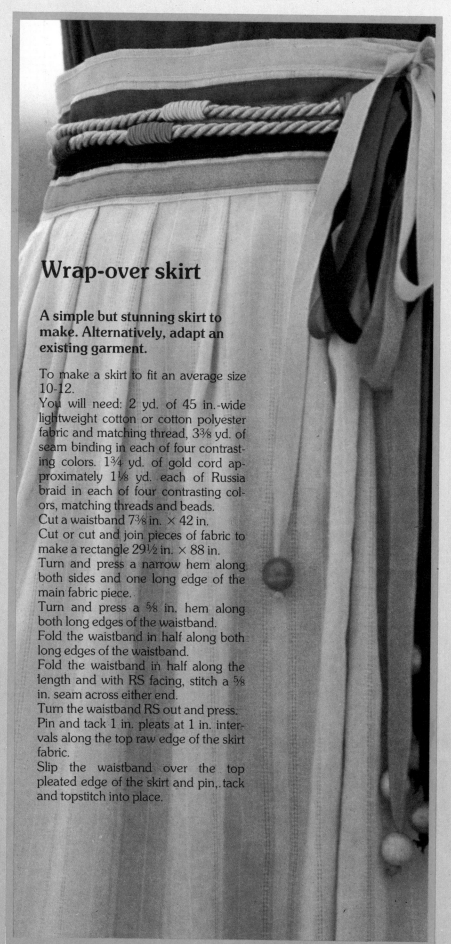

Wrap-over skirt

A simple but stunning skirt to make. Alternatively, adapt an existing garment.

To make a skirt to fit an average size 10-12.

You will need: 2 yd. of 45 in.-wide lightweight cotton or cotton polyester fabric and matching thread, 3⅜ yd. of seam binding in each of four contrasting colors. 1¾ yd. of gold cord approximately 1⅛ yd. each of Russia braid in each of four contrasting colors, matching threads and beads.

Cut a waistband 7⅜ in. × 42 in.

Cut or cut and join pieces of fabric to make a rectangle 29½ in. × 88 in.

Turn and press a narrow hem along both sides and one long edge of the main fabric piece.

Turn and press a ⅝ in. hem along both long edges of the waistband.

Fold the waistband in half along both long edges of the waistband.

Fold the waistband in half along the length and with RS facing, stitch a ⅝ in. seam across either end.

Turn the waistband RS out and press.

Pin and tack 1 in. pleats at 1 in. intervals along the top raw edge of the skirt fabric.

Slip the waistband over the top pleated edge of the skirt and pin, tack and topstitch into place.

Victor Yuan

QUILTING

English quilting

Belinda

Skills you need

* **Cutting bias strips**

If you do not know this skill, refer to page 410.

Materials

Many closely-woven fabrics are suitable for quilting. Dressweight cottons, fine linens, satins, silks and wool/cotton blends can all be used. Choose smooth, plain fabrics to show off interesting stitch patterns, back with a fabric of the same weight and finish with piping or binding in the same or a contrasting fabric.

Large projects such as quilts require strong quilting threads, although dressmaking threads can be used on smaller items. Use cotton on cotton fabric and silk on silk. Embroidery floss and pearl cotton can also be used to create bolder patterns. Beeswax will strengthen fine threads and make stitching easier, but is not recommended for thicker embroidery threads.

Special technique – making templates

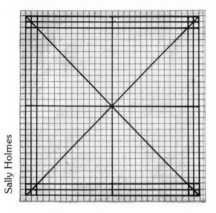
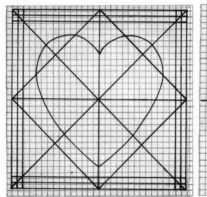
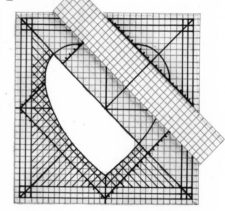

Sally Holmes

1 Using a sharp pencil and ruler, draw a 6 in. square accurately on squared paper, at a scale of 2 squares to ⅜ in. Divide into quarters, and pencil in diagonal lines from corner to corner. Next draw two lines ¼ in. apart all around the inside of the square, positioning the first ¼ in. from the edge, to leave a 5 in. square at the center.

2 Trace the heart and position, traced side down, at the center of the square, using the dividing lines as a guide. Draw over back of tracing with a hard pencil to transfer. Join the center points of each side of the square to form a diamond. Cut a strip of squared paper 1⅛ in. wide and 8⅝ in. long, following the lines of the grid. Rule line across center.

3 Place the strip along one side of the diamond, and mark off points at ¼ in. intervals along the line. Repeat for remaining three sides. Join the dots to make a diagonal grid around the heart shape, as a guide for filling patterns. Stick the drawing on thin cardboard, cut out the heart and then the outer square using a sharp knife.

The basic crib quilt

Made from a warm fabric, this pretty quilt decorated with hearts and delicate colored fillings is just the thing for a baby's crib.

Size
25¼ in. × 30¼ in.

Materials
1¾ yd. of 36 in.-wide wool/cotton blend fabric in cream
⅜ yd. of 36 in.-wide patterned wool/cotton blend fabric
⅞ yd. of 36 in.-wide polyester batting
1 skein of stranded embroidery floss in each of nine toning colors in blues and purples

Instructions
Cut the plain wool/cotton blend fabric in half, from selvege to selvege. One piece will form the backing and the other the top.

Fold the top fabric into quarters and press lightly with an iron. Tack along the two creases to mark the center lines of the quilt top. Press fabric again to remove creases and lay out on a smooth hard surface. Using masking tape, stick the fabric down at intervals to prevent it moving while marking out the pattern.

Make the template as described above and position on the fabric so that the vertical line of tacking stitches aligns with one edge and the horizontal line runs through the center of the template.

Hold the template firmly in position and using a sharp blue pencil, lightly draw around the heart shape at the center of the template and the outer edges, marking dots against the border lines. Secure in place with masking tape to prevent template moving before drawing in the grid pattern for the filling. Align a short ruler with the grid lines of the graph paper or the lines of the hand drawn diagonal grid to produce different patterns.

Move the template and butt it up against one side of the marked-out pattern. Mark out in the same way,

389

filling the heart with a different grid pattern.

Continue to mark out the hearts in the same way, until a total of 20 squares have been drawn over the surface of the fabric, to make a pattern of four hearts across the width and five along the length.

Using a ruler, mark two more lines all around the outside of the completed heart design, the first ¼ in. from the edge, and the second ⅝ in. from this line. This last line is a guide for binding. Join the dots at the edge of each square to complete the intersecting borders that run through the design.

Remove the masking tape and tacking before beginning to quilt.

Press and lay out the backing fabric on a smooth surface. Secure the corners with masking tape to prevent movement. Lay the batting squarely on top and cover the top fabric, marked side up.

First pin and then tack the three layers together from the center outward. Tack quite closely especially if working with a hoop. Finish by tacking round the edge.

Position the hoop at the center of the design and begin to quilt. Use blue thread to quilt the horizontal lines of the borders and turquoise for the vertical border lines. Use the darkest shade for the center line and work out to the palest shade at each side. Quilt all the border lines except the very outer one and fasten off thread just before this point.

Outline the heart in the darkest shade of purple and work the grid patterns in various combinations of colored threads as shown.

When all the quilting is complete, remove tacking except for the line that runs around the outer edge.

Cut four strips 1½ in. wide, on the cross of the fabric for the binding. Join into one length with diagonal seams. Place the raw edge of the binding along the line marked on the outer edge and pin, right sides together. Stitch ⅜ in. from the edge, mitering the corners as you go. Remove the last of the tacking and trim away surplus fabric. Turn the binding to the back and hemstitch in position.

Trace the outline of this heart shape to use when making the main template (described on page 389)

390

Steve Tanner

Adapting the crib quilt

Take a single design and repeat across a quilt on a square or diamond grid to give an attractive geometric pattern, or work a pretty border pattern around a quilted center.

The heart is one of many traditional designs and modern motifs that could be used in a repeat pattern over a quilt. The Peony and the Byzantine knot could both be used in the same way as the heart.

Quilted letters also make a lovely theme for a child's quilt. Repeat an intial over the whole area of the quilt, or work the letters of the alphabet.

The Art Nouveau corner would make a beautiful edging to a more stylish quilt. Continue a border from corner to corner and finish the center with rows of stitching.

Many different effects can be produced by combining fabrics and threads in different ways. Shiny fabrics show off patterns best. For a more subtle effect, use a matte fabric and matching or toning threads. Use bright colors on a pale background for a more lively result.

Quilting patterns

1 **Byzantine knot**
This attractive motif is worked in cotton quilting thread on a satin-weave cotton with 4 oz batting. Use singly or in a repeat pattern.

2 **Art Nouveau corner**
Use this stylish corner to finish a simple line border or use as a motif in its own right. Work in colored silks on glazed polyester cotton, with 2 oz batting.

2 **Peony**
Outline the flower in running stitch and give contours to petals and the center with seeding and bullion knots. Work in silk on silk, with a cotton batting.

391

Trapunto quilting
STITCHERY

The technique of trapunto quilting offers wide scope for interpreting designs from the single padded motif through free-flowing patterns and landscapes to large figurative and distinctly individual creations, used for fashion accessories and furnishings.

Skills you need

* **Buttonhole stitch**

If you do not know this skill, refer to page 397.

Materials

Supple glove leathers, kid, doeskin and fine suede, Thai silk, velvet, linen, firm cotton and upholstery satins are all suitable fabrics for trapunto quilting, and especially for the craft of bag making where the fabrics are cut, padded and stitched to specific shapes. For stitching leather, it is important to use the correct thread for both machine and hand sewing. Silk, polyester and linen threads are used and for some leathers three-sided needles are recommended.

For the padding, use polyester batting, fleece or other similar substitutes evenly teased out.

Special technique – padding trapunto quilting

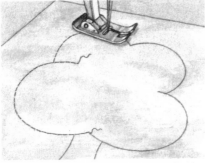

1 *With the traced design attached to the right side of the leather and the calico underneath, machine stitch around the design carefully following the traced outline. Avoid stitching beyond the lines. Fasten off the ends firmly on the wrong side.*

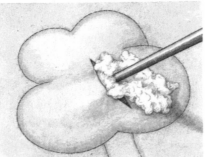

2 *Using sharp-pointed scissors make a small slit in the calico in the center of each shape to be padded. With a fine knitting needle or wool needle, insert the teased-out fleece, pushing it into the corners to make a well-padded shape. Where awkward shapes occur, make a second slit in the calico.*

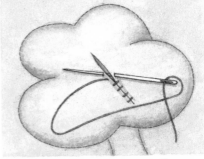

3 *Take care not to overstuff or use lumpy batting. This will show up badly on the right side where the light will reflect any uneven padding. After stuffing, loosely overcast the openings with matching sewing thread to prevent fraying.*

The basic trapunto quilted clutch bag

This smart, fully lined clutch bag made from soft glove leather and contrasting suede is quilted and padded to give a beautiful luxurious finish.

Size
5 in. × 9 in.

One pale yellow glove skin 4 in. × 31½ in. of pink suede (or another contrasting color)
⅝ yd. of pink taffeta for lining
⅝ yd. of heavy-weight bonded

interlining (sew-in)
¼ yd. of 36 in.-wide buckram
¼ yd. of 36 in.-wide calico
¼ yd. square (approximately) of synthetic fleece or similar batting
One reel of pink machine embroidery thread
One reel of pale yellow polyester

sewing thread
Tracing paper
Three pieces of brown paper each 11¾ in. × 17¾ in.
Firm cardboard 6 in. × 9¾ in.
Clear rubber cement
One snap and punch for fitting
Round-pointed wool needle

Instructions
Pattern pieces
Following the diagram given on page

Elsa Willson

394, transfer the measurements to one of the pieces of brown paper for the leather pattern. Cut out, including the curved edge – this allows for easier access into the pocket.

Then transfer the same measurements onto the second piece of brown paper for the lining pattern. Cut out and trim ¼ in. away from the outer edges.

Transfer the same outline onto the third piece of brown paper for the buckram interfacing pattern. Cut out and then cut along both fold lines. Trim ⅜ in. from around the edges and round off the corners.

From the cardboard cut a rectangle 4⅞ in. × 8½ in. and a second one 1⅛ in. × 3½ in. Cut a circular hole in the center of the small piece, slightly larger than the diameter of the snap top.

Quilting

Working directly onto tracing paper, enlarge the landscape design given on page 394 in which one square equals 1 in.

First, place the skin cutting pattern on the right side of the leather with the grain running from head to tail, choosing an unblemished area for the bag flap. Using a soft pencil, lightly draw around ⅜ in. away from the outer edge. Attach the tracing in position with adhesive tape. Place the tape on the margins of the tracing paper avoiding the top edge – this would fall on the back of the bag.

Cut out a piece of calico slightly larger than the flap section and place it underneath. Thread the sewing machine with double embroidery thread and set the

stitch length to about ½ in. Following the Special Technique, complete quilting and padding the main areas of the design. To pad the furrows in the field, thread the needle with lengths of batting and pass through each channel. Leave the sun and sky areas unpadded. Working through the leather only, embroider the tufts of grass using buttonhole stitch. Trim calico to outer edge of the design.

Cutting out

Replace the main pattern on the wrong side of the leather and with pencil, lightly mark the outline, fold lines and position of press stud. Cut out, adding a ¾ in. seam allowance. Tack along penciled outline to define edge of bag and pierce snap positions.

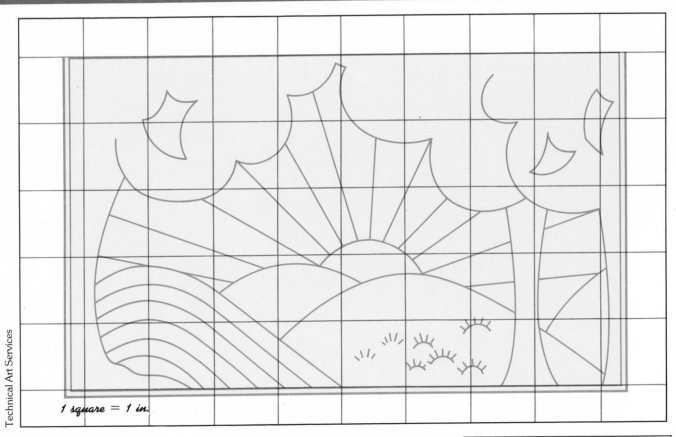

1 square = 1 in.

Place lining pattern on wrong side of taffeta on the grain of the fabric.

Transfer markings and cut out, adding a ¾ in. seam allowance. From the interlining, cut out two pieces, one from the lining pattern (A), and the second from the leather pattern (B) (without seam allowances). Mark fold lines and snap positions. Cut out buckram pieces without seam allowances. From the suede, cut one piece 1⅛ in. × 36 in. and a smaller piece 1⅛ in. × 9¾ in.

Finishing

Using the rubber cement, glue the three pieces of buckram onto the interlining (A). Reinforce the snap positions with extra buckram, about 1⅛ in. square. Crease on fold lines **a** and **b** and press (under a heavy book). Leave to dry.

Place interlining on wrong side of taffeta, clip into curved edge, fold seam allowance over edge of flap and tack. Repeat on front edge of pocket.

With wrong side outside, fold on line **b** and tack side seams together before machine stitching from top edge to fold line. Turn seam allowance over on flap sides and tack in place. Fold lining and press under heavy weight.

Cut a ¾ in wide strip of brown paper and glue it to the curved edge of interlining (B). Crease on fold lines and press under heavy weight.

394

To make the piping, take both lengths of suede and on the wrong side, apply a thin layer of adhesive to the middle of each piece. Fold in half, and when dry, tack ⅛ in. away from folded edge. Apply longer length of piping to right side of leather, around back and flap, placing folded edge inside and level with the tacked line. Tack and machine stitch in place through existing stitch line on piping. Remove tacks and trim seam allowance only.

Apply shorter length of piping in the same way to the curved front edge. Trim seam and snip into piping edges for easing around curve.

Apply a thin coat of adhesive to the cardboard, center it on the wrong side of the flap and press the flat areas of the design firmly in place. Apply adhesive to the three outer edges of the card, turn over edges of piping and press. Trim, particularly the corners.

Glue interlining (B) to the wrong side of leather, and covering the cardboard. Turn edges of piping to the inside and glue firmly in place. Fold the bag into shape and leave to dry. When dry, open out and fold right sides together. Tack and machine stitch the sides, stitching through the piping stitches. Remove tacks, trim seam and turn to the right side.

Insert the lining into the bag and slip-stitch to machine stitching inside

curved edge. Locate snap position on bag front and pierce leather with stiletto from inside. Insert snap cover with second part and hammer in place, following manufacturer's instructions. Mark snap position on flap from the inside. Press snap in place through cardboard reinforcement and hammer the two sections together.

Apply glue to cardboard then press lining and leather flap firmly together. Slip stitch flap to lining to stitches on piping to finish.

Adapting the basic clutch bag

The Pattern Library gives two further flap shapes, demonstrating quilting designs that can easily be adapted to suit handbags and a wide variety of other fashion accessories.

Though leather is one of the most luxurious fabrics from which to make a clutch bag many other fabrics can look equally impressive with stitched and padded designs. The rich textures of silks and satins reflect beautifully the padded surfaces of trapunto quilting and are ideally suited for evening and party wear.

Reflect the local color of individual motifs by machining the outlines with appropriately colored sewing threads.

Trapunto quilting designs

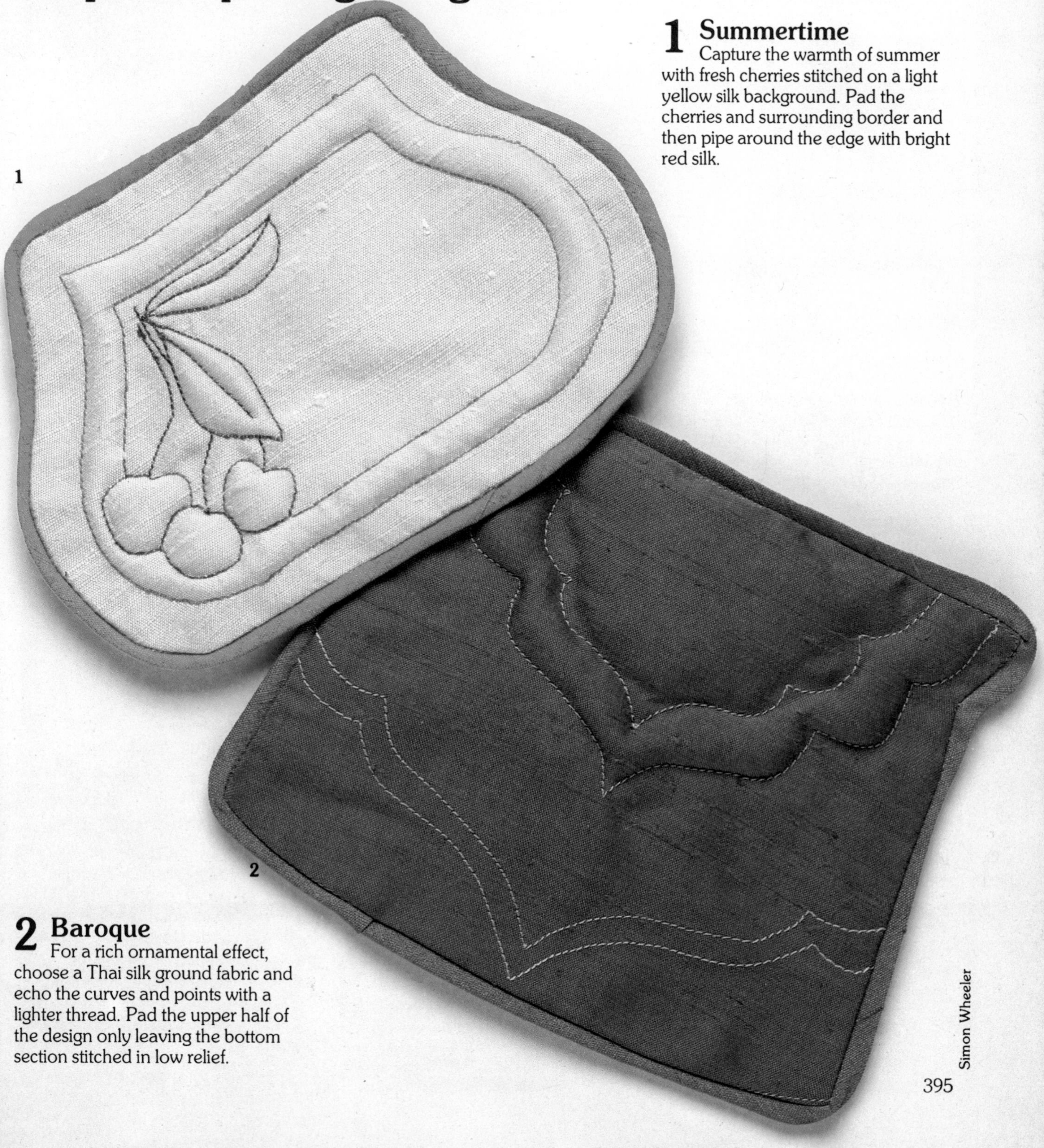

1 Summertime
Capture the warmth of summer with fresh cherries stitched on a light yellow silk background. Pad the cherries and surrounding border and then pipe around the edge with bright red silk.

2 Baroque
For a rich ornamental effect, choose a Thai silk ground fabric and echo the curves and points with a lighter thread. Pad the upper half of the design only leaving the bottom section stitched in low relief.

1

2

Simon Wheeler

These are all freestyle embroidery stitches that are particularly useful for creating painterly effects, for example when embroidering flowers or butterflies.

Choose a thread to suit the fabric and the design – silks, cottons and wools are all suitable.

Long and short stitch

Also known as shading stitch, this is worked in a similar way to satin stitch, except that the stitches are staggered.

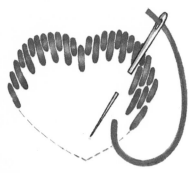

Working from the outer edge of the shape to be filled, stitch a row of alternate long and short satin stitches. Keep the outer edge even. Fill in the shape by working stitches of equal length into the spaces left in the previous row. The irregular stitching means that colors can be graduated effectively, without a strongly defined line.

Split stitch

Split stitch is mainly used for outlining, but also makes a good filling stitch.

This is worked in a similar way to stem stitch, except that the needle splits the thread of the previous stitch as it is brought out of the fabric, producing an effect rather like chain stitch.

Seeding

This delicate filling is made up of small straight stitches.

Work tiny straight stitches at random over the area to be filled. The stitches should be more or less equal in length.

Voiding

This term relates to areas of a design that are left unworked so that the color of the background fabric shows between areas of stitching and provides detail in the design.

In satin stitch embroidery, detail can be given to flowers by defining individual petals, or to leaves, by filling the shape with solid satin stitch and leaving the veins unworked.

Pekin knot

This stitch resembles a French knot, but is flatter and not as twisted.

Work as a French knot, twisting the thread two or three times around needle for a raised stitch. Vary the size by making a shorter or longer stitch.

Trellis couching

Trellis couching can be worked to secure an area of laid threads, or worked directly onto fabric as an open filling stitch.

1 *First work satin stitch over the area to be filled. To save on thread, especially if you are using silk, use a variation of satin stitch, picking up just a tiny amount of fabric at each side of the shape. Work the first row from left to right, leaving gaps, and fill these on the return journey to ensure that the stitches lie evenly on the fabric.*

2 *Lay the couching threads horizontally or diagonally across the area of laid stitches, covering the whole area. This can be done in the same color as the laid threads, or in a contrasting color if a more decorative effect is desired.*

3 *Complete the trellis by working a second set of threads across the area, at right angles to the first. Couch each of these threads at a time with a tiny back stitch or cross stitch at the point of intersection with the first set of threads.*

Machine zigzag stitching is a quick and neat way of doing appliqué, saving hours of hand-sewing. Hand embroidery can then be used for surface decoration and details such as features and foliage. Back stitch, satin stitch and running stitch are the main stitches used for "drawing" in thread. French knots and bullion stitch are useful for small details.

Machine appliqué

1 Pin the cut shape onto the background fabric, matching the grain of both fabrics so that they lie in the same direction. Tack securely in place. If the background fabric shows through the appliqué fabric, back the shape with iron-on interfacing before cutting out. Flimsy fabrics should also be backed with interfacing to keep the shape firm and stop fabric puckering.

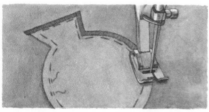

2 Attach the satin-stitch foot to the sewing machine. Set the machine to zigzag, the minimum stitch length and medium stitch width. Practice on a spare piece of fabric and adjust if necessary. The stitch should be close enough to cover the raw edges of the appliqué shapes, yet not so close that it bunches the fabric. Stitch slowly around the outline of the cut shape, making sure that the raw edge is completely covered by the line of stitching. A piece of tissue paper underneath the background fabric will prevent it from puckering.

Back stitch

Working from right to left, bring the needle up a short distance from the beginning of the line to be stitched. Put the needle back into the fabric at the beginning of the line, then bring it out an equal distance beyond the point where you started, Keep the stitches straight and of equal length. Back stitch can be worked from the wrong side of the fabric, in which case the stitches will overlap slightly on the right side.

Satin stitch

Bring the needle up on one edge of the area to be embroidered, carry the thread across to the opposite edge and return under the fabric to the starting point. Work the next stitch close to the first, making sure no background fabric shows in between. For large shapes, work several short stitches across the area rather than one long stitch.

Running stitch

Work short stitches of equal length, picking up only one or two threads of the background fabric between each stitch. Running stitch can be used to outline a shape filled with another stitch, to give it extra definition.

French knots

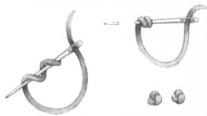

Bring the thread out at the required position and hold it down to one side with the left thumb. Twist the thread twice around the needle, then insert it back into the fabric close to the starting point. Pull the thread through to the back, tightening the knot. Bring the needle up again for next knot.

Bullion stitch

Work a back stitch to the length required but do not pull the needle right through. Twist the thread around the needle until it will cover the space. Holding the coiled thread down, pull the needle through. Now pull the thread the opposite way to flatten the stitch, and tighten by pulling gently on the thread. Still holding the stitch, put the needle back into the fabric where it was first inserted. Pull the thread until the stitch lies flat.

Buttonhole stitch

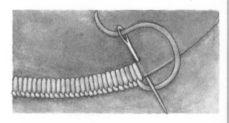

Bring the needle out of the background fabric by the edge of the appliqué. Insert the needle into the appliqué fabric above the edge, then take a downward stitch back to just beyond the edge. Loop the thread under the point of the needle and pull the needle through tightening the loop. Repeat all around the edge of the shape.

Elsa Willson

Stem stitch

Stem stitch can be worked on any fabric and as the name suggests, it is often used for the stems of flowers and leaves. The stitch is worked from left to right and can produce a broad, twisted line, or a strong, narrow one.

1 To work a broad, twisted stem stitch, bring the needle up at the beginning of the line to be worked. Take it forward and reinsert it a little to the right of the line, keeping the thread to the right of the needle. Bring the needle up again half way along the first stitch and slightly to the left, ready for the next stitch. Continue with even stitches to the end of the line.

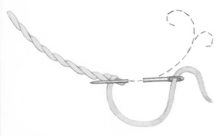

2 To produce a strong, narrow line, always bring the needle up and reinsert it along the line itself.

Stem stitch filling

Stem stitch can also be worked as a filling stitch to give a shape a solid, woven appearance.

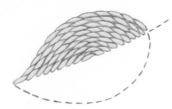

Work regular stitches, following the outline of the shape. Make the first stitch of each row slightly longer or shorter than the first stitch of the previous row.

Chain stitch

Another of the basic stitches, chain stitch can be used both as an outline stitch and, when worked in close rows, as a filling stitch. It is also used in quilting.

Bring the needle out at the beginning of the line to be worked. Reinsert it at exactly the same point, holding the thread down with the left thumb, to form a loop. Bring the needle up again a short distance ahead, inside the loop. Pull the thread through to form the first "link" in the chain. Repeat to the end of the line, making sure that the stitches are of equal length.

Open chain stitch

This stitch is one of the many variations on chain stitch, and is useful for borders and broad lines.

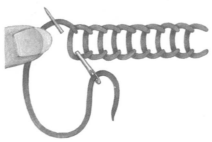

Bring the needle out at one side of the stitch and hold the thread down with the left thumb to form a loop. Reinsert the needle at the opposite side of the stitch, level with the point where it first emerged. Turn the needle back toward the opposite side of the stitch and bring it out some distance below the top of the stitch, inside the loop. Pull the thread through, keeping the loop loose. Insert the needle again opposite the point where the thread emerges. Bring the needle through inside the loop on the opposite edge, ready for the next stitch. Secure the last loop with small stitches at each side.

Cretan stitch

This stitch can be worked as a filling or as a border.

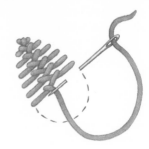

1 To work cretan stitch as a filling, bring the needle out at the top left of the shape and insert it slightly lower on the right. Bring the needle out a little toward the center and pass it over the working thread. Repeat the same movements on the left of the shape.

2 The appearance of the stitch can be varied by the amount of material picked up each time and the angle of the needle. This shows the variation known as long-armed feather stitch, where a large amount of material is picked up and the center plait is narrow.

Open Cretan stitch

This variation of Cretan stitch forms an effective border. It can be worked on its own or combined with other stitches.

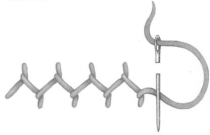

The stitch is worked in a similar way to Cretan stitch, but the needle is inserted vertically instead of at an angle, and the stitches are spaced widely apart.

Holbein stitch

Also known as double running stitch and sometimes Romanian stitch because of its popularity in Romanian embroidery, Holbein stitch is one of the most popular of the outline stitches.

It should be worked over counted threads on an even-weave fabric, and since it is completed in two stages, a complicated design should be carefully planned in order to keep the stitches an even length.

Holbein stitch is often used in cross-stitch designs and for outlines in Assisi work. It is also used in blackwork designs, where there is a continuous pattern, or in cases where the work needs to be reversible.

1 Work a row of single running stitches, making sure that the stitches and the spaces are of equal length by counting the threads. If Holbein and cross stitch are being combined in the same design, they should be worked over the same number of threads.

2 Work any side shoots in the design on the first journey as they occur. These can be worked as a satin stitch.

3 When a line of stitches is completed, turn and work back exactly along the line, filling in the spaces.

Slav stitch

Slav stitch is a simple filling stitch worked over counted threads. Worked horizontally, it is often used as a border in Balkan embroidery. If worked diagonally, it can be used to fill in large areas of fabric in a big design. Plaited Slav stitch, or long-armed cross stitch, was often used in Assisi work as a variant of basic cross stitch.

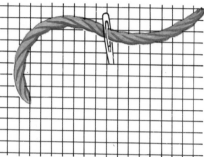

1 **Horizontal method** To work the stitch horizontally, left to right, bring the needle through to the front of the fabric and insert it eight threads along and four threads up.

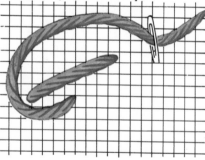

2 Bring the needle out again four threads to the left and four down. Continue to the end of the row.

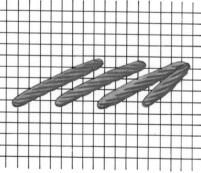

3 Finish the row with a short stitch ending at the same point as the previous stitch.

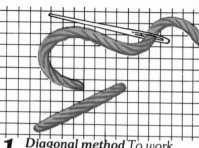

1 **Diagonal method** To work diagonally as a filling stitch, begin as above, and then bring the needle out four threads to the left, level with the top of the first stitch.

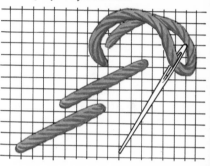

2 Continue with stitches of equal size, ending each row with a short stitch as before.

Plaited Slav stitch

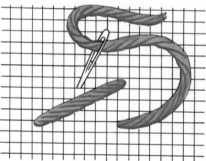

1 Begin the stitch as before and bring the needle out four threads below. Take it four threads back and up over the first stitch, to form the cross.

2 Bring the needle out four threads below this point ready for the next stitch.

Feather stitch

Feather stitch is a decorative freestyle stitch, and is often used in smocking.

1 Bring the needle out at the center top of the border to be worked. Hold the thread down with the left thumb and insert the needle a little to the right on the same level. Take a small stitch back into the center and slightly down, bringing the needle out over the working thread.

2 Next insert the needle a little to the left, level with the point where the thread emerges. Bring it out at the center, over the working thread as before. Work these two stitches alternately, as evenly as possible.

Detached chain stitch

This stitch is also known as daisy and lazy-daisy stitch.

Work as ordinary chain stitch, holding the thread down to form a loop before reinserting needle at starting point. Bring the point of the needle out a short distance away, inside the loop, at the required length of the stitch. Pull the thread through and make a small stitch over the end of the loop to

finish, bringing the needle out for next stitch. Work singly or in groups to form floral patterns.

Fly stitch

Also known as open loop stitch and Y-stitch, this stitch is worked in a similar way to feather stitch.

Bring the needle out at the left of the stitch, hold it down with the left thumb, and reinsert it a little to the right on the same level. Take a small stitch back into the center and bring the needle out over the working thread. Pull the thread through and make a small stitch at the base of the V-shape. This final stitch can vary in length to produce different effects as shown. Work singly, or in vertical or horizontal rows.

Zigzag hem stitch

Also known as serpentine hem stitch, this attractive stitch can be worked at a hem, or with other drawn-thread borders in a larger design.

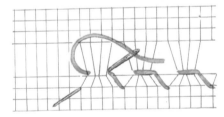

1 To work a hem, measure the required depth of hem, allowing for turnings, and withdraw threads to a depth to suit the weight of the fabric. Turn back the hem to the drawn threads and tack. Work the stitch over an even number of threads from right to left on the right side of the fabric. Bring the needle out two-four threads below the drawn threads and pass behind and then around the first two-four vertical threads. Insert the needle into the wrong side of the fabric two-four threads below and two-four threads to the left ready for the next stitch. Pull the working thread to draw the fabric threads together.

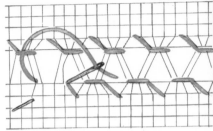

2 Turn the work and stitch the second row in a similar way, dividing the groups of threads in half to produce a zigzag pattern. Begin this row with a cluster of half the usual number of threads, and work hemstitches mid-way between stitches on the opposite side.

Twisted border

This stitch is also known as interlaced hemstitch.

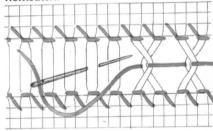

1 Hemstitch the top and bottom of the drawn-thread border, positioning the stitches in the top row immediately above those in the bottom row. Secure the thread in the middle of the border, at one side edge, then take the needle over the first two bars of threads. Slip the needle back under the second bar and over the first bar, as shown.

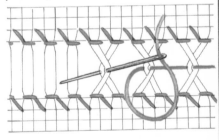

2 Point the needle back in the direction you are working and pull the thread through, so that the two bars twist over. Continue to the end of the row. Use thread withdrawn from the fabric or embroidery thread in the same or a contrasting color to interlace the bars.

Sally Holmes

Surface stitches

These are some of the stitches used on Mountmellick embroidery to give a decorative and well-raised effect. Choose thick threads, such as six-stranded cotton or silk.

Braid stitch

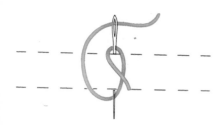

Bring the needle out on the lower line of the area to be embroidered. Loop the thread up to the left and, holding it down with the left thumb, insert the needle into the top line over the loop. Bring the needle out immediately below, looping the thread under the point of the needle as shown. Pull the needle through, drawing the thread tight. Continue working in the same way, from right to left.

Coral stitch

This stitch is most effective if worked in a double thread with the knots fairly close together.

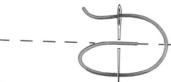

1 Bring the needle out and lay the thread along the line to be stitched. Make a small stitch at right angles to the thread.

2 Loop the thread under the point of the needle and pull it up to form a knot. Repeat for the length required.

Fern stitch

1 Bring the needle out on the stitch line, make a short vertical stitch upward and bring the needle out at the starting point. Work diagonal stitches of the same length at either side with each radiating from the same central point.

2 Repeat below, working the central stitch on the design line.

Herringbone stitch

Bring the needle out on the top stitch line. Take it diagonally down to the bottom line making a small stitch to the left with the thread above the needle. Next, insert the needle on the upper line, making a small stitch to the left with the thread below the needle. Repeat these two movements, keeping evenly spaced stitches throughout.

Porcupine stitch

Bring the needle out on the bottom stitch line. Take it diagonally across to the other side and make a short stitch back. Bring the needle out slightly to the right of the first stitch. Insert the needle on the stitch line just to the left of the first stitch, thus tieing the longer stitch with a short one at a slightly more oblique angle. Repeat, keeping the longer stitches parallel and very slightly apart.

Whipped running stitch

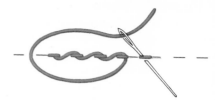

Work small even running stitches along the stitch line. Then bring the needle out just below the last stitch and work a return journey slipping the needle under the next stitch, taking care not to pierce the fabric. You may prefer to use a tapestry needle for the whipping stitch and a contrasting colored thread.

Trailing stitch

This variation of couching is made with satin stitches worked closely together over laid threads to give a raised corded effect. Useful for all curved and wavy lines.

Bring out the threads to be laid, unthreaded the needle, and place them on the stitch line. Using a smaller needle and single thread, overcast with small satin stitches worked closely together. At the end of the stitch line take the threads through to the back and neatly oversew to finish or bring out at the nearest point ready to start again.

Closed buttonhole stitch

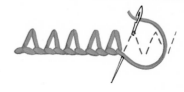

Work this variation of buttonhole stitch from left to right, inserting the needle into the same hole for each pair of stitches as shown.

Tent stitch and cross stitch are both very versatile stitches and have been used for centuries in samplers and peasant embroidery in countries all over the world. The basic principles of beginning to stitch and fastening off apply to both tent stitch and cross stitch.

Beginning to stitch

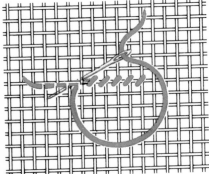

Bring the needle through to the front of the canvas, leaving 1½-2 in. of thread at the back. Work your first stitches over this end to secure. Subsequent threads can be started by running the thread through the back of completed stitches. Never use a knot as it is lumpy and tends to come undone. Do not use too long a thread when stitching as it will wear and break with the constant friction of being pulled through the canvas. 15-17 in. is a good length. The thread will twist during stitching, so let the needle hang loose every so often.

Fastening off

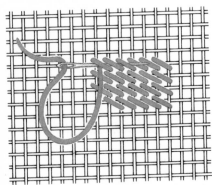

Fasten off ends by running the thread under the stitches at the back of the canvas. Trim loose ends as they occur to prevent loops and tangles at the back.

Tent stitch

(also known as petit point)
Tent stitch can be worked diagonally or horizontally. The diagonal method should be used whenever possible, especially over large areas, as the horizontal and vertical stitches at the back of the work prevent the canvas from distorting. The horizontal method is best for outlines or isolated areas of color.

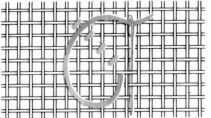

1 ***Vertical method.*** *Bring the needle through to the front of the canvas and insert it to the right of the intersection of threads above. Take the needle behind two horizontal threads of canvas so that it emerges at the bottom of the next stitch.*

2 *Work the first row from top left to bottom right and the second from bottom right to top left. Bring out the needle at the bottom of the stitch, insert it to the right of the intersection of threads above and take it horizontally behind two vertical threads of canvas, ready for the next stitch.*

Horizontal method. *Bring the needle through to the front of the canvas and insert it to the right of the intersection of threads above. Bring the needle out below the next intersection as shown. Work the rows from right to left and left to right. All stitches must slant in the same direction.*

Cross stitch

Cross stitch is used in counted thread work and all types of canvas embroidery. It can be worked on single and double thread canvas or any even-weave fabric, over a single intersection of threads or a square of several threads, according to the coarseness of the fabric and the thickness of the thread. Each cross should be thick enough to cover the fabric ground.

1 *This method of working cross stitch is the most suitable for stitching large areas. Work the first arm of the cross from right to left and complete the stitch on the return journey. Work the second row in the same way. All stitches should cross the same way.*

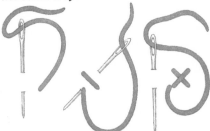

2 *This is the traditional method for working cross stitch on canvas. It is also the method most suited to shaded cottons. Work the first row from right to left, completing each stitch before progressing to the next, and the second from left to right.*

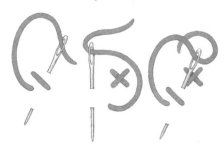

3 *To work a diagonal line of crosses each stitch must be completed in turn. Begin with step 1 and repeat steps 2 and 3 to the end of the row.*

Straight Gobelin

Sometimes known as upright Gobelin, this stitch is worked over two horizontal threads of canvas.

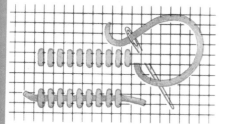

Working from left to right, bring the needle out at the bottom of the stitch and reinsert it at the top, taking it behind the threads to reemerge at the bottom of the next stitch. This stitch can be given a more solid appearance by working it over a laid thread as shown.

Plaited Gobelin

A pretty plaited effect is produced by overlapping horizontal rows of diagonal straight stitches slanting in opposite directions.

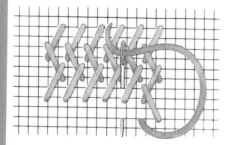

Working the first row from right to left, bring the needle out at the bottom of the stitch, take it over four horizontal and two vertical threads and reinsert it. Bring the needle out directly below as shown, ready for the next stitch. Continue to the end of the row. On the final stitch of the row bring the needle out six threads below to begin the next row. Work this row from left to right, taking the needle up over four horizontal and two vertical threads as before, but slanting the stitch in the opposite direction. The rows of stitches should overlap by two threads as shown.

Cashmere stitch

A useful stitch for large areas, it produces a rich, woven effect.

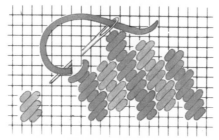

Work the first stitch of the pattern over one intersection of canvas, and the next two over two vertical and two horizontal threads as shown. Repeat from the bottom upward in diagonal rows from right to left, beginning each new row one thread lower than the last, filling in with complete or part stitches to the base line.

Scottish stitch

Groups of diagonal satin stitch are set into an outline of tent stitch. Use two contrasting tones to show the pattern to advantage.

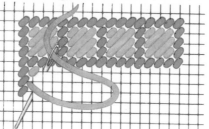

Work tent stitch outline and fill with groups of satin stitches worked diagonally over one, two, three, two and one intersections of canvas.

Fern stitch

This simple stitch produces a very distinctive solid pattern.

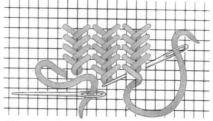

Work each row from the top downward, bringing the needle out at the left of the stitch and taking it

horizontally under a single vertical thread at the center of the stitch. Insert the needle to the right of the stitch as shown to complete. The number of threads over which the stitch is worked can be varied according to the canvas and the effect intended.

Fishbone stitch

Worked on canvas, fishbone stitch appears as regular rows of diagonal stitches, alternating in direction to produce a pile.

First work a long stitch over three horizontal and three vertical threads of canvas. Bring the needle up in the adjacent hole and work a short stitch back over the end of the first stitch. Bring the needle out as shown to begin the next stitch.

Gobelin stitch

Also known as gros point, Gobelin is another simple canvas stitch.

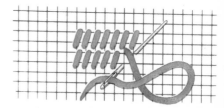

Working from left to right, bring the needle up at the top of the stitch and take it back over two horizontal and one vertical thread. Repeat to the end of the row. Work the next row from right to left, bringing the needle out at the bottom of the stitch and reinserting it at the top.

Counted satin stitch

One of the simplest filling stitches, satin stitch can be of any length, and the stitches can be the same length throughout, varied at random, or graduated according to the space to be filled. It can be worked vertically, diagonally or horizontally, and these differences in direction and length make up the variations of this stitch.

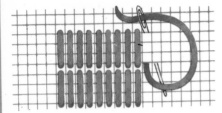

Bring the needle out of the canvas, take the thread across the area to be worked and reinsert it. Bring the needle out one thread along, ready for the next stitch.

Satin stitch variations

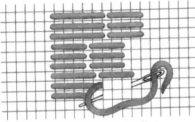

Work the stitches horizontally in a uniform way, or vary the length to create a different texture.

Hungarian stitch

This stitch produces an effective pattern if toning colors are used. It consists of vertical straight stitches, worked in groups of three graduated stitches. Each row is set alternately into the next.

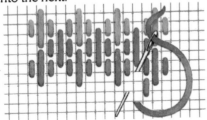

Work each group of three stitches over two, four and two horizontal threads of canvas. Leave two vertical threads free between each group.

Hungarian stitch variation

The number of stitches in the group and the threads over which they are worked can be varied according to the canvas and the effect intended.

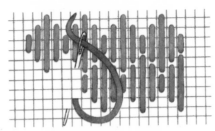

This is a slightly larger combination than the one shown below, using five stitches worked over two, four, six, four and two horizontal threads. There are no threads left between the groups of stitches, and the rows are set directly into each other.

Dutch cross stitch

A simple combination of oblong cross and vertical straight stitch.

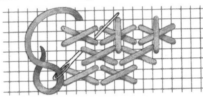

Work the oblong cross stitches first, working over four vertical and two horizontal threads. Fit the second row into the first as shown. For the overstitching, bring the needle out one horizontal thread above the center of each cross and take it down over four threads.

Encroaching Gobelin stitch

This simple canvas stitch is worked in horizontal rows from top to bottom of the area to be stitched.

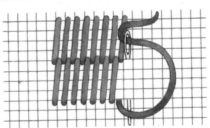

Working from right to left, bring the needle up at the top of the stitch and take it over five horizontal and one vertical thread. Begin the next row

four threads lower, and work from left to right, from the bottom to the top of each stitch.

Ridge stitch

This stitch is made up of rows of diagonal raised band stitch. The stitches must be pulled tight to produce the correct ridged effect.

Working over four threads, work vertical stitches from bottom right to top left. Make the horizontal crosses on the return journey. Work the rows directly next to each other, to cover the canvas completely.

Velvet stitch

This stitch imitates the pile of oriental carpets and produces loops that can either be cut or left as loops.

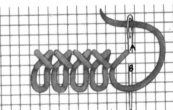

1 *Work the stitch from left to right from the bottom of the work upward. Bring the needle up at the bottom left of the stitch and make a diagonal stitch up over two horizontal threads and two vertical threads, inserting the needle at A. Bring the needle out at the starting point and repeat, leaving the thread in a loop.*

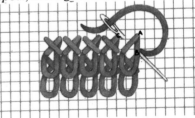

2 *Bring the needle out again two threads below at B and insert it at C to complete the cross. Bring it out again at B to begin the next stitch.*

Elsa Willson

Florentine canvaswork

This type of canvaswork, also known as Bargello or flame stitch, is worked on single thread canvas in wool or silk. Use a thread that is thick enough to cover the canvas. When the work is finished, the entire canvas should be covered with smooth, even stitches. If the thread becomes twisted during stitching, drop the needle and let the thread unwind.

Threading a needle

1 Hold the needle in one hand. Fold the yarn around the needle and pull tightly with the thumb and index finger of the other hand to form a fold.

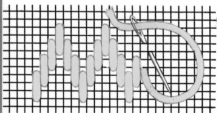

2 Keeping your fingers firmly on the folded yarn, gently withdraw the needle. Press the fold through the eye of the needle.

Florentine stitches

1 Work the stitch up over four threads, taking the needle back down under two threads.

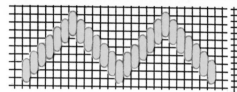

2 These stitches are worked up over three horizontal threads of canvas and back down under two, to create a solid, even, zigzag line.

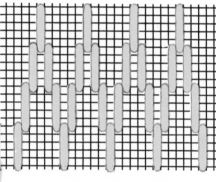

3 Sharp peaks can be achieved by working the stitches over six horizontal threads and back down under one.

Zigzag shapes

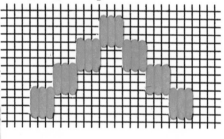

1 Stepped zigzags can be made by working groups of stitches over the same horizontal canvas threads. Here each group consists of three stitches worked over four horizontal threads and back down under one.

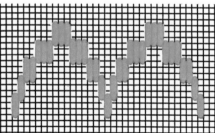

2 Scallops are made by using steps that become wider as they approach the top. Work back down under two or three threads to flatten.

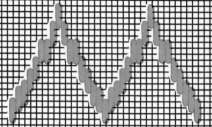

3 Pinnacles are made by using long stitches and working them back down under only one horizontal canvas thread. A sloping effect can be achieved by introducing steps and by working the stitches back down under two or more horizontal threads.

Making patterns

1 Steps, scallops and pinnacles can be combined to make many different patterns. Experiment on graph paper and then work a skeleton line on canvas.

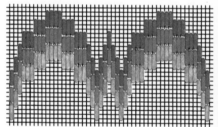

2 Once the skeleton line has been stitched, you have established the design. Stitch subsequent lines above and below it in the same way, using different colors or shades of the same color.

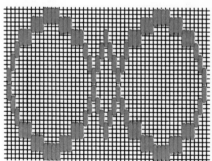

3 Alternatively, work a reversed skeleton line immediately below the first as a mirror image for a diamond or medallion effect.

Elsa Willson

Smocking stitches

Smocking stitches are both decorative and practical. They are worked over the folds of evenly gathered fabric and should be well chosen to give the right amount of control and elasticity.

Rope stitch

This is a firm control stitch.

Begin by bringing the needle up through the first fold on the left. Work stem stitch across the row, taking the needle behind one fold of fabric with the thread above the needle. Continue in this way, picking up one fold of fabric with each stitch.

To work the stitch so that it slants in the opposite direction, keep the thread below the needle.

Single cable stitch

This stitch gives firm control to the gathers.

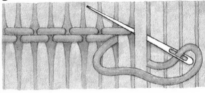

Working from left to right, bring the needle up to the left of the first fold. Make a stitch through the second fold and passing the needle behind, bring it out with the thread above the needle. Work the next stitch in the same way with the thread below the needle as shown. Continue working in this way across the row, with the thread alternating above and below the needle with each stitch.

Double closed wave stitch

This stitch is made up from two rows of wave stitch worked in a zigzag pattern and gives firm control.

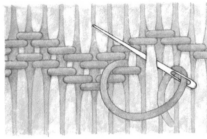

Working from left to right, and with the thread above the needle, begin by working a stitch over the second fold. Work a series of four similar stitches diagonally downward and then, with the thread below the needle, work four stitches diagonally upward. Continue in this way to the end of the row and repeat a second time as shown above.

Surface honeycomb stitch

This stitch gives a reasonably elastic finish.

1 Working from left to right and with the thread above the needle, make a stitch over the second fold. Bring the needle out in the center of the stitch between the two folds, pulling them together. With the thread still above the needle, make a similar stitch over the second fold on the line below.

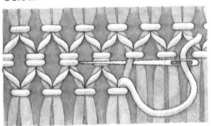

2 With the thread below the needle, stitch the second and third folds together bringing the needle out in the middle as before. Keeping the thread below the needle, make a stitch over the third fold on the first line then stitch the third and fourth

folds together with the thread above the needle. Continue in this way, working in honeycomb pattern.

Diamond stitch

This is a very elastic stitch.

1 Bring the needle out to the left of the first fold on the second line. Take it up to the first line and back stitch over the second fold. With the thread above the needle, back stitch over the third fold, bringing the needle out in the center of the two folds, pulling them together.

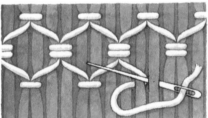

2 Take the needle down to the second line and with the thread above the needle, work a single back stitch on the fourth fold. With the thread below the needle, work another back stitch over the fifth fold, bringing the needle out just above the stitch and in the center of the two folds. Take the needle back up to the first line and repeat from the beginning to the end of the row. Work the third and fourth lines to complete the diamond pattern, with two folds in the center of each one.

Single feather stitch

Bring the needle out at the top of the stitch line. Hold the thread down with the left thumb and insert the needle in a slanting direction. Pull it through with the thread below the needle.

Smocking stitches

Smocking stitches are worked over evenly gathered fabric to secure the folds and to add colorful stitch patterns. Different stitches give varying amounts of elasticity; a point to watch when choosing stitches. See page 338 for ironing on dots for the gathers.

Honeycomb stitch

The stitch is worked over two rows for a loose elastic finish.

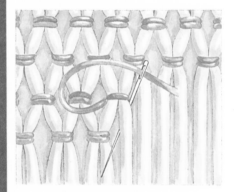

1 *Working from left to right, make a double back stitch over the first two folds, pulling them together. Slip the needle behind the fold and bring it out on the line below to the left of the second fold.*

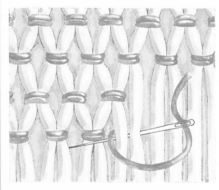

2 *Work two back stitches together over the second and third folds. Slip the needle behind the fold and bring it out on the first line to the left of the third fold. Stitch the third and fourth folds together as before. Complete the row, working alternately up and down. Work the next and subsequent rows in the same way. Use plain or variegated threads.*

Wave stitch

This stitch can be worked in either single rows or repeated in two or three rows to make a solid border, or worked in reverse to form diamonds.

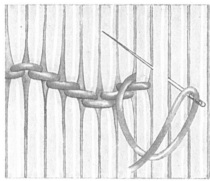

Working from left to right, and with the thread above the needle, begin by making a stitch over the second fold. Work a series of similar stitches (between four and six), diagonally downward. Then, with the thread below the needle work the same number of stitches diagonally upward. Continue in this way to the end of the row and repeat as required.

Vandyke stitch

This stitch is very like surface honeycomb stitch. The surface threads make a slightly different pattern but it produces a similar amount of elasticity.

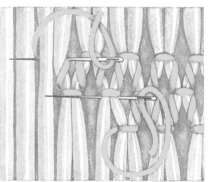

Working from right to left and with the thread above the needle, begin with a back stitch, pulling the first and second folds together. Take the needle down to the second line and with the thread to the right side of the fabric work a back stitch into the second and third folds, keeping the thread below the needle and pulling them together. Continue working alternately up and down to the end of the row. To

complete the diamond, on the next and following rows, pass the needle behind the existing stitch on the top line to work a back stitch on the bottom line as before. Can be worked in rows of different colors.

Cable trellis stitch

Cable trellis stitch makes a pretty border pattern and gives medium to firm control.

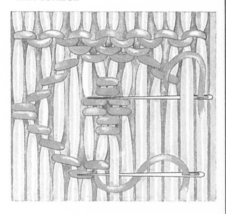

Work one row of single cable stitches across the area to be worked. Then work two rows of wave stitch to form a trellis pattern joined by five horizontal cable stitches. Using the same or contrasting thread, work four double cable stitches into the center of each diamond.

Feather stitch on smocking

This stitch is embroidered on traditional rural smocks.

Working from right to left, hold the thread below the thumb and passing the needle behind one fold at a time, make two stitches to the right and then two to the left as for ordinary feather stitch.

Buttonholed branched bars

Additional features of cutwork include bars and webs that are used to support the surrounding fabric when larger spaces have been cut away.

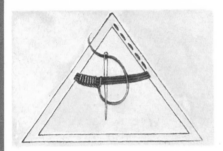

1 First take two or three threads across from right to left and buttonhole back to the center.

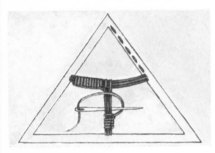

2 Take the same number of threads from the center down to the fabric below and buttonhole back up to the center.

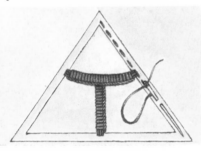

3 Work the buttonholing across to the starting point and continue the running stitch around the motif.

Loop picot

If you are right-handed, this stitch is best worked from right to left, the natural direction for shaping the picot.

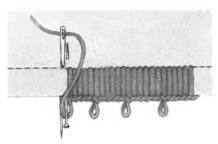

1 On fine linen mark position of picots when transfering the design. On a coarser linen count an even number of stitches between picots. Insert a pin in the fabric as shown. Pass the needle under it and make a stitch into the fabric.

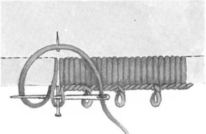

2 Pass the needle back under the loop and bring it out over the working thread as shown. Pull this buttonhole stitch firmly to secure the picot. Continue with buttonhole stitch until the next picot is required and repeat.

Outline stitch

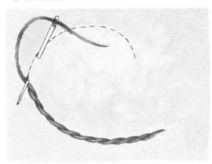

Work in a similar way to stem stitch but keep the working thread above the needle. This stitch slants in the opposite direction to stem stitch.

Ring spider web

The ring spider web is the simplest of spider webs. Use to strengthen large cut areas and produce a very delicate, lacy effect.

1 First make a small detached ring by winding the thread two or three times around a knitting needle. Slip it off the needle and finish with buttonholing.

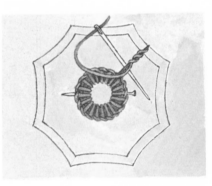

2 Pin the ring in place and attach it to the surrounding fabric with twisted bars. Take a single thread from the ring to the fabric, secure with a small stitch, and twist it back to the center ring.

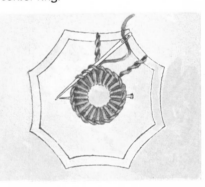

3 Run the thread through the buttonhole loops on the outside of the ring and on to the next position. Continue to work four or five bars to complete the web.

Broderie anglaise stitches

Running, satin, overcast, stem and buttonhole stitch are combined to produce this delicate work.

Raised satin stitch

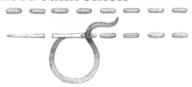

1 Work a row of running stitches along each edge of the stitch line.

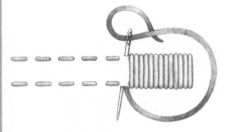

2 Work ordinary satin stitches over the whole area, covering the running stitches. Keep the stitches close and even.

Overcast stitch

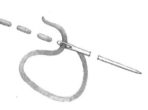

1 Work a line of running stitches along the line to be worked.

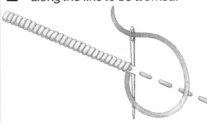

2 Work small stitches over the running stitches, picking up a tiny amount of fabric each time and keeping the stitches very close together to give a firm, raised line.

Eyelet chain

When several small eyelets come close together, it is best to work them as a chain. A chain is very effective as a border or a scroll edging.

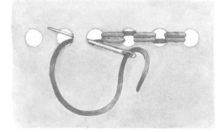

1 Use a knitting needle to make a row of holes. Working along the row, make two back stitches over the space between each hole.

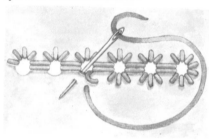

2 Work overcast stitches over the edge of each hole, keeping central thread underneath. Work all the upper halves in one journey long the row, then the lower halves.

Ladder work

Buttonhole and overcast ladders are often used in combination with broderie anglaise to give strength to cut areas.

1 Outline the edge of the shape with running stitches and work the bars as they occur from the second half of the shape. Take the thread across to the running stitch outline on the opposite edge, make a small stitch and return. Take the thread back again and buttonhole or overcast over the threads to make a bar. Continue outlining until the position of the next bar is reached and repeat.

2 Once the shape is completely outlined in running stitch, and the bars have been worked, overcast or buttonhole stitch around the edge, over the running stitches. The pearl edge of the buttonhole stitch should face the inside of the shape.

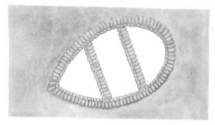

3 When the stitching is finished, cut away the material from the outline with the sharp points of embroidery scissors, leaving the delicate bars to create the impression of a ladder across the open shape.

Scallops

1 To work a simple scallop, pencil regular or irregular curves on the fabric ⅜ in. from the raw edge. Pad with running stitch and cover with buttonhole stitch. Cut away surplus fabric when completed.

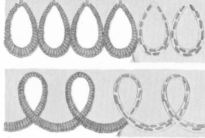

2 Pear and scroll scallops are particularly attractive. Work pear scallops as a row of oval eyelets, buttonholing the lower edges. Work the scroll scallops in a similar way, overcasting or buttonholing the eyelets.

Elsa Willson

Piping

Piping – edging a seam with fabric-covered cord – gives your work a professional touch and is well worth the extra effort involved.

On garments piping makes a feature of the chosen seam and on loose covers and pillows particularly it also adds strength and gives long wear. Piping cord is a stranded cotton cord available in several thicknesses. Choose a cord that is thick enough to give a good raised effect without the twist of the cord showing through. Be sure also that the fabric covering the cord is not too flimsy or the twist will show.

Bias strip

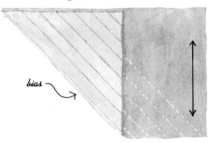

1 Find the bias by folding the fabric diagonally, then mark and cut parallel strips of fabric. The strips should be wide enough to cover the cord plus twice the width of the seam allowance.

2 Join the strips at right angles, with right sides together. Press seams open. The length of the strips will obviously depend on the width of the fabric used, but if possible, avoid having the joins in obvious places, especially on garments.

A diagonal sleeve

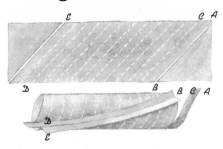

For long lengths of piping, mark the bias strips as before on a rectangular piece of fabric at least 9 in. wide. Cut off the corners. With right sides together, join the long edges so that B meets C and D meets E. Press seam open. Cut along marked spiral beginning at C.

Finishing the seam

1 Fold the bias strip with the cord inside and stitch close to the cord using a zipper foot.

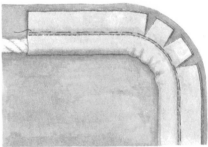

2 Pin and tack the piping to the right side of the fabric, clipping the seam allowance where necessary.

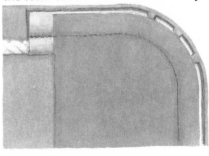

3 With the right sides together, add the second piece of fabric and complete the seam, stitching as close to the piping as possible to cover the previous row of stitching.

Alternative method

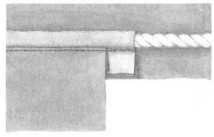

Attach the piping to the right side of one piece of fabric as shown above. Turn under the raw edges to bring the piping to the outside. Pin and tack this piece to the right side of the second piece, along the seam line. Top stitch close to the piping.

Joining ends

Overlap the ends by about 1 in. Unpick the casing at each end. Join edges of casing as for bias strips. Unravel the strands of the cord about ¾ in. Cut away two strands from one end and one from the other to reduce bulk. Twist the remaining strands together and bind securely with thread. Do not pull the cord too tightly or the ends will pull apart in wear. Fold the casing over and finish stitching. If you are using very fine cord it is sometimes enough simply to place the ends of the cord together without unraveling and bind them with thread. The important thing is to ensure that the binding is secure and will not pull apart in wear.

Cordless piping

For very fine piping no cord is used. This is particularly relevant to garments where piping is used as a decorative trim and needs to lie flat. In this case, cut the bias strips twice the width of the seam allowance, plus ¼ in. Single-fold bias tape can also be used. Stitch into the finished item as before.

These are all essential skills for successful patchwork.

Making a template

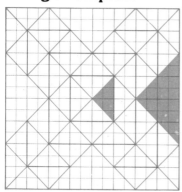

1 Draw the whole block pattern actual size on graph paper to get the exact shape and finished size of each patch needed. Drawing it on graph paper in this way ensures that all the edges and corners are exactly right, which is important when fitting the pieces together.

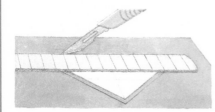

2 Cut out one shape of each template needed. Stick the graph paper shape on to stiff cardboard. Add a ¼ in. seam allowance on all edges and cut out, using a sharp cutting knife or designer's scalpel and a steel ruler. Do not use scissors as they produce inaccurate edges.

Estimating fabric

Choose a block design and work out the number of blocks needed for the quilt or item being made. Work out the number of individual pieces of each fabric required for one block and multiply by the number of blocks to calculate the total number of pieces of each fabric needed. Cut out each template, including seam allowances,

and from these measurements work out the number of pieces that will fit into the width of the fabric. Divide the total number of pieces by this number to decide the length of fabric required. Repeat for each fabric and template. Triangular pieces can be interlocked to save space, but remember that the pattern will be reversed.

Tufting or tieing

Tufting or tieing is a quick and effective alternative to quilting if patchwork is to be lined and a filling added for warmth. Use a thick, non-synthetic thread such as crochet cotton, and a darning needle, and make evenly spaced knots at intervals of about 6 in. across the patchwork. Often the position of the knots is suggested by the design of the quilt.

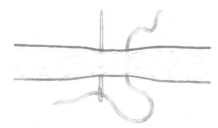

1 To make a loose double stitch, take the needle through all three layers and then back to the top.

2 Repeat the first step, drawing the three layers together by tightening the thread slightly.

3 Tie the ends with a reef knot and take them through to the back, or trim and leave as a decorative feature.

Mitreing a corner

1 Mitreing will reduce the bulk of folded material and make a neat corner. Mark a first fold line along what will be the actual edges of the finished quilt. Half way between this line and the edge, mark another fold line, parallel to the first. Mark two parallel lines diagonally across the corner: a fold line across the actual corner of the finished quilt, and a cutting line an inch or two above it.

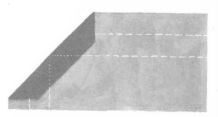

2 Cut off the corner along the cutting line and fold in the fabric along the diagonal fold line.

3 Fold in the long edges along the second fold lines and press.

4 Fold again along the first fold line so that the edges meet at the corner. Press. Hem the sides and oversew the corner seam.

Index

**This material previously
appeared as the Marshall
Cavendish partwork
Busy Needles.**

Knitting and crochet abbreviations

alt = alternate(ly)
approx = approximately
beg = begin(ning)
ch = chain(s)
cont = continu(e) (ing)
dc = double crochet
dec = decreas(e) (ing)
dtr = double triple
foll = follow(ing)
gr(s) = groups(s)
hdc = half double crochet
inc = increas(e) (ing)
K = knit
K wise = knitwise
L = left
LH = left hand
P = purl
pat = pattern
psso = pass slipped stitch over
P-wise = purlwise
rem = remain(ing)
rep = repeat
R = right
RH = right hand
RS = right side
sc = single crochet
sl = slip
sp = space(s)
sl st = slip stitch
st(s) = stitch(es)
tbl = through back of loop(s)
tog = together
tr = triple
tr tr = triple triple
WS = wrong side
Xdc = cross double crochet
ybk = yarn back
yfwd = yarn forward
yo = yarn over

Metric and British hook and needle sizes

Crochet hooks

Metric (mm)	UK Steel (fine)	UK aluminium (larger
0.60	6	
	5½	
0.75	5	
	4½	
1.00	4	
	3½	
1.25	3	
1.50	2½	
1.75	2	
	1½	
2.00	1	14
	1/0	13
2.50	2/0	12
3.00	3/0	11
		10
3.50		9
4.00		8
4.50		7
5.00		6
5.50		5
6.00		4
7.00		2

Knitting needles

Metric	British	Metric	British
2	14	5	6
2¼	13	5½	5
2½		6	4
2¾	12	6½	3
3	11	7	2
3¼	10	7½	1
3½		8	0
3¾	9	9	00
4	8	10	000
4½	7		

A guide to the pattern sizes

		10	12	14	16	18	20
Bust	cm	83	87	92	97	102	107
	in	32½	34	36	38	40	42
Waist	cm	64	67	71	76	81	87
	in	25	26½	28	30	32	34
Hips	cm	88	92	97	102	107	112
	in	34½	36	38	40	42	44